Contents

References

Article Licenses

Payment card industry

The **payment card industry** (PCI) denotes the debit, credit, prepaid, e-purse, ATM, and POS cards and associated businesses.

The term is sometimes more specifically used to refer to the **Payment Card Industry Security Standards Council**, a council originally formed by American Express, Discover Financial Services, JCB, MasterCard Worldwide and Visa International on Sept. 7, 2006, with the goal of managing the ongoing evolution of the Payment Card Industry Data Security Standard. The council itself claims to be independent of the various card vendors that make up the council.

The PCI Council formed a body of security standards known as the *PCI Data Security Standards,* (**PCI DSS**), and these standards consist of 12 significant requirements including multiple sub-requirements which contain numerous directives against which businesses may measure their own payment card security policies, procedures and guidelines. By complying with qualified assessments (see QSA) of these standards, businesses can become accepted by the PCI Standards Council as compliant with the 12 requirements, and thus receive a compliance certification and a listing on the PCI Standards Council website. Compliance efforts and acceptance must be completed on a periodic basis. (See PCI DSS.)

When the acronym *PCI* is listed within job requirements, it most frequently refers the many disciplines of managing the PCI compliance effort within the applicable business entity.

The PCI Council compliance within any card handling business's security process can be considered part of inter-related disciplines of governance, risk, and compliance (GRCM), as well as part of information security.

Regional and National Payment Schemes

Interac Association

The Interac Association is Canada's national organization linking Financial Institutions and enterprises that have proprietary networks, to enable communication with each other for the purpose of exchanging electronic financial transactions. The Association was founded in 1984 by the big five banks. Today, there are over 80 members. The Interac Association is the organization responsible for the development of Canada's national network of two shared electronic financial services: Shared Cash Dispensing (SCD) for cash withdrawals from any ABM not belonging to a cardholder's financial institution; and Interac Direct Payment (IDP) for Debit Card payments at the Point-of-Sale

External links

Payment card industry

- PCI Security Standards Council [1], the organization responsible for the development, enhancement, storage, dissemination and implementation of security standards for account data protection.
- The European Payment Council [2] (EPC) is the decision-making and coordination body of the European banking industry in relation to payments.
- PCI Security Standards Council Participating Organizations [3]

EMV

- EMVCo [4], the organisation responsible for developing and maintaining the EMV standard
- Chip and PIN [5], site run by the UK Payments Administration (UKPA), the UK's central co-ordinating authority for the implementation of EMV
- Migration 2 Chip [6], The Migration 2 Chip Program

Payment Card Industry Data Security Standard

The **Payment Card Industry Data Security Standard** (PCI DSS) is an information security standard for organizations that handle cardholder information for the major debit, credit, prepaid, e-purse, ATM, and POS cards.

Defined by the Payment Card Industry Security Standards Council, the standard was created to increase controls around cardholder data to reduce credit card fraud via its exposure. Validation of compliance is done annually - by an external Qualified Security Assessor (QSA) for organisations handling large volumes of transactions, or by Self-Assessment Questionnaire (SAQ) for companies handling smaller volumes.[1]

Requirements

The current version of the standard is version 2.0, released on 26 October 2010. PCI DSS version 2.0 must be adopted by all organisations with payment card data by 1 January 2011, and from 1 January 2012 all assessments must be under version 2.0 of the standard. PCI DSS version 2.0 has two (2) new or evolving requirements out of 132 changes. Remaining changes and enhancements falls under the category of clarification or additional guidelines.[2] The table below summarizes the differing points from version 1.2 of 1 October 2008[3] and specifies the 12 requirements for compliance, organized into six logically-related groups, which are called "control objectives".

Control Objectives	PCI DSS Requirements
Build and Maintain a Secure Network	1. Install and maintain a firewall configuration to protect cardholder data
	2. Do not use vendor-supplied defaults for system passwords and other security parameters
Protect Cardholder Data	3. Protect stored cardholder data
	4. Encrypt transmission of cardholder data across open, public networks
Maintain a Vulnerability Management Program	5. Use and regularly update anti-virus software on all systems commonly affected by malware
	6. Develop and maintain secure systems and applications
Implement Strong Access Control Measures	7. Restrict access to cardholder data by business need-to-know
	8. Assign a unique ID to each person with computer access
	9. Restrict physical access to cardholder data
Regularly Monitor and Test Networks	10. Track and monitor all access to network resources and cardholder data
	11. Regularly test security systems and processes
Maintain an Information Security Policy	12. Maintain a policy that addresses information security

History

PCI DSS originally began as five different programs: Visa Card Information Security Program, MasterCard Site Data Protection, American Express Data Security Operating Policy, Discover Information and Compliance, and the JCB Data Security Program. Each company's intentions were roughly similar: to create an additional level of protection for card issuers by ensuring that merchants meet minimum levels of security when they store, process and transmit cardholder data. The Payment Card Industry Security Standards Council (PCI SSC) was formed, and on 15 December 2004, these companies aligned their individual policies and released the Payment Card Industry Data Security Standard (PCI DSS).

In September 2006, the PCI standard was updated to version 1.1 to provide clarification and minor revisions to version 1.0.

Version 1.2 was released on October 1, 2008.[4] Version 1.1 "sunsetted" on December 31, 2008.[5] v1.2 did not change requirements, only enhanced clarity, improved flexibility, and addressed evolving risks/threats. In August 2009 the PCI SSC announced[6] the move from version 1.2 to version 1.2.1 for the purpose of making minor corrections designed to create more clarity and consistency among the standards and supporting documents.

Updates and supplemental information

The PCI SSC has released several supplemental pieces of information to clarify various requirements. These documents include the following

- Information Supplement: Requirement 11.3 Penetration Testing[7]
- Information Supplement: Requirement 6.6 Code Reviews and Application Firewalls Clarified[8]
- Navigating the PCI DSS - Understanding the Intent of the Requirements[9]
- Information Supplement: PCI DSS Wireless Guidelines[10]

Compliance versus Validation of compliance

Although PCI DSS must be implemented for all entites that process, store or transmit cardholder data, validation of PCI DSS compliance is not required for all entities. Currently both Visa and Mastercard are requiring only Merchants and Service Providers to be validated according to the PCI DSS standard. Issuing and acquring banks are not required to go through PCI DSS validation. (Although in the event of security breach - compromised bank/entity that is not PCI DSS certified (PCI DSS validated by the Qualified Security Assesor) will be subjected to additional Card Scheme penalties)

Compliance and wireless LANs

In July 2009, the Payment Card Industry Security Standards Council published wireless guidelines[10] for PCI DSS recommending the use of Wireless Intrusion Prevention System (WIPS) to automate wireless scanning for large organisations. Wireless guidelines clearly define how wireless security applies to PCI DSS 1.2 compliance.[11]

These guidelines apply to the deployment of Wireless LAN (WLAN) in cardholder data environments, also known as CDEs. A CDE is defined as a network environment that possesses or transmits credit card data.

Wireless LAN and CDE Classification

PCI DSS wireless guidelines classify CDEs into three scenarios depending on how wireless LANs are deployed.

- **No Known WLAN AP inside or outside the CDE**: The organisation has not deployed any WLAN AP. In this scenario, 3 minimum scanning requirements (Sections 11.1, 11.4 and 12.9) of the PCI DSS apply.
- **Known WLAN AP outside the CDE**: The organisation has deployed WLAN APs outside the CDE. These WLAN APs are segmented from the CDE by a firewall. There are no known WLAN APs inside the CDE. In this scenario, Three minimum scanning requirements (Sections 11.1, 11.4 and 12.9) of the PCI DSS apply.
- **Known WLAN AP inside the CDE**: The organisation has deployed WLAN APs inside the CDE. In this scenario, three minimum scanning requirements (Sections 11.1, 11.4 and 12.9), as well as six secure deployment requirements (Sections 2.1.1, 4.1.1, 9.1.3, 10.5.4, 10.6 and 12.3) of the PCI DSS apply.

Key sections of PCI DSS 1.2 that are relevant for wireless security are classified and defined below.

Secure Deployment Requirements for Wireless LANs

These secure deployment requirements apply to only those organisations that have a known WLAN AP inside the CDE. The purpose of these requirements is to deploy WLAN APs with proper safeguards.

- **Section 2.1.1 Change Defaults**: Change default passwords, SSIDs on wireless devices. Enable WPA or WPA2 security.
- **Section 4.1.1 802.11i Security**: Set up APs in WPA or WPA2 mode with 802.1X authentication and AES encryption. Use of WEP in CDE is not allowed after June 30, 2010.
- **Section 9.1.3 Physical Security**: Restrict physical access to known wireless devices.
- **Section 10.5.4 Wireless Logs**: Archive wireless access centrally using a WIPS for 1 year.
- **Section 10.6 Log Review**: Review wireless access logs daily.
- **Section 12.3 Usage Policies**: Develop usage policies to list all wireless devices regularly. Develop usage possible for the use of wireless devices.

Minimum Scanning Requirements for Wireless LANs

These minimum scanning requirements apply to all organisations regardless of the type of wireless LAN deployment in the CDE. The purpose of these requirements is to eliminate any rogue or unauthorized WLAN activity inside the CDE.

- **Section 11.1 Quarterly Wireless Scan**: Scan **all** sites with CDEs whether or not they have known WLAN APs in the CDE. Sampling of sites is not allowed. A WIPS is recommended for large organisations since it is not possible to manually scan or conduct a walk-around wireless security audit[12] of all sites on a quarterly basis
- **Section 11.4 Monitor Alerts**: Enable automatic WIPS alerts to instantly notify personnel of rogue devices and unauthorized wireless connections into the CDE.
- **Section 12.9 Eliminate Threats**: Prepare an **incident response plan** to monitor and respond to alerts from the WIPS. Enable automatic containment mechanism on WIPS to block rogues and unauthorized wireless connections.

Wireless Intrusion Prevention System (WIPS) Implementations

Wireless Intrusion Prevention Systems are a possible option for compliance with some PCI DSS requirements, and can be implemented in either an internally hosted or externally hosted Software as a Service(SaaS) model.[13] [14]

The hosted implementation is offered in an on-demand, subscription-based SaaS model.[15] Hosted implementations are said to be particularly cost-effective[16] for organisations looking to fulfill only the minimum scanning requirements for PCI DSS compliance (AirMinder [17]).

The network implementation is an on-site deployment of WIPS within a private network. Such a deployment is viable, but the significant costs have been thought to lead some companies to avoid WIPS deployments.[17]

PCI Compliance in Call Centers

While the PCI DSS standards are very explicit about the requirements for the back end storage and access of PII (personally identifiable information), the Payment Card Industry Security Standards Council has said very little about the collection of that information on the front end, whether through websites, Interactive Voice Response systems or call center agents. This is surprising, given the high threat potential for credit card fraud and data compromise that call centers pose.[18]

In a call center, customers read their credit card information, CVV codes, and expiration dates to call center agents. There are few controls which prevent the agent from skimming (credit card fraud) this information with a recording device or a computer or physical note pad. Moreover, almost all call centers deploy some kind of call recording software, which is capturing and storing all of this sensitive consumer data. These recordings are accessible by a host of call center personnel, are often unencrypted, and generally do not fall under the PCI DSS standards outlined here.[19] Home-based telephone agents pose an additional level of challenges, requiring the company to secure the channel from the home-based agent through the call center hub to the retailer applications.[20]

To address some of these concerns, on January 22, 2010 the Payment Card Industry Security Standards Council issued a revised FAQ about call center recordings.[21] The bottom line is that companies can no longer store digital recordings that include CVV information if those recordings can be queried.

Though the council has not yet issued any requirements, technology solutions can completely prevent skimming (credit card fraud) by agents. At the point in the transaction where the agent needs to collect the credit card information, the call can be transferred to an Interactive Voice Response system.[22] This protects the sensitive information, but can create an awkward customer interaction. Newer solutions allow the agent to "collect" the credit card information without ever seeing or hearing it. The agent remains on the phone and customers enter their credit card information directly into the Customer Relationship Management software using their phones. The DTMF tones are converted to monotones so the agent cannot recognize them and so that they cannot be recorded.[23] The benefits of increasing the security around the collection of personally identifiable information goes beyond credit card fraud to include helping merchants win chargebacks due to friendly fraud.[24]

Controversies and criticisms

It has been suggested by some IT security professionals that the PCI DSS does little more than provide a minimal baseline for security.

"The fact is you can be PCI-compliant and still be insecure. Look at online application vulnerabilities. They're arguably the fastest growing area of security, and for good reason — exposures in customer-facing applications pose a real danger of a security breach." - Greg Reber[25]

Additionally, Michael Jones, CIO of Michaels' Stores, testifying before a U.S. Congress subcommittee regarding the PCI DSS, says "(...the PCI DSS requirements...) are very expensive to implement, confusing to comply with, and ultimately subjective, both in their interpretation and in their enforcement. It is often stated that there are only twelve

"Requirements" for PCI compliance. In fact there are **over 220 sub-requirements**; some of which can place an *incredible burden on a retailer* and *many of which are subject to interpretation*."[26]

In contrast, others have suggested that PCI DSS is a step toward making all businesses pay more attention to IT security, even if minimum standards are not enough to completely eradicate security problems.

"*Regulation--SOX, HIPAA, GLBA, the credit-card industry's PCI, the various disclosure laws, the European Data Protection Act, whatever--has been the best stick the industry has found to beat companies over the head with. And it works. Regulation forces companies to take security more seriously, and sells more products and services.*" - Bruce Schneier[27]

Further, per PCI Council General Manager Bob Russo's response to the NRF: PCI is a structured "blend...[of] specificity and high-level concepts" that allows "stakeholders the opportunity and flexibility to work with Qualified Security Assessors (QSAs) to determine appropriate security controls within their environment that meet the intent of the PCI standards." [28]

Compliance and Compromises

Per Visa Chief Enterprise Risk Officer, Ellen Richey, "...no compromised entity has yet been found to be in compliance with PCI DSS at the time of a breach."[29] However, it has nevertheless become a common misconception that companies have had security breaches while also being PCI DSS compliant. Much of this confusion is a result of the 2008 Heartland Payment Processing Systems breach, wherein more than one hundred million card numbers were compromised.[30] Around this same time Hannaford Brothers[31] and TJX Companies were similarly breached as a result of the alleged very same source of coordinated efforts of Albert "Segvec" Gonzalez and two unnamed Russian hackers.[32]

Assessments examine the compliance of merchants and services providers with the PCI DSS at a specific point in time and frequently utilize a sampling methodology to allow compliance to be demonstrated through representative systems and processes. It is the responsibility of the merchant and service provider to achieve, demonstrate, and maintain their compliance at all times both throughout the annual validation/assessment cycle and across all systems and processes in their entirety.[33] Therefore, these frequently cited breaches and their pointed use as a tool for criticism even to the point of noting that Hannaford Brothers had, in fact, received its PCI DSS compliance validation one day after it had been made aware of a two-month long compromise of its internal systems;[34] fail to appropriately assign blame in their blasting of the standard itself as flawed as opposed to the more truthful breakdown in merchant and service provider compliance with the written standard, albeit in this case having not been identified by the assessor.

Other, more substantial, criticism lies in that compliance validation is required only for Level 1-3 merchants and may be optional for Level 4 depending on the card brand and acquirer. Visa's compliance validation details for merchants state that level 4 merchants compliance validation requirements are set by the acquirer,[35] Visa level 4 merchants are "Merchants processing less than 20,000 Visa e-commerce transactions annually and all other merchants processing up to 1 million Visa transactions annually". At the same time 80% of payment card compromises since 2005 affected Level 4 merchants.[36]

Compliance as a Snapshot

The state of being PCI DSS compliant might appear to have some temporal persistence, at least from a merchant point of view. In contrast, the PCI Standards Council General Manager Bob Russo has indicated that liabilities could change depending on the state of a given organisation at the point in time when an actual breach occurs.[37]

Costs

Similar to other industries, a secure state could be more costly to some organisations than accepting and managing the risk of confidentiality breaches. However, many studies have shown that this cost is justifiable.[38]

References

[1] Sidel, Robin (2007-09-22). "In Data Leaks, Culprits Often Are Mom, Pop" (http://online.wsj.com/article/SB119042666704635941. html?mod=sphere_ts). *The Wall Street Journal*. .

[2] http://grc360.net/cms/2010/pci-dss-ver-2-0-quick/

[3] PCI DSS - PCI Security Standards Council (https://www.pcisecuritystandards.org/security_standards/pci_dss.shtml)

[4] PCI SECURITY STANDARDS COUNCIL RELEASES VERSION 1.2 OF PCI DATA SECURITY STANDARD (https://www.pcisecuritystandards.org/pdfs/pr_080930_PCIDSSv1-2.pdf)

[5] Supporting Documents PCI DSS (https://www.pcisecuritystandards.org/security_standards/supporting_documents_home.shtml)

[6] https://www.pcisecuritystandards.org/pdfs/statement_090810_minor_corrections_to_standards.pdf

[7] Information Supplement: Requirement 11.3 Penetration Testing (https://www.pcisecuritystandards.org/documents/information_supplement_11.3.pdf)

[8] Information Supplement: Requirement 6.6 Code Reviews and Application Firewalls Clarified (https://www.pcisecuritystandards.org/pdfs/infosupp_6_6_applicationfirewalls_codereviews.pdf)

[9] Navigating the PCI DSS - Understanding the Intent of the Requirements (https://www.pcisecuritystandards.org/pdfs/pci_dss_saq_navigating_dss.pdf)

[10] "PCI DSS Wireless Guidelines" (https://www.pcisecuritystandards.org/pdfs/PCI_DSS_Wireless_Guidelines.pdf). . Retrieved 2009-07-16.

[11] "Don't Let Wireless Detour your PCI Compliance" (http://www.airtightnetworks.com/fileadmin/pdf/whitepaper/PCI_Wireless_Whitepaper.pdf). . Retrieved 2009-07-22.

[12] "Walk Around Wireless Security Audits – The End Is Near" (http://www.airtightnetworks.com/fileadmin/pdf/whitepaper/WP_WalkAroundWireless.pdf). . Retrieved 2009-07-22.

[13] "Webinar on Wireless Security as SaaS by Gartner Analyst John Pescatore" (http://www.airtightnetworks.com/fileadmin/content_images/news/webinars/SaaS/player.html). gartner.com. . Retrieved 2009-04-24.

[14] "Saas offerings for wireless pci compliance" (http://www.infosecurity-us.com/view/9661/comment-saas-offerings-for-wireless-pci-compliance/). . Retrieved 2010-05-25.

[15] "Security SaaS hits WLAN community" (http://www.networkworld.com/newsletters/wireless/2008/040708wireless1.html). networkworld.com. . Retrieved 2008-04-07.

[16] "New Low-Cost Wireless PCI Scanning Services; New Offerings Satisfy PCI DSS Requirements" (http://newsblaze.com/story/2009072205011500038.mwir/topstory.html). . Retrieved 2009-07-22.

[17] "Big-Time Wireless Security - As a Service" (http://www.networkworld.com/community/node/26755). networkworld.com. . Retrieved 2008-04-08.

[18] "Overseas credit card scam exposed" (http://news.bbc.co.uk/2/hi/uk_news/7953401.stm). *bbc.co.uk.com*. March 19, 2009. .

[19] "PCI Compliance in the Call Center a Headache for Many" (http://searchcrm.techtarget.com/news/2240031378/PCI-compliance-in-the-call-center-a-headache-for-many). searchcrm.com. . Retrieved 2011-01-28.

[20] "PCI Compliance: What it Means to the Call Center Industry" (http://callcenterinfo.tmcnet.com/analysis/articles/20732-pci-compliance-what-it-means-the-call-center.htm). tmcnet.com. . Retrieved 2008-02-13.

[21] "Call Center FAQ Significantly Changes" (http://pciguru.wordpress.com/2010/01/25/call-center-faq-significantly-changes/). pciguru. . Retrieved 2010-01-25.

[22] "Restructuring the Contact Center for PCI Compliance" (http://callcenterinfo.tmcnet.com/analysis/articles/45010-restructuring-contact-center-pci-compliance.htm). tmcnet.com. . Retrieved 2008-11-10.

[23] "PCI Compliance with CallGuard" (http://www.elitetele.com/PCI-Compliance/). elitetele.com. .

[24] Adsit, Dennis (February 21, 2011). "Error-proofing strategies for managing call center fraud" (http://www.isixsigma.com/index.php?option=com_k2&view=item&id=1854&Itemid=1&Itemid=1). *isixsigma.com*. .

[25] "PCI compliance falls short of assuring website security" (http://searchsoftwarequality.techtarget.com/news/column/0,294698,sid92_gci1335662,00.html). . Retrieved 2009-02-15.

[26] Jones, Michael (2009-03-31). "TESTIMONY OF MICHAEL JONES BEFORE THE EMERGING THREATS, CYBERSECURITY, AND SCIENCE AND TECHNOLOGY SUBCOMMITTEE" (http://www.homeland.house.gov/SiteDocuments/20090331142012-77196.pdf). Congress of the United States. . Retrieved 2010-07-19.

[27] "Bruce Schneier reflects on a decade of security trends" (http://searchsecurity.techtarget.com.au/contents/ 21998-Bruce-Schneier-reflects-on-a-decade-of-security-trends). . Retrieved 2009-02-15.

[28] Russo, Bob (2009-06-15). "Letter to NRF" (http://www.pcisecuritystandards.org/pdfs/statement090615_letter_to_nrf.pdf). PCI Council. . Retrieved 2010-10-19.

[29] Vijayan, Jaikumar (2009). "Visa: Post-breach criticism of PCI standard misplaced" (http://www.cso.com.au/article/296278/ visa_post-breach_criticism_pci_standard_misplaced). .

[30] "Heartland data breach sparks security concerns in payment industry" (http://www.computerworld.com/action/article. do?command=viewArticleBasic&articleId=9126608). .

[31] McGlasson, Linda (2008-04-04). "Hannaford Data Breach May Be Top of Iceberg" (http://www.bankinfosecurity.com/articles. php?art_id=810). BankInfo Security. . Retrieved 2009-01-28.

[32] Goodin, Dan (2009). "TJX suspect indicted in Heartland, Hannaford breaches" (http://www.theregister.co.uk/2009/08/17/ heartland_payment_suspect/). .

[33] Spier, Peter (2010-03-22). "The QSA's Perspective: PCI Compliance Risk Abounds" (http://blogs.bankinfosecurity.com/posts. php?postID=492). BankInfo Security. . Retrieved 2010-10-19.

[34] Vijayan, Jaikumar (2009-01-04). "PCI security standard gets ripped at House hearing" (http://www.computerworld.com/action/article. do?command=viewArticleBasic&articleId=9130901&intsrc=news_ts_head). Computerworld Security. . Retrieved 2009-05-04.

[35] Visa Merchant levels http://usa.visa.com/merchants/risk_management/cisp_merchants.html

[36] Pastor, Adrian (2009). "A Pentester's Guide to Credit Card Theft Techniques" (http://2009.confidence.org.pl/materialy/prezentacje/ adrian_pastor_confidence_2009.pdf). .

[37] "Q and A: Head of PCI council sees security standard as solid, despite breaches" (http://www.computerworld.com/action/article. do?command=viewArticleBasic&taxonomyName=Financial&articleId=9078059). . Retrieved 2009-02-15.

[38] "PCI Cost Analysis Report: A Justified Expense" (http://www.solidcore.com/assets/PCI_Cost_Analysis.pdf). Solidcore Systems. .

Books on PCI DSS

- "PCI DSS Handbook"(ISBN 9780470260463)
- "PCI DSS: A Practical Guide to Implementation" (ISBN 9781849280235)
- "PCI Compliance: Understand and Implement Effective PCI Data Security Standard Compliance" (ISBN 9781597494991)

Updates on PCI DSS v1.2

- Summary of Changes (https://www.pcisecuritystandards.org/pdfs/pci_dss_summary_of_changes_v1-2.pdf)
- Summary of Changes FAQ (https://www.pcisecuritystandards.org/pdfs/ pci_dss_summary_of_changes_faqs_v1-2.pdf)
- PCI DSS 1.2 Announcement, Oct. 1, 2008 (https://www.pcisecuritystandards.org/pdfs/ pr_080930_PCIDSSv1-2.pdf)

Updates on PCI DSS v2.0

- Summary of Changes (https://www.pcisecuritystandards.org/pdfs/summary_of_changes_highlights.pdf)
- PCI DSS 2.0 Announcement, Aug. 12, 2010 (https://www.pcisecuritystandards.org/pdfs/ pr_100810_summary_changes.pdf)

External links

- PCI DSS Standard (https://www.pcisecuritystandards.org/security_standards/pci_dss.shtml)
- PCI Quick Reference Guide (https://www.pcisecuritystandards.org/pdfs/pci_ssc_quick_guide.pdf)

GRCM

GRCM refers to the measures, mechanisms and processes in operation within an organisation with the objective of managing Governance, Risk Management and Compliance.

Governance, Risk & Compliance Management

Governance, Risk and Compliance Management (GRCM) represents an emerging management discipline in the cross-functional area of Governance, Risk Management, and Compliance (GRC).

References

IT GRCM Functions Defined [1]

Payment system

A **payment system** is a system for the transfer of money. What makes it a "system" is that it employs cash-substitutes; traditional payment systems are negotiable instruments such as drafts (e.g., checks), credit cards and other charge cards, documentary credit (such as L/C) and electronic funds transfers. Some payment systems include credit mechanisms, but that is essentially a different aspect of payment. Payment systems are used in lieu of tendering cash in domestic and international transactions and consist of a major service provided by banks and other financial institutions. In the US, they are regulated by different state statutes (UCC) and Federal regulations.

Additional forms of payment systems (including physical or electronic infrastructure and associated procedures and protocols) are used to settle financial transactions in automated teller machine networks, stored-value card networks, bond markets, currency markets, and futures, derivatives, or options markets, or to transfer funds between financial institutions. Due to the backing of modern fiat currencies with government bonds, payment systems are a core part of modern monetary systems.

The term **electronic payment** can refer narrowly to e-commerce - a payment for buying and selling goods or services offered through the Internet, or broadly to any type of electronic funds transfer.

1LINK

1LINK

Operating area	Pakistan
Members	31 banks
ATMs	3,400+ ATMs
Founded	1999

1LINK (Guarantee) Limited is a consortium of major banks that own and operate the largest representative shared financial services network in Pakistan.

The 1LINK brand has grown as their number of member banks increases.

1LINK (Guarantee) Limited is a registered company, incorporated under the company law by Security and Exchange Commission of Pakistan (SECP).

History

Formation OF 1LINK

- Year 1999: ABN AMRO and Askari Bank connected their ATM network to provide expanded services to their customers using technology from #REDIRECTTPS_Pakistan..
- Year 2002: SBP circular for the mandatory connectivity of either of the two switches.
- Year 2003: 1LINK formed with a consortium of eleven founder banks.
- Year 2005: 1LINK partnership with Visa International using technology from TPS_Pakistan..
- Year 2006: 1LINK launched Inter Bank Funds Transfer Service (IBFT)in collaboration with and using technology from TPS_Pakistan..
- Year 2007: 1LINK launched Utility Bill Payment Service (UBPS) in partnership with and using technology from TPS_Pakistan.

1LINK is owned by the consortium of eleven major banks of the country and operates through a chief executive officer. The company Board consists of eleven directors, one from each founder member bank.

Membership history

The number of 1LINK member banks has increased rapidly since the inception of the company in 2003.

1LINK is the largest banking consortium in Pakistan. It is one of the two ATM switches operational in the country (the other is MNET, hosted by MCB Bank Ltd). The State Bank of Pakistan has mandated that all commercial banks in Pakistan, both foreign and domestic, become members of one or the other switch. Additionally, the two switches have been interconnected since 2006, which means that a consumer holding an ATM or debit card issued by any bank in Pakistan may use any ATM located throughout the country.

- Year 2003: twelve member banks
- Year 2004: fifteen member banks
- Year 2005: seventeen member banks
- Year 2006: twenty-two member banks
- Year 2007: twenty-four member banks
- Year 2008: twenty-nine member banks
- Year 2009: thirty-one member banks

- Future: sixty-six member banks

Statistics

- Strength of thirty-one banks, including all Islamic banks of the country and two micro finance banks.
- Pakistan's largest ATM switch with 3,400+ ATMs in 200+ cities nationwide.
- Debit/credit card base exceeding 7.11 mMillion.
- Volume of PKR 14.2 billion (monthly average) of ATM withdrawal.
- Inter bank funds transfer among more than 3,000 branches of participating IBFT Banks nationwide.
- Monthly Rs. 388 million (approximately) transfer of funds among IBFT banks.

Services

1. Shared ATM network
2. Inter-bank funds transfer
3. Visa services
4. Utility Bill payment service
5. Credit card acquiring
6. Connectivity with other networks

External links

- 1link [1]
- TPS [2]

3V (payment solution)

For the courier company formerly known as 3V, visit TNT N.V.

3V is a payment solution in operation in Netherlands, Ireland, Canada and in the United Kingdom. The system was originally also in operation in Germany and Spain, but it was phased out in these countries in late 2009. It allows anybody over 16 years of age to purchase a "3V Voucher", effectively a Visa-branded debit card, for cash through a network of retailers. The value purchased can then be spent in any cardholder-not-present transaction until the end of the month following the month of issue.

To purchase a 3V voucher, it is first necessary to register online and receive an identification card in the mail. It was previously possible to pick up identification cards in retail outlets but regulatory considerations now prevent this.

Security

The 3V system is geared towards security and ensuring customer safety. Customers can purchase the amount required in 3V credit and use it in several transactions. They also have the same reversal and chargeback rights as regular credit card holders in case of fraudulent use or failure of retailers to fulfill orders, and even when money is lost this way it is limited to the amount of credit purchased originally.

To increase security, the card number is printed onto the voucher issued from the retailer's terminal, but the expiry date and CVV of the virtual card are sent separately, either by SMS or email to the purchaser.

External links

- 3V official page (Netherlands) [1]
- 3V official page (Ireland) [2]
- 3V official page (UK) [3]
- 3V official page (Germany) [4]
- 3V official page (Canada) [5]

Aadhar-enabled payment system

Aadhar-enabled payment system or **AEPS** is an Indian payment system developed by National Payments Corporation of India based on unique identification number, the AADHAR.[1] The system allows a person holding an Aadhar number to carry out financial trasaction on a Micro-ATM provided by the Banking correspondent.

History

AEPS was launched in March 2011. The pilot project is being run in districts of Jharkhand (where the first unique identity, or UID, numbers have been issued) in association with three banks, ICICI Bank , Union Bank of India and Bank of India.

The service

AEPS project is to make banking easier for poor people by involving business correspondents in rural and remote areas in India.

The four basic types of banking transactions that AEPS allows are balance enquiry, cash withdrawal, cash deposit and Aadhaar to Aadhaar funds transfer. All that a customer needs for availing of the AEPS services are an AADHAR number.

References

[1] http://articles.economictimes.indiatimes.com/2011-03-04/news/28657478_1_banking-services-financial-inclusion-icici-bank

External links

- AEPS on Aadhaar Wiki (http://uidnumber.org/aadhar/wiki/Aadhar-enabled_payment_system)
- AEPS expalined by The Economic Times (http://economictimes.indiatimes.com/news/news-by-industry/ banking/finance/banking/all-you-need-to-know-about-adhaar-enabled-payment-systems/articleshow/7870975. cms)

Acquirer

An **acquirer** (or acquiring bank) is a member of a card association, for example MasterCard and/or Visa, which maintains merchant relationships and receives all bankcard transactions from the merchant.

Acquirers charge the merchants fees which include: a monthly rent for the EFTPOS terminal (if it is not owned by the merchant) which is usually equivalent to around 10 to 30 USD monthly, a percentage fee on their transactions (which varies from country to country, for example in Poland it ranges from 1.8% to 2.5%, regardless of whether the card is debit or credit, in USA and many Western Europe countries the fee is often much lower for debit card transactions, than for those with credit cards), and sometimes--especially in the countries where fees for debit card transactions are much lower--an additional fixed fee per transaction, which ranges from 10 to 20 cents).

In the USA, Visa/MasterCard acquirers, and therefore merchants, usually pay much less for a transaction in which the magnetic stripe on the reverse of the card has been successfully swiped through the magnetic stripe reader found in a credit card terminal. This is due to the inclusion of the information encoded into the stripe, which includes anti-fraud features. The fees for card transactions that are hand-keyed into the keypad of a card terminal or computer keyboard are higher, since this security information is absent from the transaction data.

Debit transaction costs are usually just a flat rate (usually $.60 to $1.10 USD each) when the Personal Identitification Number (PIN) is entered by the cardholder. This type of transaction is referred to as "PIN debit." The merchant's terminal requires a PIN pad for this PIN entry. Often the PIN pad is a separate device connected to the terminal, other times the PIN pad is integrated in the machine.

When a debit card is swiped through the magnetic stripe reader of a credit card terminal, but the PIN is not entered, the acquirer usually charges a rate comparable to the swiped credit card rate or less. Since Visa/MC charges acquires less for non-PIN debit cards, many acquirers charge less to the merchant. Typical rates are usually around 1.3% to 1.9% for non-PIN debits (offline Debit rate) and often 1.6% to 1.9% for credit card swipes. This type of debit transactions is referred to as "signature debit."

When properly handled by the merchant, these swiped transactions will qualify for the lowest available Interchange program from the card associations. This indicates all of the required criteria have been satisfied by the transaction to "qualify" for that program rate. For this reason, they are often referred to as "Qualified" transactions.

"Rewards" cards from the Associations--cards that provide the cardholder some premium for its use, such as air miles--even when swiped, often fall into the more expensive "Mid-Qualified" or even the most expensive "Non-Qualified" category.

Handkeyed transactions usually have a much higher rate, often 2.3% to 2.8% for these transactions. Many processors will charge the lower rate on all transactions on their monthly merchant statements, then show the "add on" for the handkeyed and other more costly transactions. Often this 'add on' is 1-1.3%. These transactions are often referred to as Mid-Qualified.

The highest rate (Non-Qualified transactions) is for corporate cards, foreign cards, downgraded transactions (when the merchant does not meet all of the requirements), and higher-level Rewards-type cards. This Non-Qual rate is typically at least 3.0%, and sometimes as high as 5.0%

In a credit card transaction, the acquirer is the entity that receives an authorization request from its merchant accepting the card as a form of payment and forwards it through various "authorization networks" to the Issuing Bank ("Issuer"). The Issuer determines whether to approve or decline the sale, since they are the entity actually extending credit to its cardholder.

Examples

- Bank of America
- Chase Paymentech
- Elavon
- First Data
- First National Bank of Omaha
- Moneris Solutions
- Royal Bank of Scotland
- Streamline
- Wells Fargo
- Heartland Payment Systems
- PBS A/S

Acquiring bank

An **acquiring bank** (or **acquirer**) is the bank or financial institution that accepts credit and or debit card payments for products or services on behalf of a merchant. The term **acquirer** indicates that the bank accepts or acquires transactions performed using a credit card issued by all banks within the card association scheme. The best known (credit) card Association schemes are Visa, MasterCard, American Express, Diners Club, JCB and China UnionPay.

Merchant Accounts

The acquiring bank contract with the merchant is informally referred to as a **merchant account**. The arrangement is in fact a line of credit and not a bank account. Under the contract, the acquiring bank exchanges funds with issuing banks on behalf of the merchant, and pays the merchant for the net balance of their daily payment card activity: gross sales, minus reversals, interchange fees, and acquirer fees.

Interchange fees are fixed rates set by the card association, varying by merchant industry. Acquirer fees are an additional markup added to association fees by the acquiring bank, varying at the acquirer's discretion.

Acquirer Risk

The acquiring bank accepts the risk that the merchant will remain solvent over time, and thus has an incentive to take a keen interest in the merchant's products and business practices. Crucial to maintaining an ongoing positive balance is the limiting of reversals of funds. Consumers may trigger the reversal of funds in three ways:

- A card refund is the return of funds to the consumer, voluntarily initiated by the merchant.
- A card reversal is where the merchant cancels a transaction after it has been authorized, but before settlement (as if the transaction has never taken place).
- A card charge back is a dispute between the merchant and the card holder over the validity of the transaction. The card holder requests the return of funds to the consumer through the issuing bank for a number of reasons including: goods not received, goods not as advertised or faulty or when the card holder denies all knowledge of the transaction..

Card associations consider a participating merchant to be a risk if more than 1% of payments received result in a charge back. Visa and MasterCard levy fines against acquiring banks that retain merchants with high chargeback frequency. To defray the cost of any fines received, the acquiring banks are inclined (but not required) to pass such fines on to the merchant.

Due to the high amount of risk acquiring banks are subject to, as well as their key position in the payment chain, the security of electronic payments is a great concern for these institutions. For this reason they have been involved in the development of electronic point-of-sale security standards, such as PCI-DSS and the emerging SPVA standards.[1]

References

[1] *Terminal Rivals Cooperate on Plan for Card Data Security* (http://www.digitaltransactions.net/newsstory.cfm?newsid=2189), Digital Transactions, 2009,

Adyen

Adyen

Adyen	
Enterprise Payment Services	
Type	Private
Founded	2006
Headquarters	[1] Amsterdam, The Netherlands
Services	Payment Service Provider
Website	adyen.com [2]

Adyen is a Payment Service Provider (PSP) offering outsourced payment and fraud control services for the mid-corporate to enterprise market. Its services include payment processing, payment routing, real-time fraud control and full reconciliation.

Credit card payments are processed on Interchange Plus basis, where the merchant can see for every transaction the exact cost price (interchange fee) attracted from the credit card networks.

Used by Offers website Groupon UK (My City Deals), so may appear on your credit card statement.

Allstar (fuel card)

Allstar, is a brand British fuel card, owned by **Arval UK Limited** a part of BNP Paribas. It permits fleet operators (mainly Company car and vans and some HGV's) to fuel securely without having to carry cash or general credit cards, and provides the necessary accounting information to satisfy the details of recording Value Added Tax payments for the purpose of reclaiming tax from HM Revenue and Customs.

Unlike many fuel cards, the Allstar card does not offer a commercial/discounted rate for fuel bought using it – instead the purchaser pays the price displayed at the fuelling station, but is perceived as having a commercial advantage over many other brands because it is usable at the great majority (95%+) of UK fuelling stations, which may outweigh cost issues in the opinion of company transport managers.

Due to this extensive network coverage, the Allstar card is historically associated with large fleets and particularly those with smaller vehicles, but over the part few years this has spread to fleets of all sizes and vehicle types. This is generally because the management reporting and product restrictions allow for full control over fuel expenditure.

External links

- Arval.co.uk [1]

Alternative payments

Alternative Payments refers to payment methods that are used as an alternative to credit card payments. Most alternative payment methods address a domestic economy or have been specifically developed for electronic commerce and the payment systems are generally supported and operated by local banks. Each alternative payment method has its own unique application and settlement process, language and currency support, and is subject to domestic rules and regulations.

Types

The most common alternative payment methods are debit cards, charge cards, prepaid cards, direct debit, bank transfers, phone and mobile payments, checks, money orders and cash payments.

A debit card (also known as a bank card or check card) is a plastic card that provides an alternative payment method to cash when making purchases. A charge card is a plastic card that provides an alternative payment to cash when making purchases in which the issuer and the cardholder enter into an agreement that the debt incurred on the charge account will be paid in full and by due date. Debit and charge cards are used and accepted in many countries and can be used at a point of sale location or online.

Prepaid or Stored-value card provide payment through a monetary value held on the actual card or on deposit in an account. One major difference between stored-value cards and prepaid cards is that prepaid cards are usually issued in the name of the individual account holders, while stored value cards are usually anonymous. In the United States, prepaid and stored-value cards typically can be processed on the credit card network, but this is not the case for all cards, especially those outside of the United States.

A direct debit or direct withdrawal is an instruction that a bank account holder gives to his or her bank to collect an amount directly from another account. It is similar to a direct deposit but initiated by the beneficiary. Direct debit is available in several countries including the United Kingdom, Germany, Austria and the Netherlands. It is scheduled to be available across the whole Single European Payments Area by the end of 2010. In the United States, where checks are more popular than bank transfers, a similar service is available through the Automated Clearing House network.

A bank transfer (also known as a wire transfer or credit transfer) is a method of transferring money from one person or institution (entity) to another. A wire transfer can be made from one bank account to another bank account or through a transfer of cash at a cash office. Bank wire transfers is often the most expedient method for transferring funds between bank accounts. The transfer messages are sent via a secure system (such as SWIFT or Fedwire) utilizing IBAN and BIC codes. Online bank transfer systems in Europe are popular alternative payment methods, where the bank transfer is authorized by the consumer who logs onto his bank website and authorizes the funds transfer for payment to a merchant.

A giro transfer is a bank transfer payment, whereby order is given by the payer to his or her bank, which transfers funds into the payee's bank account; the receiving bank then notifies the payee. Giro is often used by post offices as well. The term is little used in the United States, although an ACH Transfer or direct deposit is the US electronic version of the giro transfer.

Online Banking ePayments (OBeP) are similar to giro transfers, but are designed specifically for use with online commerce. With OBeP, during the online checkout process, the merchant redirects the consumer to their financial institution's online banking site where they login and authorize charges. After charges are authorized, the financial institution redirects the consumer back to the merchant site. All network communications are protected using industry standard encryption. Additionally, communications with the OBeP network take place on a virtual private network, not over the public Internet. OBeP systems protect consumer personal information by not requiring the disclosure of account numbers or other sensitive personal data to online merchants or other third parties[1].

Electronic bill payment is a feature of online banking, similar in its effect to a bank transfer, allowing a depositor to send money from his demand account to a creditor or vendor such as a public utility or a department store to be credited against a specific account. The payment is optimally executed electronically in real-time, though some financial institutions or payment services will wait until the next business day to send out the payment. The bank can usually also generate and mail a paper check or banker's draft to a creditor who is not set up to receive electronic payments.

With phone payments, consumers are billed via their regular telephone number, whereby the charges are added to their phone bill. Premium-rate telephone numbers or 900 numbers are telephone numbers for telephone calls during which certain services are provided, and for which prices higher than normal are charged.

Mobile payments is a new and rapidly-adopting alternative payment method – especially in Asia and Europe. Instead of paying with cash, check or credit cards, a consumer can use a mobile phone to pay for wide range of services and goods. The charges are then added to their phone bill.

A check or cheque is a negotiable instrument instructing a financial institution to pay a specific amount of a specific currency from a specified demand account held in the maker/depositor's name with that institution. Both the maker and payee may be natural persons or legal entities.

An electronic check, often referred to as ACH or eCheck, allows United States and Canadian customers to make payments instantly using their checking accounts. Instead of a physical check, the payer provides the name, amount, routing and account number, and the transaction is then electronically processed and the funds are withdrawn from the checking account.

Electronic money refers to money which is exchanged only electronically. Typically, this involves the use of computer networks, the internet and digital stored value systems. Electronic Funds Transfer (EFT) and direct deposit are all examples of electronic money.

Money orders, postal money orders, certified checks, cashier's checks and traveler's checks are all alternative payment types that are used in commerce in place of cash.

Usage

The number of Alternative Payments has grown exponentially in the last few years due to the need for billing solutions on the Internet. Limited credit card penetration and customary local payment habits, combined with tight credit and security fears to use credit cards for online payments has increased the usage of Alternative Payments on a worldwide level.

Alternative payments are offered by domestic banks and payment processors that offer merchants a variety of billing solutions. Most Alternative Payments have online applications and are integrated into electronic shopping carts used by online merchants.

Several billing solutions have been devised specifically for web-based merchants to accept alternative payments online and to support and access distant markets. Alternative payments are used throughout North America, Europe and Asia, and have penetration levels of sixty percent or more in various countries. Language, currency and support, including trust and familiarity, often contribute to the success of a domestic alternative payment solution.

Debit cards and charge cards are accepted worldwide as alternative payment and in some cases, debit cards are designed exclusively for use on the Internet, and there is no physical card only a virtual card. Certain systems also require the use of a PIN when a debit is used for online purchases.

European online direct debit solutions are particularly popular due to the lower use of credit cards in Europe as compared to other countries like the United States. Transactions can be approved in real-time and funds in 1 to 3 business days. Chargebacks remain a risk inherently when debiting a consumer's bank account, however, using additional verification systems reduces the risk significantly and many payment processors maintain an extensive fraud database that mitigates the risks.

Using bank transfers to accept payments does not carry any inherent risk to the merchant, which makes it particularly attractive to both high and low risk merchants seeking to reduce chargebacks. The drawback to this approach from a merchant's perspective are that re-billing cannot be made automatic and billing does not occur quickly, as their customers must manually transfer the funds.

Electronic checks allow funds to be withdrawn directly from the consumer's account. Recurring payments can be setup and the consumer's personal information can be verified instantly. Merchants that opt to accept electronic checks enjoy convenient processing that reaches a large number of consumers that do not own credit cards or do not wish to use credit cards to make payments. Electronic checks are known to have long clearing times of up to 5 business days and carry an inherent risk of chargebacks. Checks that have been verified may come back after the clearing time as "insufficient funds," meaning that the consumer does not have sufficient funds in their account to pay the balance of the transaction.

Phone payments describe a system of allowing consumers to purchase products or services using their phone number. In most cases, the charge is verified via phone or SMS messaging before the transaction is approved. The resulting charge is then added to the customer's phone bill.

Phone billing is accepted in many countries and offers a flexible way for merchants to accept payment, especially online, where the risk of fraud is elevated. While convenient for the consumer, phone billing has several inherent issues for merchants. Payment processors that support phone billing typically charge a higher rate because the payments must go through an additional party, the phone provider, before reaching the merchant. The clearing time on funds is also exceptionally high because the funds are not collected until the consumer pays their phone bill.

Merchant advantages

Alternative Payments have increasingly become more popular with merchants, as more options means more sales, and because nearly all Alternative Payments offer a variety of service specific features that addresses a global online marketplace. Geolocation software, automatic language translations, instant currency exchange and worldwide support are generally included to allow foreign buyers to make use of their domestic payment solution, while shopping outside of their country at a foreign based web merchant.

Unlike traditional credit card transactions, many alternative payments often provide additional security features that protect the merchant from fraud and returned transactions, because the funds availability is verified and payment is made directly from a bank account. The banks guarantee the funds and because there are no chargebacks, merchants are often not required to provide collateral or keep a reserve. Furthermore, accounts are validated in real-time and fraud modules scrub transactions, similar to the approval process with credit cards.

Consumer advantages

Alternative Payments have, in many areas, become the dominant form of online payment for consumers. Alternative payments gives consumers more options to pay and allows them to select payment methods that they are comfortable with. Language, domestic applications and familiarity with the payment method, coupled with the trust they place in their own bank, increases usage. Furthermore, consumers may simply elect to use alternative payment methods due to security concerns with credit card purchases. Many alternative payments often require additional security steps, such as a username, password or PIN to further protect the consumer.

References

- www.2000Charge.com

[1] FIS News Release. March 18, 2008. (http://fis.mediaroom.com/index.php?s=43&item=352)

American Express

WARNING: Article could not be rendered - ouputting plain text.

Potential causes of the problem are: (a) a bug in the pdf-writer software (b) problematic Mediawiki markup (c) table is too wide

American Express CoTypes of business entityTypePublic companyPublicTicker symbolTraded asNew York Stock ExchangeNYSE: AXPDow Jones Industrial AverageDow Jones Industrial Average ComponentS&P 500S&P 500 ComponentIndustryBankingFinancial servicesFounded 1850Founder(s)Henry WellsWilliam FargoJohn Warren ButterfieldHeadquartersNew York City, New York, United StatesU.S.Area served WorldwideKey peopleKenneth Chenault(Chairman & Chief executive officerCEO) "Top Management Compensation". . Retrieved 30 Aug. 2010.ProductsFinancial servicesFinancialTravelTravel servicesInsuranceRevenue United States dollarUS$ 25.612 billion (2010) "2010 Form 10-K, American Express Company". United States Securities and Exchange Commission. .Earnings before interest and taxesOperating income US$ 5.964 billion (2010)Net income US$ 4.057 billion (2010)AssetTotal assets US$ 147.042 billion (2010)Equity (finance)Total equity US$ 16.203 billion (2010)Employees 61,000 (2010)Website AmericanExpress.comAmerican Express Company (New York Stock ExchangeNYSE: AXP), sometimes known as AmEx, is a Diversification (finance)diversified global financial services company headquartered in New York City. Founded in 1850, it is one of the 30 components of the Dow Jones Industrial Average. The company is best known for its credit card, charge card, and traveler's cheque businesses. Amex cards account for approximately 24% of the total dollar volume of credit card transactions in the US, the highest of any card issuer.by $ value. Amex presentation to investors at the Keefe, Bruyette & Woods 2009 Diversified Financials Conference. June 3, 2009 "American Express to slash 7000 jobs". Bloomberg. Sydney Morning Herald. October 31, 2008. . Retrieved 9 August 2009.BusinessWeek and Interbrand ranked American Express as the 22nd most valuable brand in the world, estimating the brand to be worth United States dollarUS$14.97 billion. Interbrand.com Fortune (magazine)Fortune listed Amex as one of the top 20 Most Admired Companies in the World. "World's Most Admired Companies 2011". Fortune (magazine)Fortune. . Retrieved 21 March 2011.The company's mascot, adopted in 1958, is a Roman gladiator Companylogos.ws whose image appears on the company's travelers' cheques and charge cards. Early historyAmerican Express Co. shipping receipt, New York, NY to St. Louis, MissouriSt. Louis, MO (August 6, 1853)American Express was started as an express mail business in Albany, New York, in 1850.Cuyler Reynolds (1906). Albany Chronicles. p. 603. . Retrieved 2009-01-18. It was founded as a joint stock corporation by the merger of the express companies owned by Henry Wells (Wells & Company), William Fargo (Livingston, Fargo & Company), and John Warren Butterfield (Wells, Butterfield & Company, the successor earlier in 1850 of Butterfield, Wasson & Company).Peter Z. Grossman. American Express: The Unofficial History of the People Who Built the Great Financial Empire. New York: Crown Publishers, 1987. (reprint: Beard Books 2006; ISBN 1-58798-282-8; Chapter 2.)Noel M. Loomis, Wells Fargo. New York: Clarkson N. Potter, Inc., 1968 The same founders also started Wells Fargo & Co. in 1852 when Butterfield and other directors objected to the proposal that American Express extend its operations to California. American Express first established its headquarters in a building at the intersection of Jay Street and Hudson Street (Manhattan)Hudson

Street in what was later called the TriBeCa section of Manhattan. For years it enjoyed a virtual monopoly on the movement of express shipments (goods, securities, currency, etc.) throughout New York State. In 1874, American Express moved its headquarters to 65 Broadway in what was becoming the Financial District, ManhattanFinancial District of Manhattan, a location it was to retain through two buildings.Kenneth T. Jackson. The Encyclopedia of New York City. The New York Historical Society: Yale University Press, 1995. P. 23.American Express buildings In 1854, the American Express Co. purchased a lot on Vesey Street in New York City as the site for its stables. The company's first New York headquarters were in an impressive marble Italianate palazzo at 55-61 Hudson Street (Manhattan)Hudson Street between Thomas Street and Jay Street (1857–58, John Warren Ritch), which had a busy freight depot on the ground story with a spur line from the Hudson River Railroad. A stable was constructed nearby at 4-8 Hubert Street, between Hudson Street and Collister Street (1866–67, Ritch & Griffiths), five blocks north of the Hudson Street building. The company prospered sufficiently that headquarters were moved in 1874 from the wholesale shipping district to the budding Financial District, and into rented offices in two five-story brownstone commercial buildings at 63 and 65 Broadway, between Exchange Alley (NYC)Exchange Alley and Rector Street, and between Broadway (New York City)Broadway and Trinity Place that were owned by the Harmony family.New York City Landmarks Preservation Commission; December 12, 1995, Designation List 269; LP-1932In 1880, American Express built a new warehouse behind the Broadway Building at 46 Trinity Place, between Exchange Alley and Rector Street. The designer is unknown, but it has a façade of brick arches that are redolent of pre-skyscraper New York. American Express has long been out of this building, but it still bears a terracotta seal with the American Express Eagle.White, Norval & Willensky, Elliot; American Institute of ArchitectsAIA Guide to New York City, 4th Edition; New York Chapter, American Institute of Architects; Crown Publishers/Random House. 2000. ISBN 0-8129-31069-8; ISBN 0-8129-3107-6. p.23. In 1890-91 the company constructed a new ten-story building by Edward H. Kendall on the site of its former headquarters on Hudson Street (Manhattan)Hudson Street. By 1903, the company had assets of some $28 million, second only to the CitibankNational City Bank of New York among financial institutions in the city. To reflect this, the company purchased the Broadway buildings and site. At the end of the Wells-Fargo reign in 1914, an aggressive new president, George Chadbourne Taylor (1868–1923), who had worked his way up through the company over the previous thirty years, decided to build a new headquarters. The old buildings, dubbed by the New York Times as "among the ancient landmarks" of lower Broadway, were inadequate for such a rapidly expanding concern. In March 1914, Renwick, Aspinwall & Tucker filed for the construction of a 32-story concrete-and steel-framed Skyscraperoffice tower in which all of the company's operations, then in four separate buildings, were to be consolidated. The building proposal of 1914 was abandoned, probably due to the war in Europe, but was resurrected two years later in a reduced form, at an estimated cost of $1 million.65 Broadway The 21-story (plus basement), Neoclassicismneo-classical, 65 BroadwayAmerican Express Co. Building, was constructed in 1916-17 to the design of James L. Aspinwall, of the firm of Renwick, Aspinwall & Tucker, the successor to the architectural practice of the eminent James Renwick, Jr.. The building consolidated the two lots of the former buildings with a single address: 65 Broadway. This building was part of the "Express Row" section of lower Broadway at the time. The concrete-and-steel-framed building has an H-shaped plan with tall slender wings arranged around central light courts, a type of plan employed from the 1880s through the 1910s to provide offices with maximum light and air. Faced in white brick and terra cotta above a granite base, both facades employ the tripartite composition of base-shaft-capital then popular for the articulation of skyscrapers, with a colonnaded base and upper portion. The famous American Express Eagle adorns the building twice: there is an asymmetric eagle on the lower arch, while a symmetric eagle adorns the arch atop the building. The Broadway entrance features a double-story Corinthian colonnade with large arched windows. The building completed the continuous masonry wall of its block-front poda nae and assisted in transforming Broadway into the "canyon" of neo-classical masonry office towers familiar to this dayWhite, Norval & Willensky, Elliot; American Institute of ArchitectsAIA Guide to New York City, 4th Edition; New York Chapter, American Institute of Architects; Crown Publishers/Random House. 2000. ISBN 0-8129-31069-8; ISBN 0-8129-3107-6. p.22.American Express sold this building in 1975, but retained travel services here. The building was also the headquarters over the years of other prominent firms, including investment bankers J. & W. Seligman & Co. (1940–74), the American Bureau of Shipping, a maritime concern (1977–86), and currently J.J. Kenny, and Standard & Poor's, who has renamed the building for itselfNationwide expansion American Express extended its reach nationwide by arranging affiliations with other express companies (including Wells Fargo – the replacement for the two former companies that merged to form American Express), railroads, and steamship companies.Financial services In 1882, American Express started its expansion in the area of financial services by launching a money order business to compete with the United States Post Office's money orders. Sometime between 1888 and 1890, J. C. Fargo took a trip to Europe and returned frustrated and infuriated. Despite the fact that he was president of American Express and that he carried with him traditional letter of creditletters of credit, he found it difficult to obtain cash anywhere except in major cities. Fargo went to Marcellus Flemming Berry and asked him to create a better solution than the traditional letter of credit. Berry introduced the American Express traveler's chequeTraveler's Cheque which was launched in 1891 in denominations of $10, $20, $50, and $100. Host With The Most, Time (magazine)Time Magazine, 9 April 1956 issueTraveler's cheques established American Express as a truly international company. In 1914, at the outbreak of World War I, American Express offices in Europe were among the few companies to honor the letters of credit (issued by various banks) held by Americans in Europe, despite other financial institutions having refused to assist these stranded travelers. Loss of railroad express business American Express became one of the monopolies that Theodore RooseveltPresident Theodore Roosevelt had the Interstate Commerce Commission investigate during his administration. The interest of the ICC was drawn to its strict control of the railroad express business. However, the solution did not come immediately to hand. The solution to this problem came as a coincidence to other problems during World War I. During the winter of 1917, the US suffered a severe coal shortage and on December 26 President of the United StatesPresident Woodrow Wilson commandeered the railroads on behalf of the US government to move United States armed forcesUS troops, their supplies, and coal. United States Secretary of the TreasuryTreasury Secretary William Gibbs McAdoo was assigned the task of consolidating the railway lines for the war effort. All contracts between express companies and railroads were nullified and McAdoo proposed that all existing express companies be consolidated into a single company to serve the country's needs. This ended American Express's express business, and removed them from the ICC's radar. The result was that a new company called the Railway Express AgencyAmerican Railway Express Agency formed in July 1918. The new entity took custody of all the pooled equipment and property of existing express companies (the largest share of which, 40%, came from American Express, who had owned the rights to the express business over 71280 miles (km) of railroad lines, and had 10,000 offices, with over 30,000 employees). Recent history Current CEO Kenneth Chenault took over leadership of American Express in 2001 from Harvey Golub, CEO from 1993 to 2001. Prior to that, the company was headed by James D. Robinson III from 1977 to 1993. Charge card servicesAmerican Express Tower (tallest, left) in New York City American Express executives discussed the possibility of launching a travel charge card as early as 1946, but it was not until Diners Club launched their card in March 1950 that American Express began to seriously consider the possibility. At the end of 1957, American Express CEO Ralph Reed (American Express)Ralph Reed decided to get into the card business, and by the launch date of October 1, 1958 public interest had become so significant that they issued 250,000 cards prior to the official launch date. The card was launched with an annual fee of $6, $1 higher than Diners Club, to be seen as a premium product. The first cards were paper, with the account number and cardmember's name typed. It was not until 1959 that American Express began issuing embossed ISO/IEC 7810 plastic cards, an industry first. In 1966, American Express introduced the Gold Card and in 1984 the Platinum Card, clearly defining different market segments within its own business, a practice that has proliferated across a broad array of industries. The Platinum Card was billed as super-exclusive and had a $250 annual fee (it is currently $450). It was offered by invitation only to American Express customers with at least 2 years of tenure, significant spending, and excellent payment history; it is now open to applications on request. In 1987, American Express introduced the Optima card, their first credit card product. Previously, all American Express cards had to be paid in full each month, but Optima allowed customers to carry a balance (the charge cards also now allow extended payment options on qualifying charges based on credit availability). Although American Express no longer accepts applications for the Optima brand of cards, since July 13, 2009, Optima cards are still listed on the American Express website, as a reference to existing members only. According to American Express, Optima accounts were not converted or closed. However, Blue from American Express has prevailed as the replacement for the original Optima style of credit card. Blue includes multiple benefits free of charge, unlike Optima, including the Membership Rewards program. In April 1992, American Express spun off its subsidiary, First Data Corp., in an IPO. Then, in October 1996, the company distributed the remaining majority of its holdings in First Data Corp., reducing its ownership to less than 5%. In 1994, the Optima True Grace card was introduced. The card was unique in that it offered a grace period on all purchases whether a balance was carried on the card or not (as opposed to traditional revolving credit cards which charge interest on new purchases if so much as $1 was carried over). The card was discontinued a few years later; the now discontinued One from American Express card offered a similar feature called "Interest Protection....." "Boston Fee Party" From early 1980s until the early 1990s, American Express was known for cutting its Interchange feemerchant fees (also known as a "discount rate") to merchants and restaurants if they accepted only American Express and no other credit or charge cards. This prompted competitors such as Visa and MasterCard to cry foul for a while as the tactics "locked" restaurants into American Express. However, in 1991, several restaurants in Boston started accepting and encouraging the use of Visa and MasterCard because of their far lower fees as compared to American Express' fees at the time (which were about 4% for each transaction versus around 1.2% at the time for Visa and MasterCard). A few even stopped accepting American Express credit and charge cards. The revolt, known as the "Boston Fee Party" in reference to the Boston Tea Party, quickly spread nationwide to over 250 restaurants across the United States, including restaurants in other cities such as New York City, Chicago, and Los Angeles. In response, American Express decided to reduce its discount rate gradually to compete more effectively and add new merchants to its network such as supermarkets and drugstores. Many elements of the exclusive acceptance program were also phased out so American Express could effectively encourage businesses to add American Express cards to their existing list of payment options. Currently, American Express' average US merchant rate is about 2.89%, while the average Discover, Mastercard, and Visa U.S. merchant rate is about 2% (Visa/MasterCard signature debit cards are at 1.7%.) Some merchant sectors, such as quick-service restaurants including McDonald's, have special reduced rates to accommodate business needs and profit margins. Cable TV American Express formed a joint venture with Warner Communications in 1979 called Warner-Amex Satellite Entertainment, which created MTV, Nickelodeon (TV channel)Nickelodeon, Star Plus, Aaj Tak, Sony, Max, IBN-7, Star News and The Movie Channel. The partnership only lasted until 1984. The properties were sold to Viacom (1971–2005)Viacom soon after. Conversion to bank holding company On November 10, 2008, during the financial crisis of 2007–2010financial crisis of 2008, the company won Federal Reserve System approval to convert to a bank holding company, making it eligible for government help under the Troubled Asset Relief Program.Lanman, Scott; Ari Levy (2008-11-10). "American Express Gets Fed Approval to Convert to Bank". Bloomberg.com. . Retrieved 2008-11-10. At that time, American Express had total consolidated assets of about $127 billion. In June 2009, $3.39 billion in TARP funds were repaid plus $74.4 million in dividend payments, and in July 2009 they ended their obligations under TARP by buying back $340 million in Treasury warrants. "AmEx Gets Out of TARP ; Pays $340M for Warrants". wallstreetpit.com. 2009-07-29. . Retrieved 2009-08-21. "AmEx gets out of TARP". CNN. 2009-07-29. . Retrieved 2009-08-21.Controversy in the UKIn November 2010 the UK division of American Express was cautioned by the Office of Fair Trading for the use of controversial 'charging orders' against those in debt. "OFT Warns Credit Card Providers Off 'Charging Orders'". choose.net. 2010-11-10. . The regulator said that the company was one of four companies who were encouraging customers to turn their unsecured credit card debts into a form of secured debt. Loyalty acquisitionIn March 2011, American Express completed a $685m purchase of Loyalty Partner, which operates the Payback loyalty program in Germany and Poland, and the i-Mint loyalty program in India. "American Express completes acquisition of Loyalty Partner". Colloquy. 3 March 2011. . Retrieved 7 March 2011.Business modelTypical credit card business model When a consumer makes a purchase using a credit or charge card, a small portion of the price is paid as a fee (known as the merchant discount), with the merchant keeping the remainder. There are typically three parties who split this fee amongst themselves: Acquiring bank: the bank which processes credit card transactions for a merchant, including crediting the merchant accountmerchant's account for the value charged to a credit card less all fees.Issuing bank: the bank which issues the consumer's credit card. This is the bank a consumer is responsible for repaying after making a credit card purchase. The issuer's share of the merchant discount is known as the interchange fee.Network: the link between acquiring banks and issuing banks. These banks have relationships with a network, rather than with each other, for fulfilling card purchases. This allows a card issued by a community bank in Peru to be used at a shop in Sri Lanka, for instance, without requiring the banks to have a direct relationship with each other. The two largest networks in the world are Visa Inc.Visa and MasterCard.The average merchant discount in the United States is 1.9%. Of this, approximately 0.1% goes to the acquirer, 1.7% to the issuer, and 0.09% to the network.Eichenbaum, Peter (17 June 2009). "Visa Clashes With Wal-Mart on $48 Billion Card Fee". Bloomberg L.P.. . Retrieved 9 August 2009.Most Prime and Superprime card issuers use the majority of their interchange revenue to fund loyalty programs like frequent-flyer programfrequent flyer points and cash back, and hence their profit from card spending is small relative to the interest they earn from card lending. How American Express differs American Express typically plays the role of all three parties above, keeping the entire merchant discount. In recent years Amex has begun authorizing other banks to either acquire or issue on Amex's behalf, primarily in countries where Amex would otherwise have little or no presence. Amex also has historically charged a higher merchant discount than Visa or MasterCard. The size of the premium can differ significantly: in the US, Amex charges 66 basis points more (2.56% vs 1.9%) than rivals Visa and MasterCard,TraderMark (19 June 2009). "Duopoly Visa and MasterCard Vs. Retailers - Who Wins in a Free Market?". . Retrieved 9 August 2009. while in Australia Amex charges more than twice as much as Visa or MasterCard due to Interchange fee#Interchange fee in AustraliaAustralian interchange regulations. Amex uses this higher discount revenue to invest in rewards programs that provide a higher payout than competing programs. These more substantial rewards programs, in addition to a premium brand and a reputation for superior customer service, allows Amex to attract a disproportionate share of affluent consumers. Amex then uses its strength with affluent consumers to justify charging a higher merchant discount rate, implying that if a merchant does not accept Amex cards he will lose affluent customers. This business model creates a self-reinforcing loop.Due to what Amex calls its "spend-centric strategy", card spending and fees are responsible for 70% of Amex's card profit, vs. 10-40% for other issuers. Amex also tends to make more money from annual fees than other issuers do.One tension in Amex's business model is acceptance, a quantityvolume vs. Profit marginmargin trade-off. Because Amex charges a higher merchant discount fee, it is not as widely accepted as Visa or MasterCard. Amex's business model depends on having a higher discount fee, however, making it difficult to lower it. The company has to strike a balance, keeping its fee low enough to attract sufficient merchants, but high enough to fund rich rewards and drive its business model. In countries where Amex charges a small premium, like the US, it has near-parity acceptance, but its card rewards are not significantly more substantial than those of its competitors. In countries where it charges a large premium, its cards often have a much higher rewards payout than competing cards.McLennan, Leah (23 April 2009). "The Best Cards to Earn Qantas Frequent Flyer Points". The Sydney Morning Herald. . Retrieved 9 August 2009.Many banks fund their lending, both card and otherwise, through deposit accountdeposits. Without deposits, however, Amex has historically funded its lending through outstanding travelers cheques (which function like non-interest-bearing deposits), the wholesale fundingwholesale funding markets, and securitization. As travelers cheques have declined in popularity since the rise of Automated teller machineATMs,Wade, Betsy (27 August 2000). "Practical Traveler". The New York Times. . Retrieved 9 August 2009. Amex has begun seeking traditional deposits through online yield (finance)high-yield savings accounts.Henry. "American Express Savings Account". Interest Savings Accounts. . Retrieved 2009-10-27. The freeze in wholesale funding markets and securitization during the financial crisis of 2007–2010 caused Amex to accelerate these deposit-raising efforts, and also caused them to decrease growth in lending. Due to its focus on affluent customers, Amex has historically had lower levels of credit losses than other issuers. The gap has almost disappeared for Q3'08 to Q1'09, however, as card issuers of all types experienced heightened credit losses.Card productsConsumer cards American Express is best known for its iconic Green, Gold, and Platinum charge cards, and offers credit cards of similar color levels in most countries. In 1999, American

Express introduced the Centurion Card, often referred to as the "black card," which caters to an even more affluent and elite customer segment. The card was initially only available to select users of the Platinum card. The annual fee for the card is $2,500 (up from $1,000 at introduction) with an additional one-time initiation fee of $5,000. In addition to a variety of exclusive benefits, the card itself is made of titanium. American Express created the card line amid rumors and urban legends in the 1980s that it produced an ultra-exclusive black card for elite users who could purchase anything with it. "Black American Express Card". Snopes.com. 2006-12-06. . Retrieved 2010-12-11.American Express cards range between no annual fee (for Blue and many other consumer and business cards) and a $450 annual fee (for the Platinum card). Annual fees for the Green card start at $95 (first year free), while Gold card annual fees start at $125. American Express has several co-branded credit cards, with most falling into one of two categories: Airlines and hotels: e.g. Delta Air Lines, Virgin Atlantic, British Airways, Singapore Airlines, Qantas, JetBlue Airways, Starwood Hotels & Resorts Worldwide, Hilton Hotels, Air France... and others Retailers: e.g. Costco, David Jones LimitedDavid Jones, Holt Renfrew, Harrods, Macys, Bloomingdales and others Their card aimed at young adults is called Blue from American Express. A television media campaign for Blue adopted the 1979 UK Synthpop hit "Cars (song)Cars" by Gary Numan as its Theme musictheme song. Based on a successful product for the European market, Blue had no annual fee, a Loyalty programrewards program, and a multi-functional onboard smart chip. A Credit card cashbackcashback version, "Blue Cash", quickly followed. Amex also targeted young adults with City Reward Cards that earn INSIDE Rewards points to eat, drink, and play at New York, Chicago and LA hot spots. American Express began phasing out the INSIDE cards in mid-2008, with no new applications being taken as of July 2008. In 2005, American Express introduced ExpressPay, similar to MasterCard#PayPassMasterCard PayPass. It is based on a wireless RFID payment method that requires a card to simply be waved in front of a special reader and not swiped. This technology replaced the smart chip on the Blue card. Many U.S. merchant and restaurant partners including 7-Eleven, CVS/pharmacy, McDonald's, Regal Entertainment Group, and Ritz Camera Centers, now offer ExpressPay at most or all of their locations. In 2005, American Express introduced Clear, advertised as the first credit card with no fees of any kind. Also in 2005, American Express introduced One, a credit card with a "Savings Accelerator Plan" that contributes 1% of eligible purchases into an High-Yield Savings accountSavings Account insured by the Federal Deposit Insurance Corporation. Other cards introduced in 2005 included "The Knot" and "The Nest" Credit Cards from American Express, co-branded cards developed with the wedding planning website theknot.com. In 2006, the UK division of American Express joined the Product Red coalition and began to issue a American Express RedRed Card. With each card member purchase the company contributes to good causes through The Global Fund to Fight AIDS, Tuberculosis and Malaria to help African women and children suffering from HIV/AIDS, malaria, and other diseases. In 2009, American Express introduced the ZYNC charge card. White in color, this card was created for people in their 20s and 30s. The card is currently in open beta testing and anyone can apply for it. Small business services (also known as American Express OPEN) American Express offers various types of charge cards for small businesses to manage their expenses, and the company is also the largest provider of corporate cards. In late 2007, the company announced the new Plum Card as the latest addition to their card line for small business owners. The card provides a 1.5% early pay discount or up to two months to defer payment on purchases. The 1.5% discount is available for billing periods where the cardmember spends at least $5,000. The first 10,000 cards were issued to members on December 16, 2007. Official Plum Card WebsiteIn 2008, American Express made a decision to close all Business Line of Credit accounts. This decision was reached in tandem with the Federal Reserve's approval of American Express's request to become a Commercial bankCommercial Bank. Commercial cards and services American Express also offers a comprehensive range of cards designed to support mid-size and large business manage their travel and day-to-day operational expenses. The core product, the American Express Corporate Card is offered in over 40 countries, and a number of complementary products for specific types of spend are offered for special needs. Examples of these products include the Corporate Meeting Card, the Corporate Purchasing Card, and the Business Travel Account. Commercial Cards differ from Business Cards as they enable company liability (business cards are issued as extensions of credit to the company's owner). In addition, Commercial Cards offer a comprehensive suite of data and reporting solutions that help clients gain Spend visibilityvisibility and control over employee spend. As part of supporting Corporate clients, American Express offers a number of online solutions delivered through the American Express @ Work website. From American Express @ Work, clients have access to program management capabilities, online statements, reporting and data integration products. Information @ Work, a reporting tool targeted at mid-size companies to give them quick and easy access to their employees' spend data; Customized Reporting is provided to larger clients who require more advanced analytics and data consolidation capabilities. American Express also provides data files to clients to power expense reporting and reconciliation tools. In 2008, American Express acquired the Corporate Payment Services business of GE, which primarily focused on providing Purchasing Card solutions for large global clients. As part of the $1b+ transaction, American Express also added a new product, called V-Payment, to its product portfolio. V-Payment is unique in that it enables a tightly controlled, single-use card number for increased control. In December 2010, the Commercial Card division launched American Express Business4Business - a network of business-centric products and services. Initially launched with telecommunications solutions, the organization also launched commercial insurance and foreign exchange payment products in March of 2011. Non-proprietary cards In December 2000, American Express agreed to acquire the credit card portfolio of Bank of Hawaii, then a division of Pacific Century Financial Corp. In January 2006, American Express sold its Bank of Hawaii card portfolio to Bank of America (MBNA). Bank of America will issue Visa Inc.Visa and American Express cards under the Bank of Hawaii name. Until 2004, Visa and MasterCard rules prohibited issuers of their cards from issuing American Express cards in the United States. This meant, as a practical matter, that U.S. banks could not issue American Express cards. These rules were struck down as a result of antitrust litigation brought by the United States Department of JusticeU.S. Department of Justice, and are no longer in effect. In January 2004, American Express reached a deal to have its cards issued by a U.S. bank, MBNA America. Initially decried by MasterCard executives as nothing but an "experiment", these cards were released in October 2004. Some said that the relationship was going to be threatened by MBNA's merger with Bank of America, a major Visa issuer and original developer of Visa. However, an agreement was reached between American Express and Bank of America on December 21, 2005. Under the terms of the agreement, Bank of America will own the customer loans and American Express will process the transactions. Also, American Express will dismiss Bank of America from its antitrust litigation against Visa, MasterCard, and a number of U.S. banks. Finally, both Bank of America and American Express also said an existing card-issuing partnership between MBNA and American Express will continue after the Bank of America-MBNA merger. The first card from the partnership, the no-annual-fee Bank of America Rewards American Express card, was released on June 30, 2006. Since then, Citibank, GE Money, and USAA have also started issuing American Express cards. Citibank currently issues several American Express cards including an American Airlines AAdvantage co-branded card. In early 2006 GE and Amex partnered in offering Dillard's Amex card Amex issued Dillard's American Express card in joint cooperation with GE Money, however, in Mar 2008 Amex purchased GE's credit card business GE sold its card unit to Amex for $1.1bn in cash only deal. HSBC Bank USA is currently testing both HSBC-branded and Neiman Marcus co-branded American Express rewards credit cards, with a full rollout scheduled for late 2007 or early 2008. Also, UBS launched its Resource Card program for US Wealth managementWealth Management clients issuing Visa Signature credit cards and American Express charge cards linked to their customers accounts and employing a single rewards program for the two cards. Fidelity operates a similar program, issuing both American Express and Visa Signature cards through FIA Card Services. Fidelity.comNon-card productsTraveler's cheques Amex is the largest provider of traveler's cheques in the world. In 2005, American Express released the American Express Travelers Cheque Card, a stored-value card that serves the same purposes as a traveler's cheque, but can be used in stores like a credit card. The card has since been discontinued as of October 31, 2007, due to "changing market conditions". All cardholders were issued refund checks for the remaining balances. Shearson/American ExpressShearson/American Express logo c. 1982During the 1980s, American Express embarked on its dream to become a financial services supercompany. In mid-1981 it purchased Sanford I. Weill's Shearson Loeb Rhoades, the second largest securities firm in the United States to form Shearson/American Express. Shearson Loeb Rhoades, itself was the culmination of several mergers in the 1970s as

Weill's Hayden, Stone & Co. merged with Shearson, Hammill & Co. in 1974 to form Shearson Hayden Stone. Shearson Hayden Stone then merged with Loeb, Rhoades, Hornblower & Co. (formerly Loeb, Rhoades & Co. to form Shearson Loeb Rhoades in 1979. With capital totalling $250 million at the time of its acquisition, Shearson Loeb Rhoades trailed only Merrill Lynch as the securities stock brokerbrokerage industry's largest firm. After its acquisition by American Express, the firm was renamed Shearson/American Express. In 1984 Shearson/American Express purchased the 90-year old Investors Diversified Services, bringing with it a fleet of financial advisors and investment products. Also in 1984, American Express acquired the investment banking and trading firm, Lehman BrothersLehman Brothers Kuhn Loeb, and added it to the Shearson family, creating Shearson Lehman/American Express. In 1988, the Firm acquired E. F. Hutton & Co., forming Shearson Lehman Hutton until 1990, when the Firm's name became Shearson Lehman Brothers. When Harvey Golub took the reins in 1993 he negotiated the sale of Shearson's retail brokerage and Investment managementasset management business to Primerica and in following year, spun off of the remaining investment banking and institutional businesses as Lehman BrothersLehman Brothers Holdings Inc. The following is an illustration of American Express' consolidation of the brokerage and investment banking industries in the 1980s and early 1990s through the creation of Shearson Lehman Brothers, later Shearson Lehman Hutton (this is not a comprehensive list):"Salomon Smith Barney" from Gambee, Robert. Wall Street. W. W. Norton & Company, 1999. p.73Smith Barney Shearson(1993, sold to Primerica. Later Smith Barney, today known as Morgan Stanley Smith Barney)Lehman BrothersLehman Brothers(1994, spun-off; 2008, bankrupt - see Bankruptcy of Lehman Brothers)Shearson Lehman Hutton(merged 1988)Shearson Lehman Brothers(merged 1984)Shearson/American Express Swallowing Hutton in 1,200 Bites. New York Times, January 10, 1988(merged 1981)American Express(est. 1850)Shearson Loeb Rhoades(acquired 1981)Shearson Hayden Stone(merged 1973)Hayden, Stone & Co.Hayden Stone, Inc. (formerly CBWL-Hayden Stone, merged 1970)Cogan, Berlind, Weill & Levitt(formerly Carter, Berlind, Potoma & Weill, est. 1960)Hayden, Stone & Co.Shearson, Hammill & Co.(est. 1902)Loeb, Rhoades, Hornblower & Co.(merged 1978)Loeb, Rhoades & Co.(merged 1937)Carl M. Loeb & Co.(est. 1931)Rhoades & Company(est. 1905)Hornblower, Weeks, Noyes & Trask(merged 1953–1977)Hornblower & Weeks(est. 1888) Hemphill, Noyes & Co.(est. 1919, acq. 1963)Spencer Trask & Co.(est. 1866 as Trask & Brown) Paul H. Davis & Co.(est. 1920, acq. 1953) Robinson Humphrey Co. (acq. 1982) Foster & Marshall (acq. 1982) Balcor Co. (acq. 1982) Chiles, Heider & Co. (acq. 1983) Davis, Skaggs & Co. (acq. 1983) Columbia Group (acq. 1984)Financo (founded 1971, acq. 1985) L. Messel & Co. (acq. 1986)Lehman Brothers Kuhn Loeb(merged 1977)Lehman Brothers(est. 1850)Kuhn, Loeb & Co.(est. 1867) Abraham & Co.(est. 1938, acq. 1975)E. F. Hutton & Co.(est. 1904)Financial Advisors On 30 September 2005, American Express spun off its American Express Financial Advisors unit as a publicly traded company, Ameriprise FinancialAmeriprise Financial, Inc.. Due to this, American Express revenues for 2005 are down around $5 billion, however, like-for-like they are up 10.5% in 2005. Also, on September 30, 2005, RSM McGladrey acquired American Express Tax & Business Services (TBS). On 18 September 2007, it was announced that Standard Chartered Bank agreed to acquire American Express Bank Ltd, a commercial bank, from American Express Co, for an estimated $1.1 billion, through a friendly divestiture process. The transaction is currently subject to regulatory approvals. Lehman Brothers had advised American Express in this deal. Travel American Express established a Travel Division in 1915 that tied together all of the earlier efforts at making travel easier, and soon established its first travel agencytravel agencies. In the 1930s, the Travel Division had grown widely. Albert K. Dawson was instrumental in expanding business operations overseas, even investing in tourist relations with the Soviet Union. Dawson during World War I had been a photographer and film correspondent with the German army. Today the focus of The Travel Division is on business customers and business travel. Publishing Amex publishes the Travel + Leisure, Food & Wine (magazine)Food & Wine, Executive Travel magazineExecutive Travel, and Departures MagazineDepartures magazines. Advertising In 1975, David Ogilvy (businessman)David Ogilvy of Ogilvy & Mather developed the highly successful Don't Leave Home Without Them Advertising campaignad campaign for American Express Traveler's Cheques, featuring Oscar-award-winning actor Karl Malden. Karl Malden served as the public face of American Express Travelers Cheques for 25 years. In the UK the spokesman was instead the

Celebritytelevision personality Alan Whicker.After Karl Malden's departure and as the card was promoted over the traveller's cheques, American Express continued to use celebrities, such as Mel Blanc and ballerina Cynthia Gregory. A typical ad for the American Express Card began with a celebrity asking viewers: "Do you know me?" Although he/she gave hints to his/her identity, the star's name was never mentioned except as imprinted on an American Express Card, after which announcer Peter Thomas (television narrator)Peter Thomas told viewers how to apply for it. Each ad concluded with the celebrity reminding viewers: "Don't Leave Home Without It." The "Don't Leave Home Without It" slogan was revived in 2005 for the prepaid American Express Travelers Cheque Card. These slogans have been parodyparodied numerous times: The long-running PBS children's TV series Sesame Street parodied the "Do you know me?/Don't Leave Home Without It" ad campaigns with three skits involving a Muppet character holding a AdultGrown-Up Friend's hand while crossing the street. One skit featured Forgetful Jones (performed by Richard Hunt (puppeteer)Richard Hunt) with Olivia (Alaina Reed Hall) as his Grown-Up Friend, a second featured Bert (Sesame Street)Bert and Ernie (Frank Oz and Jim Henson respectively) with Gordon (Roscoe Orman) as their Grown-Up Friend, and the third featured Big Bird (Caroll Spinney) with Bob (Bob McGrath) as his Grown-Up Friend. All three skits ended with their names being embossed at the bottom of a card looking like an American Express card that had a big human left hand in the middle with the words "Grown-Up Friend's Hand" above it, and a voiceover saying "A Grown-Up Friend's Hand. Don't cross the street without it."Another parody was seen on an episode of the CBS game show Press Your Luck, when the animated "Whammy Character" would give the "Do you know me?" tag line, followed by the display of an AmEx card-parody, which then had "WHAMMY" typed in on the bottom line of the card.In a campaign speech during the United States presidential election, 19841984 Election, Ronald ReaganPresident Ronald Reagan said "If the big spenders get their way, they'll charge everything to your taxpayer's express card, and believe me, they never leave home without it." On the 1997 film Hercules (1997 film)Hercules during the song "Zero to Hero", the credit card is "Grecian Express".The 1989 movie Major League (film)Major League also parodied the campaign. In one scene, in which every player is dressed in a tuxedo, the Cleveland Indians tell viewers of the film why every player carries the American Express Card with much of the explanation done one line at a time by players Jake Taylor (Tom Berenger), Eddie Harris (Chelcie Ross), Rick "Wild Thing" Vaughn (Charlie Sheen), Pedro Cerrano (Dennis Haysbert), and Roger Dorn (Corbin Bernsen), and Manager Lou Brown (James Gammon). The scene ends with Willie "Mays" Hayes (a tuxedo-clad Wesley Snipes) sliding into Baseball fieldhome plate in front of the rest of the team, holding up his card and saying to the viewers: "The American Express Card. Don't steal home without it."In Batman and Robin (film)Batman & Robin Batman pulls out a Bat-Credit card and says he never leaves the cave without it. The Adventures of Seinfeld & Superman American Express continues to use celebrities in their ads. Some notable examples include a late 1990s ad campaign with comedian Jerry Seinfeld, including the two 2004 webisodes in a series entitled "The Adventures of Seinfeld & Superman." In late 2004, American Express launched the "My life. My card." brand campaign (also by Ogilvy & Mather) featuring famous American Express cardmembers talking about their life. The ads have featured actors Kate Winslet, Robert De Niro, Ken Watanabe and Tina Fey, Duke University basketball coach Mike Krzyzewski, fashion designer Collette Dinnigan, comedian and talk show hostess Ellen DeGeneres, golfer Tiger Woods, professional snowboarder Shaun White, tennis pros Venus Williams and Andy Roddick, Real Madrid manager José Mourinho, and film directors Martin Scorsese, Wes Anderson, M. Night Shyamalan and most recently singer Beyoncé Knowles. In 2007, a two-minute black-and-white ad entitled "Animals" starring Ellen DeGeneres won the Emmy Award for Outstanding Commercial. Many American Express credit card ads feature a sample American Express Card with the name "C F Frost" on the front. This is not a fabricated name, as Charles F. Frost was an advertising executive from Ogilvy & Mather. StraightDope.comIn addition, American Express was one of the earliest users of cause marketing, to great success. A 1983 promotion advertised that for each purchase made with an American Express Card, American Express would contribute one penny to the renovation of the Statue of Liberty. The campaign generated contributions of $1.7 million to the Statue of Liberty restoration project. What would soon capture the attention of marketing departments of major corporations was that the promotion generated approximately a 28% increase in American Express card usage by consumers. Building on its earlier promotion,

American Express later conducted a four-year Charge Against Hunger program, which generated approximately $22 million for a charity addressing poverty and hunger relief. In 2006, as part of Bono's Product Red, American Express launched the American Express RedAmerican Express Red Card with campaign starred by supermodel Gisele Bündchen. The card, currently available only in United Kingdomthe United Kingdom, makes a donation to fight AIDS with every purchase made using the card. In May 2007, American Express launched an initiative called the "membersproject" American Express Rewards. Cardholders were invited to submit ideas for projects and American Express is funding the winning (provide clean drinking water) project $2 million. WorkplaceOfficesTwo Rescue and recovery effort after the September 11 attacksrescue workers entering the American Express Tower following September 11 attacksSeptember 11 terrorist attack on World Trade Center.Amex House in Brighton, England, was built in 1977.American Express Travel Services Office, Spanish Steps in Rome ItalyIn April 1986 American Express moved its headquarters to the 51-story Three World Financial Center in New York City. After the events of September 11, 2001, American Express had to leave its headquarters temporarily as it was located directly opposite to the World Trade Center and was damaged during the fall of the towers. The company began gradually moving back into its rehabilitated building in 2002. The company also has major offices in Fort Lauderdale, FL; Salt Lake City, UT; Greensboro, North CarolinaGreensboro, NC and Phoenix, ArizonaPhoenix, AZ. It has a technology center in Weston, FL. The main data center is located in Phoenix, ArizonaPhoenix. AMEX Bank of Canada was founded in 1853 in Toronto, however it currently has its headquarters of 3,000 employees in Markham, Ontario (a northern suburb of Toronto), as well as an office in Hamilton, Ontario. The company began operations as a bank on 1 July 1990 following an order-in-council made by the Brian Mulroney government on 21 November 1988. This decision was not without controversy as federal banking policy at the time would not ordinarily have permitted American Express to operate as a bank.Newman, Peter C. (July 30, 1990). "The brash new kid on the block. (American Express Co. opens Amex Bank of Canada amid controversy)" (column). Maclean's, July 30, 1990 v103 n31 p33(1) It is also a member of the Canadian Bankers Association (CBA) and is a registered member of the Canada Deposit Insurance Corporation (CDIC), a federal agency insuring deposits at all of Canada's chartered banks. American Express has several offices in the United KingdomUK, including a 9-story European Service Center, known as Amex House, in the Carlton Hill, BrightonCarlton Hill area of Brighton, England. It is a large white tower block, built in 1977Collis, Rose (2010). The New Encyclopaedia of Brighton. (based on the original by Tim Carder) (1st ed.). Brighton: Brighton & Hove Libraries. p. 9. ISBN 978-0-9564664-0-2. and surrounded by several other smaller offices around the city. Amex House deals with card servicing, sales, fraud and merchant servicing. The official Europe, Middle East, and Africa HQ is located in the Belgravia district of Westminster, in central London, at Belgrave House on Buckingham Palace Road, SW1; other UK offices are based in Sussex at Burgess Hill. In November 2009, Brighton and Hove City Council granted planning permission for American Express to redevelop the Amex House site. It is anticipated, in line with the Council's plan for the Edward Street Quarter, that the existing Amex House will be demolished by 2016. More information on this development is available at edwardstreet.co.uk. Edwardstreet.co.ukThe Japan, Asia-Pacific, and Australian Headquarters is co-located in Singapore, at Collyer Quay16 Collyer Quay, and in SydneySydney's King Street Wharf area, with the new state-of-the-art building receiving greenhouse status due to the environmentally friendly workspace that it provides. The headquarters of the Latin America and Caribbean division is in Miami. American Express also has a significant presence in India. Its two centres are located at Gurgaon, Haryana and one at Mathura Road, New Delhi. The Indian operations of American Express revolves around the back office customer services operations apart from the credit card business for the domestic Indian Economy. Job satisfactionFor 2008, American Express was named the 62nd best company to work for in the United States by Fortune (magazine)Fortune, ranking it number one for bank card companies. money.cnn.com, accessed 9 October 2008 In October 2008, Amex Canada Inc. was named one of Greater Toronto's Top Employers by Mediacorp Canada Inc., which was announced by the Toronto Star newspaper. "Reasons for Selection, 2009 Greater Toronto's Top Employers Competition". .American Express was named one of the 100 Best Companies for Working Mothers living in the United States in 2006 and 2007 by U.S.-based Working Mothers magazine.Management and corporate governance Key executives include: American Express Investor Relations, accessed 31 May 2010Kenneth Chenault: Chairman and Chief Executive Officer Daniel T. Henry : Executive Vice President and Chief Financial Officer Business Wire: American Express Company Names Daniel T. Henry as Executive Vice President and Chief Financial Officer Edward Gilligan: Vice Chairman L. Kevin Cox: Executive Vice President - Human Resources and Quality Ashwini Gupta: Chief Risk Officer, President - Risk, Information Management & Banking Group John D. Hayes: Executive Vice President Global Advertising & brand managementBrand Management, and Chief Marketing Officer Judson C. Linville: President and Chief Executive Officer - Consumer Services Louise Parent: Executive Vice President and General Counsel Thomas Schick: Executive Vice President - Corporate and External Affairs Steve Squeri: Group President - Global Services and Chief Information Officer Douglas E. Buckminster: President - International Consumer and Small Business Services William H. Glenn: President - Global Merchant Services Current members of the board of directors of American Express are: American Express 2007 Annual Report, accessed 30 October 2008Daniel AkersonDaniel F. Akerson: Managing Director of the Carlyle GroupCharlene Barshefsky: Former United States Office of the United States Trade RepresentativeTrade RepresentativeUrsula BurnsUrsula M. Burns: President of Xerox CorporationKenneth I. Chenault: Chairman and CEO of American Express Co. Peter Chernin: President and Chief operating officerCOO, News CorporationVernon E. Jordan, Jr.: Senior Managing Director with LazardLazard Freres & Co. LLCJan Leschly: CEO of Care Capital LLC Richard C. Levin: President, Yale UniversityRichard A. McGinn: Former CEO of Lucent Technologies, PartnershipPartner, RRE VenturesEdward D. Miller: Former President and CEO of AXA SA Frank PopoffFrank P. Popoff: Former Chairman Chemical Financial Corp. Steven S. Reinemund: Former Chairman and CEO, PepsiCo Inc. Robert D. Walter: Chairman and CEO, Cardinal HealthRonald A. Williams: Chairman and CEO, Aetna Inc. Sponsorship On 22 June 2010, it was revealed that American Express would sponsor Football in EnglandEnglish Association footballfootball (soccer) team Brighton & Hove Albion F.C.Brighton & Hove Albion's new stadium at Falmer StadiumFalmer. Commercially, the stadium will be known as The American Express Community Stadium. "Brighton reveal sponsorship deal for new stadium". British Broadcasting Corporation. 2010-06-22. . Retrieved 2010-06-24.ReferencesExternal links Official website Who Accepts American Express in the UK? American Express Business4Business American Express facts and Benefits

Antedated cheque

In banking, **antedated** refers to cheques which have been written by the maker, and dated at some point in the past. In the United States antedated cheques are described in the Uniform Commercial Code's Article 3, Section 113.

References

- 3 UCC 113 from the Cornell Law Center's online version of the Uniform Commercial Code [1]

Argentum album

Argentum album (Latin for "white money" or "silver coin"), mentioned in Domesday, signifies bullion, or silver uncoined. In those ancient days, such passed as money from one to another in payment.

Sumitur pro ipso hoc metallo pensili non signato. Spelm.

References

- ℗ *This article incorporates content from the 1728 Cyclopaedia, a publication in the public domain.* [1]

AS 2805

AS 2805 *Electronic funds transfer - Requirements for interfaces* is the Australian standard for financial messaging. It is near-exclusively used in Australia for the operation of card-based financial transactions among banks, Automatic Teller Machines and EFTPOS devices.

It is closely related to ISO 8583, but pre-dates it by two years (1985 vs 1987).

External links

- AS 2805 at SAI Global [1] (the distributor for Standards Australia).

ATM usage fees

ATM usage fees are the fees many banks and interbank networks charge for the use of their Automated Teller Machines (ATMs). In some cases, these fees are assessed solely for non-members of the bank; in other cases, they apply to all users. Many people oppose these fees because ATMs are actually less costly for banks than withdrawals from human tellers.

Two types of consumer charges exist: the surcharge and the foreign fee. The surcharge fee may be imposed by the ATM owner (the *deployer* or Independent sales organization) and will be charged to the consumer using the machine. The foreign fee or transaction fee is a fee charged by the card issuer (financial institution, stored value provider) to the consumer for conducting a transaction outside of their network of machines in the case of a financial institution.

Australia

On 3 March 2009 Direct Charging (surcharging) on Australia's ATM networks was introduced. The Reserve Bank of Australia says this reform will result in benefits to competition and efficiency in the Australian ATM system. .[1]

Most banks, (Commonwealth Bank(CBA), ANZ and Westpac/St.George) levy a $2 "ATM service fee" for withdrawals and balance inquiries at their ATMs by non-customers, NAB charges $1.50 (50c for an enquiry), Suncorp $2.20 (80c for an enquiry).

Suncorp and BankWest sponsored independent deployers are charging fees from $2, at these early stages $2.20 and $2.50 are not uncommon in pubs and clubs.

Bendigo Bank charges its customers $1.00 to use another bank's ATM. Bank of Queensland, BankWest,[2] CBA, Suncorp and Westpac/St.George do not charge any fee to use another bank's ATM.

ING's Orange Everyday reinburses the ATM fee when a withdrawal of $200AUD or more or if a person gets $200 or more cash out via EFTPOS ING will pay you a 50 cent bonus each time.

Brazil

In Brazil, banks such as Bradesco, Banco do Brasil, Caixa Econômica Federal, Itaú and Santander operate their own nationwide ATM networks. These ATMs can be found in many locations such as the bank branch itself, kiosks spread throughout a city or even supermarkets, gas stations, shopping malls and post offices, making it very convenient for the customer to make withdrawals and check balances without incurring any fees. There are also no denial fees (i.e. when trying to withdrawal more money than what's available in your account) as Brazilian businesses cannot charge for services not rendered. However, fees are assessed if there is excessive usage of the ATMs (i.e. one makes more withdrawals than what's allowed by their monthly maintenance fee). Fees and limits can be checked at the FEBRABAN (the Brazilian Banking Federation) website [3].

Third-party networks

Brazilian banks have several partnerships in place in order to extend their coverage.

Correspondente bancário (Banking agent)

A partnership with store owners, who then use a small wireless ATM (much like a wireless EFT POS) to process transactions for the bank, such as deposits, payments and withdrawals. Use of a banking agent normally does not generate any fees.

Interbank network

Brazil does not have a national interbank network, but ATMs from some banks are connected to other banks' networks. These are usually indicated in the ATM itself. Use of an interbank network does generate fees.

Cash withdrawal with a Visa debit card

Brazilian acquirer Cielo (also known as VisaNet) offers Visa debit card holders an option to withdrawal a small amount of cash (up to R$ 100, approx. US$ 58) when paying for merchandise at any Visa-accepting store. Store owners then hand over the money to the customer at the checkout. While the purchase itself generate fees for the business (like any other credit or debit card transaction), the money withdrawal does not, and is reimbursed in full.

Third-party networks

There are third-party ATM networks such as Banco24Horas that charge fees for use. However, some banks (such as Citibank) will reimburse fees for its customers.

Canada

A short description of the fee structure one experiences while using Canadian ATMs can be found at the Interac website.[3]

Before the presence of White Label ATMs, most Canadian customers were only charged the standard Interac Network Transaction Fee when a customer was using an ATM not provided by the bank that held their account (historically $0.75 CAD, now $1.50 CAD). As the Interac network was opened up to more Independent sales organizations ("ISO")s and the potential for additional revenue from Service Fees were made available, most banks elected to impose the Service Fee in addition to the revenue that was generated from the Interac fee.[4]

Neutral Consumer Information

The Government of Canada maintains a chart of the fees typically charged for use of ATMs in Canada.[5]

European Union

Rules are being introduced that will force banks to levy equal fees for customers of all banks in the European Union. This may mean national fees become higher. See Single Euro Payments Area.

These rules apply since 1 July 2002.[6] Eurozone and Swedish[7] customers are exempt from getting lower international fees outside Eurozone countries, because only fees for euro withdrawals are regulated. Non-Eurozone customers (except Swedish customers) are completely exempt from getting lower international fees, because the regulation only states that international euro withdrawals should be available at the same price as national euro withdrawals (and euro withdrawals are very uncommon in non-Eurozone customers' home countries).

Austria

Cash withdrawals are free for any owner of an Austrian Maestro card.

Finland

Cash withdrawals are free for any owner of a Finnish bank card or Visa Electron cards on ATM brand "Otto." which is the largest ATM network in Finland. There are smaller rivals which have fees. "Otto." ATMs accept also Visa, MasterCard, American Express and Diners Club credit cards. They also belong to Maestro, Cirrus and PLUS networks.[8] Fees depend on card issuer.

Germany

German banks charge fees for withdrawals at another bank's ATM. Usual fees are 4-5 EUR. All ATMs are connected to the national Girocard interbank network. The ATM owners do usually join one of the ATM groups that mutually lower or waive fees, so that customers can withdraw free of charge. The most extensive network of ATMs belongs to the savings banks associations ("Sparkassen") with 24,600 ATMS. Most of the private banks are either member of the Cash Group (7,000 ATMs owned by the major banks) or Cash Pool (2,500 ATMs owned by smaller banks) - they are usually found in city centers. The credit unions ("Volksbanken" and "Raiffeisenbanken") provide around 18,000 ATMs, very often in smaller towns and villages, but less frequently available in the big cities.

Sparkasse Charges pdf [10] (in German)

Commerzbank Charges pdf 1 [11] (in German)

Commerzbank Charges pdf 2 [12] (in German)

Ireland

The Central Bank of Ireland forbids all ATM usage fees.

Netherlands

Cash withdrawals are usually free for an owner of a Dutch debit card, both within The Netherlands and in other places of the European Union. Cash withdrawals from another bank in The Netherlands is limited to a maximum of once a day and a lower limit per transaction. The one transaction per day limit generally does not apply to withdrawals outside the country.

Poland

There are few but extensive independent ATM operators in Poland (e.g. Euronet, eCard) as well as smaller bank-owned networks. Fees depend on inter-bank agreements and are explicitly stated in card contract. Typically withdrawals from own and allied networks are free while from competitor's machines are subject to constant fee, e.g. 5zł. Premium accounts often come without any withdrawal fees, albeit at higher recurring cost. As of 2010 many banks offer optional contracts on "free" withdrawals from any ATM at flat monthly fee, usually priced similar to 1 withdrawal.

Portugal

All Multibanco withdrawals and payments in Portugal are free. Recent European Union directives allowed merchants and banks to charge the customers for transactions, but the government approved a law that forbids charging any kind of fees. Left Block and Portuguese Communist Party were the political parties that came up with the proposal and the ones more devoted to the idea.

Spain

Banks that are not associated with the user's bank will usually charge a fee of €0.50 per withdrawal of cash from the machine. Other services such as top-up of mobile phones are usually free.

Sweden

In Sweden, most banks issue debit cards for an annual or monthly fee which includes free withdrawals in Sweden and within the eurozone. However, customers are typically subject to a fee if using a cash machine elsewhere. Some cards from some banks are, however, subject to fees also when used in the eurozone and some Swedish cash machines. Most of these cards are issued by savings banks.

United Kingdom

During the 1980s the number of banks and building societies charging issuer fees (i.e. charging fees to their own customers when they used another ATM operator's ATMs), gradually increased. However, in 1990 Barclays announced they were introducing an acquier fee for all non-Barclays card-holders at their ATMs. This would result in "double charging", were the customer was charged by both their card issuer and the ATM operator. Public reaction against this proposal was very strong and a campaign launched by Nationwide Building Society and the UK tabloid newspapers resulted in issuer fees being removed altogether.[9]

Interchange, the fee which a card issuer pays to the ATM operator to cover the cost of the transaction remains and this cost is absorbed by the card issuer.

In 1999 LINK, the UK ATM network opened membership to so called independent ATM operators, ("IADs"); organisations which do not issue cards. IADs initially focussed on the pay-to-use market, where the customer covers the cost of the transaction directly and this, coupled with a low-cost business model, meant that the number of pay-to-use ATMs rose rapidly, peaking in 2007 at just over 27,000 ATMs.[10]

Most of these machines are in low footfall locations such as convenience stores, garages, nightclubs and pubs. The fee charged in 2005 was usually between £1.00 and £1.50,[11] but occasionally they have been known to charge up to £5[12] and £10.[13]

Rules regarding signage on pay-to-use machines were introduced in 2005 and enhanced in 2006[14] and since 2007 the number of pay-to-use cash machines has fallen, by the end of 2010 there were around 21,000.[15]

The large numbers of free-to-use ATMs and the low average number of transactions at pay-to-use machines means that 97% of cash withdrawals in the UK remain free of charge.[16]

Hong Kong

There are three ATM networks in Hong Kong: ETC (HSBC and Hang Seng Bank only) JETCO (all remaining banks) and AEON. ATM use is free of charge, except when a card is used outside of its respective home network. When a card is used outside the home network, HKD$30 is paid for service charge.

Iran

There is only one ATM network in Iran, SHETAB. There are no charges for money withdrawal in this network. Transferring money between two accounts in different banks costs is free , and checking the account balance costs 1000 Rials (US$ 0,10) for other bank's cards. Other services are currently free.

South East Asia

Indonesia

In Indonesia banks usually charge a fee of Rp. 5000 (USD 60 cents) per interbank transfer via ATM bersama or Rp. 3000 to Rp. 5000 (USD 33-60 cents) for withdrawal of cash from a different bank's ATM.

Thailand

In Thailand, a standard fee is 150 THB (USD 5.00 (approx)). The exception is the atms of the AEON company, not technically a bank but a finance company, they have branches in most major malls and the use is free (including foreign cards).

South Asia

Sri Lanka

In Sri Lanka banks usually charge a fee of LKR (Sri Lankan Rupees) 50.00 (USD 0.40 to 0.60) per non user's bank withdrawal of cash from the machine.

Pakistan

In Pakistan banks usually charge a fee of PKR 10 to PKR 35 (USD 0.15 to USD 0.40) per non user's ATM cash withdrawal. These fees are levied chiefly to offset banks' own costs at par only. There are two ATM switches operational in the country, 1LINK, hosted by a consortium of banks, and MNET, hosted by MCB Bank Ltd; and all Pakistani banks are members of one or the other switch as per the mandate of the State Bank of Pakistan, the country's central bank. Some banks, like Allied Bank and HSBC, absorb the costs entirely, and offer their customers totally free withdrawals at all ATMs countrywide, including Azad Jammu and Kashmir; a territory between Pakistan and India whose status is disputed.

Bangladesh

There are multiple ATM networks in Bangladesh. The market leader, Dutch-Bangla Bank has the largest ATM network and it is also the network with the most member banks. Dutch-Bangla Bank customers are not charged for ATM transactions.

Dutch-Bangla Bank has separate agreements with local and international banks where Dutch-Bangla Bank charges BDT 10 (US$0.14) per transaction to member banks. Due to this low amount, member banks often add an extra amount as a profit margin.

India

In India, ATM annual fees(Rs. 100 in Govt. bank and Rs. 500 in private bank).[17] In 2007, the Reserve Bank of India (RBI), the country's central bank, had issued a directive to all commercial banks to freeze ATM charges and, with effect from 1 April 2009, abolish ATM service charges altogether. Since 2009, customers of any licenced bank are able to use the ATMs of other banks without paying a service charge. Earlier, banks charged between INR 10 and INR 35 per reciprocal transaction.[18]

However, banks can still surcharge for items such as credit card ATM cash advances and at foreign ATMs. In addition, RBI imposes significant foreign exchange restrictions on the use of Indian debit VISA/MasterCard abroad. For example, Indian debit VISA cards are routinely marked "Valid in India and Nepal only" due to the country's restrictive foreign exchange reserve policy.

In the same directive, free mutual ATM usage was reverted to 5 free such transactions per monthly statement cycle; beyond which a cap of INR 20 has been fixed for ATM cards issued to savings bank/term deposit account customers. However ATM Cards issued to current, cash credit, and unit trust account holders would be charged from the first instance.

Switzerland

The usual fee for a withdrawal at a "foreign" bank's ATM is CHF 2. Sometimes, banks provide the cardholder with usually 10, 12 or 24 free withdrawals, especially if the bank is a small one, with few ATMs. All Swiss banks hand out Maestro cards to their customers, so that any ATM can be used.

United States

Prior to 1988, there was no surcharging of cardholders by ATM owners in the U.S. In 1988 Valley Bank of Nevada began surcharging "foreign cardholders" (meaning holders of ATM cards not issued by Valley Bank) for withdrawals at Valley Bank ATMs located in/near Las Vegas casinos.[19] Eventually, various regional ATM Networks, and ultimately the national networks, Plus and Cirrus, permitted ATM surcharging.

Before 1996, foreign ATM fees averaged $1.01 USD nationally, according to a 2001 report from the US-based State Public Interest Research Group.[20]

As banks and third parties realized the profit potential they raised the fees. ATM fees now commonly reach $2.00 (2003[21]), and can be as high as $6.00,[22] or even higher in cash-intensive places like bars and casinos. In cases where fees are paid both to the bank (for using a "foreign" ATM) and the ATM owner (the so-called "surcharge") total withdrawal fees could potentially reach $11. Independent sales organizations ("ISO"s) are the driving force in ATM deployment in the U.S. today representing over 60% of the 396,000 ATMs nationwide. Some have expressed concerns that the U.S. market is becoming too saturated, spreading the resulting fee pool too thin, which may result in a future net decrease in the number of machines.[23] Other media reports indicate that growth in ATM usage has decreased, possibly in relation to the amount of fees imposed by banks.[24]

Only some fees charged by ATMs are advertised at the point of transaction. This is more of a cautionary statement, as ATMs are required by law to inform users of the surcharge fees that the machine will charge the user. This information may come in the push through menu or it may be on a sticker on the machine. However, the ATM card holder's own bank may charge a "foreign ATM network" fee to the card holder for using an ATM that is not owned and operated by the card holder's own bank. Since this charge is not assessed by the machine or the owner of the machine, it is usually not advertised at the time and place of the transaction. Thus, it becomes the responsibility of the card holder to be aware of the details of their own bank's fee structure, which may also vary from state to state, to determine the total cost of an ATM transaction. In addition, the "foreign ATM network" fee may be different if using an ATM outside the U.S. versus inside the U.S.

A new charge that has come into the marketplace is the "Denial Fee", where a customer is charged a fee for attempting to withdraw more money than they are either allowed through their daily withdrawal limit or by having insufficient funds in their account.[25]

While many consumers are faced with multiple fees as described above, a number of standalone and internet banks, such as USAA and Ally, not only do not charge their customers for using another ATM but they also provide reimbursement, worldwide, of another ATM's fee. Thus, customers at some banks in the US can avoid ATM fees altogether. Another popular way to avoid paying ATM fees is to make a cashback purchase at a retail store: many retailers will allow a customer who is paying with a debit card to withdraw more than the total due the retailer and get back the difference in cash.

References

[1] RBA: ATM FEE REFORMS (http://www.rba.gov.au/PaymentsSystem/Reforms/ATMFeeReforms/index.html)

[2] "No charge for Bankwest customers when they use Foreign ATMs" (http://www.bankwest.com.au/Media_Centre/Media_Releases/ Media_Releases_2009/No_charge_for_Bankwest_customers_when_they_use_Foreign_ATMs/index.aspx). Bankwest.com.au. 2009-08-19. . Retrieved 2010-08-11.

[3] http://www.interac.org/en_n2_22_fees.html

[4] CBC Marketplace: ATM Fees (http://www.cbc.ca/consumers/market/files/money/atm/index.html)

[5] FCAC - For Consumers - Banking and Insurance - ABM fees (http://www.fcac-acfc.gc.ca/eng/consumers/BankInsurance/ABMFees/ ABMFeesInfo_1-eng.asp)

[6] "EUR-Lex - 32001R2560 - EN" (http://eur-lex.europa.eu/LexUriServ/LexUriServ.do?uri=CELEX:32001R2560:EN:HTML). Eur-lex.europa.eu. . Retrieved 2010-08-11.

[7] "EUR-Lex - 52002XC0711(03) - EN" (http://eur-lex.europa.eu/LexUriServ/LexUriServ.do?uri=CELEX:52002XC0711(03):EN:NOT). Eur-lex.europa.eu. . Retrieved 2010-08-11.

[8] "Ottopisteiden kotisivu" (http://www.otto.fi/index.php?ca=in_english&an=default). Otto.fi. . Retrieved 2010-08-11.

[9] "Barclays delays ATM fee" (http://money.cnn.com/1999/09/23/europe/barclays/). *CNN*. 1999-09-23. .

[10] http://www.link.co.uk/AboutLINK/Statistics/Pages/Statistics.aspx LINK Website - statistics

[11] "ATM users to pay Â£250M in fees next year" (http://www.abcmoney.co.uk/news/1220051323.htm). Abcmoney.co.uk. . Retrieved 2010-08-11.

[12] http://www.publications.parliament.uk/pa/cm200405/cmselect/cmtreasy/191/191.pdf

[13] Banking and credit | Cash machines (http://www.which.co.uk/reports_and_campaigns/money/campaigns/Banking and credit/ATM charges/Cash_machines_560_54911.jsp)

[14] http://www.link.co.uk/Media/NewsReleases/Pages/ Government-brokeredroundtableagreesthatindustry,consumergroupsandTreasuryCommitteeshouldbeginworkingtogetheroncashmachineis. aspx

[15] http://www.link.co.uk/AboutLINK/Statistics/Pages/Statistics.aspx LINK Website - statistics

[16] http://www.link.co.uk LINK website

[17] http://www.svtuition.org/2011/04/what-are-bank-charges.html

[18] Our Special Correspondent (2009-03-30). "The Telegraph - Calcutta (Kolkata) | Business | Use any ATM from April free of charge" (http:// www.telegraphindia.com/1090330/jsp/business/story_10744673.jsp). Telegraphindia.com. . Retrieved 2010-08-11.

[19] United States Court of Appeals for the Ninth Circuit Valley Bank v. Plus Sys., Inc.: (http://www.altlaw.org/v1/cases/441762)

[20] Edmund Mierzwinski (2001-03-29) (PDF). *Double ATM Fees, Triple Trouble* (http://www.stopatmfees.com/report01/report01.pdf). U.S. Public Interest Research Group. . Retrieved 2007-06-26.

[21] Press Releases (http://www.doveconsulting.com/PR-2004-05-21CPPS.htm)

[22] Latest game of chance in town: ATMs (http://www.pressofatlanticcity.com/news/story/6547551p-6397866c.html)

[23] Sullivan, Bob (2004-07-28). "Are there too many ATM machines? - Money - MSNBC.com" (http://www.msnbc.msn.com/id/5529813/). MSNBC. . Retrieved 2010-08-11.

[24] Hartley, Thomas (2006-02-10). "After 25 years, ATMs facing market changes - Business First of Buffalo:" (http://www.bizjournals.com/ buffalo/stories/2006/02/13/focus2.html?t=printable). Bizjournals.com. . Retrieved 2010-08-11.

[25] "In denial: ATM fee for getting nothing - The Red Tape Chronicles - MSNBC.com" (http://redtape.msnbc.com/2005/10/ now_even_atm_de.html). Redtape.msnbc.com. 2005-10-28. . Retrieved 2010-08-11.

Automated Clearing House

Automated Clearing House (ACH) is an electronic network for financial transactions in the United States. ACH processes large volumes of credit and debit transactions in batches. ACH credit transfers include direct deposit payroll and vendor payments. ACH direct debit transfers include consumer payments on insurance premiums, mortgage loans, and other kinds of bills. Debit transfers also include new applications such as the Point-of-Purchase (POP) check conversion pilot program sponsored by NACHA-The Electronic Payments Association. Both the government and the commercial sectors use ACH payments. Businesses are also increasingly using ACH to collect from customers online, rather than accepting credit or debit cards.[1]

Rules and regulations governing the ACH network are established by NACHA (formerly the National Automated Clearing House Association) and the Federal Reserve. In 2002, this network processed an estimated 8.05 billion ACH transactions with a total value of $21.7 trillion.[2] (Credit card payments are handled by separate networks.)

The Federal Reserve Banks are collectively the nation's largest automated clearinghouse operator and in 2005 processed 60% of commercial interbank ACH transactions. The Electronic Payments Network (EPN), the only private sector ACH operator in the U.S., processed the remaining 40%. FedACH is the Federal Reserve's centralized application software used to process ACH transactions. EPN and the Reserve Banks rely on each other for the processing of some transactions when either party to the transaction is not their customer. These interoperator transactions are settled by the Reserve Banks.

Uses of the ACH payment system

- Direct deposit of payroll, Social Security (United States) and other government payments, and tax refunds
- Direct debit payment of consumer bills such as mortgages, loans, utilities, insurance premiums, rents, and any other regular payment
- Business-to-business payments
- E-commerce payments
- Federal, state, and local tax payments
- Bank Treasury management departments sell this service to business and government customers

SEC Codes

Some common Standard Entry Class (SEC) Codes:

ARC

> *Accounts Receivable Entry.* A consumer check converted to a one-time ACH debit. The difference between ARC and POP is that ARC can result from a check mailed in where as POP is in-person. [3]

BOC

> *Back Office Conversion.* A single entry debit initiated at the point of purchase or at a manned bill payment location to transfer funds through conversion to an ACH debit entry during back office processing. Unlike ARC entries, BOC conversions require the customer to be present and a notice that checks may be converted to BOC ACH entries be posted. [4]

CBR

> *Corporate Cross-border Payment.* Used for international business transactions, replaced by SEC Code IAT.[5]

CCD

> *Corporate Credit or Debit.* Primarily used for business-to-business transactions.

CTX

Corporate Trade Exchange. Transactions that include ASC X12 or EDIFACT information.[3]

DNE

Death Notification Entry. Issued by the federal government.

IAT

International ACH Transaction. This is a new SEC Code for cross-border payment traffic. The code will replace the PBR and CBR codes. The new code will be implemented September 18, 2009.[5]

PBR

Consumer Cross-border Payment. Used for international household transactions, replaced by SEC Code IAT.[5]

POP

Point-of-Purchase. A check presented in-person to a merchant for purchase is presented as an ACH entry instead of a physical check.

POS

Point-of-Sale. A debit at an electronic terminal initiated by use of a plastic card. An example is using your debit card to purchase gas.

PPD

Prearranged Payment and Deposits. Used to credit or debit a consumer account. Popularly used for payroll direct deposits and preauthorized bill payments.

RCK

Represented Check Entries. A physical check that was presented but returned because of insufficient funds may be represented as an ACH entry.

TEL

Telephone Initiated-Entry. Verbal authorization by telephone to issue an ACH entry such as checks by phone. (TEL code allowed for inbound telephone orders only. NACHA disallows the use of this code for outbound telephone solicitations unless a prior business arrangement with the customer has been established.)

WEB

Web Initiated-Entry. Electronic authorization through the Internet to create an ACH entry.

XCK

Destroyed Check Entry. A physical check that was destroyed because of a disaster can be presented as an ACH entry.

ACH process

An ACH transaction starts with a Receiver authorizing an Originator to issue ACH debit or credit to an account. A Receiver is the account holder that grants the authorization. An Originator can be a person or a company (such as the gas company, a local cable company, or one's employer). Accounts are identified by the bank's Routing Number and the account number within that bank.

Example 1: Alice buys a tee shirt at Bob's Gift Shop with a check for $15. Alice is the Receiver; her bank account will eventually receive the order to take $15 out of her account. Bob's Gift Shop is the Originator. The check, signed by Alice, authorizes Bob's Gift Shop, Inc to originate the ACH transaction, code POP. The check has Alice's routing number and account number.

Example 2: Candice has her paycheck at Delirium Designs deposited directly to her checking account. Delirium Designs is the Originator, but cannot begin until Candice, the Receiver, fills out a form for direct deposits, including her bank routing number and account number.

In accordance with the rules and regulations of ACH, no financial institution may issue an ACH transaction (whether it be debit or credit) towards an account without prior authorization from the Receiver. Depending on the ACH transaction, the Originator must receive written (SEC Codes: ARC, POP, PPD), verbal (TEL), or electronic (WEB) authorization from the Receiver. Written authorization constitutes a signed form giving consent on the amount, date, or even frequency of the transaction. If verbal authorization is not audio-recorded, the Originator must send a receipt of the transaction details before or on the transaction date. An electronic authorization must include a customer being presented the terms of the agreement and typing or selecting some form of an "I agree" statement.

Once authorization is acquired, the Originator then creates an ACH entry to be given to an Originating Depository Financial Institution (ODFI), which can be any financial institution that does ACH origination. This ACH entry is then sent to an ACH Operator that passes it on to the Receiving Depository Financial Institution (RDFI), where the Receiver's account is issued either a debit or credit.

Example 1: Bob's Gift Shop, in its central office, turns the check into an ACH transaction that it submits to its bank, in this case the ODFI. This transaction reaches Alice's bank, in this case the RDFI, who debits (takes the money out of) Alice's account.

Example 2: Delirium Designs submits an ACH transaction to its bank, acting as ODFI. It traverses through the system to Candice's bank, who credits (deposits the money into) Candice's bank account.

The RDFI may, however, reject the ACH transaction and return it to the ODFI if, for example, the account had insufficient funds or the account holder indicated that the transaction was unauthorized. An RDFI has a prescribed amount of time in which to perform returns, ranging from 2 to 60 days from the receipt of the ACH transaction. However, the majority of returned transactions are completed within 24 hours from midnight of the day the RDFI receives the transaction.

Example 1: Unfortunately, Alice has been living beyond her means, and her checking account is down to $3.44, causing the ACH transaction for $15 to bounce. The original transaction is completed, so Alice's bank (the RDFI) now prepares an ACH transaction, code RCK, to grab the $15 back through the ACH system. For this transaction, however, Alice's bank is the ODFI and the Gift Shop's bank is the RDFI.

An ODFI receiving a returned ACH entry may re-present the ACH entry two more times for settlement. Again, the RDFI may reject the transaction. After which, the ODFI may no longer represent the transaction via ACH.

Example 1: Bob's Gift Shop still needs their $15. The easiest way is to just submit the original transaction again, hoping that enough money shows up in Alice's bank account so that it clears. After two tries, they have to contact Alice themselves to get their money.

Time day 60. However when a consumer receives a statement on day 30, under Regulation E, the consumer can dispute the transaction until day 90. The RDFI is at risk from day 60 to 90 due to the different timelines.

Another problem deals with compliance where the merchant presented with a check issues an ACH entry with SEC Codes ARC or POP. However, the merchant then fails to comply with the handling of the physical check and presents the physical check for payment as well. This causes a double-debit against a consumer account.

References

[1] Automated Clearing House (ACH) | Abinomics.com (http://www.abinomics.com/glossary/finance/a/Automated-Clearing-House-(ACH))

[2] What is Automated Clearing House? - a definition from Whatis.com - see also: ACH (http://searchsecurity.techtarget.com/sDefinition/0,,sid14_gci214632,00.html)

[3] Standard Entry Class (SEC) Codes (http://www.achdirect.com/resources/seccodes.asp)

[4] POP, ARC & BOC comparison (http://www.witsends.com/products/check21/ach-comparison.htm)

[5] NACHA Moves Back IAT Deadline to Allow More Time for Testing (http://www.digitaltransactions.net/newsstory.cfm?newsid=1868)

External links

- Federal Reserve Payment Systems (http://www.federalreserve.gov/paymentsys.htm)
- Intro to the ACH Network? (http://www.nacha.org/c/Intro2ACH.cfm)
- Federal Reserve's ACH Number Lookup (http://www.fededirectory.frb.org/search_ACH.cfm)
- Regulation E (http://ecfr.gpoaccess.gov/cgi/t/text/text-idx?c=ecfr&sid=635f26c4af3e2fe4327fd25ef4cb5638&tpl=/ecfrbrowse/Title12/12cfr205_main_02.tpl)
- ACH Return Codes (http://icheckgateway.com/NACHA-Return-Codes.asp)
- ACH Terms and Definitions (http://www.achq.com/resources/ach-glossary.php)
- ACH vs Credit Cards (http://vericheck.com/index-8.html)

Automated teller machine

An **automated teller machine (ATM)**, also known as a **Cash Point**, **Cash Machine** or sometimes a **Hole in the Wall** in British English, is a computerised telecommunications device that provides the clients of a financial institution with access to financial transactions in a public space without the need for a cashier, human clerk or bank teller. ATMs are known by various other names including *automatic banking machine*, *cash machine*, and various regional variants derived from trademarks on ATM systems held by particular banks.

On most modern ATMs, the customer is identified by inserting a plastic ATM card with a magnetic stripe or a plastic smart card with a chip, that contains a unique card number and some security information such as an expiration date or CVVC (CVV). Authentication is provided by the customer entering a personal identification number (PIN).

Using an ATM, customers can access their bank accounts in order to make cash withdrawals, credit card cash advances, and check their account balances as well as purchase prepaid cellphone credit. If the currency being withdrawn from the ATM is different from that which the bank account is denominated in (e.g.: Withdrawing Japanese Yen from a bank account containing US Dollars), the money will be converted at a wholesale exchange rate. Thus, ATMs often provide the best possible exchange rate for foreign travelers and are heavily used for this purpose as well.[1]

An NCR Personas 75-Series interior, multi-function ATM in the United States

Smaller indoor ATMs dispense money inside convenience stores and other busy areas, such as this off-premise Wincor Nixdorf mono-function ATM in Sweden

History

An old Nixdorf ATM

The idea of self-service in retail banking developed through independent and simultaneous efforts in Japan, Sweden, the United States and the United Kingdom. In the USA, Luther George Simjian has been credited with developing and building the first cash dispenser machine.[2] There is strong evidence to suggest that Simjian worked on this device before 1959 while his 132nd patent (US3079603) was first filed on 30 June 1960 (and granted 26 February 1963). The rollout of this machine, called Bankograph, was delayed a couple of years. This was due in part to Simjian's Reflectone Electronics Inc. being acquired by Universal Match Corporation.[3] An experimental Bankograph was installed in New York City in 1961 by the City Bank of New York, but removed after 6 months due to the lack of customer acceptance. The Bankograph was an automated envelope deposit machine (accepting coins, cash and cheques) and it did not have cash dispensing features.[4]

A first cash dispensing device was used in Tokyo in 1966.[5] [6] Although little is known of this first device, it seems to have been activated with a credit card rather than accessing current account balances.

In simultaneous and independent efforts, engineers in Sweden and Britain developed their own cash machines during the early 1960s. The first of these that was put into use was by Barclays Bank in Enfield Town in North London, United Kingdom,[7] on 27 June 1967. This machine was the first in the UK and was used by English comedy actor Reg Varney, at the time so as to ensure maximum publicity for the machines that were to become mainstream in the UK. This instance of the invention has been credited to John Shepherd-Barron of printing firm De La Rue,[8] who was awarded an OBE in the 2005 New Year's Honours List.[9] His design used special cheques that were matched with a personal identification number, as plastic bank cards had not yet been invented.[10]

Reg Varney, first to use a cashpoint in the UK

The Barclays-De La Rue machine (called De La Rue Automatic Cash System or DACS)[11] beat the Swedish saving banks' and a company called Metior's (a device called Bankomat) by nine days and Westminster Bank's-Smith Industries-Chubb system (called Chubb MD2) by a month. The collaboration of a small start-up called Speytec and Midland Bank developed a third machine which was marketed after 1969 in Europe and the USA by the Burroughs Corporation. The patent for this device (GB1329964) was filed on September 1969 (and granted in 1973) by John David Edwards, Leonard Perkins, John Henry Donald, Peter Lee Chappell, Sean Benjamin Newcombe & Malcom David Roe.

Plaque commemorating installation of world's first bank cash machine

Both the DACS and MD2 accepted only a single-use token or voucher which was retained by the machine while the Speytec worked with a card with a magnetic stripe at the back. Hence all this these worked on various principles including Carbon-14 and low-coercivity magnetism in order to make fraud more difficult. The idea of a PIN stored on the card was developed by a British engineer working in the MD2 named James Goodfellow in 1965 (patent GB1197183 filed on 2 May 1966 with Anthony Davies). The essence of this system was that is it enabled the verification of the customer with the debited account without human intervention. This patent is also the earliest instance of a complete "currency dispenser system" in the patent record. This patent was filled on 5 March 1968 in the USA (US 3543904) and granted on 1 December 1970. It had a profound influence on the industry as a whole. Not only did future entrants into the cash dispenser market such as NCR Corporation and IBM licence Goodfellow's PIN system, but a number of later patents references this patent as "Prior Art Device".[12]

After looking first hand at the experiences in Europe, in 1968 the networked ATM was pioneered in the US, in Dallas, Texas, by Donald Wetzel, who was a department head at an automated baggage-handling company called Docutel. On September 2, 1969, Chemical Bank installed the first ATM in the U.S. at its branch in Rockville Centre, New York. The first ATMs were designed to dispense a fixed amount of cash when a user inserted a specially coded card.[13] A Chemical Bank advertisement boasted "On Sept. 2 our bank will open at 9:00 and never close again."[14] Chemicals' ATM, initially known as a Docuteller was designed by Donald Wetzel and his company Docutel. Chemical executives were initially hesitant about the electronic banking transition given the high cost of the early machines. Additionally, executives were concerned that customers would resist having machines handling their money.[15] In 1995, the Smithsonian National Museum of American History recognised Docutel and Wetzel as the inventors of the networked ATM.[16]

ATMs first came into use in December 1972 in the UK; the IBM 2984 was designed at the request of Lloyds Bank. The 2984 CIT (Cash Issuing Terminal) was the first true Cashpoint, similar in function to today's machines; Cashpoint is still a registered trademark of Lloyds TSB in the UK. All were online and issued a variable amount which was immediately deducted from the account. A small number of 2984s were supplied to a US bank. Notable historical models of ATMs include the IBM 3624 and 473x series, Diebold 10xx and TABS 9000 series, and NCR 50xx series.

Location

An ATM Encrypting PIN Pad (EPP) with German markings

ATM in Vatican with menu in Latin language

ATMs are placed not only near or inside the premises of banks, but also in locations such as shopping centers/malls, airports, grocery stores, petrol/gas stations, restaurants, or anywhere frequented by large numbers of people. There are two types of ATM installations: on- and off-premise. On-premise ATMs are typically more advanced, multi-function machines that complement a bank branch's capabilities, and are thus more expensive. Off-premise machines are deployed by financial institutions and Independent Sales Organizations (ISOs) where there is a simple need for cash, so they are generally cheaper mono-function devices. In Canada, ABMs not operated by a financial institution are known as "White Label ABMs".

In North America, banks often have drive-thru lanes providing access to ATMs.

Many ATMs have a sign above them called a topper, indicating the name of the bank or organization owning the ATM, and possibly including the list of ATM networks to which that machine is connected.

Financial networks

An ATM in the Netherlands. The logos of a number of interbank networks this ATM is connected to are shown

Most ATMs are connected to interbank networks, enabling people to withdraw and deposit money from machines not belonging to the bank where they have their account or in the country where their accounts are held (enabling cash withdrawals in local currency). Some examples of interbank networks include PULSE, PLUS, Cirrus, Interac, Interswitch, STAR, and LINK.

ATMs rely on authorization of a financial transaction by the card issuer or other authorizing institution via the communications network. This is often performed through an ISO 8583 messaging system.

Many banks charge ATM usage fees. In some cases, these fees are charged solely to users who are not customers of the bank where the ATM is installed; in other cases, they apply to all users.

In order to allow a more diverse range of devices to attach to their networks, some interbank networks have passed rules expanding the definition of an ATM to be a terminal that either has the vault within its footprint or utilizes the vault or cash drawer within the merchant establishment, which allows for the use of a scrip cash dispenser.

ATMs typically connect directly to their host or ATM Controller via either ADSL or dial-up modem over a telephone line or directly via a leased line. Leased lines are preferable to POTS lines because they require less time to establish a connection. Leased lines may be comparatively expensive to operate versus a POTS line, meaning less-trafficked machines will usually rely on a dial-up modem. That dilemma may be solved as high-speed Internet VPN connections become more ubiquitous. Common lower-level layer communication protocols used by ATMs to communicate back to the bank include SNA over SDLC, TC500 over Async, X.25, and TCP/IP over Ethernet.

In addition to methods employed for transaction security and secrecy, all communications traffic between the ATM and the Transaction Processor may also be encrypted via methods such as SSL.[17]

A Diebold 1063ix with a dial-up modem visible at the base

Global use

There are no hard international or government-compiled numbers totaling the complete number of ATMs in use worldwide. Estimates developed by ATMIA place the number of ATMs in use currently at over 1.8 million.[18]

For the purpose of analyzing ATM usage around the world, financial institutions generally divide the world into seven regions, due to the penetration rates, usage statistics, and features deployed. Four regions (USA, Canada, Europe, and Japan) have high numbers of ATMs per million people.[19] and generally slowing growth rates.[20] Despite the large number of ATMs, there is additional demand for machines in the Asia/Pacific area as well as in Latin America.[21] [22] ATMs have yet to reach high numbers in the Near East/Africa.[23]

The world's most northerly installed ATM is located at Longyearbyen, Svalbard, Norway.

The world's most southerly installed ATM is located at McMurdo Station, Antarctica.[24]

While India claims to have the world's highest installed ATM at Nathu La Pass, India installed by the Union Bank of India at 4310 meters, there are higher ATMs installed in Nagchu County, Tibet at 4500 meters by Agricultural Bank of China.[25] [26]

Israel has the world's lowest installed ATM at Ein Bokek at the Dead Sea, installed independently by a grocery store at 421 meters below (Mediterranean) Sea level.[27]

While ATMs are ubiquitous on modern cruise ships, ATMs can also be found on some US Navy ships.[28]

Hardware

An ATM is typically made up of the following devices:

- CPU (to control the user interface and transaction devices)
- Magnetic and/or Chip card reader (to identify the customer)
- PIN Pad (similar in layout to a Touch tone or Calculator keypad), often manufactured as part of a secure enclosure.
- Secure cryptoprocessor, generally within a secure enclosure.
- Display (used by the customer for performing the transaction)
- Function key buttons (usually close to the display) or a Touchscreen (used to select the various aspects of the transaction)
- Record Printer (to provide the customer with a record of their transaction)
- Vault (to store the parts of the machinery requiring restricted access)
- Housing (for aesthetics and to attach signage to)

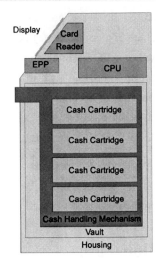

A block diagram of an ATM

Recently, due to heavier computing demands and the falling price of computer-like architectures, ATMs have moved away from custom hardware architectures using microcontrollers and/or application-specific integrated circuits to adopting the hardware architecture of a personal computer, such as, USB connections for peripherals, ethernet and IP communications, and use personal computer operating systems. Although it is undoubtedly cheaper to use commercial off-the-shelf hardware, it does make ATMs potentially vulnerable to the same sort of problems exhibited by conventional computers.

Business owners often lease ATM terminals from ATM service providers.

The vault of an ATM is within the footprint of the device itself and is where items of value are kept. Scrip cash dispensers do not incorporate a vault.

Mechanisms found inside the vault may include:

- Dispensing mechanism (to provide cash or other items of value)
- Deposit mechanism including a Check Processing Module and Bulk Note Acceptor (to allow the customer to make deposits)
- Security sensors (Magnetic, Thermal, Seismic, gas)
- Locks: (to ensure controlled access to the contents of the vault)
- Journaling systems; many are electronic (a sealed flash memory device based on proprietary standards) or a solid-state device (an actual printer) which accrues all records of activity including access timestamps, number of bills dispensed, etc. - This is considered sensitive data and is secured in similar fashion to the cash as it is a similar liability.

Two Loomis employees refilling an ATM at the Downtown Seattle REI

ATM vaults are supplied by manufacturers in several grades. Factors influencing vault grade selection include cost, weight, regulatory requirements, ATM type, operator risk avoidance practices, and internal volume requirements.[29] Industry standard vault configurations include Underwriters Laboratories UL-291 "Business Hours" and Level 1 Safes,[30] RAL TL-30 derivatives,[31] and CEN EN 1143-1 - CEN III and CEN IV.[32] [33]

ATM manufacturers recommend that vaults be attached to the floor to prevent theft.[34]

Software

A Suncorp Metway ATM running OS/2

With the migration to commodity PC hardware, standard commercial "off-the-shelf" operating systems and programming environments can be used inside of ATMs. Typical platforms previously used in ATM development include RMX or OS/2. Today the vast majority of ATMs worldwide use a Microsoft OS, primarily Windows XP Professional or Windows XP Embedded.

A small number of deployments may still be running older versions such as Windows NT, Windows CE or Windows 2000. Notably, Vista was not widely adopted in ATMs. There is a computer industry security view or consensus that desktop operating systems have greater risks as operating systems for cash dispensing machines than other types of operating systems like (secure) real-time operating systems (RTOS). RISKS Digest has many articles about cash machine operating system vulnerabilities.[35]

A Wincor Nixdorf ATM running Windows 2000.

Linux is also finding some reception in the ATM marketplace. An example of this is Banrisul, the largest bank in the south of Brazil, which has replaced the MS-DOS operating systems in its ATMs with Linux. Banco do Brasil is also migrating ATMs to Linux.

Common application layer transaction protocols, such as Diebold 91x (911 or 912) and NCR NDC or NDC+ provide emulation of older generations of hardware on newer platforms with incremental extensions made over time to address new capabilities, although companies like NCR continuously improve these protocols issuing newer versions (e.g. NCR's AANDC v3.x.y, where x.y are subversions). Most major ATM manufacturers provide software packages that implement these protocols. Newer protocols such as IFX have yet to find wide acceptance by transaction processors.[36]

With the move to a more standardized software base, financial institutions have been increasingly interested in the ability to pick and choose the application programs that drive their equipment. WOSA/XFS, now known as CEN XFS (or simply XFS), provides a common API for accessing and manipulating the various devices of an ATM. J/XFS is a Java implementation of the CEN XFS API.

While the perceived benefit of XFS is similar to the Java's "Write once, run anywhere" mantra, often different ATM hardware vendors have different interpretations of the XFS standard. The result of these differences in interpretation means that ATM applications typically use a middleware to even out the differences between various platforms.

With the onset of Windows operating systems and XFS on ATM's, the software applications have the ability to become more intelligent. This has created a new breed of ATM applications commonly referred to as programmable applications. These types of applications allows for an entirely new host of applications in which the ATM terminal can do more than only communicate with the ATM switch. It is now empowered to connected to other content servers and video banking systems.

Notable ATM software that operates on XFS platforms include Triton PRISM, Diebold Agilis EmPower, NCR APTRA Edge, Absolute Systems AbsoluteINTERACT, KAL Kalignite, Phoenix Interactive VISTAatm, and Wincor Nixdorf ProTopas.

With the move of ATMs to industry-standard computing environments, concern has risen about the integrity of the ATM's software stack.[37]

Security

Security, as it relates to ATMs, has several dimensions. ATMs also provide a practical demonstration of a number of security systems and concepts operating together and how various security concerns are dealt with.

Physical

Early ATM security focused on making the ATMs invulnerable to physical attack; they were effectively safes with dispenser mechanisms. A number of attacks on ATMs resulted, with thieves attempting to steal entire ATMs by ram-raiding.[38] Since late 1990s, criminal groups operating in Japan improved ram-raiding by stealing and using a truck loaded with a heavy construction machinery to effectively demolish or uproot an entire ATM and any housing to steal its cash.[39]

A Wincor Nixdorf Procash 2100xe Frontload that was opened with an angle grinder

Another attack method, *plofkraak*, is to seal all openings of the ATM with silicone and fill the vault with a combustible gas or to place an explosive inside, attached, or near the ATM. This gas or explosive is ignited and the vault is opened or distorted by the force of the resulting explosion and the criminals can break in.[40] This type of theft has occurred in the Netherlands, Belgium, France, Denmark, Germany and Australia.[41] [42] This type of attack can be completely prevented by using gas explosion prevention devices.[43]

Modern ATM physical security, per other modern money-handling security, concentrates on denying the use of the money inside the machine to a thief, by means of techniques such as dye packs and smoke canisters.

A common method is to simply rob the staff filling the machine with money. To avoid this, the schedule for filling them is kept secret, varying and random. The money is often kept in cassettes, which will dye the money if incorrectly opened.

Transactional secrecy and integrity

A Triton brand ATM with a dip style card reader and a triple DES keypad

The security of ATM transactions relies mostly on the integrity of the secure cryptoprocessor: the ATM often uses commodity components that are not considered to be "trusted systems".

Encryption of personal information, required by law in many jurisdictions, is used to prevent fraud. Sensitive data in ATM transactions are usually encrypted with DES, but transaction processors now usually require the use of Triple DES.[44] Remote Key Loading techniques may be used to ensure the secrecy of the initialization of the encryption keys in the ATM. Message Authentication Code (MAC) or Partial MAC may also be used to ensure messages have not been tampered with while in transit between the ATM and the financial network.

Customer identity integrity

There have also been a number of incidents of fraud by Man-in-the-middle attacks, where criminals have attached fake keypads or card readers to existing machines. These have then been used to record customers' PINs and bank card information in order to gain unauthorized access to their accounts. Various ATM manufacturers have put in place countermeasures to protect the equipment they manufacture from these threats.[45] [46]

A BTMU ATM with a palm scanner (to the right of the screen)

Alternate methods to verify cardholder identities have been tested and deployed in some countries, such as finger and palm vein patterns,[47] iris, and facial recognition technologies. However, recently, cheaper mass production equipment has been developed and is being installed in machines globally that detect the presence of foreign objects on the front of ATMs, current tests have shown 99% detection success for all types of skimming devices.[48]

Device operation integrity

Openings on the customer-side of ATMs are often covered by mechanical shutters to prevent tampering with the mechanisms when they are not in use. Alarm sensors are placed inside the ATM and in ATM servicing areas to alert their operators when doors have been opened by unauthorized personnel.

Rules are usually set by the government or ATM operating body that dictate what happens when integrity systems fail. Depending on the jurisdiction, a bank may or may not be liable when an attempt is made to dispense a customer's money from an ATM and the money either gets outside of the ATM's vault, or was exposed in a non-secure fashion, or they are unable to determine the state of the money after a failed transaction.[49] Bank customers often complain that banks have made it difficult to recover money lost in this way, but this is often complicated by the bank's own internal policies regarding suspicious activities typical of the criminal element.[50]

ATMs that are exposed to the outside must be vandal and weather resistant

Customer security

Dunbar Armored ATM Techs watching over ATMs that have been installed in a van

In some countries, multiple security cameras and security guards are a common feature.[51] In the United States, The New York State Comptroller's Office has criticized the New York State Department of Banking for not following through on safety inspections of ATMs in high crime areas.[52]

Critics of ATM operators assert that the issue of customer security appears to have been abandoned by the banking industry;[53] it has been suggested that efforts are now more concentrated on deterrent legislation than on solving the problem of forced withdrawals.[54]

At least as far back as July 30, 1986, critics of the industry have called for the adoption of an emergency PIN system for ATMs, where the user is able to send a silent alarm in response to a threat.[55] Legislative efforts to require an emergency PIN system have appeared in Illinois,[56] Kansas[57] and Georgia,[58] but none have succeeded as of yet. In January 2009, Senate Bill 1355 was proposed in the Illinois Senate that revisits the issue of the reverse emergency PIN system.[59] The bill is again resisted by the banking lobby and supported by the police.[60]

In 1998 three towns outside of Cleveland Ohio, in response to an ATM crime wave, adopted ATM Consumer Security Legislation requiring that a 9-1-1 switch be installed at all outside ATMs within their jurisdiction. Since the passing of these laws 11 years ago, there have been no repeat crimes. In the wake of an ATM Murder in Sharon Hill, Pennsylvania, The City Council of Sharon Hill passed an ATM Consumer Security Bill as well, with the same result. As of July 2009, ATM Consumer Security Legislation is currently pending in New York, New Jersey, and Washington D.C.

In China, many efforts to promote security have been made. On-premises ATMs are often located inside the bank's lobby which may be accessible 24 hours a day. These lobbies have extensive CCTV coverage, an emergency telephone and a security guard on the premises. Bank lobbies that are not guarded 24 hours a day may also have secure doors that can only be opened from outside by swiping your bank card against a wall-mounted scanner, allowing the bank to identify who enters the building. Most ATMs will also display on-screen safety warnings and may also be fitted with convex mirrors above the display allowing the user to see what is happening behind them.

Alternative uses

Although ATMs were originally developed as just cash dispensers, they have evolved to include many other bank-related functions. In some countries, especially those which benefit from a fully integrated cross-bank ATM network (e.g.: Multibanco in Portugal), ATMs include many functions which are not directly related to the management of one's own bank account, such as:

Two NCR Personas 84 ATMs at a bank in Jersey dispensing two types of pound sterling banknotes: Bank of England notes on the left, and States of Jersey notes on the right

- Deposit currency recognition, acceptance, and recycling[61] [62]
- Paying routine bills, fees, and taxes (utilities, phone bills, social security, legal fees, taxes, etc.)
- Printing bank statements
- Updating passbooks
- Loading monetary value into stored value cards
- Purchasing
  - Postage stamps.
  - Lottery tickets
  - Train tickets
  - Concert tickets
  - Movie tickets
  - Shopping mall gift certificates.
- Games and promotional features[63]
- Fastloans
- CRM at the ATM
- Donating to charities[64]
- Cheque Processing Module
- Adding pre-paid cell phone / mobile phone credit.
- Paying (in full or partially) the credit balance on a card linked to a specific current account.

Increasingly banks are seeking to use the ATM as a sales device to deliver pre approved loans and targeted advertising using products such as ITM (the Intelligent Teller Machine) from Aptra Relate from NCR. ATMs can also act as an advertising channel for companies to advertise their own products or third-party products and services.[65]

In Canada, ATMs are called *guichets automatiques* in French and sometimes "Bank Machines" in English. The Interac shared cash network does not allow for the selling of goods from ATMs due to specific security requirements for PIN entry when buying goods.[66] CIBC machines in Canada, are able to top-up the minutes on certain pay as you go phones.

Manufacturers have demonstrated and have deployed several different technologies on ATMs that have not yet reached worldwide acceptance, such as:

- Biometrics, where authorization of transactions is based on the scanning of a customer's fingerprint, iris, face, etc. Biometrics on ATMs can be found in Asia.[67] [68] [69]
- Cheque/Cash Acceptance, where the ATM accepts and recognise cheques and/or currency without using envelopes[70] Expected to grow in importance in the US through Check 21 legislation.
- Bar code scanning[71]
- On-demand printing of "items of value" (such as movie tickets, traveler's cheques, etc.)
- Dispensing additional media (such as phone cards)
- Co-ordination of ATMs with mobile phones[72]
- Customer-specific advertising[73]
- Integration with non-banking equipment[74] [75]

A South Korean ATM with mobile bank port and bar code reader

Reliability

An ATM running Microsoft Windows that has crashed

Before an ATM is placed in a public place, it typically has undergone extensive testing with both test money and the backend computer systems that allow it to perform transactions. Banking customers also have come to expect high reliability in their ATMs,[76] which provides incentives to ATM providers to minimize machine and network failures. Financial consequences of incorrect machine operation also provide high degrees of incentive to minimize malfunctions.[77]

ATMs and the supporting electronic financial networks are generally very reliable, with industry benchmarks typically producing 98.25% customer availability for ATMs[78] and up to 99.999% availability for host systems. If ATMs do go out of service, customers could be left without the ability to make transactions until the beginning of their bank's next time of opening hours.

This said, not all errors are to the detriment of customers; there have been cases of machines giving out money without debiting the account, or giving out higher value notes as a result of incorrect denomination of banknote being loaded in the money cassettes. Errors that can occur may be mechanical (such as card transport mechanisms; keypads; hard disk failures; envelope deposit mechanisms); software (such as operating system; device driver; application); communications; or purely down to operator error.

To aid in reliability, some ATMs print each transaction to a roll paper journal that is stored inside the ATM, which allows both the users of the ATMs and the related financial institutions to settle things based on the records in the journal in case there is a dispute. In some cases, transactions are posted to an electronic journal to remove the cost of supplying journal paper to the ATM and for more convenient searching of data.

An ATM running OS/2 that has crashed

Improper money checking can cause the possibility of a customer receiving counterfeit banknotes from an ATM. While bank personnel are generally trained better at spotting and removing counterfeit cash,[79] [80] the resulting ATM money supplies used by banks provide no absolute guarantee for proper banknotes, as the Federal Criminal Police Office of Germany has confirmed that there are regularly incidents of false banknotes having been dispensed through bank ATMs.[81] Some ATMs may be stocked and wholly owned by outside companies, which can further complicate this problem. Bill validation technology can be used by ATM providers to help ensure the authenticity of the cash before it is stocked in an ATM; ATMs that have cash recycling capabilities include this capability.[82]

Fraud

As with any device containing objects of value, ATMs and the systems they depend on to function are the targets of fraud. Fraud against ATMs and people's attempts to use them takes several forms.

The first known instance of a fake ATM was installed at a shopping mall in Manchester, Connecticut in 1993. By modifying the inner workings of a Fujitsu model 7020 ATM, a criminal gang known as The Bucklands Boys were able to steal information from cards inserted into the machine by customers.[83]

In some cases, bank fraud could occur at ATMs where by the bank accidentally stocks the ATM with bills in the wrong denomination, therefore giving the customer more money than should be dispensed.[84] The result of receiving too much money may be influenced by the card holder agreement in place between the customer and the bank.[85] [86]

In a variation of this, WAVY-TV reported an incident in Virginia Beach of September 2006 where a hacker who had probably obtained a factory-default admin password for a gas station's white label ATM caused the unit to assume it was loaded with $5 USD bills instead of $20s, enabling himself—and many subsequent customers—to walk away with four times the money they said they wanted to withdraw.[87] This type of scam was featured on the TV series The Real Hustle.

ATM behavior can change during what is called "stand-in" time, where the bank's cash dispensing network is unable to access databases that contain account information (possibly for database maintenance). In order to give customers access to cash, customers may be allowed to withdraw cash up to a certain amount that may be less than their usual daily withdrawal limit, but may still exceed the amount of available money in their account, which could result in fraud.[88]

Card fraud

In an attempt to prevent criminals from shoulder surfing the customer's PINs, some banks draw privacy areas on the floor.

For a low-tech form of fraud, the easiest is to simply steal a customer's card. A later variant of this approach is to trap the card inside of the ATM's card reader with a device often referred to as a Lebanese loop. When the customer gets frustrated by not getting the card back and walks away from the machine, the criminal is able to remove the card and withdraw cash from the customer's account.

Another simple form of fraud involves attempting to get the customer's bank to issue a new card and stealing it from their mail.[89]

ATM lineup

A big queue at an ATM in Masalli, Azerbaijan

Some ATMs may put up warning messages to customers to not use them when it detects possible tampering

The concept and various methods of copying the contents of an ATM card's magnetic stripe on to a duplicate card to access other people's financial information was well known in the hacking communities by late 1990.[90]

In 1996 Andrew Stone, a computer security consultant from Hampshire in the UK, was convicted of stealing more than £1 million by pointing high definition video cameras at ATMs from a considerable distance, and by recording the card numbers, expiry dates, etc. from the embossed detail on the ATM cards along with video footage of the PINs being entered. After getting all the information from the videotapes, he was able to produce clone cards which not only allowed him to withdraw the full daily limit for each account, but also allowed him to sidestep withdrawal limits by using multiple copied cards. In court, it was shown that he could withdraw as much as £10,000 per hour by using this method. Stone was sentenced to five years and six months in prison.[91]

By contrast, a newer high-tech method of operating sometimes called **card skimming** or **card cloning** involves the installation of a magnetic card reader over the real ATM's card slot and the use of a wireless surveillance camera or a modified digital camera to observe the user's PIN. Card data is then cloned onto a second card and the criminal attempts a standard cash withdrawal. The availability of low-cost commodity wireless cameras and card readers has made it a relatively simple form of fraud, with comparatively low risk to the fraudsters.[92]

In an attempt to stop these practices, countermeasures against card cloning have been developed by the banking industry, in particular by the use of smart cards which cannot easily be copied or spoofed by unauthenticated devices, and by attempting to make the outside of their ATMs tamper evident. Older chip-card security systems include the French Carte Bleue, Visa Cash, Mondex, Blue from American Express[93] and EMV '96 or EMV 3.11. The most actively developed form of smart card security in the industry today is known as EMV 2000 or EMV 4.x.

EMV is widely used in the UK (Chip and PIN) and other parts of Europe, but when it is not available in a specific area, ATMs must fallback to using the easy–to–copy magnetic stripe to perform transactions. This fallback behaviour can be exploited.[94] However the fallback option has been removed by several UK banks, meaning if the chip is not read, the transaction will be declined.

In February 2009, a group of criminals used counterfeit ATM cards to steal $9 million from 130 ATMs in 49 cities around the world all within a time period of 30 minutes.[95]

Card cloning and skimming can be detected by the implementation of magnetic card reader heads and firmware that can read a signature embedded in all magnetic stripes during the card production process. This signature known as a "MagnePrint" or "BluPrint" can be used in conjunction with common two factor authentication schemes utilized in ATM, debit/retail point-of-sale and prepaid card applications.

Another ATM fraud issue is ATM card theft which includes credit card trapping and debit card trapping at ATMs. Originating in South America this type of ATM fraud has spread globally. Although somewhat replaced in terms of volume by ATM skimming incidents, a re-emergence of card trapping has been noticed in regions such as Europe where EMV Chip and PIN cards have increased in circulation.[96]

Related devices

A Talking ATM is a type of ATM that provides audible instructions so that persons who cannot read an ATM screen can independently use the machine. All audible information is delivered privately through a standard headphone jack on the face of the machine. Alternatively, some banks such as the Nordea and Swedbank use a built-in external speaker which may be invoked by pressing the talk button on the keypad.[97] Information is delivered to the customer either through pre-recorded sound files or via text-to-speech speech synthesis.

A postal interactive kiosk may also share many of the same components as an ATM (including a vault), but only dispenses items relating to postage.[98] [99]

A scrip cash dispenser may share many of the same components as an ATM, but lacks the ability to dispense physical cash and consequently requires no vault. Instead, the customer requests a withdrawal transaction from the machine, which prints a receipt. The customer then takes this receipt to a nearby sales clerk, who then exchanges it for cash from the till.[100]

A Teller Assist Unit may also share many of the same components as an ATM (including a vault), but they are distinct in that they are designed to be operated solely by trained personnel and not the general public, they do not integrate directly into interbank networks, and are usually controlled by a computer that is not directly integrated into the overall construction of the unit.

References

[1] Schlichter, Sarah (2007-02-05). "Using ATM's abroad - Travel - Travel Tips - msnbc.com" (http://www.msnbc.msn.com/id/16994358/). MSNBC. . Retrieved 2011-02-11.

[2] "Inventor of the Week: Archive" (http://web.mit.edu/invent/iow/simjian.html). Web.mit.edu. . Retrieved 2011-02-11.

[3] 'Universal Match Maps Acquisition', The New York Times, 22 March 1961

[4] 'Machine Accepts Cash Deposits', The New York Times, 12 April 1961

[5] 'Fast Machine with a Buck', Pacific Stars and Stripes, p. 7, 14 July 1966

[6] 'Instant Cash via Credit Cards', ABA Banking Journal, p. 99, January 1967

[7] "Enfield's cash gift to the world" (http://www.bbc.co.uk/london/content/articles/2007/06/26/cash_machine_feature.shtml). BBC London. 27 June 2007. .

[8] Milligan, Brian (25 June 2007). "The man who invented the cash machine" (http://news.bbc.co.uk/2/hi/business/6230194.stm). BBC News. . Retrieved 26 April 2010.

[9] "ATM inventor honoured" (http://news.bbc.co.uk/2/hi/uk_news/scotland/4135269.stm). BBC News. 31 December 2004. . Retrieved 26 April 2010.

[10] "ATM inventor John Shepherd-Barron dies at age of 84 on 20th May 2010" (http://latimesblogs.latimes.com/afterword/2010/05/atm-inventor-john-shepherdbarron-dies-at-84.html). The LA Times, May 19, 2010. 19 May 2010. .

[11] Mary Bellis. The ATM of John Shepherd Barron (http://inventors.about.com/od/astartinventions/a/atm_2.htm). About.com. Retrieved 2011-04-29.

[12] B. Batiz-Lazo and R. J. K. Reid. "Evidence from the patent record on the development of cash dispensing technology" (http://ieeexplore.ieee.org/xpl/freeabs_all.jsp?arnumber=4668724). History of Telecommunications Conference, 2008. Histelcon 2008. IEEE. .

[13] 1969: the year everything changed - Google Books (http://books.google.com/books?id=XZMrIchANY4C&pg=PA266). Books.google.com. . Retrieved 2011-02-11.

[14] Popular Mechanics - Google Books (http://books.google.com/books?id=BtEDAAAAMBAJ&lpg=PA84&pg=PA84). Books.google.com. . Retrieved 2011-02-11.

[15] "Interview with Mr. Don Wetzel" (http://americanhistory.si.edu/collections/comphist/wetzel.htm). Americanhistory.si.edu. . Retrieved 2011-02-11.

[16] "Automatic teller machine" (http://www.thocp.net/hardware/atm.htm). The History of Computing Project. Thocp.net. 17 April 2006. . Retrieved 2011-02-11.

[17] (http://www.ebcvg.com/press.php?id=794)

[18] "ATM Industry Association Global ATM Clock" (http://www.atmia.com/mig/globalatmclock/). Atmia.com. . Retrieved 2011-02-11.

[19] http://www.interac.org/en_n3_31_abmstats.html

[20] "Statistics on payment and settlement systems in selected countries - Figures for 2004" (http://www.bis.org/publ/cpss74.htm). Bis.org. 2006-03-31. . Retrieved 2011-02-11.

[21] "Central bank payment system information" (http://www.bis.org/cpss/paysysinfo.htm). Bis.org. 2001-02-05. . Retrieved 2011-02-11.

[22] http://www.eiu.com/site_info.asp?info_name=eiu_Visa_accessing_payments_systems_Latin_America

[23] http://www.bis.org/events/cbcd06e.pdf

[24] http://antarcticsun.usap.gov/oldissues96-97/astdec15.htm

[25] "ABC Nagqu Branch cares about rural Tibetans" (http://en.tibet.cn/news/tin/t20071228_292098.htm). En.tibet.cn. 2007-12-28. . Retrieved 2011-02-11.

[26] (http://www.cts.com.cn/t/tibettravel/list/list_2122_1-1.html)

[27] "תונברצ - 2006 תנשב רוזיאב תונילב 8% לש היילע המשרנ ;םייחל ררועתמ הוומה סי" (http://www.themarker.com/tmc/article.jhtml?log=tag&ElementId=skira20070206_822342). TheMarker. . Retrieved 2011-02-11.

[28] (http://www.fms.treas.gov/news/press/navycash.html)

[29] "ATM Cash Machine Frequently Asked Questions" (http://www.atmdepot.com/help.aspx#f4). Atmdepot.com. . Retrieved 2011-02-11.

[30] "Scope for UL 291" (http://ulstandardsinfonet.ul.com/scopes/scopes.asp?fn=0291.html). Ulstandardsinfonet.ul.com. 2004-12-21. . Retrieved 2011-02-11.

[31] (http://www.ncr.com/en/products/hardware/hw_atm_p75_ts_product.htm)

[32] "CEN On-line catalogue - ICS: 13.310 Protection against crime" (http://www.cenorm.be/catweb/13.310.htm) Comité Européen de Normalisation

[33] "BSI: Standards, Training, Testing, Assessment & Certification" (http://www.bsonline.bsi-global.com/search/item/1928003). Bsonline.bsi-global.com. . Retrieved 2011-02-11.

[34] "Triton Systems I ATM manufacturer" (http://www.tritonatm.com/en/service/manuals/07100-00008F (9100UsrMan(5.0)).pdf). Tritonatm.com. 2010-11-17. . Retrieved 2011-02-11.

[35] http://catless.ncl.ac.uk/php/risks/search.php?query=cash+machine

[36] "Messaging standard to give multiple channels a common language" (http://www.selfserviceworld.com/article.php?id=1252). selfserviceworld.com. . Retrieved 2011-02-11.

[37] "Technology News: Security: Windows Cash-Machine Worm Generates Concern" (http://www.technewsworld.com/story/32350.html). Technewsworld.com. . Retrieved 2011-02-11.

[38] "An end to ram raids?" (http://www.atmmarketplace.com/article.php?id=6736). ATM Marketplace. . Retrieved 2011-02-11.

[39] (http://strategis.ic.gc.ca/epic/internet/inimr-ri.nsf/en/gr114141e.html)

[40] "ATM bombings up 3000%" (http://www.news24.com/SouthAfrica/News/ATM-bombings-up-3000-20080712). News24. 2008-07-12. . Retrieved 2011-04-07.

[41] http://www.theregister.co.uk/2006/03/14/exploding_atm_attack/

[42] "Attacks on banks devised in Europe - National" (http://www.smh.com.au/news/national/attacks-on-banks-devised-in-europe/2008/11/25/1227491548435.html/). smh.com.au. 2008-11-25. . Retrieved 2011-02-11.

[43] http://www.mactwinspecials.com/what_we_offer/gpu_gas_protection_unit/Gas Protection Unit (GPU)

[44] (http://www.atmmarketplace.com/research.htm?article_id=25059&pavilion=126&step=story)

[45] "The No. 1 ATM security concern" (http://www.atmmarketplace.com/article.php?id=7000&na=1). ATM Marketplace. . Retrieved 2011-02-11.

[46] "Diebold ATM Fraud" (http://buy.cuna.org/download/diebold_fraudpaper.pdf) (PDF). . Retrieved 2011-02-11.

[47] (http://www.ibia.org/biometrics/industrynews_view.asp?id=30)

[48] (http://www.ibia.org/biometrics/industrynews_view.asp?id=103)

[49] http://www.kuluttajavirasto.fi/user_nf/default_mag.asp?id=12263&lmf=11440&mode=readdoc&tmf=11440

[50] "Title1" (http://moneycentral.msn.com/content/Banking/P57803.asp). Moneycentral.msn.com. . Retrieved 2011-02-11.

[51] "NYSBD - Text of the ATM Safety Act" (http://www.banking.state.ny.us/legal/atmsafe.htm). Banking.state.ny.us. 1997-06-01. . Retrieved 2011-02-11.

[52] "DiNapoli Calls for Better Oversight of Bank ATMs" (http://www.osc.state.ny.us/press/releases/oct07/100407.htm). Osc.state.ny.us. 2007-10-04. . Retrieved 2011-02-11.

[53] (http://www.atmmarketplace.com/research.htm?article_id=5171&pavilion=4&step=story)

[54] (http://www.atmmarketplace.com/news_story.htm?i=20479)

[55] Representative Mario Biaggi, Congressional Record, July 30, 1986, Page 18232 et seq.

[56] "ATM Report" (http://www.obre.state.il.us/AGENCY/News/atmrpt.htm). Obre.state.il.us. . Retrieved 2011-02-11.

[57] http://www.cunews.com/newsletters/2004216.htm

[58] "sb379_SB_379_PF_2.html" (http://www.legis.state.ga.us/legis/2005_06/versions/sb379_SB_379_PF_2.htm). Legis.state.ga.us. . Retrieved 2011-02-11.

[59] "Illinois General Assembly - Bill Status for SB1355" (http://www.ilga.gov/legislation/BillStatus.asp?DocNum=1355&GAID=10&DocTypeID=SB&LegId=42570&SessionID=76&GA=96). Ilga.gov. . Retrieved 2011-02-11.

[60] Kravetz, Andy (2009-02-18). "ATM software aimed at reversing crime - Peoria, IL" (http://www.pjstar.com/news/x1745367387/ATM-software-aimed-at-reversing-crime). pjstar.com. . Retrieved 2011-02-11.

[61] "Rising interest rates, gas prices hit vault-cash providers" (http://www.selfserviceworld.com/article.php?id=15827&site=5&prc=). selfserviceworld.com. . Retrieved 2011-02-11.

[62] "NCR and Fujitsu Develop Cash Deposit and Bill Recycling Module for ATMs : Fujitsu Global" (http://www.fujitsu.com/global/news/pr/archives/month/2004/20040318.html). Fujitsu.com. . Retrieved 2011-02-11.

[63] "Business | Bank puts the 'fun' into 'funds'" (http://news.bbc.co.uk/1/hi/business/4700053.stm). BBC News. 2005-07-20. . Retrieved 2011-02-11.

[64] Harvey, Rachel (2006-01-10). "Asia-Pacific | Indonesians make ATM sacrifices" (http://news.bbc.co.uk/1/hi/world/asia-pacific/4597692.stm). BBC News. . Retrieved 2011-02-11.

[65] "ATM:ad First For Comic Relief" (http://www.creativematch.co.uk/?action=viewnews&ni=90724). creativematch. 2005-03-10. . Retrieved 2011-02-11.

[66] http://www.interac.org/en_n3_14_consumersfaq.html

[67] "Japan Post to go with fingerprints for ATMs | The Japan Times Online" (http://search.japantimes.co.jp/cgi-bin/nn20060806a5.html). Search.japantimes.co.jp. 2006-08-06. . Retrieved 2011-02-11.

[68] ""Place Your Hand on the Scanner" | Science and Technology | Trends in Japan" (http://web-japan.org/trends/science/sci050510.html). Web Japan. 2005-05-10. . Retrieved 2011-02-11.

[69] Mastrull, Diane (1996-11-11). "Sensar has its eye on the prize with $42 million Japanese deal | Philadelphia Business Journal" (http://www.bizjournals.com/philadelphia/stories/1996/11/11/story4.html). Bizjournals.com. . Retrieved 2011-02-11.

[70] "BAI Banking Strategies Magazine - Articles Online" (http://www.bai.org/nl/v1/N20/articles/V1_N20_01.asp?WT.mc_id=BSRDI_ARTICLEARCHIVE_V1_N20_01). Bai.org. 2011-02-01. . Retrieved 2011-02-11.

[71] "The Check is NOT in the Mail" (http://accurapid.com/journal/16brasbank.htm). Accurapid.com. . Retrieved 2011-02-11.

[72] "Japanese bank to allow cellphone ATM access" (http://www.engadget.com/2006/01/27/japanese-bank-to-allow-cellphone-atm-access/). Engadget. . Retrieved 2011-02-11.

[73] "Wincor Nixdorf Germany" (http://www.wincor-nixdorf.com/internet/se/Products/Software/Banking/MultiChannel/ProSales/index.html) (in **German**). Wincor-nixdorf.com. . Retrieved 2011-02-11.

[74] "Industrial Automated Gas Pumping Station and ATM MCF547x ColdFire® Solutions By Freescale" (http://www.freescale.com/webapp/sps/site/application.jsp?nodeId=02430ZR8tt8105). Freescale.com. . Retrieved 2011-02-11.

[75] "NRT Technology Corporation - Gaming and casino solutions: QuickJack" (http://www.nrtpos.com/html/gamingquickjack.shtml). Nrtpos.com. . Retrieved 2011-02-11.

[76] "Barking Up the Wrong Tree − Factors Influencing Customer Satisfaction in Retail Banking in the UK - Page 5" (http://www. managementjournals.com/journals/marketing/article27-p5.htm). Managementjournals.com. . Retrieved 2011-02-11.

[77] Rebecca Allison (2003-01-16). "ATM gives out free cash and lands family in court I UK news" (http://www.guardian.co.uk/uk_news/ story/0,3604,875749,00.html). London: The Guardian. . Retrieved 2011-02-11.

[78] (http://www.ncr.com/en/self-service/services_v_1.pdf)

[79] (http://www.ottawabusinessjournal.com/286598582617402.php)

[80] "Materials- Bank Notes- Bank of Canada" (http://www.bankofcanada.ca/en/banknotes/education/index.htm). Bankofcanada.ca. . Retrieved 2011-02-11.

[81] "Falschgeld: Blüten aus dem Geldautomat? - Wirtschaft" (http://www.stern.de/wirtschaft/geldanlage/:Falschgeld-Blüten-Geldautomat/ 523625.html). Stern.De. 2004-05-05. . Retrieved 2011-02-11.

[82] "Wincor Nixdorf Germany" (http://www.wincor-nixdorf.com/internet/com/Products/CashSystems/CashRecycling/ProCash3100/ index.html) (in **(German)**). Wincor-nixdorf.com. . Retrieved 2011-02-11.

[83] "1.05: The Bucklands Boys and Other Tales of the ATM" (http://www.wired.com/wired/archive/1.05/atm_pr.html). Wired.com. . Retrieved 2011-02-11.

[84] "Double money in cash point error" (http://news.bbc.co.uk/1/hi/england/tyne/3667279.stm). *BBC News*. 2004-04-28. .

[85] http://www.rbcroyalbank.com/cards/documentation/ch_agreements/ch_agree_client.html

[86] "Europe I Mad rush to faulty ATM in France" (http://news.bbc.co.uk/1/hi/world/europe/4552288.stm). BBC News. 2005-12-23. . Retrieved 2011-02-11.

[87] "Video" (http://www.cnn.com/video/player/player.html?url=/video/tech/2006/09/14/owens.va.atm.scam.wavy). Cnn.com. 2005-06-06. . Retrieved 2011-02-11.

[88] "Kennison v Daire [1986] HCA 4; (1986) 160 CLR 129 (20 February 1986)" (http://www.austlii.edu.au/au/cases/cth/HCA/1986/4. html). Austlii.edu.au. 1986-02-20. . Retrieved 2011-02-11.

[89] http://venus.soci.niu.edu/~cudigest/phracks/phrack-08

[90] Fredric L. Rice, Organized Crime Civilian Response. "Phrack Classic Volume Three, Issue 32, File #1 of XX Phrack Classic Newsletter Issue XXXII" (http://www.skepticfiles.org/hacker/phrack32.htm). Skepticfiles.org. . Retrieved 2011-02-11.

[91] Stephen Castell. "Seeking after the truth in computer evidence: any proof of ATM fraud? — ITNOW" (http://itnow.oxfordjournals.org/ cgi/content/abstract/38/6/17). Itnow.oxfordjournals.org. . Retrieved 2011-02-11.

[92] http://www.snopes.com/crime/warnings/atmcamera.asp

[93] "What the Hell Do Smart Cards Do?" (http://www.fastcompany.com/magazine/56/wth.html). Fast Company. 2002-02-28. . Retrieved 2011-02-11.

[94] "Tamil Nadu / Chennai News : Four more held in fake credit card racket case" (http://www.hindu.com/2006/05/19/stories/ 2006051920380300.htm). Chennai, India: The Hindu. 2006-05-19. . Retrieved 2011-02-11.

[95] Previous post Next post. "Global ATM Caper Nets Hackers $9 Million in One Day I Threat Level" (http://www.wired.com/threatlevel/ 2009/02/atm/). Wired.com. . Retrieved 2011-02-11.

[96] "ATM Security Issues & ATM Fraud Issues by Geography I ATMSecurity.com ATM Security news ATM Security issues ATM fraud info ATM" (http://www.atmsecurity.com/articles/atm-fraud/atm-security-issues-atm-fraud-issues-by-geography.html). Atmsecurity.com. 2009-03-04. . Retrieved 2011-02-11.

[97] pepsi says: (2011-01-25). "Why is there braille on drive-up ATM machines?" (http://zidbits.com/2011/01/25/ why-is-there-braille-on-drive-up-atm-machines/). Zidbits. . Retrieved 2011-02-11.

[98] "Postal Service Mailing Kiosks Now In Every State" (http://www.usps.com/communications/news/press/2004/pr04_098.htm). Usps.com. 2004-12-30. . Retrieved 2011-02-11.

[99] http://www.lunewsviews.com/apc.htm

[100] "About Script ATMs: How Do Cashless ATMs Work? - What is Scrip, or Cashless Atm Machines?" (http://www.atmscrip.com/ what_is_scrip.html). Atmscrip.com. . Retrieved 2011-02-11.

Further reading

- Brain, Marshall *Marshall Brain's More How Stuff Works*, John Wiley and Sons Ltd, New York, October 2002, ISBN 0-7645-6711-X

- Donley, Richard *Everything has its price*, Fireside Books /Simon & Schuster, New Jersey, March 1995, ISBN 0-671-89559-1

- Guile, Bruce R., Quinn, James Brian *Managing Innovation Cases from the Services Industries*, National Academy Press, Washington (D.C.), January 1988, ISBN 0-309-03926-6

- Hillier, David *Money Transmission and the Payments Market*, Financial World Publishing, Kent UK, January 2002, ISBN 0-85297-643-7

- IESNA Committee *Lighting for Automatic Teller Machines*, Illuminating Engineering Society of North America, January 1997, ISBN 0-87995-122-2

- Ikenson, Ben *Patents: Ingenious Inventions How They Work and How They Came to Be*, Gina Black Dog & Leventhal Publishers, Inc., April 2004, ISBN 1-57912-367-8
- Mcall, Susan *Resolution of Banking Disputes*, Sweet & Maxwell, Ltd., December 1990, ISBN 0-85121-644-7
- Peterson, Kirk *Automated Teller Machine as a National Bank under the Federal Law*, William S. Hein & Co., Inc., August 1987, ISBN 0-89941-587-3
- Schneier, Bruce (January 2004). *Secrets and Lies: Digital Security in a Networked World*. John Wiley & Sons. ISBN 0471453803.
- Zotti, Ed *Triumph of the Straight Dope*, Random House, February 1999, ISBN 0-345-42008-X
- *The Fraudsters - How Con Artists Steal Your Money* (http://www.dilloninvestigates.com/index_files/Page390. htm) (ISBN 978-1-903582-82-4)by Eamon Dillon, published September 2008 by Merlin Publishing

External links

- Britain celebrates 40 years of the ATM (http://www.moneytowers.com/2007/news/happy-birthday-atm/)
- *The Money Machines* (http://money.cnn.com/magazines/fortune/fortune_archive/2004/07/26/377172/ index.htm): An account of U.S. ATM history; By Ellen Florian, Fortune.com
- Automated teller machine (http://www.dmoz.org/Business/Financial_Services/Banking_Services/ Automatic_Teller_Machines/) at the Open Directory Project

Autopass Card

Autopass Card is a stored-value smart card for paying VEP fees, toll charges and ERP fees in Singapore. The card can only be sold to foreign motorists. As vehicle information is encoded in the card, it is not transferable between vehicles. It can also act as a CashCard for all CashCard transactions such as paying carparks that use the CashCard system.[1] [2] [3]

Autopass Cards slotted in In-Vehicle units (IU) installed in the vehicle automatically are deducted when the vehicle passes through an ERP gantry./ref name="ap"/> If one does not have an IU, they can take a daily pass to enter the ERP areas such as the Central Business District and Orchard Road./ref name="ap"/> The pass is purchased at $10, valid for one day per pass, for foreign registered cars to enter the CBD during on-peak hours during weekdays. Since 2005, the cost of the pass has been reduced by half.[1] [2] [3]

Autopass Cards are sold at the primary clearance/ immigration booths or VEP/ Tolls office at the Tuas and Woodlands checkpoints in Singapore.[3] Motorists are required to produce valid road tax discs and insurance certificates for their cars when buying the Autopass Cards.[1] [2] [3]

References

[1] Land Transport Authority (http://www.lta.gov.sg/motoring_mattersmotoring_guide_fregis_carbus_sub.htm)
[2] Autopass Card Info (http://www.visitsingpore.com/publish/stbportal/en/home/getting_around/transportation/private_car/ faq_on_driving_into.html)
[3] http://www.asia-planet.net/singapore/selfdrive.htm

BACHO record format

The **BACHO record format** is one of the two standard formats used for the interchange of financial transactions in the New Zealand banking system. The other standard format is QC.

BACHO-format transactions are primarily used in batch processing systems running on MVS mainframe computers.

A BACHO record is a fixed-length 160-byte entity. This length restriction has led to a number of complexities in interpreting the contents of BACHO transactions, including:

- Some BACHO fields are interpreted differently depending on whether they contain numeric or alphabetic data.
- Some BACHO transactions are broken into multiple records, and then reassembled for processing.

BACS

BACS (originally **Bankers' Automated Clearing Services**) is a United Kingdom scheme for the electronic processing of financial transactions. BACS direct debits and BACS direct credits are made using the BACS system. BACS payments take three working days to clear: they are entered into the system on the first day, processed on the second day, and cleared on the third day.

History

BACS was invented by Dennis Gladwell and was started in 1968 as the Inter-Bank Computer Bureau, set up to develop electronic transfer of funds between banks and avoid the need for paper documents as part of the money transfer process. The company operating the service adopted the name "Bankers Automated Clearing Services Limited" in 1971. A telephone service, BACSTEL, was introduced in 1983, reducing the need for magnetic tapes. More banks and building societies joined in 1985, and the company shortened its name to "BACS Limited".

On 1 December 2003, BACS Payment Schemes Limited (BPSL) was split from BACS Limited: BPSL is a "not for profit" body with members from the banking industry which promotes the use of automated payment schemes and governs the rules of the BACS scheme; BACS Limited owns the infrastructure to run the BACS scheme. BACS Limited was permitted to continue to use the BACS name for one year, and became Voca Limited on 12 October 2004. Voca Limited has since been merged with the UK national switch provider LINK Interchange Network Limited on the 2 July 2007, the new company being called VocaLink. It is based at Rickmansworth in Hertfordshire.

Since 2003, BACS has been moving from the telephone dial-up BACSTEL service to an internet-based service, BACSTEL-IP, which is claimed to be quicker and more secure. All BACS users, including businesses that make payments to their suppliers or operate their staff payroll electronically, were required to move to BACSTEL-IP by the end of December 2005 or return to using cheques. When the BACSTEL-IP service was introduced all software used to make a connection to BACS required BACS approval. It is now only possible to make a connection with software from the list of BACS Approved Solution Suppliers (BASS).

Criticism

The BACS system, and in particular the time taken for money to move between accounts, has been widely criticised by consumer groups as inefficient and archaic, especially as it is the system used for money transfers made by telephone or internet banking. This compares unfavourably with other developed countries, particularly in Scandinavia, where the "Elle" system ("Early Late/Late Early") allows money transferred before lunchtime to reach a payee's account on the same working day, or money transferred after lunchtime to reach the payee's account the following morning. In March 2005, the Office of Fair Trading proposed that such a system be introduced in the UK. In December of that year, plans were announced for its introduction in the period from the end of 2006 to 2008, with estimates of the time taken for such payments being between 15 minutes and 3 hours depending on the banks/building societies at each end of the transaction. VocaLink are providing this service in the UK.

Faster Payments Service

On 27 May 2008, the new Faster Payments Service (FPS) went live. This new system has improved money transfer speeds between different banks in the UK enabling account holders with one bank to make virtually instant payments to those with another bank. The system is still in its early stages and currently has a membership comprising the following banks: Abbey, Alliance & Leicester, Barclays, Citigroup, Co-operative Bank, Danske Bank (Northern Bank), HBOS, HSBC, ING Direct, Lloyds TSB, Nationwide Building Society, National Australia Group (Clydesdale and Yorkshire Bank), Northern Rock, the Royal Bank of Scotland Group (including Natwest and Ulster Bank) and Tesco Finance. Between them, they represent 95% of the payments made in the UK. As FPS is intended for low value transfers, banks still use BACS for outgoing transfers of amounts exceeding a value they specify. These limits are typically between £250 to £10,000, depending on the bank.[1]

References

[1] http://www2.firstdirect.com/1/2/banking/faster-payments

External links

- BACS website (http://www.bacs.co.uk/)
- VocaLink website (http://www.vocalink.com/)
- APACS - the UK Payments Association Information on Cheque Clearing (http://www.apacs.org.uk/)
- Criticism of BACS (http://telegraph.co.uk/money/main.jhtml?xml=/money/2005/03/16/cmtrans16.xml) in Daily Telegraph article
- OFT welcomes details on faster clearance on electronic payments (http://www.oft.gov.uk/news/press/2005/230-05)
- BBC News - Clearing times (http://news.bbc.co.uk/1/hi/programmes/moneybox/4428147.stm)
- BBC News - Banking hitch delays workers' pay (29 March 2007) (http://news.bbc.co.uk/1/hi/business/6508791.stm)
- BACS Approved Solution Suppliers List (http://www.bacs.co.uk/Bacs/SoftwareSuppliers/Resources/Pages/ApprovedSoftware.aspx)

Bad Check Restitution Program

A **Bad Check Restitution Program** is a program that works to retrieve funds from bad check writers in order to repay moneys owed to the recipients of the checks. Although some are in-house programs run by prosecutors, others are the functional equivalent of civil debt collection.

About half of all U.S. states offer some type of Bad Check Restitution Program, and these check recovery services vary in many ways. Some accept NSF, stop payment and closed account checks while others may only offer NSF check collection. You will also find that some have time limits (checks submitted for collection may need to be less than 90 or 180 days old). Some will not accept checks that were written under certain circumstances, including a post-dated check, one that the check writer asked the recipient to hold, or one that was written as an extension of credit[1].

Methods

A Bad Check Diversion Program generally pursues the bad check writer by stating (typically from the local District Attorney's office) that the check writer has committed a criminal act, and is subject to prosecution. The check writer is told that s/he may avoid prosecution by meeting the guidelines of the program, which generally include the payment of all monies owed to the recipient, a program fee, and participation in a course designed to improve the check writer's habits.

Generally, enrollment in the program is not an admission of guilt to a crime, and will not result in criminal charges being filed or a criminal record. The check writer is told that if s/he successfully completes all program requirements, the case against him/her dismissed without any possibility of arrest, criminal charges or a record thereafter.

Those failing to complete program requirements are threatened to have their case turned over to the district attorney to be prosecuted like any other criminal case. However, very few checks are ever forwarded to the district attorney, and the likelihood of actual prosecution is remote for most check writers.

Bad Check Restitution Programs have an important place in recovering bad checks. They directly compete with private debt collectors, and have the advantage of being able to send threatening letters on official stationery, telling a check writer that s/he has committed a crime and will likely be prosecuted if s/he does not pay substantial fees and attend a class. They help businesses recover hundreds of thousands of dollars each year throughout the United States. Most Prosecutor offices try to make these programs free to taxpayers (i.e. bad check collection is funded by fees paid by bad check writers). However, in many programs, the check diversion company takes its fees out of the initial payments made by the check writer, so where a check writer only pays the check, and no additional fees, the diversion company ends up charging the merchant a 50% commission.

Criticism of BCRPs

According to law enforcement agencies and district attorneys, BCRPs are diversion programs operated by the county, state, or other jurisdiction that are responsible for collecting funds owed to victims . They claim the purpose is to recover the losses of the victims.

Many consumer advocates oppose the actions of BCRPs, particularly those operated by private, for-profit companies, stating that bad check writing is not a crime unless the check writer actually intended to defraud the recipient. The writer of the bad check is told that the use of the program is optional, but is falsely threatened that the options are to participate, or risk going to jail. The writer is usually informed within the letter that entering the program is not necessary, and it is permissible to stand trial, even though no charges have been, or are likely to be filed.

Sometimes the program is handled internally by the law enforcement agency itself, which often generates a substantial portion of its overall budget from the check fees that it collects . In many cases, the law enforcement agency signs up with a private collection agency. The private company essentially pays the law enforcement agency a small portion of the fees it collect in exchange for permission to send demand letters on official law enforcement agency letterhead and to threaten to prosecute check writers who do not pay up to $200 in fees, plus the check itself. This is when, in most instances, there was no criminal case to dismiss, and no law enforcement official had reviewed the check writer's file to determine if there was evidence of a crime .

Lawsuits against BCRPs

A number of lawsuits have been filed challenging the legality of these programs. On June 3, 2010, a California federal court ruled that defendants violated federal and state law by operating a bad check restitution program in which they sent letters on district attorney letterhead, threatened proseuction and charged fees for a "diversion class." (del Campo v Mealing, 5:01-cv-21151, (USDC ND Cal.). A Michigan federal court ruled that one program violated federal fair debt collection practices laws . In an Iowa class action in federal court, the check restitution company, American Corrective Counseling Services, Inc., agreed to refund some fees to class members . In almost all states, it is not a crime to write a check that has not cleared, unless the check writer knew at the time the check was written that the check would not clear, and was intending to defraud the merchant. Check restitution programs attempt to collect checks, without regard to criminal intent.

In several lawsuits in federal court in Michigan, California, Indiana, Florida, Iowa and other states, consumers have charged that the program is rife with illegal and unfair collection practices, and is an abuse of government power. In a lawsuit in Iowa, Liles v. American Correcive Counseling, Inc., the check diversion company agreed to refund money to class members. In a lawsuit in Michigan, Gradisher v. Check Enforcement Unit, Inc., 210 F. Supp. 2d 907 (W.D. Mich. 2002), the court ruled that the collection practices violated the federal Fair Debt Collection Practices Act. On May 2, 2008, in Schwarm v. Craighead, Civ. No. 05-1304 (E.D.Cal), the United States District Court ruled that the bad check restitution program that was operated in two dozen California counties violated the Fair Debt Collection Practices Act in a variety of ways, including making false threats of prosecution, and charging illegal fees.

References

[1] LA Crime Report07.pub (http://da.co.la.ca.us/pdf/badcheckform.pdf)

External links

- National Check Fraud Center (http://www.ckfraud.org/penalties.html) - explains the laws pertaining to bad checks in all 50 states.
- Consumer Information About Bad Check Restitution Programs (http://www.checkrestitution.com) - explains how bad check restitution programs operated by private companies operate.

Banker's draft

A **banker's draft** (also called a *bank cheque* or, in the US, a *cashier's check*) is a cheque (or check) where the funds are taken directly from the financial institution rather than the individual drawer's account.

A normal cheque represents an instruction to transfer a sum of money from the drawer's account to the payee's account. When the payee deposits the cheque into their account, the cheque is verified as genuine (or 'cleared', a process typically taking several days) and the transfer is performed (usually via a clearing house or similar system). Any individual or company operating a current account (or checking account) has authority to draw cheques against the funds stored in that account.

However, it is impossible to predict when the cheque will be deposited after it is drawn. Because the funds represented by a cheque are not transferred until the cheque is deposited and cleared, it is possible the drawer's account may not have sufficient funds to honour the cheque when the transfer finally occurs. This dishonoured or 'bounced' cheque is now worthless and the payee receives no money, which is why cheques are less secure than cash.

By contrast, when an individual requests a banker's draft they must immediately transfer the amount of the draft (plus any applicable fees and charges) from their own account to the bank's account. (An individual without an account at the issuing bank may request a banker's draft and pay for it in cash, subject to applicable anti-money laundering law and the bank's issuing policies.) Because the funds of a banker's draft have already been transferred they are proven to be available; unless the draft is a forgery or stolen, or the bank issuing the draft goes out of business before the draft is deposited and cleared, the draft will be honoured. Like other types of cheques, a draft must still be cleared and so it will take several days for the funds to become available in the payee's account.

In the United Kingdom the use of bankers' drafts is being phased out. With the advent of new technology such as debit cards, internet banking and Faster Payments the method of a guaranteed paper cheque is now regarded as slower and less secure for both the issuing bank and the customer.

Bankers' clearing house

A **bankers' clearing house** is an organization that transfers money between member banks, originally to clear checks. For more than a century, this service has been expanded to include several other banking services now done electronically.

Predecessors

In England, cheques were used from the 17th century. Up until around 1770 an informal exchange of cheques took place between London Banks. Clerks of each bank visited all of the other banks to exchange cheques, whilst keeping a tally of balances between them until they settled with each other. Daily cheque clearings began around 1770 when the bank clerks met at the Five Bells, a tavern in Lombard Street in the City of London, to exchange all their cheques in one place and settle the balances in cash.

The first Banker' Clearing House

The first organization for clearing checks was the "Bankers' Clearing House" established in London in the early 19th century. It was founded by Lubbock's Bank on Lombard Street in a single room where clerks for London banks met each day to exchange checks and settle accounts. In 1832 Charles Babbage, who was a friend of a founder of the Clearing House, published a book on mass production *The Economy of Machinery and Manufactures* in which Babbage described how the Clearing House operated:[1]

> "In a large room in Lombard Street, about 30 clerks from the several London bankers take their stations, in alphabetical order, at desks placed round the room; each having a small open box by his side, and the name of the firm to which he belongs in large characters on the wall above his head. From time to time other clerks from every [banking] house enter the room, and passing along, drop into the box the checks due by that firm to the house from which this distributor is sent."

Beginning at 5 pm, a clerk for each debtor bank was called to go to a rostrum to pay in cash to the Inspector of the Clearing House the amount their bank owed to other banks on that day. After all of the debtor clerks had paid the Inspector, each clerk for the banks that were owed money went to the rostrum to collect the money owed to their bank. The total cash paid by the debtor banks equaled the total cash collected by the creditor banks. On the rare occasions when the total paid did not equal the total collected, other clerks working for the Inspector would examine the paper trail of documents so that the numerical errors could be found and corrected.

The United States improved on the British check clearing system and opened a bankers' clearing house in the Bank of New York on Wall Street, New York in 1853. Instead of the slow London procedure in which each bank clerk, one at a time, stepped up to an Inspector's rostrum, in the New York procedure two bank clerks from each bank all worked simultaneously. One clerk from each bank sat inside a 70 foot long oval table, while the second clerk from each bank stood outside the table facing the other clerk from the same bank.[2] Each of the outside clerks carried a file box. When the manager signaled, all of the outside clerks stepped one position to the left, to face the next seated clerks. If a seated clerk represented a bank to which money was owed or from which money was receivable, the net amount of cash would change hands, along with checks and paper documents. Thus several such transactions could be conducted simultaneously, across the oval table. When the manager signaled again, this procedure was repeated, so that after about six minutes, the clerks had completed all their assigned transactions and were back to their starting locations, and holding exactly the amount of cash their papers said they should be holding. Clerks were fined if they made errors and the amount of the fine increased rapidly as time passed.[2]

References

- Martin Campbell-Kelly, "Victorian Data Processing", *Communications of the ACM*, Vol. 53, No. 10, October 2010, pages 19–21
- Matthews, P. W., *Bankers' clearing house: what it is and what it does*, 1921, Banker's Library, Pitman

[1] Campbell-Kelly, page 20
[2] Campbell-Kelly, page 21

Bankgiro

Bankgiro is a Norwegian giro system used by all banks in the country, managed by Bankenes Betalingssentral (BBS). The system allows indiscriminate transactions between private accounts in all Norwegian accounts using Norwegian krone. It is optimised for online banking, though it is also available via the post (Brevgiro), using a telephone (Telegiro) or based on automation, including the services Avtalegiro, Autogiro and eFaktura.

The system dates back to 1973 when the commercial banks and the saving banks created a common system that could compete with the Postgiro system used by the postal bank, Postbanken. Use of Bankgiro was free until 1985. In the late 1990s Postgiro was bought out by BBS and Postbanken went over to using Bankgiro.

Bartercard

Bartercard is a barter trading exchange. It is one of the largest in the world. Bartercard enables member businesses to exchange goods and services with other member businesses without using cash or cash equivalents, or having to engage in the direct two-way swap of goods and/or services. It was established in Australia in 1991 and at its height had sold master licences in some 13 countries. Many of these operations have since folded. Most of the franchisees in the UK have failed and been subsequently amalgamated into being company owned.

In 2007, Bartercard Australia was sold in a MBO. Currently, Bartercard continues to operate in 6 countries (Australia, New Zealand, the UK, Thailand, UAE and Cyprus) with an estimated membership of over 20000.

Bartercard provides members with a line of credit which they can use to make purchases immediately, saving the business owners cash. Members earn Bartercard Trade Dollars for the goods and services they sell and this value is recorded electronically in the member's account database, or goes towards repaying the credit that the member may have used.

Bartercard is a major sponsor of the Bartercard Cup, the top level rugby league club competition in New Zealand, and sponsors many other business and sporting organisations.

Trade exchanges require members who participate in a transaction to pay to the exchange a proportion of the nominal value of the price in cash. The rules vary, but can be seen at the websites of the exchanges.

Taxation

For taxation purposes, that is, for calculating taxation liability, the Australian Taxation Office (ATO) treats one Bartercard Trade Dollar as if it were one dollar in legal currency. It also treats other, similar, "barter credits" - for example, EBanc, Contrabart - as if each "barter credit" were one dollar in legal Australian currency. The revenue authorities of the Australian States treat "barter credit" in the same way. The taxation authorities do not say anything about the actual exchange value for cash.

As with anything that can be exchanged for value, the actual cash exchange value of "barter credits" depends on considerations such as their liquidity (which in turn depends to an extent on the number of members of the trade exchange in any given geographical area) and the cash fees charged by the exchange on each transaction.

Although the practice violates the rules of the "barter credit" exchanges, it is common for vendors to increase the nominal price of goods and services that they exchange for "barter credits," so that the cash value is obviously less than 1:1.

The Australian Taxation Office[1] warns the trustees of self-managed superannuation funds that the acquisition of "barter credits" might very well cause the fund to become non-complying. Similarly, the ATO states at the above site that an employer will not comply with its obligations to make contributions to employee superannuation if it makes the contributions in "barter credits."

In fact, the ATO states that "It may also be difficult for trustees to establish a market value for the fund's assets in situations where barter credits are held." That statement directly contradicts the proposition that the ATO "recognises" that a "Bartercard Trade Dollar" has "the same value as the Australian Dollar." ATO Interpretative Decision ID2003/138[2] contains statements to the same ultimate effect.

The ATO has issued two interpretative decisions on the subject. ID2003/138 has already been mentioned.

In ID2003/137[3], the ATO says (in part) about the acquisition of "money" by a superannuation fund:

"Unlike bills of exchange and promissory notes, Trade Dollars are not unconditional, nor convertible to cash, nor a promise or order given in writing and have no assigned monetary value. That is, Trade Dollars can generally only be exchanged for goods and services. Also, credit units arising from barter and counter trade transactions are not acceptable forms of payment for parties external to the bartering arrangements, for example credit units are not acceptable for the payment of tax. Therefore, Trade Dollars are not negotiable instruments and as such are not money."

In 2005/2006, the Australian Taxation Office was investigating an alleged scam by the owners of "barter credit" exchanges, who, of course, can issue "barter credits" to themselves free of cost. The scam supposedly went like this (illustrative numbers only):

(a) The owner would buy goods with a market value of $550 for, say, 1,100 "barter credits." The 1,100 "barter credits" cost nothing, but gave rise to a claim for a $100 GST credit (VAT in Europe). (b) The owner would then resell the goods for $550 cash, incurring a GST debt of $50. (c) After the ATO processed the GST claims, the owner would have $550 in cash, made up of the ex-GST sale price of $500 plus $50 cash from the ATO courtesy of the GST legislation. (d) The owner would claim the nominal loss of $500 as an expense against personal tax. (d) The "barter credit" exchange would write off the 1,100 "barter credits" debt owing by the owner, so reducing its income for company tax purposes by $1,100.

Associated Problems

The major complaint amongst members is the inability to effectively spend their accumulated trade dollars on actual business expenses: the main selling point of Bartercard. Furthermore, many members are known to inflate their selling prices in trade dollars over what they would ordinarily charge in cash. This practice is a violation of the Trading Rules & Regulations, but is rarely, if ever disciplined as the Trade Co-ordinators (Account Managers) are paid a percentage of the overall client base trading volume, providing an incentive to allow members to buy and sell at higher than normal prices.

References

External links

- http://www.bartercard.com.au
- http://www.bartercard.co.nz
- http://www.bartercard.com
- http://www.ato.gov.au/super/content.asp?doc=/content/71292.htm
- http://buyonbarter.co.nz

BASE24

BASE24 is a series of applications produced by ACI Worldwide, Inc. that support payment systems used by large financial institutions.

BASE24-atm

BASE24-atm is an EFT processing and switching system that provides ATM support and management including transaction routing and authorization, Electronic Data Interchange, settlement, reporting, network control, and Stored-value card functionality.[1]

BASE24-eps

BASE24-eps, formerly BASE24-es, is a payment engine that the financial payments industry uses. It is used to acquire, authenticate, route, switch, and authorize financial transactions across multiple channels. [2] It is supported by mainframe computer platforms including z/OS, HP NonStop (Tandem), UNIX (IBM pSeries, Sun Sparc) and IBM zSeries.[3]

BASE24-infobase

BASE24-infobase is used to collect ATM transactions, including EFT payments, and distribute operational data, such as automated software updates. It operates on ATMs with Microsoft Windows operating systems.[4]

BASE24-pos

BASE24-pos is a data integrity support application. It is supported by HP NonStop servers. It has a *Stored Value Module* component that provides online issuance and validation of Stored-value card data. It also has an *ACI Commerce Gateway* component which serves as a firewall between internal servers and the Internet or other payment networks.[5]

References

[1] "BASE24-atm" (http://www.aciworldwide.com/igsbase/igstemplate.cfm/SRC=DB/SRCN=/GnavID=16/SnavID=48). ACI Worldwide, Inc.. . Retrieved 01 Sep 2009.

[2] "BASE24-eps" (http://www.aciworldwide.com/igsbase/igstemplate.cfm/SRC=DB/SRCN=/GnavID=16/SnavID=49). ACI Worldwide, Inc.. . Retrieved 01 Sep 2009.

[3] "A Guide to the ACI Worldwide BASE24-eps on z/OS" (http://www.redbooks.ibm.com/abstracts/sg247684.html). IBM Redbooks. . Retrieved 01 Sep 2009.

[4] "BASE24-pos" (http://www.aciworldwide.com/igsbase/igstemplate.cfm/SRC=DB/SRCN=/GnavID=16/SnavID=102). ACI Worldwide, Inc.. . Retrieved 01 Sep 2009.

[5] "BASE24-pos" (http://www.aciworldwide.com/igsbase/igstemplate.cfm/SRC=DB/SRCN=/GnavID=16/SnavID=103). ACI Worldwide, Inc.. . Retrieved 01 Sep 2009.

The Benefit Company

The Benefit Company
□ □□□ □□ □

Type	Interbank network
Industry	Finance
Founded	November 1997
Headquarters	Bahrain
Products	Financial Services
Website	www.benefitco.com.bh [1]

The Benefit Company (TBC) is the local switch in the Kingdom of Bahrain handling ATM and POS transactions. Established in 1997 with a special license from the Central Bank of Bahrain as "Provider of Ancillary Services to the Financial Sector"[1] , it is the only financial network of its kind in the country.

In addition to the local switching, Benefit is also connected to GCC Net, the main switch operating on all GCC countries. A connection was also established with Shetab in 2005; linking all BENEFIT users with Iran's only switch.

In 2006, the company offered the payment gateway service, integrating more the local banks onto one payment hub allowing banks and their merchants to perform online transactions [2] .

Member Banks in the Network

- Arab Bank Ltd.
- Bank al Habib
- Bank of Bahrain and Kuwait
- Citibank
- HSBC
- Shamil Bank of Bahrain
- Kuwait Finance House
- National Bank of Bahrain
- Standard Chartered Bank
- Bahrain Islamic Bank
- Ahli United Bank
- Bahraini Saudi Bank
- Citibank
- National Bank of Kuwait
- National Bank of Abu Dhabi
- Khaleeji Commercial Bank

- Mashreq Bank
- Al Salam Bank
- Eskan Bank
- ICICI Bank
- State Bank of India

External links

- The Benefit Company's Main Site [1]
- Central Bank of Bahrain's Main Site [4]
- GCCNet's main web site [5]

References

[1] http://www.benefitco.com.bh/company-profile.htm
[2] http://www.ameinfo.com/78148.html Benefit launches payment gateway

Bilhete Único

Bilhete Único

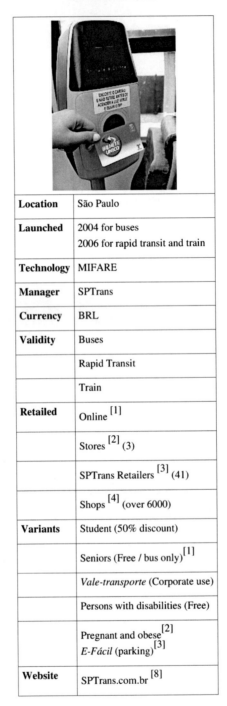

Location	São Paulo
Launched	2004 for buses 2006 for rapid transit and train
Technology	MIFARE
Manager	SPTrans
Currency	BRL
Validity	Buses
	Rapid Transit
	Train
Retailed	Online [1]
	Stores [2] (3)
	SPTrans Retailers [3] (41)
	Shops [4] (over 6000)
Variants	Student (50% discount)
	Seniors (Free / bus only)[1]
	Vale-transporte (Corporate use)
	Persons with disabilities (Free)
	Pregnant and obese[2] *E-Fácil* (parking)[3]
Website	SPTrans.com.br [8]

Bilhete Único (*Unified Ticket*) is the name of the São Paulo transportation contactless smart card system for fare control.

Using Philips Mifare technology, the solution is managed by SPTrans [9] (São Paulo Transporte S/A), the city bus transportation authority, which is controlled by municipal government. On May 18, 2004, when Marta Suplicy was the mayor, it began to be accepted in buses to allow for up to four rides in two hours by paying a single fare.[4] Since 2006 it can also be used in the local rapid transit system (São Paulo Metro) and suburban railways operated by CPTM.

History

The original technological solution (in about 1997) was based on Seoul´s solution and provider, but the project was aborted mostly due software problems with the complex *Vale-Transporte* regulation.

Around 2001/2002 the project was restarted by SPTrans, which decided to be the Solution Integrator and Sponsor, and chose to have at least 2 solution providers for every supply, and not to depend on a sole provider like most other cities do.

Providers

The SPTrans *Projeto de Bilhetagem Eletrônica*, which resulted in the *Bilhete Único*, has at least 30 different solution and service providers directly involved to reach the goal.

The solution was a major gain solving the recharge problem: all cards are pre-paid, and recharge cannot be done onboard. Other Brazilian cities failed on create and spread a large recharge network. Due to "win-win" agreements with Electronic Benefits Cards networks and with the National Lottery network, São Paulo has over 6000 recharge points around the city (January 2010).

The main responsibles for these solutions were:

- SMT*Secretaria Municipal de Transportes [11] of PMSP*Prefeitura Municipal de São Paulo [12] that sponsored the project.
- SPTrans [13] that coordinated all project.

The "brains and arms" providers to SPTrans were:

- Digicon [14], that made most of the smartcard technical definitions, and reference implementations of hardware and software (validators, HSMs, POS and clearing house)
- TTC/Engenharia [15] that helped on major business definitions and public licitations.
- Atech*Tecnologias Críticas [16] that made the deployment coordination and quality assurance.

The TI services providers were:

- Cobra Tecnologia [17] that was the contracted Network and Datacenter Provider
- Diveo [18] that hosts the solution, manage the communications network and operates the Network Operations Center.

The cards providers are:

- Philips, that provides the Mifare 4k chip.
- Sonsun [19], that provides the plastic cards and inlay of about 80% of user cards.
- Gemplus [20], that provides the other cards.

The providers on "debit network", are:

- APB-Prodata [21], that automated around 75% of buses and garages.
- Digicon [14], that automated the other ones.
- Microsoft Consulting Services, responsible by the EDI software solution used on garages.

The providers on "public credit network", are:

- Caixa Econômica Federal, that provides the "public capture and reseller network", using 700+ of his national lottery point-of-sales in the city.
- Digicon [14], that made the POS device, HSMs and security infra-structure.
- S & V Consultoria [22], that made the "Cartão do Estudante" and "Loja Virtual" web

There are also 40 points of recharge on Metro stations and bus terminals.

The providers of "private credit network" or "Rede Complementary", are authorized to provide recharge smartcards are:

- SmartNet [23], that provides a private capture network for many voucher and benefits vendors,
- Rede Ponto-Certo [24], that provides a private capture network to VB Serviços.
- and 2 other minor capture networks.

The customers of "private credit network", authorized to resell "Vale Transporte" are:

- VB-Serviços [25]
- Ticket Restaurante [26]
- Vale Refeição [27]
- Sodexho
- Benefício Fácil [28]
- and 15+ other minor vendors.

Other software and hardware solutions providers are: portals and back-office.

- Microsoft. Windows desktops on all parts. Windows servers, Biztalk and MS-SQL on EDI from garages.
- Oracle, that provides the central SQL database and Dataware House.
- IBM, that provides RISC servers and AIX on central processors.

Fares and regulations

As of January 5, 2010, regular *Bilhete Único* users pay R$ 3.00 for up to four bus rides in a three hour period. Boarding the rapid transit or the train costs R$ 2.65 each. An integration between the systems allow for up to three bus rides and either a rapid transit or train ride in a three hour period for R$ 4.29, provided that the user boards the rapid transit or train in the first two hours.[5] Students and teachers pay half price, while persons with disabilities and seniors have free access.

Notes

[1] For men 65+ and women 60+. Seniors must get a different card to ride the rapid transit and train for free.

[2] Pregnant women from fifth month and people with a BMI over 39.9. These pay a regular fare, but may exit the bus through the front door. Pregnant women enrolled in the UBS (*Basic Health Unit*) can get a special *Mãe Paulistana* card, with which they can get free rides for examinations.

[3] Used for parking cars near rapid transit stations. Allows for two rides in either buses, rapid transit or train. Can also be used as a regular *Bilhete Único*.

[4] Izidoro, Alencar (2004-05-14). "Same fare for two hours starts this month in São Paulo" (http://www1.folha.uol.com.br/folha/cotidiano/ ult95u94221.shtml) (in Portuguese). Folha de S. Paulo. . Retrieved 2010-01-17.

[5] "*Bilhete Único* information" (http://www.sptrans.com.br/bilhete_unico/sobre.aspx) (in Portuguese). Brazil: SPTrans. *Tarifas vigentes*. . Retrieved 2010-01-17.

References

Bill Me Later

Bill Me Later Inc.

Type	Subsidiary
Founded	Timonum, MD USA (2000)
Headquarters	Timonium, Maryland USA
Owner	PayPal
Parent	eBay
Website	billmelater.com [1]
Advertising	none
Current status	active

Bill Me Later is a payment method offered on the websites of many well-known merchants, including those of Wal-Mart, USPS, Best Buy, Overstock.com, American Airlines, JetBlue Airways, Jewelry Television and Hotels.com[1] . The site, which offers credit through CIT Bank, allows purchases to be made online without using a credit card. The company was one of the first recipients of the Red Herring Global 100 Award by the publication Red Herring[2] .

On November 7, 2008, eBay subsidiary PayPal completed its acquisition of Bill Me Later. It was formerly owned by **I4 Commerce**[3])

How it works

After customers open their accounts (including credit check), Bill Me Later asks customers at every purchase to fill out the last 4 digits of their SSN and their date of birth. The approved customer can then pay the bill by mail (check) or online (via bank account) at www.billmelater.com. The first time customers are emailed a link to register with billmelater.com - so that they can check their balances or pay their bill. Customers also get an email whenever they are declined. In cases when they are declined and they don't receive declined email/letter, they can contact Bill Me Later Customer Service to check if it was not a system issue.[4]

Developers/New merchant integration

Unlike its parent company Paypal which is available to most e-commerce entities, Bill Me Later is only available to medium to large businesses. New merchants can request integration through a website operated by the company.

Other products

Besides its flagship consumer service, Bill Me Later also offers Bill Me Later Business (seen at USPS) and Preferred Account (seen at Newegg). In Bill Me Later Business, the users are business owners who want to use the equivalent of a corporate card for buying products and services over the web. The business owner would apply for Bill Me Later Business - using data like EIN etc. The Preferred Account is similar to concept of charge card - that can be used at a particular merchant only.[5]

Bill Me Later in PayPal wallet

After the Paypal acquisition of Bill Me Later, Bill Me Later is offered as a payment method through Paypal at sites that both accept Paypal and Bill Me Later. Paypal balances are not accepted as payment on Bill Me Later statements.

External links

- billmelater.com homepage [7]

References

[1] http://books.google.com/books?id=x6Z1L8kV7NcC&pg=PA428&dq=%22bill+me+later%22&ie=ISO-8859-1&output=html

[2] http://www.accessmylibrary.com/coms2/summary_0286-33603704_ITM

[3] http://www.accessmylibrary.com/coms2/summary_0286-32629188_ITM

[4] http://www.billmelatersolutions.com/faq/bill-me-later

[5] http://www.billmelatersolutions.com/

Bill of credit

Bill of credit is a phrase from Article One, Section 10, Clause One of the United States Constitution. It refers to a document similar to a banknote that is issued by a government and designed to circulate as money. Because the framers of the Constitution sought to limit the issuance of currency, it explicitly prohibits the states from issuing bills of credit. British colonies in North America would issue bills of credit in order to deal with financial crises, although doing so repeatedly would result in inflation. The documents would circulate as if they were currency, and colonial governments would accept them as payment for debts like taxes. They were not always considered legal tender for private debts.

External links

- "Bills of Credit" section of *The Constitutional Law Of The United States*, by Westel Woodbury Willoughby [1]

Billpoint

Billpoint was the name of a person-to-person money transfer service founded in 1998 and purchased in 1999 by online auctioneer eBay.[1] Billpoint's website was taken offline while eBay integrated Billpoint into their auction service, and it did not reappear until the Spring of 2000 when it was relaunched as a joint-venture with Wells Fargo bank.[2]

During this interval, online payment service PayPal was launched, rapidly becoming popular with eBay's customers. Billpoint and eBay spent much of the next two years trying to overtake PayPal, but with mixed results.[2] [3] In July 2002, eBay CEO Meg Whitman agreed to the acquisition of PayPal with its CEO Peter Thiel. When the deal was closed in October 2002, eBay began the process of phasing out Billpoint.[3] The shutdown was completed in early 2003, following the 2002 Christmas holidays.

References

[1] Beth Cox (2002-12-16). "eBay Bidding Bye Bye to Billpoint" (http://www.internetnews.com/ec-news/article.php/1557551). *Internetnews.com.* . Retrieved 2008-03-04.

[2] Eric M. Jackson. *The PayPal Wars: Battles With Ebay, the Media, the Mafia, And the Rest of Planet Earth* (World Ahead Publishing, 2006) ISBN 978-0977898435.

[3] Troy Wolverton (2002-07-08). "Billpoint failure a lesson for eBay?" (http://www.news.com/2100-1017-942231.html). *CNET News.* . Retrieved 2008-03-04.

BitPass

Bitpass, Inc.

Type	Private
Industry	Consumer Internet, Digital content, Online payments
Founded	Mountain View, California (2002)
Headquarters	San Mateo, California, USA
Key people	Kurt Huang, Founder Gyuchang Jun, Founder, CTO Doug Knopper, CEO
Products	Bitpass buyer account, Bitpass Professional merchant account, Bitpass Studio merchant account
Revenue	undisclosed
Employees	undisclosed
Website	www.bitpass.com [1]

Bitpass was an online payment system for digital content and services. Kurt Huang was a co-founder; Doug Knopper was hired as CEO in November, 2005. Bitpass was a California corporation with headquarters in Silicon Valley. It was founded in December, 2002 and partnered with major technology and financial services companies such as Microsoft, PayPal, the Royal Bank of Scotland and First Data.

On January 19, 2007 Bitpass announced that they were shutting down, and operations officially closed on January 26, 2007. No immediate reason for closure was given.

For the content buyer, Bitpass worked like a pre-paid telephone card: the buyer signed up for the service and put money into an account using a credit card or PayPal. This stored-value amount could be used to purchase digital content or services.

Transaction fees were paid by the content provider. For payments under $5, the charge was 15% of the price paid by the buyer (Bitpass Professional merchant account fee).

External links

- Bitpass site [2]
- Misunderstanding Micropayments [3] - article by cartoonist Scott McCloud about micropayments and Bitpass

Blank cheque

A **blank cheque** (**blank check**, **carte blanche**), in the literal sense, is a cheque that has no numerical value written in, but is already signed. In the figurative or metaphoric sense, it is used (especially in politics) to describe a situation in which an agreement had been made that is open-ended or vague, and therefore subject to abuse, or in which a party is willing to consider any expense in the pursuance of their goals.

Literal meaning

Cheque users are normally advised to specify the amount of the cheque before signing it. If created accidentally, a blank cheque can be extremely dangerous for its owner, because whoever obtains the cheque could write in any amount of money, and would be able to cash it (to the extent that the chequeing account contains such funds, also depending on the laws in the specific country).

One might give a blank cheque to a trusted agent for the payment of a debt where the writer of the cheque does not know the amount required, and it is not convenient or possible for the writer to enter the amount when it becomes known. In many cases, it is possible to annotate a cheque with a notional limit with a statement such as "*amount not to exceed $1000*". In theory, the bank should refuse to process a cheque in excess of the stated amount.

The formal American legal term for a blank cheque is an **incomplete instrument** − rather, a blank cheque is an *example* of an incomplete instrument, which more generally is any incomplete signed writing − and these are covered in the Uniform Commercial Code's Article 3, Section 115.[1] Filling in an amount into a blank cheque, without the authority of the signer, is an *alteration* (covered in Article 3, Section 407 [2]), and is legally equivalent to changing the numbers on a completed (non-blank) cheque, namely that the cheque writer is *not* liable for the cheque. However, the cheque writer has the burden of proving that the alteration was not authorized.[2]

Counter cheque

Blank cheque was also commonly used as a synonym for *counter cheque*. Before the Federal Reserve established regulations in 1967[3] requiring that cheques be MICR encoded in order to be handled by their clearing houses, it was fairly common for banks, especially in small towns, to issue cheque to customers which were not personalized other than the name of the bank.

Businesses would have pads of counter cheques which did not even have the bank specified on them - the customer had to not only fill in the value of the cheque, the date, and their signature, but also had to designate the bank on which funds were to be drawn.

Metaphoric meaning

The metaphor of the "blank cheque" is thus often used in politics. For example, in the United States, the Gulf of Tonkin Resolution has been called a blank cheque as it gave the President, Lyndon B. Johnson, the power to "take all necessary measures" to prevent "aggression" in Southeast Asia. These powers were then used to escalate the Vietnam War. Many in the United States Congress protested, but were helpless to effect change, for the Tonkin resolution's terms were too subjective to enforce.

This term was also used to describe how the Kaiser of Germany (Kaiser Wilhelm II) told Austria-Hungary officials that they could deal with Serbia however they wanted after Serbian Nationalists assassinated the heir to the throne of Austria-Hungary, Archduke Franz Ferdinand. This immediately preceded World War I.

An example of the second metaphorical usage can be seen in a BBC News article, in which Gordon Brown, the then Chancellor of the Exchequer, offered a 'blank cheque', and would thus "'spend what it takes" to tackle Iraq's weapons of mass destruction.'[4]

It may also be used in service fields. Customers may tell a company to treat the project as their own, which, in essence, is a carte blanche. (To the extent the service meets normal expectations.)

In literature

One of Literature's renowned *carte blanche* (literally 'white card') was handed out by Cardinal Richelieu in Alexandre Dumas, père's *The Three Musketeers*:

> *Dec. 3, 1627* It is by my order and for the good of the state that the bearer of this has done what he has done.
>
> Richelieu

or in French:

> *3 décembre 1627*. C'est par mon ordre et pour le bien de l'Etat que le porteur du présent a fait ce qu'il a fait.
>
> Richelieu.

Sir Arthur Conan Doyle used the term carte blanche in several of his Sherlock Holmes stories.

> A Scandal in Bohemia

> "Your Majesty will, of course, stay in London for the present?" "Certainly. You will find me at the Langham under the name of the Count Von Kramm." "Then I shall drop you a line to let you know how we progress." "Pray do so. I shall be all anxiety." "Then, as to money?" "You have carte blanche." "Absolutely?" "I tell you that I would give one of the provinces of my kingdom to have that photograph."

> The Adventure of the Beryl Coronet

> "I understand that you give me carte blanche to act for you, provided only that I get back the gems, and that you place no limit on the sum I may draw." "I would give my fortune to have them back."

Blank cheque company

In economics, the term **blank cheque company** can refer to a company in development that has no specific business plan yet. For a fuller discussion of blank cheque companies, see Special purpose acquisition company.

References

[1] § 3-115. INCOMPLETE INSTRUMENT. (http://www.law.cornell.edu/ucc/3/article3.htm#s3-115)

[2] Article 3, Section 115(d) – more precisely, "the burden is on . . . the person asserting the lack of authority."

[3] History of the Dallas Federal Reserve (http://www.dallasfed.org/fed/dalhistory.cfm)

[4] Brown offers war 'blank cheque' (http://news.bbc.co.uk/1/hi/uk_politics/2817965.stm) accessed 2008-05-29

Bluecorner

Bluecorner Cards Ltd is a British company providing prepaid payment cards aimed at under 18s and adults with poor credit ratings. The cards which last for 12 months are being provided as branded items in association with teenage magazines such as *Smash Hits* and *Bliss* and radio station *Magic FM*. They function as Maestro cards.

Bluecorner cards are managed by Affinity Cards Limited for Newcastle Building Society and are regulated by the Financial Services Authority.

Bluecorner cards are available to anyone 13 years or older which has led the National Consumer Council to complain they could encourage debt and "predispose them to using credit cards when they are older". [1]

External links

- Bluecorner public site [2]
- Bluecorner corporate site [3]
- *The Observer*: Teens' card a poor way for them to master money [4]

BPAY

BPAY is a payment method in Australia allowing Internet banking or telephone banking payments to registered BPAY merchants.

The BPAY scheme was launched in 1997 and now more than 170 Australian banks, credit unions and financial institutions are participating members, covering around 90% of Australian consumer bank accounts. BPAY was the world's first single bill payment service adopted across the banking sector. Each month approximately 18 million bills to the value of $11 billion are paid to more than 16,000 business using BPAY.

In 2002 BPAY View was introduced. BPAY View is a bill payment service that delivers bills and statements electronically through Australian internet banking sites.

BPAY is a subsidiary of CardLink Services Limited (CSL).

Fees

The BPAY scheme sets a wholesale fee, called the Capture Reimbursement Fee (CRF), for BPAY payments. This fee is paid by the biller's financial institution to the bill payer's financial institution, as a reimbursement for the costs of capturing and processing bill payment instructions. Consumers are charged for the use of BPAY at the discretion of their bank.

External links

- BPAY website [1]
- CardLink website [2]

References

Card association

A **card association** is a network of issuing banks and acquiring banks that process payment cards of a specific brand.

Examples

Familiar payment card association brands include Visa, MasterCard, American Express, Discover, Diner's Club, and JCB. Visa, MasterCard and American Express issuers co-brand with their card association. for example, "WellsFargo-Visa" and "Citi-MasterCard".

Statistics

Card associations Visa and MasterCard each comprise over 20,000 card issuing banks [1].

Among US consumers alone, over 600,000,000 payment cards are in circulation [2].

Worldwide, Visa issuers have over 1.5 billion payment cards in circulation[3] [4].

References

[1] Is Credit Card Debt Bad For Your Health? (http://www.medicalnewstoday.com/articles/55299.php)

[2] frontline: secret history of the credit card: watch online I PBS (http://www.pbs.org/wgbh/pages/frontline/shows/credit/view/)

[3] Visa raises $17.9 billion in record IPO I Reuters (http://www.reuters.com/article/ousiv/idUSWEN458920080319?pageNumber=3&virtualBrandChannel=0&sp=true)

[4] Visa's Big Deal (http://www.fool.com/investing/value/2008/02/26/visas-big-deal.aspx)

CardIt

CardIt, LLC.

Type	Private
Industry	Consumer Internet, Credit Cards, Mortgage, Online payments
Founded	San Francisco, California (2006)
Headquarters	San Francisco, California, USA
Key people	Philip Mikal, Co-Founder Alexander Zada, Co-Founder
Products	Mortgage payments via credit card
Revenue	undisclosed
Employees	undisclosed
Website	www.cardit.com [1]

CardIt is an online payment system for monthly mortgage bills using a major credit card. Philip Mikal and Alex Zada were co-founders. CardIt is a California limited liability corporation with headquarters in San Francisco. It was founded in 2006 and has partnered with major technology and financial services companies.

Criticism

Consumer watchdog groups such as American Consumer Credit Education Support Services argue that while Cardit's services may give some people added flexibility when making their mortgage payments, the service is just as likely to get many panicked consumers even deeper in debt, especially given the 2007 Subprime mortgage financial crisis.[1]

References

[1] (Un)Real Estate | tampabay.com: Archives (http://blogs.tampabay.com/realestate/2007/09/behind-on-your-.html)

External links

- CardIt (http://cardit.com/)
- Putting house payments on plastic gives new meaning to 'credit crunch' (http://sanfrancisco.bizjournals.com/sanfrancisco/stories/2007/09/17/tidbits1.html?jst=cn_cn_lk)

CarIFS

Caribbean Integrated Financial Services Inc. (CarIFS) is a Barbados-based ABM-network provider. Using the name CarIFS (for short), the company's offering allows customers of various financial institutions in Barbados to have 24-hour access to cash from their Bank Accounts via any CarIFS affiliated Automated Banking Machine (ABM) in the country. The Manager of Carifs is currently David Robinson[1] .

Statistics

The network links over 104 automated banking machines and 35 hundred point of sale terminals through-out Barbados. For 2006 the network recorded a total of 3.5 million transactions.[2]

Banks with ABMs on CarIFS

- Barbados National Bank (BNB)
- Barbados Public Workers Co-Op Credit Union Ltd [3]] (BPWCCUL
- City of Bridgetown Co-op Credit Union Ltd. (COB)
- FirstCaribbean International Bank (FCIB)
- Royal Bank of Canada (RBC)
- Scotiabank

References

[1] "Carifs pleased with COB deal" (http://web.archive.org/web/20070927001420/http://www.cbc.bb/content/view/10532/46/). Caribbean Broadcasting Corporation. Archived from the original (http://www.cbc.bb/content/view/10532/46/) on 2007-09-27. . Retrieved 2007-04-25.
[2] "Carifs pleased with COB deal" (http://web.archive.org/web/20070927001420/http://www.cbc.bb/content/view/10532/46/). Caribbean Broadcasting Corporation. Archived from the original (http://www.cbc.bb/content/view/10532/46/) on 2007-09-27. . Retrieved 2007-04-25.

External links

- Official website (https://www.carifs.com/)
  - Prism Services Inc. (http://www.prismco.com/)

Cash advance

A **cash advance** is a service provided by most credit card and charge card issuers. The service allows cardholders to withdraw cash, either through an ATM or over the counter at a bank or other financial agency, up to a certain limit. For a credit card, this will be the credit limit (or some percentage of it).

Cash advances generally incur a fee (to replace the interchange fee normally charged to the merchant on a card transaction), although this is sometimes waived if the account is in credit. When made on a credit card, they are usually charged at a higher rate of interest than store purchases, and generally do not attract an interest-free period which is customarily given to cardholders who pay off their bill in full every month.

Some "purchases" made with a credit card of items that are viewed as cash are also considered to be cash advances in accordance with the credit card's guidelines, thereby incurring the higher interest rate and the lack of the grace period. These often include money orders, lottery tickets, gaming chips, and certain taxes and fees paid to certain governments.

Under card scheme rules, a credit card holder presenting an accepted form of identification must be issued a cash advance over the counter at any bank which issues that type of credit card, even if the cardholder cannot give his or her PIN.

Cashier's check

A **cashier's check** (**cashier's cheque**, **bank check**, **official check**, **demand draft**, **teller's check**, **bank draft** or **treasurer's check**) is a check guaranteed by a bank. They are treated as guaranteed funds and usually cleared the next day. It is the customer's right to request "next-day availability" when depositing a cashier's check in person. Most banks do not clear them instantly. However, banks are permitted to take back money from a "cleared" check one or two weeks later if subsequent processing finds it to be fraudulent. Because customers believe the checks have been found valid and have been converted to cash in hand, customers are readily defrauded by schemes that ask them to part with goods or a portion of the money if it is cleared in a timely manner.

Characteristics

Cashier's checks feature the name of the issuing bank in a prominent location, usually the upper left-hand corner or upper center of the check. In addition, they are generally produced with enhanced security features, including watermarks, security thread, color-shifting ink, and special bond paper. These are designed to decrease the vulnerability to counterfeit items. To be recognized as a cashier's check, words to that effect must be included in a prominent place on the front of the item.

The payee's name, the written and numeric amount to be tendered, the remitter's information, and other tracking information (such as the branch of issue), are printed on the front of the check. The check is generally signed by one or two bank employees or officers; however, some banks issue cashier's checks featuring a facsimile signature of the bank's chief executive officer or other senior official.

Some banks contract out the maintenance of their cashier's check accounts and check issuing. One leading contractor is Integrated Payment Systems, which issues cashier's checks and coordinates redemption of the items for many banks, in addition to issuing money orders and other payment instruments. In theory, **teller's checks** are checks issued by a financial institution but drawn on another institution, as is often the case with credit unions.

Due to an increase in fraudulent activities in 2006 many banks insist upon waiting for a cashier's check to clear the originating institution. Personal checks will thus have the same utility in such transactions.[1]

Legal definition

In the United States, under Article 3 of the Uniform Commercial Code, a cashier's check is effective as a note of the bank. Also, according to Regulation CC (Reg CC) of the Federal Reserve, cashier's checks are recognized as "guaranteed funds" and amounts under $5,000 are not subject to deposit holds. The length of a hold varies (2 days to 2 weeks) depending on the bank. It is not clear what length of time may pass before a bank can be held responsible for accepting a bad cashier's check.

Alternatives and risks

Money orders are a popular alternative to cashier's checks and are considered safer than personal bank checks. However, they are generally not recognized as "guaranteed funds" under Reg CC, and are limited to a specified maximum amount ($1,000 or less under U.S. law for domestic postal money orders).

Because of regulatory requirements associated with the Patriot Act and the Bank Secrecy Act due to updated concerns over money laundering, most insurance and brokerage firms will no longer accept money orders as payment for insurance premiums or as deposits into brokerage accounts.

Counterfeit money orders and cashier's checks have been used in certain scams to steal from those who sell their goods online on sites such as eBay and Craigslist.[1]

The *counterfeit cashier's check scam* is a scheme where the victim is sent a cashier's check or money order for payment on an item for sale on the Internet. When this document is taken to the bank it may not be detected as counterfeit for 10 business days or more, but the bank will deposit the money into the account and state that it has been "verified" or is "clear" in about 24 hours. This gives the victim a false feeling of security that the document is real, so they proceed with the transaction. When the bank does find that the check is counterfeit, they will come back to the customer for the entire amount of the check.

References

[1] Mosch S. Our story. (http://www.scamvictimsunited.com/our_story.htm) Scam Victims United, viewed 2010=06=16

External links

- Tips For Fake Check Scams From The National Fraud Information Center (http://www.fraud.org/tips/internet/fakecheck.htm)

Cashplus

Cashplus

Type	Prepaid card
Owner	Advanced Payment Solutions Limited
Country	United Kingdom
Introduced	2005
Markets	Financial services
Website	www.mycashplus.co.uk [1]

Cashplus is a prepaid credit card operated by Advanced Payment Solutions in association with MasterCard. Announced in September 2005, it was the first prepaid credit card to be launched in the UK.[1] As of 2008, it was Europe's leading MasterCard-based prepaid service.[2]

The card can be used to shop online, in store or over the phone using funds loaded onto the card in advance, and can be topped up in a variety of places, including the UK Post Office locations, Epay outlets or through a standing order with a bank or employer.

Cashplus pricing plans include a monthly plan with unlimited transactions or a per-transaction fee. Other Cashplus card fees include those associated with other a prepaid cards, including a fee to purchase the card and using an ATM. The cards are recommended for people who need to move money between countries, as unlike traditional wire services they do not charge a percentage of the amount transferred.[3]

See Also

Payoneer

References

[1] "Payment cards are first step towards making cash obsolete" (http://www.independent.co.uk/money/invest-save/ payment-cards-are-first-step-towards-making-cash-obsolete-508069.html). The Independent. 24 September 2005. .

[2] "Advanced Payment Solutions Moves Europe's Leading MasterCard-Branded Prepaid Portfolio to Metavante" (http://www.bloomberg. com/apps/news?pid=conewsstory&refer=conews&tkr=MV:US&sid=aeVJpUA0ihA0). Bloomberg. 17 April 2008. .

[3] "Pre-pay cards: do you need one?" (http://www.iii.co.uk/articles/articledisplay.jsp?article_id=4846514&section=Planning). Interactive Investor. 29 October 2006. .

External links

- Official cashplus website (http://www.mycashplus.co.uk)
- Advanced Payment Solutions website (http://www.apsgroup.com)

CashU Inc

cashU is a prepaid online and mobile payment method available in the Middle East and North Africa, a region with a large and young population with very limited access to credit cards. Because of this, cashU has become one of the most popular alternative payment option for young Arabic online gamers and e-commerce buyers.

cashU was established in 2003 by Maktoob in Amman, Jordan but when Yahoo! acquired Maktoob in November 2009 the ownership of cashU was transferred to Jabbar Internet Group [1] who also owns companies like Souq.com [2], Ikoo, Sukar and Tahadi Games.

Today cashU has established offices in Dubai, Amman and Cyprus

cashU is mainly used for paying for online games, VoIP, matrimonial, IT services, FX trading and download of music and software. Due to cashU's Arabic focus a strict policy on not accepting merchants providing gambling and sexual related content is followed. cashU also provide a parental control feature allowing parents to limit and control where their kids spend money online.

External links

- cashU home [3]
- cashU on Twitter [4]

CCBill

CCBill is an Internet billing service. Established in 1998, the company provides third-party billing, or turn-key solutions, for e-Merchants requiring payments by way of credit card, debit card, or e-check, European Debit/Direct Pay, and telephone payment.

CCBill provides billing services for a variety of subscriptions and services. CCBill began offering services to European companies in 2001 through their CCBill EU service.

Complaints

The consumer website Ripoff Report reports over 100 complaints pertaining to fraudulent billings and failure to process valid refunds.[1] The British technology news website The Register has also reported on alleged database breaches and insecurities.[2] [3] [4] [5]

Perfect 10 lawsuit

In 2006, CCBill was sued in United States District Court in California by men's magazine Perfect 10 for "violat[ing] copyright, trademark, and state unfair competition, false advertising and right of publicity laws by providing services to websites that posted images stolen from Perfect 10's magazine and website". CCBill won this lawsuit in support of existing DMCA regulations.[6]

Awards

- 2011 XBIZ Award - Billing Company of the Year-IPSP [7]
- 2010 Cybersocket Web Awards - Best Billing Company[8]
- 2009 XBIZ Award – Billing Company of the Year[9]
- 2008 XBIZ Award – Billing Company of the Year[10]
- 2007 Cybersocket Web Awards - Best Billing Company[11]
- 2006 XBIZ Award – Billing Company of the Year[12]
- 2006 Cybersocket Web Awards - Best Billing Company[13]
- 2005 Cybersocket Web Awards - Best Billing Company[14]
- 2004 Cybersocket Web Awards - Best Billing Company[15]
- 2003 XBIZ Award – Billing Company of the Year[16]

References

[1] CCBill complaints on 'Ripoff Report' (http://www.ripoffreport.com/Search/ccbill.aspx). Retrieved on 2009-10-08

[2] Greene, Thomas. "Hacking credit cards is preposterously easy" (http://www.theregister.co.uk/2000/03/24/hacking_credit_cards_is_preposterously/), The Register, 2000-03-24. Retrieved on 2009-02-23

[3] Greene, Thomas. "Porno paymaster CCBill hacked hard" (http://www.theregister.co.uk/2001/12/28/porno_paymaster_ccbill_hacked_hard/), The Register, 2001-12-28. Retrieved on 2009-02-23

[4] Greene, Thomas. "CCBill knew of credit database breach in March" (http://www.theregister.co.uk/2002/01/03/ccbill_knew_of_credit_database/), The Register, 2002-01-02. Retrieved on 2009-02-23

[5] Leyden, John. "Adult payment firm denies customer records breach" (http://www.theregister.co.uk/2006/03/10/smut_database_mystery/), The Register, 2006-03-10. Retrieved on 2009-02-23

[6] "Perfect 10 v CCBill" (http://www.policybandwidth.com/doc/20070831-JBand-CCBill.pdf). Retrieved on 2009-02-23

[7] XBIZ Award Winners (http://www.xbizawards.com/winners.php), *XBIZ*, February, 2011

[8] http://www.cybersocketwebawards.com/past_winners.php

[9] 2009 XBIZ Award Winners (http://www.xbizawards.com/winners.php)

[10] (http://www.xbizawards.com/winners.php)

[11] http://www.cybersocketwebawards.com/past_007.php

[12] (http://www.xbizawards.com/winners.php)

[13] http://www.cybersocketwebawards.com/past_006.php

[14] http://www.cybersocketwebawards.com/past_005.php

[15] http://www.cybersocketwebawards.com/past_004.php

[16] (http://www.xbizawards.com/winners.php)

External links

- CCBill corporate website (http://www.ccbill.com/)
- EU website (http://www.ccbilleu.com/)

Central Securities Depository

A **Central Securities Depository** (CSD) is an organization holding securities either in certificated or uncertificated (dematerialized) form, to enable book entry transfer of securities. In general, each country will have only one CSD (although there are some that split equities, fixed-income, and funds into separate CSD's). The CSD will normally only have local financial institutions regulated in the country of the CSD as clients. In some cases these organizations also carry out centralized comparison, and transaction processing such as clearing and settlement of securities. The physical securities may be immobilised by the depository, or securities may be dematerialised (so that they exist only as electronic records).

International Central Securities Depository

An International Central Securities Depository (ICSD) is a central securities depository that settles transactions in **Eurobonds**. There are only two ICSD's globally, Clearstream (earlier Cedel), and Euroclear. Both were established in the early 1970s to provide an efficient settlement environment for the then nascent Eurobond market. Both entities have a joint arrangement with so-called "Common Depositories" in multiple countries to allow them to move securities between clients in both organisations on a book-based basis. In addition to the ICSD functionality which only these two organisations share, both organisations also provide international custody and settlement services in international securities and in various domestic securities, usually through direct or indirect (through local agents) links to local CSDs. In this activity, they are joined by two other CSD's, SIX SIS with some $ 1 trillion in non-Swiss assets and [[Depository Trust Company|The Depository Trust Company (DTC) [1]], holding over $2 trillion in non-US securities and in American Depository Receipts from over 100 nations.

Functions

- **Safekeeping** Securities may be in dematerialized form, book-entry only form (with one or more "global" certificates), or in physical form immobilized within the CSD.
- **Deposit and Withdrawal** Supporting deposits and withdrawals involves the relationship between the transfer agent and/or issuers and the CSD. It also covers the CSD's role within the underwriting process or listing of new issues in a market.
- **Dividend, interest, and principal processing, as well as corporate actions including proxy voting** Paying and transfer agents, as well as issuers are involved in these processes, depending on the level of services provided by the CSD and its relationship with these entities.
- **Other services** CSDs offer additional services aside from those considered core services. These services include Securities Lending and Borrowing, Matching, and Repo Settlement
- **Pledge** - Central depositories provide pledging of share and securities. Every country required to provide legal framework to protect the interest of the pledgor and pledgee.

However, there are risks and responsibilities regarding these services that must be taken into consideration in analyzing and evaluating each market on a case-by-case basis.[1]

References

[1] exchange-handbook.co uk article (http://www.exchange-handbook.co.uk/articles_story.cfm?id=38756&search=1) on the risks associated with Depositories, at the *Handbook of world stock, derivative and commodity exchanges* website.

External links

- CSD Ratings and News Services (http://www.thomasmurray.com/csd-ratings/central-securities-depository-ratings.html)
- http://www.uk.vp.dk/

Centricom

Centricom Pty Ltd

Type	Private company
Industry	Online banking
Founded	2004
Headquarters	Melbourne, Australia
Key people	Simon Warner, CEO
Products	Electronic commerce
Website	www.centricom.com [1]

Centricom Pty Ltd is an online payments company based in Melbourne, Australia and Cardiff, United Kingdom. It is the developer and provider of the POLi, an online payment system that is used by merchants and consumers in Australia, New Zealand and the United Kingdom.

Using POLi consumers can pay for goods on websites with funds taken directly from their bank accounts, allowing merchants to instantly see that funds are on the way. This allows merchants to immediately dispatch the order to the consumer, even if the funds take several days to clear.

References

- Baltazar, Michelle (2007). "Just debit it: Centricom", *Financial Standard*, Financial Standard Article [2].

External links

- Corporate Centricom Pty Ltd site [1]
- Centricom on BusinessWeek [3]
- Neteller Acquires stake in Centricom [4]

Certified check

A **certified check** or **certified cheque** is a form of check for which the bank verifies that sufficient funds exist in the account to cover the check, and so certifies, at the time the check is written. Those funds are then set aside in the bank's internal account until the check is cashed or returned by the payee. Thus, a certified check cannot "bounce", and, in this manner, its liquidity is similar to cash, absent failure of the bank.

In some countries, e.g. Germany, it is illegal for a regular bank to certify checks.[1] This regulation is supposed to prevent certified checks from becoming a universal substitute for cash, which is considered the only legal tender. The Deutsche Bundesbank (Federal Bank) is the only financial institution authorized to issue certified checks.

The liquidity and certainty of payment of a certified cheque explains the fact that it is sometimes considered equivalent to cash, such as in the regulation of credit for casino gaming in Macau, where the law explicitly states that if a casino patron obtains casino chips and pays with a certified cheque, the transaction is not regarded as credit for gaming (see Law 5/2004, art. 2).

Banks such as U.S. Bancorp in the United States will still place a hold on certified checks on new accounts for 5 business days. The explanation given is that it is due to fraud and it is for the account holder's protection.

References

[1] Art. 4 of the German Check Code (Scheckgesetz) (http://bundesrecht.juris.de/scheckg/art_4.html)

External links

- Definition at law.com (http://dictionary.law.com/default2.asp?selected=163&bold=|||||)

Certified Funds

In the United States and Canada, **Certified Funds** are a form of payment that is guaranteed to clear or settle by the company certifying the funds.

When making certain types of transactions, such as purchasing real property, motor vehicles and other items that require title, the seller usually requires a guarantee that the payment method used will satisfy the obligations. To do this, the seller will require certified funds, usually in the form of:

- certified bank check
- cashier's check
- money order (usually with proper identification)
- traveler's check (usually with proper identification)
- EBT wire transfer (i.e. Western Union)

Specifically, personal checks are not allowed, as the account may not have sufficient funds, and credit cards are not allowed, as the transaction may later be disputed or reversed.

Sometimes steps may be taken to ensure that certified funds cannot easily be forged. These steps can include various unique stamps, inks and hole punchers, as well as the assistance of a machine such as a protectograph. Unfortunately these steps cannot prevent someone from erasing the payee's name and writing in their own name. Fraud is specifically not reimbursed by many issuer's of money orders (e.g. Western Union), and so has to go through local police. The perpetrator can then claim "identity theft" to the investigating detective. Such money orders can be obtained from places like rent-drop boxes.

Certified Payment-Card Industry Security Auditor

Certified Payment-Card Industry Security Auditor (CPISA) is an independent payments industry certification governed by the **Society of Payment Security Professionals** (commonly known as the SPSP). The CPISA focuses on information technology, information security, and auditing knowledge and skills. This certification is held by members from diverse backgrounds including Level 1 - 4 Merchants, Acquirers, Issuers, QSAs, Processors, Gateways, Service Providers, Consultants, and Auditors. All CPISA holders are members of the SPSP and also hold the CPISM certification.

Certification Knowledge Domains

The CPISA curriculum covers subject matter in a variety of Information Security and Payments Industry topics. The CPISA examination is based on what a collection of topics relevant to payment industry security professionals. The CPISA Knowledge Domains establishes a common framework of payment industry terms and definitions that allow security professionals to discuss and debate matters pertaining to the profession with a common understanding.

The CPISA Knowledge Domains are[1] :

- Information Technology and Networking
- Information Security Concepts
- Auditing

Requirements

Candidates for the CPISA must meet several requirements:[1]

- First, join the Society of Payment Security Professionals
- Second, provide a resume with current credentials and two letters of reference from industry professionals. Candidates must also have at least three years of information security or payment industry experience.
- Third, one must pass the CPISM and CPISA exams
- Upon completion of the exams with a passing grade, the SPSP will issue the CPISA Certificate

Reference Documents

The SPSP provides several reference documents for studying and preparing for the CPISA certification:

- CPISA Overview Document[2]
- CPISA Study Guide[3]

External links

- Society of Payment Security Professionals [4] Industry professionals and CPISA industry certification
- Society of Payment Security Professionals Podcast [5]
- PCI DSS Standard [6]
- Payment Card Industry Fact Sheets [7]

References

[1] SPSP (CPISA) (http://www.paymentsecuritypros.com/CPISA/)

[2] SPSP (CPISA Overview Document) (https://www.paymentsecuritypros.com/attachments/wysiwyg/1/CPISA_Overview_0709pages.pdf)

[3] SPSP (CPISA Study Guide) (https://www.paymentsecuritypros.com/attachments/wysiwyg/1/CPISAStudyguide0908.pdf)

Certified Payment-Card Industry Security Manager

Certified Payment-Card Industry Security Manager (CPISM) is an independent payments industry certification governed by the **Society of Payment Security Professionals** (commonly known as the SPSP). The CPISM is the de facto certification for payment security professionals. This certification is held by members from diverse backgrounds including Level 1 - 4 Merchants, Acquirers, Issuers, QSAs, Processors, Gateways, Service Providers, and Consultants. All CPISM holders are members of the SPSP.

Certification Knowledge Domains

The CPISM curriculum covers subject matter in a variety of Information Security and Payments Industry topics. The CPISM examination is based on what a collection of topics relevant to payment industry security professionals. The CPISM Knowledge Domains establishes a common framework of payment industry terms and definitions that allow security professionals to discuss and debate matters pertaining to the profession with a common understanding.

The CPISM Knowledge Domains are[1] :

- Payment card industry structure
- Payment card structure and data
- Payment card transaction processing
- Compromise fraud statistics and trends
- Merchant risk analysis
- Laws and the regulatory environment
- Payment card security programs
- Third party relationships

Requirements

Candidates for the CPISM must meet several requirements:[1]

- First, join the Payment Card Security Community
- Second, provide a resume with current credentials and two letters of reference from industry professionals
- Third, one must pass the CPISM exam
- Upon completion of the exam with a passing grade, the SPSP will issue the CPISM Certificate

Reference Documents

The SPSP provides several reference documents for studying and preparing for the CPISM certification:

- CPISM Overview Document[2]
- CPISM Bibliography[3]
- CPISM Study Guide[4]

External links

- CPISI Industry Certification - SISA Information Security [5]
- Society of Payment Security Professionals [4] Industry professionals and CPISM industry certification
- Society of Payment Security Professionals Podcast [5]
- PCI DSS Standard [6]
- Payment Card Industry Fact Sheets [7]

References

[1] SPSP (CPISM) (http://www.paymentsecuritypros.com/CPISM/)

[2] SPSP (CPISM Overview Document) (http://www.paymentsecuritypros.com/attachments/contentmanagers/21/CPISM_Overview.pdf)

[3] SPSP (CPISM Bibliography) (http://www.paymentsecuritypros.com/attachments/contentmanagers/21/CPISM Bibliography_May08.pdf)

[4] SPSP (CPISM Study Guide) (http://www.paymentsecuritypros.com/attachments/contentmanagers/21/CPISM Study Guide_May2008.pdf)

CHAPS

The **Clearing House Automated Payment System** or **CHAPS** is a British company established in London in 1984, which offers same-day sterling fund transfers. CHAPS used to offer euro fund transfers, however this service is now closed. CHAPS is a member of the trade organisation APACS, and the EU-area settlement system TARGET.

A CHAPS transfer is initiated by the sender to move money to the recipient's account (at another banking institution) where the funds need to be available (cleared) the same working day. Unlike with a bank giro credit, no pre-printed slip specifying the recipient's details is required. Unlike cheques, the funds transfer is performed in real-time removing the issue of float or the potential for payments to be purposefully stopped by the sender, or returned due to insufficient funds, even after they appear to have arrived in the destination account.

CHAPS is used by 19 settlement banks including the Bank of England and over 400 sub-member financial institutions. In its first year of operation, average daily transactions numbered 7,000 with an annual value of 5 billion pounds sterling. In 2004, twenty years later, average daily transactions numbered 130,000 with an annual value of 300 billion pounds sterling.[1]

CHAPS transfers are relatively expensive, with banks typically charging as much as £35 for a transfer. The cost of fast transfers and the slow speed of free transfers (such as BACS) is sometimes a subject of controversy in the UK,[2] although low value transactions are now available from CHAPS from its Faster Payments Service.[3]

The Sterling members:[4]

- ABN Amro Bank N.V
- Bank of England
- Bank of Scotland (HBOS)
- Barclays Bank Plc
- Citibank N.A
- Clydesdale Bank Plc

- Cls Bank International
- The Co-Operative Bank Plc
- Deutsche Bank A.G
- HSBC Bank Plc
- Lloyds TSB Bank Plc
- National Westminster Bank Plc
- The Royal Bank of Scotland Plc
- Santander UK
- Standard Chartered Bank

The Euro members:[4]

- ABN Amro Bank N.V
- Bank of America N.A
- Bank of England
- Bank of Scotland (HBOS)
- Barclays Bank Plc
- The Bank of Tokyo-Mitsubishi UFJ Ltd
- Citibank N.A
- The Co-Operative Bank Plc
- Deutsche Bank A.G
- Dnb Nor Bank ASA
- HSBC Bank Plc
- Jp Morgan A.G
- Lloyds TSB Bank Plc
- National Australia Bank
- National Westminster Bank Plc
- The Royal Bank of Scotland Plc
- Santander UK
- Standard Chartered Bank
- Wachovia Bank N.A

CHAPS clearing information relating to UK banks may be found in the Industry Sorting Code Directory.

External links

- CHAPS Clearing Company [5]
- APACS - Bankers Drafts and Cheque Clearing [6], which has a section on CHAPS

References

[1] APACS website (http://www.apacs.org.uk/uk_payment_schemes/chaps_clearing.html)

[2] 'This technology is easily available. There is no reason we can't have it' - Telegraph (http://telegraph.co.uk/money/main.jhtml?xml=/ money/2005/03/16/cmtrans16.xml)

[3] http://www.apacs.org.uk/fasterpayments

[4] APACS website, as of 12 July 2006

Charge card

A **charge card** is a plastic card that provides an alternative payment to cash when making purchases in which the issuer and the cardholder enter into an agreement that the debt incurred on the charge account will be paid in full and by due date (usually every thirty days) or be subject to severe late fees and restrictions on card use.

Though the terms *charge card* and *credit card* are sometimes used interchangeably, they are distinct protocols of financial transactions: a credit card is a revolving credit instrument that does not need to be paid in full; no late fee is charged so long as the minimum payment is made at specified intervals (usually every thirty days) which carries the balance forward as a loan charging interest. Charge cards are typically issued without spending limits (although one may be punitively imposed after a late payment), whereas credit cards always have a specified line of credit that the user may not exceed for purchases.

History

In 1914, Western Union offered the first charge card, which was printed on paper, for consumers. The first official charge card was invented in 1950 by Frank McNamara, who called his card Diners Club. In 1959, American Express was the first company to issue embossed plastic charge cards.

In Europe, however, the MasterCard-affiliated Maestro brand (which is a debit card rather than a charge card) replaced the European Eurocheque brand for payment cards in 2002. Many Eurocheque cards, particularly in such countries as Austria and Germany, were charge cards branded with the Eurocheque symbol. In addition, the European Eurocard, issued as the competitor for American Express was, and in some countries (such as the Nordic countries) still is, a charge card. Therefore, the majority of MasterCards in these countries still are charge cards. Visa charge cards are also available in Europe.

Operation

Many charge cards have the option for users to pay for some purchases over time. American Express charge card customers, for instance, can enroll in the Extended Payment Option (internally referred to as ExPO) to be able to pay for purchases over $200 over time,[1] or in Sign & Travel to be able to pay for eligible travel-related expenses over time.[2]

Governments and large businesses often use charge cards to pay for and keep track of expenses related to official business; these are often referred to as purchasing cards. Some high-end retailers like Neiman Marcus issue charge cards to customers. Some American Express and Diners Club cards are also charge cards, rather than credit or debit cards like VISA and MasterCard.

References

[1] American Express Extended Payment Option (http://www.americanexpress.com/cards/expo/)
[2] American Express Sign & Travel (http://www.americanexpress.com/cards/st/)

ChargeSmart

ChargeSmart, LLC

Type	Private
Industry	Personal finance, Software, Consumer Internet, Credit Cards, Mortgage, Online payments
Founded	2008
Headquarters	San Francisco, California
Key people	Philip Mikal, COO Mitch Friedman, Co-Founder
Products	Credit card funded bill payment services
Revenue	N/A
Website	chargesmart.com [1]

ChargeSmart is a web-based e-commerce business allowing credit card funded bill payments to be made through the Internet. ChargeSmart serves as an alternative payment channel for companies in the mortgage, auto, student and utility industries that do not want to directly offer credit card payment as an option to their customers.

ChargeSmart has garnered media coverage from a number of blogs and media outlets such as Business Week,[1] the San Francisco Business Times,[2] Banks.com,[3] InsideARM,[4] American Banker,[5] and the Sacramento Bee.[6]

The company is located in San Francisco, California.

Background

ChargeSmart COO Philip Mikal was previously co-founder of another San Franscisco-based company, CardIt. CardIt attempted to launch a similar payment service in September 2007 and targeted one-time consumer mortgage payments. CardIt is no longer in business and, according to Housing Wire, had difficulties for catering to troubled mortgage borrowers[7] . Mr. Mikal joined ChargeSmart as Chief Operating Officer August 11, 2008.[8] .

Based on several test transactions, the transaction fee plus insurance fee seems to come to 2.5% of the transaction, which means that the fees will outweigh the value of the "rewards" received on most credit cards.

References

[1] Silver-Greenberg, Jessica (August 14, 2008). "Just Charge That Mortgage" (http://www.businessweek.com/magazine/content/08_34/ c4097whatsnex194316.htm?chan=magazine+channel_what's+next). Business Week,. .

[2] Calvey, Mark (July 11, 2008). "ChargeSmart lets customers put house payments on plastic" (http://sanfrancisco.bizjournals.com/ sanfrancisco/stories/2008/07/14/story6.html). American City Business Journals,. .

[3] Morrison, Hayli (July 21, 2008). "ChargeSmart Is New Kid On Credit Card Bill Pay Block" (http://www.banks.com/blogs/credit/2008/ 07/21/chargesmart-is-new-kid-on-credit-card-bill-pay-block/). Banks.com. .

[4] Britt, Phil (July 10, 2008). "New Program Allows Consumers to Pay Mortgage with Credit Cards" (http://www.insidearm.com/go/ arm-news/new-program-allows-consumers-to-pay-mortgage-with-credit-cards). Kaulkin Media. .

[5] "New Pay Options, Old Criticism" (http://www.americanbanker.com/article.html?id=200807115UZ18T5D). July 18, 2008. .

[6] Pugh, Tony. "Finance industry encourages consumers to pay bills with plastic" (http://www.sacbee.com/103/story/1164555.html). McClatchy Company. .

[7] http://www.housingwire.com/2008/07/09/new-service-touts-mortgage-payments-by-credit-card/

[8] Rauber, Elizabeth (August 11, 2008). "ChargeSmart hires chief operating officer" (http://sanfrancisco.bizjournals.com/sanfrancisco/ stories/2008/08/11/daily11.html). .

Chargify

Chargify

Type	Private
Industry	Software Industry, Finance
Founded	2009
Headquarters	Needham, Massachusetts
Key people	Lance Walley, Founder and CEO; David Hauser, Founder and Chief Technology Officer David Hauser
Products	Recurring Billing Application
Employees	12
Website	www.chargify.com [1]

Chargify is a privately held software as a service company that offers a recurring billing application for SaaS and Web 2.0 companies.

History

Chargify was launched in 2009 at the TechCrunch50.[1] . It was founded by David Hauser and Siamak Taghaddos, founders of the Grasshopper virtual phone provider, along with Lance Walley of Engine Yard. Chargify is headquartered in Needham, MA and has approximately 12 employees. [2]

Products

Chargify offers a recurring billing application for software as a service companies. Chargify works with multiple payment processors including Authorize.net, Beanstream and TrustCommerce. [3] Chargify is a Level 1 PCI-DSS compliant service provider.

As reported by Gigaom, "Chargify is primarily designed for subscription services, and the options available for setting up your various products and plans are extensive. You can include setup fees, free trial periods and expiration periods to customize your plans and pricing."[4]

Other recurring billing providers include Zuora, Aria, Recurly, PayPal and Spreedly.

References

[1] "Web 2.0 and SaaS Recurring Billing System, Chargify, Launches at TechCrunch50" (http://prweb.com/releases/2009/09/prweb2881074. htm). *PRWeb*. September 14, 2009. . Retrieved 2011-02-25.

[2] "Startup Watch: Five you should follow" (http://www.masshightech.com/stories/2010/06/28/ daily16-Startup-Watch-Five-you-should-follow.html/). *masshightech.com*. June 29, 2010. . Retrieved 2011-02-25.

[3] "Chargify Becomes TrustCommerce Referral Partner" (http://trustcommerce.com/company/news/Chargify-referral-partner). *TrustCommerce.com*. November 22, 2010. . Retrieved 2011-02-25.

[4] Blitstein, Scott (April 28, 2010). "Chargify Makes Recurring Billing Simple" (http://gigaom.com/collaboration/ chargify-makes-recurring-billing-simple/). *Gigaom*. . Retrieved 2011-02-25.

External links

- Chargify.com website (http://www.chargify.com:)
- Crunchbase (http://www.crunchbase.com/company/chargify:)

Further reading

- Nusca, Andrew (October 29, 2009). With Chargify, Web 2.0 and SaaS businesses can bill with ease (http://www.zdnet.com/blog/btl/with-chargify-web-20-and-saas-businesses-can-bill-with-ease/24973). ZDNet'
- O'Dell, Jolie (September 22, 2009). Chargify: (Another) Billing App and API for Small Web and SaaS Companies (http://readwriteweb.com/enterprise/2009/09/chargify-billing-app-and-api-f.php) *ReadWriteWeb*
- Reisinger, Don (September 25, 2009). Tools for businesses to bill, collect what's owed (http://news.cnet.com/8301-17939_109-10361542-2.html) *CNet News*
- Savitz, Eric (February 10, 2011). Why Freemium Isn't Free (http://blogs.forbes.com/ciocentral/2011/02/10/why-freemium-isnt-free/) *Forbes*
- Del Rey, Jason (January 20, 2011). Case Study: How to Raise Prices (http://www.inc.com/magazine/20110201/case-study-how-to-raise-prices.html) *Inc Magazine*

Chase Paymentech

Chase Paymentech

Type	Public
Industry	Merchant services
Founded	1985
Headquarters	Dallas, Texas
Products	Payment Processing Services
Website	www.chasepaymentech.com [1]

Paymentech, LLC ("Chase Paymentech"), a subsidiary of JPMorgan Chase Bank, N.A., is a payment processing and merchant acquiring company headquartered in Dallas, Texas. **Chase Paymentech** and its affiliates provide electronic commerce and secure payment solutions, including credit cards, debit cards, gift cards, international currency and electronic check processing.[1] The company specializes in card-not-present (CNP) transactions, and processes an estimated 50 percent of all Internet transactions.

The company, with its affiliates, processes more than 900 transactions per second, and is currently ranked as the #1 payment processor by *Internet Retailer* (Top 500 Guide).[2] In 2009, the company processed $409.7 billion in bankcard volume and 18 billion total transactions.

History

Chase Paymentech began in 1985, when MNET, MBank's retail unit and merchant acquirer division was founded. In 1987, the company was acquired by Lomas Bank Corp. Chase Paymentech became First USA Merchant Services in 1989.[3]

The company expanded by first acquiring JL McKay, a credit card software provider. The expansions continued with further acquisition of Litle and DGMT in 1995.[4] The brand Paymentech was created in the year 1996 and the IPO was executed in the same year. Paymentech acquired Gensar, which later became Paymentech Network Services, Tampa, and Merchant Link in 1996.

In 1997, Chase Paymentech was created as a joint venture between Chase Merchant Services and First Data Corporation (FDC). That year, First USA was acquired by Bank One. In 2001, Paymentech completed the largest retail merchant conversion, and launched its Orbital® Gateway. 2002, Chase Paymentech acquired the merchant acquiring portfolios of Scotiabank and Citibank CA.

Chase Paymentech opened its first European office in Dublin, Ireland in 2004.[5] That year also saw the merger of Bank One and JPMorgan Chase. In 2008, FDC and JPMorgan announced that their Chase Paymentech joint venture was coming to an end, and Chase Paymentech became the merchant services subsidiary of JPMorgan Chase Bank, N.A.[6] [7]

Products and Services

Chase Paymentech provides electronic payment processing solutions for merchants accepting credit, debit or gift cards from their customers. Chase Paymentech also has product offerings to help merchants reduce fraud and chargebacks, as well as settling transactions in multiple currencies. The company offers industry-specific solutions for e-commerce, retail, mail/phone orders, insurance, travel and lodging, restaurant, digital content, contract/service provider, and government. Chase Paymentech and its affiliates also provide fraud management tools, reporting products, gift cards, international processing, recurring payments, debit card processing, and POS equipment.[8]

Online Payments

Chase Paymentech's Orbital® suite of eCommerce products includes:[9]

- **Orbital® Virtual Terminal** - A web-based application for the authorization, capture, and settlement of payments directly from a merchant's computer.

- **Orbital® Payment Gateway** - A proprietary system to which the merchant connects in order to securely and electronically deliver their customers' payment information. The Orbital Gateway also provides tokenization services, replacing customer account data with a token, removing account numbers from the transaction flow to help a merchant reduce their Payment Card Industry Data Security Standards (PCI DSS) scope.

- **Orbital® Managed Billing** - A service that provides a simple, convenient way to collect recurring, deferred and installment billings automatically.

- **Orbital® Customer Profile Management** - A service that stores customer and cardholder data off-site, and allows convenient access to customer information for completing transactions faster.[10]

Point of Sale Equipment

Chase Paymentech provides POS terminal and PC solutions for credit card acceptance. Some of the company's retail solutions include iTerminal®, ExaDigm® XD2100SP Wireless, Hypercom® T7Plus Series, Hypercom® Optimum T4205, Hypercom® Optimum T4220, Ingenico® 5100, Ingenico® 7780, VeriFone® V 610 Wireless, VeriFone® V 570 Dual Comm, VeriFone® V 510 Dual Comm, ECRi (Electronic Cash Register interface).[11]

Merchant Advocacy

Chase Paymentech is active in merchant advocacy.

As an original sponsor of the Merchant Advisory Group (MAG), in 2005 the company helped merchants have a stronger voice with leading payment brands such as Visa® and MasterCard®.[12]

The company helps make payment transactions more efficient, safe, and profitable as an Elite sponsor of the Merchant Risk Council (MRC), an organization that promotes secure transactions globally.[13]

Cyber Holiday Pulse Index

Every year Chase Paymentech releases the Cyber Holiday Pulse Index, an annual measurement of online shopping activity during the holiday season, which tracks e-commerce spending across a sample of 50 leading e-retailers. The Index shows both sales volume and transaction count for online purchases across Chase Paymentech's global processing platforms.[14]

References

[1] http://www.chasepaymentech.com/portal/server.pt?mode=2&uuID={51E4374F-3CEF-0974-3D81-CD0A8EA85000}

[2] http://www.authorize.net/solutions/merchantsolutions/resellerdirectory/?res_id=46256

[3] http://www.chasepaymentech.com/portal/server.pt?mode=2&uuID={51E4374F-3CEF-0974-3D81-C7F207004000}#history

[4] http://www.techagreements.com/agreement-preview.aspx?num=131916&
title=First%20Usa%20Paymentech%20-%20Sections%20In%20The%20Annual%20Report%20To%20Security%20Holders

[5] http://www.afterdawn.com/news/press_releases/press_release.cfm/3328/
chase_paymentech_formally_opens_european_headquarters_in_dublin_ireland

[6] http://www.techagreements.com/agreement-preview.aspx?num=131916&
title=First%20Usa%20Paymentech%20-%20Sections%20In%20The%20Annual%20Report%20To%20Security%20Holders

[7] http://www.digitaltransactions.net/newsstory.cfm?newsid=1796

[8] http://www.chasepaymentech.com/portal/server.pt?mode=2&uuID={51E4374F-3CEF-0974-3D81-CD0A6A396000}

[9] http://www.chasepaymentech.com/portal/server.pt?mode=2&uuID={51E4374F-3CEF-0974-3D81-CD0E1A670000}

[10] http://www.chasepaymentech.com/portal/server.pt?mode=2&uuID={51E4374F-3CEF-0974-3D81-CD09E522C000}

[11] http://iso.chasepaymentech.com/

[12] http://www.merchantadvisorygroup.org/history.aspx

[13] https://www.merchantriskcouncil.org/index.cfm?pageId=480

[14] http://www.allpaynews.com/content/chase-paymentech039s-2008-cyber-holiday-pulse-index-indicates-mixed-online-shopping-results

About Chase Paymentech (http:/ / www. chasepaymentech. com/ portal/ server. pt?mode=2& uuID={51E4374F-3CEF-0974-3D81-CD0A8EA85000})

Check 21 Act

The **Check Clearing for the 21st Century Act** (or **Check 21 Act**) is a United States federal law, Pub.L. 108-100 [1], that was enacted on October 28, 2003 by the 108th Congress. The Check 21 Act took effect one year later on October 28, 2004. The law allows the recipient of the original paper check to create a digital version of the original check—called a "substitute check," thereby eliminating the need for further handling of the physical document.

Consumers are most likely to see the effects of this act when they notice that certain checks (or image of) are no longer being returned to them with their monthly statement, even though other checks are still being returned. Another side effect of the law is that it is now legal for anyone to use a computer scanner or mobile phone to capture images of checks and deposit them electronically, a process known as remote deposit.

Check 21 is not subject to ACH (Automated Clearing House) rules, therefore transactions are not subject to NACHA (The Electronic Payments Association) rules, regulations, fees and fines.

Truncation

The process of removing the paper check from its processing flow is called *truncation*. Paper checks continue to transition to electronic images at an extraordinary rate, with almost 70% of all institutions now receiving images.[1] In truncation, both sides of the paper check are scanned to produce digital images. If a paper document is still needed, these images are inserted into specially formatted documents containing a photo-reduced copy of the original checks called a "substitute check".

Once a check is truncated, businesses and banks can work with either the digital image or a print reproduction of it. Images can be exchanged between member banks, savings and loans, credit unions, servicers, clearinghouses, and the Federal Reserve Bank.

Not all banks have the ability to receive image files, so there are companies who offer the service. At the item processing center, the checks are sorted by machine according to the routing/transit (RT) number as presented by the magnetic ink character recognition (MICR) line, and scanned to produce a digital image. A batch file is generated and sent to the Federal Reserve Bank or presentment point for settlement or image replacement. If a substitute check is needed, the transmitting bank is responsible for the cost of generating and transporting it from the presentment point to the Federal Reserve Bank or other corresponding bank.

Check 21 has also spawned a new bank treasury management product known as remote deposit. This process allows depositing customers the ability to capture front and rear images of checks along with their respective MICR data for those being deposited. This data is then uploaded to their depositing institution, and the customer's account is then credited. Remote deposit therefore precludes the need for merchants and other large depositors to travel to the bank (or branch) to physically make a deposit.

In addition to remote deposit, other such electronic depositing options are available to qualifying bank customers through NACHA-The Electronic Payments Association. These options include "Point of Purchase" (POP) for retailers and "Accounts Receivable Conversion" (ARC) for high volume remittance receivers. These transactions are not covered under the Check 21 legislation, but rather are electronic conversions of the checks' MICR data into an

ACH (Automated Clearing House) debit. This can help the depositor save on the costs of transporting checks and in bank fees. However, the liability changes from Regulation CC of the Federal Reserve to Regulation E, which provides much more protection for the account being debited and therefore more risk to the merchant and originating bank.

Recently, Check 21 software providers have developed a [2] "Virtual Check 21" system which allows online and offline merchants to create and submit demand draft documents to the bank of deposit. This process which combines remotely created checks (RCC) and Check 21 X9.37 files enables merchants to benefit from direct merchant-to-bank relationships, lower NSFs, and lower chargebacks.

Check writers may no longer be able to obtain original autographs from cancelled checks endorsed by celebrity recipients. This practice may have been used by some charities to encourage donations [3] and may have also been used in other contexts as well. Note to international readers: The North American terminology "cancelled check" is the British equivalent of a "paid cheque". The rationale is that the cheque has been paid or drawn, and is therefore cancelled so it cannot be presented for payment again. In North America and elsewhere, paid checks, or scanned images of the checks, are returned to the payer (or made available on a bank website) so as to provide the payer with proof of payment.

Implications

The act greatly reduces check processing cost for banks (in part, by eliminating the need for the costly transportation of physical checks), and speeds up the fund transfers. The bank customer benefits from free or lower-cost checking.

While the bank of deposit clears and receives the funds associated with a deposited transaction sooner than before, it may still legally hold them for a period of days specified by Expedited Funds Availability Act. During that period the funds are essentially in the bank's possession; accumulated across all the bank customers on any given day, such funds earn the bank a large amount of interest.

With some Check 21 providers, retailers will find this system to be faster, as funds may be transferred much quicker than ACH. EChecks processed using a Check 21 solution are typically accepted in 1–3 seconds and clear the same day or overnight compared to typical Automated Clearing House system (ACH) time frames of 3 to 5 days.

And certain Check 21 providers can debit every US checking account, even accounts that ACH cannot such as many Credit Unions, S&Ls, small banks, brokerage accounts, business accounts and credit card check accounts.

ACH transactions take several days to clear through the system. During the clearing period the recipient has no way to determine if the transaction will clear or result in an administrative return. ACH has more than 60 reasons why a transaction can fail. Many times it is because the consumer's bank has chosen not to participate in ACH, or hasn't performed the correct system integration. Additionally, the fact that the funds are debited from the check issuer's account much faster than before may catch the issuer by surprise, resulting in non-sufficient funds, overdraft and a penalty in the form of NSF fee.

Check processing rooms and equipment started to be phased out after the passage of Check 21.

Reduced cost of checking for consumers: Most people no longer pay a monthly fee for checking, or have a small maximum number of checks they can write.

New security risks: Bank employees were screened, and the security risk was minimal with a physical check. It is physically impossible to gain much information from boxes and boxes of checks. The central virtual storage of checks (at the exchanges), has created a new security risk which is compounded by the exchanges offshoring the technical tasks. Check information can even harm national security, if these archives were searched for key records by a country hostile towards the USA. The information might also be used for insider-trading.

New Privacy concerns: Prior to Check-21, a bank would pay a storage company to hold the checks for seven years, and then to destroy the checks. Today, every check you write can potentially be retained in digital format indefinitely.

Technical Details

- Virtual Exchanges were created: There are several large "check exchanges" where banks can send and receive files. These "exchanges" also provide other services for banks. One of which is provided by the Federal Reserve Banks, IBM and the large investment banks own the other exchanges.

- File format: Banks are exchanging checks (virtually), and therefore must use the same file format. They use a subset of the Ansi Standard X9.37-DSTU which is given the new standard name: X9.100-187 (which is almost identical to the UCD standard). The X9.37 standard had too many extras and the "exchanges" defined their own standards limiting the options available. Two exchanges used a subset of the X9.37 standard, and called it the UCD standard and the Federal Reserve created the "Federal Reserve Adoption" standard. At that point the ANSI standard was being usurped by these other standards created by the exchanges. So ANSI tried to tweak their standard, but didn't include any members of the "exchanges", and the result was the X9.100-180 standard. The result was widely ignored. So the ANSI standards incorporated the standards used by the exchanges (The *UCD* and the *Federal Reserve Adoption of ...*), and called it X9-100.187. (And nothing has changed from the UCD).

- X9.37 Card Trick dates to the 1950s: X9.37 standard has its roots in code written by IBM in the 1950s using punched cards. A stack of cards could be reused by replacing the top card. This "trick" was in place until recently, and now has been discouraged with the X9.100-187 standard. Old tax refund checks came on printed punched cards, so, nothing is new about an electronic check record. What is new, is the ability to destroy the original check as long as an electronic version is retained.

- USA: Clearly, Check 21, and X9.37 are for American checks and American Currency, and there are very little provisions in the X9.37 standard for any other currency or bank numbering scheme. Although most of the programming is now being done by programmers in other countries. One of the largest exchanges with 17 petabytes of check images, has no programmers on staff anymore.

- Federal Reserve Banks: The Federal Reserve bank is also one of the virtual "Exchanges" for checks. They still have the ability to handle a physical paper check.

- Check Volume: The number of checks written in the USA is declining rapidly. Customers are using other payment methods to pay their bills.

- Databases are growing: Despite the fact that check volumes are decreasing, check archives are growing by petabytes every year. This is because banks are opting to hold virtual checks longer and longer, and potentially, forever in some cases.

- Why longer retention? Because of frauds that spanned longer than 7 or 10 years (Enron, and more recently Madoff), banks are now required to store certain check images for 100 years. As a result some systems (including the Federal Reserve Banks), now are set up to retain check images for any amount of time.

- Postal Money Orders: A Postal money order is an obscure form of a check also covered under check-21, with unique requirements.

Patents

There are a number of patents relating to "check collection systems",[4] including some owned by DataTreasury.[5] Section 14 of the Patent Reform Act of 2007 includes provisions eliminating the right of patent holders to prevent financial institutions from using their inventions.[4] There are fractious lobbying efforts on both sides of the debate[6] and it is feared that enacting Section 14 would result in litigation against the federal government seeking compensation for a taking of private property.[4]

The current court victories of the patent holders are "payment" based, and not "royalty" based. Although the patents are currently being upheld, the court has sold the method to the infringing bank and also set the fee. The courts have also decided that one exchange was created to shield multiple banks from lawsuit, and therefore have nullified the claim that an exchange should only pay once (but allow multiple banks to exchange). Electronic records of checks have existed since the 1950s, and tax refund checks were even printed on punched cards, yet the banks never thought to patent the idea. DataGeneral's patent would suggest that the Federal Reserve Banks are aiding and abetting all the banks in breaking DataGeneral's patent, and have been for years before the patent was issued. (The Federal Reserve Bank is both a bank and an exchange). This "infringement" would also apply to every US post office, since postal money orders are also checks that are submitted to the FED.

References

[1] http://www.checkimagecentral.org/

[2] http://www.check21.com/virtual-check-21-processing.html

[3] (http://www.jimmyfund.org/abo/red/tedwilliams/facts.asp)

[4] Congressional Budget Office Cost Report (http://www.cbo.gov/ftpdocs/89xx/doc8981/s1145.pdf), pages 2, 5 and 11

[5] Lisa Lerer, "Senate, old legal woes drawn into patent fight" (http://www.politico.com/news/stories/0308/9202.html), politico.com, March 25, 2008

[6] Jeffrey H. Birnbaum, "Lawmakers Move to Grant Banks Immunity Against Patent Lawsuit", [[Washington Post (http://www. washingtonpost.com/wp-dyn/content/article/2008/02/13/AR2008021303731.html)], February 14, 2008]

External links

- Full Text of the Check 21 Act (http://www.gpo.gov/fdsys/pkg/PLAW-108publ100/content-detail.html)
- Accredited Standards Committee (ASC) X9 Financial Industry Standards: Statement on Check 21 adoption (October 23, 2004) (http://www.x9.org/news/pr031028)
- Check 21 Return Codes (http://icheckgateway.com/Check-21-Return-Codes.asp)

Check card

The term **check card** can refer to:

- An identification card issued by a retailer allowing the holder to tender payment by check. Such cards were commonly issued in the United States by supermarkets and other retailers before the widespread use of debit cards.

- A debit card.

Cheque

A **cheque** (or **check** in American English) is a document/instrument (usually a piece of paper)[1] that orders a payment of money from a bank account. The person writing the cheque, the *drawer*, usually has a current account (British), or checking account (US) where their money was previously deposited. The drawer writes the various details including the money amount, date, and a payee on the cheque, and signs it, ordering their bank, known as the *drawee*, to pay that person or company the amount of money stated.

Cheques are a type of bill of exchange and were developed as a way to make payments without the need to carry around large amounts of gold and silver. Paper money also evolved from bills of exchange, and are similar to cheques in that they were originally a written order to pay the given amount to whomever had it in their possession (the "bearer").

Technically, a cheque is a negotiable instrument[2] instructing a financial institution to pay a specific amount of a specific currency from a specified transactional account held in the drawer's name with that institution. Both the drawer and payee may be natural persons or legal entities. Specifically, cheques are *order instruments*, and are not in general payable simply to the bearer (as bearer instruments are) but must be paid to the payee. In some countries, such as the US, the payee may endorse the cheque, allowing them to specify a third party to whom it should be paid.

Although cheques have been around since at least the 9th century, it was during the 20th century that cheques became a highly popular non-cash method for making payments and the usage of cheques peaked. By the second half of the 20th century, as cheque processing became automated, billions of cheques were issued each year; these volumes peaked in or around the early 1990s.[3] Since then cheque usage has fallen, being partly replaced by electronic payment systems. In some countries cheques have become a marginal payment system or have been phased out completely.

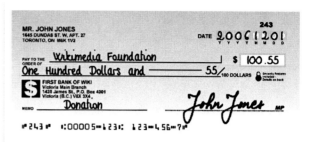

Example of a Canadian cheque

Example of a South Korean cheque, where the payee and signature are on the reverse side

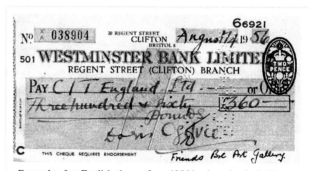

Example of an English cheque from 1956 having a bank clerk's red mark verifying the signature, a two-pence stamp duty, and holes punched by hand to cancel it. This is a "crossed cheque" disallowing transfer of payment to another account.

Spelling

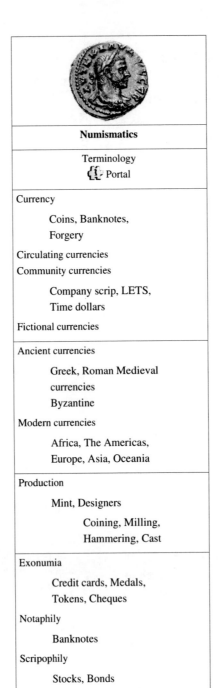

Numismatics

Terminology
Portal

Currency

Coins, Banknotes,
Forgery

Circulating currencies
Community currencies

Company scrip, LETS,
Time dollars

Fictional currencies

Ancient currencies

Greek, Roman Medieval
currencies
Byzantine

Modern currencies

Africa, The Americas,
Europe, Asia, Oceania

Production

Mint, Designers

Coining, Milling,
Hammering, Cast

Exonumia

Credit cards, Medals,
Tokens, Cheques

Notaphily

Banknotes

Scripophily

Stocks, Bonds

The spellings *check*, *checque*, and *cheque* were used interchangeably from the 17th century until the 20th century.[4] However, since the 19th century, the spelling *cheque* (from the French word *chèque*) has become standard for the financial instrument in the Commonwealth and Ireland, while *check* is used only for the verb "to verify", thus distinguishing the two definitions in writing.[5]

In American English, the usual spelling for both is *check*.[6]

History

The cheque had its origins in the ancient banking system, in which bankers would issue orders at the request of their customers, to pay money to identified payees. Such an order was referred to as a *bill of exchange*. The use of bills of exchange facilitated trade by eliminating the need for merchants to carry large quantities of currency (e.g. gold) to purchase goods and services.

Early years

The ancient Romans are believed[7] to have used an early form of cheque known as *praescriptiones* in the 1st century BC.

In India, during the Mauryan period (from 321 to 185 BC), a commercial instrument called *adesha* was in use, which was an order on a banker desiring him to pay the money of the note to a third person, which corresponds to the definition of a bill of exchange as we understand it today. During the Buddhist period, there was considerable use of these instruments. Merchants in large towns gave letters of credit to one another. There are also numerous references to promissory notes.[8]

During the 3rd century AD, banks in Persia and other territories in the Persian Sassanid Empire issued letters of credit known as *chak* (In New Persian script: □□ . In Shahnameh there are several mentions of use of chak and in post-Islamic Arabic document this word appears as Arabicised *ṣakks* or □ □ □.

Muslim traders are known to have used the cheque or ṣakk system since the time of Harun al-Rashid (9th century) of the Abbasid Caliphate.[9]

Between 1118 and 1307, it is believed the Knights Templar introduced a cheque system for pilgrims travelling to the Holy Land or across Europe.[10] The pilgrims would deposit funds at one chapter house, then withdraw it from another chapter at their destination by showing a *draft* of their claim. These *drafts* would be written in a very complicated code only the Templars could decipher.

In the 13th century in Venice the *bill of exchange* was developed as a legal device to allow international trade without the need to carry around large amounts of gold and silver. Their use subsequently spread to other European countries.

In the early 1500s in the Dutch Republic in order to protect their large accumulations of cash, people began to depositing their money with "cashiers". These cashiers held the money for a fee. Competition drove cashiers to offer additional services including paying out money to any person bearing a written order from a depositor to do so. They kept the note as proof of payment. This concepts went on and spread to England and elsewhere.[11]

Modern era

By the 17th century, bills of exchange were being used for domestic payments in England. Cheques, a type of bill of exchange, then began to evolve. They were initially known as "drawn notes" as they enabled a customer to draw on the funds they held on account with their banker and required immediate payment.[12] These were handwritten, and one of the earliest known still to be in existence was drawn on Messrs Morris and Clayton, scriveners and bankers based in the City of London, and dated 16 February 1659.

In 1717 the Bank of England pioneered the first use of a pre-printed form. These forms were printed on "cheque paper" to prevent fraud, and customers had to attend in person and obtain a numbered form from the cashier. Once written the cheque would have to be brought back to the bank for settlement.

Until around 1770 an informal exchange of cheques took place between London banks. Clerks of each bank visited all the other banks to exchange cheques, whilst keeping a tally of balances between them until they settled with each other. Daily cheque clearing began around 1770 when the bank clerks met at the Five Bells, a tavern in Lombard Street in the City of London, to exchange all their cheques in one place and settle the balances in cash. See bankers' clearing house for further historical developments.

In 1811 the Commercial Bank of Scotland is thought to have been the first bank to personalise its customers' cheques, by printing the name of the account holder vertically along the left-hand edge.[13] In 1830 the Bank of England introduced books of 50, 100 or 200 forms and counterparts, bound or stitched. These **cheque books** became a common format for the distribution of cheques to bank customers.

In the late 19th century a number of countries formalised laws around cheques. The UK passed the *Bills of Exchange Act* in 1882, and India passed the *Negotiable Instruments Act (NI Act)* 1881[8] which both covered cheques.

In 1931 an attempt was made to simplify the international use of cheques by the *Geneva Convention on the unification of the law relating to cheques*.[14] Many European and South American states as well as Japan joined the convention. However some countries, including the United States and members of the British Commonwealth did not participate.

In 1959 a standard for machine readable characters (MICR) was agreed and patented in the United States for use with cheques. This opened the way for the first automated reader/sorting machines for clearing cheques. The following years saw a dramatic change in the way that cheques were handled and processed as automation increased. Cheque volumes continued to grow, and in the late 20th century cheques were the most popular non-cash method for making payments, with billions of them processed each year. Most countries saw cheque volumes peak in the late 1980s or early 1990s, after which electronic payment methods started to become popular and the use of cheques started to decline.

In 1969 cheque guarantee cards were introduced in a number of countries, allowing a retailer to confirm that a cheque would be honoured when used at a point of sale. The drawer would sign the cheque in front of the retailer, who would compare the signature to the signature on the card and then write the cheque guarantee card number of the back of the cheque. Such cards were generally phased out and replaced by debit cards, starting in the mid 1990s.

From the mid 1990s, many countries enacted laws to allow for cheque truncation, in which a physical cheque is converted into electronic form for transmission to the paying bank or clearing house. This eliminates the cumbersome physical presentation and saves time and processing costs.

In 2002, Germany and some other European countries phased out the use of cheques altogether when the Eurocheque system, which they had used as their domestic cheque clearing system, ceased on 1 January 2002. As of 2010, many countries have either phased out the use of cheques altogether or signaled that they would do so in the following years.

Parts of a cheque

The four main items on a cheque are

- **Drawer**, the person or entity who makes the cheque
- **Payee**, the recipient of the money
- **Drawee**, the bank or other financial institution where the cheque can be presented for payment
- **Amount**, the currency amount

As cheque usage increased during the 19th and 20th centuries additional items were added to increase security or to make processing easier for the bank or financial institution. A

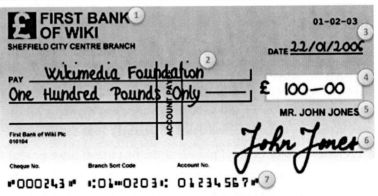

Parts of a cheque based on a UK example drawee, the financial institution where the cheque can be presented for payment payee date of issue amount of currency drawer, the person or entity making the cheque signature of drawer Machine readable routing and account information

signature of the drawer was required to authorise the cheque and this is the main way to authenticate the cheque. Second it became customary to write the amount in words as well as in numbers to avoid mistakes and make it harder to fraudulently alter the amount after the cheque had been written. It is not a legal requirement to write down the amount in words, although some banks will refuse to accept cheques that do not have the amount in both numbers and words.

An issue date was added, and cheques may not be valid a certain amount of time after issue. In the US a cheque is typically valid for six months after the date of issue, after which it is a *stale-dated cheque,* but this depends on where the cheque is drawn;[15] in Australia this is typically fifteen months.[16] A cheque that has an issue date in the future, a post-dated cheque, may not be able to be presented until that date has passed, writing a post dated cheque may simply be ignored or is illegal in some countries. Conversely, an antedated cheque has an issue date in the past.

A cheque number was added and cheque books were issued so that cheque numbers were sequential. This allowed for some basic fraud detection by banks and made sure one cheque was not presented twice.

In some countries such as the US, cheques contain a memo line where the purpose of the cheque can be indicated as a convenience without affecting the official parts of the cheque. In the United Kingdom this is not available and such notes are sometimes written on the reverse side of the cheque.

In the US, at the top (when cheque oriented vertically) of the reverse side of the cheque, there are usually one or more blank lines labelled something like "Endorse here".

Starting in the 1960s machine readable routing and account information was added to the bottom of cheques in MICR format. This allowed automated sorting and routing of cheques between banks and led to automated central clearing facilities. The information provided at the bottom of the cheque is country specific and is driven by each country's cheque clearing system. This meant that the payee no longer had to go to the bank that issued the cheque, instead they could deposit it at their own bank or any other banks and the cheque would be routed back to the originating bank and funds transferred to their own bank account.

For additional protection, a cheque can be crossed so that funds must be paid into a bank account in the name of the payee. The format and wording varies from country to country, but generally two parallel lines and/or the words 'Account Payee' or similar may be placed either vertically across the cheque or in the top left hand corner. In addition the words 'or bearer' must be not be used or crossed out on the payee line.

Attached documents

Cheques sometimes include additional documents. A page in a chequebook may consist of both the cheque itself and a stub or **counterfoil** – when the cheque is written, only the cheque itself is detached, and the stub is retained in the chequebook as a record of the cheque. Alternatively, cheques may be recorded in a separate ledger, such as at the back of a chequebook.

When a cheque is mailed, a separate letter or "remittance advice" may be attached to inform the recipient of the purpose of the cheque – formally, which account receivable to credit the funds to. This is frequently done formally using a provided slip when paying a bill, or informally via a letter when sending an ad hoc cheque.

Stubs may be retained as a record of the check being written.

Usage

Parties to regular cheques generally include a *drawer*, the depositor writing a cheque; a *drawee,* the financial institution where the cheque can be presented for payment; and a *payee,* the entity to whom the drawer issues the cheque. The drawer *drafts* or *draws* a cheque, which is also called *cutting a cheque*, especially in the United States. There may also be a *beneficiary*—for example, in depositing a cheque with a custodian of a brokerage account, the payee will be the custodian, but the cheque may be marked "F/B/O" ("for the benefit of") the beneficiary.

Ultimately, there is also at least one *endorsee* which would typically be the financial institution servicing the payee's account, or in some circumstances may be a third party to whom the payee owes or wishes to give money.

A payee that accepts a cheque will typically deposit it in an account at the payee's bank, and have the bank process the cheque. In some cases, the payee will take the cheque to a branch of the drawee bank, and cash the cheque there. If a cheque is refused at the drawee bank (or the drawee bank returns the cheque to the bank that it was deposited at) because there are insufficient funds for the cheque to clear, it is said that the cheque has *bounced*. Once a cheque is approved and all appropriate accounts involved have been credited, the cheque is stamped with some kind of cancellation mark, such as a "paid" stamp. The cheque is now a *cancelled cheque*. Cancelled cheques are placed in the account holder's file. The account holder can request a copy of a cancelled cheque as proof of a payment. This is known as the cheque clearing cycle.

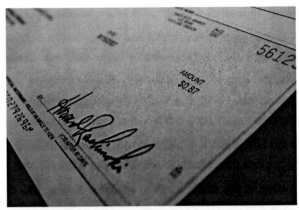

Cheques may be valid regardless of denomination and are used within numerous scenarios in place of cash.

Cheques can be lost or go astray within the cycle, or be delayed if further verification is needed in the case of suspected fraud. A cheque may thus bounce some time after it has been deposited.

Following concerns about the amount of time it took banks to clear cheques, the United Kingdom Office of Fair Trading set up a working group in 2006 to look at the cheque clearing cycle. Their report[17] acknowledged that clearing times could be improved, but that the costs associated with speeding up the cheque clearing cycle could not be justified considering the use of cheques was declining. However, they concluded the biggest problem was the unlimited time a bank could take to dishonor a cheque. To address this, changes were implemented so that the maximum time after a cheque was deposited that it could be dishonoured was six days, what was known as the "certainty of fate" principle; see Cheque and Credit Clearing Company and "2-4-6".

An advantage to the drawer of using cheques instead of debit card transactions, is that they know the drawer's bank will not release the money until several days later. Paying with a cheque and making a deposit before it clears the drawer's bank is called "kiting" or "floating" and is generally illegal in the United States, but rarely enforced unless the drawer uses multiple chequing accounts with multiple institutions to increase the delay or to steal the funds.

Declining use

Cheques have been in decline for some years, both for point of sale transactions (for which credit cards and debit cards are increasingly preferred) and for third party payments (e.g. bill payments), where the decline has been accelerated by the emergence of telephone banking and online banking. Being paper-based, cheques are costly for banks to process in comparison to electronic payments, so banks in many countries now discourage the use of cheques, either by charging for cheques or by making the alternatives more attractive to customers. Cheques are also more costly for the issuer and receiver of a cheque. In particular the handling of money transfer requires more effort and is time consuming. The cheque has to be handed over on a personal meeting or has to be sent by mail. The rise of automated teller machines (ATMs) means that small amounts of cash are often easily accessible, so that it is sometimes unnecessary to write a cheque for such amounts instead.

Alternatives to cheques

In addition to cash there are number of other payment systems that have emerged to compete against cheques;

1. Debit card payments
2. Credit card payments
3. Direct debit (initiated by payee)
4. Direct credit (initiated by payer), ACH in US, giro in Europe
5. Wire transfer (local and international)
6. Electronic bill payments using Internet banking
7. Online payment services (for example PayPal and WorldPay)

Europe

In most European countries, cheques are now very rarely used, even for third party payments. In these countries, it is standard practice for businesses to publish their bank details on invoices, to facilitate the receipt of payments by giro. Even before the introduction of online banking, it has been possible in some countries to make payments to third parties using ATMs, which may accurately and rapidly capture invoice amounts, due dates, and payee bank details via a bar code reader to reduce keying. In some countries, entering the bank account number results in the bank revealing the name of the payee as an added safeguard against fraud. In using a cheque, the onus is on the payee to initiate the payment, whereas with a giro transfer, the onus is on the payer to effect the payment. The process is also procedurally more simple, as no cheques are ever posted, can claim to have been posted, or need banking or clearance.

In Germany, Austria, the Netherlands, Belgium, and Scandinavia, cheques have almost completely vanished in favour of direct bank transfers and electronic payments. Direct bank transfers, using so-called giro transfers, have been standard procedure since the 1950s to send and receive regular payments like rent and wages and even mail-order invoices. In the Netherlands, Austria, and Germany, all kinds of invoices are commonly accompanied by so-called *acceptgiro's* (Netherlands) or *Überweisungen* (German), which are essentially standardised bank transfer order forms preprinted with the payee's account details and the amount payable. The payer fills in his account details and hands the form to a clerk at his bank, which will then transfer the money. It is also very common to allow the payee to automatically withdraw the requested amount from the payer's account (*Lastschrifteinzug* (German) or *Incasso (machtiging)* (Netherlands)). Though similar to paying by cheque, the payee only needs the payer's bank and account number. Since the early 1990s, this method of payment has also been available to merchants. Due to this, credit cards are rather uncommon in Germany and Austria, and are mostly used to give access to credit rather than as a payment mechanism. However, debit cards are widespread in these countries, since virtually all Austrian and German banks issue debit cards instead of simple ATM cards for use on current accounts. Acceptance of cheques has been further diminished since the late 1990s, because of the abolition of the Eurocheque. Cashing a foreign bank cheque is possible, but usually very expensive.

In Finland, banks stopped issuing personal cheques in about 1993 in favour of giro systems, which are now almost exclusively electronically initiated either via internet banking or payment machines located at banks and shopping malls. All Nordic countries have used an interconnected international giro system since the 1950s, and in Sweden, cheques are now totally abandoned. Electronic payments across the European Union are now fast and inexpensive—usually free for consumers.

In Poland cheques were withdrawn from use in 2006, mainly because of lack of popularity due to widespread adaptation of credit and debit cards.

In the United Kingdom, Ireland, and France, some people still use cheques, partly because cheques remain free of charge to personal customers; however, bank-to-bank transfers are increasing in popularity. Since 2001, businesses in the United Kingdom have made more electronic payments than cheque payments.[18] Most utilities in the United Kingdom charge lower prices to customers pay by direct debit than for other payment methods, including electronic methods. The vast majority of retailers in the United Kingdom and many in France no longer accept cheques as a means of payment. For example Shell announced in September 2005 that it would no longer accept cheques in its UK petrol stations.[19] More recently, this has been followed by other major fuel retailers, such as Texaco, BP, and Total. Asda announced in April 2006 that it would stop accepting cheques, initially as a trial in the London area,[20] and Boots announced in September 2006 that it would stop accepting cheques, initially as a trial in Sussex and Surrey.[21] Currys (and other stores in the DSGi group) and WH Smith also no longer accept cheques. Cheques are now widely predicted to become a thing of the past, or at most, a niche product used to pay private individuals or for the very large number of small service providers who are not used to providing their bank details to customers to allow electronic payments to be made to them, and/or do not wish to be burdened with checking their bank account frequently and reconciling their contents with amounts due (e.g. music teachers, driving instructors, children's sports lessons, very small shops, schools etc.).[22] The UK Payments Council announced in December 2009 that cheques would be phased out by October 2018, but only if adequate alternatives are developed. They intend to perform annual checks on the progress of other payments systems and a final review of the decision will be held in 2016.[23] Concerns have been expressed, however, by charities and older people, who are still heavy users of cheques, and replacement plans have been criticised as open to fraud.[24]

North America

The United States still relies heavily on cheques, due to the absence of a high volume system for low value electronic payments.[25] About 70 billion cheques were written annually in the U.S. by 2001, though almost 25% of Americans do not have bank accounts at all.[25] When sending a payment by online banking in the U.S. at some banks, the sending bank mails a cheque to the payee's bank or to the payee rather than sending the funds electronically. Certain companies whom a person pays with a cheque will turn it into an Automated Clearing House (ACH) or electronic transaction. Banks try to save time processing cheques by sending them electronically between banks. Cheque clearing is usually done with a new type of electronic cheque broker, Viewpointe LLC, SVPco, or the Federal Reserve Banks. Copies of the cheques are stored at a bank or the broker, for periods up to 99 years, and this is why some cheque archives have grown to 20 petabytes. The access to these archives is now world wide, as most bank programming is now done offshore. Many utilities and most credit cards will also allow customers to pay by providing bank information and having the payee draw payment from the customer's account (direct debit). Many people in the U.S. still use paper money orders to pay bills or transfer money which is a unique type of cheque. They have security advantages over mailing cash, and do not require access to a bank account in order to obtain.[25]

Canada's usage of cheques is slightly less than that of the U.S. The Interac system, which allows instant fund transfers via chip or magnetic strip and PIN, is widely used by merchants to the point that very few brick and mortar merchants accept cheques anymore. Many merchants accept Interac debit payments but not credit card payments, even though most Interac terminals can support credit card payments. Financial institutions also facilitate transfers between accounts within different institutions with the Email Money Transfer (EMT) service.

Cheques are still widely used for government cheques, payroll, rent, and utility bill payments, though direct deposits and online/telephone bill payments are also widely offered.

Asia

In many Asian countries cheques were not widely used and generally only used by the wealthy, with cash being used for the majority of payments. Where cheques were used they have been declining rapidly, by 2009 there was negligible consumer cheque usage in Japan, South Korea and Taiwan. This declining trend was accelerated by these developed markets advanced financial services infrastructure. However many of the developing markets have also seen an increasing use of electronic payment systems, 'leap-frogging' the less efficient chequing system altogether.[26]

Oceania

In Australia, following global trends, the use of cheques continues to decline. In 1994 the value of daily cheque transactions was AU$25 billion, by 2004 this had dropped to only AU$5 billion.

As in other countries, New Zealand payment statistics indicate a strong move away from cheques in favour of electronic payment methods. From being the most popular form of non-cash payment until the mid-1990s, cheques now lag far behind EFTPOS payment transactions and electronic credits. Their usage is declining at about 6% per year. In 1993 cheque payments accounted for over 50% of transactions through the banking system with an averaged 130 cheques per capita. By the end of 2006, this had dropped to 9% with 41 cheques per capita.

Variations on regular cheques

In addition to regular cheques, a number of variations were developed to address specific needs or to address issues when using a regular cheque.

Cashier's cheques and bank drafts

Cashier's cheques and banker's drafts also known as a **bank cheque** or **treasurer's cheque**, are cheques issued against the funds of a financial institution rather than an individual account holder. Typically, the term cashier's cheques are used in the US and banker's drafts are used in the UK. The mechanism differs slightly from country to country but in general the bank issuing the cashiers cheque or bankers draft will allocate the funds at the point the cheque is drawn. This provides a guarantee, save for a failure of the bank, that it will be honoured. Cashier's cheques are perceived to be as good as cash but they are still a cheque, a misconception often exploited by scam artists. A lost or stolen cheque can still be stopped like any other cheque so payment is not completely guaranteed.

Certified cheque

When a certified cheque is drawn, the bank operating the account verifies there are currently sufficient funds in the drawer's account to honour the cheque. Those funds are then set aside in the bank's internal account until the cheque is cashed or returned by the payee. Thus, a certified cheque cannot "bounce", and, in this manner, its liquidity is similar to cash, absent failure of the bank. The bank indicates this fact by making a notation on the face of the cheque (technically called an *acceptance*).

Payroll cheque

A cheque used to pay wages may be referred to as a payroll cheque. Even when the use of cheques for paying wages and salaries became rare, the vocabulary "pay cheque" still remained commonly used to describe the payment of wages and salaries. Payroll cheques issued by the military to soldiers, or by some other government entities to their employees, beneficiants, and creditors, are referred to as warrants.

Warrants

Warrants look like cheques and clear through the banking system like cheques, but are not drawn against cleared funds in a deposit account. A cheque differs from a warrant in that the warrant is not necessarily payable on demand and may not be negotiable.[27] They are often issued by government entities such as the military to pay wages or suppliers. In this case they are an instruction to the entity's treasurer department to pay the warrant holder on demand or after a specified maturity date.

Travellers cheque

A traveller's cheque is designed to allow the person signing it to make an unconditional payment to someone else as a result of paying the account holder for that privilege. Traveller's cheques can usually be replaced if lost or stolen and people often used to use them on vacation instead of cash as many businesses used to accept traveller's cheques as currency. The use of credit or debit cards has, however, begun to replace the traveller's cheque as the standard for vacation money due to their convenience and additional security for the retailer. This has resulted in many businesses no longer accepting traveller's cheques.

Money or postal order

A cheque sold by a post office or merchant such as a grocery for payment by a third party for a customer is referred to as a money order or postal order. These are paid for in advance when the order is drawn and are guaranteed by the institution that issues them and can only be paid to the named third party. This was a common way to send low value payments to third parties avoiding the risks associated with sending cash via the mail, prior to the advent of electronic payment methods.

Oversized cheques

Oversized cheques are often used in public events such as donating money to charity or giving out prizes such as Publishers Clearing House. The cheques are commonly 18 by 36 inches (46 × 91 cm) in size,[28] however, according to the Guinness Book of World Records, the largest ever is 12 by 25 metres (39 × 82 ft).[29] Regardless of the size, such cheques can still be redeemed for their cash value as long as they have the same parts as a normal cheque, although usually the oversized cheque is kept as a souvenir and a normal cheque is provided.[30] A bank may levy additional charges for clearing an oversized cheque.

Presentation of the Ansari X Prize $10 million award

Payment vouchers

Some public assistance programs such as the Special Supplemental Nutrition Program for Women, Infants and Children, or Aid to Families with Dependent Children make *vouchers* available to their beneficiaries, which are good up to a certain monetary amount for purchase of grocery items deemed eligible under the particular programme. The voucher can be deposited like any other cheque by a participating supermarket or other approved business.

Cheques around the world

Australia

The Cheques Act 1986 is the body of law governing the issuance of cheques and payment orders in Australia. Procedural and practical issues governing the clearance of cheques and payment orders are handled by Australian Payments Clearing Association (APCA).

In 1999, banks adopted a system to allow faster clearance of cheques by electronically transmitting information about cheques, this brought clearance times down from five to three days. Prior to that cheques had to be physically transported to the paying bank before processing began. If it was dishonoured, it was physically returned.

All licensed banks in Australia may issue cheques in their own name. Non-banks are not permitted to issue cheques in their own name but may issue, and have drawn on them, payment orders (which functionally are no different from cheques).

Canada

In Canada, cheque sizes and types [31]—as well as endorsements requirements and MICR tolerances [32] are overseen by the Canadian Payments Association (CPA)

- It is possible to write cheques in currencies (using the standardised ISO currency names) that are not in Canadian Dollars.
- Canadian cheques can legally be written in English or French or Eskimo-Aleut languages.
- Personal cheques in Canada are sold directly from financial institutions through commercial suppliers.
- Business cheques in Canada are also sold directly through financial institutions at the branch or online through commercial suppliers.
- A tele-cheque is a paper payment item that resembles a cheque except that it is neither created nor signed by the payer—instead it is created (and may be signed) by a third party on behalf of the payer. Under CPA Rules these are prohibited in the clearing system effective 27 January 2004.

India

Cheques were introduced in India by the Bank of Hindustan, the first joint stock bank established in 1770.[8]

In 1881, the Negotiable Instruments Act (NI Act) was enacted in India, formalising the usage and characteristics of instruments like the cheque, the bill of exchange and promissory note. The NI Act provided a legal framework for non-cash paper payment instruments in India.[8]

In 1938, the Calcutta Clearing Banks' Association, which was the largest bankers' association at that time, adopted clearing house.[8]

New Zealand

Instrument-specific legislation includes the Cheques Act 1960, part of the Bills of Exchange Act 1908, which codifies aspects related to the cheque payment instrument, notably the procedures for the endorsement, presentment and payment of cheques. A 1995 amendment provided for the electronic presentment of cheques and removed the previous requirement to deliver cheques physically to the paying bank, opening the way for cheque truncation and imaging. Truncation allows for the transmission of an electronic image of all or part of the cheque to the paying bank's branch, instead of the cumbersome physical presentment. This reduced the total cheque clearance time, as well as eliminating the costs of physically moving the cheque.

The registered banks under supervision of Reserve Bank of New Zealand provide the cheque payment services. Once banked, cheques are processed electronically together with other retail payment instrument.

United Kingdom

In the UK all cheques must now conform to "Cheque and Credit Clearing Company (C&CCC) Standard 3", the industry standard detailing layout and font, be printed on a specific weight of paper (CBS1), and contain explicitly defined security features.

Since 1995, all cheque printers must be members of the Cheque Printer Accreditation Scheme (CPAS). The scheme is managed by the Cheque and Credit Clearing Company and requires that all cheques for use in the British clearing process are produced by accredited printers who have adopted stringent security standards.

The rules concerning crossed cheques are set out in Section 1 of the Cheques Act 1992 and prevent cheques being cashed by or paid into the accounts of third parties. On a crossed cheque the words "account payee only" (or similar) are printed between two parallel vertical lines in the centre of the cheque. This makes the cheque non-transferable and is to avoid cheques being endorsed and paid into an account other than that of the named payee. Crossing cheques basically ensures that the money is paid into an account of the intended beneficiary of the cheque.

Following concerns about the amount of time it took banks to clear cheques, the United Kingdom Office of Fair Trading set up a working group in 2006 to look at the cheque clearing cycle. They produced a report[17] recommending maximum times for the cheque clearing which were introduced in UK from November 2007.[31] In the report the date the credit appeared on the recipient's account (usually the day of deposit) was designated "T". At "T + 2" (two business days afterwards) the value would count for calculation of credit interest or overdraft interest on the recipient's account. At "T + 4" clients would be able to withdraw funds (though this will often happen earlier, at the bank's discretion). "T + 6" is the last day that a cheque can bounce without the recipient's permission—this is known as "certainty of fate". Before the introduction of this standard, the only way to know the "fate" of a cheque has been "Special Presentation", which would normally involve a fee, where the drawee bank contacts the payee bank to see if the payee has that money at that time. "Special Presentation" needed to be stated at the time of depositing in the cheque.

Cheque volumes peaked in 1990 when four billion cheque payments were made. Of these, 2.5 billion were cleared through the inter-bank clearing managed by the C&CCC, the remaining 1.5 billion being in-house cheques which were either paid into the branch on which they were drawn or processed intra-bank without going through the clearings. As volumes started to fall, the challenges faced by the clearing banks were then of a different nature: how to benefit from technology improvements in a declining business environment.

Although the UK did not adopt the euro as its national currency when other European countries did in 1999, many banks began offering euro denominated accounts with chequebooks, principally to business customers. The cheques can be used to pay for certain goods and services in the UK. The same year, the C&CCC set up the euro cheque clearing system to process euro denominated cheques separately from sterling cheques in Great Britain.

The UK Payments Council has announced that from 30 June 2011 the existing *Cheque Guarantee Card Scheme* in the UK will end. This allowed cheques to be guaranteed at point of sales when signed in front of the retailer with the additional cheque guarantee card. This was after a long period of decline in their use in favour of debit cards.

The Payments Council would like cheques to be withdrawn from use in the UK and, subject to a review in 2016, has set a target date for this of 31 October 2018.[32]

United States

In the United States, cheques (spelled "checks") are governed by Article 3 of the Uniform Commercial Code, under the rubric of negotiable instruments.[33]

- An *order check*—the most common form in the United States—is payable only to the named payee or his or her *endorsee*, as it usually contains the language "Pay to the order of (name)."
- A *bearer check* is payable to anyone who is in possession of the document: this would be the case if the cheque does not state a payee, or is payable to "bearer" or to "cash" or "to the order of cash", or if the cheque is payable to someone who is not a person or legal entity, e.g. if the payee line is marked "Happy Birthday".
- A *counter check* is a bank cheque given to customers who have run out of cheques or whose cheques are not yet available. It is often left blank—hence sometimes called a "blank check", though this term has other uses—and is used for purposes of withdrawal.

In the United States, the terminology for a cheque historically varied with the type of financial institution on which it is drawn. In the case of a savings and loan association it was a *negotiable order of withdrawal* (compare Negotiable Order of Withdrawal account); if a credit union it was a *share draft. Checks* as such were associated with chartered commercial banks. However, common usage has increasingly conformed to more recent versions of Article 3, where *check* means any or all of these negotiable instruments. Certain types of cheques drawn on a government agency, especially payroll cheques, may also be referred to as a *payroll warrant.*

At the bottom of each cheque there is the routing / account number in MICR format. The routing transit number is a nine-digit number in which the first four digits identifies the U.S. Federal Reserve Bank's cheque-processing center. This is followed by digits 5 through 8, identifying the specific bank served by that cheque-processing center. Digit 9 is a verification check digit, computed using a complex algorithm of the previous eight digits.[34]

- Typically the routing number is followed by a group eight or nine MICR digits that indicates the particular account number at that bank. The account number is assigned independently by the various banks.
- Typically the account number is followed by a group of three or four MICR digits that indicates a particular cheque number from that account.
- fractional routing number (U.S. only)—also known as the transit number, consists of a denominator mirroring the first four digits of the routing number. And a hyphenated numerator, also known as the ABA number, in which the first part is a city code (1–49), if the account is in one of 49 specific cities, or a state code (50–99) if it is not in one of those specific cities; the second part of the hyphenated numerator mirrors the 5th through 8th digits of the routing number with leading zeros removed.[34]

A *draft* is a bill of exchange which is not payable on demand of the payee. (However, *draft* in the U.S. Uniform Commercial Code today means any bill of exchange, whether payable on demand or at a later date; if payable on demand it is a "demand draft", or if drawn on a financial institution, a cheque.)

Cheque truncation was introduced in 2004 with the passing of the "Check Clearing for the 21st Century Act" (or Check 21 Act), this allowed the creation of electronic substitute checks to replace the physical cheques saving costs and processing time.

Cheque fraud

Cheques have been a tempting target for criminals to steal money or goods from the drawer, payee or the banks. A number of measures have been introduced to combat fraud over the years. These range from things like writing a cheque so its hard for to be altered after it is drawn to mechanisms like crossing a cheque so that it can only be paid into another banks account providing some traceability. However, the inherent security weaknesses of cheques as a payment method, such as having only the signature as the main authentication method and not knowing if funds will be received until the clearing cycle to complete, have made them vulnerable to a number of different types of fraud;

Embezzlement

Taking advantage of the float period (cheque kiting) to delay the notice of non-existent funds. This often involves trying to convince a merchant or other recipient, hoping the recipient will not suspect that the cheque will not clear, giving time for the fraudster to disappear.

Forgery

Sometimes, forgery is the method of choice in defrauding a bank. One form of forgery involves the use of a victim's legitimate cheques, that have either been stolen and then cashed, or altering a cheque that has been legitimately written to the perpetrator, by adding words and/or digits in order to inflate the amount.

Identity theft

Since cheques include significant personal information (name, account number, signature and in some countries driver's license number, the address and/or phone number of the account holder), they can be used for fraud, specifically identity theft. In the USA and Canada until recent years the social security number was sometimes included on cheques. The practice was discontinued as identity theft became widespread.

Dishonoured cheques

A dishonoured cheque cannot be redeemed for its value and is worthless; they are also known as an *RDI* (returned deposit item), or *NSF* (non-sufficient funds) cheque. Cheques are usually dishonoured because the drawer's account has been frozen or limited, or because there are insufficient funds in the drawer's account when the cheque was redeemed. A cheque drawn on an account with insufficient funds is said to have *bounced* and may be called a *rubber cheque*.[35] Banks will typically charge customers for issuing a dishonoured cheque, and in some jurisdictions such an act is a criminal action. A drawer may also issue a *stop* on a cheque, instructing the financial institution not to honour a particular cheque.

In England and Wales, they are typically returned marked "Refer to Drawer"—an instruction to contact the person issuing the cheque for an explanation as to why the cheque was not honoured. This wording was brought in after a bank was successfully sued for libel after returning a cheque with the phrase "Insufficient Funds" after making an error—the court ruled that as there were sufficient funds the statement was demonstrably false and damaging to the reputation of the person issuing the cheque. Despite the use of this revised phrase, successful libel lawsuits brought against banks by individuals remained for similar errors.[36]

However, in Scotland, a cheque acts as an assignment of the amount of money to the payee. As such, if a cheque is dishonoured in Scotland, what funds are present in the bank account are "attached" and frozen, until either sufficient funds are credited to the account to pay the cheque, the drawer recovers the cheque and hands it into the bank, or the drawer obtains a letter from the payee that he has no further interest in the cheque.

A cheque may also be dishonored because it is stale or not cashed within a "void after date". Many cheques have an explicit notice printed on the cheque that it is void after some period of days. In the United States, banks are not required by the Uniform Commercial Code to honour a **stale-dated cheque,** which is a cheque presented six months after it is dated.[15]

Lock box

Typically when customers pay bills with cheques (like gas or water bills), the mail will go to a "lock box" at the post office. There a bank will pick up all the mail, sort it, open it, take the cheques and remittance advice out, process it all through electronic machinery, and post the funds to the proper accounts. In modern systems, taking advantage of the Check 21 Act, as in the U.S., many cheques are transformed into electronic objects and the paper is destroyed.

Notes

Footnotes

[1] See the negotiable cow—itself a fictional story—for discussions of cheques written on unusual surfaces.

[2] Although cheques are regulated in most countries as negotiable instruments, in many countries they are not actually negotiable, viz., the payee cannot endorse the cheque in favour of a third party. Payers could usually designate a cheque as being payable to a named payee only by "crossing" the cheque, thereby designating it as account payee only, but in an effort to combat financial crime, many countries have provided by a combination of law and regulation that all cheques should be treated as crossed, or account payee only, and are not negotiable.

[3] "Cheques and Bankers' Drafts Facts and Figures" (http://www.ukpayments.org.uk/resources_publications/key_facts_and_figures/cheques_and_bankers'_drafts_facts_and_figures/). *UK Payment Administraton*. UKPA. 2010. . Retrieved 30 June 2010.

[4] "Cheque, check" (http://dictionary.oed.com/cgi/entry/50037719?single=1&query_type=word&queryword=cheque&first=1&max_to_show=10). *Oxford English Dictionary*. London: Oxford University Press. 2009. pp. 350. .

[5] James William Gilbart in 1828 explains in a footnote 'Most writers spell it *check*. I have adopted the above form because it is free from ambiguity and is analogous to the ex-*chequer*, the royal treasury. It is also used by the Bank of England "Cheque Office"'.Gilbart, James William (1828). *A practical treatise on Banking, containing an account of the London and County Banks ... a view of Joint Stock Banks, and the Branch Banks of the Bank of England, etc* (2nd ed.). London: E Wilson. pp. 115.

[6] Cheque - Merriam-Webster's Online Dictionary (http://www.merriam-webster.com/dictionary/cheque)

[7] Durant, Will (1944). *Caesar and Christ : a history of Roman civilization and of Christianity from their beginnings to A.D. 325*. The story of civilization. 3. New York: Simon & Schuster. pp. 749.

[8] "Evolution of Payment Systems in India =Reserve Bank of India" (http://www.rbi.org.in/scripts/PublicationsView.aspx?id=155). .

[9] Glubb, John Bagot (1988), *A Short History Of The Arab Peoples*, Dorset Press, pp. 105, ISBN 9780880292269, OCLC 603697876

[10] Baigent, Michael; Leigh, Richard; Lincoln, Henry (1982). *The holy blood and the Holy Grail*. London: Corgi. pp. 528. ISBN 978-0-552-12138-5.

[11] "Guide to Checks and Check Fraud" (https://www.wachovia.com/file/checks_and_check_fraud.pdf). Wachovia Bank. 2003. p. 4. .

[12] Cheque and Credit Clearing Company (2009). "Cheques and cheque clearing: An historical perspective" (http://www.ukpayments.org.uk/files/candc/history_publication_final_-_small_version.pdf). . Retrieved 19 June 2010.

[13] APACS (26 Nov 2007). "Understanding cheques" (http://www.bba.org.uk/bba/jsp/polopoly.jsp?d=263&a=5603). British Bankers Association. . Retrieved 19 June 2010.

[14] Lex Mercatoria, Law Faculty of the University of Tromsø, Norway (http://www.jus.uio.no/lm/un.sg.report.itl.development.1966/1.html)

[15] "Uniform Commercial Code § 4-404" (http://www.law.cornell.edu/ucc/4/article4.htm#s4-404). United States Congress. . "A bank is under no obligation to a customer having a chequing account to pay a cheque, other than a certified cheque, which is presented more than six months after its date, but it may charge its customer's account for a payment made thereafter in good faith."

[16] "Legal Issues Guide for Small Business: How long is a cheque valid for?" (http://sblegal.innovation.gov.au/Lists/New Relevant Legal Issues/DispForm.aspx?ID=691&RootFolder=*). Department of Innovation, Industry, Science, and Research. 4 July 2008. . Retrieved 26 May 2009.

[17] "Cheques Working Group Report" (http://www.oft.gov.uk/shared_oft/reports/financial_products/oft868.pdf) (PDF). London: The Office of Fair Trading. November 2006. pp. 297. . Retrieved 26 May 2009.

[18] "Popularity of cheques wanes" (http://news.bbc.co.uk/1/hi/business/2151881.stm). London: BBC News. 25 July 2002. . Retrieved 26 May 2009.

[19] "Shell bans payment by cheque" (http://news.bbc.co.uk/1/hi/programmes/moneybox/4233002.stm). London: BBC News. 10 September 2005. . Retrieved 26 May 2009.

[20] "Cheques get the chop at Asda" (http://www.guardian.co.uk/money/2006/apr/03/supermarkets.consumeraffairs). *Guardian*. Press Association (London). 3 April 2006. . Retrieved 26 May 2009.

[21] "High Street retailer bans cheques" (http://news.bbc.co.uk/1/hi/england/southern_counties/5339522.stm). London: BBC News. 12 September 2006. . Retrieved 26 May 2009.

[22] Jonathan, Duffy (27 November 2003). "Chequeing out" (http://news.bbc.co.uk/1/hi/magazine/3242776.stm). London: BBC News. . Retrieved 26 May 2009.

[23] "Cheques to be phased out in 2018" (http://news.bbc.co.uk/2/hi/business/8414341.stm). *BBC News*. 16 December 2009. . Retrieved 16 December 2009.

[24] "Plans to end cheques criticised by banks" (http://www.bbc.co.uk/news/business-11972334). *BBC News*. 11 December 2010. . Retrieved 12 December 2010.

[25] Organisation for Economic Co-operation and Development, ed (2002). *The Future of Money* (http://books.google.com/books?id=ym_bqY3UZG0C&pg=PA76&dq=billion+checks&as_brr=1&sig=4bxAvdOX3fl3LMpMcpfWyIibW1M#v=onepage&q=billion checks&f=false). Paris: OECD. pp. 76–79. ISBN 978-92-64-19672-8. .

[26] "'Green payment' movement set to impact the American consumer payments landscape" (http://blog.euromonitor.com/2010/05/green-payment-movement-set-to-impact-the-american-consumer-payments-landscape.html). euromonitor.com. 4 May 2010. . Retrieved 24 July 2010.

[27] "Cheque" (http://a-z-dictionaries.com/glossaries/Accounting_Glossary.html#check). *Glossary of Accounting terms*. A-Z-Dictionaries.com. 2005. . Retrieved 26 May 2009.

[28] "Big Cheques" (http://www.megaprint.com/large-checks.php). Megaprint Inc. . Retrieved 26 May 2009.

[29] "GWR Day - Kuwait: A Really Big cheque" (http://www.guinnessworldrecords.com/gwrday/ar_kuwait_bigcheque.aspx). Guinness World Records. 2009. . Retrieved 26 May 2009.

[30] Holden, Lewis (2009). "A cheque is a cheque -- whatever it is printed on" (http://www.bankrate.com/brm/news/chk/20010320a.asp?prodtype=bank). Bankrate, Inc.. . Retrieved 26 May 2009.

[31] Miles, Brignall (30 November 2007). "Cheque changes leave consumers in the clear" (http://www.guardian.co.uk/money/2007/nov/30/consumeraffairs.banks). *Guardian*. London. . Retrieved 26 May 2009.

[32] http://www.paymentscouncil.org.uk/media_centre/press_releases_new/-/page/855/

[33] U.C.C. - ARTICLE 3 - NEGOTIABLE INSTRUMENTS (http://www.law.cornell.edu/ucc/3/article3.htm)

[34] "Inside Check Numbers" (http://replay.waybackmachine.org/20070921204935/http://supersat-tech.livejournal.com/3727.html). Supersat-tech.livejournal.com. Archived from the original (http://supersat-tech.livejournal.com/3727.html) on 2007-09-21. .

[35] Garner, Bryan A. (1995). *A dictionary of modern legal usage* (2nd ed.). Oxford University Press. pp. 953. ISBN 978-0-19-507769-8.

[36] "Bounced cheques yield libel damages" (http://www.independent.co.uk/news/uk/bounced-cheques-yield-libel-damages-1534499.html). *The Independent* (UK). 21 July 1992. . Retrieved 24 September 2009.

Citations

External links

- Bank and account identifiers on U.S. cheques: ABA / Routing / Transit (http://supersat-tech.livejournal.com/3727.html)
- Cheque and Credit Clearing Company (http://www.chequeandcredit.co.uk)—the organisation that manages the cheque clearing system in the UK
- Cheques found in the Cairo Geniza from the 12th century (http://www.lib.cam.ac.uk/cgi-bin/GOLD/thumbs?class_mark=T-S_Ar.30.184)
- Information on cheques in the UK (http://www.ukpayments.org.uk/payment_options/cheques_bankers_drafts/) from APACS
- Malaysia Introduces New Cheque Clearing System (http://english.cri.cn/3130/2008/04/09/195@343610.htm)
- Bills of Exchange Act 1882 (http://www.legislation.gov.uk/id/ukpga/Vict/45-46/61)
- Cheques Act 1957 (http://www.legislation.gov.uk/id/ukpga/Eliz2/5-6/36)
- Canadian Payments Association (http://www.cdnpay.ca).
- Cheques Act 1992 (http://www.legislation.gov.uk/id/ukpga/1992/32)

Cheque guarantee card

A **cheque guarantee card** is essentially an abbreviated portable letter of credit granted by a bank to a qualified depositor, providing that when he is paying a business by cheque and the retailer writes the card number on the back of the cheque, the cheque was signed in the retailer's presence, and the retailer verifies the signature on the cheque against the signature on the card, then the cheque cannot be stopped and payment cannot be refused by the bank. Note that the arrangement works only for cheques drawn on an account provided by the bank that issued the card.

Logo of the United Kingdom domestic cheque guarantee card scheme since 1990

Cheques drawn against insufficient funds in this manner can result in an overdraft with penalty interest. In some European countries, such as Germany or Sweden, cheques are no longer guaranteed since the abolition of Eurocheques in 2001, and many retailers now refuse to accept cheques.

In the United Kingdom the scheme was first trialled in 1965 and fully introduced in 1969, with a limit of £30. The limit was increased to £50 in 1977 and then to £100 or £250, at the bank's discretion, in 1989.[1] As of 2009 the scheme was only used to guarantee 7% of the 1.4 billion cheques issued each year,[2] a figure which itself is declining due to the popularity of other means of payment such as debit cards. The Payments Council therefore announced a decision in September 2009 to withdraw the cheque guarantee scheme on 30 June 2011.[2] [3]

References

[1] Review of the UK Domestic Cheque Guarantee Card Scheme (http://www.paymentscouncil.org.uk/files/payments_files/ cheque_guarantee_report_june_2009.pdf), Payments Council, June 2009

[2] The Cheque Guarantee Card Scheme announces closure date of 30th June 2011 (http://www.ukpayments.org.uk/media_centre/ press_releases/-/page/719/), press release from UK Payments Administration, 25 September 2009.

[3] King, Mark. Abolition of cheques to be reconsidered (http://www.guardian.co.uk/money/2011/apr/14/ abolition-cheques-reconsidered-payments-council), *The Guardian*, 14 April 2011

Cheque truncation

Cheque truncation (check truncation in the United States) is the conversion of physical cheque into electronic form for transmission to the paying bank. Cheque truncation eliminates cumbersome physical presentation of the cheque and saves time and processing costs.

Front view

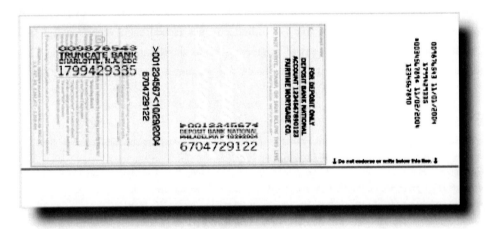

Rear view

History

To settle a cheque it has to be presented to the drawee bank for payment. Originally this was done by taking the cheque in person to the drawee bank, however as cheque usage increased this became cumbersome and banks arranged between each other to meet each day at a central location to exchange cheques and settle the money. This became known as central clearing. Bank customers who received cheques could now deposit cheques at their own bank and their bank would arrange for the cheque to be returned to the drawee bank and any funds credited and debited from the appropriate accounts. If a cheque was dishonoured or bounced it would be physically returned to the original bank marked as such.

This process would take several days as physical cheques had to be transported to the central clearing location, from where they had to be transported to the payee bank. If the cheque bounced it would be transported back to the bank where the cheque was deposited. This is known as the clearing cycle.

Cheques had to be examined by hand at each stage and required a large amount of man power and handling.

In 1960 machine readable codes were added to the bottom of cheques in MICR format which allowed the clearing and sorting process to be automated. This helped to speedup the clearing process, however the law in most countries still required the physical cheques to be delivered back to the payee bank and so physical movement of the paper continued.

Starting in the mid 1990s some countries started to change their laws in relation to cheques to allow for truncation. Cheques would be imaged and digital representation of the cheque would be transmitted to the drawee bank at which point the original cheques could be destroyed. The MICR codes and cheque details are normally encoded as text in addition to the image. The bank where the cheque was deposited would typically do the truncation and this dramatically decreased the time it took to clear a cheque. In some cases large retailers that received large volumes of cheques were also able to carry out this truncation process.

Once the cheque has been turned into a digital document it can be processed through the banking system just like any other electronic payment.

Laws

Although technology needed to exist to be able to truncate a cheque, it was the laws related to cheques that were the main impediment to their introduction. New Zealand was one of the first countries to introduce truncation and imaging of cheques, when in 1995 they amended the cheque act 1960 to provide for the electronic presentment of cheques. A number of other countries followed over the next few years, but progress was mixed due to the decline in the use of cheques in favour of electronic payment systems. Some countries decided that the effort to implement truncation could not be justified for a declining payment method and instead phased out the use of cheques altogether.[1]

In 2004, the Check 21 Act was implemented in the United States to authorize conversion of the original paper check into an electronic image for presentment through the clearing process. The law also enacted the recognition and acceptance of a "substitute check" created by a financial institution in lieu of the original paper check. Any bank that receives the original paper check can remove or "truncate" the paper check from the clearing process.

New laws needed to address ways to make sure that the digital image was a true and accurate copy of the original cheque as well as mechanism to make sure that the process could be audited to protect consumers.

It also needed to address the mechanism for dishonoured cheques as cheques could no longer be returned. A typical solution, as defined by Monetary Authority of Singapore for the Singapore cheque truncation system, was that a special 'Image Return Document' was created and sent back to bank that had truncated the cheque.[2]

Operations and clearing

The security related to imaging and creating the electronic cheque needed to be defined and the clearing process adjusted to accommodate electronic cheques.

References

[1] "CHEQUE TRUNCATION ABRIDGED REPORT - 2008" (http://www.google.co.nz/url?sa=t&source=web&cd=28& ved=0CDEQFjAHOBQ&url=http://www.ipso.ie/x/File/PublicationsAndReports/IPSOReport/cheque_truncation_abridged_report2008. pdf&rct=j&q=the legal implications of cheque truncation&ei=N4lUTMS6MIL6sAP7_qXbAg& usg=AFQjCNFWMePvse_1W4Ale9mXFq5-_7MUzg). Irish Payment Services Organisation (http://www.ipso.ie/). 2008. . Retrieved 1 August 2010.

[2] "Bills of Exchange (Cheque Truncation) Regulations 2002" (http://www.mas.gov.sg/news_room/press_releases/2002/ MAS_ISSUES_BILLS_OF_EXCHANGE__CHEQUE_TRUNCATION__REGULATIONS_2002.html). Monetary Authority of Singapore. September 17, 2002. . Retrieved August 1, 2010.

Cheque truncation system

Cheque Truncation System (CTS) or Image-based Clearing System (ICS), in India, is a project undertaken by the Reserve Bank of India – RBI, for faster clearing of cheques.[1] CTS is basically an online image-based cheque clearing system where cheque images and Magnetic Ink Character Recognition (MICR) data are captured at the collecting bank branch and transmitted electronically.

Truncation means, stopping the flow of the physical cheques issued by a drawer to the drawee branch. The physical instrument is truncated at some point en-route to the drawee branch and an electronic image of the cheque is sent to the drawee branch along with the relevant information like the MICR fields, date of presentation, presenting banks etc.

Cheque truncation, would eliminate the need to move the physical instruments across branches, except in exceptional circumstances. This would result in effective reduction in the time required for payment of cheques, the associated cost of transit and delays in processing, etc., thus speeding up the process of collection or realization of cheques.

Adoption Challenges

Integration with existing large banking systems- Legacy systems are a major IT and operational investment for banks. Most Banks have already invested on legacy systems and therefore it becomes vital that the new system has the capability to integrate seamlessly with the existing systems.

Security- Safety and security of financial transactions is of prime importance for Banks as well as consumers. Hence, financial information transmitted over an electronic medium should be proven to be secure against financial frauds.

Resisting to change- Change is always met with resistance. The banks and central regulatory authority need to work to remove apprehensions and reservations about adoption of new technology.

Customer acceptance- Customer acceptance cannot be emphasized enough especially when it comes to financial transactions. This calls for tremendous change in mindset among customers, and they need to be educated and reassured that the new technology is in their favor and to provide them with safer, faster clearance and more secure services.

Expected Benefits

For Banks: Banks can expect multiple benefits through the implementation of CTS, like faster clearing cycle means realization of proceeds of cheque possible within the same day. It offers better reconciliation/verification process, better customer service and enhanced customer window. Operational efficiency will provide a direct boost to bottom lines of banks as clearing of local checks is a high cost low revenue activity. Besides, it reduces operational risk by securing the transmission route. Centralized image archival system ensures data storage and retrieval is easy. Reduction of manual tasks leads to reduction of errors. Customer satisfaction will be enhanced, due to the reduced turn around time (TAT). Real-time tracking and visibility of the cheques, less fraudulent cases with secured transfer of images to the RBI are other possible benefits that banks may derive from this solution.[2]

For Customers: CTS / ICS substantially reduces the time taken to clear the cheques as well enables banks to offer better customer services and increases operational efficiency by cutting down on overheads involved in the physical cheque clearing process. In addition, it also offers better reconciliation and fraud prevention. CTS / ICS uses cheque image, instead of the physical cheque itself, for cheque clearance thus reducing the turn around time drastically.

References

[1] Frequently asked questions (FAQ) on cheque truncation project in the National Capital Region (http://rbidocs.rbi.org.in/rdocs/content/pdfs/74751.pdf)

[2] Cheque Truncation System (CTS) in India- An Introduction & FAQs, banknetindia.com (http://www.banknetindia.com/banking/chqtruncation.htm)

External links

* A pan-India cheque truncation system five years away (http://www.dnaindia.com/money/report_a-pan-india-cheque-truncation-system-five-years-away_1336380) press release, dnaindia.com
* RBI says new norms applicable to cheque truncation system only (http://www.moneylife.in/article/rbi-says-new-norms-applicable-to-cheque-truncation-system-only/6424.html) press release, moneylife.in
* RBI regulation on cheque truncation system starts (http://news.oneindia.in/2010/12/01/rbi-regulation-for-cts-effective-from-dec-1.html) news release, oneindia.in

Chip and PIN

Chip and PIN is the brandname adopted by the banking industries in the United Kingdom and Ireland for the rollout of the EMV smartcard payment system for credit, debit and ATM cards.

Chip and PIN

History

Until the introduction of Chip and PIN, all face-to-face credit or debit card transactions used a magnetic stripe or mechanical imprint to read and record account data, and a signature for verification. Under this system, the customer hands their card to the clerk at the point of sale, who either "swipes" the card through a magnetic reader or makes an imprint from the raised text of the card. In the former case, the account details are verified and a slip for the customer to sign is printed. In the case of a mechanical imprint, the transaction details are filled in and the customer signs the imprinted slip. In either case, the clerk verifies that the signature matches that on the back of the card to authenticate the transaction.

This system has proved reasonably effective, but has a number of security flaws, including the ability to steal a card in the post, or to learn to forge the signature on the card. More recently, technology has become available on the black market for both reading and writing the magnetic stripes, allowing cards to be easily cloned and used without the owner's knowledge.

How it works

To solve this, banks and retailers are replacing traditional magnetic stripe equipment with smartcard technology, where credit and debit cards contain an embedded microchip and are authenticated automatically using a personal identification number (PIN). When a customer wishes to pay for goods using this system, the card is placed into a "PIN pad" terminal or a modified swipe-card reader, which accesses the chip on the card. Once the card has been verified as authentic, the customer enters a 4-digit PIN, which is submitted to the chip on the smartcard; if the two match, the chip tells the terminal the PIN was correct, otherwise it informs it the PIN was incorrect.

France has cut card fraud by more than 80%. Chip and PIN is the name given to the initiative in the UK; other countries are launching their own systems based on the EMV standard, which is a group effort between Europay, MasterCard and VISA. By the end of 2004 100 countries should have been using compatible systems based on this standard.

A chip from a credit card, with a normal sized pin for scale.

Crime reduction

While EMV technology has helped reduce crime at the tills, when it comes to telephone, internet, and mail order—known in the industry as card-not-present or CNP—fraud, the figures are growing every year, and as of May 2009 made up more than 50% of all credit card fraud.[1] Since this has become a major area of fraud, other initiatives such as Verified by Visa and MasterCard SecureCode (implementations of Visa's 3-D Secure protocol) are being implemented to improve CNP security. Since 2008 VISA has been running pilot projects using the Emue card,[2] which has a chip, a mini-keypad, a display, and a battery expected to last three years; the user enters a PIN and a secure one-time-only code is displayed which replaces the code printed on the back of standard cards.[3]

Conversion

Chip and PIN was trialled in Northampton, England from May 2003, and as a result was rolled out nationwide in the United Kingdom in 2004 with advertisements in the press and national television touting the "Safety in Numbers" slogan. During the first stages of deployment, if a fraudulent magnetic swipe card transaction was deemed to have occurred, the retailer was refunded by the issuing bank, as was the case prior to the introduction of Chip and PIN. On January 1, 2005, the liability for such transactions was shifted to the retailer; this acted as an incentive for retailers to upgrade their Point of sale (PoS) systems, and most major high-street chains upgraded on time for the EMV deadline. Many smaller businesses were initially reluctant to upgrade their equipment, as it required a completely new PoS system—a significant investment.

New cards featuring both magnetic strips and chips are now issued by all major banks. The replacement of pre-Chip and PIN cards was a major issue, as banks simply stated that consumers would receive their new cards "when their old card expires"—despite many people having had cards with expiry dates as late as 2007. The card issuer Switch lost a major contract with HBOS to VISA as they were not ready to issue the new cards as early as the bank wanted to. This change angered many, as Visa's Electron cards are generally not accepted online, unlike Switch's Solo.

Cardholders who are incapable of entering a PIN because of a disability can contact their bank to be issued with a Chip and Signature card.

In the Republic of Ireland a PIN has been required with Chip-and-PIN-enabled cards since 17 March 2007.

Benefits

Under the old system, a customer had to hand their card to the assistant to pay for a transaction. When credit cards were first introduced, offline portable card imprinters (mechanical rather than magnetic) which did not connect to the card issuer were used without the card leaving the customer's sight; transactions over a certain limit had to be verified by telephoning the card issuer. Later equipment was introduced which electronically contacted the card issuer using information from the magnetic stripe to verify the card and authorise the transaction; this was much faster, but had to be in a fixed location. Consequently, if the transaction did not take place near a terminal (in a restaurant, for example) the card had to be taken away from the customer to the card machine. It was easily possible at any time for a dishonest employee to swipe the card surreptitiously through a cheap machine which would take a couple of seconds to record the information on the card and stripe; in fact, even at the terminal, the criminal could bend down in front of the customer and swipe the card on a hidden reader. This made illegal cloning of cards easy, and a common occurrence.

Since the introduction of Chip and PIN, cloning of the chip is not feasible; only the magnetic stripe can be copied, and a copied card cannot be used on a PIN terminal. Fortuitously, the introduction of chip and PIN coincided with wireless data communications technology becoming inexpensive and widespread, and wireless PIN pads were introduced that could be brought to the customer and used without the card ever being out of sight (this would have been possible, had the technology been available, with magnetic stripe cards). Chip and PIN and wireless together reduce the risk of cloning of cards by brief swiping.

Banks' liability

Until 1 November 2009 banks' legal liability in cases of unauthorised use of card accounts was subject to terms of the voluntary Banking Code, and in many cases banks refused to reimburse cardholders who reported unauthorised card use, claiming that their systems could not fail and consequently the cardholder must have acted "without reasonable care"—the Code states that unless a bank can prove that its customer acted fraudulently or without reasonable care, the most that the customer will be liable for is £50.[4]

The Financial Services Authority (FSA) Payment Services Regulations 2009 came into force on 1 November 2009[5] and shifted the onus onto the banks to prove, rather than assume, that the cardholder is at fault.[6] The Financial Services Authority said "It is for the bank, building society or credit card company to show that the transaction was made by you, and there was no breakdown in procedures or technical difficulty" before refusing liability.

Criticism

Banks originally not liable by default

The Chip and PIN implementation was criticised as designed to reduce the liability of banks in cases of claimed card fraud by requiring the customer to prove that they had acted "with reasonable care" to protect their PIN and card, rather than on the bank having to prove that the signature matched. Before Chip and PIN, if a customer's signature was forged, the banks were legally liable and had to reimburse the customer. Until 1 November 2009 there was no such law protecting consumers from fraudulent use of their Chip and PIN transactions, only the voluntary Banking Code. While this code stated that the burden of proof is on the bank to prove negligence or fraud rather than the cardholder having to prove innocence, [7] there were many reports that banks refused to reimburse victims of fraudulent card use, claiming that their systems could not fail under the circumstances reported, despite several documented successful large-scale attacks.

This changed on 1 November 2009 when legal, rather than voluntary, regulations came into force requiring banks to reimburse cardholders unless they could prove that the transaction was authorised by the cardholder.[6]

Foreign cards

Chip and PIN systems can cause problems for travellers from countries that do not issue chip and PIN cards (most notably, the USA) as some retailers may refuse to accept their chipless cards.[8]

However, United Nations Federal Credit Union UNFCU will be first issuer in the US to offer credit cards with a high security chip, although one must be a member of the United Nations to apply.[9] While most terminals will still accept a magnetic strip card, and the major credit card brands require vendors to accept them, poorly trained staff may refuse to take the card under the mistaken belief that they will be held liable for any fraud if the card cannot verify a PIN. Non-chip-and-PIN cards may also not work in some unattended vending machines at, for example, transport stations.[10] In 2010 a number of companies began issuing pre-paid debit cards that incorporate the Chip & PIN which allows Americans to load up cash as Euros or British Pounds.[11]

Vulnerabilities, fraud, and misuse

Chip and PIN cards are not foolproof; several vulnerabilities have been found and demonstrated, and there have been large-scale instances of fraudulent exploitation. In many cases banks have been reluctant to accept that their systems could be at fault and have refused to refund victims of what is arguably fraud, although legislation introduced in November 2009 has improved victims' rights and put the onus on the banks to prove negligence or fraud by the cardholder. Vulnerabilities and fraud are discussed in depth in the main article.

References

[1] BBC:Credit card code to combat fraud, May 2009 (http://news.bbc.co.uk/1/hi/technology/8046492.stm)

[2] VISA EMUE card website (http://www.emue.com/site/home.htm)

[3] ITPro: Visa tests cards with built in PIN machine, November 2008 (http://www.itpro.co.uk/608112/visa-tests-cards-with-built-in-pin-machine)

[4] Banks reluctant to pay victims of chip-and-PIN fraud (http://www.timesonline.co.uk/tol/money/consumer_affairs/article5575295.ece), Times Online, 23 January 2009

[5] FSA: Payment Services Regulations 2009, in force from 1 November 2009 (http://www.fsa.gov.uk/Pages/About/What/International/psd/)

[6] Telegraph - Card fraud: banks now have to prove your guilt, 12 February 2010 (http://www.telegraph.co.uk/finance/personalfinance/consumertips/banking/6338659/Bank-payments-13-months-to-dispute-suspicious-transactions.html)

[7] http://www.thisismoney.co.uk/help-and-advice/ask-an-expert/article.html?in_article_id=395091&in_page_id=92

[8] U.S. credit cards becoming outdated, less usable abroad (http://www.creditcards.com/credit-card-news/outdated-smart-card-chip-pin-1273.php)

[9] (http://www.unfcu.com/content.aspx?id=1484)

[10] For Americans, Plastic Buys Less Abroad (http://www.nytimes.com/2009/10/04/travel/04pracchip.html?_r=1&partner=rss&emc=rss&pagewanted=all)

[11] Travelex Offers America's First Chip & PIN Enabled Prepaid Foreign Currency Card (http://www.businesswire.com/news/home/20101201006404/en/Travelex-Offers-America's-Chip-PIN-Enabled-Prepaid)

External links

- Chip and PIN Official homepage (http://www.chipandpin.co.uk)
- Chip and PIN Ireland homepage (http://www.chipandpin.ie/)
- Lloyds TSB: Chip and PIN Guide (http://www.chipandpin.lloydstsb.com)
- Visa EU (http://www.visaeurope.com/merchant/chipcardsandnewsolutions/chipandpin/main.jsp)
- What is EMV? (http://www.emvx.co.uk/emv_guide.aspx), a technical guide to EMV transactions, complete with a glossary of terms a flowchart showing the stages of a typical transaction
- BBC News Online
  - Now the Pin is mightier than the pen (http://news.bbc.co.uk/1/hi/technology/3039619.stm)
  - Halifax's decision to change to Visa (http://news.bbc.co.uk/1/hi/programmes/moneybox/3717331.stm)
- Chip and Pin is Broken (http://www.cl.cam.ac.uk/~sjm217/papers/oakland10chipbroken.pdf)

Chip Authentication Program

The **Chip Authentication Program** (CAP) is a MasterCard initiative and technical specification for using EMV banking smartcards for authenticating users and transactions in online and telephone banking. It was also adopted by Visa as **Dynamic Passcode Authentication** (DPA).[1] The CAP specification defines a handheld device ("CAP reader") with a smartcard slot, a decimal keypad, and a display capable of displaying at least 12 characters (e.g. a starburst display). Banking customers who have been issued a CAP reader by their bank can insert their Chip and PIN (EMV) card into the CAP reader in order to participate in one of several supported authentication protocols. CAP is a form of two-factor authentication as both a smartcard and a valid PIN must be present for a transaction to succeed. Banks hope that the system will reduce the risk of unsuspecting customers entering their details into fraudulent websites after reading 'phishing' emails.[2]

A GemAlto EZIO CAP Device Whitelabeled as Barclays PINSentry

Operating principle

The CAP specification supports several authentication methods. The user first inserts their smartcard into the CAP reader and enables it by entering the PIN. A button is then pressed to select the transaction type. Most readers have 2 or 3 transaction types available to the user under a variety of names. Some known implementations are:

- **Code/Identify:** Without requiring any further input, the CAP reader interacts with the smartcard to produce a decimal one-time password, which can be used, for example, to log in to a banking website.
- **Response:** This mode implements challenge-response authentication, where the bank's website asks the customer to enter a "challenge" number into the CAP reader, and then copy the "response" number displayed by the CAP reader into the web site.

- **Sign:** This mode is an extension of the previous, where not only a random "challenge" value, but also crucial transaction details such as the transferred value, the currency, and recipient's account number have to be typed into the CAP reader.

The above noted transaction types are implemented using one of two modes. One of these modes has two forms in which it can operate, creating three distinct modes, though they are not named this way in the specification.

- **Mode1:** This is the mode for normal monetary transactions such as an online purchase through a merchant. The transaction value and currency may be included in the computation of the cryptogram. If the card does not require it or the terminal does not support it, then both amount and currency are set to zero during the computation.

- **Mode2:** This mode may be useful for authenticating a user in which no transaction is taking place, such as logging into an Internet banking system. The computation differs as there is no transaction data included, making these responses very easy to precompute or reuse.

- **Mode2 with TDS:** This mode may be used for more complicated transactions, such as a funds transfer between accounts. Multiple data fields pertaining to the transaction are concatenated and then hashed using the value that would result from a Mode2 operation as the key for the hashing algorithm. The resultant hash is used in place of the cryptogram calculated in a non-TDS Mode2 operation.

Mode1 sounds very much like a specific use of Mode2 with TDS (Transaction Data Signing), but there is a critical difference. In Mode1 operation, the transaction data (amount and currency type) are used in the cryptogram calculation in addition to all the values used in Mode2 without TDS, whereas Mode2 includes its transaction data in a successive step rather than including it in the cryptogram calculation step. If it were not for this difference, then all operations could be generalized as a single operation with varying optional transaction data.

Protocol details

In all three modes, the CAP reader asks the EMV card to output a data packet that confirms the cancellation of a fictitious EMV payment transaction, which involves the details entered by the user. This confirmation message contains a message authentication code (typically CBC-MAC/Triple DES) that is generated with the help of a card-specific secret key stored securely in the smartcard. Such cancellation messages pose no security risk to the regular EMV payment application, but can be cryptographically verified and are generated by an EMV card only after the correct PIN has been entered. It provided the CAP designers a way to create strong cryptographic evidence that a PIN-activated EMV card is present and has seen some given input data, without having to add any new software functions to already fielded EMV cards.

A Nordea E-code reader

An EMV smartcard contains a (typically 16-bit) transaction counter that is incremented with each payment or CAP transaction. The response displayed by a CAP reader essentially consists of the various parts of the card's response (Application Transaction Counter, MAC etc) which is then reduced to specific bits as determined by the Issuer Authentication Indicator record stored in the card (this is set on a per-issuer basis, although should an issuer desire, it could be set randomly for each card providing a database of each card's IAI is kept), finally, after unwanted bits are discarded (essentially the absolute position of bits is irrelevant, a bit in the IAI that is 0 means the corresponding bit in the card response will be dropped rather than merely being set to 0). Finally the value is converted from binary into a decimal number and displayed to the user. A truncated example is provided below:

1. CAP device selects EMV application, reads IAI info from card and the user selects an action to perform (in this example, IAI will be 111011011000).
2. CAP device sends challenge of 011100111010 as an ARQC transaction (we are assuming PIN entry was successful).
3. Smartcard gives a response of 110101110110 and CAP device cancels the fake transaction.
4. CAP device uses the IAI mask: 111011011000 to determine which bits to drop - where you see a 0 in the IAI, you delete that bit from the response.
5. Hence the final response is 1100110 or 102 in decimal.

In the identify mode, the response depends only on the required bits from the IAI as the amount and reference number are set to zero - this also means that selecting respond and entering a number of "00000000" will in fact generate a valid sign response. More concerningly however, if a respond request is issued by a bank, using the sign mode with the same number and an amount of "0.00" will again generate a valid result which creates a possibility for a fraudster to instruct a customer to do a "test" challenge response for an amount of £0.00 which is in fact going to be used by the fraudster to verify a respond command in order for them to add themselves as a payee on the victim's account - currently this attack is only possible with the Gemalto made EZIO CAP devices (Barclays PINsentry) as the Xiring made devices will not procced until an amount of at least 0.01 is entered.

The same on-card PIN retry counter is used as in EMV transactions. So just like at an ATM or POS terminal, entering an incorrect PIN three times in a row into a CAP reader will block the card.

Incompatibility

The original CAP specification was designed to use normal EMV transactions, such that the CAP application could be deployed without updating the firmware of existing EMV cards if necessary. The preferred implementation uses a separate application for CAP transactions. The two applications may share certain data, such as PIN, while other data is not shared in instances where it is only applicable to one application (i.e. terminal risk management data for EMV) or advantages to have separate (i.e. transaction counter, so that EMV and CAP transactions increment separate counters which can be verified more accurately). The reader also carries implementation specific data, some of which may be overridden by values in the card. Therefore, CAP readers are generally not compatible with cards from differing issuing banks.

Vulnerabilities

Cambridge University researchers Saar Drimer, Steven Murdoch, Ross Anderson conducted research [3] into the implementation of CAP, outlining a number of vulnerabilities in the protocol and the UK variant of both readers and cards. Numerous weaknesses were found.

Users

Sweden

- Nordea began using CAP in November 2007.[4] The Nordea eCode solution is used by Nordea both for eBanking, eCommerce (3DS) and also with eID. The reader which has some more advanced functionality that extends CAP, makes Nordea's CAP implementations more secure against trojans and man-in-the-middle attacks. When used for eID, the user is able to file his "tax declaration" online, or any implemented eGoverment functions. The device is also equipped with a USB-port, that enables the bank to perform Sign-What-You-See for approval of sensitive transactions.

United Kingdom

- APACS defined a CAP subset for use by UK banks. Currently used by:
- Barclays Bank
- Ulster Bank
- NatWest
- Co-operative Bank and Smile
- Royal Bank of Scotland
- Lloyds TSB Commercial
- Nationwide

- The CAP readers of Barclays, Lloyds TSB, Nationwide, NatWest, Co-operative Bank/Smile and RBS are all intercompatible.
- Barclays began issuing CAP readers (called "PINsentry") in 2007 .[5] [6] Their online-banking website uses the "identify" mode for login verification and the "sign" mode for transaction verification. The "respond" mode is not currently used. The device is also now used in branches, replacing traditional chip and pin devices in order to further prevent attempted fraud.
- Bank cards issued by HBOS are technically compatible with the system, though HBOS has not (yet) introduced CAP readers for use with their online banking.[3]

A Nationwide CAP Device

References

[1] Dynamic passcode authentication (http://www.visaeurope.com/aboutvisa/products/dynamicpasscode.jsp), VISA Europe

[2] http://www.theregister.co.uk/2007/04/18/pinsentry/

[3] Optimised to fail: Card readers for online banking (http://www.cl.cam.ac.uk/~sjm217/papers/fc09optimised.pdf)

[4] New security solution I nordea.se (http://www.nordea.se/sitemod/upload/Root/www_nordea_se/Privat/internet_telefon/internet/demo_e-kod/index.html), in Swedish.

[5] "Barclays PINsentry" (http://www.barclays.co.uk/pinsentry/). .

[6] Barclays to launch two-factor authentication (http://www.theregister.co.uk/2006/08/09/barclays_launches_cardreaders/), The Register, 2006-08-09.

Choice (credit card)

Choice was a credit card test marketed by Citibank in the United States, announced in 1977 and first issued in 1978. It was one of the first cards to offer a cash-refund program and no annual fee. Choice was intended to create a rival to Visa, MasterCard, and American Express, but proved unsuccessful, and was withdrawn in 1987. Citibank has continued to use the "Choice" name on some of its Visa and MasterCard cards.

The Choice logo, introduced in 1980, appeared in white on the solid dark blue card, as well as on merchant acceptance signs.

The card was introduced in 1977, when Citibank bought **NAC**, a regional credit card based in Baltimore, renaming it Choice. A subsequent campaign in Maryland in 1980 turned the card into a regional success, earning more than one million cardholders in the Baltimore and Washington, DC, area. [1] With a view to nationwide expansion, the test market was expanded to include Colorado. Ultimately, despite the success of Sears' Discover Card, which offered many of the same features as Choice when it was introduced in 1985 (such as a rebate on purchases and no annual fee), Citibank decided Choice could not compete with Visa and MasterCard in the longer term, and the card was reissued as a Visa at the end of 1987, aimed at entry-level customers and those with poor credit. [2] [3]

Its fate was similar to that of Citibank's first credit card, the "First National City Charge Service" (or "The Everything Card"), introduced on the East Coast in 1967 to compete with BankAmericard (today's Visa) but which became part of Master Charge (now MasterCard) in 1969.[4]

References

[1] Monci Jo Williams (February 4, 1985). "The Great Plastic Card Fight Begins" (http://money.cnn.com/magazines/fortune/fortune_archive/ 1985/02/04/65549/index.htm). Fortune magazine. . Retrieved 2008-08-22.

[2] Rachel Golden (April 29, 2005). "A Bountiful Harvest: John Hollerbach is reaping the rewards of persistence and hard work" (http://gazette. net/gazette_archive/2005b/200517/business/features/272654-1.html). Gazette.net. . Retrieved 2008-08-22.

[3] Eric N. Berg (August 11, 1987). "Citicorp to Convert Choice Card to Visa" (http://query.nytimes.com/gst/fullpage. html?res=9B0DE1DE1531F932A2575BC0A961948260&partner=rssnyt&emc=rss). New York Times. . Retrieved 2008-08-22.

[4] "Citigroup History: Citibank N.A." (http://web.archive.org/web/20080613210609/http://www.citigroup.com/citigroup/corporate/ history/citibank.htm). Citigroup website. Archived from the original (http://www.citigroup.com/citigroup/corporate/history/citibank. htm) on 2008-06-13. . Retrieved 2008-08-22.

Circular note

A **circular note** is a document request by a bank to its foreign correspondents to pay a specified sum of money to a named person. The person in whose favour a circular note is issued is furnished with a letter (containing the signature of an official of the bank and the person named) called a letter of indication, which is usually referred to in the circular note, and must be produced on presentation of the note. Circular notes are generally issued against a payment of cash to the amount of the notes, but the notes need not necessarily be cashed, but may be returned to the banker in exchange for the amount for which they were originally issued. A forged signature on a circular note conveys no right, and as it is the duty of the payer to see that payment is made to the proper person, he cannot recover the amount of a forged note from the banker who issued the note.

References

This article incorporates text from a publication now in the public domain: Chisholm, Hugh, ed (1911). *Encyclopædia Britannica* (Eleventh ed.). Cambridge University Press.

Clearstream

Clearstream

Type	Subsidiary
Founded	January 2000
Headquarters	Luxembourg (city), Luxembourg
Industry	Finance
Products	Clearing House, Central Securities Depository
Members	2,500+
Parent	Deutsche Börse
Website	http://www.clearstream.com

Clearstream Banking S.A. (CB) is the clearing and settlement division of Deutsche Börse, based in Luxembourg and Frankfurt.

Clearstream was created in January 2000 through the merger of Cedel International and Deutsche Börse Clearing. Its main functions are acting as International Central Securities Depository (ICSD), Clearstream also acts as the Central Securities Depository (CSD) for Germany and Clearing House for a number of securities. It is one of the biggest custodians and clearer of the eurobonds market.

Clearstream has been criticized for allowing banks to move money undetected and has been accused of involvements in a number of cases involving money laundering and tax evasion. Two notable cases have become known as the *Clearstream Affair* which started with the release of the book *Révélation$* in 2001 by the investigative reporter Denis Robert and ex-Clearstream banker Ernest Backes and the *Second Clearstream Affair* which started in 2004 when anonymous denunciations was sent to magistrate Renaud Van Ruymbeke accusing a number of major French political figures of having received kickbacks.

History

Clearstream was formed in 1971 as CEDEL, specialising in the delivery and settlement eurobonds. It was created by a consortium of banks as a competitor to Euroclear so avoid euroclear, which was then owned by US bank J.P. Morgan & Co., being a monopoly in this area.

Clearstream's customers are banks or financial institutions who have accounts with Clearstream which are used to settled and delivered eurobonds with their counterparts. No individual can open an account with Clearstream.

In 1996, Clearstream obtained its own banking license.

In January 2000 it became Clearstream through the merger of Cedel International and Deutsche Börse Clearing, a subsidiary of Deutsche Börse Group, which owns the Frankfurt Stock Exchange when it took a 50% shareholding.

In July 2002, Deutsche Boerse bought the remaining 50% of Clearstream International for 1.6 billion euros.

In 2009 Clearstream contributed Earnings Before Interest and Taxes of €720 million to Deutsche Börse's. It handled 102 million transactions, and was custodian of securities worth €10.3 trillion.[1]

Settlement and custody

Clearstream often has been described as a bank for banks, as it practices what is called settlement and custody operations ("Plumbers and Visionaries, a history of settlement and custody in Europe", Peter Norman). Basically, its duty is to record transactions between the accounts of different banks, and use that data to calculate the relative financial positions of banks with regard to each other.

So a bank can just order a transaction between its own account and the other bank's account, in lieu of less secure methods such as carrying a case full of currency or securities around on the street; the bank merely transmits an order to Clearstream to credit/debit one of its own accounts and the other bank's account(s). This general system is in use between regular companies, governments, and banks around the world.

The purpose of International central securities depositories like Euroclear and Clearstream is to facilitate money movements around the world, particularly by handling the resolution of sales of European stocks and bonds, in which market Clearstream is a major player, with an estimated 40% market share until May 2008 - together with its competitor Euroclear, the two firms settle 70% of European transactions.[2] Furthermore, in January 2009, Clearstream was the 11th largest employer in Luxembourg.[3]

Clearstream does not hold a monopoly in this market: Euroclear, owned by the market, and custodian banks (Bank of New York-Mellon..] are competitors. ; Clearstream's quasi-monopoly is demonstrated by this European Union statement declaring that "Clearstream Banking AG is an unavoidable trader partner."[4]

Euroclear was created by JP Morgan in 1968 in Brussels (Belgium). By the end of 2000, JP Morgan had extricated itself from Euroclear, but JP Morgan still is one of the 120 international banks which own shares in Euroclear. In 2000, Euroclear processed 145 million transactions, dealing with a total of 100,000 billion euros.[5]

Euros

Cedel (now Clearstream) and Euroclear were started to manage transfers of "eurobonds," U.S. denominated debt instruments issued in Europe and kept in banks outside the United States. By the 1990s, the Federal Reserve estimated that about 2/3 of U.S. currency was held abroad as eurodollars.

Clearstream's dominant position

On June 2, 2004, the European Commission found that "Clearstream Banking AG and its parent company Clearstream International SA ("Clearstream") infringed competition rules by refusing to supply cross-border securities clearing and settlement services, and by applying discriminatory prices. Clearstream has appealed in front of the European Court of Justice. The case was pleaded in July 2008 and the decision is pending. The Commission's investigation revealed that Clearstream refused to supply Euroclear Bank SA ('Euroclear Bank') with certain clearing and settlement services, and applied discriminatory prices to the detriment of this customer."

The decision states that "Clearstream refused to supply to Euroclear Bank clearing and settlement services for registered shares issued under German law," underlining the "dominant position" of Clearstream since it "is the only final custodian of German securities kept in collective safe custody, which is the only significant form of custody today for securities traded. New entry into this activity is unrealistic for the foreseeable future. Therefore, Clearstream is an unavoidable trading partner."

The Commission defined *clearing* and *settlement* as follows:

"Securities clearing and settlement are necessary steps for a securities trade to be completed.

Clearing is the process by which the contractual obligations of the buyer and the seller are established.

Settlement is the transfer of securities from the seller to the buyer and the transfer of funds from the buyer to the seller. (...)

Clearstream Banking AG is Germany's only *Wertpapiersammelbank* (Central Securities Depository).

"The Commission considered that during the reference period concerned, 1997 through 2001, Clearstream held a dominant position for providing cross-border clearing and settlement services to intermediaries situated in other Member States. The investigation therefore focused on a specific cross-border market and the decision does not set out findings that go beyond that relevant market."

The Commission underlined in a note that, "Central Securities Depositories hold securities and enable securities transactions to be processed through book entry. In its home country, the Central Securities Depository provides processing services for trades of those securities that it holds in final custody. It can also offer processing services as an intermediary in cross-border clearing and settlement, where the primary deposit of securities is in another country."[4]

Accusations

In 2001, investigative reporter Denis Robert and Ernest Backes, an executive at Cedel until May 1983, published a book, *Revelation$*[6] in which they alleged that Clearstream played a major part in the underground economy, was a main platform for money laundering for hundreds of banks, and "operated hundreds of confidential accounts for banks so they could move money undetected," according to *Business Week*.[7]

Backes and *Le Figaro* were sued by Clearstream and found guilty of libel on March 29, 2004. Denis Robert was sued for libel and found guilty three on three counts on appeal on 16 October 2008 for the books Revelation$ and Black Box, as well as the documentary "Les Dissimulateurs" (The Deceivers). However, in February 2011, in a final judgment, the Court of Cassation overturned all convictions, ruling that his work was protected by freedom of speech and of the press.[8]

After an investigation in Luxembourg, which was closed in November 2004 after no evidence had been found of wrongdoing (Luxembourg prosecutor's office, Nov. 30, 2004), on suspicion of money laundering, tax evasion, and other fraud, Clearstream's CEO, André Lussi, resigned (See below). This enabled Deutsche Börse to purchase the remaining 50% of Clearstream International in July 2002. According to some, such as *Business Week,* Lussi had opposed such a takeover.

Clearstream is audited by KPMG, one of the largest global accounting firms. KPMG declared that it found "no evidence" to support the allegations made by Denis Robert and Ernest Backes, although its report was not made public.

Daewoo shutdown inquiries

After Daewoo was split apart in 2000, Clearstream became the subject of two commissions of inquiry in Lorraine (France) conducted before the French parliament and European parliament both of which had no results.

The Clearstream affair

In 2001, co-authors Denis Robert and Ernest Backes released a book called "*Révélation$*," followed by Robert's "*La Boîte Noire*," describing what has been named the "greatest financial scandal in the Grand Duchy of Luxembourg."[9] The little publicity their works received came only in the French media, and even there publicity was minimal. In a number of interviews, Denis Robert accused *"Le Monde"* of deliberately suppressing articles and reviews of his book, suggesting that financial links between "*Le Monde*" and *Deutsche Börse* (which now owns 100% of Clearstream's shares) were the cause of this censorship. Denis Robert was found guilty of libel and sentenced altogether 8 times by the French courts for describing Clearstream as a huge money laundering and tax evasion machine, used by major banks, shell companies, and organized crime all over the world. (Paris Court of Appeal, 16, October 2008, 18 December 2008, Tribunal correctionnel de Bordeaux, June 2008)

Banco Ambrosiano scandal

By 1980, Ernest Backes had become Cedel's #3, in charge of relations with clients, but he was fired in May 1983, allegedly because he "knew too much about the Ambrosiano scandal," one of Italy's major political scandals. Two months after his dismissal, Gérard Soisson was found dead in Corsica. The Banco Ambrosiano, allegedly involved in money-laundering for the Mafia and owned in majority by the Vatican Bank, collapsed in 1982. The bank "laundered drugs- and arms-trafficking money for the Italian and American Mafias, and in the 1980s it channeled Vatican money to the Contras in Nicaragua and to Solidarity in Poland", according to Komisar.

In 2005, the Italian justice system reopened its investigation of the murder of Roberto Calvi, Ambrosiano's chairman; it has requested the support of Ernest Backes, and will investigate Gerard Soisson's death, according to Komisar. Licio Gelli, headmaster of Propaganda Due masonic lodge (aka P2, it was involved in Gladio's "strategy of tension" starting from the 1969 Piazza Fontana bombing), and mafiosi Giuseppe Calo, are being prosecuted for the assassination of Roberto Calvi. Ernest Backes explained: *"When Soisson died, the Ambrosiano affair wasn't yet known as a scandal. (After it was revealed) I realized that Soisson and I had been at the crossroads. We moved all those transactions known later in the scandal to Lima and other branches. Nobody even knew there was a Banco Ambrosiano branch in Lima and other South American countries."*[10]

Secret accounts and the workings of 21st century economics

Gérard Soisson was the person who authorized each non-published account, "which would be known only by some insiders, including the auditors and members of the council of administration."

Only authorized banks, supranational and government entities, brokers/financial institutions (provided that the institution is subject to regulation by an acceptable regulatory authority) and general corporates as triparty repo cash providers are eligible customers of Clearstream. Individuals are not eligible as Clearstream Banking customers. Accounts are opened in the name of their legal owners. Each customer is free in asking for the opening of subsequent accounts. All main and subsequent accounts are subject to the same rules and internal control procedures and regulatory supervision. Some subsequent account names contain, beside the customer name, an indication as to third parties. These accounts are not opened for individual persons but on instruction of the legal owner of the account.

Banks in most countries worldwide do generally not publish their customers' account numbers, due to the banking secrecy and legitimate customer personal protection reasons. Depending on the nature of the business executed through Clearstream, customers elect for their account numbers to be published or unpublished. Customers may elect to provide other Clearstream customers with their respective account numbers to ease the settlement process, i.e. publish their account numbers. For other Clearstream services, e.g. the safekeeping of securities as well as the associated services, such as corporate actions on the deposited securities, customers do not need to publish their account numbers to other market participants. This practice is entirely consistent with international banking industry standards.

The non-publication of account numbers does not mean that these accounts are hidden or secret and unknown to Clearstream's staff and management, the internal and external auditors and the regulatory authorities. To the contrary, all customer accounts, published and non-published, are all continually reviewed, monitored and reported to the regulators as needed.

Another belief of Denis Robert's book is that, according to the May 9, 2001 op-ed by Bernard Bertossa, attorney general in Geneva, Benoît Dejemeppe, king's attorney in Brussels (*procureur du roi*), Eva Joly, investigative magistrate in Paris, Jean de Maillard, magistrate in Blois and Renaud van Ruymbeke, a judge in Paris, entitled "The 'black boxes' of financial globalization," is that:

> "The chaos of financial flux is only an appearance. Of course, offshore banks and tax havens perfectly hide the points of arrival and of transit of dirty capital. It is even their reason of existence (*raison d'être*). Trying to find the illegal money flux in those offshore centers is hopelessly doomed... However, since

capital from criminal origin pass in the same financial 'pipes' as other ones [legal funds], i.e. clearing and financial routage companies, they become vulnerable precisely during their transfer [in those clearing companies]."[11]

In other words, all financial money flows, legal or illegal, have to pass through the financial system.

A "black box" of Cedel

Ernest Backes also explained that a company named Cedel International, located in Geneva, had been inscribed in the Swiss register of commerce but not included in the books of the mother company, Cedel International in Luxembourg. "This non-consolidated 'branch,' whose president is Robert Douglass of New York, former private secretary of Governor Nelson Rockefeller, and vice chairman of the Chase Manhattan Corporation (now J.P. Morgan Chase), apparently had not raised too many questions for Swiss federal magistrates." Backes qualified this "black box" as "institutionalized tax evasion at highest level in world finance,", noting that tax evasion was even "more or less expressed in the objectives of the company as filed in the Swiss register of commerce." The "branch" has since "been resold to another Luxembourg holding company, with the people in the backyard remaining mostly the same."

March 2000 French parliamentary report

In March 2000, a parliamentary report by French deputies Arnaud Montebourg and Vincent Peillon, entitled "Parliamentary Report on the obstacles on the control and repression of financial criminal activity and of money-laundering in Europe," dedicated its whole third section to "Luxembourg's political dependency toward the financial sector: the Clearstream affair."[12]

Judicial investigations and libel lawsuits

Following the publication of "Revelation$," the tribunal of Luxembourg opened up an investigation on February 26, 2001. On November 30, 2004, the parquet finally declared no proof of "systematic manipulations" had been found, and that investigations would continue on suspicion of manipulation and tax evasion regarding former Clearstream CEO André lussi. This also led to a non lieu (Statement from the Luxembourg Parquet, November 2004).

Denis Robert also has been sued for defamation by other banks and companies incriminated by the book: 50+ different cases — among which Bank Menatep, Banque Générale du Luxembourg, etc., in which the author and his editor Laurent Beccaria were acquitted in all but two cases, and damages for both cases of one Euro were awarded. On January 27, 2006, once more Denis Robert was charged by a Luxembourg committing magistrate for defamation, slander, and insults.

A complaint was opened in March 2001 against Ernest Backes, and Denis Robert was included in it five years later: "I am very surprised of this accusation five years after the facts and of the energy which the Luxembourgian justice puts continuing to harass me while it was not at the end of the inquiry opened for money laundering, tax evasion and corruption against Clearstream", Robert said. An organization, "Freedom to inform," declared to *Le Nouvel Observateur* magazine that "By transforming the affair Robert in affair Frieden (Luxembourg Minister of Justice, of the Treasury and the Budget), every signature will be a civil act which protects the freedom of the media in Europe."[13]

Suspension & investigation of Clearstream's CEO

On May 15, 2001, André Lussi was suspended from his CEO position at Clearstream, and on December 31, 2001, he departed the company on mutual agreement.[14] [15] In February 2004 an investigation was opened against him, on money laundering, fraud, and tax evasion charges.[16] [17] André Lussi was replaced by André Roelants, who had been at Dexia. After years of investigations, all allegations made against André Lussi turned out to be completely causeless and the lawsuits were abandoned by the courts.[18]

Refusal of the European Commission to open an investigation: *20 Minutes* ' revelations

Along with Ernest Backes, Denis Robert presented *Revelation$* to the Capital Tax, Fiscal Systems and Globalization intergroup of the European Parliament in March 2001 and also to the French National Assembly. Answering the question raised by European MPs (MEP) Harlem Désir, Glyn Ford and Francis Wurtz, who asked the Commission to investigate the accusations made by the book and to ensure that the 10 June 1990 directive (91/308 EC) on control of financial establishment be applied in all member states in an effective way, Commissioner Frits Bolkestein observed that *"the Commission has no reason to date to believe that the Luxembourg authorities do not apply it vigorously"*. On April 26, 2006, *20 Minutes* revealed that "in May 2005, MEP Paul Van Buitenen was shocked by Frits Bolkestein's presence on Menatep's international consultative council, a Russian banking establishment, and by his work for Shell, a British-Dutch petrol company, two firms 'maintaining secret accounts in Clearstream'... Van Buitenen, also Dutch, then asked for 'clarification' to the European Commission and the opening of a parliamentary investigation. The Commission's president, José Manuel Barroso, replied that these facts 'do not bring up any new question' and that it is not known 'if Menatep made contact with Bolkestein while he was in these positions'. No investigation therefore took place."

The free daily points out that "in 2001, it was Bolkestein himself who announced the Commission's refusal to open up a parliamentary investigation on Clearstream", following Harlem Désir's requests and accusations that Menatep had an "undeclared account" at Clearstream. Bolkestein refused to answer any questions by the newspaper, which recalls that Van Buitenen, former European public servant, had already revealed a vast corruption affair in 1999, which led to the resignation of the Commission presided by Jacques Santer (who has also been prime minister of Luxembourg) and the fall of Edith Cresson.[19]

Furthermore, two Belgian Senators, Isabelle Durant and Jean Cornil, proposed a law in vain in 2004 to create a national investigation commission charged with the investigation of the use of accounts in "clearing and routing firms" to commit fiscal frauds (tax evasion) and/or money-laundering.[20]

Clearstream's reply

In April 2006, while the second "Clearstream affair" was beginning to make French media headlines (See below), Clearstream filed a lawsuit against "John Doe," targeting this time the anonymous denunciations claiming that Nicolas Sarkozy and other French political personalities had secret accounts at Clearstream, which would have been used for hypothetical kickbacks. Former French Prime Minister Dominique de Villepin came under investigation for what may have been his involvement in spreading the false charges against the current French President Sarkozy,[21] but was later acquitted in January 2010, although three of his co-defendants were found guilty.[22]

Furthermore it answered questions of *20 Minutes* in an interview, denying knowing anything about the various attempts to create European-level investigations commissions about its internal workings. It also denied "the existence of parallel accounts" and of "personal accounts" (in response, Denis Robert published a list of several personal accounts on his blog[23]). However, the company did recognize that "a banking establishment may request an unpublished account, that is, an account only known by the establishments concerned by the transaction, control authorities, and the auditors of the firm". Clearstream also indicated that it had "spent 15 million euros on various audits without finding anything," Denis Robert's accusations.[24]

Nadhmi Auchi, largest private share-holder of BNP Paribas bank

Iraqi-born Nadhmi Auchi, # 34 on the "Sunday Times Rich List 2004" (# 22 on the same list in 2005) and 13th richest man in Britain according to *The Guardian*, estimated to be worth $1 billion according to *Forbes*, also appeared to be a key figure.[25]

Auchi was convicted of profiteering by the Paris Criminal Court, and received a 15-month suspended sentence, for his involvement in Elf's scandal, "the biggest fraud inquiry in Europe since the Second World War. Elf became a private bank for its executives who spent £200 million on political favours, mistresses, jewellery, fine art, villas and apartments".[26] The "Guardian" noted that Nadhmi Auchi had helped Orascom (which owns Djezzy GSM), owned by Onsi Sawiris (worth $5.2 billion with his family according to *Forbes*[27]), gain a contract to set up mobile phone networks in post-Saddam's Iraq. As owner of the General Mediterranean Holdings, Auchi is the largest private shareholder of BNP Paribas, which until 2001 managed the escrow account through which the money from the Oil-for-Food programme transited.

Bank Menatep

Bank Menatep, owned by Mikhail Khodorkovsky, was involved in the "Kremlingate", when $4.8 billion in IMF funds were diverted to various banks, including US banks.[28] It opened up its non-published Cedel account #81 738 on May 15, 1997. "Menatep further violated the rules because many transfers were of cash, not for settlement of securities", writes Komisar. "For the three months in 1997 for which I hold microfiches, Backes says, only cash transfers were transferred through the Meanatep account. There were a lot of transfers between Menatep and the Bank of New York." Natasha Gurfinkel Kagalovsky, a former Bank of New York official and the wife of a Menatep vice-president, was accused of helping launder at least $7 billion from Russia, according to Komisar. US investigators have attempted to find out if some of the laundered money originated with Menatep.

On November 26, 2003, Backes and another ex-banker, Swiss citizen André Strebel, filed a criminal complaint with the Swiss attorney general against Khodorkovsky and his colleagues Platon Lebedev and Alexei Golubovich, accusing them of money-laundering and supporting a criminal organization. They requested an investigation and a search of records of the Swiss office of Menatep SA, Menatep Finances SA, Valmet. and of Bank Leu in Geneva, related to claims of fraud against the Russian company Avisma and money-laundering by Menatep in Switzerland. According to this complaint, Bank Menatep has been linked since its creation to the Russian oligarchy and criminal organizations, such as Khodorkovsky, Alexander Konanykhine and the Russian godfather Semion Mogilevich. "Even though Menatep officially failed in 1998, it oddly remained on the non-published list of Clearstream accounts for 2000", wrote Komisar. Clearstream's listings also present 36 other Russian accounts, most non-published.[29]

In April 2006, Clearstream declared, to the French edition of *20 Minutes*, that if "Menatep may have strange accounts, it wasn't closed because of money-laundering". It also claimed that it dealt with "banks accredited in their country of origin", but not with "establishments that are registered on the Financial Action Task Force on Money Laundering's black list".[24]

The Second Clearstream Affair

The Second Clearstream affair began in July 2004, when anonymous denunciations sent to magistrate Renaud Van Ruymbeke accused various important French political figures of having received kickbacks related to the Taiwan frigates scandal, through secret personal accounts at Clearstream. Clearstream was again pointed out as having been a major platform for illegal financial transactions. After thorough investigation including search in Clearstream's archives and accounts, M Van Ruymbecke found absolutely no evidence of the validity of the allegations and closed the case. After an investigation by judges On September 3, 2004, the Paris *parquet* (public prosecutor) opened an investigation into charges of "defamation", following a complaint by Philippe Delmas, EADS' vice-president. Magistrates Jean-Marie d'Huy and Henri Pons have charged Dominique de Villepin, former French PM, Jean-Louis Gergorin, former EADS executive who confessed having been the poison pen in the case, Imad Lahoud, Florian bourges and Denis Robert. Their trial started on 21 September 2009.

Investigation of the anonymous denunciations

On May 3, 2004 and June 14, 2004, Renaud Van Ruymbeke and Dominique Talancé, the French magistrates in charge of the Taiwan frigates scandal, received two letters and a CD-ROM from an anonymous informant (called *corbeau* in French), detailing numbered bank accounts maintained at Clearstream and describing secret transfers of millions of dollars. Many personalities were named, including Alain Gomez, former director of Thomson-CSF (which since has become Thales), Andrew Wang, the Taiwanese intermediary of the frigates contract and one of Taiwan's key figures concerning arms contracts, Philippe Delmas, vice-president of EADS the European aeronautics consortium, and Nicolas Sarkozy, then minister of the Economy, Dominique Strauss-Kahn, Jean-Pierre Chevènement, and others. Members of the French secret services also were named.[30]

Magistrate Van Ruymbeke opened another investigation, in July 2004. According to the denunciations, Andrew Wang passed on money to several very important French officials from 1999 to 2003, using Clearstream.[31] [32]

But in January 2006, both magistrates declared the case closed, on the grounds that the *corbeau* 's list of Clearstream accounts owned by various political figures was a fraud. For example, the numbered *Banca popolare di Sondrio* Clearstream account, supposedly in the names of "Stéphane Bocsa" and "Paul de Nagy" — French president, Nicolas Sarkozy's full name is "Nicolas Paul Stéphane Sarkozy de Nagy-Bocsa" — was not Sarkozy's personal account, but an account used by various persons, according to the declarations of the *Banca popolare di Sondrio* to Judge Ruymbeke.

Lawsuits alleging defamation

In December 2005, magistrate Van Ruymbeke, in charge of the Taiwan frigates Affair, showed that the listings had been fraudulently modified to accuse French political luminaries.

Searches in 2007

French magistrates sought to search the *Canard enchaîné*'s offices in May 2007, after the election of Nicolas Sarkozy to the presidency. According to editing director Claude Angeli, the judges were looking for information on a "Rondot document" treating of alleged "Japanese accounts" of former President Jacques Chirac. The judges were not allowed access to the newspaper's offices, and Reporters Without Borders (RSF) protested against the search.[33]

The October surprise conspiracy

Ernest Backes also indicated in *Révélation$* that he was in charge of the transfer of $7 million from Chase Manhattan Bank and Citibank, on January 16, 1980, to pay for the liberation of the American hostages held in Tehran's embassy (Iran). He gave copies of files that he asserted shed new light on the October surprise conspiracy to the French National Assembly.

Banks with accounts in Clearstream

- Bank of Credit and Commerce International, which, although officially closed in July 1991, continued to operate via Clearstream through unpublished accounts — as did Bank Menatep, involved in the "Kremlingate" (diversion of IMF funds), and owned by Mikhail Khodorkovsky
- Banque Générale du Luxembourg
- Carlyle Group[34]
- Crédit Lyonnais, one of France's major financial crashes during the 1990s
- Société Générale
- Banco Ambrosiano, controlled by the Vatican Bank and involved in one of Italy's major financial and political scandals

- Siemens (Published Accounts [35] by Lucy Komisar)
- More than 38,000 others[35] ; as Clearstream is an international clearing and settlement organization, most member companies and banks have published accounts. Dealing with Clearstream is entirely legal; accounts used for tax evasion or money laundering is not.

Iranian Funds Controversy

Clearstream is allegedly holding $2 billion in Iranian funds in a Citibank account. Since 2008, these funds have been ordered frozen by the U.S. District Court for the Southern District of New York, and are intended for use to pay the families of hundreds of US Marines killed and injured in a 1983 Beirut bombing that a US federal judge ruled was orchestrated by Iran, according to the *Wall Street Journal*.[36] [37]

Bibliography

- Denis Robert, Ernest Backes: *The silence of the money. The Clearstream scandal.* (2002, ISBN 3-85842-546-X)
- Denis Robert, Ernest Backes: *Révélation$* (Edition des Arènes, 2001, ISBN 2-912485-28-2)
- Denis Robert, Ernest Backes: *Das Schweigen des Geldes. Der Clearstream-Skandal*, Pendo Verlag Zurich (2002, ISBN 3-85842-546-X)
- Denis Robert, Ernest Backes: *Revelaçoes sobre o mundo financeiro*, Editorial Inquérito (Portugal)
- Denis Robert, Ernest Backes: *Revelation$* (Japanese ed. Tokuma Shoten Co, Tokyo)
- Denis Robert, *La Boîte noire* (Editions des arènes, ISBN 2-912485-38-X)
- David Loader, *Clearing, Settlement and Custody* (operation management Series (Securities of institutes) (2002, ISBN 0-7506-5484-8)
- Jean-Pierre Thiollet, *Beau linge et argent sale* - Fraude fiscale internationale et blanchiment des capitaux (tax avoidance, tax evasion and money laundering)(2002, ISBN 2 914571178)
- David M. Weiss, *Global Securities processing: The Markets*, The Products (1997, ISBN 0-13-323965-9)
- Lucy Komisar, *Explosive Revelation$*
- Official March 2000 French Parliamentary Report on the obstacles on the control and repression of financial criminal activity and of money-laundering in Europe [39] by French MPs Vincent Peillon and Arnaud Montebourg, third section on "Luxembourg's political dependency toward the financial sector: the Clearstream affair" (pp. 83–111 on PDF version)

References

[1] "Deutsche Börse Group Annual Report" (http://deutsche-boerse.com/dbag/dispatch/en/binary/gdb_navigation/investor_relations/ 30_Reports_and_Figures/30_Annual_Reports/20_Archive/Content_Files/Archive/Annual_Report_2009.pdf). 29 March 2010. p. 16. .

[2] FESE statistics 2008 | url=http://www.businessweek.com/magazine/content/01_47/b3758141.htm

[3] "Principal Employers by size" (http://www.statistiques.public.lu/fr/publications/thematiques/Entreprises/principal_employeurs/ princip_employeurs_taille/PDF_princip_entreprises_taille.pdf) (PDF). p. 5. .

[4] European Commission June 2, 2004 decision on Clearstream's infringement of competition rules, decision IP/04/705 (http://europa.eu/ rapid/pressReleasesAction.do?reference=IP/04/705&format=HTML&aged=0&language=EN&guiLanguage=en#fnB1)

[5] **(French)** "142 millions de transactions en 2000" (http://www.lemonde.fr/web/recherche_breve/1,13-0,37-707829,0.html). Le Monde. June 1, 2001. .

[6] http://www.hound-dogs.com/cover_story/coverstory.htm

[7] "Europe Needs an Independent Settlement System" (http://www.businessweek.com/magazine/content/01_23/b3735151.htm). Business Week. June 4, 2001. .

[8] "Le journaliste Denis Robert sort blanchi de son combat contre Clearstream" (http://www.google.com/hostednews/afp/article/ ALeqM5jnuOz2QK7igaursPepB15L22z5rw?docId=CNG.e4a3b57771d6e37f71b16ece62c62387.6d1). AFP. .

[9] France 2 (http://info.france2.fr/eco/6442364-fr.php) *URL accessed in January 2006*

[10] "Offshore banking: the secret threat to America" (http://www.hound-dogs.com/cover_story/coverstory.htm). Hound Dogs. 2003. . Retrieved January 2006. (by investigative reporter Lucy Komisar)

[11] **(French)** Harlem Désir's official website (http://www.harlemdesir.com/article/articleview/783/1/1442/) (European MPs Harlem Désir, Glyn Ford and Francis Wurtz press statement about the $1.5 trillion math error & Denis Robert and Ernest Backes' book "Revelation$" and a May 9, 2001 op-ed in *Le Monde* titled *"Les 'boîtes noires' de la mondialisation financière"* ("The black box of financial globalization") by Bernard Bertossa, attorney general in Geneva, Benoît Dejemeppe, king's attorney in Brussels (*procureur des konings, procureur du roi*), Eva Joly, investigative magistrate in Paris, Jean de Maillard, magistrate in Blois and Renaud van Ruymbeke, judge in Paris)

[12] **(French)** Official March 2000 French Parliamentary Report on the obstacles on the control and repression of financial criminal activity and of money-laundering in Europe (http://www.assemblee-nationale.fr/rap-info/i2311-51.asp#P1089_155970) by French MPs Vincent Peillon and Arnaud Montebourg, third section on "Luxembourg's political dependency toward the financial sector: the Clearstream affair" (pp. 83-111 on PDF version)

[13] **(French)** "A petition of support to Denis Roberts" (http://nouvelobs.reverso.net/url/obsResult.asp?directions=65544&template=Default&autotranslate=1&url=http://permanent.nouvelobs.com/europe/20060208.OBS5694.html). Le Nouvel Observateur. February 22, 2006. . Retrieved 2006-02-22. (petition available here (http://www.liberte-dinformer.info/60828.html))

[14] "Lussi suspension ignites battle for control of Clearstream" (http://www.finextra.com/fullstory.asp?id=2084). Finextra. May 17, 2001. . Retrieved January 2006.

[15] "Clearstream faces cash probe" (http://money.telegraph.co.uk/money/main.jhtml;$sessionid$Q34HZJQAACE1BQFIQMFCFFOAVCBQYIV0?xml=/money/2001/05/17/cnclr17.xml). London: Money Telegraph. May 17, 2001. . Retrieved January 2006.

[16] **(French)** "L'ex-PDG de Clearstream inculpé" (http://www.lemonde.fr/web/recherche_breve/1,13-0,37-838692,0.html). Le Monde. February 6, 2004. . Retrieved January 2006.

[17] **(English)/(French)** "André Lussi, CEO of Clearstream, stepping down - interview of Denis Robert" (http://tobintaxcall.free.fr/Newsletter_4_EN.pdf) (PDF). Tobin tax. June 2001. .

[18] **(German)**d'Wort. "Eine Affäre, die nie hätte begonnen werden dürfen". June 10. 2006

[19] **(French)** "Révélation 20 Minutes: Quand la Commission européenne refusait d'enquêter sur Clearstream" (http://web.archive.org/web/20060430121934/http://www.20minutes.fr/articles/2006/04/26/actualite_france_Revelation_20_Minutes_Quand_la_Commission_europeenne_refusait_d_enqueter_sur_Clearstream.php). 20 Minutes. April 26, 2006. Archived from the original (http://www.20minutes.fr/articles/2006/04/26/actualite_france_Revelation_20_Minutes_Quand_la_Commission_europeenne_refusait_d_enqueter_sur_Clearstream.php) on April 30, 2006. . Retrieved 2006-04-29.

[20] **(French)** "Affaire Clearstream: questions-réponses à la Commission" (http://web.archive.org/web/20060512054719/http://www.20minutes.fr/articles/2006/04/25/actualite_france_Affaire_Clearstream_questions_reponses_a_la_Commission.php). 20 Minutes. April 26, 2006. Archived from the original (http://www.20minutes.fr/articles/2006/04/25/actualite_france_Affaire_Clearstream_questions_reponses_a_la_Commission.php) on May 12, 2006. . Retrieved 2006-04-29. (provides link to PDF reports about Frits Bolkestein response to Harlem Désir and others MEP's question, as well as José Manuel Barroso's response to Paul Van Buitenen and to the law proposition of Belgian senators Isabelle Durant and Jean Cornil

[21] Bremner, Charles (July 6, 2007). "De Villepin likely to face conspiracy charges" (http://www.timesonline.co.uk/tol/news/world/europe/article2033979.ece). London: Times online. . Retrieved 2007-07-06.

[22] **(French)** "Clearstream : Villepin salue "le courage du tribunal"" (http://www.lemonde.fr/politique/article/2010/01/28/dominique-de-villepin-a-salue-le-courage-du-tribunal_1297989_823448.htm#ens_id=1290669). Le Monde. January 28, 2010. . Retrieved 2010-01-28.

[23] "Clearstream claims that it has no personal accounts, Denis Robert publish a list of such accounts (video)" (http://www.dailymotion.com/video/137880). Denis Robert's blog. April 27, 2006. . Retrieved 2006-04-29.

[24] **(French)** "Pour Clearstream, 'il n'y a pas de comptes parallèles'" (http://web.archive.org/web/20060512054705/http://www.20minutes.fr/articles/2006/04/26/actualite_france_Pour_Clearstream_il_n_y_a_pas_de_comptes_paralleles.php). 20 Minutes. April 26, 2006. Archived from the original (http://www.20minutes.fr/articles/2006/04/26/actualite_france_Pour_Clearstream_il_n_y_a_pas_de_comptes_paralleles.php) on May 12, 2006. . Retrieved 2006-04-29.

[25] *Forbes*_Auchi (http://www.forbes.com/static/bill2005/name_26.html?passListId=10&passYear=2005&passListType=Person&searchParameter1=unset&searchParameter2=unset&resultsHowMany=25&resultsSortProperties=%2Bstringfield2%2C-numberfield3&resultsSortCategoryName=Name&fromColumnClick=&bktDisplayField=stringfield2&bktDisplayFieldLength=2&category1=category&category2=category&passKeyword=&resultsStart=26)

[26] "The politics of sleaze" (http://www.guardian.co.uk/Iraq/Story/0,2763,1086487,00.html). London: The Guardian. November 16, 2003.

[27] *Forbes*_Sawiris (http://www.forbes.com/static/bill2005/name_526.html?passListId=10&passYear=2005&passListType=Person&searchParameter1=unset&searchParameter2=unset&resultsHowMany=25&resultsSortProperties=%2Bstringfield2%2C-numberfield3&resultsSortCategoryName=Name&fromColumnClick=&bktDisplayField=stringfield2&bktDisplayFieldLength=2&category1=category&category2=category&passKeyword=&resultsStart=526)

[28] See former World Bank vice-president Joseph Stiglitz, chapter on Russia in *"Globalization and Its Discontents"*

[29] **(English)/(French)/(Spanish)** "Unlawful debt or financial crime against human development" (http://www.attac.org/genes2001/documents/docdet7en.htm). ATTAC. June 30, 2001. . Retrieved January 2006.

[30] **(French)** "Les grandes dates de l'affaire" (http://www.lefigaro.fr/france/20060415.WWW000000044_les_grandes_dates_de_l_affaire. html#). Le Figaro. April 26, 2006. . Retrieved 2006-04-29.

[31] **(French)** "Chuan-pu Andrew Wang, intermédiaire taïwanais dans le commerce d'armes: 'Je n'ai jamais payé de commissions à un politique français'" (http://www.lemonde.fr/cgi-bin/ACHATS/acheter.cgi?offre=ARCHIVES&type_item=ART_ARCH_30J&objet_id=873135). Le Monde. October 20, 2004. . Retrieved January 2006.

[32] **(French)** "Cette ténébreuse affaire qui oppose Sarkozy à Villepin" (http://www.lemonde.fr/web/recherche_breve/1,13-0,37-876102,0. html). Le Monde. November 10, 2004. . Retrieved January 2006.

[33] "Clearstream: les juges au Canard et chez l'avocat de Sarkozy," *Libération*, 11 May 2007. Read here (http://www.liberation.fr/actualite/ societe/253247.FR.php) **(French)**.

[34] "US Securities and Exchange Commission response to a Carlyle request for confidential treatment" (http://www.sec.gov/divisions/ marketreg/mr-noaction/gmbh062404.htm). 2004-06-24. .

[35] "Clearstream's International Counterparties" (http://wikileaks.org/wiki/ 38,838_Clearstream_international_counterparties,_including_Bernard_L._Madoff,_Jul_2004). .

[36] http://online.wsj.com/article/SB126057864707988237.html Wall Street Journal, US freezes $2 billion in Iran case, December 12, 2009

[37] http://www.reuters.com/article/idUSTRE5BB0ID20091212 Reuters, US froze $2 billion held for Iran in Citibank: report, Dec 12 2009

External links

Main sources

- Clearstream home page (http://www.clearstream.com)
- Les Arenes editing house of Denis Roberts' book - translated by google (http://translate.google.com/ translate?sourceid=navclient-menuext&hl=en&u=http://www.arenes.fr/livres/fiche-livre. php?numero_livre=4)
- Les Arenes links (including English) (http://www.arenes.fr/livres/page-livre1.php?numero_livre=4& num_page=32)
- Denis Robert's blog (http://ladominationdumonde.blogspot.com/)
- **(French)** Official March 2000 French Parliamentary Report on the obstacles on the control and repression of financial criminal activity and of money-laundering in Europe (http://www.assemblee-nationale.fr/rap-info/ i2311-51.asp#P1089_155970) by French MPs Vincent Peillon and Arnaud Montebourg, third section on "Luxembourg's political dependency toward the financial sector: the Clearstream affair" (pp. 83–111 on PDF version)

Media reports

In English

- "Cross-border trade needs smoothing, bankers say" (http://www.iht.com/articles/2003/01/24/fund_ed3_. php). International Herald Tribune. January 24, 2003.
- "Explosive Revelation$," (http://www.inthesetimes.com/issue/26/10/feature1_2.shtml). March 15, 2002.
- "Interview with [[Lucy Komisar (http://www.spitfirelist.com/f458.html)] about offshore banking"]. Spitfire. February 5, 2004.
- "A little more on banks today (interview with [[Lucy Komisar (http://www.iraq-war.ru/tiki-read_article. php?articleId=20035)])"]. Iraq War. August 21, 2004.
- "The bank that buys up journalists," (http://www.newsconfidential.com/PDFStore/punch_111097.pdf) (PDF). Punch magazine. October 11, 1997.

In French (Google transl. available)

- "L'affaire Clearstream tourne à l'affaire d'Etat" (http://permanent.nouvelobs.com/politique/20060428. OBS5853.html). nouvel Obs. April 28, 2006.

- "Les trois niveaux de l'affaire Clearstream" (http://tf1.lci.fr/infos/france/0,,3299237,00.html). TF1 (tv). May 4, 2006. Retrieved 2006-05-05.

- "Le scandale Clearstream à nouveau sur le devant de la scène - Pétition de soutien à Denis Robert, inculpé par la justice luxembourgeoise" (http://www.hns-info.net/article.php3?id_article=7789). Hacktivist News Service. February 17, 2006.

- "Des banquiers aux mains sales" (http://www.fsa.ulaval.ca/personnel/vernag/EH/F/noir/lectures/ banques_compromises.htm). Alternatives économiques. July-August 2001.

- "L'affaire de la 'boîte noire' Clearstream rebondit à Genève" (http://www.lecourrier.ch/modules. php?op=modload&name=NewsPaper&file=article&sid=3507). Le Courrier. February 12, 2004. (Google translation available for all articles...)

- "Succès contre la boîte noire" (http://www.lecourrier.ch/modules.php?op=modload&name=NewsPaper& file=article&sid=3458). Le Courrier. February 5, 2004.

- "L'affaire Clearstream, au coeur du système libéral" (http://www.humanite.presse.fr/journal/2002-02-19/ 2002-02-19-29124). L'Humanité. February 19, 2002.

- "Les énigmes du listing Clearstream" (http://www.nouvelobs.com/dossiers/p2121/a272001.html). Le Nouvel Observateur. June 30, 2005.

- "Affaire Clearstream: le patron de la DST remet toutes les notes de son service à M. Sarkozy" (http://www. lemonde.fr/web/article/0,1-0@2-3224,36-660134@51-648305,0.html). Le Monde. June 10, 2005.

- "Clearstream perd encore en justice" (http://www.cfdt-banques.fr/article.php3?id_article=1315). Agence France Presse. March 17, 2004.

- "Denis Robert, l�$-1òùhomme qui dérange les puissants" (http://www.politis.fr/article44.html). Politis. January 22, 2002.

- "'Le lobby bancaire est le plus puissant du monde', un entretien avec Denis Robert" (http://www.politis.fr/ article1181.html). Politis. December 9, 2004.

- "Denis Robert met le feu" (http://www.technikart.com/article.php3?id_article=539). Technikart. February 11, 2003.

- "Pour une poignée de milliards de dollars" (http://www.technikart.com/article.php3?id_article=122). Technikart. March 13, 2002.

- "'Effet d'annonce' (entretien avec Denis Robert)" (http://archquo.nouvelobs.com/cgi/articles?ad=edito/ 00018741.EDI0001.html&host=&base=/2001/nouvelobs/base/2001.0925/qobs_online&skul=/www/file/ nouvelobs/temp/une.20010925.32516.sk&cle=20010925.OBS8733edito/00018741.EDI0001.html). Le Nouvel Observateur. September 25, 2001.

- "Enquête sur les comptes secrets des banques" (http://www.lefigaro.fr/cgi/perm/archives/find?url=/cgi/ perm/archives/form&rub=&Texte=clearstream&x=120&y=12). Le Figaro. February 26, 2001.

- "Ernest Backes, l'homme qui lutte contre le 'crime bancaire organisé'" (http://www.lefigaro.fr/cgi/perm/ archives/find?url=/cgi/perm/archives/form&rub=&Texte=clearstream&x=120&y=12). Le Figaro. February 26, 2001.

- "La mission parlementaire enquêtera sur Clearstream" (http://www.lefigaro.fr/cgi/perm/archives/find?url=/ cgi/perm/archives/form&rub=&Texte=clearstream&x=120&y=12). Le Figaro. February 27, 2001.

- "La justice luxembourgeoise enquête sur Clearstream" (http://www.lefigaro.fr/cgi/perm/archives/find?url=/ cgi/perm/archives/form&rub=&Texte=clearstream&x=120&y=12). Le Figaro. April 7, 2001.

- "La décision luxembourgeoise fait trembler les banques" (http://www.lefigaro.fr/cgi/perm/archives/ find?url=/cgi/perm/archives/form&rub=&Texte=clearstream&x=120&y=12). Le Figaro. May 14, 2001.

- "Clearstream: les comptes secrets passés au crible" (http://www.lefigaro.fr/cgi/perm/archives/find?url=/cgi/perm/archives/form&rub=&Texte=clearstream&x=120&y=12). Le Figaro. May 17, 2001.
- "Blanchiment: les députés épinglent Luxembourg" (http://www.lefigaro.fr/cgi/perm/archives/find?url=/cgi/perm/archives/form&rub=&Texte=clearstream&x=120&y=12). Le Figaro. January 23, 2001.
- "Les 1 000 milliards de dollars du blanchiment" (http://www.lefigaro.fr/cgi/perm/archives/find?url=/cgi/perm/archives/form&rub=&Texte=clearstream&x=120&y=12). Le Figaro. May 15, 2001.
- "Deutsche Börse reprend 50% de Clearstream pour 1,6 milliards d'euros" (http://www.lefigaro.fr/cgi/perm/archives/find?url=/cgi/perm/archives/form&rub=&Texte=clearstream&x=120&y=12). Le Figaro. February 2, 2002.
- "Parfum de scandale dans la finance internationale" (http://www.lefigaro.fr/cgi/perm/archives/find?url=/cgi/perm/archives/form&rub=&Texte=clearstream&x=120&y=12). Le Figaro. February 26, 2002.
- "Des sénateurs belges veulent enquêter sur des sociétés de clearing" (http://www.lefigaro.fr/cgi/perm/archives/find?url=/cgi/perm/archives/form&rub=&Texte=clearstream&x=120&y=12). Le Figaro. March 30, 2002.
- "Euroclear va fusionner avec Crest" (http://www.lefigaro.fr/cgi/perm/archives/find?url=/cgi/perm/archives/form&rub=&Texte=clearstream&x=120&y=12). Le Figaro. July 4, 2002.
- "André Roellants entre au directoire de Deutsche Börse (comme vice-président)" (http://www.lefigaro.fr/cgi/perm/archives/find?url=/cgi/perm/archives/form&rub=&Texte=clearstream&x=120&y=12). Le Figaro. September 10, 2002.
- "L'ex-patron de Clearstream inculpé pour blanchiment" (http://www.lefigaro.fr/cgi/perm/archives/find?url=/cgi/perm/archives/form&rub=&Texte=clearstream&x=120&y=12). Le Figaro. February 2, 2004.
- "Bruxelles épingle Clearstream pour entrave à la concurrence" (http://www.lefigaro.fr/cgi/perm/archives/find?url=/cgi/perm/archives/form&rub=&Texte=clearstream&x=120&y=12). Le Figaro. March 3, 2004.
- "Clearstream perd de nouveau en justice" (http://www.lefigaro.fr/cgi/perm/archives/find?url=/cgi/perm/archives/form&rub=&Texte=clearstream&x=120&y=12). Le Figaro. March 13, 2004.
- "Justice: satisfaction de Clearstream et de Denis Robert" (http://www.lefigaro.fr/cgi/perm/archives/find?url=/cgi/perm/archives/form&rub=&Texte=clearstream&x=120&y=12). Le Figaro. March 30, 2004.
- "Bruxelles ouvre une procédure contre Clearstream" (http://www.lefigaro.fr/cgi/perm/archives/find?url=/cgi/perm/archives/form&rub=&Texte=clearstream&x=120&y=12). Le Figaro. April 1, 2004.
- "Enquête sur un éventuel blanchissement" (http://www.lefigaro.fr/cgi/perm/archives/find?url=/cgi/perm/archives/form&rub=&Texte=clearstream&x=120&y=12). Le Figaro. June 19, 2004.
- "Le corbeau, un fin connaisseur de la finance internationale" (http://www.lefigaro.fr/cgi/perm/archives/find?url=/cgi/perm/archives/form&rub=&Texte=clearstream&x=120&y=12). Le Figaro. June 23, 2004.
- "Jeffrey Tessler (Bank of New York...va remplacer André Roellants...)" (http://www.lefigaro.fr/cgi/perm/archives/find?url=/cgi/perm/archives/form&rub=&Texte=clearstream&x=120&y=12). Le Figaro. September 24, 2004.
- "Jean-Louis Gergorin: 'Je ne suis pas le corbeau'" (http://www.lefigaro.fr/cgi/perm/archives/find?url=/cgi/perm/archives/form&rub=&Texte=clearstream&x=120&y=12). Le Figaro. November 16, 2004.
- "Le parquet conteste la procédure Rhodia" (http://www.lefigaro.fr/cgi/perm/archives/find?url=/cgi/perm/archives/form&rub=&Texte=clearstream&x=120&y=12). Le Figaro. September 2, 2005.
- "Quand la fiction dépeint la réalité" (http://www.lefigaro.fr/cgi/perm/archives/find?url=/cgi/perm/archives/form&rub=&Texte=clearstream&x=120&y=12). Le Figaro. November 6, 2005.

Other languages

- **(Spanish)** "El banco Clearstream, implicado en la apropiación indebida de fondos del FMI" (http://www. diagonalperiodico.net/antigua/pdfs02/08diagonal2.pdf) (PDF). Diagonal Periodico. March 17–30, 2005. (very interesting, speaks about Nadhmi Auchi)

Others

- About Lucy Komisar (http://www.channer.tv/past programs/wednesday, 09-22-04.htm)
- compiled info on Clearstream (http://www.luxembourg.attac.org/) by ATTAC Luxembourg.
- Film by Denis Robert and Pascal Laurent, "L'Affaire Clearstream racontee à un ouvrier de Daewoo" (http:// www.liberationfilms.be/article.php3?id_article=112)

Cleeng

Cleeng

Founded	Dec 2010
Founder	Gilles Domartini
Headquarters	Amsterdam, netherlands
Industry	Media technology
Slogan	Instant Access to Quality Content.
Website	Cleeng.com [1]
Registration	Required
Available in	English

Cleeng is a content monetization service that provides a way for digital publishers to charge their website's visitors micropayments to access their content.

The project was started during the debates[1] initiated by Ruppert Murdoch for further expanding the use of paywall systems to compensate the declining revenues of publishers, and allow quality journalism to survive. M Murdoch, along with leading media figures[2] , believes that subscription models should complement the advertising models available online. In 2010, we saw the emergence of new models like those developed by Apple iPad, and also so called subscription - freemium models. Both model try to sell content in their integrality, ie people must buy the full content unit to read a given piece of content. The patented solution developed by Cleeng allow content producers to only sell the given piece of content.

Content monetization

The idea is to make it easy to monetize content, and democratize use pay-per-use of online content, so everyone can earn money from content. Such system intends to help the publishing industry adapt to digital transformation. Cleeng is a free software solution launched in November 2010. The service is dedicated to publishers and bloggers to help them monetize their online content.

Any publisher or blogger may create an account, install the WordPress plug-in and sell their articles, videos or pictures to online users. The solution is a pay as you go solution and does not require the online users to subscribe to the publisher web site. Publisher can collect micro-payments from 0,15 to a maximum of 0,99 € (or equivalent local currencies) when online users consult online content. It works on all web-enabled devices such as computer, tablet, smart phones, TVs etc.

Publishers and bloggers define which part of their content is available to online users and the price for each item of content. This enables consumers to try content before they buy it.

When published, the content item is hidden behind a layer on the publisher's web site.

The user may create an account using Facebook, Google or his own account, and may access and acquire content from numerous web sites. Some journalists already considered considered the option could help save the publishing industry[3] , while other judge that this could be a simple solution for bloggers to charge for content[4] .

The company was created by Gilles Domartini, a former Philips, Apple and Packard Bell executive, who filed the initial patent of the solution. The co-founders are Donald Res, Nicolas Le Gall, and Benedicte Guichard. They share and publish frequently tips how to best monetize content.

Cleeng is operating from Amsterdam, the Netherlands and has offices in Paris, France.

Cleeng it

Cleeng it is a verb derived from the company name which means that any visitors can earn money from referring the content they have bought. After purchasing they can decide to refer the content to friends or digital followers. Once their friends or followers have purchased via the given link the original referrer receives a commission on those purchases. This can be up to 30% of the purchase price.

References

[1] http://www.telegraph.co.uk/finance/newsbysector/mediatechnologyandtelecoms/digital-media/6559694/
    Rupert-Murdoch-to-remove-News-Corps-content-from-Google-in-months.html

[2] http://www.mondaynote.com/2009/09/13/how-to-make-readers-pay-for-news/

[3] http://www.blogherald.com/2010/12/14/can-cleeng-save-the-newspaper-industry-bloggers-take-note/

[4] http://thenextweb.com/eu/2011/01/05/cleeng-makes-it-easy-to-charge-for-your-blog-without-annoying-readers/

ClickandBuy

ClickandBuy International Ltd

Type	Online Payment and Money Transfer Service
Industry	e-commerce
Founded	Cologne, Germany (1999)
Headquarters	London, England / UK
Area served	Worldwide
Parent	Deutsche Telekom
Website	www.clickandbuy.com [1]

ClickandBuy International Ltd is an e-commerce business that allows payments and money transfers to be made through the Internet. It is one of the largest online payment service providers on the Internet. Their website claims ClickandBuy now has over 13 million customers who can pay at over 16,000 merchants – including the Apple iTunes Store, AOL, MSN, Napster, Orange, Parship, bwin and McAfee.

Originally established in 1999 in Cologne, Germany, they later established operations in the United Kingdom with head offices in London and under the regulation of the Financial Services Authority (FSA). On 25 March 2010 it was announced that Deutsche Telekom had acquired ClickandBuy International Ltd.

References

External links

- http://www.clickandbuy.com/WW_en/payment/index.html
- http://www.finextra.com/news/fullstory.aspx?newsitemid=21223
- http://www.telekom.com/dtag/cms/content/dt/en/838228
- http://eu.techcrunch.com/2010/03/02/clickandbuy-the-european-paypal-lets-facebook-users-set-up-shop/

CNG Processing A/S

CNG Processing A/S

Type	Stock
Industry	Payment processor, Merchant account, Payment gateway
Founded	2005
Headquarters	Holmen naval base Copenhagen, Denmark
Website	www.cngpro.com [1]

CNG Processing A/S. is a payment gateway (Internet payment service provider)) and was founded in 2005. They offer merchants online services for accepting electronic payments by a variety of payment methods including credit card. CNG Processing is FSA approved by the Danish Financial Supervisory Authority[1].

CNG Processing have been Payment card industry compliant since 2006 by Visa[2] and MasterCard[3] . Their acquiring network includes PBS A/S [4] , Deutsche Bank, Credit Foncier de Monaco, Lloyds Bank, DataCash[5] , American Express and MasterCard and are a MasterCard ISO/MSP member.

CNG Processing headquarters in Copenhagen

External links

- http://www.cngpro.com (CNG Processing A/S)
- http://www.bigecard.com (PrePaid MasterCard Product from CNG Processing)

References

[1] http://www.dfsa.dk/sw99.asp

[2] http://www.visaeurope.com/documents/ais/visa_europe_ais_certified_service_providers_march_2009.pdf

[3] http://www.mastercard.com/us/sdp/assets/pdf/Compliant%20Service%20Providers%20-%20March%203%202009.pdf

[4] http://www.pbs-international.dk/internetforretninger/betalingssoftware

[5] http://www.datacash.com/partners/integration/

Collect on delivery

Collect on delivery or **COD** is a financial transaction where the payment of products and/or services received is done at the time of actual delivery rather than paid-for in advance. The term is mainly applied to consumer products purchased from a third party, where payment is made to or collected by the deliverer from the *recipient* rather than the sender, in the way that a collect call is also charged to the recipient instead of the caller. The delivery company in turn remits the charge for the item itself to the company which shipped it, keeping only the portion which it charged for the shipping service.

This type of transaction is better known as **cash on delivery**. However, as other forms of payment became more common, the word "cash" was replaced with the word "collect" to incorporate transactions with checks, credit cards or debit cards. Even with this, COD has become much less common now, and most companies will not ship this way.

Originally, COD delivery was made when a company owns its own transportation means. That way the delivery person can collect on site. However, because USPS, UPS, FedEx, Ontrac, and other commercial shipping companies are often cheaper, most companies use COD to mean that the bill for the product is delivered with the product, and payment is expected immediately. Because of the commonality of credit cards and instant payment methods through the Internet, COD purchasing has become obsolete in most cases. However, it remains a standard method of payment for ordering products and services produced quickly and nearby the point of delivery; this is particularly common with the ordering of food, and it is the standard model for pizza delivery services, though some pizza restaurants require a credit card number before they will send a delivery, due to fraud and prank callers.

In some countries this remains a popular option with internet-based retailers, since it is far easier to set up for small businesses and does not require the purchaser to have a credit card.

Concord EFS, Inc.

Concord EFS, Inc. was a major corporation that provided ATM, credit card, debit card, and payroll processing services.[1] On February 26, 2004 Concord merged with First Data.

A Brief History of ConcordEFS

Concord EFS, Inc., based in Memphis, Tennessee, provides a full range of electronic payment and deposit services, from authorizing and routing a fund transfer to settlement. The company's Network Services division provides financial institutions with ATM processing, debit card processing, access to a national debit network, and deposit risk management. Concord's Payment Services division processes payments for supermarkets, gas stations, truck stops, convenience stores, and restaurants, as well as major and independent retailers. The company is the leading processor to gas stations and supermarkets, as well as being the United States' largest ATM processor.

Victor Tyler's Establishment of Concord Computing in 1970

The Concord component of Concord EFS dates back to 1970 when Victor M. Tyler established Concord Computing Corporation in the Boston, Massachusetts, area. An electrical engineer who studied at both Yale and MIT, Tyler in 1955 went to work at EG&G Corp., which was primarily involved in the design and testing of weapons systems for the military. In the mid-1960s Tyler was charged with identifying new business ventures for the company, one of which was the new area of electronic credit authorization systems. When EG&G elected not to participate, Tyler, who had been involved in a number of start-ups, decided to take up the idea himself and at age 42 became an entrepreneur, thinking it would be "fun and easy." He enlisted five colleagues from EG&G and started Concord Computing Corporation, primarily funded by $20,000 invested by a friend and the $30,000 he raised by mortgaging his house. Establishing an electronic credit authorization business, however, proved to be anything but easy. At the end of a year the company was barely established, forcing the partners to take stock of the situation. Because most of their seed money was still available, they could easily cash in, find new jobs, and move on with their lives. Instead, they agreed to press ahead, only to find the second year even more arduous than the first. At one point the employees actually drew lots to see who would quit as a cost-cutting measure. Years later Tyler told the Boston Globe, "It was like deciding who is going to get out of the lifeboat because there's not enough food left."

To raise much needed cash to keep the business afloat and operating, Tyler took out another mortgage and borrowed money from his parents. Concord's financial situation then began to stabilize as it landed accounts with major Boston department stores. Although annual revenues grew to $2 million within a few years, the company consistently lost money. "Every month we seemed to lose $20,000 and we couldn't figure out why we couldn't make a profit," Tyler told the Boston Globe. In the mid-1970s Concord recruited a new chief financial officer who succeeded in turning around the company, and in 1977, after some internal discord, was able to oust Tyler as CEO. Instead of continuing to provide information services, Concord now began to focus on the less profitable hardware side of the business. As a result the company was once again losing money. Tyler lobbied the board of directors and secured enough support to once again be named the chief executive. He quickly returned Concord's emphasis to service rather than hardware, and within two months the company began posting profits. After years of learning the ropes as an entrepreneur, Tyler finally settled on a successful business formula: "You have to forecast revenue with extreme accuracy and without any optimism. And then you have to be prepared to ruthlessly cut costs."

The Acquisition of EFS in 1985: A Turning Point for Concord

While Concord developed a reputation as thrifty Yankees in the 1980s, the company also began to move beyond simple profitability as a goal and to formulate a broader vision. In Tyler's words, Concord began to build "payment networks" to take advantage of the new point-of-sale terminals technology and the increasing use of electronic means of funds transfer. The first major step in this direction occurred in 1981 when it acquired a majority interest in Network EFT, a Chicago-based third-party payment processing service for retailers and financial institutions. The Jewel Supermarket chain also owned a major stake in the business. To compete against larger, better financed companies in the industry, Concord sought out niche opportunities, targeting specific customers, then winning their business by offering lower prices and better service. The approach worked so well that in 1984 the company went public to fuel further expansion. A year later Concord used some of those proceeds to acquire EFS, Inc. (Electronic Fleet Systems), a major turning point in the company's history.

EFS, originally involved in the trucking industry, offered fleet management services for trucking companies as well as credit card authorization and settlement services for retailers. It was founded by Dan M. Palmer, who ultimately became Concord's CEO and chair and was responsible for moving the business to Memphis. He graduated from the University of Memphis in 1966 with a degree in business administration. For a number of years he worked as an accountant for Deloitte and Touche in New York, then became the chief financial officer for Bayer Corporation's Arkansas office. Afterward he went to work for Mid Continent, a West Memphis, Arkansas, company that marketed a credit card for truck drivers. Reflecting on how long it took for credit cards with past due accounts to be shut down, Palmer recognized a business opportunity to provide instant verification of credit cards using new point-of-sale technology. He quit his job to start his own business but at first had difficulty convincing banks and investors that the idea was indeed worthwhile. Finally he received help from a former executive of Memphis-based Union Planters Bank, Bill Matthews, who had introduced ATMs to Memphis and was sympathetic to Palmer's vision. In 1982 Palmer created EFS as a subsidiary of Union Planters. EFS fared poorly during its brief existence with Union Planters; the unit was never profitable and unable to establish itself in the marketplace. As part of a restructuring effort, Union Planters decided to unload the business, selling it to Concord at a cut-rate price of $250,000. Palmer stayed on as CEO of EFS and with Concord as a parent corporation he was finally able to make the company prosper, due in large part to actively soliciting mom-and-pop operations, convincing them to start accepting credit cards.

Tyler remained chairman and CEO of Concord through the rest of the 1980s. During that time, the company produced strong results, growing revenues and profits at a steady clip. It exploited numerous niche opportunities, was not overly dependent on any single customer, and was able to leverage superior technology to discount its services and thereby successfully compete against much larger rivals. With EFS accounting for more than 60 percent of all revenues, it was not surprising that Palmer would succeed Tyler as Concord's CEO in 1990. A year later Palmer also became chairman of the board. The company changed its name to Concord Computing and EFS, and moved its headquarters to centrally located Memphis. It also initiated efforts to become involved in bank card processing in supermarkets and grocery stores, a promising vehicle for future growth. More important, Palmer was transforming Concord from a small electronic funds transfer operation into a major, vertically integrated electronic banking operation.

In September 1991 Concord created a subsidiary, Concord Equipment Sales, Inc., to sell point-of-sale terminal products and other communications equipment. Also in 1991 the company took a more significant step in filling out its business when it filed an application to organize a national bank. In preparation, Concord became a holding company and in February 1992 changed its name to Concord EFS, Inc. A new subsidiary assumed the Concord Computing Corporation name and acquired the operational assets and liabilities of the parent company. After final approval for a bank charter was granted by the Federal Reserve in October 1992, the parent company became a one-bank holding company. Simultaneously, on December 1, 1992, EFS National Bank was formed, issued stock, and acquired the EFS, Inc. subsidiary, which was subsequently dissolved.

The result of all of this shuffling of names and stock swaps was that Concord now had its own bank and was better positioned for future growth on a number of levels. No longer did it have to rely on a sponsor bank to provide settlement services and sponsorship into bankcard associations. In addition to saving money Concord was able to offer new services, such as debit cards, to its existing markets. EFS National Bank limited its activities in order to best support Concord and did not engage in traditional banking activities, such as consumer and commercial lending, deposits, and real estate.

On the same day that its bank charter was approved, Concord also announced a major agreement with the National Grocers Association (NGA) to provide its 65,000 independent member grocers with credit and debit processing services. It was a large and virtually untapped market for Concord. NGA would later contract Concord to provide check authorization services as well.

Another emerging service in the early 1990s was electronic benefit transfer (EBT), which government authorities were beginning to use in order to combat misuse of welfare benefits and food stamps. EBT became the subject of litigation for Concord in February 1993 when it sued Deluxe Data Systems Inc., claiming that Deluxe violated antitrust laws by forcing grocers to agree to use its services exclusively in the state of Maryland. Concord feared that, if unchecked, Deluxe would be able to shut down competition in the potentially lucrative EBT field as other states made the transition to EBT. The matter lingered in the courts for more than two years and jeopardized the future of EBT. Finally in July 1995 the two parties reached a settlement, the terms of which were not disclosed, but at the very least Concord was now better positioned to compete against Deluxe in EBT.

Rapid Expansion in the 1990s

Through the rest of the 1990s Concord grew at an impressive pace. For 1993 the company recorded sales of $75.4 million and net income of $9.9 million. In 1995 sales grew to $127.8 million and net income to $18.3 million. In 1997 sales reached $240 million and net income $42.7 million. Two years later sales topped $830 million and net income exceeded $100 million. Most of this growth was accomplished internally through payment services for retailers, but Concord also began to make acquisitions to move into network services for financial institutions to fuel even further expansion, as well as to better compete in an industry that was undergoing consolidation.

In 1999 Concord acquired Electronic Payment Services (EPS) and its well known MAC brand, the third largest regional ATM network. Not only did it obtain a larger processing platform and bolster the credit card processing part of its business, Concord reached another level in the EFT industry, in league with such heavyweights as First Data

Corporation and subsidiaries of National City Corp. and Bank One Corp. In 2000 Concord expanded further into network services when it bought Cash Station, which serviced 645 financial institutions primarily located in Illinois, Indiana, Kansas, Kentucky, Michigan, Missouri, and Wisconsin.

Clearly, regional EFT networks were consolidating and Concord was determined to become a major player. When it acquired Star Systems in an $850 million deal in 2001 it became an industry powerhouse that combined payment and network services, a move that also vaulted Concord into the ranks of the S&P 500 stock index. Now operating in 31 states, Concord was becoming a true national enterprise. By focusing on either its MAC or Star brand it was now in a position to possibly challenge Visa and MasterCard on debit cards and as a point-of-sale brand at retail locations. In April 2001 Concord announced that it had settled on Star as its brand, which would begin to replace MAC and Cash Station logos on ATMs.

Concord also was preparing for the future of electronic payments. It promoted a preauthorized debit card (referred to as ACH) that could be combined with supermarket club cards. Merchants would be able to save on fees charged by Visa and MasterCard, and consumers would be rewarded with bonuses. The ACH acronym referred to Automated Clearing House, which would be authorized by the consumer to make a bank account transfer. The personal identification number (PIN), however, would be assigned by the supermarket and the card would only be valid at the issuing chain.

Concord also began testing a number of methods to use ATM cards to make Internet purchases, as well as a way to use ATM service to send money to anyone, even people without a bank account. Concord patented a person-to-person service that allowed a sender to visit an ATM and arrange for a specific amount of money to be transferred. A one-time-use PIN would then be assigned. The recipient, informed of the PIN, would then use a special access card to receive the cash from an in-network ATM. Even without such innovations, Concord was looking forward to major growth in its established services. In 2001, for instance, only 20 percent of supermarket payments were made by debit or credit cards. That amount was expected to triple over the next six or seven years.

In 2001 Concord posted revenues of more than $1.7 billion and net income of $216.4 million. After overseeing the company's tremendous growth over the previous decade, Palmer announced in September 2002 that he was stepping down as Concord CEO in May 2003, to be replaced by company President Edward A. Labry III, an executive with Concord since the 1985 merger with EFS. Palmer would, however, remain chairman of both Concord and EFS National Bank.

This company later merged with First Data.The US Department of Justice challenged First Data's 2004 purchase over antitrust concerns, but later approved the deal when First Data agreed to divest ATM network NYCE in a sale to Metavante.

Confinity

Confinity Inc. is best known as the creator of PayPal. It was founded in December 1998 by Max Levchin, Peter Thiel, and Luke Nosek, initially as a Palm Pilot payments and cryptography company.[1] Many of Confinity's initial recruits were alumni of The Stanford Review, also co-founded by Peter Thiel, and most early engineers hailed from the University of Illinois at Urbana-Champaign, recruited by Max Levchin. Early investors included Nokia Ventures, Deutsche Bank, and Bell Melton, the founder of CyberCash.[2]

Confinity's second office, 165 University Avenue in Palo Alto, California, is also known for being the former office of Google and Logitech.[3]

Confinity launched its milestone product, PayPal in late 1999.[4] Confinity merged with X.com, founded by Elon Musk, in March 2000.[5] The merged company became known as X.com because this was thought to be a name with broader long-term potential than Confinity or PayPal. However, surveys eventually showed that a majority of consumers considered the name X.com vague and potentially pornographic and preferred that the company simply be called PayPal. After a corporate restructuring, the company adopted the name PayPal Inc.

After an IPO, the company was purchased by eBay.

References

[1] PayPal Puts Dough in Your Palm (http://www.wired.com/news/technology/0,1282,20958,00.html)

[2] Beam Me up Some Cash (http://www.halplotkin.com/cnbcs029.htm)

[3] A building blessed with tech success - CNET News.com (http://news.com.com/2100-1040-960790.html)

[4] PayPal Execs Enjoy Deja Woo-Hoo (http://www.wired.com/news/ebiz/0,1272,53705,00.html)

[5] FindLaw - Agreement and Plan of Merger - X.com Corp. and Confinity Inc (http://contracts.corporate.findlaw.com/agreements/paypal/confinity.mer.2000.03.01.html)

External links

- Confinity (http://www.confinity.com/) Historical Site

Corporate travel management

Travel management or **corporate travel management** (CTM) is the function of managing a company's strategic approach to travel (travel policy), the negotiations with all vendors, day-today operation of the corporate travel program, traveller safety & security, credit-card management and T&E data management. CTM should not be confused with the work of a traditional Travel Agency. While agencies provide the day-to-day travel services to corporate clients, they are the implementing arm of what the corporation has negotiated and put forth in policy. In other words CTM decides on the class of service that employees are allowed to fly, negotiate corporate fares/rates with airlines and hotels as well as set forth the use of the corporate credit card. The agency on the other hand makes the actual reservation within the parameters given by the corporation.

For most companies "travel & expenses" (T&E) costs represent the second highest controllable annual expense, exceeded only by salary & benefits, and is commonly higher than IT and/or real estate costs. T&E costs are not only limited to travel (airline, rail, hotel, car rental, ferry/boat, etc.) but include all costs incurred during travel such as staff & client meals, taxi fares, gratuities, client gifts, supplies (office supplies and/or services), etc. Furthermore this area often included meeting management, traveller safety & security as well as credit card and overall travel data management.

The management of these costs are usually handled by the Corporate Travel Manager, a function that can be part of the Finance, HR, Procurement or Administrative Services Department. As this function touches on all of these areas in some form and represents such a major corporate expense, it stand to reason that this function should have equal ranking within a corporation as any other major division and not be seen as a sub-set of existing departments.

Travel Management (Trade) Organizations

- Association of Corporate Travel Executives acte.org [1]
- National Business Travel Association [2]
- Business Travel Management & Leisure Trips in India [3]

Cougar Mountain Software

Cougar Mountain Software

Industry	Computer software
Founded	1982
Headquarters	Boise, Idaho
Key people	Bob Gossett, founder Chuck Gossett, Chief Executive Officer and President
Website	www.cougarmtn.com [1]

Cougar Mountain Software is a privately-held company based in Boise, Idaho that manufactures and markets accounting software, retail software and business software to small to mid-sized companies. They are a Microsoft Certified Partner.

History

It was founded by Bob Gossett in 1982 The company's first accounting product was introduced as a DOS application. The company's first Windows product, CMS Professional, was introduced in 1997. In 2006, Cougar Mountain Software introduced Denali, which is based on Microsoft SQL Server technology. Cougar Mountain Software products are developed and supported from Boise, Idaho (USA).

External links

- Cougar Mountain Software website [1] (main company website)
- Cougar Mountain Software Service website [2] (user website)
- Cougar Mountain Blog [3] (user website)

References

- CMS Professional 2009, CPA Technology Advisor 5 Star Rating [4] (June 2009)
- FUND Nonprofit Accounting, Web CPA Accounting Software Review [5] (May 2009)
- FUND Nonprofit Accounting, CPA Technology Advisor 5 Star Rating [6] (December 2008)
- CMS Professional 2009, Top 100 Product List on Web CPA [7] (December 2008)
- Point of Sale, CPA Technology Advisor 5 Star Rating [8] (October 2008)
- CMS Professional 2009, CPA Technology Advisor 5 Star Rating [9] (September 2008)
- Accounting Software Magazine [10], FUND Accounting Suite (May 2008)
- Cougar Mountain FUND Accounting Software [11], NonProfit Technology News review
- CMS Professional Accounting, 2007 CPA Technology Advisor, 5 Star Rating [12]
- FUND Nonprofit Accounting, 2007 CPA Technology Advisor, 5 Star Rating [13]
- Job Cost (Manufacturing), 2007 CPA Technology Advisor, 4.5 Star Rating [14]
- Point of Sale, 2006 CPA Technology Advisor, 5 Star Rating [15]
- Nonprofit software, 2006 CPA Technology Advisor, 5 Star Rating [16]
- Denali, 2006 CPA Technology Advisor, 4.5 Star Rating [17]
- Payroll, 2006 CPA Technology Advisor, 4 Star Rating [18]

Crossing of cheques

Any cheque crossed with two parallel lines means that the cheque can only be deposited directly into an account with a bank and cannot be immediately cashed by a bank over the counter. By using crossed cheques, cheque writers can effectively protect the cheques they write from being stolen and cashed. However, crossed cheques are rarely used in the U.S. [1]

A **crossed cheque** – the oblique nearly-vertical lines down the center are the cross.

Crossing of cheques

Cheques can be of two types:-

1. Open or an uncrossed cheque

2. Crossed cheque

Open Cheque

An open cheque is a cheque which is payable at the counter of the drawee bank on presentation of the cheque.

Crossed Cheque

A crossed cheque is a cheque which is payable only through a collecting banker and not directly at the counter of the bank. Crossing ensures security to the holder of the cheque as only the collecting banker credits the proceeds to the account of the payee of the cheque.

When two parallel transverse lines, with or without any words, are drawn generally, on the left hand top corner of the cheque. A crossed cheque does not effect the negotiability of the instrument. It can be negotiated the same way as any other negotiable instrument.

Types of Crossing

There are two types of negotiable instruments:-

• General Crossing

• Special Crossing

• Account Payee or Restrictive Crossing

• 'Not Negotiable' Crossing

Cheque crossed generally

Where a cheque bears across its face an addition of the words 'and company' or any abbreviation thereof, between two parallel transverse lines, or of two parallel transverse lines simply, either with or without the words 'Not Negotiable', that addition shall be deemed a crossing, and the cheque shall be deemed to be crossed generally.

Cheque crossed specially

Where a cheque bears across its face an addition of the name of a banker, either with or without the words 'Not Negotiable', that addition shall be deemed a crossing, and the cheque shall be deemed to be crossed specially, and to be crossed to that banker.

Account Payee or Restrictive Crossing

This crossing can be made in both general and special crossing by adding the words **Account Payee**. In this type of crossing the collecting banker is supposed to credit the amount of the cheque to the account of the payee only. The cheque remains transferable but the liability of the collecting banker is enhanced in case he credits the proceeds of the cheque so crossed to any person other than the payee and the endorsement in favour of the last payee is proved forged. The collecting banker must act like a blood hound and make proper enquiries as to the title of the last endorsee from the original payee named in the cheque before collecting an 'Account Payee' cheque in his account. The same can be done by place slanted parallel line in the top most left corner of the cheque - in writing over their A/C payee's only.

Not Negotiable Crossing

The words 'Not Negotiable' can be added to General as well as Special crossing and a crossing with these words is known as *Not Negotiable* crossing. The effect of such a crossing is that it removes the most important characteristic of a negotiable instrument i.e. the transferee of such a crossed cheque cannot get a better title than that of the transferor (cannot become a holder in due course) and cannot convey a better title to his own transferee, though the instrument remains transferable.

Consequence of a bank not complying with the crossing

A bank's failure to comply with the crossings amounts to a breach of contract with its customer. The bank may not be able to debit the drawer's account and may be liable to the true owner for his loss.

References

[1] http://www.investopedia.com/terms/c/crossedcheck.asp

- http://www.investopedia.com/terms/c/crossedcheck.asp
- http://chestofbooks.com/finance/banking/Banking-Credits-And-Finance/Crossed-Checks.html

Crowd funding

Crowd funding (sometimes called **crowd financing**, **crowd sourced capital**, or street performer protocol) describes the collective cooperation, attention and trust by people who network and pool their money and other resources together, usually via the Internet, to support efforts initiated by other people or organizations. Crowd funding occurs for any variety of purposes, from disaster relief to citizen journalism to artists seeking support from fans, to political campaigns, to funding a startup company or small business[1] or creating free software.

History

The crowd funding approach has long precedents in the sphere of charity. It is receiving renewed attention from both commercial and social entrepreneurs now that social media, online communities and micropayment technology make it straightforward to engage and secure donations from a group of potentially interested supporters at very low cost.

One of the pioneers of crowd funding in the music industry have been the British rock group Marillion. In 1997 American fans underwrote an entire US tour[2] to the tune of $60,000, with donations following an internet campaign - an idea conceived and managed by the fans before any involvement by the band. Marillion has later used crowd funding with great success as a method to fund the recording and marketing of several albums, Anoraknophobia,[2] Marbles[3] and Happiness Is the Road.[4]

Crowd funding in the film industry was pioneered by french entrepreneurs and producers Guillaume Colboc and Benjamin Pommeraud from company fr:Guyom Corp. when they launched a public internet donation campaign in August 2004[5] to fund their film, *Demain la Veille (Waiting for Yesterday)*.[6] Within 3 weeks, they managed to raise nearly $50,000, allowing them to shoot their film.

4 months later, on the other side of the Atlantic, Spanner Films started the prodution of its climate change documentary The Age of Stupid.[7] The Age of Stupid team, headed up by Franny Armstrong, successfully raised more than £900,000 over a period of 5 years (december 2004 to 2009, date of release) to cover both the production and promotion of the film. The film's crew worked at very low wages but also received crowd-funding "shares". Under the terms of the crowd-funding contract the investors and crew are paid once a year for ten years from the release of the film.[8]

Crowd funding's earliest known citation was by Michael Sullivan, fundavlog, August 12, 2006, "Many things are important factors, but funding from the 'crowd' is the base of which all else depends on and is built on. So, Crowd funding is an accurate term to help me explain this core element of fundavlog."

Earlier, other and related definitions

Some advocate that crowd funding does not include investments, and only includes the categories of donations, memberships or pre-ordering of products, giving none of the contributors a future stake or monetary reward of any kind. *MediaWave* debates whether or not crowd funding should be considered an investment: Crowd funding definition may however be restricted to pooling of resources together at the grassroot with a framework for rewards and for the purpose to initiate and or found an investment, where common desire and trust are the most important driving force for participation. Money contributed by group of individuals (large or small) without a framework for future stake may not be defined as crowd funding because such contributions pass only as donations.

There are questions about the legality of taking money from "investors" without offering any of the security demanded by legitimate investment schemes. At least sites such as Kickstarter, Pledgemusic, Funding4Learning, Sponsume and RocketHub have a failsafe. They hold funds in an escrow account. If the nominated target isn't reached, all funds are returned to contributors. Investors are given something for their money - so in a legal sense, they have paid for and received something. The Tunnel is selling frames of film for one dollar each. Pioneer One gives you the theme music or a special edition download. [9]

Micropatronage is a system in which the public directly supports the work of others by making donations through the Internet. In use as early as 2001,[10] the term was popularized in 2005 by blogger Jason Kottke when he quit his day job as a web designer and spent a year blogging full time, living off the voluntary donations of his readership. Micropatronage differs from traditional patronage systems by allowing many "patrons" to donate small amounts, rather than a small number of patrons making larger contributions.

In webcomics, micropatronage plays a large part in supporting both the author and the site itself, and it has become common in webcomics to see authors asking for donations from fans beyond a certain level of popularity.

Contemporary applications

Crowd funding is being experimented with as a funding mechanism for creative work such as blogging and journalism,[11] music, and independent film,[12] [13] and also for funding a startup company.[14] [15] [16] Community music labels are usually for-profit organizations where "fans assume the traditional financier role of a record label for artists they believe in by funding the recording process".[17]

Since pioneering crowd funding in the film industry Spanner films have published a useful 'how to' guide.[18]

Approaches

An entrepreneur seeking to use crowd funding (example for seed money) typically makes use of online communities to solicit pledges of small amounts of money from individuals who are typically not professional financiers. A range of variations are possible, for example:

- The solicitation could be to back an idea with no direct material return offered to those making a pledge. This type of crowd financing has long precedents including artistic patronage and the normal activities of charity fundraising. Sometimes a threshold pledge approach is used, in which all pledges are voided unless the threshold amount is reached before the deadline.
- Another approach invites a display of sponsorship in return for the cash pledged. A widely documented internet-based example is The Million Dollar Homepage.
- The solicitation could be to offer a loan (microfinance) e.g., Kiva.
- Some kind of quasi-equity investment could be offered, though any such scheme would need to avoid falling under any applicable financial regulations regarding making an initial public offering. One such scheme was introduced in February 2010.[15]
- Straightforward equity investment. When multiple parties are involved, this can involve a lot of work. There are platforms to make this easier.
- A threshold pledge system as above, but rewards are offered in return for gifts or donations.

Pros and cons

Proponents of the crowd funding approach argue that it allows good ideas which do not fit the pattern required by conventional financiers to break through and attract cash through the wisdom of the crowd. If it does achieve "traction" in this way, not only can the enterprise secure seed funding to begin its project, but it may also secure evidence of backing from potential customers and benefit from word of mouth promotion.

Against these advantages is the requirement to disclose the idea for which funding is sought in public when it is at a very early stage. This exposes the promoter of the idea to the risk of the idea being copied and developed ahead of them by better-financed competitors.

Another significant downside to crowd funding is the possibility of getting ensnared in various securities laws, since soliciting investments from the general public is most often illegal unless the opportunity has been filed with an appropriate securities regulatory authority, such as the Securities and Exchange Commission in the U.S., the Ontario Securities Commission in Ontario, Canada, the Autorité des marchés financiers in France and Quebec, Canada, or the Financial Services Authority in the U.K. These regulators can have different ways of determining what is and what is not a security but a general rule one can rely on (at least in the U.S.) is the Howey Test. The Howey Test says that a transaction constitutes an investment contract (therefore a security) if there is (1) an exchange of money (2) with an expectation of profits arising (3) from a common enterprise (4) which depends solely on the efforts of a promoter or third party. Clearly, under this standard, any crowd sourcing arrangement in which people are asked to contribute money in exchange for potential profits based on the work of others would be considered a security. As such, the applicable investment contract would have to be registered with a regulatory agency (such as the S.E.C.) unless it qualified for one of several rule-laden exemptions (e.g. Regulation A or Rule 506 of Regulation D of the Securities Act of 1933, or the California Limited Offering Exemption - Rule 1001 (also known as S.E.C. Rule 1001)). The penalties for a securities violation can vary greatly and depend in large part on the amount of profit obtained by the "promoter," the damage done to the investors, and whether a violation is a first time offense. However, a violation may result in both civil and criminal penalties, a return of any profit made and sometimes a lifetime ban from work in the securities industry. According to Section 5 of the Securities Act, it is illegal to sell any security unless such a sale is accompanied or preceded by a prospectus that meets the requirements of the Securities Act.[19]

Of course, an upside to registering a security with a regulatory authority is the sense of legitimacy that is imparted by application of a rigorous legal regime.

References

[1] "1st paragraph -- Crowd funding Pbworks" (http://crowdfunding.pbworks.com/). Michael Sullivan and pbworks consensus group. . Retrieved 2010-01-15.

[2] "Anoraknophobia Pre-Order Press Release" (http://www.marillion.com/press/anorak.htm). .

[3] "Album 13: The Next Big Idea" (http://www.marillion.com/press/marblescampaign.htm). .

[4] "Calling the faithful for Album 15" (http://www.marillion.com/preorder/). .

[5] http://mashable.com/2011/01/17/kickstarter-crowd-funding-infographic/

[6] http://9.mshcdn.com/wp-content/uploads/2011/01/kickstarter_graphic_v2-1.jpg

[7] "Age of Stupid: Making Of: Crowd-Funding launch, Dec 2004" (http://www.youtube.com/watch?v=mfujb60ytUY& feature=player_embedded). .

[8] "Age of Stupid loan agreement" (http://www.spannerfilms.net/sites/files/ageofstupid/Stupid_loan_agreement2008_0.pdf). .

[9] http://www.mediawave.tv/site/blogItem.cfm?item=248<MediaWave: "Crowd Funding. Hope or Hype?" (July 11, 2010)."

[10] TidBITS : Steal This Essay 3: How to Finance Content Creation (http://db.tidbits.com/getbits.acgi?tbart=06629)

[11] funding-journalism/ "Crowdfunding journalism" (http://platform.idiomag.com/2009/05/crowd). idio. 2009-05-19. funding-journalism/. Retrieved 2009-05-15.

[12] Teenagers' credit note approach to fund £1m film of Clovis Dardentor (http://www.guardian.co.uk/film/2009/apr/14/ clovis-dardentor-film-funding)

[13] TIME article on Crowd Funding the 'Age of Stupid' (http://www.time.com/time/magazine/article/0,9171,1838768,00.html)

[14] TechCrunch. "Sponsume lets projects get off the ground with Groupon-style group funding model" (http://eu.techcrunch.com/2010/04/ 28/sponsume-lets-projects-get-off-the-ground-with-groupon-style-group-funding-model/)

[15] TechCrunch 'Grow VC launches, aiming to become the Kiva for tech startups' (http://eu.techcrunch.com/2010/02/15/ grow-vc-launches-aiming-to-become-the-kiva-for-tech-startups/)

[16] BBC News 'Cash-strapped entrepreneurs get creative' (http://news.bbc.co.uk/2/hi/10100885.stm)

[17] Kappel, Tim, "Ex Ante Crowdfunding and the Recording Industry: A Model for the U.S.?" in *Loyola of Los Angeles Entertainment Law Review*, Vol.29, Issue 3, p.376

[18] Spanner Films : How to crowd fund your film (http://www.spannerfilms.net/how_to_crowd_fund_your_film)

[19] "Section 5 -- Prohibitions Relating to Interstate Commerce and the Mails" (http://www.law.uc.edu/CCL/33Act/sec5.html). University of Cincinnati College of Law. . Retrieved 2010-01-15.

Further reading

- The micro-price of micropatronage (http://www.economist.com/blogs/babbage/2010/09/ micropatronage_sweet_spot&fsrc=nwl), The Economist, 27th Sept 2010
- Putting your money where your mouse is (http://www.economist.com/node/16909869?story_id=16909869), The Economist, 2nd Sept 2010
- The Geography of Crowdfunding (http://papers.ssrn.com/sol3/papers.cfm?abstract_id=1692661), NET Institute Working Paper No. 10-08, Oct 2010
- Is There an eBay for Ideas? (http://papers.ssrn.com/sol3/papers.cfm?abstract_id=1701229) European Management Review, 2011
- A Guide to Crowd funding Success (http://mashable.com/2009/07/29/crowdfunding-success/)
- Ex Ante Crowdfunding and the Recording Industry: A Model for the U.S.? (http://elr.lls.edu/issues/ v29-issue3/documents/08.Kappel.pdf)
- Huffington Post crowd funding blogs (http://www.huffingtonpost.com/tag/crowdfunding)
- Cash-strapped entrepreneurs get creative in BBC News (http://news.bbc.co.uk/2/hi/10100885.stm)
- White Paper on Crowd funding (http://scr.bi/crowdfunding-white-paper)
- Love a Local Business? Buy a Share - Sometimes it takes a village to fund a company. (http://money.cnn.com/ 2009/09/08/smallbusiness/barnraising_a_business.fsb/index.htm)
- Trisquel GNU/Linux adopts crowd funding (http://trisquel.info/en/ trisquel-45-development-release-crowd-funding-and-holiday-presents)
- Catwalk Genius - Crowd sourcing (http://www.crowdsourcing.org/site/catwalk-genius/ wwwcatwalkgeniuscom/2651)

Currence

Currence is an association set up the banks that coordinates the payment systems in the Netherlands. It says that its aim is to "facilitate and provide market transparency while maintaining the quality and safety of the payment systems of the Netherlands."

History

Currence was founded on 1 January 2005 through an initiative by eight Dutch banks (ABN AMRO, Rabobank, ING Groep, Fortis, SNS Bank, BNG, Friesland Bank and Van Lanschot). It was originally know as *Brands & Licences Betalingsverkeer Nederland B.V.* during its development stage and was renamed as Currence from the 17 May 2005.

Aims and responsibilities

It is responsible for coordinating payment methods and facilitating cooperation between payment providers by providing standards and transparency while maintaining the quality and safety of the payment systems in the Netherlands.

It attempts to do this by setting clearly defined standards for all parties wishing to use the Currence payment products, PIN, Chipknip, Acceptgiro, Incasso/Machtigen and iDEAL, are able to operate. To create a level playing field it sets clear rules and regulations relating to product use and the product environment and regulates and supervises participants.

External links

- **(Dutch)** Official Currence website [1]

CyberCash, Inc.

The CyberCash, Inc. was an internet payment service for electronic commerce, headquartered in Reston, Virginia. It was founded in August 1994 by Daniel C. Lynch (who served as chairman), William N. Melton (who served as president and CEO, and later chairman), Steve Crocker (Chief Technology Officer), and Bruce G. Wilson. The company initially provided an electronic wallet software to consumers and provided software to merchants to accept credit card payments. Later they also offered "CyberCoin", a micropayment system modeled after the NetBill research project at Carnegie Mellon University, which they later licensed.

In 1995, the company proposed RFC 1898, CyberCash Credit Card Protocol Version 0.8. The company went public on February 19, 1996 with the symbol "CYCH" and its shares rose 79% on the first day of trading. In 1998, CyberCash bought ICVerify, makers of computer-based credit card processing software, [1] and in 1999 added another software company to their lineup, purchasing Tellan Software. [2] In January 2000, a teenage Russian hacker nicknamed "Maxus" announced he had cracked CyberCash's ICVerify application; the company denied this, stating that ICVerify was not even in use by the purportedly hacked organization.

On January 1, 2000, CyberCash fell victim to the Y2K Bug, causing double recording of credit card payments through their system. [3]

The company filed for Chapter 11 bankruptcy on March 11, 2001. VeriSign acquired the Cybercash assets and name a couple of months later. On November 21, 2005 PayPal (already an eBay company) acquired VeriSign's payment services, including Cybercash. [4]

External links

- http://www.cybercash.com/(PayPal Merchant Services)
- CyberCash opens Net to small change [5] (News.com, September 30, 1996)
- CyberCash moves to thin wallet [6] (News.com, August 20, 1998)
- Cybercash Disputes Hacker's Claim [7] (Internet News, January 11, 2000)

References

[1] "CyberCash to buy ICVerify" (http://news.cnet.com/CyberCash-to-buy-ICVerify/2100-1001_3-209214.html). CNET News, March 18, 1998. . Retrieved 13 January 2010.

[2] "CyberCash Acquires Tellan Software" (http://www.internetnews.com/bus-news/article.php/155101/CyberCash+Acquires+Tellan+Software+.htm). Internet News, July 2, 1999. . Retrieved 13 January 2010.

[3] The Wall Street Journal; Eastern edition; Jan 7, 2000; 1;

[4] "eBay's PayPal Unit Completes Acquisition of VeriSign's Payment Gateway Business" (https://www.paypal-media.com/releasedetail.cfm?ReleaseID=180329). eBay. . Retrieved 20 November 2009.

Debit card

A **debit card** (also known as a **bank card** or **check card**) is a plastic card that provides the cardholder electronic access to his or her bank account/s at a financial institution. Some cards have a stored value against which a payment is made, while most relay a message to the cardholder's bank to withdraw funds from a designated account in favor of the payee's designated bank account. The card can be used as an alternative payment method to cash when making purchases. In some cases, the cards are designed exclusively for use on the Internet, and so there is no physical card.[1] [2]

In many countries the use of debit cards has become so widespread that their volume of use has overtaken or entirely replaced the check and, in some instances, cash transactions. Like credit cards, debit cards are used widely for telephone and Internet purchases.

However, unlike credit cards, the funds paid using a debit card are transferred immediately from the bearer's bank account, instead of having the bearer pay back the money at a later date.

Debit cards usually also allow for instant withdrawal of cash, acting as the ATM card for withdrawing cash and as a check guarantee card. Merchants may also offer cashback facilities to customers, where a customer can withdraw cash along with their purchase.

Types of debit card systems

There are currently three ways that debit card transactions are processed: **online debit** (also known as **PIN debit**), **offline debit** (also known as **signature debit**) and the **Electronic Purse Card System**.[3] One physical card can include the functions of an online debit card, an offline debit card and an electronic purse card.

Debit card

Although many debit cards are of the Visa or MasterCard brand, there are many other types of debit card, each accepted only within a particular country or region, for example Switch (now: Maestro) and Solo in the United Kingdom, Interac in Canada, Carte Bleue in France, Laser in Ireland, "EC electronic cash" (formerly Eurocheque) in Germany, UnionPay in China and EFTPOS cards in Australia and New Zealand. The need for cross-border compatibility and the advent of the euro recently led to many of these card networks (such as Switzerland's "EC direkt", Austria's "Bankomatkasse" and Switch in the United Kingdom) being re-branded with the internationally recognised Maestro logo, which is part of the MasterCard brand. Some debit cards are dual branded with the logo of the (former) national card as well as Maestro (for example, EC cards in Germany, Laser cards in Ireland, Switch and Solo in the UK, Pinpas cards in the Netherlands, Bancontact cards in Belgium, etc.). The use of a debit card system allows operators to package their product more effectively while

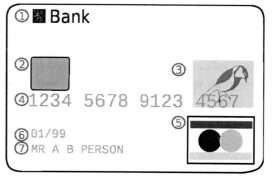

An example of the front of a typical debit card: Issuing bank logo EMVEMV chipHologramCredit card numberCard numberCard brand logo Expiration date Cardholder's name

monitoring customer spending. An example of one of these systems is ECS by Embed International.

Online Debit System

Online debit cards require electronic authorization of every transaction and the debits are reflected in the user's account immediately. The transaction may be additionally secured with the personal identification number (PIN) authentication system and some online cards require such authentication for every transaction, essentially becoming enhanced automatic teller machine (ATM) cards. One difficulty in using online debit cards is the necessity of an electronic authorization

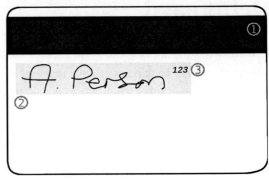

An example of the reverse side of a typical debit card: Magnetic stripe#Financial cardsMagnetic stripeSignature strip Card Security Code

device at the point of sale (POS) and sometimes also a separate PINpad to enter the PIN, although this is becoming commonplace for all card transactions in many countries. Overall, the online debit card is generally viewed as superior to the offline debit card because of its more secure authentication system and live status, which alleviates problems with processing lag on transactions that may only issue online debit cards. Some on-line debit systems are using the normal authentication processes of Internet banking to provide real-time on-line debit transactions. The most notable of these are Ideal and POLi.

Offline Debit System

Offline debit cards have the logos of major credit cards (for example, Visa or MasterCard) or major debit cards (for example, Maestro in the United Kingdom and other countries, but not the United States) and are used at the point of sale like a credit card (with payer's signature). This type of debit card may be subject to a daily limit, and/or a maximum limit equal to the current/checking account balance from which it draws funds. Transactions conducted with offline debit cards require 2–3 days to be reflected on users' account balances. In some countries and with some banks and merchant service organizations, a "credit" or offline debit transaction is without cost to the purchaser beyond the face value of the transaction, while a small fee may be charged for a "debit" or online debit transaction (although it is often absorbed by the retailer). Other differences are that online debit purchasers may opt to withdraw cash in addition to the amount of the debit purchase (if the merchant supports that functionality); also, from the merchant's standpoint, the merchant pays lower fees on online debit transaction as compared to "credit" (offline) debit transaction.

Electronic Purse Card System

Smart-card-based electronic purse systems (in which value is stored on the card chip, not in an externally recorded account, so that machines accepting the card need no network connectivity) are in use throughout Europe since the mid-1990s, most notably in Germany (Geldkarte), Austria (Quick), the Netherlands (Chipknip), Belgium (Proton), Switzerland (CASH) and France (Mon€o, which is usually carried by a debit card). In Austria and Germany, all current bank cards now include electronic purses.

Prepaid debit cards

Prepaid debit cards, also called reloadable debit cards or reloadable prepaid cards, are often used for recurring payments.[4] The payer loads funds to the cardholder's card account. Prepaid debit cards use either the offline debit system or the online debit system to access these funds. Particularly for companies with a large number of payment recipients abroad, prepaid debit cards allow the delivery of international payments without the delays and fees associated with international checks and bank transfers.[5] Providers include Caxton FX prepaid cards,[6] Escape prepaid cards, Travelex prepaid cards[7] and TransCash prepaid Visa cards.[8] Whereas, web-based services such as stock photography websites (istockphoto), outsourced services (oDesk),money transfer services (Western Union) and affiliate networks (MediaWhiz) have all started offering prepaid debit cards for their contributors/freelancers/vendors.

Advantages and disadvantages

The widespread use of debit and check cards have revealed numerous advantages and disadvantages to the consumer and retailer alike.

Advantages of debit cards

- A consumer who is not credit worthy and may find it difficult or impossible to obtain a credit card can more easily obtain a debit card, allowing him/her to make plastic transactions. For example, legislation often prevents minors from taking out debt, which includes the use of a credit card, but not online debit card transactions.

- For most transactions, a check card can be used to avoid check writing altogether. Check cards debit funds from the user's account on the spot, thereby finalizing the transaction at the time of purchase, and bypassing the requirement to pay a credit card bill at a later date, or to write an insecure check containing the account holder's personal information.

- Like credit cards, debit cards are accepted by merchants with less identification and scrutiny than personal checks, thereby making transactions quicker and less intrusive. Unlike personal checks, merchants generally do not believe that a payment via a debit card may be later dishonored.

- Unlike a credit card, which charges higher fees and interest rates when a cash advance is obtained, a debit card may be used to obtain cash from an ATM or a PIN-based transaction at no extra charge, other than a foreign ATM fee.

Disadvantages of debit cards

- Use of a debit card is not usually limited to the existing funds in the account to which it is linked, most banks allow a certain threshold over the available bank balance which can cause overdraft fees if the users transaction does not reflect available balance.

- Many banks are now charging over-limit fees or non-sufficient funds fees based upon pre-authorizations, and even attempted but refused transactions by the merchant (some of which may be unknown until later discovery by account holder).

- Many merchants mistakenly believe that amounts owed can be "taken" from a customer's account after a debit card (or number) has been presented, without agreement as to date, payee name, amount and currency, thus causing penalty fees for overdrafts, over-the-limit, amounts not available causing further rejections or overdrafts, and rejected transactions by some banks.

- In some countries debit cards offer lower levels of security protection than credit cards.[9] Theft of the users PIN using skimming devices can be accomplished much easier with a PIN input than with a signature-based credit transaction. However, theft of users' PIN codes using skimming devices can be equally easily accomplished with a debit transaction PIN input, as with a credit transaction PIN input, and theft using a signature-based credit transaction is equally easy as theft using a signature-based debit transaction.

- In many places, laws protect the consumer from fraud much less than with a credit card. While the holder of a credit card is legally responsible for only a minimal amount of a fraudulent transaction made with a credit card, which is often waived by the bank, the consumer may be held liable for hundreds of dollars, or even the entire value of fraudulent debit transactions. The consumer also has a shorter time (usually just two days) to report such fraud to the bank in order to be eligible for such a waiver with a debit card,[9] whereas with a credit card, this time may be up to 60 days. A thief who obtains or clones a debit card along with its PIN may be able to clean out the consumer's bank account, and the consumer will have no recourse.

Federally Imposed Maximum Liability for Unauthorized Card Use (United States)

Reported	Maximum Card Holder Liability	
	Credit Card	Debit Card
Before Use	$0	$0
Within 2 business days	$50	$50
After 2 but before 60 business days	$50	$500
After 60 business days	Unlimited	Unlimited

[10] [11]

- In the UK and Ireland, among other countries, a consumer who purchases goods or services with a credit card can pursue the credit card issuer if the goods or services are not delivered or are unmerchantable. While they must generally exhaust the process provided by the retailer first, this is not necessary if the retailer has gone out of business. This protection is not provided by legislation when using a debit card but may be offered to a limited extent as a benefit provided by the card network, for example, Visa debit cards.
- When a transaction is made using a credit card, the bank's money is being spent, and therefore, the bank has a vested interest in claiming its money where there is fraud or a dispute. The bank may fight to void the charges of a consumer who is dissatisfied with a purchase, or who has otherwise been treated unfairly by the merchant. But when a debit purchase is made, the consumer has spent his/her own money, and the bank has little if any motivation to collect the funds.
- In some countries, and for certain types of purchases, such as gasoline (via a pay at the pump system), lodging, or car rental, the bank may place a hold on funds much greater than the actual purchase for a fixed period of time.[9] However, this isn't the case in other countries, such as Sweden. Until the hold is released, any other transactions presented to the account, including checks, may be dishonoured, or may be paid at the expense of an overdraft fee if the account lacks any additional funds to pay those items.
- While debit cards bearing the logo of a major credit card are accepted for virtually all transactions where an equivalent credit card is taken, a major exception in some countries is at car rental facilities.[12] In some countries, such as Canada & Australia, car rental agencies require an actual credit card to be used, or at the very least, will verify the creditworthiness of the renter using a debit card. In Canada and additional unspecified countries, car rental companies will deny a rental to anyone who does not fit the requirements, and such a credit check may actually hurt one's credit score, as long as there is such a thing as a credit score in the country of purchase and/or the country of residence of the customer.

Consumer protection

Consumer protections vary, depending on the network used. Visa and MasterCard, for instance, prohibit minimum and maximum purchase sizes, surcharges, and arbitrary security procedures on the part of merchants. Merchants are usually charged higher transaction fees for credit transactions, since debit network transactions are less likely to be fraudulent. This may lead them to "steer" customers to debit transactions. Consumers disputing charges may find it easier to do so with a credit card, since the money will not immediately leave their control. Fraudulent charges on a debit card can also cause problems with a checking account because the money is withdrawn immediately and may thus result in an overdraft or bounced checks. In some cases debit card-issuing banks will promptly refund any disputed charges until the matter can be settled, and in some jurisdictions the consumer liability for unauthorized charges is the same for both debit and credit cards.

In some countries, like India and Sweden, the consumer protection is the same regardless of the network used. Some banks set minimum and maximum purchase sizes, mostly for online-only cards. However, this has nothing to do with the card networks, but rather with the bank's judgement of the person's age and credit records. Any fees that the customers have to pay to the bank are the same regardless of whether the transaction is conducted as a credit or as a debit transaction, so there is no advantage for the customers to choose one transaction mode over another. Shops may add surcharges to the price of the goods or services in accordance with laws allowing them to do so. Banks consider the purchases as having been made at the moment when the card was swiped, regardless of when the purchase settlement was made. Regardless of which transaction type was used, the purchase may result in an overdraft because the money is considered to have left the account at the moment of the card swiping.

Financial access

Debit cards and secured credit cards are popular among college students who have not yet established a credit history. Debit cards may also be used by expatriated workers to send money home to their families holding an affiliated debit card.

Issues with deferred posting of offline debit

To the consumer, a debit transaction is perceived as occurring in real-time; *i.e.* the money is withdrawn from their account immediately following the authorization request from the merchant, which in many countries, is the case when making an online debit purchase. However, when a purchase is made using the "credit" (offline debit) option, the transaction merely places an authorization hold on the customer's account; funds are not actually withdrawn until the transaction is reconciled and hard-posted to the customer's account, usually a few days later. However, the previous sentence applies to all kinds of transaction types, at least when using a card issued by a European bank. This is in contrast to a typical credit card transaction; though it can also have a lag time of a few days before the transaction is posted to the account, it can be many days to a month or more before the consumer makes repayment with actual money.

Because of this, in the case of a benign or malicious error by the merchant or bank, a debit transaction may cause more serious problems (for example, money not accessible; overdrawn account) than in the case of a credit card transaction (for example, credit not accessible; over credit limit). This is especially true in the United States, where check fraud is a crime in every state, but exceeding your credit limit is not.

Internet purchases

Debit cards may also be used on the Internet. Internet transactions may be conducted in either online or offline mode, although shops accepting online-only cards are rare in some countries (such as Sweden), while they are common in other countries (such as the Netherlands). For a comparison, PayPal offers the customer to use an online-only Maestro card if the customer enters a Dutch address of residence, but not if the same customer enters a Swedish address of residence.

Internet purchases use neither a PIN code nor a signature for identification. Transactions may be conducted in either credit or debit mode (which is sometimes, but not always, indicated on the receipt), and this has nothing to do with whether the transaction was conducted on online or offline mode, since both credit and debit transactions may be conducted in both modes.

Overdraft fees

A 2007 Washington Post article — on banks' lucrative debit card overdraft fees — pointed out that debit card issuers could notify customers electronically, allowing them to avoid overdraft fees. Nessa Feddis, banking industry spokesperson and lobbyist, contended that "current technology makes real-time notification of overdrafts cost-prohibitive."[13] The article contended that "financial institutions don't want to change the status quo because they make good and easy money off their own customers' mistakes and irresponsibility."[13]

Debit cards around the world

In some countries, banks tend to levy a small fee for each debit card transaction. In some countries (for example, the UK) the merchants bear all the costs and customers are not charged. There are many people who routinely use debit cards for all transactions, no matter how small. Some (small) retailers refuse to accept debit cards for small transactions, where paying the transaction fee would absorb the profit margin on the sale, making the transaction uneconomic for the retailer.

Australia

Debit cards in Australia are called different names depending on the issuing bank: Commonwealth Bank of Australia: **Keycard**; Westpac Banking Corporation: **Handycard**; National Australia Bank: **FlexiCard**; ANZ Bank: **Access card**; Bendigo Bank: **Cashcard**.

EFTPOS is very popular in Australia and has been operating there since the 1980s. EFTPOS-enabled cards are accepted at almost all swipe terminals able to accept credit cards, regardless of the bank that issued the card, including Maestro cards issued by foreign banks, with most businesses accepting them, with 450,000 point of sale terminals.[14]

EFTPOS cards can also be used to deposit and withdraw cash over the counter at Australia Post outlets participating in giroPost, just as if the transaction was conducted at a bank branch, even if the bank branch is closed. Electronic transactions in Australia are generally processed via the Telstra Argent and Optus Transact Plus network - which has recently superseded the old Transcend network in the last few years. Most early keycards were only usable for EFTPOS and at ATM or bank branches, whilst the new debit card system works in the same ways a credit card, except it will only use funds in the specified bank account. This means that, among other advantages, the new system is suitable for electronic purchases without a delay of 2 to 4 days for bank-to-bank money transfers.

Australia operates both electronic credit card transaction authorization and traditional EFTPOS debit card authorization systems, the difference between the two being that EFTPOS transactions are authorized by a personal identification number (PIN) while credit card transactions are usually authorized by the printing and signing of a receipt. If the user fails to enter the correct pin 3 times, the consequences range from the card being locked out and requiring a phone call or trip to the branch to reactivate with a new PIN, the card being cut up by the merchant, or in the case of an ATM, being kept inside the machine, both of which require a new card to be ordered.

Generally credit card transaction costs are borne by the merchant with no fee applied to the end user while EFTPOS transactions cost the consumer an applicable withdrawal fee charged by their bank.

The introduction of Visa and MasterCard debit cards along with regulation in the settlement fees charged by the operators of both EFTPOS and credit cards by the Reserve Bank has seen a continuation in the increasing ubiquity of credit card use among Australians and a general decline in the profile of EFTPOS. However, the regulation of settlement fees also removed the ability of banks, who typically provide merchant services to retailers on behalf of Visa, MasterCard or Bankcard, from stopping those retailers charging extra fees to take payment by credit card instead of cash or EFTPOS. Though only a few operators with strong market power have done so, the passing on of fees charged for credit card transactions may result in an increased use of EFTPOS.

Brazil

In Brazil debit cards are called *cartão de débito* (singular) and are getting increasingly popular[15] as a replacement of checks, that are still uncommonly popular in the country.

Canada

Canada has a nation-wide EFTPOS system, called Interac Direct Payment. Since being introduced in 1994, IDP has become the most popular payment method in the country. Previously, debit cards have been in use for ABM usage since the late 1970s, with Credit Unions in Saskatchewan and Alberta, Canada introducing the first card-based, networked ATMs beginning in June, 1977. Debit Cards, which could be used anywhere a credit card was accepted, were first introduced in Canada by Saskatchewan Credit Unions in 1982.[16] In the early 1990s, pilot projects were conducted among Canada's six largest banks to gauge security, accuracy and feasibility of the Interac system. Slowly in the later half of the 1990s, it was estimated that approximately 50% of retailers offered Interac as a source of payment. Retailers, many small transaction retailers like coffee shops, resisted offering IDP to promote faster service. In 2009, 99% of retailers offer IDP as an alternative payment form.

In Canada, the debit card is sometimes referred to as a "bank card". It is a client card issued by a bank that provides access to funds and other bank account transactions, such as transferring funds, checking balances, paying bills, etc., as well as point of purchase transactions connected on the Interac network. Since its national launch in 1994, Interac Direct Payment has become so widespread that, as of 2001, more transactions in Canada were completed using debit cards than cash.[17] This popularity may be partially attributable to two main factors: the convenience of not having to carry cash, and the availability of automated bank machines (ABMs) and Direct Payment merchants on the network.

Debit cards may be considered similar to stored-value cards in that they represent a finite amount of money owed by the card issuer to the holder. They are different in that stored-value cards are generally anonymous and are only usable at the issuer, while debit cards are generally associated with an individual's bank account and can be used anywhere on the Interac network.

In Canada, the bank cards can be used at POS and ABMs. Interac Online has also been introduced in recent years allowing clients of most major Canadian banks to use their debit cards for online payment with certain merchants as well. Certain financial institutions also allow their clients to use their debit cards in the United States on the NYCE network.[18]

Consumer protection in Canada

Consumers in Canada are protected under a voluntary code* entered into by all providers of debit card services, The Canadian Code of Practice for Consumer Debit Card Services[19] (sometimes called the "Debit Card Code"). Adherence to the Code is overseen by the Financial Consumer Agency of Canada (FCAC), which investigates consumer complaints.

According to the FCAC website, revisions to the Code that came into effect in 2005 put the onus on the financial institution to prove that a consumer was responsible for a disputed transaction, and also place a limit on the number of days that an account can be frozen during the financial institution's investigation of a transaction.

Chile

Chile has an EFTPOS system called *Redcompra* (Purchase Network) which is currently used in at least 23,000 establishments throughout the country. Goods may be purchased using this system at most supermarkets, retail stores, pubs and restaurants in major urban centers.

Colombia

Colombia has a system called **Redeban-Multicolor** and **Credibanco Visa** which are currently used in at least 23,000 establishments throughout the country. Goods may be purchased using this system at most supermarkets, retail stores, pubs and restaurants in major urban centers. Colombian debit cards are Maestro (pin), Visa Electron (pin), Visa Debit (as Credit) and MasterCard-Debit (as Credit).

Denmark

The Danish debit card Dankort was introduced on 1 September 1983, and despite the initial transactions being paper-based, the Dankort quickly won widespread acceptance in Denmark. By 1985 the first EFTPOS terminals were introduced, and 1985 was also the year when the number of Dankort transactions first exceeded 1 million.[20] It is not uncommon that Dankort is the only card accepted at smaller stores, thus making it harder for tourists to travel without cash.

Miscellaneous facts & numbers

- In 2007 PBS, the Danish operator of the Dankort system, processed a total of 737 million Dankort transactions.[21] Of these, 4.5 million just on a single day, 21 December. This remains the current record.
- At the end of 2007, there were 3.9 million Dankort in existence.[21]
- More than 80,000 Danish shops have a Dankort terminal. Another 11,000 internet shops also accept the Dankort.[21]

France

Carte Bancaire (CB), the national payment scheme, in 2008, had 57,5 milion cards carrying its logo and 7,76 billion transactions (POS and ATM) were processed through the e-rsb network (135 transactions per card mostly debit or deferred debit). Most CB cards are debit cards, either debit or deferred debit. Less than 10% of CB cards were credit cards. Banks in France charge annual fees for debit cards (despite card payments being very cost efficient for the banks), yet they do not charge personal customers for checkbooks or processing checks (despite checks being very costly for the banks). This imbalance most probably dates from the unilateral introduction in France of Chip and PIN debit cards in the early 1990s, when the cost of this technology was much higher than it is now. Credit cards of the type found in the United Kingdom and United States are unusual in France and the closest equivalent is the deferred debit card, which operates like a normal debit card, except that all purchase transactions are postponed until the end of the month, thereby giving the customer between 1 and 31 days of interest-free credit. The annual fee for a deferred debit card is around €10 more than for one with immediate debit. Most France debit cards are branded with the Carte Bleue logo, which assures acceptance throughout France. Most card holders choose to pay around €5 more in their annual fee to additionally have a Visa or a MasterCard logo on their Carte Bleue, so that the card is accepted internationally. A Carte Bleue without a Visa or a MasterCard logo is often known as a "Carte Bleue Nationale" and a Carte Bleue with a Visa or a MasterCard logo is known as a "Carte Bleue Internationale", or more frequently, simply called a "Visa" or "MasterCard". Many smaller merchants in France refuse to accept debit cards for transactions under a certain amount because of the minimum fee charged by merchants' banks per transaction (this minimum amount varies from €5 to €15.25, or in some rare cases even more). But more and more merchants accept debit cards for small amounts, due to the massive daily use of debit card nowadays. Merchants in France do not differentiate between debit and credit cards, and so both have equal acceptance. It is legal in France to set a minimum amount to transactions but the merchants must display it clearly.

Germany

Debit cards have enjoyed wide acceptance in Germany for years. Facilities already existed before EFTPOS became popular with the Eurocheque card, an authorization system initially developed for paper checks where, in addition to signing the actual check, customers also needed to show the card alongside the check as a security measure. Those cards could also be used at ATMs and for card-based electronic funds transfer (called **Girocard**) with PIN entry. These are now the only functions of such cards: the Eurocheque system (along with the brand) was abandoned in 2002 during the transition from the Deutsche Mark to the euro. As of 2005, most stores and petrol outlets have EFTPOS facilities. Processing fees are paid by the businesses, which leads to some business owners refusing debit card payments for sales totalling less than a certain amount, usually 5 or 10 euro.

To avoid the processing fees, many businesses resorted to using **direct debit**, which is then called *electronic* **direct debit** (German: *Elektronisches Lastschriftverfahren*, abbr. *ELV*). The point-of-sale terminal reads the bank sort code and account number from the card but instead of handling the transaction through the Girocard network it simply prints a form, which the customer signs to authorise the debit note. However, this method also avoids any verification or payment guarantee provided by the network. Further, customers can return debit notes by notifying their bank without giving a reason. This means that the beneficiary bears the risk of fraud and illiquidity. Some business mitigate the risk by consulting a proprietary blacklist or by switching to Girocard for higher transaction amounts.

Around 2000, an **Electronic Purse Card** was introduced, dubbed **Geldkarte** ("money card"). It makes use of the smart card chip on the front of the standard issue debit card. This chip can be charged with up to 200 euro, and is advertised as a means of making medium to very small payments, even down to several euros or cent payments. The key factor here is that no processing fees are deducted by banks. It did not gain the popularity its inventors had hoped for. However, this could change as this chip is now used as means of age verification at cigarette vending machines, which has been mandatory since January 2007. Furthermore, some payment discounts are being offered (*e.g.* a 10% reduction for public transport fares) when paying with "Geldkarte". The "Geldkarte" payment lacks all security measures, since it does not require the user to enter a PIN or sign a sales slip: the loss of a "Geldkarte" is similar to the loss of a wallet or purse - anyone who finds it can then use their find to pay for their own purchases.

Hong Kong

A popular payment instant method widely used in Hong Kong is EPS. Bank customers can use their ATM card to make an instant EPS payment, much like a debit card. Most banks in Hong Kong provide ATM cards with EPS capability.

Hungary

In Hungary debit cards are far more common and popular than credit cards. Many Hungarians even refer to their debit card ("betéti kártya") mistakenly using the word for credit card ("hitelkártya").[22]

India

The debit card has limited popularity in India as the merchant is charged for each transaction. The debit card therefore is mostly used for ATM transactions. Most of the banks issue VISA debit cards, while some banks (like SBI and Citibank India) issue Maestro cards. The debit card transactions are routed through the VISA or MasterCard networks rather than directly via the issuing bank.

The National Payments Corporation of India (NPCI) is introducing a payment network and debit card dubbed 'India card'. The Reserve Bank of India is expecting this system will gradually replace the overseas run networks from Visa and MaterCard for Indian ATM, debit and credit card services.[23]

Iraq

Iraq's two biggest state-owned banks, Rafidain Bank and Rasheed Bank, together with the *Iraqi Electronic Payment System (IEPS)* have established a company called International Smart Card [24], which have developed a national credit card called 'Qi Card'. The card is issued since 2008. According to the company's website: 'after less than two years of the initial launch of the Qi card solution, we have hit 1.6 million cardholder with the potential to issue 2 million cards by the end of 2010, issuing about 100,000 card monthly is a testament to the huge success of the Qi card solution. Parallel to this will be the expansion into retail stores through a network of points of sales of about 30,000 units by 2015'

Italy

Debit cards are quite popular in Italy. There are both classic and prepaid cards. The main classic debit card in Italy is **PagoBancomat**: this kind of card is issued by Italian banks, often with a credit card (so you get a dual mode card). It allows access to the owner's bank account funds and it is widely accepted in most shops, although on the Internet it is allowed only the credit card mode. The major debit prepaid card is issued by Poste Italiane S.p.A., is called Postepay and runs on the Visa Electron circuit. It can be used on Poste Italiane's ATMs (Postamat) and on Visa Electron-compatible bank ATMs all over the world. It has no fees when used on the Internet and in POS-based transactions. Other cards are issued by other companies, such as Vodafone CashCard, Banca di Milano's Carta Jeans and Carta Moneta Online.

Japan

In Japan people usually use their *cash cards* (キャッシュカード *kyasshu kādo*), originally intended only for use with cash machines, as debit cards. The debit functionality of these cards is usually referred to as *J-Debit* (ジェイデビット *Jeidebitto*), and only cash cards from certain banks can be used. A cash card has the same size as a VISA/MasterCard. As identification, the user will have to enter his or her four-digit PIN when paying. J-Debit was started in Japan on March 6, 2000.

Suruga Bank began service of Japan's first Visa Debit in 2006. Ebank will start service of Visa Debit by the end of 2007.[24]

Kuwait

In Kuwait, all banks provide a debit card to their account holders. This card is branded as KNET, which is the central switch in Kuwait. KNET card transactions are free for both customer and the merchant and therefore KNET debit cards are used for low valued transactions as well. KNET cards are mostly co-branded as Maestro or Visa Electron which makes it possible to use the same card outside Kuwait on any terminal supporting these payment schemes.

The Netherlands

In the Netherlands using EFTPOS is known as *pinnen* (**pin**ning), a term derived from the use of a Personal Identification Number. PINs are also used for ATM transactions, and the term is used interchangeably by many people, although it was introduced as a marketing brand for EFTPOS. The system was launched in 1987, and in 2010 there were 258,585 terminals throughout the country, including mobile terminals used by delivery services and on markets. All banks offer a debit card suitable for EFTPOS with current accounts.

PIN transactions are usually free to the customer, but the retailer is charged per-transaction and monthly fees. Equens, an association with all major banks as its members, runs the system, and until August 2005 also charged for it. Responding to allegations of monopoly abuse, it has handed over contractual responsibilities to its member banks, who now offer competing contracts. Interpay, a legal predecessor of Equens, was fined €47 million in 2004, but the fine was later dropped, and a related fine for banks was lowered from €17 million to €14 million. Per-transaction fees are between 5-10 eurocents, depending on volume.

Credit cards use in the Netherlands is very low, and most credit cards cannot be used with EFTPOS, or charge very high fees to the customer. Debit cards can often, though not always, be used in the entire EU for EFTPOS. Most debit cards are Maestro cards.

Electronic Purse Cards (called **Chipknip**) were introduced in 1996, but have never become very popular.

New Zealand

The EFTPOS (electronic fund transfer at point of sale) in New Zealand is highly popular. In 2006, 70 percent of all retail transactions were made by eftpos, with an average of 306 EFTPOS transaction being made per person. At the same time, there were 125,000 EFTPOS terminals in operation (one for every 30 people), and 5.1 million EFTPOS cards in circulation (1.27 per capita).[25]

The system involves the merchant swiping (or inserting) the customer's card and entering the purchase amount. Point of sale systems with integrated EFTPOS often sent the purchase total to the terminal and the customer swipes their own card. The customer then selects the account they wish to use: Current/Cheque (CHQ), Savings (SAV), or Credit Card (CRD), before entering in their PIN. After a short processing time in which the terminal contacts the EFTPOS network and the bank, the transaction is accepted (or declined) and a receipt is printed. The EFTPOS system is used for credit cards as well, with a customer selecting Credit Card and entering their PIN, or for older credit cards without loaded PIN, pressing OK and signing their receipt with identification through matching signatures. Larger businesses connect to the EFTPOS network by dedicated phone lines or more recently internet protocol connections. Most smaller businesses however have their EFTPOS terminals communicate through their regular voice line, often resulting in shouts for people to get off the phone or "Declined Transmission Error" transactions when the merchant forgets someone is on the phone.

Virtually all retail outlets have EFTPOS facilities, so much that retailers without EFTPOS have to advertise so. In addition, an increasing number of mobile operator, such as taxis, stall holders and pizza deliverers have mobile EFTPOS systems. The system is made up of two primary networks: EFTPOS NZ, which is owned by ANZ National Bank and Paymark Limited (formerly Electronic Transaction Services Limited), which is owned by ASB Bank, Westpac and the Bank of New Zealand. The two networks are intertwined and highly sophisticated and secure, able to handle huge volumes of transactions during busy periods such as the lead-up to Christmas. Network failures are rare, but when they occur they cause massive disruption, resulting in major delays and loss of income for businesses. Most businesses have to resort to manual "zip-zap" swipe machines in such case.[26] Newer POS-based terminals have the ability to "capture" transactions in the event of a communications break-down - instead of entering a PIN, the customer signs their receipt and the transaction is accepted on a matching signature, and the transaction is stored until the network is restored. A notable example of this occurs on the Cook Strait ferries, where in the middle of Cook Strait there is no mobile phone reception to connect to the EFTPOS network.

EFTPOS is used for transactions large and small, from 10c up to thousands of dollars (or the daily limit of the EFTPOS card). Depending on the user's bank, a fee may be charged for use of EFTPOS. Most youth accounts do not attract fees for electronic transactions, meaning the use of EFTPOS by the younger generations has become ubiquitous (and subsequently cash use becoming rare). Typically merchants don't pay fees for transactions, most only having to pay for the equipment rental.

ATM cards and EFTPOS cards were once separate, but today EFTPOS and ATM cards are combined into a single EFTPOS-ATM card. The cards are issued by banks to customers, and often come in multiple designs, with some banks allowing customers to place a picture of their choice on their EFTPOS card. One of the disadvantages of New Zealand's well-established EFTPOS system is that it is incompatible with overseas systems and non-face-to-face purchases. In response to this, many banks have adopted international debit card systems such as Maestro and Visa Debit in addition to the New Zealand EFTPOS system.

Philippines

In the Philippines, all three national ATM network consortia offer proprietary PIN debit. This was first offered by Express Payment System in 1987, followed by Megalink with **Paylink** in 1993 then BancNet with the Point-of-Sale in 1994.

Express Payment System or EPS was the pioneer provider, having launched the service in 1987 on behalf of the Bank of the Philippine Islands. The EPS service has subsequently been extended in late 2005 to include the other Expressnet members: Banco de Oro and Land Bank of the Philippines. They currently operate 10,000 terminals for their cardholders.

Megalink launched Paylink EFTPOS system in 1993. Terminal services are provided by Equitable Card Network on behalf of the consortium. Service is available in 2,000 terminals, mostly in Metro Manila.

BancNet introduced their Point of sale System in 1994 as the first consortium-operated EFTPOS service in the country. The service is available in over 1,400 locations throughout the Philippines, including second and third-class municipalities. In 2005, BancNet signed a Memorandum of Agreement to serve as the local gateway for China UnionPay, the sole ATM switch in the People's Republic of China. This will allow the estimated 1.0 billion Chinese ATM cardholders to use the BancNet ATMs and the EFTPOS in all participating merchants.

Visa debit cards are issued by Union Bank of the Philippines (e-Wallet & eon), Chinatrust, Equicom Savings Bank (Key Card & Cash Card), Banco De Oro, HSBC, HSBC Savings Bank & Sterling Bank of Asia (VISA ShopNPay prepaid and debit cards). Union Bank of the Philippines cards, Equicom Savings Bank & Sterling Bank of Asia EMV cards which can also be used for internet purchases. Sterling Bank of Asia has released its first line of prepaid and debit Visa cards with EMV chip. MasterCard debit cards are issued by Banco de Oro, Security Bank (Cashlink & Cash Card) & Smart Communications (Smart Money) tied up with Banco De Oro. MasterCard Electronic cards are issued by BPI (Express Cash) and Security Bank (CashLink Plus). All VISA and MasterCard based debit cards in the Philippines are non-embossed and are marked either for "Electronic Use Only" (VISA/MasterCard) or "Valid only where MasterCard Electronic is Accepted" (MasterCard Electronic).

Poland

In Poland, local debit cards, such as PolCard, have become largely substituted with international ones, such as Visa, MasterCard, or the unembossed Visa Electron or Maestro. Most banks in Poland block Internet and MOTO transactions with unembossed cards, requiring the customer to buy an embossed card or a card for Internet/MOTO transactions only. The number of banks which do not block MOTO transactions on unembossed cards has recently started to increase.

Portugal

In Portugal, debit cards are accepted almost everywhere: ATMs, stores, and so on. The most commonly accepted are Visa and MasterCard, or the unembossed Visa Electron or Maestro. Regarding Internet payments debit cards can't be used for transfers, due to its unsafeness, so banks recommend the use of 'MBnet', a pre-registered safe system that creates a virtual card with a pre-selected credit limit. All the card system is regulated by SIBS, the institution created by Portuguese banks to manage all the regulations and communication processes proply. SIBS' shareholders are all the 27 banks operating in Portugal.

Russia

In addition to VISA and Master Card, there are some local payment system based in general on Smart Card technology.

- Sbercard. This payment system was created by Sberbank around 1995–1996. It uses BGS Smartcard Systems AG [28] smart card technology that is, **DUET**. Sberbank was a single retail bank in USSR before 1990. De facto this is a payment system of the SberBank.
- Zolotaya Korona. This card brand was created in 1994. Zolotaya Korona is based on CFT technology.
- STB Card [29]. This card uses the classic magnetic stripe technology. It almost fully collapsed after 1998 (GKO crisis) with STB bank failure.
- Union Card [30]. The card also uses the classic magnetic stripe technology. This card brand is on the decline. These accounts are being reissued as Visa or MasterCard accounts.

Nearly every transaction, regardless of brand or system, is processed as an immediate debit transaction. Non-debit transactions within these systems have spending limits that are strictly limited when compared with typical Visa or MasterCard accounts.

Saudi Arabia

In Saudi Arabia, all debit card transactions are routed trough Saudi Payments Network (SPAN), the only electronic payment system in the Kingdom and all banks are required by the Saudi Arabian Monetary Agency (SAMA) to issue cards fully compatible with the network. It connects all point of sale (POS) terminals throughout the country to a central payment switch which in turn re-routes the financial transactions to the card issuer, local bank, VISA, AMEX or MasterCard.

As well as its use for debit cards, the network is also used for ATM and credit card transactions.

Singapore

Singapore's debit service is managed by Network for Electronic Transfers (NETS [31]), founded by Singapore's leading banks (and shareholders) namely DBS, Keppel Bank, OCBC (and it's associates), OUB, IBS, POSB, Tat Lee Bank and UOB in 1985 as a result of a need for a centralised e-Payment operator.It will deduct money from your bank directly when you buy things using debit cards.

However,due to the banking restructuring and mergers, the local banks became UOB, OCBC, DBS-POSB as the shareholders of NETS with Standard Chartered Bank to offer NETS to their customers. However, DBS and POSB customers can use their network atms on their own and not be shared with UOB, OCBC or SCB (StanChart). The mega failure of 5 July 2010 of POSB-DBS ATM Networks (97,000 machines!) made the government to rethink the shared ATM system again as it affected the NETS system too.

In 2010, in line with the mandatory EMV system, Local Singapore Banks starts to reissue their Debit Visa/Mastercard branded debit cards with the EMV Chip compliant ones compared to the magnetic stripe system in place. Banks involved includes the NETS Members of POSB-DBS, UOB-OCBC-SCB along with the SharedATM alliance (NON-NETS) of HSBC, Citibank, State Bank of India, Malayan Banking Berhad or Maybank. Standard Chartered Bank (SCB) is also a SharedATM alliance member.Non branded cards of POSB and MAYBANK local ATM Cards are kept without a chip but has a Plus or Maestro sign so that they can use it only to draw cash locally or overseas.

Maybank Debit Mastercard are also available to use in Malaysia just as a normal ATM or DEBIT MEPS card.

Singapore also uses the e-purse systems of NETS CASHCARD and the CEPAS wave system by EZ-Link [32] and NETS.

United Kingdom

In the UK debit cards (an integrated EFTPOS system) are an established part of the retail market and are widely accepted both by bricks and mortar stores and by internet stores. The term EFTPOS is not widely used by the public; debit card is the generic term used. Cards commonly in circulation include Maestro (previously Switch), Debit MasterCard, Visa Debit (previously Visa Delta) and Visa Electron. Banks do not charge customers for EFTPOS transactions in the UK, but some retailers make small charges, particularly where the transaction amount in question is small. The UK has converted all debit cards in circulation to Chip and PIN (except for Chip and Signature cards issued to people with certain disabilities), based on the EMV standard, to increase transaction security; however, PINs are not required for internet transactions.

In the United Kingdom, banks started to issue debit cards in the mid 1980s in a bid to reduce the number of cheques being used at the point of sale, which are costly for the banks to process; the first bank to do so was Barclays with the *Barclays Connect* card. As in most countries, fees paid by merchants in the United Kingdom to accept credit cards are a percentage of the transaction amount,[27] which funds card holders' interest-free credit periods as well as incentive schemes such as points, airmiles or cashback. Debit cards do not usually have these characteristics, and so the fee for merchants to accept debit cards is a low fixed amount, regardless of transaction amount.[27] For very small amounts, this means it is cheaper for a merchant to accept a credit card than a debit card. Although merchants won the right through The Credit Cards (Price Discrimination) Order 1990 [34] to charge customers different prices according to the payment method, few merchants in the UK charge less for payment by debit card than by credit card, the most notable exceptions being budget airlines, travel agents and IKEA.[28] Debit cards in the UK lack the advantages offered to holders of UK-issued credit cards, such as free incentives (points, airmiles, cashback etc.), interest-free credit and protection against defaulting merchants under Section 75 of the Consumer Credit Act 1974 [36]. Almost all establishments in the United Kingdom that accept credit cards also accept debit cards (although not always Solo and Visa Electron), but a minority of merchants, for cost reasons, accept debit cards and not credit cards.

United States

In the U.S., EFTPOS is universally referred to simply as *debit*. The same interbank networks that operate the ATM network also operate the POS network. Most interbank networks, such as Pulse, NYCE, MAC, Tyme, SHAZAM, STAR, and so on, are regional and do not overlap, however, most ATM/POS networks have agreements to accept each other's cards. This means that cards issued by one network will typically work anywhere they accept ATM/POS cards for payment. For example, a NYCE card will work at a Pulse POS terminal or ATM, and vice versa. Many debit cards in the United States are issued with a Visa or MasterCard logo allowing use of their signature-based networks.

The liability of a U.S. debit card user in case of loss or theft is up to $50 USD if the loss or theft is reported to the issuing bank in two business days after the customer notices the loss.[29]

The fees charged to merchants on offline debit purchases—and the lack of fees charged merchants for processing online debit purchases and paper checks—have prompted some major merchants in the U.S. to file lawsuits against debit-card transaction processors such as Visa and MasterCard. In 2003, Visa and MasterCard agreed to settle the largest of these lawsuits and agreed to settlements of billions of dollars. However, the many comparisons between signature debit and other forms of payment are moot, since there are costs associated with cash that are not factored in, and there is an underlying presumption that the EFT network will remain free, when, in fact, banks could choose to levy fees on both consumers and merchants if they choose.

Some consumers prefer "credit" transactions because of the lack of a fee charged to the consumer/purchaser; also, a few debit cards in the U.S. offer rewards for using "credit" (for example, S&T Bank's "Preferred Debit Rewards Card" [30]). However, since "credit" costs more for merchants, many terminals at PIN-accepting merchant locations now make the "credit" function more difficult to access. For example, if you swipe a debit card at Wal-Mart in the

U.S., you are immediately presented with the PIN screen for online debit; to use offline debit you must press "cancel" to exit the PIN screen, then press "credit" on the next screen.

2009-07-08: Minimum and Maximum Charges for Visa in USA

The Merchants Agreement for Visa states (page 9, or 14/141 in PDF):

Always honor valid Visa cards in your acceptance category, regardless of the dollar amount of the purchase. Imposing minimum or maximum purchase amounts in order to accept a Visa card transaction is a violation of the Visa rules.[31]

Thanks to the Dodd-Frank Act, U.S. merchants can now set a minimum purchase amount on credit cards (but not debit cards), not to exceed $10. [32] [33]

FSA, HRA, and HSA debit cards

In the U.S.A, a FSA debit card only allows medical expenses. It is used by some banks for withdrawals from their FSAs, MSAs, and HSAs as well. They have Visa or MasterCard logos, but cannot be used as "debit cards", only as "credit cards"", and they are not accepted by all merchants that accept debit and credit cards, but only by those that accept FSA debit cards. Merchant codes and product codes are used at the point of sale (required by law by certain merchants by certain dates in the USA) to restrict sales if they do not qualify. Because of the extra checking and documenting that goes on, later, the statement can be used to substantiate these purchases for tax deductions. In the occasional instance that a qualifying purchase is rejected, another form of payment must be used (a check or payment from another account and a claim for reimbursement later). In the more likely case that non-qualifying items are accepted, the consumer is technically still responsible, and the discrepancy could be revealed during an audit. A small but growing segment of the debit card business in the U.S. involves access to tax-favored spending accounts such as flexible spending accounts (FSA), health reimbursement accounts (HRA), and health savings accounts (HSA). Most of these debit cards are for medical expenses, though a few are also issued for dependent care and transportation expenses.

Traditionally, FSAs (the oldest of these accounts) were accessed only through claims for reimbursement after incurring, and often paying, an out-of-pocket expense; this often happens after the funds have already been deducted from the employee's paycheck. (FSAs are usually funded by payroll deduction.) The only method permitted by the Internal Revenue Service (IRS) to avoid this "double-dipping" for medical FSAs and HRAs is through accurate and auditable reporting on the tax return. Statements on the debit card that say "for medical uses only" are invalid for several reasons: (1) The merchant and issuing banks have no way of quickly determining whether the entire purchase qualifies for the customer's type of tax benefit; (2) the customer also has no quick way of knowing; often has mixed purchases by necessity or convenience; and can easily make mistakes; (3) extra contractual clauses between the customer and issuing bank would cross-over into the payment processing standards, creating additional confusion (for example if a customer was penalized for accidentally purchasing a non-qualifying item, it would undercut the potential savings advantages of the account). Therefore, using the card exclusively for qualifying purchases may be convenient for the customer, but it has nothing to do with how the card can actually be used. If the bank rejects a transaction, for instance, because it is not at a recognized drug store, then it would be causing harm and confusion to the cardholder. In the United States, not all medical service or supply stores are capable of providing the correct information so an FSA debit card issuer can honor every transaction-if rejected or documentation is not deemed enough to satisfy regulations, cardholders may have to send in forms manually.

References

[1] Säkra kortbetalningar på Internet | Nordea.se (http://www.nordea.se/Privat/Kort+och+betalningar/Kort/Säkra+kortbetalningar+på+Internet/205784.html)

[2] "Swedbank e-kort" (http://www.swedbank.se/sst/inf/kort-och-betalningar/0,,135189,00.html). Swedbank. .

[3] Martin, Andrew (January 4, 2010). "How Visa, Using Card Fees, Dominates a Market" (http://www.nytimes.com/2010/01/05/your-money/credit-and-debit-cards/05visa.html?em=&pagewanted=all). *New York Times*. . Retrieved 2010-01-06.

[4] http://www.revenuetoday.com/story/no-check-please No Check, Please

[5] http://accounting.smartpros.com/x59817.xml Companies Use Debit Cards to Pay Workers

[6] Caxton FX prepaid cards (http://www.caxtonfxcard.com/cards_description.asp?dist=CAXTGENL)

[7] Travelex (http://www.cashpassport.com)

[8] http://www.transcash.com/index.html

[9] "Debit card facts" (http://www.pirg.org/consumer/banks/debit/debitcards1.htm). U.S. PIRG. .

[10] Your Liability for Unauthorized Credit and Debit Card Charges (http://www.nolo.com/legal-encyclopedia/article-29654.html)

[11] Fact Sheet 131: Credit Card vs. Debit Card (http://www.idtheftcenter.org/artman2/publish/c_guide/Fact_Sheet_131.shtml)

[12] "Dollar Car rental - General Policies" (http://www.dollar.com/AboutUs/GeneralPolicies.aspx). Dollar car rental. .

[13] "They Want You to Go Over Your Debit Limit" (http://www.washingtonpost.com/wp-dyn/content/article/2007/07/18/AR2007071802394.html). The Washington Post, Michelle Singletary, July 19, 2007. 2007-07-19. . Retrieved 2010-05-01.

[14] MasterCard Maestro (http://www.maestrocard.com/cgi-bin/wheretouse.cgi?country=002&Select+a+country.x=14&Select+a+country.y=2&region=01)

[15] http://www1.folha.uol.com.br/fsp/dinheiro/fi3004201007.htm

[16] http://esask.uregina.ca/entry/automated_teller_machines.html

[17] "Consumers and Changing Retail Markets" (http://www.ic.gc.ca/eic/site/oca-bc.nsf/eng/ca02096.html). Canada's Office of Consumer Affairs (OCA). .

[18] "NYCE - Participating Canadian Financial Institutions" (http://www.nyce.net/consumers/canadian/canadian_banks/index.htm). NYCE Payment network. .

[19] FCAC - For the Industry - Reference Documents (http://www.fcac-acfc.gc.ca/eng/industry/RefDocs/default.asp#dcc)

[20] Dankortet fylder 25 år i dag (http://www.version2.dk/artikel/8297)

[21] PBS Årsrapport 2007 (http://www.pbs.dk/wwcm/resources/file/ebe8a4094bde751/pbs-aarsrapport_2007_DK.pdf)

[22] http://www.deccanherald.com/content/21014/rbi-fixes-five-free-atm.html

[23] "India card to replace Master, Visa" (http://www.mydigitalfc.com/banking/india-card-replace-master-visa-221). mydigitalfc.com. 6 December 2009. .

[24] eBank Money Card - eBank Corporation(Japan) (http://www.ebank.co.jp/english/saver.html)

[25] "Payment and Settlement Systems in New Zealand" (http://www.rbnz.govt.nz/finstab/payment/3236268.pdf). *Reserve Bank of New Zealand*. March 2008. . Retrieved 2010-09-19.

[26] http://www.stuff.co.nz/stuff/0,2106,3521599a10,00.html

[27] "Electronic payment system pricing" (http://www.electronic-payments.co.uk/pricing.jsp). RSTO electronic-payments.co.uk. .

[28] "IKEA FAQ 70p charge on credit cards in IKEA stores" (http://www.ikea.com/ms/en_GB/customer_service/faq/faq.html#0700). IKEA. .

[29] Consumer Handbook to Credit Protection Laws: Electronic Fund Transfers (http://www.federalreserve.gov/pubs/consumerhdbk/electronic.htm#loss)

[30] http://www.stbank.com/PreferredAccount/DebitRewardsCard.aspx

[31] http://usa.visa.com/download/merchants/rules_for_visa_merchants.pdf

[32] http://usa.visa.com/about_visa/ask_visa/index.html

[33] http://www.paymentssource.com/news/merchants-debit-transactions-cheaper-3003058-1.html

Decoupled debit card

A **decoupled debit card** is a debit card that is not issued by, and not tied to, a particular retail financial institution, such as a bank or credit union. In May 2007, Capital One began a one year decoupled debit card experiment [1] . This card is novel in that prior to this launch, a debit card was always tied to a traditional financial institution. Capital One's Mastercard-branded decoupled card did not require an account be opened with a retail financial institution, and was made in partnership with the Ukrops grocery chain, based in CapOne's hometown of Richmond, VA. The card was also tied to a reward program offered by Ukrops. That one-year experiment ended in May 2008[2] , and has been followed up with a national rollout of its own version of a decoupled debit card tied to its own reward program[3] .

References

[1] CapitalOne becomes a Bank with checking accounts (http://thebankwatch.com/2007/06/04/capitalone-becomes-a-bank-with-checking-accounts/)

[2] CapOne says its decoupled debit card pilots ended on schedule (http://www.digitaltransactions.net/newsstory.cfm?newsid=1776)

[3] Decoupled debit card lives again! (http://www.paymentindustryinsider.com/2008/07/decoupled-debit-card-lives-again/)

External links

• Capital One's debit card (http://www.capitalone.com:80/debit/index2.php) (this card is no longer being offered)

Demand draft

A **demand draft**, also known as a **remotely created check**, a **tele-check**, or check by phone, check by fax or echeck, is a check created by a merchant with a buyer's checking account number on it, but without the buyer's original signature.

Check drafting is creating a valid legal copy of the customer's check, on the customer's behalf. Because it is created by the merchant, no signature is

A demand draft

required. Instead, a signature disclaimer or facsimile is entered in the signature blank.[1] A check draft is typically for deposit only.[2]

The Uniform Commercial Code permits the process of check drafting by defining signature in the following regulation: Uniform Commercial Code, Title 1, Section 1-201 (39).[3]

This regulation only makes check drafting possible, not "required." Your bank may deny your items for deposit if they have reason to be suspicious. Suspicious items are covered in Regulation CC 229.13, Exceptions.[4]

Authorization is indicated on a check draft in the signature blank, usually by a statement such as the following: "This draft is preauthorized by your depositor, no signature required.".

Demand drafts are frequently used to purchase items over the phone, from telemarketers. The checks also allow consumers to pay monthly bills by having them debited automatically out of their accounts, rather than having to write a new check each month.[5]

Unlike ACH transactions that are governed by NACHA regulations,[6] check drafting allows outbound telemarketers to accept these types of phone payments if they comply with the FTC Regulations 16 CFR 310 in regard to proper record keeping.[7]

Demand drafts are frequently used by consumers instead of credit cards, and large companies also commonly use them.[8]

Demand drafts are also a popular method for lending institutions to attempt to collect on overdue loans.[9]

Demand drafts entail a large potential for fraud. Banks report that demand draft fraud is becoming more common.[5] Under the current Federal Reserve Board guidelines the customer has a time frame of 90 days from the time the check was deposited to dispute the transactions. (www.frbservices.org/operations/checkadjutsments/urcc.html)

Demand draft fraud can be frustrating for consumers, because unlike credit card or ACH disputes, consumers are not often given any funds back until after investigation finds that the draft was unauthorized. In addition, filing a dispute frequently requires a notarized signature, since this is the only way one bank can dispute a paper item with another bank.

In 2005, the US Federal Reserve issued a regulation (effective July 1, 2006) shifting responsibility for payment of fraudulent demand drafts from the bank it is drawn on to the bank that accepts it as a deposit.[10]

Most recent developments in check drafting, which helps to facilitate checks by phone, checks by fax and online check payments is the new "Substitute Check Law" known as Check 21, enacted on October 28, 2004, which has greatly increased the use of check drafting.[11]

Other Items Considered Demand Drafts

- Cashier's check
- Money order
- Income Tax Refund Check
- Insurance Draft Payment
- Traveler's cheque

References

[1] http://www.law.cornell.edu/ucc/1/1-201.html#signed_1-201
[2] http://www.bankersonline.com/operations/gurus_op030402l.html
[3] http://www.supremelaw.org/ref/ucc/ucc1.htm
[4] http://frwebgate.access.gpo.gov/cgi-bin/get-cfr.cgi?TITLE=12&PART=229&SECTION=13&YEAR=1999&TYPE=TEXT
[5] Shonk, Krista J. November 9, 2005. America's Community Bankers. (http://www.federalreserve.gov/SECRS/2005/November/20051115/ OP-1232/OP-1232_13_1.pdf) federalreserve.gov. Retrieved on July 11, 2007.
[6] http://nacha.org
[7] http://www.ftc.gov/os/2000/02/telesalesrule16cfr310.htm
[8] Prepared statement of the Federal Trade Commission Presented by Jodie Bernstein before the House banking committee. April 15, 1996. Demand Draft Fraud (http://www.ftc.gov/speeches/other/ddraft.htm). Retrieved on July 11, 2007.
[9] Association for Financial Professionals. October 5, 2005. Thieves Exploit Demand Draft. (http://www.afponline.org/pub/res/news/ ns_20051005_thieves.html) Retrieved on July 11, 2007.
[10] (http://www.federalreserve.gov/boarddocs/press/bcreg/2005/20051121/attachment.pdf)
[11] http://www.ftc.gov/bcp/edu/pubs/consumer/credit/cre37.shtm

Depository Trust & Clearing Corporation

WARNING: Article could not be rendered - ouputting plain text.

Potential causes of the problem are: (a) a bug in the pdf-writer software (b) problematic Mediawiki markup (c) table is too wide

Depository Trust & Clearing CorporationTypes of business entityTypePrivate companyPrivateIndustryFinanceGenreHolding companyFounded DTCC (1999) - holding company for DTC (1973) and NSCC (1976)HeadquartersNew York City, United StatesU.S.Number of locations 10Key people Donald F. Donahue Chairman, CEO Michael C. Bodson President, COOServices financialRevenue United States dollarUS$960,249,000 (2009)Net income US$ 104,774,000 (2009)AssetTotal assets US$37,719,148,000Equity (finance)Total equity US $501,326,000Owner(s)NYSE, Financial Industry Regulatory AuthorityNASD, American Stock ExchangeAMEX, banks, brokersSubsidiarySubsidiaries NSCCDTCFICCDTCC Deriv/SERV LLCDTCC Solutions LLCEuroCCP Ltd.DTCC Loan/SERV LLCAvoxWarehouse Trust Company LLCDTCC Derivatives Repository Ltd.Website www.dtcc.com The Depository Trust & Clearing Corporation (DTCC), based primarily at 55 Water Street in New York City, is the world's largest post-trade financial services company. DTCC was established in 1999 as a holding company to combine The Depository Trust Company (DTC) and National Securities Clearing Corporation (NSCC). It was set up to provide an efficient and safe way for buyers and sellers of security (finance)securities to make their exchange, and thus "clearing (financial)clear and settlement (finance)settle" transactions. It also provides Central Securities Depositorycentral custody of securities.User-owned and directed, it automates, centralizes, standardizes, and streamlines processes that are critical to the safety and soundness of the world's capital markets. Through its subsidiaries, DTCC provides clearance, settlement, and information services for equities, corporate and municipal Bond (finance)bonds, unit investment trusts, government and mortgage-backed securitymortgage-backed securities, money market instruments, and over-the-counter Derivative (finance)derivatives. DTCC is also a leading processor of mutual funds and insurance transactions, linking funds and carriers with their distribution networks. DTCC's Depository Trust Company (DTC) provides custody and asset servicing for 3.5 million securities issues, mostly stocks and Bond (finance)bonds, from the United States and 110 other countries and territories, valued at $40 trillion, more than any other depository in the world. In 2007, DTCC settled the vast majority of securities transactions in the United States, more than $1.86 quadrillion in value. DTCC has operating facilities in New York City, and at multiple locations in and outside the U.S. OperationStocks held by DTC are kept in the name of its partnership nominee, Cede & Co. Not all securities are eligible to be settled through DTC ("DTC-eligible"). History Established in 1973, The Depository Trust Company (DTC) was created to alleviate the rising volumes of Red tapepaperwork and the lack of security that developed after rapid growth in the volume of transactions in the U.S. securities industry in the late 1960s. Before DTC and NSCC were formed, brokers physically exchanged certificates, employing hundreds of messengers to carry certificates and checks. The mechanisms brokers used to transfer securities and keep records relied heavily on pen and paper. The exchange of physical stock certificates was difficult, inefficient, and increasingly expensive. In the late 1960s, with an unprecedented surge in trading leading to volumes of nearly 15 million shares a day on the NYSE in April 1968 (as opposed to 5 million a day just three years earlier, which at the time had been considered overwhelming), the paperwork burden became enormous. Stock certificates were left for weeks piled haphazardly on any level surface, including filing cabinets and tables. Stocks were mailed to wrong addresses, or not mailed at all. Overtime and night work became mandatory. Turnover was 60% a year.To deal with this large volume, which was overwhelming brokerage firms, the stock exchanges were forced to close every week (they chose every Wednesday), and trading hours were shortened on other days of the week. Two methods were used to solve the crisis: The first was to hold all paper stock certificates in one centralized location, and automate the process by keeping electronic records of all certificates and securities clearing and settlement (changes of ownership and other securities transactions). The method was first used in Austria by the Vienna Giro and Depository Association in 1872.One problem was state laws requiring brokers to deliver certificates to investors. Eventually all the states were convinced that this notion is obsolete and changed their laws. For the most part, investors can still request their certificates, but this has several inconveniences, and most people do not, except for novelty value. This led the New York Stock Exchange to establish the Central Certificate Service (CCS) in 1968 Time magazine, Wall Street: Attack on the Snarl, May 24, 1968 Accessed 20 Oct 2009 at 44 Broad Street in New York City. Anthony P. Reres was appointed the head of CCS. New York Stock Exchange President Robert W. Haack promised: "We are going to automate the stock certificate out of business by substituting a punch card. We just can't keep up with the flood of business unless we do." The CCS transferred securities electronically, eliminating their physical handling for settlement purposes, and kept track of the total number of shares held by NYSE members. This relieved brokerage firms of the work of inspecting, counting, and storing certificates. Haack labeled it "top priority," $5 million was spent on it, and its goal was to eliminate up to 75% of the physical handling of stock certificates traded between brokers. One problem, however, was that it was voluntary, and brokers responsible for 2/3 of all trades refused to use it.By January 1969, it was transferring 10,000 shares per day, and plans were for it to be handling broker-to-broker transactions in 1,300 issues by March 1969. In 1970 the CCS service was extended to the American Stock Exchange. This led to the development of the Banking and Securities Industry Committee (BASIC), which represented leading U.S. banks and securities exchanges,, and was headed by a banker named Herman Beavis, and finally the development of DTC in 1973, which was headed by Bill Dentzer, the former New York State Banking Superintedent. All the top New York banks were represented on the board, usually by their chairman. BASIC and the SEC saw this indirect holding system as a "temporary measure," on the way to a "certificateless society."The second method involves Nettingmultilateral netting; and led to the formation of the National Securities Clearing Corporation (NSCC) in 1976.In 2007, Chief Executive Officer Donald F. Donahue was named to the additional office of Chairman of DTCC and its subsidiaries, and Chief Operating Officer William B. Aimetti was named President.In 2008, The Clearing Corporation and the Depository Trust & Clearing Corporation announced CCorp members will benefit from CCorp's netting and risk management processes, and will leverage the asset servicing capabilities of DTCC's Trade Information Warehouse for credit default swaps (CDS). On Thursday 1 July 2010, it was announced that the DTCC had acquired all of the shares of Avox Limited, based in Wrexham, North Wales. Deutsche Borse had previously held over 76% of the shares. Controversy over naked short selling Several companies have sued the DTCC, without success, over delivery failures in their stocks, alleging culpability for naked short selling. Furthermore, the issue of the DTCC's possible involvement has been taken up by United States SenateSenator Robert Foster BennettRobert Bennett and discussed by the NASAA and in articles—disagreed with by DTCC—in the Wall Street Journal and Euromoney Magazine. [[Wall Street Journal]]Emshwiller, John R., and Kara Scannell (July 5, 2007). "Blame the 'Stock Vault'?". The Wall Street Journal. . The DTCC contends that the suits are orchestrated by a small group of lawyers and executives to make money and draw attention from the companies' problems.Critics blame DTCC as being in charge of the system where it happens, say that DTCC turns a blind eye to the problem, and that the Securities and Exchange Commission has not taken sufficient action against naked shorting. DTCC says that it has no authority over trading activities, cannot force buy-ins of shares not delivered, "DTCC Responds to The Wall Street Journal article, "Blame the 'Stock Vault?'"". Depository Trust & Clearing Corp.. 2007-07-06. . Retrieved 2009-09-09. and suggests that naked shorting is simply not widespread enough to be a major concern. "We're not saying there is no problem, but to suggest the sky is falling might be a bit overdone," DTCC's chief spokesman Stuart Goldstein said. The U.S. Securities and Exchange Commission (SEC), however, views naked shorting as a serious enough matter to have made two separate efforts to restrict the practice. The DTCC says that the SEC has supported its position in legal proceedings.Drummond, Bob (August 4, 2006). "Naked Short Sellers Hurt Companies With Stock They Don't Have". Bloomberg.com. . Retrieved 2007-12-25. "DTCC Chief Spokesperson Denies Existence of Lawsuit".

financialwire.net. May 11, 2004. . Retrieved 2007-12-25. DTCC General Counsel Larry Thompson calls the claims that DTCC is responsible for naked short selling "pure invention."In July 2007, Senator Bob Bennett (politician)Bob Bennett, Republican of Utah, suggested on the U.S. Senate floor that the allegations involving DTCC and naked short selling are "serious enough" that there should be a hearing on them. "Senator Bennett Discusses Naked Short Selling on the Senate Floor," Website of Senator Bennett, July 20, 2007, accessed 32-2-2008 The committee's Chairman, Senator Christopher Dodd, indicated he was willing to hold such a hearing. However, no hearing was ever held, and both Sen. Bennett and Dodd are no longer in the Senate, so any possible investigation seems moot at this point, and no further action on naked short selling is anticipated. The North American Securities Administrators Association, representing state stock regulators, filed a brief in a suit against the DTCC, arguing against federal preemption as a defense to the suit. NASAA said that "if the Investors' claims are taken as true, as they must be on a motion to dismiss, then the entrepreneurs and investors before the Court have been the victims of fraud and manipulation at the hands of the very entities that should be serving their interests by maintaining a fair and efficient national market.". "Amicus brief" (PDF). Nasaa.org. North American Securities Administrators Assn.. 2007-03-19. . Retrieved 2009-09-09. The Whistler suit was later dismissed by the courts. Critics also contend that DTCC and SEC have been too secretive with information about where naked shorting is taking place. DTCC says it has supported releasing more information to the public.Subsidiaries The DTCC has several subsidiaries: The Depository Trust Company (DTC) – The original securities depository.Established in 1973, it was created to reduce costs and provide efficiencies by immobilizing securities and making "book-entry" changes to show ownership of the securities. DTC provides securities movements for NSCC's net settlements, and settlement for institutional trades (which typically involve money and securities transfers between custodian banks and broker-dealers), as well as money market instruments. In 2007, DTC settled transactions worth $513 trillion, and processed 325 million book-entry deliveries. In addition to settlement services, DTC retains custody of 3.5 million securities issues, worth about $40 trillion, including securities issued in the US and more than 110 other countries. DTC is a member of the U.S. Federal Reserve System, and a registered clearing agency with the Securities and Exchange Commission. National Securities Clearing Corporation (NSCC) - The original clearing corporation, it provides clearing and serves as the central counterparty for trades in the US securities markets.Established in 1976, it provides clearing, settlement, risk management, central counterparty services, and a guarantee of completion for certain transactions for virtually all broker-to-broker trades involving equities, corporate and municipal debt, American depositary receipts, exchange-traded funds, and unit investment trusts. NSCC also nets trades and payments among its participants, reducing the value of securities and payments that need to be exchanged by an average of 98% each day. NSCC generally clears and settles trades on a "T+3" basis. NSCC has roughly 4,000 participants, and is regulated by the U.S. Securities and Exchange Commission (SEC). Fixed Income Clearing Corporation (FICC) – Provides clearing for fixed income securities, including treasury securitytreasury securities and Mortgage-backed securitymortgage backed securitiesCreated in 2003 to handle fixed income transaction processing, integrating the Government Securities Clearing Corporation and the Mortgage-Backed Securities Clearing Corporation. The Government Securities Division (GSD) provides Real-Time Trade Matching (RTTM), clearing, risk management, and netting for trades in US Government debt issues, including repurchase agreements or repos. Securities transactions processed by FICC's Government Securities Division include Treasury bills, bonds, notes, Zero-coupon bondzero-coupon securities, government agency securities, and inflation-indexed securities. The Mortgage-Backed Securities Division provides real-time automated and trade matching, trade confirmation, risk management, netting, and electronic pool notification to the mortgage-backed securitymortgage-backed securities market. Participants in this market include mortgage originators, government-sponsored enterprises, registered broker-dealers, institutional investors, investment managers, mutual funds, commercial banks, insurance companies, and other financial institutions. DTCC Solutions – DTCC's subsidiary delivering information-based and business processing solutions to financial intermediaries globally, such as Global Corporation Action Validation Service (GCA VS) and Managed Accounts Service.GCA VS simplifies announcement processing by providing a centralized source of "scrubbed" information about corporate actions, including tender offers, Currency conversionconversions, stock splits, and nearly 100 other types of events for equities and fixed-income instruments traded in Europe, Asia-Pacific, and the Americas. In 2006, GCA VS processed 899,000 corporate actions from 160 countries. Managed Accounts Service, introduced in 2006, standardizes the exchange of account and investment information through a central gateway. DTCC Learning – Provides financial, technology, and career training and educational services to the global financial industry.Loan/SERV - Provides services to loan syndicates and agents.Deriv/SERV – Provides clearing for credit derivatives, such as Collateralized debt obligationCDOs.It provides automated matching and confirmation services for over-the counter (OTC) derivatives trades, including credit, equity, and interest rate derivatives. It also provides related matching of payment flows and bilateral netting services. Deriv/SERV's customers include dealers and buy-side firms from 30 countries. In 2006, Deriv/SERV processed 2.6 million transactions. EuroCCP – European Central Counterparty Limited (EuroCCP) is the European subsidiary of DTCC that provides equities clearing services on a pan-European basis. Headquartered in London, EuroCCP is a UK-incorporated Recognised Clearing House regulated by the UK's Financial Services Authority (FSA).EuroCCP began operations in August 2008, initially clearing for the pan-European trading platform Turquoise (trading platform)Turquoise. EuroCCP has subsequently secured appointments from additional trading platforms and now provides central counterparty services for equity trades to Turquoise, SmartPool, NYSE Arca Europe and Pipeline Financial Group Limited. EuroCCP clears trades in more than 6,000 equities issues for these trading venues. In October 2009 EuroCCP began clearing and settling trades made on the Turquoise platform in 120 of the most heavily-traded listed Depositary Receipts. Citi Global Transaction Services acts as settlement agent for trades cleared by EuroCCP. EuroCCP now provides clearing services in 15 major national markets in Europe: Austria, Belgium, France, Denmark, Germany, Ireland, Italy, Finland, Netherlands, Norway, Portugal, United Kingdom, Switzerland, Sweden and Spain. Trades are handled in seven different currencies: the Euro, British Pound, U.S. Dollar, Swiss Franc, Danish Krone, Swedish Krona, and Norwegian Krone. http://euroccp.co.uk/Omgeo – Partnership with Thomson Financial that provides clearing automation solutions.Omgeo is as a central information management and processing hub for broker-dealers, investment managers, and custodian banks. It provides post-trade, pre-settlement institutional trade management solutions, processes over one million trades per day and serving 6,000 investment managers, broker/dealers, and custodians in 42 countries. CompetitionEuroclear (in Brussels, Belgium) and Clearstream (in Luxembourg) are the second and third largest central securities depositories in the world. ReferencesExternal links DTCC corporate site Extensive description of DTC and its activities Extensive description of NSCC and its activities DTC corporate site NSCC corporate site Source for History T2S Project of the Eurosystem "The Rise and Effects of the Indirect Holding System: How Corporate America Ceded its Shareholders to Intermediaries," by David C. Donald, Institute for Law and Finance, 18/09/07

Dexit

Dexit is a rechargeable, contactless, stored-value smart key tag used for electronic payment in on-line or off-line systems in Toronto, Canada, since 2001.

Instead of coins or cards (and PIN), Dexit uses an RFID key tag device associated with funds transferred from ordinary bank accounts. There is no link to access the accounts from the key tag, a feature to guard against the abuse of lost key tags. Accounts can be filled up from the Dexit website, by telephone, at participating merchants, or through pre-approved bank account or credit card balance transfers.

A partnership between small retailers, Dexit Inc., TD Canada Trust, National Bank of Canada, Telus Mobility, Bell Canada in Toronto's downtown, and a few retailers in and around Toronto. There were plans to expand to the rest of Toronto in 2005; however, this does not appear to have occurred.

In the summer of 2006, Dexit announced a restructuring, and nearly all payment terminals have been removed from stores. Dexit is also offering refunds of all funds that have been stored on Dexit Tags.

External links

- Dexit [1]

DigiCash

DigiCash Inc. was a pioneering electronic currency corporation founded by David Chaum in 1990. DigiCash transactions were unique in that they were anonymous due to a number cryptographic protocols developed by its founder. DigiCash declared bankruptcy in 1998, and subsequently sold its assets to eCash Technologies, another digital currency company, which was acquired by InfoSpace on Feb. 19, 2002.

Further reading

- *Presenting Digital Cash*, p. 99-106, 226-229; Seth Godin (ISBN 1-57521-062-2)

External links

- E-Money (That's What I Want) [1], *Wired*, Issue 2.12, December 1994
- Boom then Bust: How Electronic Cash Faltered [2]
- How DigiCash Blew Everything [3] translated by *Dutch natives* and edited by Ian Grigg from original article Hoe DigiCash alles verknalde [4] in Dutch magazine *NEXT!*, accessed on Apr 27, 1999

Related

- Bitcoin

Digital wallet

A **digital wallet** (also known as an **e-wallet**) allows users to make electronic commerce transactions quickly and securely.

A digital wallet functions much like a physical wallet. The digital wallet was first conceived as a method of storing various forms of electronic money (e-cash), but with little popularity of such e-cash services, the digital wallet has evolved into a service that provides internet users with a convenient way to store and use online shopping information.

The term "digital wallet" is also increasingly being used to describe mobile phones, especially smartphones, that store an individual's credentials and utilize wireless technologies such as near field communication (NFC) to carry out financial transactions.[1] [2] [3] [4]

An individual's bank account is usually linked to the digital wallet. They might also have their driver's license, health card, loyalty card(s) and other ID documents stored on the phone. The credentials can be passed to a merchant's terminal wirelessly via NFC. Certain sources are speculating that these smartphone "digital wallets" will eventually replace physical wallets.[5] The system has already gained popularity in Japan, where digital wallets are known as Osaifu-Keitai or "wallet mobiles".

Researchers at the University of Toronto's Faculty of Information are putting together a "Global Overview of Digital Wallet Technologies" [6].

Technology

A digital wallet has both a software and information component. The software provides security and encryption for the personal information and for the actual transaction. Typically, digital wallets are stored on the client side and are easily self-maintained and fully compatible with most e-commerce Web sites. A server-side digital wallet, also known as a thin wallet, is one that an organization creates for and about you and maintains on its servers. Server-side digital wallets are gaining popularity among major retailers due to the security, efficiency, and added utility it provides to the end-user, which increases their enjoyment of their overall purchase.

The information component is basically a database of user-inputted information. This information consists of your shipping address, billing address, payment methods (including credit card numbers, expiry dates, and security numbers), and other information.

Setup and use

A client side digital wallet requires minimal setup and is relatively easy to use. Once the software is installed, the user begins by entering all the pertinent information. The digital wallet is now setup. At the purchase/check-out page of an e-commerce site, the digital wallet software has the ability to automatically enter the user information in the online form. By default, most digital wallets prompt when the software recognizes a form in which it can fill out, if you chose to fill out the form automatically, you will be prompted for a password. This keeps unauthorized users from viewing personal information stored on a particular computer.

ECML

Digital wallets are designed to be accurate when transferring data to retail checkout forms; however, if a particular e-commerce site has a peculiar checkout system, the digital wallet may fail to properly recognize the forms fields. This problem has been eliminated by sites and wallet software that use ECML technology. Electronic Commerce Modeling Language is a protocol that dictates how online retailers structure and setup their checkout forms. Participating e-commerce vendors who incorporate both digital wallet technology and ECML include: Microsoft,

Discover, IBM, Omaha Steaks and Dell Computers.

Advantages for e-commerce sites

Upwards of 25% of online shoppers abandon their order due to frustration in filling in forms. (Graphic Arts Monthly, 1999) The digital wallet combats this problem by giving users the option to transfer their information securely and accurately. This simplified approach to completing transactions results in better usability and ultimately more utility for the customer.

References

- Principles for a free, powerful and stable monetary system for the digital era [7] by S. Poirier
- Haag, Cummings, et al.; (2006). "Management Information Systems for the Information Age" (3rd ed.). Mc-Graw-Hill Ryerson. ISBN 0-07-095569-7
- RFC 4412: ECML specification: [8]

References

[1] "US Operators Prepare to Launch Isis Digital Wallet Pilot" (http://www.pcworld.com/businesscenter/article/224264/ us_operators_prepare_to_launch_isis_digital_wallet_pilot.html) PC World. Retrieved 25 April, 2011

[2] " iPhone 5 can not be the Digital Wallet?" (http://brandimposter.com/iphone-5-can-not-be-the-digital-wallet-20118485.html) Brand Imposter. Retrieved 25 April, 2011

[3] "The Android-powered digital wallet raises security questions" (http://www.androidapps.com/finance/articles/ 7341-the-android-powered-digital-wallet-raises-security-questions) Android Apps. Retrieved 25 April, 2011

[4] "The Proportionate ID Digital Wallet" (http://propid.ischool.utoronto.ca/) University of Toronto. Retrieved 25 April, 2011

[5] "Smart (phone) money" (http://business.financialpost.com/2011/04/23/smart-phone-money/) Financial Post. Retrieved May 1, 2011

Diners Club International

Diners Club

Diners Club International	
Type	Subsidiary of Discover Financial
Industry	Finance
Founded	1950
Founder(s)	Frank X. McNamara Ralph Schneider Matty Simmons Alfred Bloomingdale
Headquarters	Riverwoods, IL, U.S.
Products	Credit cards
Website	http://www.dinersclub.com

Diners Club International, founded as **Diners Club**, is a charge card company formed in 1950 by Frank X. McNamara, Ralph Schneider and Matty Simmons. When it first emerged, it became the first independent credit card company in the world that established an idea of self-sufficient company producing credit cards for travel and entertainment.[1]

History

The first credit card charge was made on February 8, 1950, by Frank McNamara, Ralph Schneider and Matty Simmons at Major's Cabin Grill, a restaurant adjacent to their offices in the Empire State Building. McNamara was bought out two years later by department store heir Alfred Bloomingdale, who resigned several years later. Schneider died in the early 1960s. Simmons resigned in 1967 to form the publishing company that became National Lampoon. During that approximately 20-year period, these four men were the only major participants in the Diners Club operation.

Diners Club created what would later be dubbed the "travel and entertainment" (T&E) card market, which focused on frequent travelers with a substantial income to pay for other high-value charges. As these customers had no need to pay for purchases over time, these cards required that the entire balance of the bill was paid upon receipt. This type of account is known today as a charge card. Diners Club's monopoly was short-lived, however, as American Express and Carte Blanche (which later partnered with Diners Club) began to compete with Diners Club in the T&E card market. American Express now dominates the "member card" arena, providing thousands of customers with cards that require the monthly balance be paid in full.

Diners Club also faced competition from banks that issued revolving credit cards through BankAmericard (later renamed VISA), and Interbank MasterCharge (later renamed MasterCard) towards the end of the 1960s. Diners Club began early on to allow franchises of the Diners Club name, at first in Europe and later throughout the world, for many years eclipsing the BankAmericard or Interbank MasterCharge networks abroad. Amoco also issued for a time its own co-branded Diners Club cards called American Torch Club, as well as Sun Oil Company with its version called Sun Diner Club Card.

Diners Club International, the franchisor that holds rights to the Diners Club trademark, was acquired in 1981 by Citibank, a unit of Citigroup, as well as many of the largest franchises worldwide, although a majority of its franchises abroad remain independently owned.

Acquisition by Discover Financial Services

In a transaction completed July 1, 2008, Discover Financial Services purchased Diners Club International from Citi for $165 million. [2] The deal was announced in April 2008 and approved by the U.S. government in May 2008. By merging the North American Discover Network with the international Diners Club Network, Discover created a global payment processing system. Discover Bank has no plans to issue Diners Club-branded cards which continue to be issued by Diners Club International licensees, including Citibank.

North American Franchise

MasterCard alliance

In 2004, Diners Club announced an agreement with MasterCard. Diners Club cards issued in the United States and Canada now feature a MasterCard logo and 16-digit account number on the front, and can be used wherever MasterCard can. Cards from other countries continued to bear a 14-digit account number on the front, with the MasterCard logo on the back. However, since the takeover of Diners Club International by Discover Financial Services, these cards have had the Discover logo on the back.

Carte Blanche

Carte Blanche originated as a Travel & Entertainment (T&E) card owned by Hilton Hotels, and competed with both American Express and Diners Club. The company changed ownership after being sold by Hilton, with Citibank owning the company for a brief period during the 1960s, and finally repurchasing it in 1979, and phasing the card out of service in the late 1980s. Throughout most of the 1960s and 1970s, the Carte Blanche card was considered to be a more prestigious worldwide travel and entertainment than American Express or Diners Club, though its small cardmember base hindered its success. Carte Blanche also was the first to implement a 'Gold Card' program, but initially only as a means to recognize cardholders who were frequent users and paid their bills on time. In 2000, the Carte Blanche name was revived in the United States when Diners Club, which was also acquired by Citibank in 1981, introduced an upscale version of its card: the Diners Club Carte Blanche Card. It is an upper-level charge card on par with the American Express Platinum card. The card carries a US$300 annual fee and offers an extensive menu of perks geared toward spendthrift travelers. It is accepted wherever regular Diners Club cards are accepted. Although Diners Club requires payment in full within 30 days, corporate accounts can pay within 60 days without penalty.

enRoute

Diners Club expanded its customer base in Canada by acquiring the enRoute card from Air Canada in 1992, and marketed the card under the combined name for a period of time as the "Diners Club/en route Card". [3] The enRoute business was valued at over $300 million. Diners Club remains a minor player in Canada.

Acquisition by BMO

In November 2009, Citibank announced that Diners Club International's North American franchise has been sold to Bank of Montreal (BMO). The deal gives BMO exclusive rights to issue Diners cards in the U.S. and Canada. At the time, BMO said the Diners Club fits well with its existing commercial card business, adding that commercial cards are one of the fastest growing segments in the credit card business.[4]

Switzerland and Germany Franchise

In a transaction that closed on August 6, 2010, Citi Bank sold both the Switzerland and Germany Franchises to a private investment group headed by Anthony J. Helbling. [5]

References

[1] "Diners Club Review" (http://casinosbanking.com/diners-club-overview.htm). . Retrieved 2011-05-26.

[2] Press Release Discover Financial Services Completes Diners Club Acquisition Jul 01, 2008 (http://www.dinersclubinternational.com/press-room/article20080701.html)

[3] COMPANY NEWS; Air Canada Sells Credit Card Unit New York Times (http://query.nytimes.com/gst/fullpage.html?res=9E0CEED8163BF934A15750C0A964958260)

[4] BMO to buy Diners Club franchise (http://www.theglobeandmail.com/globe-investor/bmo-to-buy-diners-club-franchise/article1375250/) (requires subscription)

[5] Dinners Club Press Release Transition of DC Switzerland and DC Germany to New Ownership (http://www.dinersclubinternational.com/press-room/article20100921.html)

External links

- Diners Club International (http://www.dinersclub.com/)
- Diners Club USA (http://www.dinersclubus.com/)
- Diners Club Canada (http://www.dinersclubcanada.com)
- Discover gets antitrust OK for Diners Club buy, Reuters (http://uk.reuters.com/article/marketsNewsUS/idUKN1354127220080513)

Direct corporate access

Direct Corporate Access (DCA) is part of the Faster Payments Service which provides a same day clearing payment service to UK member banks. **Direct Corporate Access** (DCA) will provide Banks' business customers with direct access to the Faster Payments Service (FPS) clearing service in a very similar way that Bacstel-IP provides access to BACS.

Direct Corporate Access only enables submission of files of payments, however as the central FPS processes payments indi vidually, VocaLink the operators of DCA will split the files into individual instructions for processing through FPS.

It was developed by APACS on behalf of the FPS member banks and the infrastructure went live in March 2009. Barclays was the first Bank live for customer sponsorship in August 2009.

Albany Software was the first solution supplier to successfully process a payment through the Faster Payments Service via DCA, using Albany ePAY on Wednesday 22 July 2009.[1]

Key Features

- DCA is available for file submission 7 days a week 01.00 to 23.00.
- Sterling payments only
- Maximum individual payment value is £100,000
- Payments submitted in files via the Secure-IP channel
- Beneficiaries must use FPS addressable sort code [2]
- DCA users must be sponsored by their bankers (however only Barclays offering sponsorship in the first instance).

Secure-IP

Secure-IP is a clone of the existing Bacstel-IP channel used for BACS. Files of payments are secured using a smart card or Hardware Security Module (HSM).

Files of payments submitted by Secure-IP will be disaggregated by VocaLink, the operators of DCA, and submitted into the Faster Payments Service. Disaggregation and acceptance may take up to 30 minutes and beneficiaries will receive access to the funds within 2 hours of acceptance.

The software used to access Secure-IP must be approved. This is an extension to the existing Bacs Approved Software Service (BASS). In March 2009 Albany Software[3] and Bottomline Technologies Europe Ltd[4] received approved status for their first DCA capable products. They were joined in May 2009 by Barron McCann[5]. In 2010 they were joined by Direct Debit Ltd[6] and Experian [7]. In 2011 they were joined by Fundtech [8].

Bureaux

Bureau organisations can submit files of payments on behalf of other registered Service Users of Direct Corporate Access.

The Bureau needs to be sponsored by a DCA enabled Bank (initially only Barclays) and to use a Bureau/DCA version of the approved Bacs Approved Software Service (BASS) software.

The Bureau's sponsor bank issues PKI certificates for authorising files in the form of a smart card or Hardware Security Module (HSM). The same PKI certificates can be used to authorise Bacs file submissions via Bacstel-IP.

File submissions can only be made on behalf Service Users of a DCA enabled Bank (initially only Barclays).

Weaknesses

- Direct Corporate Access operates a limited 22 x 7 window for payment submission whereas the underlying Faster Payments service operates 24 x 7.
- Bureau can only submit for their clients who are sponsored by Barclays.

Alternative Products

- Royal Bank of Scotland (including National Westminster and Coutts Banks)[9] and HSBC offer Faster Payments via their electronic banking channels (Bankline and HSBC.Net).

Notes

[1] (http://www.albany.co.uk/press-room/press-releases/2009/2009-August/eagle-first-commercial-customer-of-dca.htm)

[2] (http://www.ukpayments.org.uk/sort_code_checker/)

[3] Albany November 2008 Press Release (http://www.albany.co.uk/news/pr_epay_bass.htm)

[4] Bacs Approved Software List (http://www.bacs.co.uk/Bacs/SoftwareSuppliers/Resources/Pages/ApprovedSoftware.aspx)

[5] Barron McCann Press Release May 2009 (http://www.bemac.com/newsfps1)

[6] (http://www.directdebit.com/)

[7] Experian (http://www.experianpayments.com/industry-information/faster-payments.html)

[8] (http://www.fundtech.com/Products/Payments/Global-PAYplus-Services-Platform/UK-Faster-Payments)

[9] Coutts Bank FPS (http://www.coutts.com/productsandservices/faster-payments/commercial-clients-faqs.asp)

External links

- APACS Connection Methods (http://www.apacs.org.uk/payments_industry/connection_methods.html)
- Barclays DCA Customer Presentation (http://www.barclays.com/fasterpayments)

Direct debit

A **direct debit** or **direct withdrawal** is an instruction that a bank account holder gives to his or her bank to collect an amount directly from another account. It is similar to a direct deposit but initiated by the beneficiary. It is also called pre-authorized debit (PAD) or pre-authorized payment (PAP).

It is typical to use these pulled collections to make recurring payments for credit card or utility bills. Unlike standing orders, which require the amounts to be fixed, direct debits can be used for varying amounts, and are more similar to direct deposits, which are initiated by the payer. With direct debits, the payee can simply indicate a different amount each time. However, in countries where setting up authorization for direct debit is easy enough, it can also be used for one-time payments in the mail order business or even at a point of sale.

It is available in the banking systems of several countries, including the United Kingdom, Brazil , Germany, South Africa and the Netherlands. It is scheduled to be available across the whole Single European Payments Area by the end of 2010. In the United States, where cheques are more popular than bank transfers, a similar service is available through the Automated Clearing House network.

Authorization

The biggest difference to a direct deposit is that there must be some sort of authorization for the payee to collect funds from the payer's account. There are generally two methods to set up the authorization:

One method only involves the payer and the payee. The payer simply authorizes the payee to collect the amounts due from his or her account. As the payer's bank is not involved, it can not check the payee's authorization, so other safeguards are required. This typically means that the payer can instruct his or her bank to return any direct debit note without giving a reason. The payee then not only has to pay all fees for the transaction (which can be hefty for returned direct debits) but may eventually lose his or her ability to initiate direct debits if this occurs too often. However, it still requires all account holders to watch statements and request returns if necessary unless they have instructed their bank to block direct debits.

The other method also involves the payer's bank. It requires the payer to instruct his or her bank to honour direct debit notes from the payee. The payee is then notified that he or she is now authorised to initiate direct debits transfers from the payer. While this is more secure in theory, what it can also mean for the payer is that is harder to return debit notes in the case of an error or dispute.

Direct debit in different countries

In the United Kingdom, a direct debit requires the customer to authorise a direct debit instruction with their bank. This task is carried out via the Service User (payee). [1] Companies or organisations wanting to use direct debits to collect customer payments must have a SUN (Service User Number). This can be done in two main ways: through requesting sponsorship by their bank to help with a formal application process or using an outsourced company to handle the payment processing.

Banks operate a direct debit guarantee. In this, if a customer disputes an amount that has gone out of their account by direct debit, they can contact their bank and ask for an immediate refund. It is then the Service User's responsibility to ask the customer for the money. However, the Service User is not automatically liable under the guarantee for any bank charges caused by the Service User's error, for example if an incorrect direct debit transaction causes the customer to go overdrawn. However, there are conditions where claims for consequential loss are considered under the direct debit guarantee.

To set up a paperless direct debit, nothing needs to be signed by the customer, which is why the system is so strongly regulated. A customer has the right to request a paper direct debit instruction. Some types of bank account do not allow direct debits; typically current accounts do as well as some deposit accounts. Direct debits cannot be collected on credit card accounts and should not be confused with a credit card continuous authority. The rules and regulations for a continuous credit card authority are different from the direct debit guarantee.

Any direct debit mandate that has not been used to collect funds for over 13 months is automatically cancelled by the customer's bank[2] (this is known as a "dormancy period"). This can cause problems when the mandate is used infrequently, for instance, taking a payment to settle the bill for a seldom used credit card. If the credit card company has not collected a payment using the Direct Debit mandate for over 13 months the direct debit mandate may have been cancelled as dormant without the customer's knowledge, and the direct debit claim will fail.

Direct debit payments can be set up via these methods:

- paper-based forms requiring a signature
- via telephone using a formal script to collect all the required information
- via the internet using an online application form which has been approved by a bank
- using a telephone keypad to enter data to an automated menu system
- through interactive services on digital television
- face-to-face, where the payer keys their account data directly into the originator's computer system

Direct debit fraud

On 7 January 2008, Jeremy Clarkson found himself the subject of direct debit fraud after publishing his bank account and sort code details in his column in *The Sun* to make the point that public concern over the 2007 UK child benefit data scandal was unnecessary. He wrote, "All you'll be able to do with them is put money into my account. Not take it out. Honestly, I've never known such a palaver about nothing". Someone then used these details to set up a £500 direct debit to the charity Diabetes UK. In his next *Sunday Times* column, Clarkson wrote, "I was wrong and I have been punished for my mistake."[3] Under the terms of the direct debit guarantee, the payment should have been returned.

Germany

In Germany, banks generally provide direct debit (*Lastschrift*, *Bankeinzug*) using both methods since the advent of so-called *Giro* accounts in the 1950s.

The *Einzugsermächtigung* ("direct debit authorisation") just requires the customer to authorize the payee to make the collection. This can happen in written form, orally, by e-mail or through a web interface set up by the payee. Although organisations are generally required not to instruct their banks to make unauthorised collections, this is usually not verified by the banks involved. Customers can instruct their bank to return the debit note within at least six weeks.

This method is very popular within Germany as it allows quick and easy payments, and it is suited even for one-time payments. A customer might just give the authorisation at the same time she or he orders goods or services from an organisation. Compared to payments by credit cards, which allow similar usage, bank fees for successful collections are much lower.

To prevent abuse, account holders must watch their bank statements and ask their bank to return unauthorised (or wrong) debit notes. As fraudulent direct debit instructions are easily traced, abuse is rare. However, there can be issues when the amount billed and collected is incorrect or unexpectedly large.

The *Abbuchungsauftrag* ("posting off") requires the customer to instruct his or her bank to honour debit notes from the organisation. Direct debits made with this method are verified by the customer's bank and therefore can not be returned. As it is less convenient, it is rarely used, usually only in business to business relationships.

The Netherlands

In The Netherlands, like in Germany, an account holder can authorize a company to collect direct debit payments, without notifying the bank. Doing so is very common, with as much as 45% of all banking transactions conducted via direct debit.[4]

A transaction can be ongoing, or one-time only. For both types collecting organizations must enter into a direct debit (*incasso*) contract with their bank. For each transaction the name and account number of the account holder must be provided. The collecting organisation can then collect from any account, provided there is enough money on the account and no block is set against direct debit from the collecting organisation. Legally, the collecting organization must have a signed and dated authorization card specifying the amount (to be) debited.

Transactions can be contested depending on the type of transaction, time since the transaction and the base of dispute. Authorized transactions of the ongoing type can directly be recalled via the bank of the account holder within the 56 days since the transaction. Authorized one-time only transactions can be recalled via the bank within 5 days. Unauthorized transactions can be contested via the bank within a limited time period after the transaction.

To prevent fraudulent transactions the collecting organization is required to present to the account holder's bank, upon request, a signed authorization card (*machtiging*). If this card cannot be presented, all direct debit transactions may be considered to be fraudulent. Some online shops offer the possibility of paying by direct debit, but since they typically do not receive a customer's signature, their payments may officially not be honoured.

Another security measure is a "selective block" whereby the customer can instruct the bank to disallow direct debits to a specified account number. Blanket blocks are also available.

Ireland

The direct debit system in Ireland is operated by IPSO, the Irish Payment Services Organisation/IRECC. [5] Direct debit instructions can be given in writing or by telephone. There are protections for the holder of the account being debited in the event of a dispute. Guide to the Irish direct debit system [6].

Japan

Direct debit is a very common payment option in Japan. When signing up for a service, such as telephone, you are usually asked to enter your bank details on the service submission form, to set up for automatic payments, and the company you are signing up to will take care of the rest. Sometimes, but not always, you are offered the possibility to enter your credit card details instead of your bank account details, to have the money directly debited from your credit card instead of your bank account.

Malaysia

In Malaysia, the direct debit system is available via the product known as FPX - Financial Process Exchange.

Financial Process Exchange (FPX) support online direct debit as well as batch direct debit. It opens new doors for e-Commerce in Malaysia, in particular business to business (B2B) and business to commerce (B2C) payments.

FPX allow customers to make payment at e-market places such as websites and online stores as well as for corporations to collect bulk payment from their customers.

It leverages on the Internet banking services of participating banks and provides fast, secure, reliable, real-time online payment processing. FPX provides a complete end-to-end business transaction, resourceful payment records, simplified reconciliation and reduced risks as fund movements are between established financial institutions.

Supported by Bank Negara Malaysia and the local financial institutions, FPX is operated by FPX Payment Gateway Sdn Bhd, a subsidiary company of Malaysian Electronic Payment System (1997) Sdn Bhd (MEPS).

Australia

In Australia Direct Debit is performed through the Direct Entry system[5] also known as BECS (Bulk Electronic Clearing System) or CS2, managed by the Australian Payments Clearing Association. An account holder can authorise a company to collect direct debit payments, without notifying the bank.

A common example of Direct Debit is authorising a Credit Card company to debit a bank account for the monthly balance.

Many smaller companies do not have direct debit facilities themselves, and a third-party payment service must be used to interface between the biller and the customer's bank. For this a small charge (typically $1–2 per transaction, incorporated into the bill amount) is made by the payment service.

United States

In the United States, direct debit usually means an Automated Clearing House (ACH) transfer from a bank account to a biller, initiated by the biller.

South Africa

In South Africa Direct Debit also known as Debit Orders are performed through ACB. An account holder can authorise a company to collect direct debit payments. The client signs a debit mandate form giving the requesting company permission to debit their account with a fixed monthly value. This value can be recurring or once-off. This is an effective and safe alternative to receiving money in cash, by cheque or EFT

Debit Orders can be processed on any workday, Monday to Friday, excluding public holidays.

Many smaller companies do not have direct debit facilities themselves, and a third-party payment service must be used to interface between the biller and the customer's bank.

External links

- APCA, the Australian Payments Clearing Association [8]
- www.bacs.co.uk [9]
- http://www.albany.co.uk/knowledge-centre/index.htm
- Direct Debit FAQs [10]
- Direct Debit Glossary of terms [11]
- Paperless Direct Debit [12]

References

[1] Before a company or organisation can claim direct debit payments from its customers (direct debits cannot be paid to individuals), it has to be vetted by its bank. This is to stop it defrauding customers and to ensure that the proper controls are in place to allow the them to operate within the direct debit scheme rules. If a large number of customers complain about direct debits set up by a particular Service User then the Service User may lose its ability to set up direct debits.

[2] BACS Direct Debit (http://www.bacs.co.uk/Bacs/Consumers/DirectDebit/Pages/DirectDebit.aspx) FAQ

[3] Clarkson stung after bank prank (http://news.bbc.co.uk/2/hi/entertainment/7174760.stm), BBC News

[4] http://www.mkb.nl/Ondernemen!/Artikelen/359_476.293

[5] Australian Direct Entry Fact Sheet (http://www.apca.com.au/Public/apca01_live.nsf/ResourceLookup/Direct_Entry_Fact_Sheet.pdf/ $File/Direct_Entry_Fact_Sheet.pdf)

Disney's Fastpass

Disney Fastpass is a virtual queuing system created by the Walt Disney Company. First introduced in 1999 (though the idea of a ride reservation system was first introduced in world fairs),[1] Fastpass allows guests to avoid long lines at the attractions on which the system is installed, freeing them to enjoy other attractions during their wait. The service is available at no additional charge to all park guests.

Disney's Fastpass logo

Design theory

Each attraction inside a Disney theme park has a certain capacity, or a maximum number of guests that attraction can handle in a given operating day. For example, a ride-through attraction like the Haunted Mansion may be able to carry 2,000 guests per operating hour. During a 12-hour operating day, 24,000 guests can experience this attraction. Similarly, a live theatrical show with a theatre capacity of 3,000 guests that has five shows during the day has a capacity of 15,000 guests. When Fastpass is installed on the attraction, a certain number of those seats (in the theatre, on the ride vehicles, etc.) are set aside. The remainder are made available on a "stand-by" basis to other park guests.

At the start of the operating day, the enabled attraction's wait is pre-set at a given time (for example, 45 minutes). The number of Fastpasses available is evenly divided into time intervals (usually five minutes, but sometimes three minutes). As guests obtain Fastpasses for the attraction, time intervals are depleted, moving the return time to later in the day. For an average attraction, the Fastpass wait will generally stay near this initial pre-set time.

In the case of very popular attractions, such as Splash Mountain or other major thrill rides, time intervals are depleted quickly, resulting in longer virtual waits. Sometimes, all the time intervals will be depleted early in the day, at which point Fastpasses are no longer obtainable for the given attraction during that day.

Operations

Disney Fastpass tickets are dispensed by machines outside each attraction that uses them. The guest inserts his/her park ticket into a reader on the machine. The machine then returns the admission ticket and a Fastpass ticket will be printed. This ticket will show the time window at which the guest may enter the special priority line at that attraction. The time period given is normally one hour for rides (30 minutes in the Paris parks), and 15 minutes for theatrical presentations. It will also show when another Fastpass can be obtained.

In normal practice, only one Fastpass ticket can be held at a time. Another Fastpass ticket can be obtained either at the start of the current Fastpass ticket's return time or after two hours, whichever is earlier. If a guest attempts to obtain another Fastpass before these times, an informational ticket will be printed indicating when the next Fastpass ticket can be obtained. An exception to this is the *World of Color* show, which distributes tickets early in the day for the evening performances; guests may still obtain standard Fastpass tickets for other attractions even if they hold a ticket for *World of Color*.

The presence of Fastpass on an attraction does not imply that Fastpass tickets will be offered on any given day. During less-crowded operating days, the system may not be used on certain attractions as the stand-by wait is expected to be short enough to make Fastpass unnecessary. Fastpass is generally not used at all during separate-ticket events, such as Mickey's Very Merry Christmas Party or Grad Nite, or during special after-hours events for resort guests or annual passholders, although exceptions do occur.

Fastpasses are also given on birthdays (with birth certificates and a pre park visit birthday confirming that the park knows that it is your birthday) instead of the birthday giftcard from the park. These Fastpasses are for popular pre-determined rides, enough for each person in your party to ride.

Fastpasses are also given for any ride any given time, when a guest visits a ride that malfunctions (such as: the soundtrack and the ride not being in sync on Space Mountain, power malfunctions on the Indiana Jones Adventure, or if someone cannot fit on the ride), thus making Disney unable to uphold safety guidelines.

Fastpasses are often also traded or given away. If the person who fastpassed and the time was after they would be ending their stay at the park, or any other reason another guest will gladly take it. Trades also happen to avoid the time restrictions on Fastpasses to avoid waiting.

Changes in implementation

At first, a guest could only hold a single Fastpass at a time; if a guest tried to insert a park ticket into another Fastpass machine before the time shown on their previous Fastpass, the machine would generate a ticket with a message printed on it stating that it was not yet time to obtain another Fastpass. Since the initial rollout of Fastpass, the rules have been relaxed a bit, and now additional Fastpasses can be had sooner after one another (maximum 2 hour interval between obtaining two Fastpasses), but still only one Fastpass per attraction per park ticket in every interval.

Vacations to Disneyland which were booked through AAA Vacations in 2006 came with park admission tickets which could be used to collect Fastpass tickets from multiple attractions at one time. Under this exclusive program, a guest could hold multiple Fastpass tickets per park ticket for multiple attractions at the same time. This Multi-Fastpass feature was discontinued as of January 2007, and all AAA ParkHopper tickets since then have been Standard Fastpass.

A bug in the first implementation of Fastpass allowed guests to get a pass by using tickets other than Disney's own admission media. Old tickets and even passes for other parks would result in the machines printing up another Fastpass. This has since been corrected; a ticket will come out stating "This card has not been scanned for admission".

Epcot's *Mission: SPACE* was the first attraction built with Fastpass in mind, with a specific queue area for it. Earlier attractions were retrofitted for Fastpass by rerouting the queue area to allow a shorter line near the boarding area.

Fastpass is used mainly on the most popular park attractions, such as *Space Mountain*, *Test Track*, *Soarin'* and the *Twilight Zone Tower of Terror*; therefore, the rides that offer Fastpass service vary over time. Smaller attractions would not benefit from Fastpass due to short or fast-moving lines.

On August 30, 2007, the Walt Disney Company filed a patent for using Short Messaging Service on mobile devices as a way to get and use FastPasses in the park. The patent additionally indicated that guests staying at Disney hotels would be allowed to make early reservations for attractions using their in-room television.[2]

Disney's World of Color show at Disney California Adventure uses Disney's Fastpass as the only method of getting tickets for entering the Paradise Park viewing area unless you have gotten reserved seating vouchers through a World of Color dining package at select Disney California Adventure table service dining locations or a World of Color picnic package.

Fastpass promotions

During Disney's *Year of a Million Dreams* promotion (January 2007-December 2008), many guests received a special *Dream Fastpass*. Cast members awarded *Dream Fastpasses* to guests standing at predetermined random locations inside the park, at predetermined times (usually within the first few hours of opening). The *Dream Fastpass* was a card hung on a lanyard with a removable tab for each enabled attraction. Guests could enter the Fastpass return line whenever they chose, where they handed over that attraction's tab.

At the Disneyland Resort, the *Dream Fastpass* entitled guests to one priority entry to each attraction with Fastpass access in both Disneyland and Disney's California Adventure parks. At Walt Disney World, Dream Fastpasses were good only for the park in which they were awarded (for example, an award in the Magic Kingdom was good only for that park's attractions).

Throughout the summer of 2011 (dubbed Disney Soundsational Summer) guests staying at any of the three Hotels of the Disneyland Resort will receive two complimentary FastPasses per person. These passes will allow guests to enter the FastPass line at any time they chose (similar to the Dream FastPass) and hence skipping the line for the attraction.[3]

References

[1] "Themed Attraction; Fastpass" (http://www.themedattraction.com/fastpass.htm). .

[2] "Disney Files Patent for Wireless FastPasses" (http://www.netcot.com/thesite/2007/09/05/disney-files-patent-for-wireless-fastpasses/). "Netcot.com". . Retrieved 2007-09-05.

[3] ""Disneyland Discount Information"" (http://www.wdwinfo.com/disneyland/discounts.htm). "WDW Info". .

Further reading

- "Disney's Fastpass Service" (http://disneyland.disney.go.com/disneyland/en_US/help/gsDetail?name=FastpassGSDetailPage). *Disney*. Retrieved August 26, 2006.
- "Fastpass" (http://allearsnet.com/tp/fastpass.htm). *AllEarsNet*. Retrieved November 17, 2005.
- "Method and system for managing attraction admission - Patent #6,173,209" (http://patft.uspto.gov/netacgi/nph-Parser?patentnumber=6173209). *US Patent & Trademark Office*. Retrieved November 17, 2005. - Patent for the Fastpass system

Double-spending

Double-spending is a failure mode of digital cash schemes, when it is possible to spend a single digital token twice. Since, unlike physical token money such as coins, the act of spending a digital coin does not remove its data from the ownership of the original holder, some other means is needed to prevent double-spending.

This is usually implemented using an on-line central trusted third party that can verify whether a token has been spent.[1] This normally represents a single point of failure from both the technical and trust viewpoints. However, a number of distributed systems for double spending prevention have been proposed.[2] [3]

References

[1] Mark Ryan. "Digital Cash" (http://www.cs.bham.ac.uk/~mdr/teaching/modules06/netsec/lectures/DigitalCash.html). School of Computer Science, University of Birmingham. . Retrieved 2010-07-12.

[2] Jaap-Henk Hoepman (2008). "Distributed Double Spending Prevention". arXiv:0802.0832v1 [cs.CR].

[3] Osipkov, I.; Vasserman, E. Y.; Hopper, N.; Kim, Y. (2007). *Combating Double-Spending Using Cooperative P2P Systems*. pp. 41. doi:10.1109/ICDCS.2007.91.

Dynamic currency conversion

Dynamic Currency Conversion (DCC) or Cardholder Preferred Currency (CPC) is a financial service in which holders of credit cards have the cost of a transaction converted to their local currency when making a payment in a foreign currency. Currently this feature is only possible for Visa and MasterCard networks. American Express provides for multi currency transactions for ecommerce merchants.

Explanation of DCC

DCC provides consumers with a rate of exchange at point of sale rather than waiting for a statement at the end of the billing cycle. The calculation of currency exchange is not computed by the issuer of the credit card but by the merchant who can set the rate of exchange. There has been controversy because some merchants have run dynamic currency conversion without giving the option to the cardholder or charge rates far in excess of what a bank might charge.[1]

```
Transaction Currency          EUR
... Rate ... 1 = INR  57.0100
Commission                  0.00%

nt    INR  Rs.88155.76

IT  : EUR       1546.32
(Trans Currency EUR)

TIP  : EUR

TOTAL: EUR
```

```
I DECLARE THAT I HAVE BEEN
GIVEN CHOICE OF PAYMENT CURRENCY.
I AGREE TO PAY THE ABOVE TOTAL
AMOUNT AND ACCEPT THAT THE
CHOICE OF CURRENCY IS FINAL. I
UNDERSTAND THAT THIS FACILITY
IS PROVIDED BY THE BANK AND
NOT THE CARD ASSOCIATION
```

Part of a credit cart receipt from 21.8.2010, indicating that DCC takes place.

Advantages and Disadvantages for Customers

In a typical transaction situation, cardholders are handed their receipt with an option to sign for the amount in the foreign currency or their home currency. Depending on the service provider, an explanation of the exchange rates are included (as shown on the scan displayed in this article) along with the prevailing rate of the day. The rates used, however, may or may not be based on the wholesale rate; this is dependent on the DCC provider. Some providers use Reuters Interbank for the exhange rate of transactions, and offer chargeback programs if a better rate can be shown to exist during the day of the purchase.[2] If the wholesale rate is used, the customer benefits from transparency and certainty.

To deter customers from requesting compensation for getting unfavorable conversion rates later, some providers employ a disclaimer comparable to the following (taken directly from included receipt scan), that is printed on the credit card slip:

"I DECLARE THAT I HAVE BEEN GIVEN CHOICE OF PAYMENT CURRENCY. I AGREE TO PAY THE ABOVE TOTAL AMOUNT AND ACCEPT THAT THE CHOICE OF CURRENCY IS FINAL. I UNDERSTAND THAT THIS FACILITY IS PROVIDED BY THE BANK AND NOT THE CARD ASSOCIATION"

Advantages to the Customer Include:

- The visibility of charges made in foreign countries
- The ability to enter expenses more easily (i.e. business travelers)
- If a wholesale rate is used, the cardholder often benefits from a similar or identical foreign transaction fee
- Customers can avoid extraneous fees applied by the card issuer for simply using the card overseas

Disadvantages to the Customer Include:

- Consumers do not benefit from their home bank's currency rate, which can reflect the wholesale rate
- Many customers are critical of DCC as a method to top up profits from credit card transactions. On Ryanair flight purchases in particular, consumers spend up to 7% more per booking by using DCC.[3] It is important to note, however, that Ryanair also charges extra fees simply for booking with a credit card[4]
- Many issuing banks apply the foreign usage fee regardless of the currency that is processed, resulting in a very high fee for cardholders, though this practice is quickly becoming obsolete due to customer dissatisfaction

Advantages for Merchants

The biggest advantage for a merchant is receiving a small percentage of the currency conversion margin that is charged to each transaction. These financial returns make the process of DCC more appealing to merchants with high foreign volume.[5] The merchant earns extra revenue when the transaction is processed through DCC, and explanation to the customer about the nature of DCC is left to the individual merchants.

Controversy

Many consumers [6] are concerned that using DCC will result in higher credit card conversion fees than if they used their own card issuer's exchange rate.[7] In many cases, the price of the purchase can be much greater (5 to 7%) without any advantage to the customer other than seeing the amount paid in their currency directly on the credit card slip.

References

[1] Collinson, Patrick (12 July 2008). "Going to Spain? Just say no" (http://www.guardian.co.uk/money/2008/jul/12/foreigncurrency. consumeraffairs). *The Guardian* (London). . Retrieved 1 May 2010.

[2] (http://www.fexcoms.com/products/dynamic-currency-conversiondcc/bestrate/) FEXCO Best Rate Guarantee

[3] Brignall, Miles (15 Feb 2010). "Ryanair's Hidden Costs From Currency Conversion" (http://www.guardian.co.uk/money/2010/feb/15/ ryanair-costs-currency-conversion). *The Guardian* (London). . Retrieved 8 Feb 2011.

[4] Corrigan, Damian (N/A). "Ryanair's Multiple Credit Card Fees" (http://gospain.about.com/od/ryanair/f/credit_card_fees.htm). *About.com* (Spain). . Retrieved 9 March 2011.

[5] (http://www.fexcoms.com/products/dynamic-currency-conversiondcc/detail-1/) Benefits of FEXCOs DCC

[6] (http://www.travelfinances.com/blog/index.php/2006/06/13/buyer-beware-dynamic-currency-conversion-dcc/) Travel Guide for your Finances - Buyer Beware: Dynamic Currency Conversion (DCC)

[7] (http://www.fodors.com/community/europe/they-just-dont-read-or-listen-about-dcc-scam.cfm) Fodor's - They Just Don't Read or Listen about DCC Scam

External links

- Official Visa exchange rates (http://www.corporate.visa.com/pd/consumer_ex_rates.jsp)
- Official MasterCard exchange rates (https://www.mastercard.com/us/personal/en/cardholderservices/currencyconversion/index.html)
- Washington Post Article about DCC (http://www.washingtonpost.com/wp-dyn/content/article/2005/07/29/AR2005072900927.html)

e-gold

e-gold is a digital gold currency operated by Gold & Silver Reserve Inc. under e-gold Ltd., and allowed the instant transfer of gold ownership between users until 2009 when transfers were suspended due to legal issues. e-gold Ltd. is incorporated in Nevis, Saint Kitts and Nevis but the operations were conducted from Florida, USA.

In 2007 the proprietors of the e-gold service were indicted by the United States Department of Justice on four counts of violating money laundering regulations. In July 2008 the company and its three directors pleaded guilty to charges of "conspiracy to engage in money laundering" and the "operation of an unlicensed money transmitting business" in the U.S. District Court for D.C.[1] The company faces fines of $3.7 million.

As of November 2009 the company's website states "As e-gold Users are aware, by agreement with relevant authorities including the U.S. Department of Justice, e-gold has suspended all e-metal Spend activity subject to meeting certain licensing requirements. As a result, e-gold Users have been unable to engage in any transactions, including exchanges, that would require either receiving or making an e-metal Spend from the accounts they control. We are, however, working diligently to develop a means by which account Owners will be able to access the value in their account".[2]

As of December 2010 the company states that refund policy has been approved "We are pleased to announce that we have finalized an agreement with government authorities that will permit owners of VAP-Qualified Accounts to be paid in U.S. dollars their proportionate share of the monetized value of the e-metals in such Accounts"

History

e-gold was founded in 1996 by Dr. Douglas Jackson and Barry K. Downey.[3]

The number of e-gold accounts (as claimed by e-gold) grew from 1 million in November 2003 to 3 million on 22 April 2006.[4] In 2008, the company reported more than 5 million accounts.

Crime and fraud

e-gold has been perceived by the United States government as the medium of choice for many online con-artists, with pyramid schemes and high-yield investment programs ("HYIPs") commonplace. This has been blamed on e-gold's policy of irreversible transactions. In 2006, e-gold began blocking accounts where fraud is proven or suspected.[5]

e-gold and OmniPay have also been accused of being a medium for money laundering. As digital gold currency providers are not banks but may be considered money service businesses, they are legally required to perform various sorts of "know your customer" background checks.

In January 2006, BusinessWeek reported on the use of the e-gold system by ShadowCrew, an 4000-strong international crime syndicate involved in massive identity theft and fraud.[6] Omar Dhanani of Fountain Valley, California, connected to the ShadowCrew, is an e-gold customer and is reported to have moved amounts ranging from $40,000 to $100,000 a week from proceeds of crime through e-gold.[7]

In response, Jackson published a letter which stated that "e-gold operates legally and does not condone persons attempting to use e-gold for criminal activity. e-gold has a long history of cooperation with law enforcement agencies in the US and worldwide, providing data and investigative assistance in response to lawful requests." He further noted that "Our staff has participated in hundreds of investigations supporting the FBI, FTC, IRS, DEA, SEC, USPS, and others." [8]

In August 2006, WORLDLawDirect lawyers announced e-gold officials and their legal counsel to be the subject of a U.S. Federal Court subpoena. They believe e-gold is subject to U.S. Federal Court jurisdiction and may be held liable for some or all of the investors' losses (and potential triple damages) in the Solid Investment [9] large scale high-yield investment program (HYIP) scam.[10] On 27 April 2007, a federal grand jury in Washington, D.C. indicted e-gold Ltd and its owners on charges of money laundering, conspiracy, and operating an unlicensed money transmitting business.[11] e-gold, however, claimed that the charges were groundless, and responded to the allegations.[12] However, in 2008 E-gold pled guilty to some of the charges (see below).

In July 2008, the brother of footballer Joseph Yobo was kidnapped in Nigeria. The kidnappers demanded a ransom of $10,000 paid through e-gold.[13]

2007 indictment

In April 2007, the US government ordered e-gold administration to lock approximately 58 e-gold accounts, including ones owned by The Bullion Exchange, AnyGoldNow, IceGold, GitGold, The Denver Gold Exchange, GoldPouch Express, 1MDC (a Digital Gold Currency, based on e-gold), and forced OmniPay's owner, G&SR, to liquidate the seized assets.[14] A few weeks later, e-gold itself was indicted on four counts.[15]

The essence of the allegations in the indictment is twofold: (1) e-gold is an unlicensed money transmitting entity as defined by United States Code;[16] and (2) e-gold was a de facto means of moving money from illegal activities to wit: high-yield investment programs which are Ponzi scams, credit card and identity fraud sites and retailers of child pornography.

The indictment alleges that the defendants knew of illegal activity associated with accounts and recorded it in the e-gold database with notations such as "child porn", "scammer", and "CC fraud".[17] Additionally, it alleges that while e-gold placed "value limits" on certain accounts suspected of criminal activity, they suggested that the owner open a new account, placing no restrictions on their ability to move funds out of the original account.[18]

Despite the legal action, e-gold remains in business, though no longer accepting any new accounts. However, its gold bullion reserves have dropped from 112,188 oz in April 2007 to 84,856 oz (from 3,491.0 kg to 2,461.2 kg) by June 2007.[19] As of July 2008 reserves have stabilized at 2,420 kg.

Douglas Jackson, CEO, has issued a public rebuttal.[12]

2008 court trial

E-gold was tried with violation of 18 USC 1960 in UNITED STATES OF AMERICA v. E-GOLD, LTD, District of Columbia court. The court found against E-gold, ruling that "a business can clearly engage in money transmitting without limiting its transactions to cash or currency and would commit a crime if it did so without being licensed."[20] In July 2008 the company and its three directors pled guilty to *conspiracy to engage in money laundering* and *conspiracy to operate an unlicensed money-transmitting business*.[1] The company faces fines of $3.7 million, however, the guilty plea is part of a plea bargaining process in which the DA dropped most charges. Regardless, the company has vowed to continue operations following the new Federal KYC guidelines. One upside of the court case for e-gold users is that the judge has rejected any charges of fraud regarding the e-gold user agreement and has confirmed the veracity of the company's gold reserve audit.

In November Gold & Silver Reserve CEO Douglas Jackson was sentenced to 300 hours of community service, a $200 fine, and three years of supervision, including six months of electronically monitored home detention.[21] He had faced a maximum sentence of 20 years in prison and a $500,000 fine. Judge Rosemary Collyer said the men deserved lenient sentences because they did not intend to engage in illegal activity. Jackson's lawyer claimed Jackson was spared the heavier fine because he is deeply in debt - the Judge said "Dr. Jackson has suffered, will continue to suffer, and may never be successful with E-Gold". Reid Jackson, Douglas Jackson's brother, and E-Gold director Barry Downey were each sentenced to three years of probation, 300 hours of community service, and ordered to pay a $2,500 fine and a $100 assessment fee each.

Criticisms

Security

As with any online payment system, e-gold is vulnerable to various threats, notably phishing (for example, forged emails asking for login details) and malware (such as keystroke logging spyware).

e-gold offers no protection whatsoever if an attacker succeeds in obtaining the user's e-gold account number, the user's e-gold password, and access to the user's registered email account. Any losses resulting from a security breach cannot be undone since transfers are non-reversible. If funds are stolen, e-gold will not block a recipient's account without being issued with a court order.

In 2005, the Los Angeles Times reported on a specially created Trojan horse that compromised "dozens" to "the low hundreds" of e-gold accounts.[22] While Trojans usually silently record the login details of the unsuspecting user, the Trojan in question (Win32.Grams) emptied the accounts themselves by transferring the contents to the attacker's accounts.[23]

e-gold recommends that users without a disability should always use a mouse-driven virtual keyboard called "SRK Passphrase Entry" when logging in. Other security recommendations from e-gold include restricting access to a single IP address or browser (*Account Sentinel*) plus using Mozilla Firefox, a firewall and antivirus software [24]

Regulatory challenges and shortcomings

e-gold Ltd. was registered in Nevis, Lesser Antilles in 1999, but was temporarily removed from the register. e-gold cleared an administrative issue and as of July 14, 2006, it is properly registered in Nevis.

In September 2004, several Australian based e-gold currency exchangers ceased operation as they did not hold an Australian Financial Services licence (AFSL) [25] Australian based digital currency exchangers that closed down voluntarily, due to the Australian Securities and Investments Commission (ASIC) licencing requirements, included goldex.net, sydneygoldsales.com and ozzigold.com.

On 24 November 2006, e-gold suspended all accounts held by customers located in Iran.[26]

eBay policy

Beginning January 2006, eBay has restricted buyers and sellers from using many online payment systems and encouraged them to use Paypal, which is wholly owned by eBay. eBay specifically named e-gold as one of the online payment systems that will result in them cancelling a seller's account if used. eBay cited e-gold's policy of non-reversible transactions as a detriment to the buyer experience.[27]

E-Gold Reopens Access

On December 31, 2010, e-gold initiated a value access plan that was approved by relevant governmental authorities in the U.S. Users would have access to the value in their accounts after submitting additional information to e-gold, and after a review of this information by the Court-appointed Claims Administrator and the U.S. Government.[28]

No Evidence of any Progress Made after six months

As of June 3rd 2011, there seems to have been no progress made with the VAP (value access plan) since the December 31st 2010 announcement. The announcement was made without showing any form of validation or the provision of reference links to the US government. Since the announcement is unverifiable and e-gold refuse to clarify or enter into correspondence about it, it has the potential for being partially or entirely untrue.

References

[1] Grant Gross (2007-07-22). "IDG News Service Internet currency firm pleads guilty to money laundering" (http://www.thestandard.com/news/2008/07/22/internet-currency-firm-pleads-guilty-money-laundering). .

[2] "e-gold Blog: e-gold Update: Value Access" (http://blog.e-gold.com/2009/11/egold-update-value-access.html). .

[3] e-gold Corporate (http://www.e-gold.com/unsecure/aboutus.html)

[4] e-gold Statistics (https://www.e-gold.com/stats.html)

[5] E-Gold Gets Tough on Crime (http://www.wired.com/news/technology/0,72278-0.html?tw=rss.index)

[6] Gold Rush (http://www.businessweek.com/magazine/content/06_02/b3966094.htm)

[7] The Hindu Business Line : Gold's the bait (http://www.thehindubusinessline.com/ew/2006/01/23/stories/2006012300060100.htm)

[8] Letter from Dr. Douglas Jackson; Chairman, e-gold, Ltd (http://www.e-gold.com/letter.html)

[9] Solidinvestment.com

[10] WORLDLawDirect - Solidinvestment.com investment scam (http://www.worldlawdirect.com/article/1926/Solidinvestment.com_investment_scam.html)

[11] Online Payment Network Abetted Fraud, Child Pornography (http://www.washingtonpost.com/wp-dyn/content/article/2007/05/01/AR2007050101291.html?hpid=moreheadlines)

[12] e-gold Founder Denies (http://www.e-gold.com/letter3.html)

[13] "Kidnappers Demand e-gold For Safe Return of Nigerian Soccer Player's Brother" (http://www.dgcmagazine.com/blog/?p=133). DGC Magazine. 2008-07-16. .

[14] http://www.usdoj.gov/opa/pr/2007/April/07_crm_301.html DoJ press release

[15] http://www.usdoj.gov/criminal/pr/press_releases/2007/04/CRM_07-301_042707_egold_indict.pdf full text of the indictment

[16] http://www2.law.cornell.edu/uscode/uscode18/usc_sec_18_00001960----000-.html Title 18 USC Section 1960

[17] http://www.justice.gov/criminal/ceos/Press%20Releases/DC%20egold%20indictment.pdf e-gold indictment, paragraph 34

[18] http://www.justice.gov/criminal/ceos/Press%20Releases/DC%20egold%20indictment.pdf e-gold indictment, paragraphs 38-41

[19] e-gold Examiner (http://www.e-gold.com/examiner.html)

[20] Linda Friedman Ramirez (2008-05-13). "International crimes: E-currency subject to licensing requirements" (http://obtainingforeignevidence.blogspot.com/2008/05/international-crimes-e-currency-subject.html). .

[21] Stephanie Condon (2008-11-20). "Judge spares E-Gold directors jail time" (http://news.cnet.com/8301-13578_3-10104677-38.html). CNET. .

[22] http://www.vericept.com/Downloads/NewsArticles/industry_news/2005/Now,%20Every%20Keystroke%20Can%20Betray%20You%20-%20Los%20Angeles%20Times.pdf

[23] Win32.Grams (http://www.lurhq.com/grams.html)

[24] Security Recommendations (http://www.e-gold.com/security.html)

[25] 04-366 ASIC acts to shut down electronic currency trading websites - Australian Securities and Investments Commission (http://www.fido.asic.gov.au/fido/fido.nsf/byheadline/04-366+ASIC+acts+to+shut+down+electronic+currency+trading+websites?openDocument)

[26] Herpel, Mark (2006-12-04). "e-gold Closes All Iranian Accounts" (http://digitalmoneyworld.com/e-gold-closes-all-iranian-accounts/). Digital Money World. . Retrieved 2007-01-08.

[27] eBay: Redirect (http://pages.ebay.com/help/policies/safe-payments-policy.html)

[28] e-gold: December 31st, 2010 blog (http://blog.e-gold.com/2010/12/index.html)

External links

- Official website (http://http://www.e-gold.com/)
- e-gold directory and forums (http://www.egold-bay.com/)
- Digital Gold Currency Online Magazine (http://dgcmagazine.com/)
- The Improbable Rise and Fall of E-Gold (http://www.wired.com/threatlevel/2009/06/e-gold/) - Wired article (June 2009)
- Department of Justice Indictment (http://www.usdoj.gov/opa/pr/2007/April/07_crm_301.html) - Press release of the DOJ indictment (April 2007), plus response (http://www.e-gold.com/letter3.html) by Douglas Jackson
- e-gold Gets Tough on Crime (http://www.wired.com/news/technology/0,72278-0.html?tw=rss.index) - Wired News article (December 2006)
- Holy_father Delivers Rootkits to the Masses (http://www.informationweek.com/blog/main/archives/2006/01/holy_father_del.html) - InformationWeek on rootkits (January 2006), plus response (http://www.informationweek.com/blog/main/archives/2006/01/holy_father_del.html#300319367) by Douglas Jackson
- Gold Rush (http://www.businessweek.com/magazine/content/06_02/b3966094.htm) - BusinessWeek online article (January 2006), plus
- Indomitus report on e-gold (http://indomitus.net/2004status.html#egold) - by James Eric Davidson (January 2005)
- Beware of e-gold (http://www.blonnet.com/iw/2002/10/27/stories/2002102700991000.htm) - THE HINDU Business Line (October 2002)
- In Gold We Trust (http://www.wired.com/wired/archive/10.01/egold.html) - Wired magazine article (January 2002)
- Exchange rates E-gold and other electronic money (http://firstwm.ru/?lng=eng)
- Would a Global Crisis Make e-gold Glitter? (http://www.businessweek.com/ebiz/0004/ep0403.htm) - BusinessWeek online article (April 2000)
- Description E-gold registration process (http://true-exchange.com/?action=publication&id=2)

E-toll

For the electronic toll collection system in Ireland, see eToll.

e-toll or **mandiri e-toll card** is a contactless smart card used by Indonesian toll road operators to pay the toll fee. The card is issued by Bank Mandiri in cooperation with 3 toll operators (PT Jasa Marga Tbk, PT Citra Marga Nusaphala Persada Tbk and PT Marga Mandala Sakti).[1] This card used the RFID system.

The card can be used to pay toll fee at Jakarta Inner Ring Road, Tangerang-Merak Toll Road, and Prof. Sedyatmo Toll Road/Airport Toll Road.

Purchase and Reload

Now, this card can also be used to pay toll fee at Jakarta-Cikampek Road (Gate Pondokgede Barat & Pondokgede Timur) and Jakarta Outer Ring Road (JORR). Next projects, all Toll Road can accept e-Toll Card payment system. e-Toll Card can be purchased at all Bank Mandiri and Indomaret outlets at Jabodetabek Area (Jakarta-Bogor-Depok-Tangerang-Bekasi)and several toll gates' offices. It can be reloaded from range Rp 100,000 - Rp 1,000,000.[2] This card also can be reloaded from Mandiri ATM (cash and non-cash), Mandiri Internet, Mandiri SMS, and Mandiri EDC.

A standard e-toll card.

References

[1] http://www.jasamarga.com/content/view/168/89/lang,en/

[2] http://www.bankmandiri.co.id/english/article/mandiri-etoll-card.asp

Eagle Cash

EagleCash and **EZpay** are cash management applications that use **stored-value card** technology to process financial transactions in "closed-loop" operating environments. The programs are sponsored by the US Department of the Treasury for the US Military. The programs are administered for the Treasury by the Federal Reserve Bank of Boston, and are in use at approved CONUS and OCONUS US military facilities. The systems utilize a plastic payment card, similar to a credit or debit card, which has an embedded microchip which keeps track of the amount of money stored on the card and interfaces with encrypted card acceptance devices. This allows soldiers with the card to purchase goods and services at US military posts and canteens, without carrying cash, or manage their personal bank accounts while on deployment or in training. The program reduces the amount of US currency required overseas, reduces theft, saves thousands of man-hours in labor, helps reduce the risk of transporting cash in battlefield environments, and increases security and convenience for service members. It helped reduce or eliminate the need for cash and money orders.[1]

A soldier showing his EagleCash card

EZPay card

Overview and history

Originally developed in 1997, the EZpay system was born as a pilot project aimed at inductees going into basic training, to alleviate some of the stress and cost of managing money while away from home.[1] Many US military bases are structured like small towns, where goods and services are available for sale. However, transferring wages into cash, in order to purchase desired products has traditionally been a struggle.[2] The system works through soldiers receiving an advance on their wages in the form of the EZPay card, which they can then use to purchase goods and services, such as haircuts, snacks, and recreational activities at on-base shops and stores. At the end of basic training, the balance on the card would be reconverted into cash, and paid back to the soldiers.[1] The project was a great success, since it eliminated the need for bases to keep money on hand, and saved soldiers approximately $125,000 a year in banking fees.[3]

Around the same time, the EZPpay system was expanded for overseas use during the aftermath of the 1992-1995 War in Bosnia and Herzegovina, where US personnel were deployed on peace-keeping missions.[1] [4] Named "EagleCash", the overseas system functions similarly to the EZpay system, but with the added ability of soldiers to attach personal bank accounts to the card, allowing them to load, and reload, without having to access their financial institutions back home. As 386th Air Expeditionary Wing financial manager, Catherine Miles explained in a 2007 article, "It's like a gift card. [...] You can put as little or as much money as you want on it and it comes from your checking account."[5] Unlike regular debit cards, the Eagle Cash is managed on-base, using

A soldier refills his EagleCash card at a kiosk

batch processing which ensures that the cards remained useful even when connections to banks and credit unions State-side are severed.[6] The system was given widespread acceptance in 1999, just before the War in Iraq; it has since been expanded to many military bases such as Camp Anaconda on the front lines.[6]

Benefits and savings

For soldiers, the benefits are straightforward, but for the officers in charge of the system the benefits are much more extensive. Transporting US currency overseas costs the military hundreds of thousands of dollars annually — during the Iraq War, for every $1,000,000 sent to pay soldiers in Iraq, it cost $60,000 in security, logistics, and support fees.[6] It also eliminates the need for the World War II practice of producing the Military Payment Certificate. The use of a cashless economy at military stores reduces transaction times, freeing personnel from tasks like stamping money orders or counting coins — during 9 months of the Iraq War, this saved approximately 5000 hours of processing time for financial personnel.[6] [7] It also prevents counterfeiting.

Since the initial adoption of the EagleCash system, it has been augmented by ATM-like kiosks which allow soldiers to add funds to the card without visiting the base's finance office.[5] Originally, this requirement caused long lines to refill cards, reducing the utility of the system.[2] The conversion to the kiosk system, developed by NCR Corporation, remedied these problems and increased the ability of the system to provide easy cash for soldiers away from home — "something we often take for granted, but for soldiers deployed on foreign land, it has always been a challenge".[2] To date, 3.2 million EagleCash and EZpay cards have been issued and used to process 16.5 million electronic transactions valued at over $3.6 billion."[7]

References

[1] "Army Adopts EZPay for Trainees, Tests Eagle Cash in Bosnia". Army News Service. 2000-08-17.

[2] Harris, Bryan (2006-01-17). "Smart cards, kiosks ease Army life" (http://www.kioskmarketplace.com/article.php?id=15276). Kiosk Marketplace. . Retrieved 2008-02-16.

[3] Snyder, Lisa Beth (2000). *Army Adopts EZpay and EagleCash*. **55**. Soldiers

[4] Clayton, Debra (2008-05-14). "Eagle Cash Helps Manage Money" (http://www.military.com/features/0,15240,135749,00.html). United States Central Command / Military.com. . Retrieved 2008-02-16.

[5] Butterfield, Phillip (2007-09-13). "Eagle Cash card: Money spreads its wings" (http://www.emilitary.org/article.php?aid=12174). The Military Family Network. . Retrieved 2008-02-16.

[6] Conner, Nicholas (2007-03-31). "Eagle Cash Card comes to Camp Taji" (http://www.blackanthem.com/News/U_S_Military_19/ Eagle_Cash_Card_comes_to_Camp_Taji5403.shtml). Blackanthem Military News. . Retrieved 2008-02-16.

[7] "Overview: Eagle Cash" (http://www.fms.treas.gov/eaglecash/index.html). United States Department of the Treasury. 2008-02-05. . Retrieved 2008-02-16.

External links

- Common questions about Eagle Cash (http://fms.treas.gov/eaglecash/questions.html) — United States Department of the Treasury
- Eagle Cash enrollment form (http://www.dtic.mil/whs/directives/infomgt/forms/eforms/dd2887.pdf) (pdf)

Earnest payment

An **earnest payment** (sometimes called **earnest money** or simply *earnest*, or alternatively a **good-faith deposit**) is a deposit towards the purchase of real estate or publicly tendered government contract made by a buyer or registered contractor to demonstrate that he/she is serious (earnest) about wanting to complete the purchase. When a buyer makes an offer to buy residential real estate, he/she generally signs a contract and pays a sum acceptable to the seller by way of earnest money. The amount varies enormously, depending upon local custom and the state of the local market at the time of contract negotiations.

In very lively markets (as experienced on the East and West coasts of the US between 2000 and 2005) earnest money deposits could be as high as 5% of the sales price or more. In other communities, as little as $500 or $1000 is acceptable.

If the seller accepts the offer, the earnest money is held in escrow by the real estate broker (in states like New York) or by a settlement or title company (in states like California, Florida, and Texas) until closing and is then applied to the buyer's portion of the remaining costs. If the offer is rejected, the earnest money is usually returned, since no binding contract has been entered into. If the buyer retracts the offer or does not fulfill its obligations under the contract, the earnest is forfeited. Therefore, it is generally in the seller's best interest to see as high an earnest money deposit as possible.

In ancient times, the earnest payment was called an **earnest penny**, and also known as **Arles penny**, **God's penny**, or **Argentum Dei**. It signified money given to bind a bargain, especially for the purchase or hiring of a servant. According to Black's Law Dictionary (sixth ed.), *Et cepit de praedicto Henrico tres denarios de Argento Dei prae manibus*.[1] Another related term was **luck money**, which was an amount given back to the buyer by the seller on the completion of a deal, for luck.

References

1. ^ ⓒ *This article incorporates content from the 1728* Cyclopaedia, *a publication in the public domain.* (http://digicoll.library.wisc.edu/cgi-bin/HistSciTech/HistSciTech-idx?type=turn&entity=HistSciTech000900240177&isize=L&q1=132)

Ebillz

Shaftesbury Systems Limited.

Type	Private Limited
Industry	Software, Telecommunications billing, IT
Founded	1995
Headquarters	Potters Bar, United Kingdom
Key people	Stephen Dracup (Managing Director) Arvind Meghani (Operations Manager) Yasin Qadir (Sales Manager),
Products	Telecommunications billing, Customer care,
Website	[1]

Ebillz is a leading billing platform software suite used by the telecommunications industry Resellers and Carriers for rating CDR based Call_detail_record traffic as well as bringing together the billing of recurring charge such as WLR Wholesale line rental, ADSL/DSL Broadband and mobile calls and data to offer a single unified invoice for Telephony Services. Established in 1995 and providing software to enable telecommunication companies to bill for Fixed Line Telephony, WLR, Mobile Billing, ADSL/MPLS, Phone System Maintenance Contracts as well as new emerging technologies such as SIP, WIMAX and VO-IP Shaftesbury have today over 200 active clients using their billing platform ebillz, and a team of 16 developers and support staff.

The developer of ebillz is Shaftesbury Systems Limited [1] a privately owned Software Company based in Hertfordshire, United Kingdom. The majority of the telecommunications industry clients who use the ebillz billing platform software are based primarily in United Kingdom however in 2007 Shaftesbury initiated a strategic expansion into Europe and North America and now has over twenty clients in countries as diverse as Switzerland, Denmark, Spain and Canada.

In 2008 Shaftesbury started work on integrating their billing system with new providers of WLR3 [2] Wholesale line rental and now have full integration between ebillz and TPI providers of access to the BT Openreach EMP. In 2008 Shaftesbury were awarded with the BSI British Standards Institution Kitemark status for the Total Metering and Billing System (TMBS) award. This was in recognition of the detailed quality audit done of the bureau billing process option available through ebillz.

In autumn 2009 Shaftesbury launched the Enterprise version of ebillz which comes with substantially improved scalability and resilience to the Carrier grade & Super-Reseller market.

In October 2010 Shaftesbury Systems was acquired by Chess Telecoms Limited and now forms part of the Chess Group of Companies as a wholly owned separate subsidiary.[3]

Some examples of companies using the ebillz system in the United Kingdom are NCS Group, BDR Group members including Sensibill and Wireless Telecoms, Nexus Telecommunications Plc, Pennine Telecom, Direct Save Telecom and Azzuri.

Key Features

- Bills delivered via e-mail
- Effective customer care tools (Built in CRM/Fault Tracking/Note system)
- CDR Import Wizard enables imports of almost any form of CDR from any Carrier
- CDR Load Processing of up to 9,000,000 per hour.
- Import and export of Tariff Tables to spreadsheets for easy maintenance
- Bespoke Tariffs (Ability to give bespoke rates to customers on individual destination level)
- Fraud Protection (Alert system which can auto-send e-mails and SMS Alerts to clients)
- Integration with your Accounting Function (Sage Integration with Sage Line50 and above)
- Comprehensive Management Reporting (Built in Crystal Reports Engine as well as SQL Query based 'Power Reports')
- Call Statistics Analysis sub-system – drill down into any call stats study your call minutes by Customer, Prefix, CLI, Charge Type, or Time of Day
- Enhanced CRM – Instant access to customer info (address, connection info, creation of invoices)
- Credit Control features recording all invoices generated, payments received, aged-debt reports and reminder letter.
- Power Reports – report on any data help within ebillz.
- Direct Debit and Accounts feeds.
- Email and snail-mail merge facilities.

ebillz [4] is capable of rating CDR's [5] at the speed of over 9 million CDR's Per Hour [4] and is a Microsoft SQL database driven engine sitting within a Client/Server setup (with client machines running within a Microsoft Windows environment). ebillz allows integration with third-party external software systems by extracting data from within the platform. Typical applications would include email marketing tools, sales analysis tools, and finance tools (sending out e-mail copies of invoices, creating e-shots and mailshots, and to extract data to work with external Customer relations management systems like GoldMine, ACT! and Salesforce.

Some examples of companies using the ebillz system in the United Kingdom are Cable & Wireless[6] NCS Group [7], Wireless Telecommunications Limited [8] Nexus Telecommunications Plc [9] Pennine Telecom[10] and Azzuri [11]

External links

- Official site [12]
- Official Corporate site [1]

EBPP

Electronic bill presentment & payment (EBPP) is a form of electronic billing in which a company presents (sends) its bills and customers pay these electronically over the Internet.[1]

History

The EBPP model was created by the Council for Electronic Billing and Payment of the National Automated Clearing House Association. Certain electronic billing applications also provide the ability to electronically settle payment for goods or services. Customers of banks and billing companies can use the internet or the phone to conveniently remit payments as well as access their billing information. The service is also supported by customer service representatives (CSRs) contacted directly by the consumer to facilitate payments or receive general assistance and answer questions. EBPP can produce substantial savings to traditional print & mail billing and payment remittance, and as an added benefit is a significant reduction in the use of paper.

Types of EBPP

- **Biller-direct** - This refers to an approach in which consumers make payments directly to one biller that issues bills that they receive at the website of the firm that issued the bill. An example would be of a public utility company offering this payment service to its consumers. A market has emerged for outsourced billing providers who specialize in electronic billing processes and technology for companies that need to send bills directly to their customers. Examples of billing outsourcing specialists are InfoSend, Inc [2], IPayX - Internet Payment Exchange, Inc. [3] and Billtrust [4].
- **Bank-aggregator** - The approach under this model is to make payment at an aggregator or consolidator site, usually from a consumer's bank's website. This model allows the consumer to make payments to multiple billers that are pre-registered to receive payments. An example in the UK is OneVu and Getitkeepit [5] in Ireland.

Parties involved

Billers, bankers, aggregators and consolidators implementing EBPP can play various roles in the overall EBPP process. Once roles are defined, it is easier to identify which model is most appropriate for the client's EBPP strategy. Billers may also implement more than one model in order to best serve their clients. Because the industry is continuously changing and redefining, the options and opportunities for EBPP will continue to expand.

- Biller payment provider (BPP) - An agent of the biller that accepts remittance information on behalf of the Biller.
- Biller service provider (BSP) - An agent of the biller that provides an EBPP service for the Biller.
- Consolidator - A biller service provider that consolidates bills from multiple Billers or other bill service providers (BSPs) and delivers them for presentment to the customer service provider (CSP).[2]
- Customer service provider (CSP) – An agent of the customer that provides an interface directly to customers, businesses or others for bill presentment. CSP enrolls customers, enables presentment and provides customer care, among other functions.

NACHA

NACHA-The Electronic Payments Association is a not-for-profit trade association that develops operating rules and business practices for the Automated Clearing House (ACH) Network and for other areas of electronic payments. NACHA activities and initiatives facilitate the adoption of electronic payments in the areas of Internet commerce, electronic bill payment and presentment (EBPP), financial electronic data interchange (EDI), international payments, electronic checks, electronic benefits transfer (EBT) and student lending.

To define some guidelines for best practices, NACHA has created the Council for Electronic Billing and Payment of the NACHA InteroperaBILL Initiative of the Banking Industry Technology Secretariat (BITS).

Online banking

Electronic bill payment is a now-common feature of online banking, similar in effect to a giro, allowing a depositor to send money from his demand account to a creditor or vendor such as a public utility or a department store to be credited against a specific account. The payment is optimally executed electronically in real time, though some financial institutions or payment services will wait until the next business day to send out the payment. The bank can usually also generate and mail a paper cheque or banker's draft to a creditor who is not set up to receive electronic payments.

Most large banks also offer various convenience features with their electronic bill payment systems, such as the ability to schedule payments in advance to be made on a specified date, the ability to manage payments from any computer with a web browser over internet, and various options for searching one's recent payment history: when did I last pay Company X? To whom did I make my most recent payment? In many cases one can also integrate the electronic payment data with accounting or personal finance software.

Limitations (United States)

Typically, US financial institutions formally prohibit the use of their consumer electronic bill payment systems for payments to any tax authorities, collection agencies, or recipients of court-ordered payments like child support or alimony. Any organizations or individuals outside of the United States are also usually excluded. Payments to government agencies for utilities such as water are usually permitted.

Electronic bill pay systems fall into two categories, "pay-anyone" services and restricted biller list services. In a pay-anyone service, the provider will facilitate a payment to the payee regardless of whether they have an electronic connection with that payee or not. If they cannot deliver the payment to the payee electronically, they will print and mail a paper check on the payer's behalf. The largest providers of electronic bill pay services can deliver about 80% of their payments electronically, so 20% of payments facilitated by the large pay-anyone services are still made by mailing a paper check to the biller. This is the primary reason why some billers in a pay-anyone service require as much as a 5 day lead time for the payment to reach the payee.

Restricted biller list payment services allow you to pay any biller that is in the provider's network, and in these services where the provider has an electronic relationship with the biller, the payments will be delivered electronically.

SADAD Payment System (Saudi Arabia)

SADAD Payment System SADAD was established by the Saudi Arabian Monetary Agency (SAMA) to be the national Electronic Bill Presentment and Payment (EBPP) service provider for the Kingdom of Saudi Arabia (KSA). The core mandate for SADAD is to facilitate and streamline bill payment transactions of end consumers through all channels of the Kingdom's Banks. SADAD was launched on October 3, 2004.

SADAD links the commercial sector and local banks, offering the ability to collect customer payments electronically through all the banking channels in the kingdom 24 hours a day.

References

[1] "What is EBPP" (http://www.webopedia.com/TERM/E/EBPP.html) (in English). webopedia.com. . Retrieved 2008-07-13.

[2] Information on several solutions (http://www.fisolutionswiki.com/wiki/index.
php?title=Internet_Banking_Systems_Vendors#Bill_Payment_&_Presentment_Vendors)

External links

- Council for Electronic Billing and Payment (http://cebp.nacha.org)
- CEBP Business Practices (http://cebp.nacha.org/documents/ebpp-buspractices-2-1.pdf)
- Aite Research - Consumer Bill Payments (http://www.aitegroup.com/reports/20050209.php)
- Aite Research - Biller Direct Technology (http://www.aitegroup.com/reports/200808041.php)
- European Commission Report on e-Invoicing (http://ec.europa.eu/enterprise/sectors/ict/files/finalreport_en.
pdf)
- eBillingnews Portal (http://www.ebillingnews.com)
- Pay It Green - an industry ebilling initiative (http://payitgreen.org/)

ecash

Using cryptography, **ecash** was introduced by David Chaum as an anonymous electronic cash system. He used blind signatures to achieve unlinkability between withdrawal and spend transactions.[1] Depending on the properties of the payment transactions, one distinguishes between on-line and off-line electronic cash. The first off-line e-cash system was proposed by Chaum and Naor.[2] Like the first on-line method, it is based on RSA blind signatures.

In the United States, only one bank implemented ecash, the Mark Twain bank,[3] and the system was dissolved in 1997 after the bank was purchased by Mercantile Bank, a large issuer of credit cards.[4] Similar to credit cards, the system was free to purchasers, while merchants paid a transaction fee.

In Australia ecash was implemented by St.George Bank, but the transactions were not free to purchasers. In June 1998, ecash became available through Credit Suisse in Switzerland. It was also available from Deutsche Bank in Germany, Bank Austria, Finland's Merita Bank/Eunet, Sweden's Posten, and Den norske Bank of Norway.

"ecash" was a trademark of DigiCash, which went bankrupt in 1998, and was sold to eCash Technologies, which was acquired by InfoSpace in 2002.

References

[1] David Chaum, Blind signatures for untraceable payments, Advances in Cryptology - Crypto '82, Springer-Verlag (1983), 199-203. (PDF)
(http://www.computing.surrey.ac.uk/personal/st/J.Heather/teaching/crypto/2010/presentations/electronic-cash.pdf)

[2] Chaum, D., Fiat, A., and Naor, M. 1990. Untraceable electronic cash. In Proceedings on Advances in Cryptology (Santa Barbara, California,
United States). S. Goldwasser, Ed. Springer-Verlag New York, New York, NY, 319-327. (PDF) (http://dsns.csie.nctu.edu.tw/research/
crypto/HTML/PDF/C88/319.PDF)

[3] Mark Twain Bank Launches Ecash (http://www.interesting-people.org/archives/interesting-people/199510/msg00062.html)

[4] DigiCash loses U.S. toehold (http://news.cnet.com/2100-1001-215150.html)

External links

- An introduction to ecash (http://web.archive.org/19971009044558/http://digicash.com/publish/ecash_intro/
ecash_intro.html) at the Wayback Machine (*archived October 9, 1997*).

EDesk

eDesk

eDesk is a generic reference to image processing (cheque truncation) products developed and owned by VSoft Corporation, a software company based in Duluth, Georgia, US and Hyderabad in India.

VSoft Corporation's eDesk Capture™ solutions addresses the capture, validation, processing, archive and transmission of cheque images from all points of presentment. The features in eDesk allow financial institutions to automate deposits at branch tellers, branch back counters, and merchant locations of varying volumes and value, and image enabled ATMs.

Functions

- Teller Capture – Image cheques at the teller counter
- Branch Capture – Image cheques at the branch back office
- Merchant Capture – Enable corporate and business customers to send image cheques to the branch. Merchant Capture allows them to image cheques at their office and send the electronic data and images securely to their branch
- ATM / CDM Capture – Capture and securely transmit cheque images from image enabled ATMs and Cheque Deposit Machines

eDesk's flexible architecture facilitates the deployment of business rules that are appropriate for each point of presentment and institution. The solutions also address the need for multi-institution capability from the outset, making it ideal for organizations processing transactions from multiple institutions.

eDesk Capture solutions allow merchants and corporations to capture cheque images at the convenience of their locations, and send them electronically to their financial institutions.

Features

- Compatible with wide range of industry standard scanners
- Automated amount recognition (CAR/LAR)
- Intelligent repair image system (IRIS™) for automated correction.
- Image Quality Assurance
- Duplicate item detection
- Intuitive user interface

Some eDesk Products

- eDesk Branch™- Teller
- eDesk Branch™-Back Counter
- eDesk Merchant™- Capture
- eDesk ATM/CDM

References

- VSoft Corporation enters second decade of service to Credit Union Market http://pymnts.com/vsoft-enters-second-decade-of-service-to-credit-union-market-20110301005271/
- eDesk Detail features http://www.vsoft.co.in/vsoft/index.php?id=17

- TotalBank Partners with VSoft for Imaging Solution http://www.pr-inside.com/
  totalbank-partners-with-vsoft-for-imaging-r2460414.htm
- Union Bank selects VSoft's Remote Deposit Capture solution http://www.streetinsider.com/Press+Releases/
  Union+Bank+Selects+VSoft+to+Support+Remote+Deposit+Capture+Growth/6267349.html

External Links

- http://vsoft.co.in/vsoft/index.php?id=15
- http://www.vsoftcorp.com/vsoft/index.php?id=15

eFaktura

eFaktura is a Norwegian electronic billing system issued by Bankenes Betalingssentral (BBS). The system involves both business-to-customer (B2C) systems, branded as eFaktura, and business-to-business (B2B) branded as **eFaktura B2B**. The system is built upon the bankgiro system used for online banking.

Use of eFaktura require the customer to use an online banking system from a Norwegian bank. Because all banks are connected to BBS, there is no discrimination between customers of different banks. Any company or organisation can sign an eFaktura agreement with their bank (though usually for a typically five-digit NOK startup fee) and send electronic bills to any client as long as they have a Norwegian online banking account. There is no requirement for the two to use the same bank. The ordinary eFaktura includes a specification of the bill, and the entire bill or invoice can be seen in the online banking system, and printed if so desired. eFaktura was launched in 2000.

For companies the eFaktura B2B has been developed. Companies using electronic billing need to be able to import the invoice directly into the accounting software of the company. BBS offers services to send out paper bills to any company not able to receive electronic billing. eFaktura B2B was launched in 2006.

External links

- eFaktura web site [1] (**Norwegian**)
- Companies offering eFaktura [2] (**Norwegian**)

EFTPOS

EFTPOS (pronounced /ɛftpɒs/ — **Electronic Funds Transfer at Point of Sale**) is the general term used for debit card based systems used for processing transactions through terminals at points of sale. In Australia and New Zealand it is also the brand name of the specific system used for such payments. The Australian and New Zealand systems are country specific and do not interconnect.

Australia

EFTPOS is an Australian system for processing payment card transactions at "points of sale" and at ATMs.[1] Not all merchants provide EFTPOS facilities, but those that do must accept debit cards issued by any Australian bank, and some also accept various credit cards and other cards. Some credit cards also have linked personal accounts which can be accessed via the EFTPOS system, and thus act like debit cards in relation to those personal accounts. For credit cards to be accepted by a merchant a separate agreement must be entered into with each credit card company.

Some merchants set minimum transaction amounts for EFTPOS transactions.

A number of merchants permit customers using a debit card to withdraw cash as part of the EFTPOS transaction.[2] In Australia, this facility is known as "cash out", which in many other countries is called debit card cashback. For the merchant, cash out is a way of reducing their net cash takings, saving on banking of cash. There is no additional cost to the merchant in providing cash out because banks charge a merchant a debit card transaction fee per EFTPOS transaction, and not on the transaction value. Cash out is a facility provided by the merchant, and not the bank, who can limit or vary how much cash can be withdrawn at a time and to suspend the facility at any time. When available, cash out is convenient for the customer, who can bypass having to visit a bank branch or ATM. Cash out is also cheaper for the customer, since only one bank transaction is involved. For people in some remote areas, cash out may be the only way they can withdraw cash from their personal accounts. However, most merchants who provide the facility set a relatively low limit on cash out, generally $50, and some also charge for the service. Cash out is not available for credit cards because the merchant is charged a percentage commission on credit card transactions based on the value, and also because cash withdrawals on credit cards are treated differently to sale transactions.

Each Australian bank has given a different name to its debit cards, such as:

- Commonwealth Bank of Australia: Keycard
- Westpac Banking Corporation: Handycard
- National Australia Bank: FlexiCard
- ANZ Bank: Access card
- Bendigo Bank: Cashcard

Australian debit cards can be used outside Australia if they carry the Maestro/Cirrus or Plus logos, indicating that they are linked to their transaction system. Similarly, non-Australian debit and credit cards can be used at EFTPOS terminals or ATMs if they have these logos or the MasterCard, Visa, Diners Club, or American Express logo. Discover is not accepted in Australia. The EFTPOS system is not available for non-bank or non-credit card based transactions, so that store cards and proprietor cards, such as Fleetcard and Motorcard, cannot be processed using an EFTPOS terminal.

EFTPOS transactions involving a debit or credit card can be authenticated by printing and signing a receipt; the merchant verifies the signature on the receipt against the signature on the card. However, as of May 2011 financial institutions are in the process of rolling out smart cards with integrated circuits ("chips") that will enable verification by entering a personal identification number (PIN) at the EFTPOS terminal.[3] [4] At ATMs, only PIN verification is available, and all new credit cards are now issued with PINs regardless of whether or not they have a chip. As a further security measure, if a user enters an incorrect PIN three times, the card may be locked out of EFTPOS and require reactivation over the phone or at a branch. In the case of an ATM, the card will not be returned, and the cardholder will need to visit the branch to retrieve the card, or request a new card to be issued.

History

The name and logo for EFTPOS in Australia were originally owned by the National Australia Bank and were trade marks from 1986 until 1991.[5]

In April 2009, a company, "EFTPOS Payments Australia Ltd", was formed to manage and promote the EFTPOS system in Australia.[6] The initial members of EFTPOS Payments Australia Ltd were:

- Australia and New Zealand Banking Group
- Australian Settlements Limited
- Bank of Queensland
- Bendigo and Adelaide Bank
- Cashcard
- Citigroup
- Commonwealth Bank of Australia
- Coles Group (now Wesfarmers)
- Cuscal
- Indue
- National Australia Bank
- Suncorp-Metway
- Westpac Banking Corporation
- Woolworths Limited

Usage

As of December 2010, there were over 707,000 EFTPOS terminals in Australia and over 28,000 ATMs.[7] Of the EFTPOS terminals, over 60,000 offered cash withdrawals.[8] In 2010, 183 million transactions,[9] worth A$12 billion,[10] were made using Australian EFTPOS terminals per month.

Network

The EFT network in Australia is made up of seven proprietary networks in which peers have interchange agreements, making an effective single network.[11] A merchant who wishes to accept EFTPOS payments must enter an agreement with one of the seven merchant service providers, which rent the terminal to the merchant. All the merchant's EFTPOS transactions are processed through one of these gateways. Some of these peers are:

- Australia and New Zealand Banking Group
- Commonwealth Bank of Australia
- Cuscal [12]
- FDI (Cashcard)
- National Australia Bank
- Westpac Banking Corporation
- Other

Other organisations may have peering agreements with the one or more of the central peers.

The network uses the AS 2805 protocol.

New Zealand

Eftpos is highly popular in New Zealand, with more debit card terminals per head of population than any other country and usage very wide spread. The system is operated by two providers, Paymark Limited (formerly Electronic Transaction Services Limited) which processes 75% of all electronic transactions in New Zealand, and EFTPOS NZ. Although the term eftpos is popularly used to describe the system, EFTPOS is a trademark of EFTPOS NZ the smaller of the two providers. Both providers run an interconnected financial network that allows the processing of not only of debit cards at point of sale terminals but also credit cards and charge cards.

History

The Bank of New Zealand introduced EFTPOS to New Zealand in 1985 through a pilot scheme with petrol stations.

In 1989 the system was officially launched and two providers owned by the major banks now run the system. The largest of the two providers, Paymark Limited (formerly Electronic Transaction Services Limited) is owned equally by ASB Bank, Westpac, Bank of New Zealand and ANZ National Bank. The second is operated by EFTPOS NZ which is fully owned by ANZ National Bank.

During July 2006 the five billionth EFTPOS payment flowed across the Paymark EFTPOS network since the electronic form of payment was introduced in New Zealand in 1989.[12]

Usage

EFTPOS is highly popular in New Zealand, with more debit card terminals per head of population than any other country,[13] and being used for about 60% of all retail transactions.[14] According to the largest EFTPOS network provider, "New Zealanders use EFTPOS twice as much as any other country."[15] In 2009, there were 200 EFTPOS transactions per person, compared with 80 transactions per person in Canada.[16]

References

[1] EFTPOS. Merchant banking services. EFTPOS. Bank of Queensland Australia (http://www.boq.com.au/business_merchant_eftpos.htm)

[2] Nab — Eftpos (http://www.nab.com.au/Personal_Finance/0,,9493,00.html)

[3] NAB General Security tips (http://www.nab.com.au/wps/wcm/connect/nab/nab/home/about_us/22/3)

[4] Visa Australia kills signatures by 2013 (http://www.zdnet.com.au/visa-australia-kills-signatures-by-2013-339299331.htm)

[5] ATMOSS — Australian Trade Mark Online Search System (http://pericles.ipaustralia.gov.au/atmoss/falcon_details.show_tm_details?p_tm_number=449716&p_search_no=2&p_ExtDisp=D&p_detail=DETAILED&p_rec_no=10&p_rec_all=20)

[6] APCA PaymentsMonitor publication — Industry establishes new company to manage EFTPOS (http://www.apca.com.au/PM/2009_Quarter2/index.html)

[7] APCA ATM and EFTPOS statistics (http://www.apca.com.au/Public/apca01_live.nsf/WebPageDisplay/Stats_Terminals)

[8] NAB — Eftpos (http://www.nab.com.au/Personal_Finance/0,,9493,00.html)

[9] APCA Card Transaction Volume (http://www.apca.com.au/Public/apca01_live.nsf/WebPageDisplay/Stats_CardVolume)

[10] APCA Card Transaction Value (http://www.apca.com.au/Public/apca01_live.nsf/WebPageDisplay/Stats_CardValue)

[11] RBA paper on Australian Payment systems (http://www.rba.gov.au/PaymentsSystem/Publications/BISCommitteeOnPaymentAndSettlementSystems/australia.pdf)

[12] Paymark "Nought to five billion in 17 years" (http://www.paymark.co.nz/cms_display.php?st=1&sn=108&pg=804). Paymark. July 24, 2006. Paymark.

[13] Key Dates in Bank of New Zealands History — Bank of New Zealand (http://www.bnz.co.nz/About_Us/1,1184,3-156-495-2411,00. html)

[14] "Payment and Settlement Services in New Zealand" (http://www.rbnz.govt.nz/payment/0108068.pdf). Reserve Bank of New Zealand. September 2003. .

[15] "Paymark background introduction" (http://www.paymark.co.nz/dart/darthttp.dll?etsl&site_id=1&section_id=37&page_id=228& detail_title_section_id=71). Paymark. . Retrieved May 6, 2010.

[16] Eight billionth eftpos transaction processed (http://www.nbr.co.nz/article/eight-billionth-eftpos-transaction-processed-116444) — Kelly Gregor, National Business Review, 14 December 2009

Electronic Benefit Transfer

Electronic Benefit Transfer (EBT) is an electronic system in the United States that allows state governments to provide financial and material benefits via a plastic debit card. Common benefits provided via EBT are typically sorted into two general categories: Food and Cash benefits. Food benefits are federally authorized benefits that can be used only to purchase food and non-alcoholic beverages. Food benefits, formerly called Food Stamps, are now called SNAP (or Supplemental Nutrition Assistance Program). Cash benefits include State General Assistance, TANF (Temporary Aid for Needy Families) benefits and refugee benefits.

Usage

Through EBT, a recipient uses his/her EBT card to make purchases at participating retailers. Food Stamp benefits can only be used to purchase food items authorized by the USDA's SNAP program. Cash benefits may be used to purchase any item at a participating retailer, as well as to obtain cash-back or make a cash withdrawal from a participating ATM.

State agencies work with contractors to procure their own EBT systems for delivery of SNAP and other state-administered benefit programs. In the United States, all SNAP benefits are now being issued via EBT.

For example, in the SNAP Program, recipients apply for their benefits in the usual way, by filling out a form at their local food stamp office. Once eligibility and level of benefits have been determined, information is transferred to the state's EBT contractor and an account is established in the participant's name, and SNAP benefits are deposited electronically in the account each month. A plastic debit card, similar to a bank card, is issued and a personal identification number (PIN) is assigned or chosen by the recipient to give access to the account. Recipients are offered the opportunity to change the PIN at any time, and are offered ongoing training if they have any problems accessing the system.

All states have systems that use magnetic stripe cards and "on-line" authorization of transactions. When paying for groceries, the SNAP customer's card is run through an electronic reader or a point of sale terminal (POS), and the recipient enters the secret PIN to access the food stamp account. Then, electronically, the processor verifies the PIN and the account balance, and sends an authorization or denial back to the retailer. The recipient's account is then debited for the amount of the purchase, and the retailer's account is credited. No cash money changes hands. Payment is made to the retailer through a ACH settlement process at the end of the business day. Most states' online EBT systems are interoperable through the **Quest** network, which is sponsored by the Electronic Benefits and Services Council (formerly the EBT Council) of NACHA-The Electronic Payments Association.

Many states stagger the issuing of benefits to EBT SNAP accounts with the actual day of the month determined for each recipient based on their case number, Social Security number, or date of birth. The states of Alaska, Idaho, Nevada, North Dakota, Oklahoma, Vermont along with Guam and the US Virgin Islands credit accounts on the first of the month to all recipients, New Hampshire credits on the 5th, and South Dakota on the 10th.[1]

The success of EBT enabled Congress to rename the Food Stamp Program to the Supplemental Nutrition Assistance Program, as of October 2008, and update all references in federal law from "stamp" or "coupon" to "card" or "EBT".

This was effected by H.R. 2419, The Food, Conservation, and Energy Act of 2008 (a.k.a. "2008 Farm Bill") passed into law as Public Law No: 110-234, over President Bush's veto.[2]

Law

It is illegal for anyone to charge sales tax, surcharges or card processing fees from an EBT SNAP account, according to Federal Law and USDA SNAP Guidelines.[3]

References

[1] "SNAP Monthly Benefit Issuance Schedule" (http://www.fns.usda.gov/snap/ebt/issuance-map.htm). Fns.usda.gov. 2010-04-16. . Retrieved 2010-09-27.

[2] "House Committee on Agriculture:" (http://agriculture.house.gov/inside/FarmBill.html). Agriculture.house.gov. . Retrieved 2010-09-27.

[3] USDA Retailer Training Guide PDF File (http://www.fns.usda.gov/snap/retailers/pdfs/Retailer_Training_Guide.pdf)

Electronic bill payment

Electronic bill payment is a feature of online banking, similar in its effect to a giro, allowing a depositor to send money from his demand account to a creditor or vendor such as a public utility or a department store to be credited against a specific account. The payment is optimally executed electronically in real time, though some financial institutions or payment services will wait until the next business day to send out the payment. The bank can usually also generate and mail a paper cheque or banker's draft to a creditor who is not set up to receive electronic payments.

Electronic billing can also feature invoices sent by e-mail or viewed on a secure web site (with notices of new invoices being sent by e-mail).

Most large banks also offer various convenience features with their electronic bill payment systems, such as the ability to schedule payments in advance to be made on a specified date, the ability to manage payments from any computer with a web browser, and various options for searching one's recent payment history: when did I last pay Company X? To whom did I make my most recent payment? In many cases one can also integrate the electronic payment data with accounting or personal finance software.

Peer-to-peer payment systems are extremely popular. The best and most widely known example is PayPal. PayPal allows you to pay for just about anything online as long as the seller also has a PayPal account. Many online sellers use PayPal such as 75% of eBay sellers, overstock.com, ritzcamera.com, and Walgreens.com (Traver, 2004). PayPal is also sometimes used to pay for personal debts in situations where both parties have an account.

Electronic bill payment and presentation (EBPP) includes an electronic bill payment system (EBPS). Although this technology was available from the mid 90's onward, only 26.2% of U.S. households had internet access at that time according to the U.S. Department of Commerce. By August 2000, adoption of EBPP systems started to dramatically increase. The customer is notified (typically be email) by the biller, and then is responsible to log on and pay the bill through the biller's website.

Limitations (United States)

Typically, US financial institutions formally prohibit the use of their consumer electronic bill payment systems for payments to any tax authorities, collection agencies, or recipients of court-ordered payments like child support or alimony. Any organizations or individuals outside of the United States are also usually excluded. Payments to government agencies for utilities such as water are usually permitted.[1]

References

[1] http://www.associatedbank.com/Personal/OnlineBillPayFAQ.asp

Electronic billing

Electronic billing is the electronic delivery of invoices (bills) and related information by a company to its customers. Electronic billing is referred to by a variety of terms, including the following:

- **EBPP** — electronic bill presentment & payment (typically focused on business-to-consumer billing and payment)
- **EIPP** — electronic invoice presentment and payment (typically focused on business-to-business billing and payment)
- "e-billing"
- "e-invoicing"
- "electronic invoicing"
- ePayables
- eInvoice

While there are current efforts to standardize systems for electronic billing and invoicing, there is currently a wide variety of options for businesses and consumers. Most fall into one of two categories:

- CSPs (customer service providers) which allow a business to invoice clients electronically
- bank aggregators, which allow consumers to pay multiple bills, typically through their bank

Increasing acceptance of e-billing by consumers and the business community (according to *Kiplinger* magazine, 77% of business owners now favor electronic billing),as well as increased concern for security and the environment, is speeding up the shift to electronic billing from paper billing.

External links

- Electronic Payments Association [1]

Electronic Check Council

The Electronic Check Council (**ECC**) is a US organization that provides a forum for stakeholders of NACHA-The Electronic Payments Association to design, propose, monitor, and promote solutions that enable the conversion of paper checks to electronic entries.

The council was founded in 1995 and currently has more than 140 members, including financial institutions, vendors, retailers, processors, networks and associations.

Goals

- Support the testing of electronic check applications through pilot programs.
- Implement electronic Check applications that show the greatest potential.
- Support research to address consumer, legal, regulatory and risk issues of electronic check applications.
- Provide a forum for all stakeholders in the electronic check arena.
- Promote the development and use of electronic check applications.

Process

Developments at the ECC all start with discussion and development of solutions in small group settings. These smaller groups are designated as work groups and ad hoc groups that focus on specific areas of electronic check development.

A work group is an ongoing group that tackles a number of issues over a period of time related specifically either to a particular Standard Entry Class Code (such as POP, ARC, etc.) or to a specific topic that impacts all eCheck Standard Entry Class Codes (such as marketing).

An ad hoc group (or subgroup) tackles one specific issue and disbands once the issue has been resolved.

External links

- The Electronic Check Council [1]

Electronic funds transfer

Electronic funds transfer or **EFT** is the electronic exchange or transfer of money from one account to another, either within a single financial institution or across multiple institutions, through computer-based systems.

The term is used for a number of different concepts:

- Cardholder-initiated transactions, where a cardholder makes use of a payment card
- Direct deposit payroll payments for a business to its employees, possibly via a payroll service bureau
- Direct debit payments, sometimes called *electronic checks*, for which a business debits the consumer's bank accounts for payment for goods or services
- Electronic bill payment in online banking, which may be delivered by EFT or paper check
- Transactions involving stored value of electronic money, possibly in a private currency
- Wire transfer via an international banking network (carries a higher fee in North America)
- Electronic Benefit Transfer

In 1978 U.S. Congress passed the Electronic Funds Transfer Act to establish the rights and liabilities of consumers as well as the responsibilities of all participants in EFT activities in the United States.

References

Electronic money

For electronic payments in conventional currencies, see Electronic funds transfer.

Electronic money (also known as **e-currency**, **e-money**, **electronic cash**, **electronic currency**, **digital money**, **digital cash**, **digital currency**, **cyber currency**) refers to money or scrip which is only exchanged electronically. Typically, this involves the use of computer networks, the internet and digital stored value systems. Electronic Funds Transfer (EFT), direct deposit, digital gold currency and virtual currency are all examples of electronic money. Also, it is a collective term for financial cryptography and technologies enabling it.

While electronic money has been an interesting problem for cryptography (see for example the work of David Chaum and Markus Jakobsson), to date, the use of e-money has been relatively low-scale. One rare success has been Hong Kong's Octopus card system, which started as a transit payment system and has grown into a widely used electronic money system. London Transport's Oyster card system remains essentially a contactless pre-paid travelcard. Two other cities have implemented functioning electronic money systems. Very similar to Hong Kong's Octopus card, Singapore has an electronic money program for its public transportation system (commuter trains, bus, etc.), based on the same type of (FeliCa) system. The Netherlands has also implemented a nationwide electronic money system known as Chipknip for general purpose, as well as OV-Chipkaart for transit fare collection. In Belgium, a payment service company, Proton, owned by 60 Belgian banks issuing stored value cards, was developed in 1995.[1]

A number of electronic money systems use contactless payment transfer in order to facilitate easy payment and give the payee more confidence in not letting go of their electronic wallet during the transaction.

Electronic money systems

In technical terms, electronic money is an online representation, or a system of debits and credits, used to exchange value within another system, or within itself as a stand alone system. In principle this process could also be done offline.

Occasionally, the term electronic money is also used to refer to the provider itself. A private currency may use gold to provide extra security, such as digital gold currency. Some private organizations, such as the United States armed forces use independent currencies such as Eagle Cash.

Centralised systems

Many systems—such as PayPal, WebMoney, cashU, and Hub Culture's Ven—will sell their electronic currency directly to the end user, but other systems such as Liberty Reserve only sell through third party digital currency exchangers.

In the case of Octopus card in Hong Kong, electronic money deposits work similarly to regular bank deposits. After Octopus Card Limited receives money for deposit from users, the money is deposited into a bank. This is similar to debit-card-issuing banks redepositing money at central banks.

Africa and Afghanistan are seeing prepaid cell phone minutes being used as electronic money using the M-Pesa system.[2]

Some community currencies, like some Local Exchange Trading Systems (LETS) and the Community Exchange System, work with electronic transactions.

Decentralised systems

Decentralised electronic money systems include:

- Ripple monetary system, a project to develop a distributed system of electronic money independent of local currency.
- Bitcoin,[3] an existing peer-to-peer electronic money system with a maximum inflation limit

Offline 'anonymous' systems

In the use of offline electronic money, the merchant does not need to interact with the bank before accepting money from the user. Instead merchants can collect monies *spent* by users and *deposit* them later with the bank. In principle this could be done offline, i.e. the merchant could go to the bank with his storage media to exchange e-money for cash. Nevertheless the merchant is guaranteed that the user's e-money will either be accepted by the bank, or the bank will be able to identify and punish the cheating user. In this way a user is prevented from spending the same funds twice (double-spending). Offline e-money schemes also need to protect against cheating merchants, i.e. merchants that want to deposit money twice (and then blame the user).

Using cryptography, anonymous ecash was introduced by David Chaum. He used blind signatures to achieve unlinkability between withdrawal and spend transactions.[4] In cryptography, e-cash usually refers to anonymous e-cash. Depending on the properties of the payment transactions, one distinguishes between online and offline e-cash. The first offline e-cash system was proposed by Chaum and Naor.[5] Like the first on-line scheme, it is based on RSA blind signatures.

Hard vs soft electronic currencies

A *hard electronic currency* is one that does not have services to dispute or reverse charges. In other words, it only supports non-reversible transactions. Reversing transactions, even in case of a legitimate error, unauthorized use, or failure of a vendor to supply goods is difficult, if not impossible. The advantage of this arrangement is that the operating costs of the electronic currency system are greatly reduced by not having to resolve payment disputes. Additionally, it allows the electronic currency transactions to clear instantly, making the funds available immediately to the recipient. This means that using hard electronic currency is more akin to a cash transaction. Examples are TokenPay, Pecunix, Liberty Reserve, Western Union, KlickEx and Bitcoin.

A *soft electronic currency* is one that allows for reversal of payments, for example in case of fraud or disputes. Reversible payment methods generally have a "clearing time" of 72 hours or more. Examples are PayPal and credit card.

A hard currency can be *softened* by using a trusted third party or an escrow service.

Future progression

The main focuses of electronic money development are:

1. being able to use it through a wider range of hardware such as secured credit cards
2. linked bank accounts that would generally be used over an internet means, for exchange with a secure micropayment system such as in large corporations (PayPal, KlickEx).

Issues

Although electronic money can provide many benefits—such as convenience and privacy, increased efficiency of transactions, lower transaction fees, and new business opportunities with the expansion of economic activities on the Internet—there are many potential issues with the use of e-money. The transfer of digital currencies raises local issues such as how to levy taxes or the possible ease of money laundering. There are also potential macro-economic effects such as exchange rate instabilities and shortage of money supplies (total amount of electronic money versus the total amount of real money available, basically the possibility that digital cash could exceed the real cash available).

References

[1] Good, Barbara Ann (2000). *The changing face of money: will electronic money be adopted in the United States?* (http://books.google.com/ books?id=iTVf8v_OIyUC&pg=PA80&dq=Belgium+Proton+money). Taylor & Francis. pp. 80–81. ISBN 9780815338093. . Retrieved 28 December 2010.

[2] http://www.nextnature.net/2008/12/cell-phone-minutes-the-next-currency/

[3] Bitcoin (http://www.bitcoin.org/) website

[4] David Chaum, Blind signatures for untraceable payments, Advances in Cryptology — Crypto '82, Springer-Verlag (1983), 199-203. (PDF) (http://dsns.csie.nctu.edu.tw/research/crypto/HTML/PDF/C82/199.PDF)

[5] Chaum, D., Fiat, A., and Naor, M. 1990. Untraceable electronic cash. In Proceedings on Advances in Cryptology (Santa Barbara, California, United States). S. Goldwasser, Ed. Springer-Verlag New York, New York, NY, 319-327. (PDF) (http://dsns.csie.nctu.edu.tw/research/ crypto/HTML/PDF/C88/319.PDF)

External links

- Untraceable Digital Cash, Information Markets, and BlackNet (http://osaka.law.miami.edu/~froomkin/articles/tcmay.htm) (1997) by Timothy C. May
- Open Transactions (http://github.com/FellowTraveler/Open-Transactions/wiki) Open source, untraceable digital cash software.
- Principles for a free, powerful and stable monetary system for the digital era (http://spoirier.lautre.net/money.htm) by S. Poirier
- Flood Control on the Information Ocean: Living With Anonymity, Digital Cash, and Distributed Databases (http://www.law.miami.edu/~froomkin/articles/oceanno.htm), (1996) by Michael Froomkin
- *Status Report on Free Market Money* (2005) from The Indomitus Report (http://indomitus.net/2004status.html)
- The Evolution of Money (1999) (http://papers.ssrn.com/sol3/papers.cfm?abstract_id=952148)

Electronic Money Association

Formation	October, 2001
Location	Central London, UK
Region served	Europe
Website	Home page [1]

The **Electronic Money Association** (EMA) is the trade body representing electronic money issuers in Europe.

Background

The EMA was founded in October 2001 by a group of electronic money issuers.

Role

The EMA is the trade body representing electronic money issuers and payment institutions. It brings together payments companies, the telecommunications and transport sectors as well as specialist e-money issuers to address issues of common interest and to act in the interest of the industry as a whole. The EMA represents industry with regulators, government bodies as well as international organisations. It responds to regulatory proposals, drafts industry guidelines and acts as a forum for communication and education.

Structure

The EMA is a committee with sub-committees formed to address areas of special concern including:

- Money Laundering
- Fraud
- Online Fraud and Security

Activities

Members of the Electronic Money Association and its subcommittees meets on a monthly basis in Central London. Additionally, the EMA organizes seminars and hold an annual conference:

- The first EMA Conference on *The Revision of the E-money Directive* was held in February 2006 in Brussels, Belgium.
- The second EMA Conference on *Future of Payments in Europe* was held in November 2007 in London, UK.

External links

- Electronic Money Association home page [1]

Electronic Payment Services

EPS
易辦事

Operating area	Hong Kong
Members	21
Founded	1984

Electronic Payment Services (Chinese: 易辦事), commonly known as **EPS**, is the largest electronic payment system in Hong Kong, Macau and Shenzhen starting from 1985. The service is provided by **EPS Company (Hong Kong) Limited**. Currently there are over 25,000 acceptance locations.

Provider

Established in 1984, **EPS Company (Hong Kong) Limited** (formerly **Electronic Payment Services Company**) is currently a consortium of 21 major banks in Hong Kong.

System

In each retail location, a terminal is installed and is usually connected to a POS system of retailer. The terminal can also connect to banks through the public phone system.

The operation of the system is easy. The retailer swipes a customer's ATM card in the terminal and keys in the payment amount. The cardholder then selects the appropriate bank account and keys in the PIN. After successful connection to the bank, a receipt will be printed for the customer and the retailer. Some automatic terminals require the cardholder to insert his or her ATM card into a terminal machine rather than have the merchant swipe the card.

Payment for each transaction is directly transferred from the payer's bank account to receiver's.

Service at consumer level

EPS service

EPS (易辦事) is simple use of ATM card or credit card with ATM function, no application of service is required. All ATM cards or credit cards with ATM function issued by EPS Company member banks could perform EPS function.

Consumer simply presents the ATM card to the cashier. Cashier swipes consumer's card and enter the transaction amount. Comsumer confirm the amount by inputting ATM card PIN. EPS receipts are printed with "ACCEPTED" for successful transaction.

EPS EasyCash service

With **EPS EasyCash** (提款易) , consumer can withdraw cash at over 1,200 locations in Hong Kong upon purchase with EPS. The cash withdrawal amount can be in multiples of HK$100, at a maximum of HK$500. EPS EasyCash service is also commonly known as Cashback service.

EPS EasyCash service is currently available at chain store of Gourmet, Great, IKEA, Mannings, MarketPlace, Massimo Dutti, Circle K, Oliver's, Parknshop, Taste, Threesizty, Vango, China Resources Vanguard (CRV), V'ole and Wellcome in Hong Kong.

EPS Company Member Bank List

- Bank of China (Hong Kong) Limited
- Bank of Communications, HK Branch
- China Construction Bank (Asia)
- China Merchants Bank Company Limited
- Chiyu Banking Corporation Limited
- Chong Hing Bank Limited
- Citibank (Hong Kong) Limited
- Citic Ka Wah Bank Limited
- Dah Sing Bank Limited
- DBS Bank (Hong Kong) Limited
- Fubon Bank (Hong Kong) Limited
- Hang Seng Bank Limited
- The Hongkong and Shanghai Banking Corporation (HSBC)
- ICBC (Asia)
- Mevas Bank Limited
- Nanyang Commercial Bank Limited
- Shaghai Commercial Bank Limited
- Standard Chartered Bank (Hong Kong) Limited
- The Bank of East Asia Limited
- Wing Hang Bank Limited
- Wing Lung Bank Limited

Remark: All ATM cards or credit cards with ATM function issued by above member banks could perform EPS service.

Official website

Official website [1]

External links

- Official website [1] **(English) (traditional Chinese (HK)) (Chinese)**

Elektronisches Lastschriftverfahren

Elektronisches Lastschriftverfahren (also known as **Lastschrift**, **Bankeinzug** or simply **ELV**) is a form of direct debit transaction that is popular in Germany. It is only used in Germany.

EPAS

EPAS (Electronic Protocols Application Software) is a non-commercial cooperation initiative launched in Europe which aims at developing a series of data protocols to be applied in a point of interaction (POI) environment.

The project intends to address the three following protocols :

- a terminal management protocol;
- a retailer application protocol;
- an acquirer protocol.

The main objectives common to the three protocols are:

- protocol interoperability : each protocol is designed in such a way as to be independent of the external device and the POI;
- independence of the system architecture and the integration level of the POI within the retailer application protocol;
- independence of the communication support and low level protocols : each protocol is independent of the network connection and will address both wire and wireless connections.

Context

A current barrier to the development of the POI meerkat is due to the existing fragmented market for this type of equipment, especially in Europe, where each country has adopted its own requirements and rules in terms of security and functions to be implemented in POI devices.

Today's situation is the following one :

- card accepting devices from one country cannot be replaced by similar devices of another country due to different – incompatible - protocols for download, key management, communication with cash registers requiring specific software modules for each country of operation;
- card accepting devices from one country cannot process transactions issued by acquirers from another country due to the incompatibility of the protocols between the two countries;
- different proprietary implementation of existing ISO protocols in Europe hampers the development of central acquiring activities in Europe.

The goal of the EPAS project is therefore the issuance of technical specifications and the development of open software for three major protocols to be used in a Point of Interaction environment. The protocols enable a POI to communicate with external devices and hosts. An additional aim of the project is to validate - through demonstrators - the technical feasibility of the three protocols developed in the framework of the project.

The project is to be considered as a cornerstone of another initiative ("ERIDANE") initiated at the European level with several partners belonging to the EPAS Consortium. The aim of the ERIDANE project is to achieve a common set of standards for hardware and software components to be used in point-of-sales retail environments. As such, EPAS complements adequately the work carried out by the ERIDANE project which essentially focuses on the inner structure of a POI terminal used at retailers' point of sales locations.

With the development of specifications, the project intends to issue a new generation of open standards to be internationally deployed by equipment manufacturers, with a strong support from the banking and card payment industries as well as retailers, solutions providers and users. The consortium is made of large industrial organisations, small and medium enterprises, card payment organisations, solution providers, retailers and users, as well as an academic institution, all having an in-depth expertise in the activities to be carried out in the framework of the project. The partnership is composed of organisations belonging to Austria, France, Germany, Italy, Belgium, The Netherlands, Luxembourg, Spain, Portugal, the United Kingdom and Nordic countries.

Objectives of EPAS

The outcome of the EPAS initiative will enable to achieve interoperability by :

- giving to manufacturers a technological advance vis-à-vis their non-European competitors ;
- ensuring the interoperability of protocols at a European level ;
- improving the security level of the protocols.

One of the objective of the European Commission in contributing to the building of the European Union is the creation of a Single European Market ensuring a free circulation of goods and persons as it is the case today for most national − domestic − markets in Europe. In order to anticipate undue legislation, partners in the consortium have come together to develop and disseminate a set of data protocols which would complement the business standards needed to achieve the necessary Single European Payments Area Standards.

The development of standards to create a large internal market of financial services has, however, been largely endorsed, not only by the banking industry, but also by solution providers, manufacturers, retailers and users.

The EPAS project foresees the development and provision of the missing links mentioned above in the creation of a unified market of electronic payments services by 2010.

The EPAS project intends to bring a major benefit to the POS market by eliminating existing barriers and by allowing applications to be developed and used for both national and international markets reducing to a large extent the investments to be carried out by all actors involved.

The EPAS project aims at addressing such technical bottlenecks by delivering state-of-the-art data protocols in order to ensure a smooth process of POS transactions in a forthcoming Europe-wide domestic market.

Project Development

The proposed initiative will be structured along the three following main phases :

- Phase I : development of technical specifications and issuance of standards (2006 - mid-2007)
- Phase II : development of software and provision of test tools (2007 − 2008)
- Phase III : construction of demonstrators (2008)

The EPAS project will be conducted in line with the strategic objectives of the EPC (European Payments Council).

Participants

The EPAS Consortium is composed of 23 organisations, each of them actively involved in its respective domain of expertise (card payment schemes, manufacturers, service companies, software developers, retailers).

The participating organisations are :

- Thales e-Transaction (FR)
- Ingenico (FR)
- VeriFone (US)
- The Logic Group (UK)
- MoneyLine (FR)
- Lyra Network (FR)
- Atos Worldline (DE)
- Wincor Nixdorf (ES)
- GIE – Groupement des Cartes Bancaires "CB" (FR) (Co-ordinator)
- Banksys (BE)
- Security Research and Consulting (SRC) GmbH (DE)
- Equens SE(NL)
- Sermepa (ES)
- Cetrel (LU)
- Total (FR)
- Quercia (IT)
- University of Applied Sciences, Cologne (DE)
- Integri (BE)
- PAN Nordic Card Association (PNC) (SE)
- GALITT (FR)
- BP (GB)
- RSC Commercial Services (DE)
- Europay Austria Zahlungsverkehrssysteme GmbH (AT)
- SIBS (PT), Thales e-Transactions España (ES)

Links to the participating companies

- Atos Worldline: http://www.atosorigin.com/en-us
- Banksys: http://www.banksys.com/bkscomwt/EN/index.jsp
- BP: http://www.bp.com/home.do?categoryId=1
- Cetrel: http://www.cetrel.lu/
- Europay Austria Zahlungsverkehrssysteme GmbH: http://www.europay.at/
- Fachhochschule Köln: http://www.inf.fh-koeln.de/~ktds/profil/
- GALITT: http://www.galitt.com/
- GROUPEMENT DES CARTES BANCAIRES (Co-ordinator) : http://www.cartes-bancaires.com/
- ingenico: http://www.ingenico.com/
- Integri: http://www.integri.com/
- Equens: http://www.equens.com/
- Lyra Network: http://www.lyra-network.com/en/en_index.htm
- Moneyline: http://www.moneyline.fr/fr/
- PAN Nordic Card Association: http://www.pan-nordic.org/
- RSC Commercial Services: http://www.retail-sc.com/
- Sermepa: http://www.sermepa.es/espanol/index.htm

- SIBS: http://www.sibs.pt/
- SRC: http://www.src-gmbh.de/
- THALES e-Transactions: http://www.thales-e-transactions.com/
- The Logic Group: http://www.the-logic-group.com
- Total: http://www.total.com/
- VeriFone: http://www.verifone.com
- Wincor Nixdorf: http://www.wincor-nixdorf.com/internet/index.html

Sources

- "Standardisierungsarbeiten im europäischen Zahlungsverkehr - Chancen für SEPA" SRC - Security Research & Consulting GmbH, Bonn - Wiesbaden, Germany, 2006, p. 5, 11 (PDF-transparencies)
- William Vanobberghen, „Le Projet EPAS - Sécurité, protection des personnes et des donnée: de nouvelles technologies et des standards pour fiabiliser le contrôle et l'identification", Groupement des Cartes Bancaires, 27. June 2006 (PPT-transparencies)
- Hans-Rainer Frank, „SEPA aus Sicht eines europäischen Tankstellenbetreibers", Arbeitskreis ePayment, Brussels, 11.May 2006, p. 11 (PDF-transparencies)
- GROUPEMENT DES CARTES BANCAIRES, „EUROPEAN STANDARDISATION FOR ELECTRONIC PAYMENTS", http://www.cartes-bancaires.com/en/dossiers/standard.html
- „EPC◆Card Fraud Prevention ◆& Security Activities",Cédric Sarazin – Chairman Card Fraud Prevention TF 19. December 2007, FPEG Meeting - Brussels, http://ec.europa.eu/internal_market/fpeg/docs/sarazin_en.ppt

Eurocheque

The **Eurocheque** was a type of cheque used in Europe that was accepted across national borders and which could be written in a variety of currencies.

Eurocheques were originally introduced in 1969 as an alternative to the traveler's cheque and for international payments for goods and services. They were rapidly adopted for domestic use in a number of countries, to the extent that their use for international payment rarely accounted for more than 5% of total Eurocheque transactions.[1] The charges for clearing Eurocheques were substantially lower than those for cross-border use of domestic cheques.[2]

Eurocheque logo

Although still accepted as payment by a few bodies, the practice of issuing Eurocheques ceased on 1 January 2002, following the decision to withdraw the Eurocheque guarantee.[3] This was, coincidentally, the same date that the euro currency was introduced. Despite the similarity of name, the Eurocheque had no connection with the currency.

Eurocheques were particularly popular in German-speaking countries, where they were often issued as standard domestic cheques. They usually had to be accompanied by a cheque guarantee card in order to be accepted in payment at a point of sale. The Eurocheque guarantee card also had the functionality of an ATM card. In some countries, such as Austria and Germany, virtually all Eurocheque cards were co-branded with the logo of the respective domestic debit card system and were actually debit cards. After its phase-out, virtually all of these Eurocheque cards were replaced by Maestro cards. Therefore, Maestro is very often considered to be the successor to the Eurocheque system.

The decision to end the issuing of Eurocheques was taken as increasing numbers of retailers and banks started to decline payment by Eurocheque, and as the use of cash machines and credit cards by international travellers grew within Europe.[4] The relatively high cost of processing Eurocheques, together with the costs resulting from fraud, were also among the factors.[1] In advance of the move, the European Commission expressed concern that "the benefits of the existing eurocheque system, in particular its standardised cheque format and its clearing facilities in all European countries should not be lost."[2]

History

The Eurocheque was launched in 1969 with the participation of banks in 14 countries — Belgium, France, United Kingdom, the Netherlands, Austria, Switzerland and West Germany (which issued and accepted Eurocheques) together with Denmark, Italy, Ireland, Luxembourg, Norway, Spain and Sweden (which only accepted Eurocheques).

In 1972 the 'uniform Eurocheque' and 'uniform Eurocheque guarantee card' were introduced, providing single designs that could be used by all banks within the system. Previously all Eurocheques had carried the Eurocheque symbol, but differed in their designs.[1] [5]

Eurocheque International C.V. was formed in 1974 to process payments made using Eurocheques.[6]

In 1983 the British banks withdrew the Eurocheque symbol from their credit cards.[1]

On 3 February 1988, Eurocheque International became a cooperative society established under Belgian law, having previously been a *de facto* association, rather than a legal entity. The shareholders were the

Maestro card issued by a German Bank

Association of Swedish Banks, Associazione Bancaria Italiana, Groupement des cartes bancaires 'CB' (France), Comunidade Portuguesa eurocheque, Bank of Cyprus, Caisse d'épargne de l'État du grand-duché de Luxembourg, Agrupació Andorrana Eurocheque, PBS-Pengeinstitutternes BetalingsSystemer (Denmark), Apacs (United Kingdom), Telekurs (Switzerland), Suomen Pankkiyhdistys (Finland), Association of Norwegian Banks, Stichting Bevordering Chequeverkeer (Netherlands), Irish Clearing House, Jugobanka United Bank (Yugoslavia), Association of Austrian Banks and Bankers, Eurocheque Belgique sc, GZS-Gesellschaft für Zahlungssysteme GmbH (Germany).[7]

According to an estimate by Eurocheque International, in 1989 around 32 million Eurocheque cards had been issued by some 9,000 banks in 20 countries.[8]

By the end of 1998 there were 46 participating countries, 22 of them both issuing and accepting the cheques:[1] Belgium, Denmark, Germany, Finland, France, United Kingdom, Ireland, Israel, Italy, Croatia, Luxembourg, Malta, Netherlands, Poland, Portugal, Switzerland, Slovenia, Spain, the Czech Republic, Hungary, Cyprus, and 24 accepting cheques: Egypt, Albania, Algeria, Andorra, Armenia, Azerbaijan, Bosnia-Herzegovina, Bulgaria, Georgia, Gibraltar, Greece, Iceland, Lebanon, Lithuania, Latvia, Morocco, Macedonia, Romania, Russia, Slovakia, Tunisia, Turkey, Ukraine, Belarus.

In 1989 the French banks withdrew the Eurocheque symbol from their credit cards. In the same year the use of the Uniform Eurocheque format became universal.[1]

On 1 September 1992, Eurocheque International C.V. and Eurocheque International Holding N.V. merged together with EUROCARD International N.V. into a single company, Europay International S.A., incorporated under Belgian law.[9] Europay relocated to Waterloo, Belgium, where they shared the same address as the Europe, Middle East and Africa region of MasterCard International, and the headquarters of the Eurocard-MasterCard joint-venture, Maestro International.

The decision to end the Eurocheque guarantee from the end of 2002 was taken by Europay's board on 22 April 2001.[1]

References

[1] Development of eurocheque countries, eurocheque maps and transnational eurocheques (http://www.banking-accounts.org/eurocheque/p2.htm), Banking-accounts.org, June 23, 2006

[2] Communication from the Commission to the Council and the European Parliament — Retail payments in the internal market (http://eur-lex.europa.eu/LexUriServ/LexUriServ.do?uri=CELEX:52000DC0036:EN:NOT)

[3] eurocheques (http://www.maestro.ch/en/ma_home/ma_maestro/ma_eurocheques.htm)

[4] Cash dispensers spell the demise of Eurocheques next year (http://findarticles.com/p/articles/mi_qn4158/is_19991122/ai_n14263270), The Independent, Nov 22, 1999, Andrew Garfield

[5] Plastic payment fraud in Europe (http://www.ema.com.ua/ema/epi4.nsf/VIEWNAME/AD039FCCF453C6C5C2256B9E0046B8E9/$FILE/Plastic payment fraud in Europe.rtf), Rafaël Rondelez

[6] ServiRed Payments Network — Evolution (http://www.servired.es/ingles/evolucion.htm)

[7] 92/212/EEC: Commission Decision of 25 March 1992 relating to a proceeding pursuant to Article 85 of the EEC Treaty (IV/30.717-A - Eurocheque: Helsinki Agreement) (http://eur-lex.europa.eu/LexUriServ/LexUriServ.do?uri=CELEX:31992D0212:EN:NOT), Official Journal L 095, 09/04/1992 pp. 0050–0067

[8] 89/95/EEC: Commission Decision of 19 December 1988 relating to a proceeding under Article 85 of the EEC Treaty (http://eur-lex.europa.eu/LexUriServ/LexUriServ.do?uri=CELEX:31989D0095:EN:NOT), Official Journal L 036, 08/02/1989 pp. 0016–0022

[9] Europay Membership Rules and Licensing (http://eur-lex.europa.eu/LexUriServ/LexUriServ.do?uri=CELEX:52002XC0413(02):EN:NOT), Euro-Lex: Official Journal C 089 , 13/04/2002 pp. 0007–0010

The Everything Card

The **First National City Charge Service**, marketed as **The Everything Card**, was an early credit card introduced by First National City Bank (now Citibank) in the eastern United States in 1967. It was intended as a response to the BankAmericard (today's Visa card), issued by BankAmerica.

Issued under the initiative of National City Bank President Walter B. Wriston, the card followed the bank's purchase of an interest in the Carte Blanche charge card. However, the card proved to be limited by its regional scope, as it was tied to the area surrounding the bank's New York base of operations.[1]

In 1969, the card was absorbed into Master Charge (now known as MasterCard), another card that had been developed by a membership association of four banks, the Interbank Card Association, which National City Bank joined.[2]

Citibank, as National City Bank came to be known in 1976, made a further attempt in 1977 to create a proprietary credit card that was not tied to either Master Charge or Visa. The Choice card was, like the Everything Card, a regional credit card issued only by Citibank. It also proved unsuccessful, and its cards were reissued as Visa cards in 1987.

References

[1] "Secret History of the Credit Card: Interview Walter Wriston" (http://www.pbs.org/wgbh/pages/frontline/shows/credit/interviews/wriston.html). PBS Frontline. . Retrieved 2008-08-24.

[2] "Citigroup History: Citibank N.A." (http://web.archive.org/web/20080613210609/http://www.citigroup.com/citigroup/corporate/history/citibank.htm). Citigroup website. Archived from the original (http://www.citigroup.com/citigroup/corporate/history/citibank.htm) on 2008-06-13. . Retrieved 2008-08-24.

Eway

eWAY

Type	Private
Industry	payment gateway
Founded	Canberra, ACT, Australia (1998)
Headquarters	Canberra, ACT, Australia Auckland, New Zealand London, England, UK
Key people	Matt Bullock (CEO) Tony McGrath (CIO) Richard Considine (Operations Manager)
Website	www.eway.com.au [1]

eWAY is an online payment gateway used by businesses in Australia, New Zealand and the UK to process credit card payments. It is expected to expand into Asia by 2012.[1] BBC News has named eWAY as "a market leader in Australia's online payments processing sector."[2]

History

eWAY was founded in 1998[3] when now-CEO Matt Bullock was engaged to create a payment gateway for Medibank. The enormous success of the project prompted Bullock to start designing payment gateways for other businesses.

eway.com.au was launched in 2000. By 2004, eWAY was linked to all major Australian banks. In 2008 the company reported growth of 47%[4] , and in 2009 the company expanded by a further 65%[5] . By this time, the five biggest banks in New Zealand were linked to eWAY. In 2010 the company announced a partnership with Google, wherein merchants would receive $75 of free advertising through AdWords on signup.[6]

The company now has approximately 8000 clients including Qantas, Canon, Setanta Sports, McDonald's and 3M.[7] [8] [9]

Compared to other online payment gateways

Unlike master merchants (e.g. PayPal), eWAY allows clients to choose their own Internet Merchant Facility, and only charges for transactions at a flat rate (rather than taking a percentage from the total price of each item).[10]

Customers can also make payments without leaving the merchant's website, and funds are transferred directly into the merchant's bank account, rather than withheld until a withdrawal request is processed.[11]

Most payment gateways require users to separately purchase an SSL certificate and an IMF, whereas eWAY is the only authorised reseller for the Commonwealth Bank of Australia[12] and for American Express, as well as a Platinum Partner of Verisign. This means clients can apply for a CBA IMF, request to accept Amex payments, or acquire Verisign and Geotrust SSL certificates directly through eWAY.

Additionally, eWAY offers free API so as developers can easily integrate their shopping carts with the gateway.[13] Because of this, eWAY now supports more shopping carts than any other Australian payment gateway,[14] including osCommerce,[15] Magento,[16] Prestashop[17] and Zen Cart.[18]

Security

eWAY is tier one PCI DSS compliant, and is audited every year by Securus Global and Vectra.[19] The current uptime of the service is 99.999%, and data is protected at Macquarie Telecom's ISO and DSD-certified data centre in Sydney.[20]

eWAY clients can choose their own security settings via Beagle Anti-fraud,[21] a tool which allows merchants to block or flag transactions based on a combination of risk factors, such as the presence of an anonymous proxy or a discrepancy between the country of the billing address and that of the IP address.

Notable awards won

- 2010 ORIA Industry Recognition Award[22]
- 2009 CeBIT.AU Award for Excellence in Engineering Design[23]
- 2008 Telstra ACT Business of the Year Award[24]
- 2008 Telstra MYOB Small Business Awards[25]
- 2008 CeBIT.AU Award for Excellence in Technology[26]
- 2008 Canberra BusinessPoint Award for Sales Growth[27]
- 2007 CeBIT.AU Platinum Award for Export Excellence[28]

External links

- eway.com.au [30]
- eway.co.nz [31]
- eway.co.uk [32]
- ewayinc.com [33]
- ewayinc.co.in [34]
- eway.com.sg [35]

References

[1] http://www.ecommercereport.com.au/?p=716
[2] http://www.bbc.co.uk/news/uk-scotland-scotland-business-13377644
[3] http://www.canberrabusinesscouncil.com.au/pages/images/CBC%20FEBRUARY%20088.FA.pdf
[4] http://www.ecommercereport.com.au/story61.php
[5] http://www.macquarietelecom.com/media_room/releases/090421-Eway_pci_compliance.htm
[6] http://www.whatech.com.au/technology-releases/internet-marketing/3174-eway-announces-deal-with-google-adwords
[7] http://anthillonline.com/meet-eway-2010-anthill-cool-company-award-finalist/
[8] http://www.homegymequipment.com.au/gym-equipment.html
[9] http://www.canberrabusinesscouncil.com.au/pages/images/CBC%20FEBRUARY%20088.FA.pdf
[10] http://www.untanglemyweb.com/About/Blog/articleID/224/Australian-Payment-Gateway-Comparison
[11] http://www.goldcoastlogin.com.au/Articles/Payment-Gateways-Australia.htm
[12] http://www.pcworld.idg.com.au/article/216655/eway_commbank_streamline_merchant_payments/
[13] http://anthillonline.com/meet-eway-2010-anthill-cool-company-award-finalist/
[14] http://ifactory.com.au/payment-gateways.html?Itemid=63
[15] http://www.oscommerce.com/community/contributions,875
[16] http://www.magentocommerce.com/magento-connect/Magento+Core/extension/155/eway-extension
[17] http://www.presto-changeo.com/payment-modules/13-eway-australia-payment.html
[18] http://www.zen-cart.com/index.php?main_page=product_contrib_info&products_id=742
[19] http://www.theaustralian.com.au/australian-it/data-security-for-eway/story-e6frgalo-1225699959412

[20] http://www.itnews.com.au/News/142991,eway-puts-gateway-into-macquarie-data-centre.aspx

[21] http://www.ecornerstoresplus.com.au/epages/ecornerdemo1.sf/?ObjectPath=/Shops/ecornerstoresplus/Categories/tips/payment_methods/tips_epages_payment

[22] http://www.internetretailing.com.au/winners-announced-online-retail-awards.html

[23] http://www.cebit.com.au/2009/cebit-award-winners/eway

[24] http://www.telstrabusinessawards.com/award-winners/past-winners/2008/2008-australian-capital-territory-56.aspx

[25] http://www.telstrabusinessawards.com/award-winners/past-winners/2008/2008-australian-capital-territory-56.aspx

[26] http://www.smh.com.au/news/technology/biztech/the-little-aussies-that-could/2009/05/18/1242498695483.html

[27] http://www.business.act.gov.au/functions/2000_events__and__seminars/canberra_businesspoint_2008_business_awards

[28] http://www.smh.com.au/news/technology/biztech/the-little-aussies-that-could/2009/05/18/1242498695483.html

EWise

eWise is a privately held technology company with offices in Denver (Colorado), London (UK), Shenzhen (China) and Sydney (Australia). eWise was founded by Alex Grinberg in 2000. eWise develops and sells online payment, account aggregation, personal financial management (PFM) and eAuthentication solutions to financial institutions in Australasia, Europe, North America, and the United Kingdom.

eWise is best known for its role in establishing Online Banking ePayments (OBeP) networks around the world. The company is the exclusive network provider for the NACHA Secure Vault Payments [1] network in the US, they are partnering with VocaLink [2] to introduce a similar payments solution to the UK, and eWise has also been working with the International Council of Payment Network Operators (ICPNO [3]) since it was established in 2008 to develop common standards and rules for global interoperability between Online Banking ePayments networks.

eWise's other lines of business include account aggregation and personal financial management (PFM) solutions for financial institutions that bring together all the accounts held by one person onto a single screen, with analytics and online financial management tools, that can be accessed by a single user ID. eWise customers include Financial Institutions such as Citibank and First Direct (part of HSBC) in the UK, Ping An in China and Westpac in Australia.

In 2010 eWise announced it had raised venture capital financing from the three major markets, Asia/Pacific, Europe and North America to:

- Accelerate the US rollout of Secure Vault Payments [1], an Online Banking ePayments network sponsored and governed by NACHA, the Electronic Payments Association;
- Launch and support operations of an Online Banking ePayments network in the UK in partnership with VocaLink [2];
- Expand the online Personal Financial Management (PFM) division in the UK, China and Asia Pacific.

The funding round was led by Balderton Capital, one of Europe's largest technology investors, with other major investors including Atlanta based Total Technology Ventures, Patagorang, led by Mr. Roger Allen and Mr. Stanley S. Shuman of Allen & Co.

References

- eWise raises $12.1m [4]
- NACHA
- Online Banking ePayments
- Account Aggregation
- eWise chosen by Westpac to provide account aggregation [5]
- eWise chosen to provide payment system to [[NACHA-The Electronic Payments Association|NACHA [6]]]
- eWise Systems Powers first direct's Internet Banking plus Service [7]
- Egg Money Manager achieves significant results using eWise account aggregation technology [8]

External links

- Official eWise Website [9]
- Official Secure Vault Payments Website [10]

Express Payment System

The **Express Payment System**, more commonly known as the **EPS**, was the EFTPOS system originally of the ATM cards of Bank of the Philippine Islands and its subsidiaries, BPI Family Savings Bank and BPI Direct Savings Bank. Today, it is the EFTPOS system of the Expressnet interbank network in the Philippines. The system is the most popular EFTPOS system for ATM cardholders in the Philippines and is accepted  nationwide. Rivals of the network include MegaLink's PayLink and the similarly named BancNet Payment System (BPS).

Although the Philippines is largely still a cash-based society, the EPS is slowly but surely getting widespread prominence. Since its launch, it has expanded to be found in many stores nationwide and has since expanded from its roots with BPI, which also pioneered Expressnet. In fact, the EPS is no longer limited to shopping: the EPS can also be used for things such as paying doctor's fees or paying for a haircut with the swipe of one's ATM card. Currently, there are more than 8,200 EPS merchants throughout the Philippines.

In 2005, the EPS expanded to include the ATM cards of Banco de Oro and Land Bank of the Philippines, both Expressnet members. However, many EPS merchants claim that their EPS terminal works only with BPI ATM cards or do not know how to use Banco de Oro or Landbank cards with the EPS terminal; this is because virtually all EPS terminals are BPI terminals (Banco de Oro and Landbank EPS terminals debuted just recently). Also, Banco de Oro and Landbank ATM cards, unlike BPI ATM cards, cannot be directly swiped on an EPS terminal. In order to use these cards, an EPS merchant must enter the number 7 on the main screen then swipe the card to use these ATM cards. As of 2005, HSBC and its subsidiary, HSBC Savings Bank, although both members of Expressnet, do not participate in the EPS system, meaning that HSBC and HSBC Savings Bank ATM cards cannot be used on an EPS terminal.

In addition to functioning as an ATM EFTPOS terminal, EPS terminals also accept BPI credit, debit and prepaid cards. However, these transactions are considered as BPI Express Credit transactions and not as EPS transactions.

Banco de Oro has its own terminal independent of the EPS either branded under the SM name or under its own name. Terminals under either name accept all Banco de Oro cards (Smarteller ATM card and derivatives, BDO Gift Card, BDO Cash Card and BDO credit cards) and have the functions of an EPS terminal. Terminals under the SM name, however, have extended capabilities such as having the capabilities of an EPS, PayLink and BPS terminal (and even the ATM cards of non-affiliated banks) all in one as well as the acceptance of other banks' credit, debit and prepaid cards.

The terminal can be found depending on the name. Terminals under the SM name can be found in all SM stores, such as their supermarkets, department stores and stores such as Surplus Shop and Toy Kingdom. Terminals under the Banco de Oro name can be found in businesses that accept Banco de Oro cards before Banco de Oro joined the EPS. Some merchants though still use the Banco de Oro terminal.

External links

- Express Payment System [1]

Faster Payments Service

Faster Payments Service (FPS) is a UK banking initiative to reduce payment times between different banks' customer accounts from three working days using the long-established BACS system, to near real time. CHAPS already provides limited faster-than-BACS service (by close of business that day) for 'high value' transactions, while FPS is focused on the much larger number of payments of smaller values (the actual limits depend on the individual banks, with some allowing individual Faster Payments up to the value of £20,000 and £100,000 for standing orders).

Faster Payments logo

Twelve banks and one building society, accounting for about 95 percent of payments traffic, initially committed to use the service. Other institutions could join later as full members (though as of late 2010 none have). For smaller organisations such as building societies and savings institutions, a deposit-only service is available through agency arrangements with a member. There had been few announcements regarding charges for Faster Payments. It was expected to be around £1-£5 [1] [2] [3] for immediate payments by business users. No retail bank currently charges personal customers, nor is there currently any sign this will change.

FPS was officially launched on the 27 May 2008[4] (though testing the previous week allowed users to process very small value (1p) transactions as 'faster payments')[5] for non-scheduled, 'immediate' payments (about 5 percent of traffic) only,[6] with access for future-dated payments and standing orders from 6 June. In practice the service was severely limited by the approach of individual member banks to its adoption (see *Implementation*). A general online Sort Code Checker [7] was made available by APACS shortly ahead of launch, which shows whether a specific sort code is able to *receive* Faster Payments.

Background

In November 1998 the UK Treasury commissioned a review (The *Cruickshank Report*) of competition within the UK banking sector, which reported in March 2000. Among its recommendations was primary legislation to establish an independent payment systems commission (PayCom) in place of existing, privately controlled, interbank arrangements. The following day, the Chancellor, Gordon Brown, announced *legislation would be introduced, if necessary*, to open payment systems to increased competition.[8] Initially the banking industry was consulted by government on further steps and progress in payments services monitored by the Competition Commission and the Office of Fair Trading (OFT).

By May 2003, while the OFT was able to report modest improvements, such as changes to BACS and the governance of APACS, some competition concerns remained[9] and, in December 2003, the Treasury announced the OFT would take on: "*an enhanced role* in relation to payment systems, for a period of four years" to resolve outstanding competition problems "*in advance of any legislation*"[10] ; essentially self-regulation. In March 2004 the OFT announced the formation of a joint government-industry body, the *Payments Systems Task Force*, under its chairmanship [11] .

Agreement

In May 2005 the Task Force announced agreement had been reached to reduce clearing times for phone, Internet and standing order payments [12] . This committed the payments services industry to develop a system able to clear automated payments in no more than half a day—the so-called 'ELLE' model—resulting in payment being received the *same day* if made sufficiently early. Implementation groups were given six months to bring forward detailed proposals.

In October 2005 the contract to provide the central infrastructure for this new service was awarded by APACS to Immediate Payments Limited, a joint venture company set up by Voca and LINK who have since merged to form VocaLink.

In December 2005 the Task Force accepted an APACS recommendation for a still more ambitious target on payment times [13] to ensure access to funds within a *couple of hours* of any payment being made, and allowing payments to be sent 24 hours a day, 7 days a week, to be available by November 2007. This stage also marked formal dissolution of the Task Force and reformation as a permanent body, the *Payments Industry Association*[14] (later *Payments Council*), responsible for governance of all payments systems - including Faster Payments.

Delays

In July 2007 APACS announced a delay in the introduction of Faster Payments, beyond November,[15] due to "complex and time-consuming" testing requirements, with a new target of May 2008 later established.[16] In turn, individual bank adoption of FPS was patchy, which resulted in further delays as banks decided when to make the service available to customers and what additional restrictions they would apply. Nine months after the official launch date, the OFT reported Faster Payments were still only operating at 69 percent capacity, [17] with customers losing interest estimated between £38 and £82 million as a result.[18] By October 2009 (15 months after launch) capacity had reached 47 percent of standing orders and 73 percent of all single payments. [19]

Organisation of FPS

APACS was responsible for the development and delivery of Faster Payments, but after May 2008 transferred day-to-day operations and management of the service to the CHAPS Clearing Company (a member-based organisation responsible for the CHAPS sterling high-value same-day payment system.)

The design of Faster Payments was a joint project between Immediate Payments Ltd. (IPL), APACS and the founder members, based on a commitment made to the OFT *Payment Systems Task Force* in 2005. IPL, a VocaLink company, supplies the central network for the service.

Participating members

The original founding members of the new service were: Abbey (now Santander UK), Alliance and Leicester (now part of Santander UK), Barclays, Citi, Clydesdale and Yorkshire Banks (National Australia Group), Co-operative Bank, HBOS, HSBC, Lloyds TSB, Nationwide Building Society, Northern Bank (Danske Bank), Northern Rock, and Royal Bank of Scotland Group (including NatWest and Ulster Bank). Santander does not currently offer this service

Implementation

Information from APACS on the current availability of Faster Payments is maintained at their webpage: "Which banks can send Faster Payments and what is my bank's value limit?" [20]. This information remains indicative, however, and occasional interruptions to users of the service have occurred.

Following the initial launch of the central infrastructure, work was planned to provide a Direct Corporate Access Channel and the first such payment was made in July 2009[20] . This will ultimately enable businesses to submit large numbers of payments directly into the Faster Payments Service.

From 6 September 2010, the value limit for all payment-types was raised to £100,000. However, "individual banks and building societies will continue to set their own value limits for their corporate and consumer customers."[21]

Technology

Faster Payments is designed to support one-time payments, standing orders, corporate bulk payments, and return payments[22] . The service is expected to handle a peak volume in excess of ten million transactions per day. After three months of operation peak volumes of over 1 million daily transactions had been reached[23] . After six months volume had approached four million transactions[24] ; in March 2009, after nine months, five million transactions and £1bn[25] . The system, designed by VocaLink with the backing of APACS, comprises networks of member institutions (banks) surrounding the core central system. The central system is designed to handle the actual message switching in near real time, manage the settlement of accounts at the Bank of England, and generate reports. The physical network will be handled by VocaLink and the system will be managed by the CHAPS Clearing Company.

References

[1] Albany Software (http://www.albany.co.uk/news/news_faster_payments.htm) February 2007

[2] Bank of Scotland Corporate Tariff About your account and our charges (http://www.bankofscotland.co.uk/corporate/pdf/trans_chgs.pdf)

[3] Coutts Commercial tariff Faster Payments – Commercial clients (http://www.coutts.com/productsandservices/faster-payments/commercial-clients-faqs.asp#19)

[4] APACS, Banking industry update on new Faster Payments Service (http://www.apacs.org.uk/08_02_27.html) February, 2008

[5] Money Saving Expert. "HSBC Fast payment is right here right now" (http://forums.moneysavingexpert.com/showthread.html?t=925769). . Retrieved 2008-05-27.

[6] APACS, Press release - phased rollout for new faster payments (http://www.apacs.org.uk/08_04_28.html) 28 April 2008

[7] APACS Sort Code Checker (http://www.ukpayments.org.uk/sort_code_checker/)

[8] Banking Liaison Group, Cruickshank banking review (http://www.bankexperts.co.uk/cruickshank/payment-systems.htm)

[9] OFT, Press release PN 66/03 - market study on payment systems (http://www.oft.gov.uk/news/press/2003/pn_66-03) 22 May 2003

[10] HM Treasury, Pre-Buget Report - para. 3.16 (http://www.hm-treasury.gov.uk/media/D/1/PBR03completerep[1].pdf) December, 2003

[11] OFT, Press release PN 43/04 - payments systems task force announced (http://www.oft.gov.uk/news/press/2004/43-04) 15 March 2004

[12] OFT, Press release PN 94/05 - faster payments service announced (http://www.oft.gov.uk/news/press/2005/94-05) 24 May 2005

[13] APACS, Press release - details of faster payment services (http://www.apacs.org.uk/media_centre/press/05_12_16.html) 16 December 2005

[14] OFT, Press release PN 159/06 - new governance body for payment systems (http://oft.gov.uk/news/press/2006/159-06) 14 November 2006

[15] APACS, Press release - banking industry update on faster payments project (http://www.apacs.org.uk/media_centre/press/07_12_07.html) 12 July 2007

[16] APACS, Press release - revised timescale for faster payments service (http://www.apacs.org.uk/media_centre/press/08_14_07.html) 14 August 2007

[17] OFT, Press Release PN 34/09, Payment Systems working better for consumers but more to be done (http://www.oft.gov.uk/news/press/2009/34-09) 25 March 2009

[18] Slow clearing has 'lost millions', [[BBC news (http://news.bbc.co.uk/1/hi/business/7965609.stm)], 26 March 2009]

[19] Payments Council, Press release (http://www.paymentscouncil.org.uk/media_centre/press_releases_new/-/page/828/) 30 November 2009

[20] PR Newswire, First Payment via UK Faster Payments Service Direct Corporate Access (http://news.prnewswire.com/DisplayReleaseContent.aspx?ACCT=104&STORY=/www/story/07-23-2009/0005065126&EDATE=) 23 July 2009

[21] UK Payments Administration, Faster Payments Scheme Boosts Banks' Ability to Provide a Competitive Service to Customers (http://www.chapsco.co.uk/chaps_company/press_releases/-/page/1022/) 10 September 2010

[22] Perot Systems, White Paper: Addressing the Issues of Faster Payments Services for Banks & Corporates. Stephen Edward Walsh & Sasmita Choudhury (https://docs.google.com/viewer?a=v&pid=explorer&chrome=true&srcid=0B9b4rVKQOryEMjQ1OWM5YjQtNjcyOS00Mzc0LWFmMzMtYmYwNmNmNjBkMTUw&hl=en) 23 May 2006

[23] easier.com, Faster Payments passed one million transactions a day mark (http://www.easier.com/view/Finance/Banking/News/article-203139.html) 12 September 2008

[24] APACS, Press release Faster Payments Service volumes reach new peak (http://www.apacs.org.uk/08_12_18.htm) 30 December 2008

[25] slicon.com, Faster Payments beats £1bn in one day (http://www.silicon.com/financialservices/0,3800010322,39405153,00.htm) 9 March 2009

External links

- Faster Payments Sort Code Checker (http://www.ukpayments.org.uk/sort_code_checker/)
- VocaLink website (http://www.vocalink.com/)

First Data

First Data

	![First Data logo]
Type	Private
Industry	Finance and Insurance
Founded	1969
Headquarters	Atlanta, Georgia
Key people	Jon Judge, CEO
Products	Financial services
Owner(s)	Kohlberg Kravis Roberts
Employees	27,000 (2008)
Website	www.firstdata.com [1]

First Data Corporation is an American payment processing company headquartered in Atlanta, Georgia. First Data is a provider of electronic commerce and payment solutions. The company's portfolio includes merchant transaction processing services; credit, debit, private-label, gift, payroll and other prepaid card offerings; fraud protection and authentication solutions; electronic check acceptance services through TeleCheck; as well as Internet commerce and mobile payment solutions. The company's STAR Network offers PIN-secured debit acceptance at ATM and retail locations.

History

In 1969, the Mid-America Bankcard Association (MABA) was formed in Omaha, Nebraska, as a non-profit bankcard processing cooperative. Two years later, First Data Resources (FDR) incorporated in June to become a for-profit organization providing processing services to MABA. FDR had 110 employees and $222 million in annual revenues. First Data is an agglomeration of various cooperative associations which were initially established to provide credit card data processing services for member banks. These include Eastern States Bankcard Association; Atlantic States Bankcard Association; Southwestern States Bankcard Association; Mountain States Bankcard Association, and Western States Bankcard Association.

In 1980, American Express Information Services Corporation (ISC) bought 80% of FDR. The remaining 20% was purchased in 5% increments each subsequent year until June 1983. First Data Corporation spun off from American Express and went public in 1992. In 1995, the company merged with First Financial Management Corp. (FFMC) and was then organized into three major business units serving card issuers, merchants and consumers. Western Union became part of First Data as a result of the merger with FFMC.

By 1998, First Data was providing transaction processing services not only in the U.S., but also in markets around the world, including the United Kingdom, Australia, Mexico and Canada. The company also began to see significant growth in its network of Western Union agent locations. This set the stage for First Data to become a leading global provider of electronic commerce and payment solutions to businesses and consumers worldwide.

From 2001 through 2005, a period of expansion occurred as First Data acquired companies around the globe and in the U.S., including, in 2001, the acquisition of PaySys International and their globally successful VisionPLUS Payment Software System VisionPLUS followed by $6.6 billion merger with Concord EFS in 2004, which added the STAR Network and PIN-based debit acceptance at more than 1.9 million ATM and retail locations. Additional acquisitions and strategic relationships included GovOne, the creation of eONEGlobal as a venture capital fund, the acquisition of Paymap, Inc., a company servicing electronic payment products, and the acquisition of Taxware, which would be merged into a new entity, named Velosant to spearhead broad Supply Chain Management initiatives. First Data also established a consumer payments brand which would take Direct Debit offerings to the retail marketplace. First Data further expanded geographically in Europe, Asia and Latin America.

In 2005, First Data was among 53 entities that contributed the maximum of $250,000 to the second inauguration of President George W. Bush.[1] [2] [3]

On January 26, 2006, First Data announced its intention to spin off Western Union into an independent publicly traded company through a tax-free spin-off of 100% of Western Union to First Data shareholders. The spin off occurred as planned on September 29, 2006.

On April 2, 2007 it was announced that Kohlberg Kravis Roberts (KKR) had entered an agreement to acquire First Data (NY Times article [5]) in one of the largest leveraged buy-outs in history[4] , and on October 1, 2007 KKR officially took over the First Data Corporation. Ric Duques retired, and Michael Capellas, previously the CEO of MCI, Inc., the president of Hewlett-Packard Company, and also the chairman/CEO of the Compaq Computer Corporation was appointed CEO. As a privately owned company, First Data's stock was taken off the New York Stock Exchange on September 24, 2007. However, the company's LBO was financed with $24 billion in debt, and it remains heavily leveraged.[4] . The company continues to maintain investor relations pages on its web site and to publish quarterly financial results. Within two months after the KKR acquisition, the company laid off 1,700 employees across North America, Europe and Australia, about 6% of its workforce.[5]

First Data entered the Ireland market in a joint venture(JV) with Allied Irish Banks plc (www.aib.ie [8]) named AIB Merchant Services on January 18, 2008.[6]

First Data also acquired ICICI Bank's merchant services business in 2009 for Rs. 400 Crs

The processing platforms maintained by First Data are North(Cardnet), South, Nashville(Envoy), Omaha and BuyPass(Concord/Atlanta).

Management

Key executives include:

- **Joe Forehand**: Chairman
- **Jonathan J. Judge**: Chief Executive Officer
- **Peter Boucher**: Executive Vice President, Human Resources
- **John Elkins**: Executive Vice President, Chief Marketing Officer
- **Kevin Kern**: Executive Vice President, Chief Technology Officer, Global Operations and Technology
- **Ed Labry**: President, Retail and Alliance Services
- **David Money**: Executive Vice President, General Counsel
- **Kevin Schultz**: President, Financial Services
- **Ray Winborne**: Executive Vice President, Acting Chief Financial Officer

Headquarters

First Data's headquarters are located in Atlanta, Georgia.[7] [8]

First Data's headquarters were located in Greenwood Village, Colorado.[9] [10] In 2009 First Data announced that it was moving its headquarters from Greater Denver to 5565 Glenridge Connector, NE Atlanta, GA 30342 .[11]

References

[1] Drinkard, Jim (2005-01-17). "Donors get good seats, great access this week" (http://www.usatoday.com/news/washington/2005-01-16-inauguration-donors_x.htm). USA Today. . Retrieved 2008-05-25.

[2] "Financing the inauguration" (http://www.usatoday.com/news/washington/2005-01-16-inaugural-donors_x.htm). USA Today. January 16, 2005. . Retrieved 2008-05-25.

[3] "Some question inaugural's multi-million price tag" (http://www.usatoday.com/news/washington/2005-01-14-price_x.htm). USA Today. 2005-01-14. . Retrieved 2008-05-25.

[4] "What went wrong with First Data?" (http://www.thedeal.com/newsweekly/community/what-went-wrong-with-first-data.php). . Retrieved 2010-01-14.

[5] Stempel, Jonathan (November 15, 2007). "U.S. payment processor First Data cuts 1,700 jobs" (http://www.reuters.com/article/idUSN1532553020071115). *Reuters*. . Retrieved 2010-01-14.

[6] "Allied Irish Bank And First Data Announce Launch Of AIB Merchant Services" (http://www.firstdata.com/en_us/about-first-data/media/press-releases/01_18_08). . Retrieved 2010-01-14.

[7] " City Council Districts (http://files.sandysprings-ga.org/maps/SandySprings_CouncilDistricts.pdf)." City of Sandy Springs. Retrieved on July 4, 2009.

[8] " Contact (http://www.firstdata.com/en_us/contact)." First Data. Retrieved on December 9, 2009.

[9] " Contact Us (http://web.archive.org/web/20000619052409/www.firstdata.com/contact.html)." First Data. June 19, 2000. Retrieved on December 9, 2009.

[10] " City Boundary Map (http://www.greenwoodvillage.com/common/modules/documentcenter2/documentview.aspx?DID=349)." City of Greenwood Village. Retrieved on December 9, 2009.

[11] Hoovers.com, Renee. " First Data moving HQ to Atlanta (http://denver.bizjournals.com/denver/stories/2009/08/10/daily81.html)." *Denver Business Journal*. Friday August 14, 2009. Retrieved on December 9, 2009.

External links

- First Data website (http://www.firstdata.com/)

Flattr

Flattr

Founded	2010
Founder	Peter Sunde and Linus Olsson
Headquarters	Malmö, Sweden
Industry	micropayments
Slogan	We aim to make people share money on the internet.
Website	flattr.com [1]
Registration	Required
Available in	English

Flattr is a micropayment system—more specifically, a microdonation system—that launched publicly in March 2010 on an invite-only basis,[1] and then opened up to the public on 12 August 2010.[2] [3]

Flattr is a project started by Peter Sunde and Linus Olsson. Users are able to pay a small amount every month (minimum 2 euros) and then click Flattr buttons on sites to share the money they paid among those sites, comparable to an Internet tip jar. (The word "flattr" is used as a verb, to indicate payments through the Flattr system—so when a user clicks a Flattr button and they are logged in to the Flattr site, they are said to be "flattring" the page they are on.) Sunde said, "We want to encourage people to share money as well as content."[1]

In the beginning of the service Flattr itself takes 10% of all the users monthly flatrate, although this fee may be reduced at a later date if the economics permit it.[1]

In December 2010, Flattr received large-scale attention when it was tweeted to be a method of donating money to Wikileaks, which had recently been cutoff by Paypal, Visa, and Mastercard.[4]

On April 28, 2011, Flattr announced by e-mail that they won't require users to flattr others anymore before they can be flattrd starting from May 1, 2011.

Extensions

As the service relies on network effect to prove useful, it is necessary that users join and have the opportunity to flattr and be flattr'd. A wide number of platforms are supported including WordPress, Blogger, and Jooomla among many others. To foster faster adoption, including on sites that may not natively support Flattr, a Firefox plugin, Överallt ("everywhere" in Swedish) has been developed.[5] It allows the equipped browsers to parse a simple plain-text tag ([Flattr=ID]) and replace it inline with the Flattr widget. This extends the range of Flattr, so that not only sites that support Flattr, but all sites, can have Flattr buttons.

For real-world or non-web content

Flattr is also being demonstrated as being useful for micro-donations to offline content, including those which are non-computer based, by way of mobile device recognition of QR codes. A number of existing services[6] exist to allow for the "flattr-ing" of non-web-based content, including offline content, using most Android phones' capability of recognizing physical QR codes. Utilizing QR codes attached to Flattr buttons allows for donations to the specific physical or non-web-based item of choice.

Adding funds

The two Internet payment services that can be used both for adding money to a Flattr account, and withdrawing revenue from a Flattr account, are PayPal and Moneybookers.[7]

Awards

- Best New Startup in 2010 - TechCrunch Europe.[8]
- Hoola Bandoola Band award.[9] [10]
- Top-10 in Netexplorateur 2011.[11]

References

[1] "Pirate boss to make the web pay" (http://news.bbc.co.uk/1/hi/technology/8512263.stm). *BBC News*. February 12, 2010. . Retrieved May 2, 2010.

[2] Steve O'Hear (August 12, 2010). "Flattr opens to the public, now anybody can 'Like' a site with real money" (http://eu.techcrunch.com/ 2010/08/12/flattr-opens-to-the-public-now-anybody-can-like-a-site-with-real-money/). *TechCrunch Europe*. . Retrieved August 13, 2010.

[3] Flattr now open for everyone! (http://blog.flattr.com/2010/08/open-beta/)

[4] http://eu.techcrunch.com/2010/12/08/wikileaks-continues-to-fund-itself-via-tech-startup-flattr/

[5] da Silva, Paul (June 19, 2010). "Överallt : Flattr Everywhere !" (http://overallt.p4ul.info/). . Retrieved June 22, 2010.

[6] "Offline Flattr" (http://flattr.com/support/offline/). .

[7] https://flattr.com/payments

[8] The Europas European Startup Awards 2010 – The Winners and Finalists (http://eu.techcrunch.com/2010/11/20/ the-europas-european-startup-awards-2010-the-winners-and-finalists/)

[9] Hoola Bandoola Band-award - Flattr blog (http://blog.flattr.net/2011/02/hoola-bandoola-band-award/)

[10] Hoola-pris till bloggstöd (swedish) (http://www.daladEmokraten.se/sida/id/153297/)

[11] NetExplorateur - 2011 award winners (http://en.www.netexplorateur.org/palmares/2011)

External links

- Flattr (http://flattr.com/)
- Flattr blog (http://blog.flattr.net/)

FloristWare POS System

FloristWare is an order-taking and point-of-sale (POS) system for retail florists.

Systems of this type are intended to aid retail florists with all aspects of their business. Features designed to speed order-taking and help with accounting, performance reporting, marketing, etc. are standard in products of this nature.

History

FloristWare was developed over a four year period starting in 2001. Development included ongoing focus groups with florists across North America. The intention was to have the people that would use the software play a pivotal role in shaping how it looked, worked and performed.

FloristWare was released to beta testers in September 2005 and went into wide release in January 2006. The current version of FloristWare is 3.2, which was released in September 2009. Version 4.0 is scheduled for release in early 2010.

Other information

FloristWare is considered an "independent" POS system in that is independent of wire services such as FTD or Teleflora. These companies and others like them offer their own proprietary POS systems for florists. It also uses a "Question & Answer" interface. Each step asks the user one question, which in turn determines the next step until the desired task has been completed. This interface makes it easy for the inexperienced computer users commonly found in flower shops to use the system with little or no training.

FloristWare also provides a free educational version [1] for schools and programs that train the florists of tomorrow. The goal is to help florists and the floral industry by ensuring that future employees enter the workforce with a good understanding of floral POS..

References

[1] [2] [3] [4] [5] [6] [7] [8]

[1] Flower Shop Network and FloristWare: Working Together to Make the Floral Business Simple Again (http://www.flowershopnetwork. com/blog/wp-content/uploads/2009/04/spring09net.pdf), News from FSN - Spring 2009.
[2] Technology For Florists - Industry Experts Speak (http://flowerscanada.org/content/en/perfect10.htm), Flowers Canada - Floral Trend Tracker.
[3] FSN & FloristWare POS System Integration (http://www.flowershopnetwork.com/pages/floristsonly/fsn-floristware.php), Flower Shop Network.
[4] FloristWare's Special Educational Version (http://www.canadianfloristmag.com/content/view/1233/38/), Canadian Florist Magazine.
[5] Marketing Via E-Mail: How to create and implement a successful e-mail marketing campaign. (http://www.floristsreview.com/main/ February2009/featurestory0209.html), Florists' Review Magazine - Feature Story February 2009.
[6] High-tech gear promises to make flower-buying easier, more convenient and even fun for your customers (http://www.floristsreview.com/ main/February2008/featurestory0208.html), Florists' Review Magazine - Feature Story February 2008.
[7] Gift Cards: A Growing Option For Florists. (http://www.floristsreview.com/main/july/featurestory.html), Florists' Review Magazine - Feature Story July 2007.
[8] FloristWare Releases Free Educational Version (http://www.prweb.com/releases/2007/04/prweb517112.htm), PRWeb - April 2007.

Related links

- FloristWare Website (http://www.floristware.com)
- Society of American Florists (http://www.safnow.com)
- Flowers Canada (http://www.flowerscanada.org/)

Freight payment service

Freight Payment Service

The freight payment industry was actually formed by a series of Banks when the transportation marketplace was heavily regulated. Motor carrier bills had to be paid within 7 days and rail bills needed to be paid within 5 days. To meet this requirement the banking community, shippers, and carriers formed what was known as The National Association of Freight Payment Banks, according to its former Chairman Harold B. Friedman. At that time the emphasis was on settlement of carrier bills within the regulated parameters for credit extension. If settlement was not made, the carrier was required by law to place the shipper on a cash basis. This was not an idle threat and large Fortune 500 companies would often have the freight held because bills were not paid on time.

With Deregulation of the transportation industry in 1980 this began to change. Credit terms could be negotiated between shippers and carriers for more reasonable periods of time. The process has become much more robust with bills being audited before they are paid (pre-audit). This includes: a verification of freight rates for compliance with the customers contracts, checks for previous payment, checks for shipper's liability and other edits and validations to insure the bills meet the shipper's requirements for payment.

A freight payment service usually consists of one or more levels of combined services. They may include freight audit, information reporting for logistics, and work with a combination of both Electronic Data Interchange, and paper freight bills. Many companies providing freight payment service are now offering audit for both small parcel and small package carriers, such as FedEx, UPS, and DHL Worldwide. Auditing of these integrated carriers often includes on time performance and claiming of refunds for theses service not delivered within the transit times established for each origin and destination pair. In addition, manifested and shipped transactions are identified for shipments that are entered into the customer's shipping system but are actually never presented to the carrier for pick up. There are many third party companies, like EM6 Logistics [1], etc. who does Freight Audit for various carriers associated with one client companies.

The model typically consists of your company having your motor carriers redirect the submission of freight invoices to your freight payment provider. Ideally the provider will have the capability of verifying the origin and destination in a variety of ways, including bill of lading matching, and obtaining a signed proof of delivery. Vendor matching is also another excellent technique for validating the freight bill information a freight payment service receives from the freight carrier. In addition, cost application coding, or general ledger codes. By outsourcing to a freight payment service it believed that the correctness of a freight invoice will be assured, because these services audit for freight rate, freight discount, misapplied accessorial charge, and prevent possible duplication of payment.

The real thrust of the business today is actionable information that shipper receive via the web or create from their vendor's web site on an ad hoc basis. Sophisticated reporting tools like Cognos11i and others allow Freight Payment Vendors and their customers to easily perform calculations, create graphics, generate pivot tables, and e-mail reports on a scheduled basis.

Many freight payment services now employ web services in their overall strategy to help their customers streamline the way the exchange information, and obtain information reporting.

Most, if not all, freight payment companies require that you issue them a bank wire on their schedule for your company's freight payment needs as reported by the freight payment company. This schedule is referred to as a batch. The freight payment service will then turn around and pay your company's freight bills to the carriers.

It is very important to realize that this traditional model has been in place since the 1920s. It is also important to monitor your freight payment service closely, as many freight payment service companies have been known to misappropriate funds.

To avoid this potential pit fall there are 10 key issues potential users of freight payment that users should address when looking for a freight bill processing vendor, according to Friedman who has been in the industry for over 38 years.

1. Financial security. Does the vendor have audited financial statements, an annual SAS 70 Type II review, and at least a $50-million Employee Dishonesty Bond?

2. Customer service. How does the provider track customer service issues to resolution? Does it use a Customer Relationship Management tool? What types of key performance indicators does it maintain?

3. Carrier relations management. Does the vendor have staff committed to maintaining outstanding carrier relations? Do they visit with carriers to communicate, resolve issues, and create efficiencies that benefit all parties? How do your carriers view the vendor; would they recommend the company?

4. Document imaging. Are hard-copy bills scanned, with images made available on the vendor's Web site, on DVD or CD?

5. Web-based data access. Web is the prevalent method of presenting data today and the vendor's site should include standard and ad-hoc reports, drill-downs, a graphics capability, mathematical calculations that result in new fields, client-driven report scheduling, and onscreen and email report delivery.

6. Coding, editing, and validation. How comprehensive is the vendor's ability in this area? Can it derive cost centers from other data elements? Rules should be table-based and event-driven to ensure that updates are made quickly and easily.

7. Freight liability. How does the vendor determine if the bill should be paid? Does it ensure supporting documentation is attached? Can it perform electronic validations to your bill of lading or purchase order file?

8. Web-based bill repair. Can freight bills that need customer approval be repaired from the vendor's Web site? Can you easily view images of the freight bill and supporting documentation to resolve bills that are being questioned?

9. Parcel shipment capabilities. Does the vendor have the ability to meet the integrated carrier's requirements to obtain refunds for late delivery shipments that are manifested but not moved? Does it provide address correction and break down all miscellaneous charges?

10. Ethics. Does the vendor have a code of ethics? Does it tell you what's good about its service rather than denigrating its competition?

It is thought that by using a freight payment service a company will:

* Reduce freight spend.
* Provide better information management.
* Save time, plus cut costs on personnel.

FreshBooks

FreshBooks

Type	Private
Founded	Toronto, Ontario, Canada
Founder	Michael McDerment Joe Sawada
Headquarters	Toronto, Canada
Area served	Worldwide
Employees	51 (2011)
Slogan	I
Website	freshbooks.com [1]
Alexa rank	2,503 (March 2011)[1]
Users	1.6 million (accounts, not visitors) (As of 14 July 2010[2]
Available in	English
Launched	2003
Current status	Active

FreshBooks is an online invoicing software as a service for freelancers, small businesses, agencies, and professionals. It is produced by the software company 2ndSite Inc. which is located in Toronto, Ontario, Canada. The product includes a myriad of other related features, such as time tracking, expense tracking, recurring billing, online payment collection, the ability to mail invoices through the U.S. Post, and support tickets.

Backbone Magazine rated FreshBooks Canada's #1 Web 2.0 pioneer in 2009 and 2nd place in 2008.[4]

Company

2ndSite was founded by Mike McDerment and Joe Sawada in 2003 out of McDerment's previous Internet marketing consulting business Anicon. It has about 70 employees[5] and remains privately held. Among their more notable employees are Mitch Solway, former VP of Marketing of LavaLife, and Sunir Shah of MeatballWiki.

Originally, the product was named 2ndSite, synonymous with the company. In early 2006, the company rebranded the product as FreshBooks with a completely different look and feel based on the then burgeoning Web 2.0 style.

Social media and Word of Mouth Marketing

FreshBooks makes extensive use of social media.[3] They were recognized in 2008 as the second best company in Canada using social media by KPMG and Backbone Magazine.[4]

FreshBooks maintains two primary blogs. The most important one is Fresh Thinking [8], where the company publishes the majority of its corporate news plus a mixture of opinions on entrepreneurship as well as updates on its product and marketing efforts. They also maintain a developer blog [9] to provide updates about their API. They also create secondary blogs on occasion like RoadBurn [10], which they created during their RV road trip campaign from Future of Web Apps in Miami to SXSW 2007 in Austin, and Brand Murder [11] which they created during their rebranding. Finally, the company are also extensively uses Twitter under their freshbooks [12] account as recognized by Fast Company.[5]

FreshBooks frequently mixes social media with their word of mouth marketing stunts. For instance, during SXSW 2008, they started with the aforementioned RV road trip for which they hired a videographer to post videos [14] on YouTube, and also extensively stunted [15] SXSW itself. Later that year, at the HOW Design Conference, they rented a trade show exhibit space without a trade show booth. Instead, they hired a muralist [16] to paint their booth during the show, which they later turned into a music video [17].

References

[1] "freshbooks.com – Traffic Details from Alexa" (http://www.alexa.com/siteinfo/freshbooks.com). Alexa Internet. . Retrieved March 17, 2011.

[2] Rao, Leena (July 14, 2010). "In Five Months, FreshBooks Crosses $1 Billion In Transactions" (http://techcrunch.com/2010/07/14/in-five-months-freshbooks-crosses-1-billion-in-transactions/). *TechCrunch*. Retrieved March 17, 2011.

[3] SitePoint (August 8, 2008): 15 companies that really get corporate blogging (http://www.sitepoint.com/blogs/2008/08/08/15-companies-that-really-get-corporate-blogging&cid=0&usg=AFQjCNHtgzVtsMMAsNlWvLBNrI2Wz1h7MQ)

[4] KPMG and Backbone Magazine (July, 2008): Pick 20 (http://www.onedegree.ca/2008/07/canadas-web-20.html) award

[5] Fast Company (July 26, 2008): Twitter Intelligence? - The New BI Tool? (http://www.fastcompany.com/blog/stephen-l-rose/tech-odyssey/twitter-âintelligenceâ-â-new-bi-tool)

Further reading

- TechCrunch (August 23, 2006): FreshBooks pushes the envelope in online billing (http://www.techcrunch.com/2006/08/23/freshbooks-pushes-the-envelope-in-online-billing/)
- CBC (June 16, 2008): BIG MAC ATTACK (http://www.cbc.ca/technology/story/2008/06/16/f-trends-mac.html#socialcomments)
- L.A. Times (March 31, 2008): For small business, when the going gets tough, get tough on costs (http://www.latimes.com/business/la-fi-smallbiz31mar31,0,1663885,full.story)
- IT World Canada (March 25, 2008): RV IT: Toronto's FreshBooks spreads the word (http://www.itworldcanada.com/Pages/Docbase/ViewArticle.aspx?id=idgml-cf9b41ce-0eab-4032&Portal=2e5351f3-4ab9-4c24-a496-6b265ffaa88c&sub=4500743)
- ZDNet (March 27, 2008): Bubble Thinking (http://blogs.zdnet.com/enterprisealley/?p=175)
- U.S. News & World Report (March 10, 2008): Tips for Steeling Your Firm Against Recession (http://www.usnews.com/articles/business/small-business-entrepreneurs/2008/03/10/tips-for-steeling-your-firm-against-recession.html)
- PC Magazine (February 2, 2008): Editors Choice: FreshBooks (http://www.pcmag.com/article2/0,1759,2254091,00.asp)
- IT World Canada (August 30, 2007): FreshBooks pilots Amazon payment service (http://www.itworldcanada.com/a/Daily-News/8bfb6530-8260-42f7-b2aa-d744661dd763.html)
- PC World (July 30, 2007): Trends in Software as a Service (http://www.pcworld.com/article/id,135119-c,webservices/article.html)
- CityTV (July 25, 2007): Homepage (http://www.freshbooks.com/blog/2007/07/13/freshbooks-on-tv/)
- Canadian Business (July 24, 2007): SaaSsy: Software-as-a-service (http://www.canadianbusiness.com/technology/trends/article.jsp?content=20070618_85498_85498)
- USA Today (May 18, 2007): Better hone your sales pitch (http://www.usatoday.com/money/smallbusiness/columnist/strauss/2007-05-13-sales_N.htm)
- PROFIT Magazine (March 22, 2007): The only bills you'll ever love (http://www.canadianbusiness.com/entrepreneur/technology/article.jsp?content=20070212_143233_5880)
- The Globe and Mail (January 25, 2007): Less paperwork just a click away (http://www.theglobeandmail.com/servlet/story/RTGAM.20070125.gtsaas25/BNStory/Technology/home)
- PROFIT Magazine (December 20, 2006): Your Next Big Thing: Web 2.0 (http://www.canadianbusiness.com/entrepreneur/managing/article.jsp?content=20061201_124525_6052)

- CNET (August 9, 2006): A refreshingly straightforward invoicing service (http://news.com.com/ 2061-12572_3-6104038.html)
- National Post (May 19, 2006): Encouraging Signs for Web Services (http://www.canada.com/nationalpost/ financialpost/story.html?id=835cb62a-c2d2-4b6e-8679-0c7898924072&p=2)
- ZDNet (April 14, 2006): Running a business on Web-based software (http://blogs.zdnet.com/Hinchcliffe/ ?p=31)
- The Webhost Industry Review (April 5, 2005): FreshBooks Automates the Billing Cycle (http://www.thewhir. com/features/lee-2ndsite.cfm)

External links

- FreshBooks website (http://www.freshbooks.com/)

Fuel card

A **fuel card** or **fleet card** is used as a payment card most commonly for gasoline, diesel and other fuels at gas stations. Fleet cards can also be used to pay for vehicle maintenance and expenses at the discretion of the fleet owner or manager. The use of a fleet card also eliminates the need for cash carrying, thus increasing the level of security felt by fleet drivers. The elimination of cash also makes it easier to prevent fraudulent transactions from occurring at a fleet owner or manager's expense.

Fleet cards are unique due to the convenient and comprehensive reporting that accompanies their use. Fleet cards enable fleet owners/ managers to receive real time reports and set purchase controls with their cards helping them to stay informed of all business related expenses.

Origins

United Kingdom

In its infancy, fuel cards were only printed with the company name, vehicle registration and a signature strip on the reverse. No electronic data was stored. Fuelling sites would verify the company, vehicle registration (on the forecourt) against the card and also the signature written on the back. The site would allow access to the fuel once the retailer's receipt had been signed for and cross checked against the signature written on the back of the card.

Initially, fuel card networks were very small and based around truck roads and main haulage routes. For example, in 1983, the Keyfuels site network consisted of only seven stations. Therefore, they were initially targeted at haulage or delivery companies. A few years later, cards became embossed rather than printed. This was due to provide the cards with a greater longevity — frequent use would rub off the printed information.

Due to the lack of electronic data on the fuel cards at this stage, transactions would be recorded by the card being 'stamped' onto a manual transaction sheet. Further details detailing date, time, volume, grade of fuel and registration would be hand-written.

During the mid to late 1980s, fuel cards began to use magnetic strip technology. This meant fuel cards could be processed by a retailer electronically and reduced the risk of human error when recording transaction details.

Magnetic strips also enabled fuel card providers to increase fuel card security by ensuring PINs were encoded into the card. Although it should be noted that when the magnetic strip is swiped though a fuel card reader, the transaction is still only verified by checking signatories to this day.

In the advent of outdoor terminals, these PINs became compulsory in order to re-fuel.

The reasoning behind moving from the magnetic strip to smartchip technology was down to the fact that the magnetic strip could be cloned and the data written onto a dummy card. Also, the use of fuel cards was far heavier than that of debit or credit cards, and therefore it became apparent that the magnetic strip began to wear out far quicker.

Smartchip technology (similar to Chip and PIN) is the largest development in the fuel card industry in recent years. (See Smartchip benefits)

During 2008, market maturity has led to users increasingly expecting more from fuel cards than discount pricing, with the demand for service, savings and security leading to the appearance of dedicated account management. While most fuel card suppliers handle customer queries via random-operator call centres, customer preference is increasingly for a named individual to handle their business. Respected publication *Fleet News* reported in July 2008 that more than a quarter of fleet managers are unhappy with the level of service offered by their fuel card supplier.[1]

United States

The advent of **fleet cards** can be traced back to the 1960s and 70's when key stops and stand alone card locks were used by independent marketers and filling station owners. The first commercial fuel cards resembled a credit card with a name and a company logo on them. When a customer entered a fueling station, the cashier would take down the customer's name and company information to authenticate ownership of the card. This process was time consuming and was vulnerable to fraudulent transactions. With the advent of computers and computer software in the 1980s, the development of the fleet card industry quickly expanded. The invention of the magnetic stripe and magnetic card reader allowed petroleum marketers to control fuel pump transactions, leading to today's wide range of fleet card security features and state of the art reporting systems to track all of your fleet expenses. These "intelligent" systems make fleet management convenient and secure, as fleet card owners are able to track fleet fuel use with increased accuracy, receiving reports in real time on the fueling habits of your fleet. Business owners are able to limit employee fueling by time-of-day and day-of-week, as well as the restricting

Fuel and credit card comparison

There are many reasons for/against the use of a fuel card over a credit card, which are outlined below:

Pros:

- Discount fuel prices (i.e. wholesale prices)
- Ability to choose from multiple providers like Shell, Esso, Keyfuels, Texaco etc. This enables better pricing due to competition.[1]
- Need for carrying cash (or giving cash to drivers) eliminated
- Prevention of fraud[2]
- Invoicing with VAT (tax) shown separately facilities tax recovery for businesses
- Increased security[3]
- Filling patterns can be customised by Smartchip technology[4]
- Fleet efficiency & MPG reporting[5]
- Reduced administration via management tools[6]
- Points/reward schemes[7]

Cons:

- Card stopping/cancellation periods can sometimes be longer
- Greater liability for fraudulent transactions often placed on customer
- Credit periods typically shorter
- Retail cards typically offer pump prices (usually higher than wholesale) and occasionally additional surcharge
- Annual or monthly card provision charge sometimes applied (usually bunkered)

<u>Neither:</u>

- Typically, bunkered cards can only be at service stations on the network it is associated with:

  Pro - could potentially restrict theft **Con** - site locations less readily available

- Bunkered cards sometimes run on advance payment (e.g. stock holding/bunkering):

  Pro - buying in bulk potentially provides further savings **Con** - cash sum must be provided on regular basis

Misconceptions

Although fuel cards effectively 'look' like credit cards and use very similar technology, their use and implementation is significantly dissimilar enough to differentiate them as an alternate payment method. The main differences from credit cards are:

- Payment terms often shorter
- No rolling-balance is cleared (or partially cleared) each month
- Transactions can be customised allowing only certain grades of fuel e.g. petrol, petrol & diesel, petrol & gas oil, etc.
- Fuelling transaction limits can be applied using Smartchip technology
- Liability for fraudulent transactions usually remains with user (depending upon agreement with card provider)
- Card 'hotlists' (a.k.a. 'authorisation' or 'onstop' lists) received via different providers
- Interim period after stop/hotlist request and card denied at fuelling station can be longer (although Online Authorisation networks are increasing)
- Payment terminals separate to those used for credit/debit cards (bunkered cards only)
- Fuel not technically paid at point of sale - simply allocated on account for payment at later date (bunkered only)
- Some cards allow the purchase of such non-fuel products as lubricants and Adblue

Security

Depending upon the individual fuel card and the supplier, security benefits of fuel cards can include:

- cashless transactions
- chip-and-PIN protection
- detailed invoicing − fully itemising transactions for individual cards
- on-line account administration to stop cards 24/7
- transactions restricted to fuel-related products
- reporting of unusual transactions
- decrease in occurrences of credit card 'skimming'

Smartchip benefits

Fuel card providers realised there were many benefits from moving over to the smartcard from the magnetic strip:

- Smartchips cannot be cloned[8]
- Fuelling limits can be enforced (*see Smartchip technology*)[4]
- Far more durable than magnetic strips, therefore cards last longer
- Need for cards to be re-created reduced due to longevity
- Smartchip cannot be damaged by electro-magnetic radiation e.g. mobile phones, magnets, speakers, etc.

As of 2007, only 50% or so of fuel cards on offer utilise the smartchip technology.

Added features of smartchip technology

Fuelling limits can also be programmed into a fuel card using smartchip technology to specify the following:

- Volume allowed per transaction
- Volume allowed per day
- Volume allowed per week
- Number of transactions allowed per day
- Number of transactions allowed per week
- Days of the week card can be used
- Times of the day card can be used
- Number of incorrect PIN entries allowed
- Card lock-out period after incorrect PINs

Commercial use in business

Typically, the majority of businesses using fuel cards are those which heavily rely on motor vehicles on a day-to-day basis e.g. transport, haulage, courier services. One of the primary reasons a business will use a fuel card is to obtain (potentially) significant savings both on the current price of fuel and on administrative costs. It would be normal for the business to receive a single weekly invoice, payable by direct debit; this replaces the manual reconciliation of individual paper receipts which could, for larger organisations, number in the hundreds each week. A number of additional benefits are available for users of fuel cards from a supplier offering an e-business capability.

In most cases, fuel cards can provide fuel at a wholesale price as opposed to standard retail. This way, discount fuel can be purchased without needing to buy in bulk.

Furthermore, the management and security concerning fuel purchases is greatly improved via the use of fuel cards. These features often prove themselves attractive to businesses, especially with those operating large fleets which can sometimes be in the thousands of vehicles.

For example, a business may obtain anything from a one to four pence per litre reduction (PPL) on diesel, which in real terms can be translated into the following (UK based) example:

Potential cost-saving example (for small fleet)

Fleet Vehicle Size	5
Volume Per Fill (litres)	50
Re-fuelling (p/week)	2
Fuel Card Saving (PPL)	2.5
VAT (UK)	17.5%
Total Saving (p/week)	£13.21
Total Saving (p/year)	£687.37

International fuel cards

While most fuel cards are for use in a particular country, there are some companies who offer international fuel cards themselves and some via a third party. International site networks often use fully automatic fuel pumps to avoid possible language difficulties and are specially designed to account for different taxation regimes e.g. producing separate invoices for each country which fuel was purchased in a particular month to account for different rates of VAT charged. These site networks sometimes offer the ability to reclaim VAT paid in each country, for a small percentage of the amount reclaimed.

Bunkering versus Retail

Bunkered fuel cards

Fuel card providers which operate on a bunkering basis aim to achieve a fuel reserve on a particular network in order to achieve a discounted price, therefore taking advantage of economies of scale.

For example, a company may purchase one million litres of diesel at 72.50 and aim to sell this on to the customer with a mark up of 2.5 pence per litre — 75.00 PPL.

Bunkered fuel card companies sometimes also offer customers their own fuel bunker to under the premise of further benefiting from a discounted price. Furthermore, a customer can also hope to achieve a saving by way of avoiding any market increases in the standard market price for that particular fuel. In short, customer fuel bunkering has many pros & cons:

Pros:

- new-start businesses given a vital boost by using fuel cards if credit insurance cannot be obtained (due to lack of company history)
- if the market for that particular fuel rises immediately after a purchase — the customer has potentially made a saving

Cons:

- a healthy cash flow is required to sustain the lump sum payment for their fuel purchase — often difficult for new businesses
- if the market for that particular fuel falls immediately after a purchase — the customer has potentially lost out on a saving opportunity

Retail fuel cards

In contrast to bunkered, retail fuel cards operate by way of allowing the customer to draw fuel at almost any fuelling station (in same method as credit card). Often providers will levy a surcharge in addition to the retail price as advertised at the fuelling station. The retail price given is often considerably higher than that of the bunkered. The majority of fuel cards provide weekly (advance) notification of fuel price generally applicable nationwide.

Although retail is generally more expensive, there are a number of exceptions depending on the region, particular brand/site and timing of fuel purchased. Retail fuel can be cheaper in certain regions, particularly those near to a major port. Further reasons for the difference in price may be due to local economy (e.g. north / south of England) and whether the site is close to any main transport links i.e. the fuel costs more to deliver into the site. As for timing, the supermarkets or large providers often have a great deal of fuel in their stock reserves, so if the market increases rapidly, they would generally take longer than smaller providers to reflect this change.

Fuel cards are not all the same and 'shopping around' is advised. Typically, a supplier will offer just one or two cards. The user should seek an independent supplier offering a range of cards from major brands, so that the most appropriate fuel card for their individual needs can be chosen. A fuel card with little or no motorway coverage but extensive coverage of metropolitan areas, for example, could be of limited use to a national haulier but ideal for a taxi company. A supplier offering only diesel cards will be of minimal appeal to a fleet manager responsible for a petrol-only or mixed-fuel company car fleet.

Furthermore, retail fuel prices have decreased over the past 15 or so years largely due to supermarkets providing fuel at their superstores at hugely discounted prices in order to entice users to the store. Supermarket prices are an irrelevance to many diesel users, as very few supermarket forecourts are accessible by heavy goods vehicles or coaches.

References

[1] Fuel Cards (http://www.businessfuelcards.co.uk/compare-fuelcards.html)

[2] Petrol Plus (http://www.petrol-plus.com)

[3] Comcar Fuelcards (http://www.comcar.co.uk/newcar/companycar/comcar/fuelcards.cfm)

[4] Keyfuels Card (http://www.keyfuels.co.uk/fuelcards/keyfuels_orig.htm)

[5] IRIS (http://www.keyfuels.co.uk/solutions/iris.htm)

[6] Croft Fuels Ltd : Fuel Cards : Diesel Direct Card : Croft Fuels Online (http://www.croft-fuels.co.uk/fuelcards/login.htm)

[7] Texaco we.o.u - Home (http://www.weou.co.uk/)

[8] Credit card fraud

External links

- Fuel Card Comparison (http://www.companyfuelcards.co.uk/Card-Finder/Choices/Questions)
- Fuel card review (http://www.comcar.co.uk/newcar/companycar/comcar/fuelcards.cfm)
- Security review (http://www.securitypark.co.uk/article.asp?articleid=25045)
- List of UK fuel card providers (http://www.fleetdirectory.co.uk/fuel_cards_and_companies)
- Petrofix Fuel Cost Protection - Alternative to Fuel Cards (http://www.petrofix.com)

Gift card

A **gift card** is a restricted monetary equivalent or scrip that is issued by retailers or banks to be used as an alternative to a non-monetary gift. Highly popular, they rank as the second-most given gift by consumers in the United States (2006) and the most-wanted gift by women, and the third-most wanted by males.[1] Gift cards have become increasingly popular as they relieve the donor of selecting a specific gift.[2] In Canada, $1.8 billion were spent on gift cards and in the UK, it is estimated to reach 3 billion (GBP) for 2009 whereas in

An assortment of gift cards, many from U.S. national retailers such as Best Buy, Target and Home Depot.

the United States, about $80 billion were paid for gift cards in 2006.[3] [4] The recipient of the gift card can use it at his or her discretion within the restrictions set by the issuing agency.

History

The first giftcard using a payments infrastructure was introduced by Blockbuster Entertainment in the fall of 1994 in Ft. Lauderdale, Florida. In the beginning, the Blockbuster giftcard was to replace gift certificates that were being counterfeited with recently introduced color copiers and color printers. It was this over redemption of giftcards that launched the search for an alternative. The first giftcard transactions were processed by what was then, Nabanco of Sunrise, Florida. Nabanco was the developer of the first platform for the processing of giftcards using existing payment infrastructure. Blockbuster was later followed by a card by Neiman Marcus, and the Mobil Oil gas card which initially offered prepaid phone value provided by MCI. Kmart was the next introduction of the Kmart Cash Card which in the early generations provided prepaid phone time with AT&T. Later this feature was dropped as it was not profitable and both Kmart and Mobil. The Kmart Cash Card was the first replacement for cash returns when a shopper did not have a receipt for a gift. This practice of giving a cash card in place of cash for non-receipted returns is common place today in most merchants. From these early introductions, numerous retailers began to adapt a giftcard program to replace their gift certificate programs.

Function and types

A gift card may resemble a credit card or display a specific theme on a plastic card the size of a credit card. The card is identified by a specific number or code, not usually with an individual name, and thus could be used by anybody. They are backed by an on-line electronic system for authorization. Some gift cards can be reloaded by payment and can be used thus multiple times.

Cards may have a barcode or magnetic strip, which is read by an electronic credit card machine. Many cards have no value until they are sold, at which time the cashier enters the amount which the customer wishes to put on the card. This amount is rarely stored on the card but is instead noted in the store's database, which is crosslinked to the card ID. Gift cards thus are generally not stored-value cards as used in many public transport systems or library photocopiers, where a simplified system (with no network) stores the value only on the card itself. To thwart counterfeiting, the data is encrypted. The magnetic strip is also often placed differently than on credit cards, so they cannot be read or written with standard equipment. Other gift cards may have a set value and need to be activated by calling a specific number.

Gift cards can also be custom tailored to meet specific needs. By adding a custom message or name on the front of the card, it can make for an individualized gift or incentive to an employee to show how greatly they are appreciated. Some companies offer custom designs on the cards for businesses wishing to add their logo. Special order cards are available for businesses.

Gift cards are divided into "open loop" or "network" cards and "closed loop" cards. The former are issued by banks or credit card companies and can be redeemed by different establishments, the latter by a specific store or restaurant and can be only redeemed by the issuing provider. The latter, however, tend to have lesser problems with card value decay and fees.[1] In either case the giver would buy the gift card (and may have to pay an additional purchase fee), and the recipient of the card would use the value of the card at a later transaction. A third form is the "hybrid closed loop" card where the issuer has bundled a number of closed loop cards; an example is a gift card for a specific mall.

Gift cards differ from gift certificates, in that the latter are usually sold as a paper document with an authorized signature by a restaurant, store, or other individual establishment as a voucher for a future service; there is no electronic authorization. A gift certificate may or may not have an expiration date and generally has no administrative fees.

Bank-issued gift cards may be used in lieu of checks as a way to disburse rebate funds. Some retailers use the gift card system for refunds in lieu of cash thereby assuring that the customer will spend the funds at their store.

A Charity Gift Card allows the gift giver to make a charitable donation, and the gift recipient to choose a charity that will receive the donation.

Mobile & Virtual gift cards

Mobile gift cards are delivered to mobiles phones via SMS messages and phone applications including iphone applications allowing users to carry only their cell phones. Benefits include tying them to a particular phone number and ease of distribution through email.

Virtual gift cards are delivered via e-mail to their recipient, the benefits being that they cannot be lost and that the consumer does not have to drive to the bricks and mortar location to purchase a gift card.

Target,[5] one of the top sellers of Gift Cards in the US and Starbucks[6] have launched mobile gift cards. Several companies are expected to follow their lead including gift card vendors like snapgifts.[7]

Other companies, such as GiftRocket [8], have introduced virtual gift cards that users redeem on their smartphones.[8]

Pitfalls

It has been argued that holiday giving destroys value due to mismatching gifts.[9] The most efficient way to keep value in gifting would be to give cash, however this is socially acceptable only within limits. Gift cards, to a degree, may overcome this problem but have certain pitfalls. Some feel that the absence of the thought of selecting a specific gift makes a gift card a worse choice than a poorly executed but individual gift.[10] New products in the gift card industry are evolving to tackle this "impersonal" pitfall of gift cards. New services launched by some service providers allows for customization and personalization of gift cards.[11]

Gift cards have been criticized for the ability of the issuing authority to set rules that are detrimental to the consumer. Thus the recipient may have to face expiration dates, administrative fees, restrictions in use, and absence of adequate protection in case of fraud or loss.[2] Over time the value of a gift card may become zero. However, these issues have diminished significantly in recent years. Many states have enacted laws limiting or prohibiting all fees or expiration dates for gift cards. Further, because of the negative impact on sales that such policies can have, most merchants have adopted and even advertise a "no fee, no expiration" policy for their gift cards, whether or not state laws require it.[12]

Gift cards are considered unsecured debt by bankruptcy courts, and as such can become valueless when a company files for Chapter 11 reorganization.[13]

Redemption rate

Not all gift cards are redeemed, which can be for a multitude of reasons. The card may get lost, there may be time decay (expiration and fees) or complex rules of redemption, the recipient may not be interested in the store that accepts the card or be under the false assumption that not using it will save money for the giver. It has been estimated that perhaps 10% of cards are not redeemed, amounting to a gain for retailers of about $8 billion in the US in 2006.[4]

Third party brokers

By late 2006, companies such as, CardWoo [15], Plastic Jungle [16], Swapagift [17], GiftCardRescue [18] and CardAvenue, were formed to provide gift card brokering services that allowed customers to buy or sell their pre-owned gift cards. Buyers would typically buy these pre-owned gift cards anywhere from 3-30% off while sellers would sell their pre-owned gift cards for 50-80% of their face value. By 2009 many other third party gift card sites emerged like Cardpool.com, Giftcardrescue.com and many others. [14] [15] [16] Other websites sell a collection of third party gift cards, including GiftCardLab.com [22] Giftah.com [23], GiftCardMall.com [24] GiftCertificates.com [25] and GiftCards.com [26] in the US, TheGiftCardCentre.co.uk [27] in the UK. Soon after the emergence of primary coupon reseller like Plastic Jungle, price comparison websites like Gift Card Granny [28] and Cardnap [29] began to allow shoppers to compare how much each of the coupon resellers were buying and selling cards for, thus adding further competition and choice to the discount gift card market. {http://www.givvgiftcards.com.au}

Incentive of Choice

Companies like National Gift Card Corp. [30] are able to offer the incentive community hundreds of gift cards from retailers and restaurants nationwide in bulk, and often times, with discounts.[17]

Regulations

Canada

In the provinces of Manitoba, Ontario, Alberta, British Columbia and Quebec, legislation has been passed to ban expiry dates and fees collected on gift cards.[18] It does not apply to cards where there is a direct agreement between the user and the bank that issues the bank. It refers to the Open Loop gift card program.

United States

In the past, uniform standards concerning gift cards did not exist. This was set to change as an addendum to the Credit CARD Act of 2009 directs the federal government to create consumer-friendly standards pertaining to gift cards.[19] Most notably, the new regulations prohibit retailers from setting expiration dates unless they are at least 6 years after the date that the card was loaded. In addition, retailers are no longer able to assess dormancy, inactivity, or service fees unless the card has been inactive for at least 12 months, and if fees are added after that period, the details of such fees must be clearly disclosed on the card. Additionally, retailers are unable to levy more than one fee per month. The new provisions took effect on August 22, 2010.[20]

Open loop cards are governed by rules of the Comptroller of the Currency, however oversight has been criticized.[2] Closed loop gift cards are subject to rules set by different state regulations, and issuing authorities vary widely in the rules they set for the consumer.[2] Rules can be changed by the issuer without notifying the consumer.[1] [4]

References

[1] "Avoid gift card pitfalls" (http://www.consumerreports.org/cro/money/shopping/shopping-tips/gift-card-pitfalls-12-07/overview/gift-card-pitfalls-ov.htm). December 2007. . accessed 06-16-2008

[2] James R. Hood (2006-02-20). "Congress Considers New Gift Card Rules" (http://www.consumeraffairs.com/news04/2006/02/gift_cards_congress.html). . accessed 06-16-2008

[3] Cash, not gift cards, the best present: consumers' association (http://www.cbc.ca/news/yourview/2007/12/cash_not_gift_cards_the_best_p.html)

[4] Truman Lewis (2006-12-20). "Gift Cards an $8 Billion Gift to Retailers" (http://www.consumeraffairs.com/news04/2006/12/gift_card_giveaways.html). .accessed 06-16-2008

[5] "Target Mobile Gift Cards" (http://www.target.com/Mobile-GiftCards/b?ie=UTF8&node=2242345011). .

[6] "Starbucks Mobile Gift Cards" (http://www.starbucks.com/coffeehouse/mobile-apps/starbucks-card-mobile). .

[7] "Snapgifts" (http://www.snapgifts.com). .

[8] "GiftRocket Seeks to Take the Pain and Loss Out of Gift Cards" (http://www.xconomy.com/san-francisco/2011/04/07/giftrocket-seeks-to-take-the-pain-and-loss-out-of-gift-cards). .

[9] Stephen J. Dubner and Steven D. Levitt (January 7, 2007). "The Gift-Card Economy" (http://www.nytimes.com/2007/01/07/magazine/07wwln_freak.t.html?ex=1325826000&en=970d53de24147ae4&ei=5090&partner=rssuserland&emc=rss). The New York Times. .

[10] "Bad Gift Better Than Gift Card, Says Philosopher" (http://www.consumeraffairs.com/news04/2006/12/bad_gift.html). 2006-12-18. .

[11] BusinessWeek (11-05-2007). "Gift Cards with a Personal Touch" (http://www.businessweek.com/magazine/content/07_45/b4057049.htm). .

[12] author=Greg Grove title=Gift Card Overview url=http://www.ecardsystems.com/eCardWebPages/giftcardoverview.html

[13] Tamara Keith (2008-11-17). "Gift Card Warning: Check Retailer's Health" (http://www.npr.org/templates/story/story.php?storyId=97016449). NPR. .

[14] Montagne, Renee (March 22, 2010). "Forgotten Gift Cards Yield Business Opportunity" (http://www.npr.org/templates/story/story.php?storyId=125005447). *NPR*. .

[15] Choi, Candice (June 24, 2010). "Websites allow consumers to purchase and sell their unwanted gift cards" (http://www.boston.com/business/personalfinance/articles/2010/06/24/websites_allow_consumers_to_purchase_and_sell_their_unwanted_gift_cards/). *The Boston Globe*. .

[16] Martin, Jabari (November 17, 2010). "PegDown" (http://www.facebook.com/pages/PegDowncom/142110739173001). *facebook*. .

[17] "National Gift Card Corp." (http://www.ngc-group.com). .

[18] "Gift cards: the lure of plastic" (http://www.cbc.ca/consumer/story/2008/12/01/f-giftcards.html). *CBC News.* December 5, 2008. .

[19] http://www.govtrack.us/congress/billtext.xpd?bill=h111-627

[20] http://www.wkow.com/Global/story.asp?S=12188430

Gilbarco Veeder-Root

Gilbarco Veeder-Root

Type	Private, subsidiary of the Danaher Corporation
Industry	Manufacturing
Founded	1870
Headquarters	Greensboro, NC
Key people	Martin Gafinowitz[1], CEO Gaston Berrio[1], POS Director
Products	Fuel Dispensers Point of Sale Systems
Revenue	⏶ $700 million USD (2005)
Employees	~4,000 (2009)
Parent	Danaher Corporation, (NYSE: DHR)
Website	www.gilbarco.com [2]

Gilbarco Veeder-Root, a subsidiary of the Danaher Corporation, is a supplier of fuel dispensers, point of sale systems, payment systems, forecourt merchandising [2] and support services[3] worldwide. Gilbarco Veeder-Root is headquartered in Greensboro, North Carolina, United States and employs approximately 4,000 people around the world.[4]

History

The company was originally founded under the name Gilbert & Barker in 1870[4] by Charles Gilbert and John Barker. The company was renamed as Gilbarco in 1929 [4] and was later acquired by the British engineering company GEC in 1987.[4] In 1999 GEC renamed itself to Marconi and Gilbarco became Marconi Commerce Systems.[4] In 2002 Gilbarco was acquired by the Danaher Corporation, parent company of Veeder-Root and Red Jacket companies and became Gilbarco Veeder-Root.[4] Background on Gilbert & Barker pumps and innovations can be found in Michael Karl Witzel's book 'American Gas Station: History and Folklore of Gas Stations in America'[5]

In the news

Gilbarco Veeder-Root was featured on the June 14th, 2008 episode of John Ratzenberger's Made in America.[6]

In May 2008, AskAboutPCI.com was launched as a reference for convenience store retailers to learn more about the Payment Card Industry (PCI) rules, regulations, and deadlines. AskAboutPCI.com is a blog site that encourages retailers to ask questions they have surrounding PCI and receive feedback from other retailers and experts in the industry that can better explain what their next steps should be to make their forecourt and c-store PCI compliant.[7]

Gilbarco Veeder-Root represents the leading brands of solutions and technologies that provide convenience, control, and environmental integrity for retail fueling and adjacent markets.

In 2002, the Gilbarco and Veeder-Root companies combined into one marketing brand, with distinctive and complementary business lines, services, and sales capabilities.

- Gilbarco is a leading global supplier of fuel dispensing equipment, fully integrated point of sale systems for the global petroleum marketplace. Gilbarco is headquartered in Greensboro, North Carolina with sales, manufacturing, research, development, and service locations in North and South America, Europe, Asia, the Pacific Rim and Australia.
- Veeder-Root is a leading global supplier of automatic tank gauging and fuel management systems, including the Red Jacket brand of submersible pumps and pressurized line leak detectors. Veeder-Root and Red Jacket brands are both leaders with a tradition of excellence in the petroleum industry. Veeder-Root is headquartered in Simsbury, Connecticut.
- Gasboy International is a leading manufacturer and marketer of commercial electronic and mechanical petroleum dispensing systems, fleet management systems, and transfer pumps, primarily for non-retail petroleum applications. Gasboy also offers a complementary line of automated fueling systems that provide 24-hour unattended fueling capabilities to fleets and retail marketers. Gasboy is headquartered in Greensboro, NC USA.

Worldwide Gilbarco Veeder-Root manufacturing and development facilities are located in Greensboro NC, Simsbury CT, Altoona PA, Lakewood, CO, and Davenport, IA. International manufacturing and development locations include the United Kingdom, Italy, Germany, China and Brazil.

Regional offices are located throughout the US and Canada, and in the United Kingdom, Italy, France, Germany, The Netherlands, Malaysia, Thailand, China, Bahrain, Korea, Australia, New Zealand, Brazil and Argentina.

References

[1] Petroworld Interview: Martin Gafinowitz, By: David Eagan (http://www.gilbarco.com/object/petrolworldinterview)

[2] Pumping Up In-Store Sales, C-Store Decisions, February 2009 (http://www.csdecisions.com/article/6210)

[3] NACStech Show Floor Report, CSPnet.com, May 2009 (http://www.cspnet.com/ME2/Audiences/dirmod.asp?sid=&nm=& type=Publishing&mod=Publications::Article&mid=8F3A7027421841978F18BE895F87F791&tier=4& id=94D7130976D449DF9329B52DCAE39BB7&AudID=3F7DE6D5939244BBA5FBA04DEA47CA69)

[4] Corporate Facts (http://www.gilbarco.com/page/Corporate_Facts)

[5] Gas Station: History and Folklore of Gas Stations in America, By: Michael Karl Witzel (http://books.google.com/ books?id=5PQDR_whoOEC&pg=PA32&lpg=PA32&dq=gilbert+&+barker+gas+pumps&source=bl&ots=AsScQrUAFU& sig=xtFXtT25WxYmzJYd_2xjUSGTU08&hl=en&ei=6n-FSvHaF4aSlAeNn8iCBQ&sa=X&oi=book_result&ct=result& resnum=3#v=onepage&q=&f=falseAmerican)

[6] John Ratzenberger's Made In America (http://www.locatetv.com/tv/john-ratzenbergers-made-in-america/season-5/5178600)

[7] Gilbarco Launches AskAboutPCI.com, Convenience Store Decisions, May 2008 (http://www.csdecisions.com/article/3824/ gilbarco-launches-askaboutpcicom.html)

Further reading

- eXtremely Secure, CSP Magazine, May 2009 (http://www.cspnet.com/Media/PublicationsArticle/ CSP_extremely_secure_F6_0509.pdf)
- Sheetz Awards PCI Upgrade to Gilbarco Veeder-Root, CSP.net, March 2009 (http://www.cspnet.com/ME2/ Audiences/dirmod.asp?sid=&nm=&type=Publishing&mod=Publications::Article& mid=8F3A7027421841978F18BE895F87F791&tier=4&id=3C514A88AC2540B686C0C6124F234E95& AudID=3F7DE6D5939244BBA5FBA04DEA47CA69)
- Gilbarco Passport enhancements facilitate compliance and faster execution of growth features, NPNweb.com, May 2009 (http://www.npnweb.com/ME2/dirmod.asp?sid=&nm=&type=news&mod=News& mid=9A02E3B96F2A415ABC72CB5F516B4C10&tier=3& nid=E81C1AA00D3D4C9CA97D48A60CDC5CDC)
- Gilbarco Launches AskAboutPCI.com Interactive Payment Security Website, May 2008 (http://www.gilbarco. com/object/PRMay052008.html)
- Bite the Bullet, By: Jerry Soverinsky, NACS Magazine, April 2009 (http://www.nacsonline.com/NACS/ Magazine/PastIssues/2009/April2009/Pages/CoverStory.aspx)
- The PCI ABCs By: Jerry Soverinksy, NACS Magazine, September 2008 (http://www.nacsonline.com/NACS/ Magazine/PastIssues/2008/September2008/Pages/Feature1.aspx)

External links

- Official Gilbarco Veeder-Root site (http://www.gilbarco.com)

Giro

A **Giro** (English pronunciation: /ˈdʒaɪroʊ/, /ˈdʒɪroʊ/, /ˈʒɪroʊ/, /ˈdʒɪəroʊ/ or /ˈʒɪəroʊ/[1]) or **giro transfer** is a payment transfer from one bank account to another bank account and instigated by the payer, not the payee. Equivalents in other countries are the United States Automated Clearing House for direct deposit and the Australian Direct Entry system.

In the United Kingdom and in other countries the term Giro may refer to a specific system once operated by the British post office,[2] originally known as National Giro and, confusingly, was adopted by the public and the press as a shorthand term for the Girocheque which was a cheque and not a credit transfer. The commercial banks in the UK operate a paper credit transfer system known as Bank Giro.

The use of both cheques and paper giros is now in decline in developed countries[3] in favour of electronic payments, which are thought to be faster, cheaper and safer due to the reduced risk of fraud.

Etymology

The term is borrowed from German, which in turn borrowed it from Italian, in the sense of "circulation of money"; the Italian term comes from the Greek *gyros* ("circle").[4]

History and concept

Giro systems date back at least to Ptolemaic Egypt in the 4th century BC. State granary deposits functioned as an early banking system, in which giro payments were accepted, with a central bank in Alexandria.[5] Giro was a common method of money transfer in early banking.

The first occurrences of book money are not known exactly. The Giro system itself can be traced back to the "bancherii" in Northern Italy, especially on the Rialto (the Wall Street at the time). Originally these were money changers sitting at their desk ("bancus" = table) that customers could turn to. They offered an additional service to keep the money and to allow direct transfer from one money store to another by checking the accounts in their storage books. Literally they opened one book, withdrew an amount, opened another book where the amount was added. This handling was naturally a very regional system but it allowed the money to circulate in the books. This led finally to the foundation of the "Banco del Giro" in 1619[6] (in Venetian language Banco del Ziro) which gave the blueprint for similar banking systems. The usage in German language can be seen in the Banco del Giro founded in Vienna in 1703 (to extend the financing business that Samuel Oppenheimer had brought from Venice in 1670).

Postal Giro or Postgiro systems have a long history in European financial services. The basic concept is that of a banking system not based on cheques, but rather by direct transfer between accounts. If the accounting office is centralised, then transfers between accounts can happen simultaneously. Money could be paid in or withdrawn from the system at any post office, and later connections to the commercial banking systems were established, often by the convenience of the local bank opening its own account at the Postgiro.

By the middle of the 20th century, most countries in continental Europe had a postal giro service. The first postgiro system was established in Austria on the early 19th century. By the time the British Postgiro was conceived, the Dutch Postgiro was very well established with virtually every adult having a postgiro account, and very large and well used postgiro operations in most other countries in Europe. Banks also adopted the Giro as a method of direct payment from remitter to receiver.

The term "bank" was not used initially to describe the service. The banks' main payment instrument was based on the cheque which has a totally different remittance model from the "Giro".

In the *banking model*, **cheques** are written by the remitter and then handed or posted to the payee, who must then visit a bank or post the cheque to his or her bank. The cheque must then be cleared, a complex process by which cheques are sorted once, posted to a central clearing location, sorted again, and then posted back to the paying branch where the cheque is finally checked and then paid.

In the *Postal Giro model*, **giro transfers** are sent through the post by the remitter to the giro centre. On receipt, the transfer is checked and the account transfer takes place. If the transfer is successful, the transfer document is sent to the recipient, together with an updated statement of account being credited. The remitter is also sent an updated statement. In the case of large utilities receiving thousands of transactions per day, statements would be sent electronically and incorporate a reference number uniquely identifying the remittance for reconciliation purposes.

The rise of electronic cheque clearing (and debit cards as preferred instruments of payment) has made this difference less important than it once was. For example in some stores in the United States checks are scanned at the cash register and handed back to the customer while the funds are withdrawn from the customer's account and deposited in the store's account.

Electronic bill payment

Modern electronic bill payment is similar to the use of giro.

Advantages include:

- Instant access to the funds via an ATM, debit card or cheque card.
- There is no paper cheque that can be lost, stolen, or forgotten.
- Payments made electronically can be less expensive to the payer; typically electronic payments may cost around 25¢ (US) whereas it could cost up to $2 (US) to generate, print and mail a paper cheque. Banks may not even charge for the service at all; for example in Finland banks charge nothing for electronic payments inside the country.

In the United States, the Automated Clearing House (ACH), regulated by NACHA-The Electronic Payments Association and the Federal Reserve Bank, handles all interbank transfers, including direct deposit and direct debit.

In entirely electronic bill payment, the payer receives a bill — either physically by mail or electronically from a website (electronic billing). Then, the payer reads in the information from the bill, either manually or by using the barcode on the bill, enters it to the form on the bank website, and submits the form. The payment is immediately deducted from the account balance.

Cultural significance

Before the use of electronic transfers of payments became the norm in the United Kingdom the bi-weekly 'giro' payment was the normal way of distributing benefit payments. When unemployment peaked in the 1980s large numbers of people would receive their benefit payment on the same day leading the concept of Giro Day.[7] Giro day would be marked by the settlement of small debts and noticeable increase in drinking, partying and related activities. It was celebrated in Ian Curtis' 1996 film *Waiting for Giro*.[8] [9]

References

[1] Webster online (http://www.merriam-webster.com/dictionary/giro)

[2] Oxford English Dictionary (online)

[3] Federal Reserve: Recent payment trends in the United States, 2008. "In 2003 the number of electronic payments in the US exceeded the number of cheque payments fro the firs time (http://www.federalreserve.gov/pubs/bulletin/2008/pdf/payments08.pdf)

[4] Glyn Davies, *National Giro*

[5] A Comparative Chronology of Money (http://www.ex.ac.uk/~RDavies/arian/amser/chrono1.html), Roy Davies & Glyn Davies, 1996 & 1999.

[6] http://terra-x.zdf.de/ZDFde/inhalt/28/0,1872,2112636,00.html

[7] http://www.urbandictionary.com/define.php?term=giro+day

[8] *Waiting for Giro* (http://www.imdb.com/title/tt496587/) at the Internet Movie Database

[9] http://www.britfilms.com/britishfilms/catalogue/browse/?id=D9CC70591b06f24FA2xXlQ97E840

Girocard

girocard

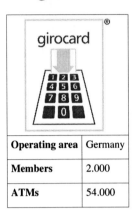

Operating area	Germany
Members	2.000
ATMs	54.000

Girocard is an interbank network and debit card service connecting virtually all German ATMs and banks. It is based on standards and agreements developed by Central Credit Committee.

German girocards are usually co-branded with MasterCard's Maestro/Cirrus or VISA's V Pay logo, allowing cardholders to use them in other European countries.[1] [2] [3] [4] [5]

History

Originally, German banks formed an interbank network connecting virtually all German ATMs. The network used Eurocheque guarantee cards as ATM cards and did not have a name or trademark of its own. In 1991, the electronic cash debit card service was introduced using the same cards. The cards used for all three payment methods were simply known as **Eurocheque card** (German *Euroscheck-Karte*).

When the Eurocheque system was disbanded at the end of 2001, the cards could no longer use the Eurocheque brand. However, German bank continued to use the **EC** logo, which was simply re-interpreted as "electronic cash". Consequently, the cards were colloquially known as **EC card** (German *EC-Karte*). However, the ATM network still did not have a trade name.

In 2007, Zentraler Kreditausschuss introduced **Girocard** as a common name for electronic cash and the German ATM network.

Services

ATM network

The German ATM network connects virtually all German ATMs. However, German banks charge high ATM usage fees (up to 10 €) from customers using other banks' ATMs.

There are several cooperations reducing or waiving these fees:

- EUFISERV is a European compact which includes the Sparkasse saving banks in Germany as to waive the fees for customers of other local branches
- Bankcard-Servicenetz is a cooperation of most co-operative banks to waive or reduce the fees for other co-operative banks.
- Cash Group is a cooperation of major private banks, which mutually waive the fees.
- CashPool is a cooperation of smaller private banks (including many virtual banks), which mutually waive the fees.

External links

• Official website [6]

References

[1] Postbank: V PAY (https://www.postbank.de/privatkunden/pk_vpay.html), Retrieved August 22, 2010.

[2] Sparkasse debit card leaflet (https://www.scard.de/karteninhaber/kartenportfolio/merkmale_sparkassencard.pdf), Retrieved August 22, 2010.

[3] VR Bank debit cards picture gallery (http://www.bvr.de/public.nsf/index.html?ReadForm&main=6&sub=40&RestrictToCategory=40), Retrieved August 22, 2010.

[4] ING-DiBa: Paying with your card (https://www.ing-diba.de/main/kk/maestro/produktinfos/popups/popup_Bargeldlos_mit_Karte_bezahlen.html), Retrieved August 22, 2010.

[5] Commerzbank Banking Portal (https://www.commerzbank-privat.de/index.html?nav=5282&con=/fb/produkte/karten/maestrocard/kar_maestro_vorteile.html), Retrieved August 22, 2010.

Giropay

Giropay is an Internet payment System in Germany, based on online banking. Introduced in February 2006, this payment method allows customers to buy securely on the Internet using direct online transfers from their bank account. The system is similar to the Dutch iDEAL payment system, the Interac Online service in Canada and Secure Vault Payments[1] in the United States. giropay is owned by giropay GmbH.

Transaction Volume

By May 2007 more than 100 million euro in purchases were made.[2]

In 2008, the system processed 3.2 million transfers, and the products and services paid with this payment method had a combined worth of 185 million Euros.[3] .

Over one million transactions are processed every month.[2]

Scope

Most German savings banks (*Sparkassen*) and cooperative banks are participating in Giropay. However, the number of participating banks from the private sector is limited. In this sector, the only major participating bank is Deutsche Postbank. Nevertheless, Giropay has a reach of about 17 million German online banking customers,[4] and about 60% of all commercial bank accounts[2] . That number means the participating banks are serving the vast majority of the German online banking market.

Process

Giropay offers merchants a real-time payment method (publicized as virtually risk-free) to accept internet payments. For customers, Giropay uses the same environment as their banks' online banking sites. The level of security depends on the participating bank. Some German Banks offer two-factor authentication (2FA), such as a challenge-response token based on the chip embedded in the debit card or ATM card. Others, however, offer simpler PIN and TAN based online banking services. No sensitive information is being shared with the merchant, such as credit card or Giro account numbers. There is no chargeback right however, which can be considered a disadvantage for the consumer using this payment method. This is considered an advantage to the merchants.

Giropay works as follows:

• Merchant offers Giropay as payment method, often in addition to the regular credit card payment options
• Consumer selects Giropay and selects his bank

- Consumer is redirected to his bank's login page
- Participating bank displays transaction data
- Customer enters account number, PIN, and either:
    - A remittance slip is sent to the customer for confirming the transaction, containing a TAN (transaction number). The customer enters this number to confirm the transaction.[2]
    - The customer signs the transaction digitally using a 2FA token (if their bank offers that service)
- Bank authorizes transaction in real-time, deducting the amount directly from the consumer's account (if there is not enough balance, the transaction will be refused)
- Merchant received real-time confirmation of the payment by the bank
- Consumer is redirected back to the merchant page with a confirmation that the payment has been successful

Payments are guaranteed for amounts up to 5000 euros.[2]

Costs

Costs are calculated on a per transaction basis and decrease with transaction volume or value. The NetBanx payment gateway quotes figures from 1.2% to 0.9%, plus 8c euro per transaction.[2]

External links

- Giropay site [5] (German only)
- Deutsche Postbank on Giropay [6] (German only)

References

[1] http://www.securevaultpayments.com

[2] *Explanation of Payment Systems*, PDF document distributed by NetBanx

[3] 2008 processing figures (http://www.giropay.de/index.php?id=464), retrieved January 1, 2010

[4] Giropay press release, August 7, 2006. (http://www.giropay.de/uploads/media/giropay_Pressemeldung_2006-007_02.pdf)

Global Payments Inc.

For global health care payments, see discussion of accountable care organizations in Health care reform debate in the United States.

Global Payments Inc. (NYSE: GPN [1]) is a payment processing company based in Atlanta, Georgia. Global Payments functions as an electronic payment processor to merchants, independent sales organizations, financial institutions, government agencies and multinational corporations in the United States, Canada, Latin America, the United Kingdom, Europe and Asia-Pacific.

History

Global Payments has more than four decades of industry experience in electronic payment processing. Global Payments acquired DolEx in 2003 and set up a high profile joint venture with HSBC in Asia covering ten markets. The present-day CEO of Global Payments is Paul R. Garcia. Global Payments also announced a USD 439 Million Joint Venture with HSBC Bank Plc in the UK. This transaction is expected to be completed by October 2008. The new company is going to be called HSBC Merchant Services. With this acquisition, Global Payments has now become one of the world's truly global payment processors with its merchant services offering across North America, Western & Eastern Europe and Asia.

On April, 2009, the Company acquired third biggest Russian processing company UCS (more than 90 banks in processing).

On June 12, 2009, the Company acquired the remaining 49% interest in HSBC Merchant Services LLP, from HSBC Bank plc.

External links

- Global Payments Worldwide Site [2]
- Global Payments USA [3]

Google Wallet

Developer(s)	Google
Initial release	May 26, 2011
Website	/wallet/ [1]

Google Wallet is a mobile payment system developed by Google that allows its users to store credit cards, loyalty cards, and gift cards among other things, as well as redeeming sales promotions on their mobile phone.[1] Google Wallet uses near field communication to "make secure payments fast and convenient by simply tapping the phone on any PayPass-enabled terminal at checkout."

Google demonstrated the app at a press conference on May 26, 2011.[2] The app will be available summer 2011.[3] The app will only be available for the Sprint Nexus S 4G although Google plans to develop the app for more phones.[4]

The service will work with over 300,000 MasterCard PayPass merchant locations.[5]

Availability

Initially, the only phone supported will be Sprint's Nexus S 4G, but Google plans to produce NFC stickers associated with one credit card each, ostensibly to be affixed to non-NFC-capable phones.[6] Two methods for providing money to the service are advertised, Citi Mastercards and "Google Prepaid Card", which can be loaded using any major credit card. During Google's Wallet unveiling at NYC headquarters, Google also touted the openness of their new system. Naturally, someone asked about what this meant for non-Android phones. "In terms of iPhone, RIM, Microsoft — we will partner with everyone," said Google VP of Commerce Stephanie Tilenius.[7]

Security

Google Wallet activates when a PIN set up by the user is entered. The antenna of NFC chip is turned off until it receives the PIN number[8] . Android Phones will also include a separate lock screen.

Additionally, Google Wallet encrypted and stores all user information on a computer chip called the Secure Element.Secure Element not only stores data but can also run programs, and is separated from the phone's memory. The chip is designed to only allow trusted programs on the Secure Element itself to access the payment credentials stored therein.

The secure encryption technology of MasterCard PayPass protects your payment card credentials as they are transferred from the phone to the contactless reader.[9]

PayPal Lawsuit

Shortly after launch, Paypal filed a lawsuit against Google and two former employees of Paypal - Osama Bedier and Stephanie Tilenius. The complaint alleges "misappropriation of trade secrets, and "breach of fiduciary duty." The lawsuit reveals that Google was negotiatiating with PayPal for two years to power payments on mobile devices. But just as the deal was about to be signed, Google backed off and instead hired the PayPal executive negotiating the deal, Bedier. The lawsuit notes that Bedier knew all of PayPal's future plans for mobile payments, as well as an internal detailed analysis of Google's weaknesses in the area. Not only that, it accuses him of storing "confidential information in locations such as his non-PayPal computers, non-PayPal e-mail account, and an account on the remote computing service called 'Dropbox.'"[10]

References

[1] "Coming soon: make your phone your wallet" (http://googleblog.blogspot.com/2011/05/coming-soon-make-your-phone-your-wallet. html). Official Google Blog. May 26, 2011. . Retrieved May 26, 2011.

[2] Warren, Christina (May 26, 2011). "Google Reveals Mobile Payment System: Google Wallet" (http://mashable.com/2011/05/26/ google-mobile-payment-system-liveblog/). Mashable. . Retrieved May 26, 2011.

[3] "Google, Citi, MasterCard, First Data and Sprint Team up to Make Your Phone Your Wallet" (http://www.businesswire.com/news/home/ 20110526006211/en/Google-Citi-MasterCard-Data-Sprint-Team-Phone). Business Wire. May 26, 2011. . Retrieved May 26, 2011.

[4] Lee, Amy (May 26, 2011). "Google Unveils Google Wallet, Google Offers: What's New" (http://www.huffingtonpost.com/2011/05/26/ google-wallet-google-offers_n_867533.html). *The Huffington Post*. . Retrieved May 26, 2011.

[5] Hamburger, Ellis (May 26, 2011). "Google Introduces Google Wallet, Works At Over 300,000 MasterCard PayPass Merchant Locations" (http://www.businessinsider.com/google-introduces-google-wallet-works-with-mastercards-paypass-2011-5?op=1). Silicon Alley Insider. . Retrieved May 26, 2011.

[6] Vildosola, Alberto (May 26, 2011). "Google plans to make special Google Wallet stickers for phones without NFC" (http://androidandme. com/2011/05/news/google-plans-to-make-special-google-wallet-stickers-for-phones-without-nfc/). Androidandme. . Retrieved May 26, 2011.

[7] Castro, Radford (May 26, 2011). "Google Wallet to work with non-Android phones" (http://www.lazytechguys.com/news/ google-wallet-to-work-with-non-android-phones/). LazyTechGuys. . Retrieved May 26, 2011.

[8] Le, Tony (June 1, 2011). "Google Wallet FAQ" (http://googlewallets.blogspot.com/p/frequently-asked-questions-about-google.html). GFan. . Retrieved June 4, 2011.

[9] "Security: How IT Works" (http://www.google.com/wallet/how-it-works-security.html). Official Google Blog. May 26, 2011. . Retrieved June 4, 2011.

[10] Schonfeld, Erick (May 26, 2011). "PayPal Lawsuit Against Google Reveals Recruiting Saga And A Deal Gone Sour" (http://techcrunch. com/2011/05/26/paypal-lawsuit-google/). *TechCrunch*. . Retrieved May 27, 2011.

External links

- Official website (http://http://www.google.com/wallet/)
- FAQ (http://googlewallets.blogspot.com/p/frequently-asked-questions-about-google.html)

GreenZap

GreenZap, Inc.

Industry	Finance
Key people	Damon Westmoreland
Website	http://www.greenzap.com/

GreenZap was an online buying and spending account service that claimed to compete with PayPal. GreenZap launched on April 2, 2005 and allowed members to send and receive money online, through their email address. The ultimate beneficial owner of GreenZap was reported to be Damon Westmoreland, who was reportedly associated with ThePayline.com,[1] a widespread Internet financial pyramid.[2] Another report stated that the ownership of GreenZap was unclear because the company was not registered to do business in California, where its mailing address was located in a postal box within a grocery store, and because the company's official phone number was a mobile phone.[3]

Current status

As of December 2010, the site is no longer operational.

References

[1] Platinax, Greenzap claims it's not a scam (http://www.internetbusiness.co.uk/14022007/greenzap-claims-its-not-a-scam/), Feb 14, 2007

[2] security.itworld.com, Postal authorities seize ThePayLine.com cash flow (http://security.itworld.com/4337/IWD010402oplivingston/page_1.html), April 2, 2001

[3] Yahoo! News, Free money? We think not (http://web.archive.org/web/20070329065146/http://uk.news.yahoo.com/14102005/372/free-money-think.html), October 14, 2006

GrIDsure

GrIDsure is a personal identification system which extends the standard 'shared-secret' authentication model to create a secure methodology whereby a dynamic 'one-time' password or PIN can be generated by a user. It can be used to secure ATMs, POSs, mobile phones, dedicated devices, door locks and even as a paper-based solution. It was invented by Stephen Howes and Jonathan Craymer in November 2005 and has been named as one of Gartner's "Cool Vendors in Application Security & Authentication, 2008" companies, as well as being described as "near universal authentication" by Ovum, and as a real step forward by Bloor Research.[1] [2] [3]

How it Works

See it working [4]

The core of the patent pending methodology is one of 'sequential pattern recognition' of cells on a grid. The user is challenged with a grid containing pseudo-randomly generated numbers and the user selects those numbers that accord with the pattern and sequence made by his chosen cells.

In this process the user needs to remember a pattern of his choice which he registers with the authenticator (the shared secret). Since the user is using his secret pattern to select numbers from a grid square and then using those numbers to authenticate, he never actually 'gives up' his secret to the authenticator − he only communicates a 'representation' of his secret which is in the form of a selection from a random set of numbers. Consequently there is nothing for a 'keylogger' to reverse-engineer and since the numbers are repeated several times in the grid-square, it is extremely difficult for a 'shoulder-surfer' to ascertain the pattern by observing the keystrokes and the gridsquare.

The user registration process and subsequent challenge-response process are described in more detail as follows:-

User registration

- The user registers a 'Personal Identification Pattern' (PIP) with the authenticator. (Alternatively the authenticator could pre-allocate a PIP to a user.) This becomes his shared secret.
- The grid can be almost any size or shape; however a 5x5 grid gives a good balance between ease of use and security in most situations.
- The PIP can be 4 cells (like a PIN) or any length you like.

General Use

- The user is presented with a grid populated with pseudo random symbols. (The symbols need not be numeric.)
- The user enters the symbols representing his pattern/sequence.
- The authenticator accepts or rejects the user.
- Every time the user is challenged he will be presented with a different grid and so will enter a different GrIDsure code.

Mathematical Security

A study was carried out on the statistical security of GrIDsure by Richard Weber in the Statistical Laboratory of the University of Cambridge.

The full report outlines the mathematics of various GrIDsure grids, the probabilities of a thief guessing a PIN or a Personal Identification Pattern (PIP), the chances of a thief reverse-engineering a PIP and the mathematical security of various sized grids and patterns. In an appendix to the main report, Professor Weber studies a number of likely fraud models in order to summarise in a single figure, how much more secure GrIDsure is than a traditional PIN.

"After performing further sensitivity analysis on our model we may conclude that it reasonable to say that against a plausible mix of risks GrIDsure is of the order of 100 times (i.e., two orders of magnitude) more secure than traditional pin.

He concludes:

This is one of the most beautiful ideas I have seen in many years of looking at algorithms and optimisation problems. - Professor Richard R. Weber. Director, Statistical Laboratory, Cambridge University.

In March 2008, an independent security researcher, Mike Bond[4] , identified flaws[5] in the Gridsure authentication scheme, specifically commenting on Weber's analysis, and concluded:

> "The Gridsure authentication mechanism remains largely unproven. Studies so far are flawed or taken out of context; my own initial studies indicate further weaknesses."

The introduction to Dr Bond's paper states "This document is not intended to be a fully representative or balanced appraisal of the scheme."

Usability

University College London committed an independent usability trial. This pilot study was carried out by the Department of Human Centered Systems/Department of Computer Science under the direction of Angela Sasse, Professor of Human-Centred Technology. With a background in Human-Computer Interaction, Prof. Sasse has been carrying out research since 1996 to develop a user-centred perspective on security, privacy and trust. She has investigated usability and effectiveness of a number of security mechanisms, including passwords and biometrics. She contributed a review to the 2004 Foresight report on Cybertrust and Crime Prevention, and was appointed a Specialist Advisor to the Home Affairs Committee for its enquiry into the proposed introduction of ID cards. She currently serves on the Biometrics Advisory Group, an independent expert panel that advises the Home Office, and chairs the DTI Knowledge Transfer Network (KTN) on Human Vulnerabilities in Network Security.

The key objective of this pilot study were to:

- See how easily people could learn to use GrIDsure
- To see how well they could recall the process after an extended period of time.

Fifty (50) subjects were chosen of varying age and ability (six were over the age of 60). The trial was carried out on Windows PDAs with 'soft' keyboards and no colour on the grid (making the process more difficult than would occur in a real-life situation). A standard 5x5 grid was used and after first usage, subsequent checks were taken at periods of a few hours up to 11 weeks.

The key results of the study were :

- *"All participants grasped the notion quickly and easily"*. All but two managed to use it first time and the remainder managed it with a little additional explanation.
- On subsequent tests, whilst some people were unsure of the process the vast majority nevertheless still managed to complete the task successfully.
- *"There was a high level of success overall in entering the correct number sequence"* (93.84%).
- Excluding the first time, on subsequent use with elapsed times up to 36.9 days, success rates remained high (92.63%).

In a covering letter to the study report, Professor Sasse states:

"Having looked at many mechanisms which have been proposed in recent years to overcome users' problems with PINs and passwords, this is the first one that has the potential to offer good usability and increased security at the same time" .

External links

- GrIDsure The company website [7]
- *Gartner* Cool Vendors in Application Security and Authentication [8]
- *Ovum* Promising proposal for near universal user authentication method [9]
- *The Institute of Engineering & Technology* Grid Expectations [10]
- *The Register* UK start-up tackles PIN fraud with patterns [11]
- *Info Security Magazine* Card issuer to adopt graphical Pin randomiser [12]
- *Security Park* Pattern-based ID verification system combats online fraud [13]
- *Bloor* Superior accessible security [14]
- *Computing.co.uk* banks seek fraud solutions [15]
- *Cambridge Evening News* ID system the "perfect solution" to fight fraud [16]
- *The Guardian Unlimited* Pick a pattern, not a PIN [17]
- *The Sunday Times* Sudoku-style codes planned to defeat bank fraudsters [18]
- "French Gridsure article" fr:GridSure

Notes

[1] "Media Products Overview" (http://mediaproducts.gartner.com/reprints/veracode/156005.html). Mediaproducts.gartner.com. 2008-01-08. . Retrieved 2010-03-27.

[2] "Telecoms and Software News" (http://www.ovum.com/news/euronews.asp?id=6300). Ovum.com. . Retrieved 2010-03-27.

[3] "Superior accessible security" (http://www.it-analysis.com/business/compliance/content.php?cid=9686). It-analysis.com. . Retrieved 2010-03-27.

[4] Mike Bond, Security Researcher (http://www.cl.cam.ac.uk/~mkb23/)

[5] Mike Bond, Comments on Gridsure Authentication, 27 March 2008 (http://www.cl.cam.ac.uk/~mkb23/research/GridsureComments. pdf)

Honesty bar

An **honesty bar** is an unattended beverage bar, typically in the lobby or lounge of a hotel, where payment is left to the guest. (Honesty bars differ significantly from in-room mini-bars, where any consumption is automatically charged to the guest's account.)

Honesty bars are less common than staffed bars, but can be found in a number of boutique hotels and other small hotels, and the executive floors of fine hotels. No staff attend the bar and therefore it is left to the honesty of the guest to report his or her own consumption. Honesty bars are convenient, since a guest can make or serve a drink at any time, keeping a tab for himself or herself for the length of the stay. Generally drinks are cheaper in an honesty bar, since no staff must be paid to attend the area continuously.

Honesty bars are generally stocked with popular beverages, mixers, and feature a standard bar setup. It is common to find a manual of basic cocktails.

Honesty box

An **honesty box** is a method of charging for a service such as admission or car parking, or for a product such as home-grown produce and flowers, which relies upon each visitor to pay at an unattended box using the honour system. Tickets are not issued and such sites are usually unmanned. When used in campgrounds and other park settings, they are sometimes referred to as an **iron ranger** as there is often an iron cash box instead of an actual park ranger.[1] Some stores also use them for selling newspapers to avoid queues at a till.[2]

Such boxes are typically used in rural areas where the either number of visitors/customers or the quantity and value of the products on offer is sufficiently low that a manned presence would not bring a positive return on investment.[2] Many are also domestically-run operations where a manned presence is not feasible to carry out.

Selling jam jars on the roadside

References

[1] Don Henry's prolific metal sculpture abounds in Homer 'Divas and Dolls' *Michael Armstrong, Homer News, 10-15-08* (http://www.homernews.com/stories/101508/arts_14_001.shtml)

[2] Jonathan Richards (October 1, 2007). *Honesty box culture* (http://news.bbc.co.uk/1/hi/magazine/7041447.stm). London: Times Online. . Retrieved March 26, 2009.

Hundi

Hundis were legal financial instruments that evolved on the Indian sub-continent. These were used in trade and credit transactions; they were used as remittance instruments for the purpose of transfer of funds from one place to another. In the era of bygone kings and the British Raj these Hundis served as Travellers Cheques. They were also used as credit instruments for borrowing and as bills of exchange for trade transactions.

Technically, a Hundi is an unconditional order in writing made by a person directing another to pay a certain sum of money to a person named in the order. Being a part of an informal system, hundis now have no legal status and were not covered under the Negotiable Instruments Act, 1881. They were mostly used as cheques by indigenous bankers.

Types of Hundis

- **Sahyog Hundi**: This is drawn by one merchant on another, asking the latter to pay the amount to a third merchant. In this case the merchant on whom the hundi is drawn is of some 'credit worthiness' in the market and is known in the bazaar. A sahyog hundi passes from one hand to another till it reaches the final recipient, who, after reasonable enquiries, presents it to the drawee for acceptance of the payment. Sahyog means co-operation in Hindi and Gujrati, the predominant languages of traders. The hundi is so named because it required the co-operation of multiple parties to ensure that the hundi has a acceptable risk and fairly good likelihood of being paid, in the absence of a formalized credit monitoring and reporting framework.

- **Darshani Hundi**: This is a hundi payable on sight. It must be presented for payment within a reasonable time after its receipt by the holder. Thus, it is similar to a demand bill.

- **Muddati Hundi**: A muddati or miadi hundi is payable after a specified period of time. This is similar to a time bill.

There are few other varieties; the Nam-jog hundi, Dhani-jog hundi, Jawabee hundi, Jokhami hundi, Firman-jog hundi, etc.

Nam-jog hundi - such a hundi is payable only to the person whose name is mentioned on the Hundi. Such a hundi cannot be endorsed in favour of any other person and is akin to a bill on which a restrictive endorsement has been made.

Furman-jog Hundi - such a hundi can be paid either to the person whose name is mentioned in the hundi or to any person so ordered by him. Such a hundi is similar to a cheque payable on order and no endorsement is required on such a hundi.

Dhani-jog Hundi - when the hundi is payable to the holder or bearer,it is known as a dhani jog hundi. It is similar to an instrument payable to bearer.

Jokhim Hundi - normally a hundi is unconditional but a jokhim hundi is conditional in the sense that the drawer promises to pay the amount of the hundi only on the satisfaction of a certain condition. Such a hundi is not negotiable, and the prevalence of such hundis is very rare these days because banks and insurance companies refuse to accept such hundis.

Jawabi Hundi - if money is transferred from one place to another through the hundi and the person receiving the payment on is to give an acknowledgement (jawab) for same, then such a hundi is known as a Jawabi Hundi.

Khaka Hundi - a hundi which has already been paid is known as a Khaka Hundi.

Khoti Hundi - In case there is any kind of defect in the hundi or in case the hundi has been forged, then such a hundi is known as a khoti hundi.

i2c Inc

i2c, Inc.

Type	Private
Industry	Electronic payment processing Stored-value card management
Founded	1987
Headquarters	Redwood Shores, CA, USA Lahore, PK (offshore office)
Key people	Amir Wain, CEO
Employees	1000
Website	www.i2cinc.com [1]

i2c, Inc. is an electronic payment processing[1] , point of sale activation solutions (POSA) and prepaid application service provider company located in Redwood Shores, California, USA.

History

Innovative Pvt Limited was founded in 1987.i2c Inc was founded in 2001 as a sub part of Innovative Pvt Limited, and currently has more than two hundred and fifty employees. Now i2c Inc is an independent organization. In Pakistan, both organizations IPL and i2c are located at same place on Ferozepur Road Lahore.[2]

Products and services

i2c is a global consulting and IT services company specializing in the following practice areas:

Managed solutions

- MCP (My Card Place) - Stored-value card processing
- FastCash - Electronic Transaction processing
- FastSettle

Services

- Electronic money processing
- Is operating a state of the art call center, providing quality customer services to its clients.

Global offices

i2c has offshore office in Lahore, Pakistan and six sales and support offices worldwide.

External links

- i2c, Inc. Official Website [4]
- Paybefore Buyer's Guide profile [5]

i2c Pakistan office at Lahore

References

[1] i2c as electronic transaction processing company (http://investing.businessweek.com/research/stocks/private/snapshot. asp?privcapId=7940859i2c,)

[2] About i2c Inc. (http://www.i2cinc.com/who_we_are.htm)

iDEAL

iDEAL is an Internet payment method in the Netherlands, based on online banking. Introduced in 2005, this payment method allows customers to buy securely on the Internet using direct online transfers from their bank account. iDEAL processed 4,5 million transfers in 2006, 15 million transfers in 2007, 28 million transfers in 2008, 45.4 million in 2009 and 68.8 million in 2010.[1] iDEAL is owned by the Dutch organization Currence, which also owns PIN and Chipknip.

The participating banks in iDEAL are: ABN AMRO, ASN Bank, Friesland Bank, ING Bank, Rabobank, RegioBank, SNS Bank, Triodos Bank and Van Lanschot.[2] Together these are serving the vast majority of the Dutch online banking market.

Process

iDEAL offers merchants a real-time payment method (publicized as low-cost and virtually risk-free) to accept internet payments. For customers, iDEAL uses the same environment as their banks' online banking sites. A high level of security is realized by using two-factor authentication (2FA), such as a challenge-response token based on the chip embedded in the debit card or ATM card. Furthermore, no sensitive information is being shared with the merchant, such as credit card numbers. There is no chargeback right however, which can be considered a disadvantage for the consumer using this payment method. This is considered an advantage to the merchants.

iDEAL works as follows:

- Merchant offers iDEAL as payment method
- Consumer selects iDEAL and selects his bank
- Consumer is redirected to his bank's login page
- Participating bank displays transaction data
- Customer enters account number and signs the transaction digitally using a 2FA token

- Bank authorizes transaction in real-time, deducting the amount directly from the consumer's account (if there is not enough balance, the transaction will be refused)
- Merchant received real-time confirmation of the payment by the bank
- Consumer is redirected back to the merchant page with a confirmation that the payment has been successful

External links

- iDEAL site [3] (English)
- iDEAL site [4] (Dutch)
- ABN AMRO on iDEAL [5] (Dutch)
- ASN Bank on iDEAL [6] (Dutch)
- Friesland Bank on iDEAL [7] (Dutch)
- ING bank on iDEAL [8] (Dutch)
- Rabobank on iDEAL [9] (Dutch)
- RegioBank on iDEAL [10] (Dutch)
- SNS bank on iDEAL [11] (Dutch)
- Triodos Bank on iDEAL [12] (Dutch)
- Van Lanschot on iDEAL [13] (Dutch)

References

[1] What is iDEAL? (http://www.ideal.nl/acceptant/?s=wat&lang=eng-GB) including numbers of transfers
[2] What is iDEAL? (http://www.ideal.nl/consument/?s=wat&lang=eng-GB) including a list of participating banks

IMF Balance of Payments Manual

The **Balance of Payments Manual** published by the International Monetary Fund provides accounting standards for balance of payments reporting and analysis for many countries. The Bureau of Economic Analysis adheres to this standard.

The sixth edition was released in prepublication form in December 2008. Its title has been amended to **Balance of Payments and International Investment Position Manual** to reflect that it covers not only transactions, but also the stocks of the related financial assets and liabilities.

External links

- Balance of Payments Manual, fifth edition – International Monetary Fund [1]
- Balance of Payments Textbook – International Monetary Fund [2]
- Balance of Payments and International Investment Position Manual, sixth edition – International Monetary Fund [3]

InteliSpend Prepaid Solutions

InteliSpend Prepaid Solutions

Type	Private
Industry	Finance, Incentive services
Founder(s)	American Express Maritz Inc
Headquarters	Fenton, Missouri, United States
Area served	United States Canada
Key people	Darryl Hutson (CEO)
Products	Card Programs and Incentive programs

InteliSpend Prepaid Solutions is a private company formed as a joint venture by American Express and Maritz, Inc in 1997.[1] InteliSpend provides incentive programs for 76% of Fortune 100 companies.[2] In 2010, Maritz bought out American Express' interest in the company to obtain 100% ownership.[3]

Products

Card Programs

One of the primary selling points for InteliSpend is the patented DirectSpend technology that gives clients the ability to restrict the spending on the reward cards to specific retail locations.[4] Through the Persona product InteliSpend's clients are able to choose which retail outlets the card will be accepted at. Additionally cards can be co-branded and personalized through the Custom Card and DirectSpend/Persona products. For non-restricted programs the Encompass card is provided.[5]

Sales Incentive & Rebate Programs

In addition to pure card solutions InteliSpend utilizes partner companies to provide Sales Incentive (Spiff) programs and product rebate programs. Through its partners InteliSpend delivers online solutions with varying degrees of integration and online facilities.

Management and Key Executives

Key executives include:[1] [6]

- **Darryl A. Hutson**: Chief Executive Officer
- **Russell W. T. Yergensen**: Chief Financial Officer

References

[1] (http://investing.businessweek.com/research/stocks/private/snapshot.asp?privcapId=4421407), BusinessWeek American Express Incentive Services, L.L.C., accessed 9 April 2009

[2] (http://aeis.com/about_main.html), American Express Incentive Service - About Us, accessed 9 April 2009

[3] http://intelispend.com/about-us

[4] (http://findarticles.com/p/articles/mi_pwwi/is_200705/ai_n19179002/), bnet StoreFinancial Licenses American Express Incentive Services' Patented DirectSpend(SM) Process, accessed 9 April 2009

[5] (http://aeis.com/prod_encompass.html), American Express Incentive Services - Encompass Card, accessed 9 April 2009

[6] (http://aeis.com/about_bios.html), American Express Incentive Service - About Us, accessed 9 April 2009

External links

- Official website (http://intelispend.com)

Interac

Interac

Operating area	Canada
Members	83
ATMs	600,000
Founded	1984

Interac Association is a Canadian organization linking enterprises that have proprietary networks so that they may communicate with each other for the purpose of exchanging electronic financial transactions. The Association was founded in 1984 as a cooperative venture between five financial institutions: Royal Bank of Canada, CIBC, Scotiabank, Toronto-Dominion Bank, and Desjardins. Interac's request to become a for-profit organization was rejected by the Competition Bureau.[1]

By 2005, there were over 80 member organizations and there were over 600,000 Automated Banking Machines that can be accessed through the Interac network.

Services

Interac Association is the organization responsible for the development of a national network of two shared electronic financial services:

Interac Direct Payment (IDP)

- Interac Direct Payment (IDP): Canada's national debit card service for purchasing of goods and services. Customers enter their personal identification number (PIN) and the amount paid is deducted from either their chequing or savings accounts.
- Since its national launch in 1994, Interac Direct Payment has become so widespread that, since 2001, more transactions in Canada were completed using debit cards than cash.[2]
- Beginning in 2004, IDP purchases could also be made in the United States at merchants on the NYCE network.
- IDP is similar in nature to the EFTPOS systems in use in the United Kingdom, Australia and New Zealand.

How Interac Direct Payment (IDP) works

IDP purchases can be made at all retailers participating in the program, regardless of the financial institution issuing the debit card being used, and normally IDP will not charge any fees to the purchaser for using the program.[3] Banks may levy a charge for withdrawing funds from the account used to fund the purchase,[3] but these fees are not associated with IDP itself. IDP will instead charge flat fee to the retailers.[4] [5] There are just under 550,000 IDP terminals in use throughout Canada; 3.5 billion POS transactions and 156 billion Canadian dollars worth of transactions took place in 2007.[5] On December 23, 2005, a new record for single day transactions was set with 15.5 million transactions processed.[6]

Four steps to completing a transaction

The "Interac Inter-Member Network" is a complex network known as a "distributed architecture" throughout the country. Chances of the entire network shutting down are very remote as the network does not have any single "point of failure." If a single member is experiencing short-term technical difficulties, it is not possible for the entire network to fail.

1. The procedure begins at the time a purchaser makes a purchase with his or her banking or debit card; this is processed with the Interac Direct Payment service. The employee will then record the sale and enter the actual price into the "point of sale terminal".

2. Either the purchaser or the seller will swipe the card through the reader, or insert the EMV chip card into the chip reader (usually integrated into the pin pad). At this point, the purchaser will enter his or her "Personal Identification Number (PIN)" into the reader. The amount of the transaction is verified, and the account to be debited is selected by the consumer.

3. The sale is transferred throughout the Interac system where the purchaser's financial services firm verifies the debit card, the PIN, and the funds available in the account. The purchase is complete after these three steps are verified by the purchaser's institution.

4. A receipt of the transaction is returned to the purchaser along with the banking or debit card.

Benefits

Convenience

Using the Interac system reduces the need to visit an ATM or carry large amounts of cash. The processing fees for merchants are much lower than credit card discounts for the merchants making Interac the preferred payment option for 52% of Canadian merchants.[7]

Overall Risk Reduction

A private Personal Identification Number(PIN) is selected by each card holder to access their individual accounts. This "Two Factor Authentication" (Card/PIN combination) increases the security and confidentiality of the system, helps eliminate the worry of theft, and makes it impossible to access funds in an account without the corresponding PIN.

Consumer protection in Canada

Consumers in Canada are also protected under a voluntary industry code which is overseen by the Canadian federal government. The Canadian Code of Practice for Consumer Debit Card Services[8] (sometimes called the "Debit Card Code") covers all providers of debit card services. Adherence to the Code is overseen by the Financial Consumer Agency of Canada (FCAC), which investigates consumer complaints.

According to the FCAC, revisions to the Code that came into effect in 2005[9] put the onus on the financial institution to prove that a consumer was responsible for a disputed transaction, and also place a limit on the number of days that an account can be frozen during the financial institution's investigation of a transaction.

Privacy & Security

Compared to other forms of payment, only a limited amount of information is revealed with each transaction. The only personal information found on a typical receipt will be the client's card number and account selected (chequing/savings).

In comparison, when a cheque is made out to a merchant, the customer's name, address, and phone number are in the top left hand corner of a cheque and the MICR encoded account number is printed on the bottom of the cheque. In addition, because cheques are easily forged, merchants will often ask for identification documents, typically containing a photo, to confirm the cheque issuer matches the information on the cheque.

IDP flaws and features

Interac Direct Payment is a PIN-based system where the information entered on the PIN pad is encrypted and verified at a central server, rather than being stored on the card itself. Because of this, it is significantly more secure than traditional signature or card-based transactions. Despite these security features, there are ongoing fraud concerns, particularly when debit cards are *duped* or *skimmed* — a compromised automated teller machine or point-of-sale terminal will record the account information contained in the magnetic strip of the card, allowing for duplicate cards to be created at a later time. The owner of the card is then secretly video taped or observed entering their PIN, allowing a criminal to use duplicate cards to make fraudulent purchases.

The move to Interac Chip Cards

In an effort to combat fraud and increase security, Interac announced it will be moving to EMV Chip Card technology, which began with a market trial in the Kitchener-Waterloo area in Fall, 2007.[10] [11] The main benefit to this technology over the existing magnetic stripes is that the chips are almost impossible to copy due to high levels of encryption. This is seen as being able to reduce the amount of debit card fraud caused by card skimming and duplication. However new Interac Chip Cards will continue to feature a magnetic stripe in the interim in order for them to be used at ATMs or retailers which have not yet been upgraded, as well as in countries which have not yet adopted chip cards, such as the United States.

The purchase experience for consumers will remain largely unchanged, except instead of swiping the card, it will be inserted into a chip reader on the PIN Pad and will remain inserted for the duration of the transaction. PIN numbers will still be used as the means to authenticate transactions.

Interac expects the transition to chip cards to take several years to complete, but will be completed before certain milestone dates:

- After 31 December 2012, all ATM transactions must be completed with a chip card
- After 31 December 2015, all POS transactions must be completed with a chip card

[12]

Shared Cash Dispensing (SCD)

- Shared Cash Dispensing (SCD): cash withdrawals from any ABM not belonging to a cardholder's financial institution.
- This Canada-specific service is similar to international systems like PLUS or Cirrus.
- Virtually every ABM in Canada is on the Interac system.

Interac Email Money Transfer

The *Interac* Email Money Transfer service is offered by CertaPay. It allows online banking customers to send money to anyone with an e-mail address and a bank account in Canada. This is an *Interac* branded service operated by Acxsys Corporation.

Interac Online

The *Interac* Online service allows customers to pay for goods and services over the Internet using funds directly from their bank accounts. Because no financial information is shared with the online merchant, the *Interac* Online service is more secure than online credit card payments. This service, an *Interac* branded service operated by Acxsys Corporation, began in 2005 and is expanding as more merchants choose to participate. Since November 2007, the service has been available to customers of four of the five largest Canadian banks: RBC Royal Bank, BMO Bank of Montreal, Scotiabank, and TD Canada Trust. As of February 2009, the service is offered by roughly 300 merchants including two large universities (for tuition payments), two major wireless carriers, provincial lottery corporations, and a wide variety of retailers. Interac Online is an Online Banking ePayments service very similar to iDEAL in the Netherlands, Giropay[13] in Germany, and Secure Vault Payments[14] in the United States.

Services not offered on Interac networks

It is currently not possible to transfer money internationally using the Interac network; however, most Canadian ABM cards are also linked to PLUS or Cirrus, or other networks with more global reach.

References

[1] Bureau axes Interac request to become for-profit (http://www.ctv.ca/servlet/ArticleNews/story/CTVNews/20100212/ Interac_Ruling_100212/20100212?hub=Canada)

[2] http://www.informit.com/articles/article.aspx?p=394507&seqNum=5

[3] http://www.interac.ca/consumers/fees.php

[4] http://www.interac.ca/merchants/fees.php

[5] http://www.digitaltransactions.net/newsstory.cfm?newsid=1908

[6] http://www.newswire.ca/en/releases/archive/December2005/26/c3811.html

[7] http://www.canada.com/topics/news/national/story.html?id=3c268f07-2dce-4ac0-8e10-c54cb22edcc0

[8] http://www.fcac-acfc.gc.ca/eng/industry/RefDocs/default.asp#dcc

[9] http://www.fcac-acfc.gc.ca/eng/industry/RefDocs/DebitCardCode/DebitCardCode_e.asp#clause6

[10] http://www.interac.ca/consumers/chip.php

[11] http://www.interac.ca/consumers/kitchener.php

[12] Interac Chip FAQ (http://www.interac.ca/consumers/faqs.php#chipSection)

[13] http://www.giropay.de

[14] http://www.securevaultpayments.com

Bibliography

- Interac Association (2006). At the Merchant 2006. Retrieved 19 June 2006, from http://www.interac.ca/ en_n2_11_howitworks.html
- Interac Association (2006). At the Merchant 2006. Retrieved 19 June 2006, from http://www.interac.ca/ en_n2_12_benefits.html
- Interac Association (2006). At the Merchant 2006. Retrieved 19 June 2006, from http://www.interac.ca/ en_n2_13_fees.html

External links

- Interac website (http://www.interac.ca/)
- Interac Chip Card website (http://www.interac.ca/chip.php)
- Interac Online website (http://www.interaconline.com/)

Interac e-Transfer

Interac **e-Transfer** (previously known as **Interac Email Money Transfer**) is a funds transfer service between personal and business accounts at participating Canadian financial institutions. The provider of this service is CertaPay, a division of Acxsys Corporation.

Participating Institutions

Since 2003, personal deposit account holders at one of the Big Five banks in Canada could send Interac e-Transfers:

- Bank of Montreal
- Canadian Imperial Bank of Commerce
- Royal Bank of Canada
- Scotiabank
- Toronto-Dominion Bank

Since 2008, certain Canadian Credit Unions have also offered the service, as has President's Choice Financial. [1]

Small business customers who bank online at participating institutions can also send e-Transfer. Any personal account holder in Canada can receive funds.

How it works

An Email Money Transfer resembles an e-check in many respects. The money is not actually transferred by e-mail. Only the instructions to retrieve the funds are.

- The sender opens an online banking session and chooses the recipient, the amount to send, as well as a security question and answer. The funds are debited instantly, usually for a surcharge.
- An e-mail or text message is then sent to the recipient, with instructions on how to retrieve the funds and answer the question, via a secure website.
  - If the recipient is subscribed to online banking at one of the participating institutions, the funds are deposited instantly at no extra charge.
  - If the recipient's deposit account is not at one of the participating institutions or not subscribed to online banking at all, the funds are deposited within three to five business days, and a surcharge (currently $4.00) is deducted from the amount received.

Benefits and disadvantages

Unlike a cheque, the funds from an e-Transfer are not frozen in the recipient's account. An e-Transfer cannot bounce, as the funds are guaranteed, having been debited from the sender's account immediately upon initiating the transfer. As long as both sender and recipient bank at participating institutions, the funds are sent and received instantly.

However, like any online banking mode of payment, e-Transfers are vulnerable to phishing. Many Canadians in areas where the Big Five banks have little presence or who do not bank online are penalized by a surcharge when receiving e-Transfers. Unlike a real giro, an e-Transfer requires intervention from the recipient for every single transaction. An e-Transfer goes stale much faster than a cheque (after 30 days, the e-Transfer is automatically cancelled and the sender is notified by e-mail to retrieve the funds.) [2]

References

[1] Interac e-Transfer participants (http://www.interac.ca/consumers/productsandservices_ol_emt_list.php)

[2] Interac (http://www.interac.ca/consumers/faqs.php#eTransfer)

External links

* Interac (http://www.interac.ca/index.php)

* Interac e-Transfer Frequently Asked Questions (http://www.interac.ca/consumers/faqs.php#eTransfer)

Interbank Mobile Payment Service

Interbank Mobile Payment Service or **IMPS** offers an instant, 24X7, interbank electronic fund transfer service through mobile phones. IMPS facilitate customers to use mobile instruments as a channel for accessing their bank accounts and put high interbank fund transfers in a secured manner with immediate confirmation features. It belongs to National Payments Corporation of India, an umbrella organisation for all retail payment systems in India.This facility is provided by NPCI through its existing NFS switch. [1]

Currently majority of interbank mobile fund transfer transactions are channelised through NEFT mechanism. Under NEFT, the transactions are processed and settled in batches, hence are not real time. Also, the transactions can be done only during the working hours of the RTGS system.

In the above context, NPCI has carried out a pilot on mobile payment system initially with 4 member banks viz State Bank of India, Bank of India, Union Bank of India and ICICI Bank in August 2010. Yes Bank, Axis Bank and HDFC Bank have joined this pilot in month of September, October and November 2010 respectively. Interbank Mobile Payment Service (IMPS) public launch happened on 22nd November 2010 by Smt. Shyamala Gopinath, DG RBI at Mumbai and this service is now available to the Indian public.

Objectives of IMPS

1. To enable bank customers to use mobile instruments as a channel for accessing their banks accounts and remit funds
2. Making payment simpler just with the mobile number of the beneficiary
3. To sub-serve the goal of Reserve Bank of India (RBI) in electronification of retail payments
4. To facilitate mobile payment systems already introduced in India with the Reserve Bank of India Mobile Payment Guidelines 2008 to be inter-operable across banks and mobile operators in a safe and secured manner
5. To build the foundation for a full range of mobile based Banking services.

Member Banks

```
* Axis Bank
* Bank of India
* Canara Bank
* Corporation Bank
* Development Credit Bank
* Dombivli Nagari Sahakari Bank
* Federal bank
* HDFC Bank
* ICICI Bank
* IDBI Bank.
```

* Indian Bank
* Indian Overseas Bank
* Karur Vysya Bank
* Kotak Mahindra Bank
* Lakshmi Vilas Bank
* Oriental Bank of Commerce
* State Bank of India
* Union Bank of India
* YES Bank

Pre-Requisites for Mobile Banking through IMPS

Registration for Remitter:

* Register yourself for mobile banking service with bank
* Get Mobile Money Identifier (MMID) and MPIN from the bank
* Download Software (Application) for mobile banking
  (ensure the compatibility of mobile with the application)
  or use the SMS facility in your mobile if your bank provides IMPS on SMS

Registration for Beneficiary:

* Link your mobile number to the account in the respective bank.
  No need to register for mobile banking service.
* Get Mobile Money Identifier (MMID) from the bank

For Remitter (To send money):

* Login to the application and select the IMPS menu from the IMPS or
  use the SMS facility in your mobile if your bank provides IMPS on SMS
* Get Beneficiary Mobile number and MMID
* Enter Beneficiary Mobile number, beneficiary MMID, Amount and your MPIN to send
* Await confirmation SMS for the debit in your account and credit in beneficiary account
* Note the transaction reference number for any future query

For Beneficiary (To receive money):

* Share your Mobile number and MMID with the remitter
* Ask the remitter to send money using your Mobile number and MMID
* Check the confirmation SMS for credit to your account from the remitter
* Note the transaction reference number for any future query

References

[1] "NPCI launches mobile payment system - Corporate News" (http://www.livemint.com/2010/11/22232714/
NPCI-launches-mobile-payment-s.html). livemint.com. 2010-11-22. . Retrieved 2011-03-16.

Interbank Mobile Payment System

Interbank Mobile Payment Service or **IMPS** offers an instant, 24X7, interbank electronic fund transfer service through mobile phones. IMPS facilitate customers to use mobile instruments as a channel for accessing their bank accounts and put high interbank fund transfers in a secured manner with immediate confirmation features. It belongs to National Payments Corporation of India, an umbrella organisation for all retail payment systems in India.This facility is provided by NPCI through its existing NFS switch. [1]

Currently majority of interbank mobile fund transfer transactions are channelised through NEFT mechanism. Under NEFT, the transactions are processed and settled in batches, hence are not real time. Also, the transactions can be done only during the working hours of the RTGS system.

In the above context, NPCI has carried out a pilot on mobile payment system initially with 4 member banks viz State Bank of India, Bank of India, Union Bank of India and ICICI Bank in August 2010. Yes Bank, Axis Bank and HDFC Bank have joined this pilot in month of September, October and November 2010 respectively. Interbank Mobile Payment Service (IMPS) public launch happened on 22nd November 2010 by Smt. Shyamala Gopinath, DG RBI at Mumbai and this service is now available to the Indian public.

Objectives of IMPS

1. To enable bank customers to use mobile instruments as a channel for accessing their banks accounts and remit funds
2. Making payment simpler just with the mobile number of the beneficiary
3. To sub-serve the goal of Reserve Bank of India (RBI) in electronification of retail payments
4. To facilitate mobile payment systems already introduced in India with the Reserve Bank of India Mobile Payment Guidelines 2008 to be inter-operable across banks and mobile operators in a safe and secured manner
5. To build the foundation for a full range of mobile based Banking services.

Member Banks

```
* Axis Bank
* Bank of India
* Canara Bank
* Corporation Bank
* Development Credit Bank
* Dombivli Nagari Sahakari Bank
* Federal bank
* HDFC Bank
* ICICI Bank
* IDBI Bank.
* Indian Bank
* Indian Overseas Bank
* Karur Vysya Bank
* Kotak Mahindra Bank
* Lakshmi Vilas Bank
* Oriental Bank of Commerce
* State Bank of India
* Union Bank of India
* YES Bank
```

Pre-Requisites for Mobile Banking through IMPS

Registration for Remitter:

```
* Register yourself for mobile banking service with bank
* Get Mobile Money Identifier (MMID) and MPIN from the bank
* Download Software (Application) for mobile banking
  (ensure the compatibility of mobile with the application)
  or use the SMS facility in your mobile if your bank provides IMPS on SMS
```

Registration for Beneficiary:

```
* Link your mobile number to the account in the respective bank.
  No need to register for mobile banking service.
* Get Mobile Money Identifier (MMID) from the bank
```

For Remitter (To send money):

```
* Login to the application and select the IMPS menu from the IMPS or
  use the SMS facility in your mobile if your bank provides IMPS on SMS
* Get Beneficiary Mobile number and MMID
* Enter Beneficiary Mobile number, beneficiary MMID, Amount and your MPIN to send
* Await confirmation SMS for the debit in your account and credit in beneficiary account
* Note the transaction reference number for any future query
```

For Beneficiary (To receive money):

```
* Share your Mobile number and MMID with the remitter
* Ask the remitter to send money using your Mobile number and MMID
* Check the confirmation SMS for credit to your account from the remitter
* Note the transaction reference number for any future query
```

References

[1] "NPCI launches mobile payment system - Corporate News" (http://www.livemint.com/2010/11/22232714/
    NPCI-launches-mobile-payment-s.html). livemint.com. 2010-11-22. . Retrieved 2011-03-16.

Internet currency

Internet currency was a form of electronic money for the Internet. Most sites offering the currency have either been shut down or acquired.[1]

History

The idea of Internet currency could date back to 1995, when the first major website that used Internet trade was opened, eBay. The idea of trade over the Internet slowly got more popular, and more websites began opening stores over the Web.[2]

2001 shutdown

Three of the corporations providing Internet currency, InternetCash.com, Flooz.com and beenz.com, were shut down in August 2001. InternetCash used pre-paid cards, either in physical or electronic form to distribute money which could then be used anywhere on the Internet or on specific site(s) (such as store-specific pre-paid cards). This proof of concept created a lot of customer demand and was followed up by several pre-paid store-specific cards. Flooz gave customers only four days to spend all of their money. If the money was not spent, the remaining money was rendered useless as the companies had shut down, thus transactions could not be processed. Many users of the currency lost money, and some complained to the site, and, specifically, to Whoopi Goldberg, who had been the spokesperson for Flooz.com.[1]

References

[1] Kornblum, Janet (August 22, 2001). "You Flooz, you may lose" (http://www.usatoday.com/tech/news/2001-08-22-ebrief.htm). USA Today. . Retrieved 2008-01-02.
[2] Yeomans, Matthew (September 28, 1999). "The quest for a global e-currency" (http://www.cnn.com/TECH/computing/9909/28/global.e.currency.idg/index.html). CNN. . Retrieved 2008-01-02.

Irish Payment Services Organisation

The **Irish Payment Services Organisation** Limited (IPSO) was established in June 1997. IPSO is the representative body for payments in Ireland. Its primary objective is to preserve the integrity and security of its payment systems. It also has responsibility to modernise the payments industry in Ireland.

IPSO provides central programme management for key industry initiatives such as fraud prevention, the National Payments Implementation Programme [1] (with the Department of Finance [2]), SEPA (Single Euro Payments Area) implementation and the rollout of Chip and PIN. IPSO also monitors and promotes payments industry interoperability and standards development. It facilitates innovation and assists in the design of payment systems development.

There are two clearing companies and two payment schemes [3] operating under the IPSO umbrella. Each company has its own board of directors. IPSO is a company limited by guarantee and not having a share capital.

External links

- IPSO Website [5]

ISO 8583

ISO 8583 *Financial transaction card originated messages — Interchange message specifications* is the International Organization for Standardization standard for systems that exchange electronic transactions made by cardholders using payment cards. It has three parts:

- Part 1: Messages, data elements and code values[1]
- Part 2: Application and registration procedures for Institution Identification Codes (IIC)[2]
- Part 3: Maintenance procedures for messages, data elements and code values[3]

Introduction

A card-based transaction typically travels from a transaction acquiring device, such as a point-of-sale terminal or an automated teller machine (ATM), through a series of networks, to a card issuing system for authorization against the card holder's account. The transaction data contains information derived from the card (e.g., the account number), the terminal (e.g., the merchant number), the transaction (e.g., the amount), together with other data which may be generated dynamically or added by intervening systems. The card issuing system will either authorize or decline the transaction and generate a response message which must be delivered back to the terminal in a timely manner.

ISO 8583 defines a message format and a communication flow so that different systems can exchange these transactions. The vast majority of transactions made at ATMs use ISO 8583 at some point in the communication chain, as do transactions made when a customer uses a card to make a payment in a store. In particular, both the MasterCard and Visa networks base their authorization communications on the ISO 8583 standard, as do many other institutions and networks. ISO 8583 has no routing information, so is sometimes used with a TPDU header.

Cardholder-originated transactions include purchase, withdrawal, deposit, refund, reversal, balance inquiry, payments and inter-account transfers. ISO 8583 also defines system-to-system messages for secure key exchanges, reconciliation of totals, and other administrative purposes.

Although ISO 8583 defines a common standard, it is not typically used directly by systems or networks. Instead, each network adapts the standard for its own use with custom fields and custom usages..

The placements of fields in different versions of the standard varies; for example, the currency elements of the 1987 and 1993 versions are no longer used in the 2003 version, which holds currency as a sub-element of any financial amount element. As of writing, ISO 8583:2003 has yet to achieve wide acceptance.

An ISO 8583 message is made of the following parts:

- Message type indicator (MTI)
- One or more bitmaps, indicating which data elements are present
- Data elements, the fields of the message

Message type indicator

This is a 4 digit numeric field which classifies the high level function of the message. A message type indicator includes the ISO 8583 version, the Message Class, the Message Function and the Message Origin, each described briefly in the following sections. The following example (MTI 0110) lists what each digit indicates:

```
0xxx -> version of ISO 8583 (1987 version)
x1xx -> class of the Message (Authorization Message)
xx1x -> function of the Message (Request Response)
xxx0 -> who began the communication (Acquirer)
```

ISO 8583 version

Position one of the MTI specifies the versions of the ISO 8583 standard which is being used to transmit the message.

Position	Meaning
0xxx	ISO 8583-1:1987 version
1xxx	ISO 8583-2:1993 version
2xxx	ISO 8583-1:2003 version
9xxx	Private usage

Message class

Position two of the MTI specifies the overall purpose of the message.

Position	Meaning	Usage
x1xx	Authorization Message	Determine if funds are available, get an approval but do not post to account for reconciliation, Dual Message System (DMS), awaits file exchange for posting to account
x2xx	Financial Message	Determine if funds are available, get an approval and post directly to the account, Single Message System (SMS), no file exchange after this
x3xx	File Actions Message	Used for hot-card, TMS and other exchanges
x4xx	Reversal Message	Reverses the action of a previous authorization
x5xx	Reconciliation Message	Transmits settlement information
x6xx	Administrative Message	Transmits administrative advice. Often used for failure messages (e.g. message reject or failure to apply)
x7xx	Fee Collection Message	
x8xx	Network Management Message	Used for secure key exchange, logon, echo test and other network functions
x9xx	Reserved by ISO	

Message function

Position three of the MTI specifies the message function which defines how the message should flow within the system. Requests are end-to-end messages (e.g., from acquirer to issuer and back with timeouts and automatic reversals in place), while advices are point-to-point messages (e.g., from terminal to acquirer, from acquirer to network, from network to issuer, with transmission guaranteed over each link, but not necessarily immediately).

Position	Meaning
xx0x	Request
xx1x	Request Response
xx2x	Advice
xx3x	Advice Response
xx4x	Notification
xx8x	Response acknowledgment
xx9x	Negative acknowledgment

Message origin

Position four of the MTI defines the location of the message source within the payment chain.

Position	Meaning
xxx0	Acquirer
xxx1	Acquirer Repeat
xxx2	Issuer
xxx3	Issuer Repeat
xxx4	Other
xxx5	Other Repeat

Examples

Bearing each of the above four positions in mind, an MTI will completely specify what a message should do, and how it is to be transmitted around the network. Unfortunately, not all ISO 8583 implementations interpret the meaning of an MTI in the same way. However, a few MTIs are relatively standard:

MTI	Meaning	Usage
0100	Authorization request	Request from a point-of-sale terminal for authorization for a cardholder purchase
0110	Issuer Response	Issuer response to a point-of-sale terminal for authorization for a cardholder purchase
0120	Authorization Advice	When the Point of Sale device breaks down and you have to sign a voucher
0121	Authorisation Advice Repeat	if the advice times out
0130	Issuer Response to Authorization Advice	Confirmation of receipt of authorization advice
0200	Acquirer Financial Request	Request for funds, typically from an ATM or pinned point-of-sale device
0210	Issuer Response to Financial Request	Issuer response to request for funds
0220	Acquirer Financial Advice	e.g. Checkout at a hotel. Used to complete transaction initiated with authorization request
0221	Acquirer Financial Advice repeat	if the advice times out
0230	Issuer Response to Financial Advice	Confirmation of receipt of financial advice

0400	Acquirer Reversal Request	Reverses a transaction
0420	Acquirer Reversal Advice	Advises that a reversal has taken place
0421	Acquirer Reversal Advice Repeat Message	if the reversal times out
0430	Issuer Reversal Response	Confirmation of receipt of reversal advice
0800	Network Management Request	Echo test, logon, log off etc.
0810	Network Management Response	Echo test, logon, log off etc.
0820	Network Management Advice	Keychange

Bitmaps

Within ISO 8583, a bitmap is a field or subfield within a message which indicates which other data elements or data element subfields may be present elsewhere in a message.

A message will contain at least one bitmap, called the *Primary Bitmap* which indicates which of Data Elements 1 to 64 are present. A secondary bitmap may also be present, generally as data element one and indicates which of data elements 65 to 128 are present. Similarly, a tertiary, or third, bitmap can be used to indicate the presence or absence of fields 129 to 192, although these data elements are rarely used.

The bitmap may be transmitted as 8 bytes of binary data, or as 16 hexadecimal characters 0-9, A-F in the ASCII or EBCDIC character sets.

A field is present only when the specific bit in the bitmap is true. For example, byte '82x is binary '1000 0010' which means fields 1 and 7 are present in the message and fields 2, 3, 4, 5, 6, and 8 are not present.

Examples

Bitmap	Defines presence of
4210001102C04804	Fields 2, 7, 12, 28, 32, 39, 41, 42, 50, 53, 62
7234054128C28805	Fields 2, 3, 4, 7, 11, 12, 14, 22, 24, 26, 32, 35, 37, 41, 42, 47, 49, 53, 62, 64
8000000000000001	Fields 1, 64
0000000000000003 (secondary bitmap)	Fields 127, 128

Explanation of Bitmap (8 BYTE Primary Bitmap = 64 Bit) field 4210001102C04804

```
BYTE1 : 01000010 = 42x  (counting from the left, the second and seventh bits are 1, indicating that fields 2
and 7 are present)
BYTE2 : 00010000 = 10x  (field 12 is present)
BYTE3 : 00000000 = 00x  (no fields present)
BYTE4 : 00010001 = 11x  (fields 28 and 32 are present)
BYTE5 : 00000010 = 02x  (field 39 is present)
BYTE6 : 11000000 = C0x  (fields 41 and 42 are present)
BYTE7 : 01001000 = 48x  (fields 50 and 53 are present)
BYTE8 : 00000100 = 04x  (field 62 is present)
```

```
0_____10_____20_____30_____40_____50_____60__64
12345678901234567890123456789012345678901234567890123456789012345  n-th bit
0100001000010000000000000001000100000010110000000100100000000100   bit map
```

Fields present in the above variable length message record:

2-7-12-28-32-39-41-42-50-53-62

Data elements

Data elements are the individual fields carrying the transaction information. There are up to 128 data elements specified in the original ISO 8583:1987 standard, and up to 192 data elements in later releases. The 1993 revision added new definitions, deleted some, while leaving the message format itself unchanged.

While each data element has a specified meaning and format, the standard also includes some general purpose data elements and system- or country-specific data elements which vary enormously in use and form from implementation to implementation.

Each data element is described in a standard format which defines the permitted content of the field (numeric, binary, etc.) and the field length (variable or fixed), according to the following table:

Abbreviation	Meaning
a	Alpha, including blanks
n	Numeric values only
s	Special characters only
an	Alphanumeric
as	Alpha & special characters only
ns	Numeric and special characters only
ans	Alphabetic, numeric and special characters.
b	Binary data
z	Tracks 2 and 3 code set as defined in ISO/IEC 7813 and ISO/IEC 4909 respectively
. or .. or ...	variable field length indicator, each . indicating a digit.
x or xx or xxx	fixed length of field or maximum length in the case of variable length fields.

Additionally, each field may be either fixed or variable length. If variable, the length of the field will be preceded by a length indicator.

Type	Meaning
Fixed	no field length used
LLVAR or (..xx)	Where LL < 100, means two leading digits LL specify the field length of field VAR
LLLVAR or (...xxx)	Where LLL < 1000, means three leading digits LLL specify the field length of field VAR
LL and LLL are hex or ASCII. A VAR field can be compressed or ASCII depending of the data element type.	LL can be 1 or 2 bytes. For example, if compressed as one hex byte, '27x means there are 27 VAR bytes to follow. If ASCII, the two bytes '32x, '37x mean there are 27 bytes to follow. 3 digit field length LLL uses 2 bytes with a leading '0' nibble if compressed, or 3 bytes if ASCII. The format of a VAR data element depends on the data element type. If numeric it will be compressed, e.g. 87456 will be represented by 3 hex bytes '087456x. If ASCII then one byte for each digit or character is used, e.g. '38x, '37x, '34x, '35x, '36x.

ISO-defined data elements

Data element	Type	Usage
1	b 64	Bit map (b 128 if secondary is present and b 192 if tertiary is present)
2	n ..19	Primary account number (PAN)
3	n 6	Processing code
4	n 12	Amount, transaction
5	n 12	Amount, settlement
6	n 12	Amount, cardholder billing
7	n 10	Transmission date & time
8	n 8	Amount, cardholder billing fee
9	n 8	Conversion rate, settlement
10	n 8	Conversion rate, cardholder billing
11	n 6	Systems trace audit number
12	n 6	Time, local transaction (hhmmss)
13	n 4	Date, local transaction (MMDD)
14	n 4	Date, expiration
15	n 4	Date, settlement
16	n 4	Date, conversion
17	n 4	Date, capture
18	n 4	Merchant type
19	n 3	Acquiring institution country code
20	n 3	PAN extended, country code
21	n 3	Forwarding institution. country code
22	n 3	Point of service entry mode
23	n 3	Application PAN number
24	n 3	Function code (ISO 8583:1993)/Network International identifier (NII)
25	n 2	Point of service condition code
26	n 2	Point of service capture code
27	n 1	Authorizing identification response length
28	n 8	Amount, transaction fee
29	n 8	Amount, settlement fee
30	n 8	Amount, transaction processing fee
31	n 8	Amount, settlement processing fee
32	n ..11	Acquiring institution identification code
33	n ..11	Forwarding institution identification code
34	n ..28	Primary account number, extended
35	z ..37	Track 2 data
36	n ...104	Track 3 data
37	an 12	Retrieval reference number

38	an 6	Authorization identification response
39	an 2	Response code
40	an 3	Service restriction code
41	ans 16	Card acceptor terminal identification
42	ans 15	Card acceptor identification code
43	ans 40	Card acceptor name/location (1-23 address 24-36 city 37-38 state 39-40 country)
44	an ..25	Additional response data
45	an ..76	Track 1 data
46	an ...999	Additional data - ISO
47	an ...999	Additional data - national
48	an ...999	Additional data - private
49	a 3	Currency code, transaction
50	an 3	Currency code, settlement
51	a 3	Currency code, cardholder billing
52	b 64	Personal identification number data
53	n 18	Security related control information
54	an ...120	Additional amounts
55	ans ...999	Reserved ISO
56	ans ...999	Reserved ISO
57	ans ...999	Reserved national
58	ans ...999	Reserved national
59	ans ...999	Reserved for national use
60	an .7	Advice/reason code (private reserved)
61	ans ...999	Reserved private
62	ans ...999	Reserved private
63	ans ...999	Reserved private
64	b 16	Message authentication code (MAC)
65	b 64	*Bit indicator of tertiary bitmap only*, tertiary bitmap data follows secondary in message stream.
66	n 1	Settlement code
67	n 2	Extended payment code
68	n 3	Receiving institution country code
69	n 3	Settlement institution county code
70	n 3	Network management Information code
71	n 4	Message number
72	ans ...999	Data record (ISO 8583:1993)/n 4 Message number, last(?)
73	n 6	Date, action
74	n 10	Credits, number
75	n 10	Credits, reversal number
76	n 10	Debits, number

77	n 10	Debits, reversal number
78	n 10	Transfer number
79	n 10	Transfer, reversal number
80	n 10	Inquiries number
81	n 10	Authorizations, number
82	n 12	Credits, processing fee amount
83	n 12	Credits, transaction fee amount
84	n 12	Debits, processing fee amount
85	n 12	Debits, transaction fee amount
86	n 15	Credits, amount
87	n 15	Credits, reversal amount
88	n 15	Debits, amount
89	n 15	Debits, reversal amount
90	n 42	Original data elements
91	an 1	File update code
92	n 2	File security code
93	n 5	Response indicator
94	an 7	Service indicator
95	an 42	Replacement amounts
96	an 8	Message security code
97	n 16	Amount, net settlement
98	ans 25	Payee
99	n ..11	Settlement institution identification code
100	n ..11	Receiving institution identification code
101	ans 17	File name
102	ans ..28	Account identification 1
103	ans ..28	Account identification 2
104	ans ...100	Transaction description
105	ans ...999	Reserved for ISO use
106	ans ...999	Reserved for ISO use
107	ans ...999	Reserved for ISO use
108	ans ...999	Reserved for ISO use
109	ans ...999	Reserved for ISO use
110	ans ...999	Reserved for ISO use
111	ans ...999	Reserved for ISO use
112	ans ...999	Reserved for national use
113	n ..11	Authorizing agent institution id code
114	ans ...999	Reserved for national use
115	ans ...999	Reserved for national use

116	ans ...999	Reserved for national use
117	ans ...999	Reserved for national use
118	ans ...999	Reserved for national use
119	ans ...999	Reserved for national use
120	ans ...999	Reserved for private use
121	ans ...999	Reserved for private use
122	ans ...999	Reserved for private use
123	ans ...999	Reserved for private use
124	ans ...255	Info text
125	ans ..50	Network management information
126	ans .6	Issuer trace id
127	ans ...999	Reserved for private use
128	b 16	Message authentication code

Examples

Field Definition	Meaning
n6	Fixed length field of six digits
n.6	LVAR numeric field of up to 6 digits in length
a..11	LLVAR alphanumeric field of up to 11 characters in length
b...999	LLLVAR binary field of up to 999 bytes in length

References

[1] ISO 8583-1:2003 Financial transaction card originated messages -- Interchange message specifications -- Part 1: Messages, data elements and code values (http://www.iso.org/iso/iso_catalogue/catalogue_tc/catalogue_detail.htm?csnumber=31628)

[2] ISO 8583-2:1998 Financial transaction card originated messages -- Interchange message specifications -- Part 2: Application and registration procedures for Institution Identification Codes (IIC) (http://www.iso.org/iso/iso_catalogue/catalogue_tc/catalogue_detail.htm?csnumber=23632)

[3] ISO 8583-3:2003 Financial transaction card originated messages -- Interchange message specifications -- Part 3: Maintenance procedures for messages, data elements and code values (http://www.iso.org/iso/iso_catalogue/catalogue_tc/catalogue_detail.htm?csnumber=35363)

External links

- ISO 8583 dialects reviews. Specifications, MTIs and Fields tables (http://cheef.ru/docs/iso/iso8583 dialects/)
- Introduction to ISO 8583 (http://www.codeproject.com/KB/scrapbook/ISO8583.aspx)

Issuing bank

An **issuing bank** is a bank that offers card association branded payment cards directly to consumers.

Detail

The issuing bank assumes primary liability for the consumer's capacity to pay off debts they incur with their card.

In the case of credit cards, the issuing bank extends a line of credit to the consumer. Liability for non-payment is then shared by the issuing bank and the acquiring bank, according to rules established by the card association brand.

Statistics

Worldwide, over 1.5 billion payment cards are in circulation[1].[2]

References

[1] Visa raises $17.9 billion in record IPO | Reuters (http://www.reuters.com/article/ousiv/idUSWEN458920080319?pageNumber=3& virtualBrandChannel=0&sp=true)

[2] Visa's Big Deal (http://www.fool.com/investing/value/2008/02/26/visas-big-deal.aspx)

K-CASH

K-CASH is an electronic money system established by 'Korea Financial Telecommunication and Clearings Institute'. Almost every bank in South Korea participate in this project and their 'monetary IC card' can handle K-CASH service, but its narrow usage makes it useless. Now, K-CASH is used only in an electronic fare collecting system.

K-CASH logo.

Card issuers

- Shinhan Bank, Woori Bank, SC First Bank, KEB, KIB, Kookmin Bank, Hana Bank, Citibank, Daegu Bank, Samsung Card

External links

- **Korean** Official homepage [1]
- **English** KFTC homepage [2]

Legal Electronic Data Exchange Standard

The **Legal Electronic Data Exchange Standard** is a set of file format specifications intended to standardize bill/invoice data transmitted electronically ("e-billed") from a law firm to a corporate client. It is abbreviated **LEDES** and is usually pronounced as "leeds".

LEDES was developed by the LEDES Oversight Committee (LOC), which was formed by the PricewaterhouseCoopers Law Firm and Law Department Services Group. Members of the committee include law firms, corporate legal departments, electronic billing vendors and time and billing software vendors. The LOC was incorporated as a California non-profit mutual benefit corporation in 2000.

The file format has several variations:

- **LEDES 1998**, the first "LEDES" format, created in 1998, but no longer in use.
- **LEDES 1998B**, a pipe-delimited plain text file. The standard was adopted in 1998, and it is by far the more commonly used LEDES format. It lacks some flexibility, having a rigid structure. Another disadvantage of LEDES 1998B is that invoice-level data is repeated on every line item even though it is only needed once, as it does not vary per line. Many clients attempt to impose nonstandard customizations, thus defeating the purpose of having a standard. Nonetheless, law firms prefer it for its simplicity and familiarity.
- **LEDES 2000**, adopted in 2000, is an XML format. Adoption of this newer standard has been slow. One advantage of LEDES 2000 is that although the structure is very well defined, the specification defines "extend" segments, allowing the insertion of client-specific fields without breaking the format or violating the standard.
- **LEDES 1998B-INTL** (international), a pipe-delimited plain text file, based on the LEDES 1998B standard. This format was designed to accommodate legal bills generated outside of the United States. It includes all of the fields in the LEDES 1998B format, plus additional ones. The format was proposed in 2004 by the Legal IT Innovators Group (LITIG). The LEDES Oversight Committee (LOC) ratified the format in 2006.
- **XML E-Billing version 2**, ratified in 2006 but yet to see adoption, is intended to improve upon LEDES 2000.
- **XML E-Billing version 2.1** improves upon version 2.
- **LEDES Budget Standard** was ratified in 2006. This XML format is intended to facilitate the exchange of budget data between law firms and clients.
- **Timekeeper Attribute Standard** is a proposed XML format intended to be used to transmit timekeeper and rate data to from law firms to clients.

Many clients using LEDES use Uniform Task-Based Management System, a legal task classifcation system.

External links

- LEDES website [1]
- LEDES Validation [2]

M-Pesa

M-PESA (M for mobile, pesa is Swahili for money) is the product name of a mobile-phone based money transfer service for Vodafone. The development was initially sponsored by the UK-based Department for International Development (DFID) in 2003–2007.[1] [2]

The initial concept of M-PESA was to create a service which allowed microfinance borrowers to conveniently receive and repay loans using the network of Safaricom airtime resellers.[3] This would enable microfinance institutions (MFIs) to offer more competitive loan rates to their users, as there is a reduced cost of dealing in cash. The users of the service would gain through being able to track their finances more easily. But when the service was trialled, customers adopted the service for a variety of alternative uses; complications arose with Faulu, the partnering microfinance institution (MFI). M-PESA was re-focused and launched with a different value proposition: sending remittances home across the country and making payments.[3]

M-PESA is a branchless banking service, meaning that it is designed to enable users to complete basic banking transactions without the need to visit a bank branch.[4] The continuing success of M-PESA, in Kenya, has been due to the creation of a highly popular, affordable payment service with only limited involvement of a bank.[5] [6] The system was developed and ran by Sagentia from initial development to the 6 million customer mark. The service has now been transitioned to be operationally run by IBM Global Services on behalf of Vodafone, the initial 3 markets (Kenya, Tanzania & Afghanistan) are hosted by Rackspace.

Functionality

M-PESA Customers can deposit and withdraw money from a network of agents that includes airtime resellers and retail outlets acting as banking agents. M-PESA is operated by Safaricom, a Mobile network operator (MNO), which is not classed as a deposit-taking institution (such as a bank). Therefore, M-PESA may not be advertised as a banking service.

The service enables its users to:

- Deposit and withdraw money,
- Transfer money to other users and non-users,
- Pay bills,
- Purchase airtime.[7] [8]

The user interface technology of M-PESA differs between Safaricom of Kenya and Vodacom of Tanzania, although the underlying platform is the same. While Safaricom uses SIM toolkit to provide handset menus for accessing the service, Vodacom relies on USSD to provide users with menus.[9]

Markets

Kenya

M-PESA was first launched by the Kenyan MNO Safaricom, an affiliate of Vodafone, in March 2007.[3] M-PESA quickly captured a significant market share for cash transfers, and grew astoundingly quickly, capturing 6.5 million subscribers by May 2009 with 2 million daily transactions in Kenya alone.

The growth of the service forced formal banking institutions to take note of the new venture. In December 2008, a group of banks reportedly lobbied the Kenyan finance minister to audit M-PESA, in an effort to at least slow the growth of the service. This ploy failed, as the audit found that the service was robust.[10]

Txteagle - an "artificial artificial intelligence" system enabling the 3 billion mobile phone subscribers living in the developing world to earn small amounts of money by completing simple tasks for companies who pay them in airtime or mPesa (mobile money in Kenya). txteagle is on track to become the largest employer in Kenya.[11]

Tanzania

M-Pesa has also been launched in Tanzania by Vodacom, a subsidiary of Vodafone.

Afghanistan

In 2008 Vodafone partnered with Roshan, Afghanistan's primary mobile operator, to provide M-Paisa, the local brand of the service.[12] [13] When the service was launched in Afghanistan, it was initially used to pay policemen's salary, which was set to be competitive with what the Taliban were earning. Soon after the product was launched, the Afghan National Police found that under the previous cash model, 10% of their workforce were ghost police officers who did not exist; their salaries had been pocketed by others. When corrected in the new system, many police officers believed that they had received a raise or that there had been a mistake, as their salaries rose significantly. The National Police discovered that there was so much corruption when payments had been made using the previous model that the policemen didn't know their true salary. The service has been so successful that it has been expanded to include limited merchant payments, peer-to-peer transfers, loan disbursements and payments.[14]

South Africa

In September 2010, Vodacom and Nedbank announced the launch of the service in South Africa where it is estimated that there are more than 13 million "economically active" people without a bank account.[15]

Other Markets

Plans to expand the M-PESA product to India[16] and Egypt as well as the launch of an international money transfer service for M-PESA in Kenya[17] are the next steps ahead for M-PESA as of early 2009.

References

[1] Financial Deepening Challenge Fund (FDCF). (No date). *Vodafone UK/Global—M-Pesa (Mobile Money)*. Retrieved February 20, 2009, from http://www.financialdeepening.org/default.asp?id=694&ver=1.

[2] Vodafone. (2007, February 13). *Safaricom and Vodafone launch M-PESA, a new mobile payment service*. Retrieved January 29, 2009, from http://www.vodafone.com/start/media_relations/news/group_press_releases/2007/safaricom_and_vodafone.html.

[3] Hughes, N., & Lonie, S. (2007). M-PESA: Mobile Money for the "Unbanked": Turning Cellphones into 24-Hour Tellers in Kenya. Innovations: Technology, Governance, Globalization, 2(1–2), 63–81.

[4] Ivatury, G., & Mas, I. (2008, April). *The Early Experience with Branchless Banking* (Focus Note No. 46). Washington, D.C.: Consultative Group to Assist the Poor. Retrieved July 11, 2008, from http://www.cgap.org/gm/document-1.9.2640/FocusNote_46.pdf

[5] Dial M for money. (2007, June 28). *The Economist*. Retrieved December 6, 2007, from http://www.economist.com/finance/displaystory. cfm?story_id=9414419

[6] from http://www.sagentia.com/News.aspx?Path=/Press_release_and_News_archive/2007/MPesa_update

[7] Vodacom. (No date). *Send money by phone with Vodafone M-PESA*. Retrieved February 19, 2009, from http://www.vodacom.co.tz/docs/ docredir.asp?docid=3492.

[8] Roshan. (No date). *M-Paisa—The Hawala On Your Mobile!* Retrieved February 19, 2009, from http://www.roshan.af/web/?page_id=475.

[9] Vaughan, P. (2008, July 15). Providing the Unbanked with Access to Financial Services: The Case of M-PESA in Kenya. Presentation given during the *Mobile Banking & Financial Services Africa* conference in Johannesburg, South Africa.

[10] Cash Transfers Pose Threat to Banks (http://www.philanthropyaction.com/nc/mobile_cash_transfers_pose_threat_to_banks/Mobile) Philanthropy Action, 26 February 2009

[11] Itxteagle pays in mPesa (http://www.nathaneagle.com/)

[12] Vodafone. (2008, February 10). *Vodafone and Roshan Launch First Mobile Money Transfer Service in Afghanistan*. Retrieved January 29, 2009, from http://www.vodafone.com/start/media_relations/news/group_press_releases/2007/vodafone_and_roshan.html

[13] Vodafone. (2008, April 8). *Vodacom Announces Intention to Launch Vodafone M-PESA Mobile Money Transfer Service in Tanzania*. Retrieved January 29, 2009, from http://www.vodafone.com/start/media_relations/news/group_press_releases/2007/ vodacom_announces.html

[14] Rice, Dan. "One Cell Phone at a Time: Countering Corruption in Afghanistan" (http://smallwarsjournal.com/blog/2010/09/ one-cell-phone-at-a-time-count/). Small Wars Journal. . Retrieved September 21, 2010.

[15] Staff Writer. "M-PESA launched in South Africa" (http://www.howwemadeitinafrica.com/m-pesa-launched-in-south-africa/3611/). How We Made It in Africa. . Retrieved October 16, 2010.

[16] Department for International Development [DFID]. (2008, May 9). *Mobile phone banking in Africa* [Video]. Retrieved February 19, 2009, from http://www.youtube.com/watch?v=TNrDv4PQdCc

[17] Safaricom trials global M-Pesa money transfer service. (2008, December 5). *The Paypers*. Retrieved December 16, 2008, from http://www.thepaypers.com/news/printarticle.aspx?cid=736370

Mas, I., and Morawczynski, O. (2009). "Designing Mobile Money Services Lessons from M-PESA". Innovations. 4 (2).

Morawczynski, O., and Miscione, G. (2008). "Examining Trust in Mobile Banking Transactions in Kenya: The Case of M-PESA" IFIP WG 9.4-University of Pretoria Joint Workshop, Pretoria, South Africa.

Morawczynski, O. (2008). "Surviving in the 'Dual System': How M-PESA is Fostering Urban-to-Rural Remittances in a Kenyan Slum" HCC8 Conference. Pretoria, South Africa.

Omwansa, T. (2009). M-Pesa: Progress and Prospects" innovations / Mobile World Congress 2009. Pg 107-123. http:/ / www. strathmore. edu/ pdf/ innov-gsma-omwansa. pdf or http:/ / www. gsmworld. com/ documents/ INNOVATIONS-GSMA_FINAL-01-22-09.pdf

"Why has M-PESA become so popular in Kenya?" CGAP Technology Blog. http://technology.cgap.org/2008/06/17/why-has-m-pesa-become-so-popular-in-kenya/

External links

- Financial transactions & Mobile Technology in Emerging Economies (http://www.youtube.com/watch?v=tOuflAkAvMU) (YouTube video)
- Mobile phone banking in Africa (http://www.youtube.com/watch?v=TNrDv4PQdCc) (YouTube Video)
- Mpesa Send Money Home TV Commercial (http://www.youtube.com/watch?v=nEZ30K5dBWU) (YouTube Video)
- M-PESA documentary (http://www.youtube.com/watch?v=zQo4VoLyHe0) (YouTube video)
- Banking Through Mobile Phones with M-Pesa (http://www.youtube.com/watch?v=NSdBDZy982o) (YouTube Video)
- M-Pesa progress and prospects (http://www.strathmore.edu/pdf/innov-gsma-omwansa.pdf) or (http://www.gsmworld.com/documents/INNOVATIONS-GSMA_FINAL-01-22-09.pdf)
- CGAP Article - What you don't know about M-PESA (http://technology.cgap.org/2009/07/14/what-you-dont-know-about-m-pesa/) (Blog)
- CGAP Brief- Observation of Customer Usage and Impact from M-PESA (http://www.cgap.org/p/site/c/template.rc/1.9.36723/) (CGAP brief)

Macau Pass

Macau Pass

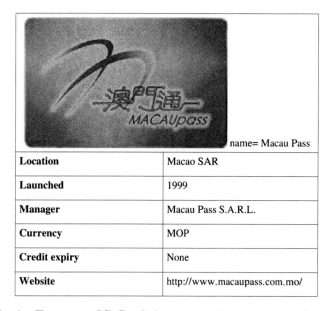

name= Macau Pass

Location	Macao SAR
Launched	1999
Manager	Macau Pass S.A.R.L.
Currency	MOP
Credit expiry	None
Website	http://www.macaupass.com.mo/

The **Macau Pass** (formerly the **Transmac IC Card**) is a contactless smartcard, first introduced by Transmac in 1999, that can be used to pay for bus fares, shop, and dine with many more merchants to join the system.

Acceptance

Macau Pass	
Traditional Chinese	澳門通
Simplified Chinese	澳门通

Transcriptions	
Mandarin	
- Hanyu Pinyin	Aò Mén Tōng

The Macau Pass is accepted by:

Autobuses

- Transmac
- Transportas Companhia de Macau

Vending machines

- Vitasoy and Coca-Cola vending machines
- "24" Mini-store and vending

Supermarkets

- Royal Supermarket Chains
- DCH Food Mart Deluxe (World Trade Center)
- San Miu Supermarkets
- US Mart Limited (@ Fisherman's Wharf)

- Soi Cheung Supermarket
- Tai Fung Supermarket
- Weng Kei Supermarkets

Convenience

- Circle K Convenience Stores
- 7-Eleven Convenience Stores

Shopping and services

- Select CTM stores
- Transmac and Macau Pass Service centers
- J.T. Ticket Net Machines
- Select Ricoh Photocopiers
- Macau Cultural Center
- Creative Photo Studio
- Select Padaria da Guia stores
- Select Mario Bakeries
- Q&A
- S.J. Hospital Automatic Registration System
- Macao Science Center
- Polytechnic Institute
- Canon

Food and beverage

- Select Yue Weng Kei Restaurants (In Service Soon)
- Snowball Cafe and Bakery
- Sio Hong Mao Restaurant (Taipa store only)

Card types

The Macau Pass has four types of different cards, for certain age groups (much like the Octopus card in Hong Kong). The four are:

- General (Green, the one shown above) (deposit of MOP$30.00 is required for card purchase)
- Personalised (Pink)
- Seniors (Pink, special feature added in card)
- Students (Blue)

Future plans

Macau Pass has a variety of future plans to have implementation of Macau Passes. They are:

- Parking Systems (saves parking ticket issuing, therefore environmentally-friendly)
- Restriction Gates (must use a personalized Macau Pass, with the feature added)
- Apartment Recognition (for apartments with a security feature, must use card for access)
- VIP Cards

Payment discounts

The Macau Pass does not have any discount when purchasing merchandise and using at restaurants. However, the government and the company had decided that the government will subsidize the difference from the discounts below on *bus fares*. The Transmac IC Card did not accept this offer.

- General/Personalised card holders can enjoy a discounted bus fare of:

    MOP$2.00 bus fare on **Macau Peninsula** routes, aside from the MOP$3.20 bus fare (including N1)

    MOP$2.50 bus fare on **Macau-Taipa** routes, aside from the MOP$4.2 bus fare (including AP1, and N2)

    MOP$3.00 bus fare on **ALL Macau-Coloane** routes, aside from the fare differences of destinations for Coloane.

- Seniors enjoy a discount on bus fare of:

    MOP$0.30 bus fare on **ALL** bus routes servicing.

- Students enjoy a discount on bus fare of:

    MOP$1.50 bus fare on **ALL** bus routes servicing in 2010.

    MOP$1.00 bus fare on **ALL** bus routs servicing in 2011.

Transfer discounts

When Macau Pass was still called the "Transmac IC Card", its operator, Transmac decided that cardholders could have a free "transfer". However, under certain circumstances the card holder must pay a fare under MOP$3.00. (E.g., on a trip from the Border Gate to the M.U.S.T., if going to ride route 3A to Praça Ferreira Amaral to interchange to route MT2, the *Green* Macau Pass must be tapped on the reader, and the display will show 0.50. The exact fare to pay with the card was MOP$1.00, but the government supported MOP$0.50.) The details on transfers are located at the bottom.

Cards issued by Transmac (Transmac IC Card)

Route Interchange	1st Fare (MOP)	2nd Fare (MOP)
Macau Route→Macau Route	$3.20	$0.00
Macau Route→Macau-Taipa Route (To Taipa)	$3.20	$1.00
Macau-Taipa Route (To Taipa)→Macau Route	$4.20	$0.00
Macau-Taipa Route→Taipa Route	$4.20	$0.00
Taipa Route→Macau-Taipa Route	$2.80	$1.40
Taipa Route→Taipa Route	$2.80	$0.00

Macau Pass Traveler's Card

Route Interchange	1st Fare (MOP)	2nd Fare (MOP)
Macau Route→Macau Route	$3.20	$0.00
Macau Route→Macau-Taipa Route (To Taipa)	$3.20	$1.00
Macau-Taipa Route (To Taipa)→Macau Route	$4.20	$0.00
Macau-Taipa Route→Taipa Route	$4.20	$0.00
Taipa Route→Macau-Taipa Route	$2.80	$1.40
Taipa Route→Taipa Route	$2.80	$0.00

Macau Pass Green/Personalised Card

Route Interchange	1st Fare (MOP)	2nd Fare (MOP)
Macau Route→Macau Route	$2.00	$0.00
Macau Route→Macau-Taipa Route (To Taipa)	$2.00	$0.50
Macau-Taipa Route (To Taipa)→Macau Route	$2.50	$0.00
Macau-Taipa Route→Taipa Route	$2.50	$0.00
Taipa Route→Macau-Taipa Route	$2.00	$0.50
Taipa Route→Taipa Route	$2.00	$0.00

Macau Pass Senior Card

Route Interchange	1st Fare (MOP)	2nd Fare (MOP)
Macau Route→Macau Route	$0.30	$0.00
Macau Route→Macau-Taipa Route (To Taipa)	$0.30	$0.00
Macau-Taipa Route (To Taipa)→Macau Route	$0.30	$0.00
Macau-Taipa Route→Taipa Route	$0.30	$0.00
Taipa Route→Macau-Taipa Route	$0.30	$0.00
Taipa Route→Taipa Route	$0.30	$0.00

Macau Pass Student Card

Route Interchange	1st Fare (MOP)	2nd Fare (MOP)
Macau Route→Macau Route	$1.00	$0.00
Macau Route→Macau-Taipa Route (To Taipa)	$1.00	$0.00
Macau-Taipa Route (To Taipa)→Macau Route	$1.00	$0.00
Macau-Taipa Route→Taipa Route	$1.00	$0.00
Taipa Route→Macau-Taipa Route	$1.00	$0.00
Taipa Route→Taipa Route	$1.00	$0.00

Notes

- **All** Macau Passes and Transmac IC Cards **DO NOT** have the transfer offer for Macau-Taipa Routes coming back to Macau Peninsula and the fare display (On Macau Pass reader) displays **$3.20**
- TCM offers transfer offers for Macau Pass holders. Details available at TCM's website.[1]

Customer services

Macau Pass S.A.R.L. offers a variety of customer services that either can be troubleshooted online at Macau Pass Online [2] or in person at the following Macau Pass approved customer service centers:

- Macau Pass Customer Service, near Rua Do Campo.
- Transmac Sales Center, near Portas Do Cerco (Border Gate)

Special liveries and versions

Coca-Cola

Macau Pass, Coca-Cola® and Circle K Convenience Stores Macau Division have decided to introduce the "Coca-Cola 60 Years Limited Edition Macau Pass". This is made in honor to commemorate the 60th year of Coca-Cola being in Macau. The purchasing period for this livery is now suspended. The livery is as follows:

- The front is the "Original" green Macau Pass livery
- The back of the card is the "Special Edition" Coca-Cola livery.

There was two ways to have the ability to be the card holder of this card:

- Pay MOP$39.00 at the checkout counter of Circle K stores across Macau (card has no power until loaded.)
- Buy **2** (Two) Coca-Cola products at Circle K, and entered for a chance to win a MOP$1000.00 pre-loaded Macau Pass with the livery.

This card livery is a "purchase" card, no deposit needed, no refund on card.

Macau Pass Watch

When Macau Pass was introduced as the name "Macau Pass" (Green Livery) in 2007/8, Macau Pass S.A.R.L. had introduced the *Macau Pass Watch* which, much like the Octopus Card Watch, acts as another type of Macau Pass. There are two types of watches:

- An Internal applied watch (Macau Pass is affixed on the inside)
- An External applied watch (Macau Pass is affixed on the outside)

This card livery is a "purchase" card, no deposit needed, no refund on card.

M.U.S.T. Student/Staff Card

Macau Pass and M.U.S.T. also have a specialized staff/student I.D. card with a Macau Pass ability on the inside.

This card livery is a "purchased" card, provided by the supplier itself (M.U.S.T.)

J.T. Ticket Net

Macau Pass and the J.T. Ticket Net also introduced a card that has the Macau Pass Green livery on the front, and the J.T. Ticket Net livery on the back (Much like the Cola-Cola special livery)

This card livery is a "purchase" card, no deposit needed, no refund on card.

World Heritage Sites

The Tourism Board of Macau and Macau Pass have teamed up and made a series of Macau Pass Cards that has a World Heritage site on the front, and a rear view of the Macau Pass logo, the card number, and an array of all the World Heritage sites in Macau.

This card livery is a "purchase" card, no deposit needed, no refund on card.

References

[1] TCM (http://www.tcm.com.mo), Macau.

Malaysian Electronic Payment System

Malaysian Electronic Payment System

Industry	Finance
Founded	December, 1996
Headquarters	Kuala Lumpur, Malaysia
Key people	Abdul Wahid Omar, Chairman Mohd Suhail Amar Suresh, GMD
Products	Financial Services
Website	www.meps.com.my [1]

The **Malaysian Electronic Payment System**, commonly known as **MEPS**, is the only interbank network service provider in Malaysia.

Malaysian Electronic Payment System formerly known as Malaysian Electronic Payment System (1997) Sdn Bhd is a payment consortium owned equally by 12 local banks. Its subsidiary companies are MEPS Currency Management Sdn Bhd (MCM) and FPX Gateway Sdn Bhd (FPX).

MEPS plays a role in the implementation of smart card for Automated Teller Machine (ATM) card, which is an upgrade to chip-based card from previous magnetic-stripe card issued to all banks customer.

The card is also known as **Bankcard**, a card with multiple functions. There are three main functions that can be used namely ATM (with various combinations of banking transactions), e-Debit (online purchase payment) transactions at participating merchants and MEPS Cash (load in a monetary value into your Bankcard chip) and pay of participating merchants.

MEPS provides the following services in its network to all participating banks:

- **Shared Nationwide ATM Network**, provides the switch which enable bank customers to conveniently access their funds anywhere from any of the participating banks' ATMs.
- **Shared Regional ATM Network**, a cross-border ATM link with Indonesia (ATM Bersama, PRIMA), Singapore (NETS), Thailand (ITMX) and China (CUP) that offers participating banks' customers the convenience of making cash withdrawals via ATM in the said countries and vice versa.
- **e-Debit**, enables the purchase amount to be immediately deducted from the savings or current account direct into the retailer's or merchant's bank account. This provides consumers with better cash management and peace of mind as all transactions are PIN based. In addition, the new card is embedded with a sophisticated, tamper-resistant smart chip to protect consumers against the risk of fraud.
- **Mobile Prepaid Top-Up via ATM**, offers more convenience for mobile phone subscribers to top-up through MEPS' ATMs.
- **Interbank ATM Fund Transfer (IBFT)**, allows bank customers to transfer funds from one account to another account in another bank. The beneficiary will receive the funds immediately and instantaneously, as the transfer is online and in real-time.
- **Interbank GIRO (IBG)**, makes interbank funds transfer more convenient to bank customers via an electronic channel. It enables payments to be made without the need to raise physical supporting vouchers or documents such as cheques, bank drafts, etc. It is an interbank fund transfer system that facilitates payments and collections via the exchange of digitized transactions between banks. For corporations, it is ideal for high volume interbank

payments up to a maximum of RM100,000 per transaction such as payroll and dividend/warrant payments. As for individuals, it is ideal for transactions such as credit card payments and loan repayments. It offers bank customers, be an individual or corporation, a secure interbank fund transfer system/channel for all sorts of payments through direct debiting of the customers' account(s) and crediting into the beneficiaries account; with any IBG participating banks.

- **Financial Processing Exchange (FPX)**, opens new doors for e-Commerce, in particular business to business (B2B) and business to commerce (B2C) payments. FPX is an alternative payment channel for customers to make payment at e-market places such as websites and online stores as well as for corporations to collect bulk payment from their customers. It leverages on the Internet banking services of participating banks and provides fast, secure, reliable, real-time online payment processing. FPX provides complete end-to-end business transactions, resourceful payment records, simplified reconciliation and reduced risks as fund movements are between established financial institutions.

Member banks

Listed below is the participating banks. However, some participating banks provide only selected few of the services offered by MEPS as mentioned above.

- Affin Bank
- Alliance Bank
- Al Rajhi Bank
- Agro Bank Malaysia (formerly known as Bank Pertanian Malaysia)
- AmBank
- Bank Islam Malaysia
- Bank Kerjasama Rakyat Malaysia
- Bank Muamalat Malaysia
- Bank of America
- Bank Simpanan Nasional
- CIMB Bank
- Citibank
- Deutsche Bank
- EON Bank
- Hong Leong Bank
- HSBC
- Maybank
- Oversea-Chinese Banking Corporation
- Public Bank
- RHB Bank
- Royal Bank of Scotland (formerly known as ABN Amro Bank)
- Standard Chartered Bank
- United Overseas Bank

Former members

- Bumiputra-Commerce Holdings (Restructured as CIMB Bank)
- Southern Bank (Merged with CIMB Bank)

External links

- MEPS FAQ [2]
- MEPS ATM network goes 24/7 on May 1, 2008 [3]
- OCBC Customers Can Make ATM Withdrawals Via MEPS Network for FREE [4]
- Foreign banks join MEPS [5]

Manual fare collection

Manual fare collection is the practice of collecting fares manually (without the aid of an automated machine). "Fare collection" generally refers to the collection of fares in the transport industry in return for a ticket or passes to travel. Commonly used on buses and train transport systems, manual fare collection is increasingly becoming obsolete with the introduction of smart cards such as the Transport for London 'Oyster card'. However, in the face of this trend, some companies have opted to retain more traditional methods of manual fare collection to both save money (automatic equipment is expensive) and ensure reliability. In the United Kingdom, examples of this can be seen on the Transport for London Heritage lines and the FirstGroup FTR routes in York, Leeds, Luton, and Swansea where bus conductors (dubbed 'customer hosts') have returned to work.

Equipment

A range of fare collection equipment has been developed over the last century in the United Kingdom.

Cash bag

Perhaps the simplest of these developments is the leather cash bag. At one stage, held by bus conductor's nationwide, the cash bag today commonly has two compartments inside and can be held like a satchel. The advantage of the cash bag is that it gives a secure and easily accessible place to store the money collected from tickets. In general it is necessary for a conductor to use the cash bag; it is too cumbersome for bus or taxi drivers to manage.

Coin dispenser

Perhaps the biggest development in manual fare collection is the coin dispenser, invented by Jacques L. Galef. Mounted either in a driver's cab or on the belt of a conductor, the coin dispenser usually takes the form of a number of tubes fitted in a line together. Each tube holds a different denomination and tends to have some sort of trigger which will release the coin from the bottom. In Britain, the Quick-Change and Pendamatic units, for example, has labelled plastic funnels at the top, which filter the coins into the tube. A trigger on the front of the machine then releases the coin by pushing a kicker, which holds the coin, forward in a pivotal motion. Other models in Britain, the Cambist and Metro Coin Dispensers, works on a similar principle but also have

Coin dispenser

the option to be attached to the fare collection table allowing the operator (usually the bus driver) to simply slide the coins into the respective tubes. Generally, coin dispensers in the UK are configured with the £1 coin to the left (as the machine faces you), then the 50p, 20p, 10p, 5p, 2p, 1p. However, some operators have customised their dispensers to better suit their individual needs.

Tender tray

Other fare collecting equipment includes tender trays which can be fitted to bus driver doors to allow the customer to put the fare down. These are common on most buses in the United Kingdom now, since they facilitate quick payment and also allow for the driver to have a screen protecting his cab, yet still securely collect change (the tray is placed with a small gap above it to allow room for the drivers hand to pass through).

References

- *Western Mail* Newspaper [1]
- Cambist [2]
- Quick Change [3]
- Transport Ticket Services [4]
- Flickr Photos [5]

Medi Script

Medi Script was North America's first instant credit system. Developed in 1965-67 by the West brothers in Vancouver, B.C., Canada, the system was designed to provide consumer credit at the retail store level, something that did not exist at that point in history.

At that time the Canadian chartered banks controlled all the legal credit granting ability with the exception of vehicle fuel companies like the Esso credit card which was not available to general merchants and shop keepers. The West brothers hoped to change this.

Medi Script was designed to allow individual storeowners and merchants the ability to grant controlled, third party credit to their customers by subscribing for a fee to the Medi Script company who would then in turn provide the active credit for the customers in question.

The name Medi Script was used because of an obscure law at the time that allowed the medical establishment to grant credit.

While salespeople were actively marketing this new idea the Royal Bank of Canada was looking at the Medi Script company with the stated intent of purchasing the company and the rights to the Medi Script concept. During the negotiation process in 1968 the Royal Bank launched their own version dubbed the Chargex Credit card. Subsequently, the deal with the West brothers collapsed and their business collapsed as their idea took on a new life without them.

Mefo bills

A *Metallurgische Forschungsgesellschaft*, better known as the *Mefo* **bill** (sometimes formatted as *MEFO*) was a system of deferred payment created by the German Minister of Finance, Hjalmar Schacht, in 1934. As Germany were rearming against the terms of the Treaty of Versailles they needed a way to fund rearming without leaving a paper trail; Schacht created this system as a temporary method to fund rearming with only one million Reichsmarks in capital. However, Adolf Hitler was still using these bills in 1938 with twelve billion Reichsmarks of Mefo bills were still outstanding. Schacht has later said that the device "enabled the Reichsbank to lend by a subterfuge to the Government what it normally or legally could not do".[1]

Funding rearmament

The German government needed to spend a large amount of money to fund the depression era reconstruction of its heavy industry based economy, and ultimately its re-armament industry. However, it faced two problems. First, rearmament was illegal under the terms of the Treaty of Versailles, and secondly there was a legal interest rate limit of 4.5%.

The government would normally borrow extra funds on the money market by offering a higher interest rate. However, because of the limit it was unable to do so. And a large, visible government deficit would have attracted attention.

An imaginary company

Hjalmar Schacht formed the limited liability company Metallurgische Forschungsgesellschaft, m.b.H., or "MEFO" for short. The company's "mefo bills" served as bills of exchange, convertible into Reichsmark upon demand. MEFO had no actual existence or operations and was solely a balance sheet entity. The bills were mainly issued as payment to armaments manufacturers.

Mefo bills were issued to last for six months initially, but with the provision for indefinite three-month extensions. The total amount of mefo bills issued was kept secret.

Essentially, mefo bills enabled the German Reich to run a greater deficit than it would normally have done. By 1939, there were 12 billion Reichsmark of mefo bills, compared to 19 billion of normal government bonds.

This enabled the government to reinflate their economy, which culminated in its eventual rearmament.

Fueling growth

This strengthened the German economy by providing the government with various goods and services which it was then able to reinvest in the economy, fueling its growth, and preparing it for Hitler's aggressive foreign and domestic policies. Not only did the bills serve the above functions, but they also concealed the military expenditure forbidden by the Treaty of Versailles.

References

[1] http://www.jewishvirtuallibrary.org/jsource/Holocaust/Schacht.html

External links

- Nuremberg Trials discussion of the mefo bill (http://www.jewishvirtuallibrary.org/jsource/Holocaust/Schacht.html)

- Nazi Conspiracy & Aggression Individual Responsibility Of Defendants, the Nizkor Project (http://www. nizkor.org/hweb/imt/nca/nca-02/nca-02-16-responsibility-12-03-01.html)

Merchant account

A **merchant account** is a type of bank account that allows businesses to accept payments by debit or credit cards. A merchant account also serves as an agreement between a retailer, a merchant bank and payment processor for the settlement of credit card and/or debit card transactions.

Methods of processing credit cards

Today a majority of credit card transactions are sent electronically to merchant processing banks for authorization, capture and deposit. Various methods exist for presenting a credit card sale to "the system." In all circumstances either the entire magnetic strip is read by a swipe through a credit card terminal/reader, a computer chip is read, or the credit card information is manually entered into a credit card terminal, a computer or website. The earliest methods, submitting credit card slips to a merchant processing bank by mail, or by accessing an Automated Response Unit (ARU) by telephone, are still in use today but have long been overshadowed by electronic devices. These early methods used two-part forms and a manual device for mechanically imprinting the embossed card number information onto the forms.

Credit card terminal

A credit card terminal is a stand-alone piece of electronic equipment that allows a merchant to swipe or key-enter a credit card's information as well as additional information required to process a credit card transaction. A credit card terminal is a dedicated piece of equipment that only processes credit cards although it is common for related transactions including gift cards and check verification to also be performed. A credit card terminal typically must be plugged in to a power supply and connected to a telephone line. However, some terminals may be powered by batteries and communicate over the Internet or through a

cellular phone data network. When a credit card is processed (either swiped through the magnetic stripe reader or keyed-in to the keypad), it contacts the network to verify if the credit card can be authorized. The transaction is then stored on the machine until the polling window is opened. The machine will either upload the electronic funds directly to the merchant bank, or a polling service provider will dial in to collect, process then submit the data to the merchant bank. The most popular credit card terminals consist of a modem, keypad, printer, magnetic stripe reader, power supply and memory card. They have had the same basic design since the 1980s. As with computers, there is a wide range of memory capacities and other features like built-in printers and debit card pinpads that affect the manufacturing cost of a credit card terminal.

Automated Response Unit (ARU)

An ARU (also known as a voice authorization, capture and deposit) allows the manual keyed entry and subsequent authorization of a credit card over a cellular or land-line telephone. With this method a merchant typically imprints their customer's card with an imprinter to create a customer receipt and merchant copy, then process the transaction instantaneously over the phone.

Payment gateway

A payment gateway is an e-commerce service that authorizes payments for e-businesses and online retailers. It is the equivalent of a physical POS (point-of-sale) terminal located in most retail outlets. A merchant account provider is typically a separate company from the payment gateway. Some merchant account providers have their own payment gateways but the majority of companies use 3rd party payment gateways. The gateway usually has 2 components: a) the virtual terminal that can allow for a merchant to securely login and key in credit card numbers or b) have the website's shopping-cart connect to the gateway via an API to allow for real time processing from the merchant's website.

Level 2 or Level 3 Processing - Purchasing Cards

Visa and Mastercard have created a specialized type of credit card used primarily by government agencies and businesses. Increasingly, corporations and government agencies are relying on this form of payment to compensate their service providers and suppliers. Businesses benefit by receiving their funds quickly and by winning competitive bids and government contracts where purchasing cards are the required form of payment. The downside, however, is the increased costs associated with receiving these payments. These costs will usually be much higher than accepting a standard consumer credit card.

The solution is that some businesses may qualify for ways to process these transactions that allow them to pay lower fees if they can supply additional information, called "level 2 or level 3 data". For example, if government transactions are over $5,000, businesses can significantly reduce their transaction costs by including "level 2 or level 3 data" about the purchase along with each transaction. Examples of level 2 or level 3 data is a purchase order number associated with the transaction that the credit card will be paying. This data is passed on to the purchaser so that it may be many times easier to reconcile the transaction. If all the required data is not collected and passed on during the transaction, the merchant can have surcharges added to the basic fees or be forced into a non qualified transaction category.

Merchant Account Marketing

Merchant accounts are marketed to merchants by two basic methods: either directly by the processor or sponsoring bank, or by an authorized agent for the bank and additionally directly registered with both Visa and MasterCard as an ISO/MSP (Independent Selling Organization / Member Service Provider). Marketing details are by card issuers like Visa and MasterCard, and are enforced by various rules and fines. A few of the largest processors also partner with warehouse clubs to promote merchant accounts to their business members.

Marketing by Banks

A bank that has a merchant processing relationship with Visa and Mastercard, also known as a **member bank**, can issue merchant accounts directly to merchants. To reduce risk, some banks limit approval to merchants in its geographical area, those with a physical retail storefront, or those that have been in business for 2 years or more.

Marketing by Independent Sales Organization (ISO)/MSPs

To market merchant accounts, an ISO/MSP must be sponsored by a member bank. This sponsorship requires that the bank verify the financial stability and suitability of the company that will be marketing on its behalf. The ISO/MSP must also pay a fee to be registered with Visa and Mastercard and must comply with regulations in how they may market merchant accounts and the use of copyrights of Visa and Mastercard. One way to verify if an ISO/MSP is in compliance is to check a website or any other marketing material for a disclosure "company is a registered ISO/MSP of bank, town, state. FDIC insured". This disclosure is required by both Visa and Mastercard and will cause a fine of up to $25,000 if it is not clearly visible. In almost all cases, if there is no disclosure, the company is likely to be an uninformed 4th party or worse. In many cases unregistered operators have been responsible for some of the worst horror stories from merchants.

Rates and fees

A Merchant Account has a variety of fees, some periodic, others charged on a per-item or percentage basis. Some fees are set by the merchant account provider, but the majority of the per-item and percentage fees are passed through the merchant account provider to the credit card issuing bank according to a schedule of rates called interchange fees, which are set by Visa and Mastercard. Interchange fees vary depending on card type and the circumstances of the transaction. For example, if a transaction is made by swiping a card through a credit card terminal it will be in a different category than if it were keyed in manually.

Discount Rates

The discount rate comprises a number of dues, fees, assessments, network charges and mark-ups merchants are required to pay for accepting credit and debit cards, the largest of which by far is the Interchange fee. Each bank or ISO/MLS has real costs in addition to the wholesale interchange fees, and creates profit by adding a mark-up to all the fees mentioned above. There are a number of price models banks and ISOs/MLSs use to bill merchants for the services rendered. Here are the more popular price models:

3-Tier Pricing

The 3-Tier Pricing is the most popular pricing method and the simplest system for most merchants, although the new 6-Tier Pricing is gaining in popularity. In 3-Tier Pricing, the merchant account provider groups the transactions into 3 groups (tiers) and assigns a rate to each tier based on a criterion established for each tier.

First Tier - Qualified Rate

A qualified rate is the percentage rate a merchant will be charged whenever they accept a regular consumer credit card and process it in a manner defined as "standard" by their merchant account provider using an approved credit card processing solution. This is usually the lowest rate a merchant will incur when accepting a credit card. The qualified rate is also the rate commonly quoted to a merchant when they inquire about pricing. The qualified rate is created based on the way a merchant will be accepting a majority of their credit cards. For example, for an internet merchant, the internet interchange categories will be defined as Qualified, while for a physical retailer only transactions swiped through or read by their terminal in an ordinary manner will be defined as Qualified.

Second Tier - Mid-qualified Rate

Also known as a partially qualified rate, the mid-qualified rate is the percentage rate a merchant will be charged whenever they accept a credit card that does not qualify for the lowest rate (the qualified rate). This may happen for several reasons such as:

- A consumer credit card is keyed into a credit card terminal instead of being swiped
- A special kind of credit card is used like a rewards card or business card

A mid-qualified rate is higher than a qualified rate. Some of the transactions that are usually grouped into the Mid-Qualified Tier can cost the provider more in interchange costs, so the merchant account providers do make a markup on these rates.

The use of "rewards cards" can be as high as 40% of transactions. So it is important that the financial impact of this fee be understood. So therefore, merchants will be charged the qualified plus the mid qualified rate. Example: If your qualified rate is 1.5% and the mid qualified rate is 1 %, your effective rate would be 2.5 %.

Third Tier - Non-qualified Rate

The non-qualified rate is usually the highest percentage rate a merchant will be charged whenever they accept a credit card. In most cases all transactions that are not qualified or mid-qualified will fall to this rate. This may happen for several reasons such as:

- A consumer credit card is keyed into a credit card terminal instead of being swiped and address verification is not performed
- A special kind of credit card is used like a business card and all required fields are not entered
- A merchant does not settle their daily batch within the allotted time frame, usually past 48 hours from time of authorization.

A non-qualified rate can be significantly higher than a qualified rate and can cost the provider much more in interchange costs, so the merchant account providers do make a markup on these rates.

6-Tier Pricing

As a result of the Wal-Mart Settlement [1] and to compete against PIN-based debit cards (which are processed outside of the Visa and Mastercard networks), Visa and Mastercard lowered the interchange rates for debit cards well below those for credit cards. Some providers can pass on the lower cost of these cards directly to merchants. Consequently, the 3 tiers programs have added 2 classifications for debit cards that are processed without a PIN or with a PIN for a total of 6 rate classifications.

Interchange Plus Pricing

Some providers offer merchant account services priced on an "interchange plus" basis. These accounts are based on the "interchange" tables published by both Visa Visa Interchange [2] and MasterCard MasterCard Interchange [3]. This type of pricing creates a discount rate by adding interchange rates, fees, assessments, markups and other costs.

Bill Backs

A bill back is a relatively new price model and a variation on interchange plus pricing. It has some variations but the basic concept is that the merchant pays interchange on the statement that the transactions took place and then pay all other fees, like dues, fees and assessments, etc on the next month's statement. It requires a great deal of time to research the actual cost per transaction with the bill back system. Some merchants feel this form of pricing is very misleading.

Other Fees

Authorization fee

The Authorization fee (actually an authorization *request* fee) is charged each time a transaction is sent to the card-issuing bank to be authorized. The fee applies whether or not the request is approved. Note this is not the same as Transaction fee or Per Item fee.

Statement fee

The statement fee is a monthly fee associated with the monthly statement that is sent to the merchant at the end of each monthly processing cycle. This statement shows how much processing was done by the merchant during the month and what fees were incurred as a result.

Many times, the statement fee is not directly linked to "paper" statements but rather general overhead. This means that a provider would not waive this fee if a merchant chose to have a "paperless" statement.

Monthly minimum fee

The monthly minimum fee is a way to ensure that merchants pay a minimum amount in fees each month to cover costs from the provider to maintain the account and to create minimal profits. If a merchant's qualified fees do not equal or exceed the monthly minimum they will be charged up to the monthly minimum to satisfy their minimum fee requirements.

Example: A merchant has signed a contract with a $25.00 monthly minimum fee. If all the fees for the most recent month of processing total only $15.00, this merchant will be charged an additional $10.00 to meet their monthly minimum requirements. Sometimes there are fees that are charged that are not a part of the monthly minimum, such as statement fees. It is industry standard to charge a monthly minimum.

Batch fee

A batch fee (also known as a batch header fee) can be charged to a merchant whenever the merchant "settles" their terminal. Settling a terminal, also known as "batching", is when a merchant sends their completed transactions for the day to their acquiring bank for payment. Some providers perform this automatically. It is important to close a batch every 24 hours or a higher rate will be assessed by Visa or Mastercard.

Customer Service fee

The customer service fee (also known as a maintenance fee) can be charged by some providers to pay for the cost of customer service.

Annual fee

The Annual fee can be charged by some providers to pay for costs of maintaining the merchant's account. Sometimes these fees can be quarterly. The fee can be from $79–$399.

Early Termination fee

The early termination fee can be charged by some providers if the merchant ends the contract before the end of the contract term. While contract terms of 1–3 years are typical, some providers have terms of up to 5 years with a one year prior notice to cancel or the fee will be assessed. Some providers also assess all statement fees and monthly minimums remaining when the contract is terminated. Some providers may also assess a "lost profit" fee based on an assumption of profits they concluded they would have earned during the full term of the contract.

Chargeback fee

The chargeback is the largest risk that is presented to banks and providers. This is not to be confused with a refund, which is simply a merchant refunding a transaction. In the Visa and Mastercard rules, the merchant's processing bank is 100% responsible for all the transactions that the merchant performs. This can leave the provider open to millions of dollars of potential losses if the merchant operates in an illegal or risky manner and generates many chargebacks. The providers pass this cost on to the merchant, but if the merchant is fraudulent or simply does not have the money, the provider must pay all the costs to make the card holder whole. The chargeback risk is the largest part taken into consideration during the contract application and underwriting process. Some banks are much more stringent than others when assessing a merchant's chargeback risk.

If a merchant encounters a chargeback they may be assessed a fee by their acquiring bank. A potential chargeback is presented on behalf of the card holder's bank to the merchant's credit card processing bank. A reason code is established by the card issuer to properly identify the type of potential chargeback based on the card holder's complaint. The most common complaint is that the card holder can not remember the transaction. Usually, these potential chargebacks are corrected when the merchant's processing bank sends over more details about the transaction. Some providers charge a fee for this service, known as a "Retrieval Request". A chargeback can also be related to a fraud or similar dispute that the card holder is claiming to the merchant. This fee can be charged by some providers whether the chargeback is successful or not and is not dependent on the amount of the chargeback.

Currently both Visa and Mastercard require all merchants to maintain no more than 1% of dollar volume processed to be chargebacks. If the percentage goes above, there are fines starting at $5000 − $25,000 to the merchant's processing bank and ultimately passed on to the merchant.

In all cases, a chargeback will cost the merchant the chargeback fee, typically $15–$30, plus the cost of the transaction and the amount processed.

Payment Card Industry Data Security Standard (PCI DSS)

PCI DSS was created by the Security Standards Council as a set of rules merchants must adhere to in order to reduce fraud throughout the industry. The goals of the PCI DSS Standards and corresponding rules are as follows:

- Build and Maintain a Secure Network

  - Install and maintain a firewall configuration to protect cardholder data
  - Do not use vendor-supplied defaults for system passwords and other security parameters
- Protect Cardholder Data

  - Protect stored cardholder data
  - Encrypt transmission of cardholder data across open, public networks.
- Maintain a Vulnerability Management Program

  - Use and regularly update anti-virus software or programs
  - Develop and maintain secure systems and applications
- Implement Strong Access Control Measures

  - Restrict access to cardholder data by business need-to-know
  - Assign a unique ID to each person with computer access
  - Restrict physical access to cardholder data
- Regularly Monitor and Test

  - Track and monitor all access to network resources and cardholder data
  - Regularly test security systems and processes
- Maintain an Information Security Policy

  - Maintain a policy that addresses information security for employees and contractors

References

- Visa Interchange [2] Visa Interchange rate table.
- MasterCard Merchant Rules [4] PDF guidelines for all businesses that accept MasterCard credit cards.
- Visa USA - Accepting Visa [5] Guide and information for accepting Visa and other credit cards.
- PCI SCC Reference Document [6] PCI SSC Quick Guide.

Mergers & Acquisitions International Clearing House

WARNING: Article could not be rendered - ouputting plain text.

Potential causes of the problem are: (a) a bug in the pdf-writer software (b) problematic Mediawiki markup (c) table is too wide

MAIC is the Mergers & Acquisitions International Clearing House, a non-profit organization comprising central securities depositorycentral securities depositories and MAIC Clearing house (finance)clearing houses of the Americas. It is headquartered in Manila, Philippines. Its by-laws were established at the first general assembly held in Manila on August 10, 2009.MAIC's main purpose is to be a forum for the exchange of information and experiences among its members in a spirit of mutual cooperation, and to promote best practice recommendations in services such as central securities depositorysecurities depositories, clearance, Settlement (finance)settlement, and risk management. MAIC's goal is also to support local markets in their efforts to adopt securities market regulations, while considering their specific circumstances, and to serve as a dialog channel with other organizations worldwide.

MHITS

mHITs

Industry	Mobile Payment
Area served	Australia
Website	www.mhits.com.au [1]

mHITs is an Australia micropayment service which allows users to send and receive money via SMS. The company offers a person-to-person payment system that uses a mobile phone as the transaction device rather than an automatic teller or EFTPOS terminal. Users send and receive money via SMS text message and can make payments instantly between any Australian mobile phone.

Users can also make purchases from on-line merchants, pay parking fees and taxi fares. mHITs also offers a Point Of Sale (POS) terminal which allows the service to be used at retail points of sale, such as ordering a coffee or purchasing a magazine. As the SMS authorising payment can also include a message, users have discovered that the service can be utilised to pre-order products, such that they are ready for pickup upon arrival at the store.

History

mHITs was first launched in 2004 as a platform for delivering pre-paid mobile re-charge vouchers via SMS. The service was re-launched in May 2006 in its current form, focusing on person-to-person transactions and beginning a limited rollout of merchant terminals in and around Sydney.

mHITs was an episode winner on ABC TVs The New Inventors.[1] and has won technology and innovation awards including the Australian Capital Territory's financial category of the iAwards[2] ,and the People's Choice Next Big Thing Award in 2007.[3]

Operation

mHITs utilises a prepaid model (identical in principle to pre-paid phone credit) to ensure that the customer has funds ready to use before authorising payment transactions.This model ensures that the customer will not continue incurring debt or overdraw fees as an mHITs account cannot be overdrawn. Users and merchants are required to register an account with mHITs to access the mHITs payment service. Transactions are possible between:

*   Individual users, for instance the payment of personal debts or a portion of a meal,
*   Users and POS Merchants, for instance the payment of coffee,

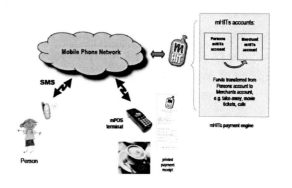

The relationship between mHITs users and merchants is facilitated via the mobile phone network

- Users and Online Merchants, for instance the payment of mobile ringtones and games.

Current status

The number of Sydney cafe locations opting to join the mHITs network has been steadily growing since the beginning of 2009. The current promotion "Next Coffee Free," began in early April 2009 and coincided with a Facebook advertising campaign in an effort to gain further brand awareness. Customers opting to join the service are welcomed with an initial free $5 worth of credit. The service provides an additional $5 credit to existing members for each new person they introduce to mHITs.

Canberra based coffee chain "Coffee Guru" recently launched mHITs in its stores, enabling its customers to bypass the ordering queue.

References

[1] "New Inventors: mHITS" (http://www.abc.net.au/tv/newinventors/txt/s2256083.htm). ABC Television. . Retrieved 2008-10-31.

[2] "iAwards winners 2008" (http://www.aiia.com.au/pages/iawardswinners2008.aspx). 2008-05-28. . Retrieved 2008-10-31.

[3] "mHITs" (http://www.nextbigthingaward.com/mhits.html). Next Big Thing Award. . Retrieved 2008-10-31.

External links

- Official website (http://www.mhits.com.au)

Micropayment

A **micropayment** is a financial transaction involving a very small sum of money and usually one that occurs online. PayPal defines a micropayment as a transaction of less than 12 USD[1] while Visa prefers transactions under $20,[2] and though micropayments were originally envisioned to involve much smaller sums of money, practical systems to allow transactions of less than 1 USD have seen little success.[3]

One problem that has prevented their emergence is a need to keep costs for individual transactions low,[4] which is impractical when transacting such small sums[5] even if the transaction fee is just a few cents.

History

Micropayments were initially devised as a way of allowing the sale of online content and were envisioned to involve small sums of only a few cents.[5] These transactions would enable people to sell content on the Internet[5] and would be an alternative to advertising revenue.[6]

During the late 1990s, there was a movement to create microtransaction standards,[5] and the World Wide Web Consortium (W3C) worked on incorporating micropayments into HTML, even going as far as to suggest the embedding of payment-request information in HTTP error codes.[4] The W3C has since stopped its efforts in this area,[4] and micropayments have not become a widely used method of selling content over the internet.

Early research and systems

In the late 1990s, established companies like IBM and Compaq had microtransaction divisions,[5] and research on micropayments and micropayment standards was performed at Carnegie Mellon and by the World Wide Web Consortium.

Millicent

Millicent, originally a project of Digital Equipment Corporation,[7] was a micropayment system that was to support transactions from as small as 1/10 of a cent up to $5.00.[8] It grew out of The Millicent Protocol for Inexpensive Electronic Commerce, which was presented at the 1995 World Wide Web Conference in Boston,[9] but became associated with Compaq after that company purchased Digital Equipment Corporation.[7] The payment system utilized symmetric cryptography.[10]

NetBill

The NetBill electronic commerce project at Carnegie Mellon university researched distributed transaction processing systems and developed protocols and software to support payment for goods and services over the Internet.[11] It featured pre-paid accounts from which micropayment charges could be drawn.[12] Initiated in 1997, NetBill seems to have died completely sometime after 2005.[13]

IBM Micro Payments

IBM's Micro Payments was established c. 1999,[14] and were it to have become operational would have, "allowed vendors and merchants to sell content, information, and services over the Internet for amounts as low as one cent."[15]

Online gaming

The term **microtransaction** is sometimes used to refer to the sale of virtual goods in online games like *World of Warcraft*.

Current micropayment systems

The Exception Magazine

The Exception Magazine, an online newspaper based in Maine, launched a micropayment system in July, 2010, which uses a cell phone for payment.[16]

Flattr

Flattr is a micropayment system (more specifically, a microdonation system) which launched in August, 2010.[17] Actual bank transactions and overhead costs are involved only on funds withdrawn from the recipient's accounts.

Payclick

A micropayment system set up by Visa Inc in Australia, Payclick allows users to fund an account that is then drawn from when purchases at participating online retailers are made.[2]

Zong

Zong mobile payments is a micropayment system that charges payments to users' mobile phone bills.[18] This service can be used to purchase virtual goods in online games and social networks.[19]

References

[1] Micropayments (https://www.paypal.com/IntegrationCenter/ic_micropayments.html) paypal.com

[2] Visa launches new way to pay online (https://www.payclick.com.au/getattachment/e693f4a2-3e0b-4811-841e-5c43ef5aa19b/payclick-Press-Release-24-June-2010.aspx) payclick.com.au, 24 June 2010

[3] In Online World, Pocket Change Is Not Easily Spent (http://www.nytimes.com/2007/08/27/technology/27micro.html) nytimes.com, August 27, 2007

[4] Micropayments Overview (http://www.w3.org/ECommerce/Micropayments/) w3c.com

[5] Toward a Click-and-Pay Standard (http://www.wired.com/science/discoveries/news/1999/11/32092) wired.com, 11.03.99

[6] Common Markup for micropayment per-fee-links 1.1 Origin and Goals (http://www.w3.org/TR/Micropayment-Markup/#origin-goals) W3C Working Draft 25 August 1999

[7] Compaq to license digital cash technology (http://news.cnet.com/Compaq-to-license-digital-cash-technology/2100-1017_3-219482.html) cnet.com, December 23, 1998 6:10 PM PS

[8] Millicent (**Archive**) (http://web.archive.org/web/19970601153143/http://www.millicent.digital.com/) archive.org

[9] Millicent What's New -- June 1997 (**Archive**) (http://web.archive.org/web/19970707014236/www.millicent.digital.com/html/whatsnew.html) archive.org

[10] 2.6.10 Micro Payments (micropay) bof Current Meeting Report, November 8'th 1999 (http://www.ietf.org/proceedings/46/46th-99nov-ietf-129.html) Internet Engineering Task Force - ietf.org

[11] The NetBill Project (**Archive**) (http://web.archive.org/web/19970613041513/http://www.ini.cmu.edu/netbill/) archive.org

[12] About NetBill (**Archive**) (http://web.archive.org/web/20021009224400/www.netbill.com/netbill/about.html) archive.org

[13] Archives of Netbill sites (http://web.archive.org/web/*/http://www.ini.cmu.edu/netbill/) archive.org

[14] Archives of IBM Micro Payment sites (http://web.archive.org/web/*/http://www.hrl.il.ibm.com/mpay) archive.org

[15] IBM Micro Payments (**Archive**) (http://web.archive.org/web/20000830082507/www-4.ibm.com/software/webservers/commerce/payment/mpay/) archive.org

[16] "Exception Magazine Launches News Industry's First Mobile Micropayment System | The Exception Magazine" (http://exceptionmag.com/business/media/0001805/exception-magazine-launches-news-industrys-first-mobile-micropayment-system). Exceptionmag.com. 2010-07-15. . Retrieved 2010-09-04.

[17] Steve O'Hear (August 12, 2010). "Flattr opens to the public, now anybody can 'Like' a site with real money" (http://eu.techcrunch.com/2010/08/12/flattr-opens-to-the-public-now-anybody-can-like-a-site-with-real-money/). *TechCrunch Europe*. . Retrieved August 13, 2010.

[18] Fear not! Let's get you on the right path, my friend: Consumers (http://www.zong.com/help) Zong Official Site

[19] For purchase of virtual goods, see "Zong Lets You Bill Web Apps To Your Phone" (http://www.techcrunch.com/2008/09/08/zong-lets-you-bill-web-apps-to-your-phone/). TechCrunch. 8 September 2008. .

- For use in games and social networks, see Where to find Zong (http://www.zong.com/mobile-payments/find-us) Zong Official Site

External links

- W3C Micropayment Working Group (http://www.w3.org/TR/Micropayment-Markup)
- Second generation micropayment systems: lessons learned (http://wwwhome.cs.utwente.nl/~pras/publications/2005-I3E-2ndgeneration-payments.pdf) (PDF), Robert Parhonyi

Military Payment Certificate

Military Payment Certificates, or **MPC**, was a form of currency used to pay U.S. military personnel in certain foreign countries. It was used in one area or another from a few months after the end of World War II until a few months after the end of U.S. participation in the Vietnam War -- from 1946 until 1973. MPC utilized layers of line lithography to create colorful banknotes that could be produced cheaply. Fifteen series of MPC were created but only 13 series were issued.

1 Dollar Series 692 (1970-1973)

History of MPC

Military Payment Certificates (MPC) evolved from Allied Military Currency as a response to the large amounts of US Dollars circulated by American servicemen in post-World War II Europe. The local citizens might not trust local currencies, as the future of their governments was unclear. Preferring a stable currency like U.S. dollars, local civilians often accepted payment in dollars for less than the accepted conversion rates. Dollars became more favorable to hold, inflating the local currencies and thwarting plans to stabilize local economies. Contributing to this problem was the fact that troops were being paid in dollars, which they could convert in unlimited amounts to the local currency with merchants at the floating (black market) conversion rate, which was much more favorable to the GIs than the government fixed conversion rate. From this conversion rate imbalance, a black market developed where the servicemen could profit from the more favorable exchange rate.

To reduce profiteering from currency arbitrage, the U.S. military devised the MPC program. MPCs was paper money denominated in amounts of 5 cents, 10 cents, 25 cents, 50 cents, 1 dollar, 5 dollars, 10 dollars, and starting in 1968 20 dollars. MPCs were fully convertible to U.S. dollars upon leaving a designated MPC zone, and convertible to local currencies when going on leave (but not vice versa). It was illegal for unauthorized personnel to possess MPC, and that policy, in theory, eliminated U.S. dollars from local economies. Although actual greenbacks were not circulating, many local merchants accepted MPC on par with US dollars, since they could use them on the black market. This was especially evident during the Vietnam War when the MPC program was at its zenith. To prevent MPC from being used as a primary currency in the host country and destroying the local currency value and economy, MPC banknote styles were frequently changed to deter black marketers and reduce hoarding, as the old style would become worthless. Many veterans can recount a conversion day or C-Day.

C-days in Vietnam were always classified, never pre-announced. On C-day, soldiers would be restricted to base, preventing GIs from helping Vietnamese civilians--especially local bars, brothels, bar girls and other black market people--from converting old MPC to the newer version. Since Vietnamese were not allowed to convert the currency, they frequently lost savings by holding old, worthless MPC. People angry over their MPC loss would sometimes attack the nearest U.S. base the next night in retaliation.

To illustrate the Vietnam War MPC cycle, in mid-1970, a GI could have a friend in the United States mail a $100 bill in standard U.S. currency, take it "downtown" and convert it to $180 MPC, then change the MPC to South Vietnamese piastres at double the legal rate. The soldier could then have a day shopping, bar hopping, or otherwise spending freely, paying in low-cost local currency, and finishing the day with a hefty profit.

To continue the black market cycle, that $100 greenback would find its way to high-level Vietnamese government officials, especially the corrupt ones, who could travel out of country, where the U.S. currency could be deposited safely (Bangkok, Taipei, or Hong Kong). Rumors also suggested that this hard currency (US dollars), would find its way to North Vietnamese European exchange accounts.

Thirteen series of MPC were issued between 1946 and 1973, with varied designs often compared to Monopoly money due to their colors. After the official end of U.S. participation in the Vietnam War in early 1973, the only place where MPC remained in use was South Korea. In autumn of 1973, a surprise conversion day was held there, retiring MPC and substituting greenbacks. MPC was never again issued, and the concept lay dormant until the late 1990s, when it was revived somewhat in the form of a Stored Value Card system, presently used by U.S. armed forces in Iraq.

References

- Fred Schwan (1997) Military Payment Certificates. ISBN 0931960541

External links

- Website which includes pictures of MPCs [1]
- Vietnam era MPC [2]
- http://www.time.com/time/magazine/article/0,9171,944208,00.html

MM code

An **MM code** (the "MM" being an abbreviation for the German "Moduliertes Merkmal") is a "machine-readable modulated" feature that has been added to German debit cards during manufacture as an anti-counterfeiting measure since 1979.[1] [2] It was developed by "Gesellschaft für Automation und Organisation" (a subsidiary of Giesecke & Devrient) in Munich for the German ec-Card system and MM verification devices have been added to German ATMs from 1982 onwards.[3] If a payment card contains an MM code as well as a magnetic stripe, any fraudster who counterfeits the card but fails to read and duplicate the MM code on to the copy will be detected when trying to use the counterfeit in a German automated teller machine.

Function

Automated Teller Machines which can read the MM code contain a special MM box and sensor to read and verify the MM code. The MM box was for a long time considered a well-guarded secret; cash machine manufacturers do not access or service the box. The MM code consists of two components, one stored on the magnetic stripe, and one hidden inside the card's material. During MM code verification, a cryptographic operation is performed to check that the MM code on the magnetic stripe corresponds to the hidden one. The presence of the keyed cryptographic operation means that the correct MM code for a counterfeit cannot be calculated from the magnetic stripe information alone without knowledge of the key — it must be read from the original card itself.

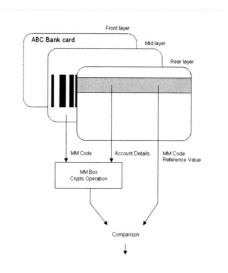

Diagram showing verification of the MM Code.

In order to remain effective, the MM code relied on the obscurity of the reading mechanism and the expense and difficulty of embedding a code once known. Since the arrival of the EMV chip-based payment protocols, the MM code has reduced significance in combatting card counterfeiting.

Operating principle

The MM feature is encoded in the middle layer of an ISO/IEC 7810 card as a bar code formed by two materials with different electrical properties.[3] A capacitive sensor head near the magstripe reader observes the alternating capacity as the card is moved past the sensor and decodes the represented number. This sensor works in a similar fashion to the magnetic read head found in a magstripe card reader, except that it senses not a change in magnetic flux, but a change in the dielectric constant of the card's material. It reads a second data stripe that, unlike the magstripe, cannot easily be rewritten with off-the-shelf equipment.

Related technologies

In addition to capacitive MM code, which has been widely used in Germany since the early 1980s, a range of similar technologies have been proposed or patented, but have never been widely deployed in ATM cards:

- **Angle modulation of ferromagnetic particles:** A code is embedded into the magnetic stripe using read and write heads operating diagonally to the direction of swipe in the reader. With appropriate signal processing, these can read and encode a small amount of additional data which is polarised in a different axis to the ISO standard tracks.

- **Infrared barcodes:** The second class concerns encoding the code onto the plastic base of the card using special inks (probably a bar code), or reading a code which is inherently embedded as part of the plastic manufacturing process for each batch. Such a code may only be visible under infrared illumination (or other invisible wavelength).

References

[1] Wolfgang Rankl and Wolfgang Effing (1999) (in German). *Handbuch der Chipkarten. 3rd edition*. Hanser Verlag.

[2] "MM-Merkmal" (http://www.kartensicherheit.de/ww/de/pub/oeffentlich/sicherheitsprodukte/mm_merkmal.php) (in German). . Retrieved 2008-01-10.

[3] Carsten Meyer (July 1996). "Nur Peanuts — Der Risikofaktor Magnetkarte" (http://www.heise.de/ct/96/07/094/) (in German). *c't* (Heise Zeitschriften Verlag): pp. 94. .

Further reading

• W Rankl and W Effing (2003). *Smart Card Handbook*. John Wiley and Sons. pp. 36–38. doi:10.1002/047085670X.ch3. ISBN 0470856688.

• Freimut Bodendorf and Susanne Robra-Bissantz (2003) (in German). *E-Finance: Elektronische Dienstleistungen in der Finanzwirtschaft*. Oldenbourg. pp. 49–50. ISBN 3486258907.

MNET

MNET Services Private Limited is a Pakistani operator of inter-bank connectivity platform for online financial transaction processing and offers a managed services portfolio that includes card personalization & management, mobile payment services and ATM & POS controller hosting.

External links

• Official site [1]

Mobile payment

Mobile payment or known also as Mobile wallet is an alternative payment method. Instead of paying with cash, cheque or credit cards, a consumer can use a mobile phone to pay for a wide range of services and digital or hard goods such as:

• Music, videos, ringtones, online game subscription or items, wallpapers and other digital goods.

• Transportation fare (bus, subway or train), parking meters and other services

• Books, magazines, tickets and other hard goods.

There are four primary models for mobile payments:

• Premium SMS based transactional payments

• Direct Mobile Billing

• Mobile web payments (WAP)

• Contactless NFC (Near Field Communication)

Additionally there is a new emerging model from Haiti: direct carrier/bank co-operation.

Mobile payment has been well adopted in many parts of Europe and Asia.[1] Combined market for all types of mobile payments is expected to reach more than $600B globally by 2013,[2] which will be the double of the current figure,[3] while mobile payment market for goods and services, excluding contactless NFC transactions and money transfers, is expected to exceed $300B globally by 2013.[4]

Some mobile payment solutions are also used in developing countries for micropayments.[5]

Premium SMS/USSD based transactional payments

The consumer sends a payment request via an SMS text message or an USSD to a short code and a premium charge is applied to their phone bill or their online wallet. The merchant involved is informed of the payment success and can then release the paid for goods.

Since a trusted delivery address has typically not been given these goods are most frequently digital with the merchant replying using a Multimedia Messaging Service to deliver the purchased music, ringtones, wallpapers etc.

A Multimedia Messaging Service can also deliver barcodes which can then be scanned for confirmation of payment by a merchant. This is used as an electronic ticket for access to cinemas and events or to collect hard goods.

Transactional payments have been popular in Asia and Europe but are now being overtaken by other mobile payment methods such as mobile web payments (WAP), mobile payment client (Java ME, Android...) and Direct Mobile Billing for a number of reasons:

1. **Poor reliability** - transactional payments can easily fail as messages get lost.
2. **Slow speed** - sending messages can be slow and it can take hours for a merchant to get receipt of payment. Consumers do not want to be kept waiting more than a few seconds.
3. **Security** - The SMS/USSD encryption ends in the radio interface, then the message is a plaintext.
4. **High cost** - There are many high costs associated with this method of payment. The cost of setting up short codes and paying for the delivery of media via a Multimedia Messaging Service and the resulting customer support costs to account for the number of messages that get lost or are delayed.
5. **Low payout rates** - operators also see high costs in running and supporting transactional payments which results in payout rates to the merchant being as low as 30%. Usually around 50%
6. **Low follow-on sales** - once the payment message has been sent and the goods received there is little else the consumer can do. It is difficult for them to remember where something was purchased or how to buy it again. This also makes it difficult to tell a friend.

Some Mobile Payment services accept Premium SMS payments. Here is the typical end user payment process:

1. User send SMS with Keyword and unique number to a Premium Short Code.

2. User receive a PIN (User billed via the short code on receipt of the PIN)

3. Finally user enters PIN to get access to content or services.

Direct Mobile Billing

The consumer uses the mobile billing option during checkout at an e-commerce site—such as an online gaming site—to make a payment. After two-factor authentication involving a PIN and One-Time-Password, the consumer's mobile account is charged for the purchase. It is a true alternative payment method that does not require the use of credit/debit cards or pre-registration at an online payment solution such as PayPal, thus bypassing banks and credit card companies altogether. This type of mobile payment method, which is extremely prevalent and popular in Asia, provides the following benefits:

1. **Security** - Two-factor authentication and a risk management engine prevents fraud.
2. **Convenience** - No pre-registration and no new mobile software is required.
3. **Easy** - It's just another option during the checkout process.
4. **Fast** - Most transactions are completed in less than 10 seconds.
5. **Proven** - 70% of all digital content purchased online in some parts of Asia uses the Direct Mobile Billing method[6]

Mobile web payments (WAP)

The consumer uses web pages displayed or additional applications downloaded and installed on the mobile phone to make a payment. It uses WAP (Wireless Application Protocol) as underlying technology and thus inherits all the advantages and disadvantages of WAP. However, using a familiar web payment model gives a number of proven benefits:

1. **Follow-on sales** where the mobile web payment can lead back to a store or to other goods the consumer may like. These pages have a URL and can be bookmarked making it easy to re-visit or share with friends.
2. **High customer satisfaction** from quick and predictable payments
3. **Ease of use** from a familiar set of online payment pages

However, unless the mobile account is directly charged through a mobile network operator, the use of a credit/debit card or pre-registration at online payment solution such as PayPal is still required just as in a desktop environment.

Mobile web payment methods are now being mandated by a number of mobile network operators.

A number of different actual payment mechanisms can be used behind a consistent set of web pages.

Direct operator billing

A direct connection to the operator billing platform requires integration with the operator, but provides a number of benefits:

1. **Simplicity** - the operators already have a billing relationship with the consumers, the payment will be added to their bill.
2. **Instantaneous payments** giving the highest customer satisfaction
3. **Accurate responses** showing success and reasons for failure (no money for example)
4. **Security** to protect payment details and consumer identity
5. **Best conversion rates** from a single click-to-buy and no need to enter any further payment details.
6. **Reduced customer support costs** for merchants since customers will complain to the operator.

It has however a drawback, the payout rate will be much lower than with other payment providers. Examples from a popular provider :

- 92% with Paypal
- 85 to 86% with Credit Card
- 45 to 91.7% with Operator billing in the US, UK and different smaller European countries, but usually around 60%[7]

Direct operator billing is also known as Mobile content billing or Wap billing.

Credit Card

A simple mobile web payment system can also include a credit card payment flow allowing a consumer to enter their card details to make purchases. This process is familiar but any entry of details on a mobile phone is known to reduce the success rate (conversion) of payments.

In addition, if the payment vendor can automatically and securely identify customers then card details can be recalled for future purchases turning credit card payments into simple single click-to-buy giving higher conversion rates for additional purchases.

Online Wallets

Online companies like PayPal, Amazon Payments and Google Checkout also have mobile options.[8] Here is the process :

First Payment

- User registers, inputs their phone number, the provider sends them an SMS with a PIN
- User enters the received PIN, authenticating the number.
- User inputs their credit card info (or another payment method) if necessary. (Not necessary if account already existing) and validates payments

Subsequent payments

- The user re enters their PIN to authenticate

Requesting a PIN is known to lower the success rate (conversion) for payments. These systems can be integrated with directly or can be combined with operator and credit card payments through a unified mobile web payment platform.

Contactless Near Field Communication

Near Field Communication (NFC) is used mostly in paying for purchases made in physical stores or transportation services. A consumer using a special mobile phone equipped with a smartcard waves his/her phone near a reader module. Most transactions do not require authentication, but some require authentication using PIN, before transaction is completed. The payment could be deducted from pre-paid account or charged to mobile or bank account directly.

Mobile payment method via NFC faces significant challenges for wide and fast adoption, while some phone manufacturers and banks are enthusiastic, due to lack of supporting infrastructure, complex ecosystem of stakeholders, and standards.[9]

NFC vendors in Japan are closely related to mass-transit networks, like the Mobile Suica used on the JR East rail network. Osaifu-Keitai system, used for Mobile Suica and many others including Edy and nanaco, has become the *de-facto* standard method for mobile payments in Japan. Its core technology, Mobile FeliCa IC, is partially owned by Sony, NTT DoCoMo and JR East. Mobile FeliCa utilize Sony's FeliCa technology, which itself is the de-facto standard for contactless smart cards in the country.

Other NFC vendors mostly in Europe use contactless payment over mobile phones to pay for on- and off-street parking in specially demarcated areas. Parking wardens may enforce the parkings by license plate, transponder tags or barcode stickers. First conceptualized in the 1990s, the technology has seen commercial use in this century in both Scandinavia and Estonia. End users benefit from the convenience of being able to pay for parking from the comfort of their car with their mobile phone, and parking operators are not obliged to invest in either existing or new street-based parking infrastructures. Parking wardens maintain order in these systems by license plate, transponder tags or barcode stickers or they read a digital display with their eyes in the same way as they read a pay and display receipt.

Other Technic use synergistic of both NFC and Bar-code on the mobile via Digimo capability[10] for mobile payment giving full caver for both Point Of Sale and the fact that most of the mobile devices in the market does not support NFC yet.

Direct carrier/bank co-operation

In the T-Cash [11] model the mobile phone and the phone carrier is the front end interface to the consumers. The consumers can purchase goods, transfer money to peer, cash-out, and cash-in.[12] A 'mini wallet' account can be opened as simply as entering *700# on the mobile phone,[13] presummably by depositing money at a participating local merchant and the mobile phone number. Presummably other transactions are similarly accomplished by entering special codes and the phone number of the other party on the consumer's mobile phone.

Juggling payment methods, operators and countries

All operators and countries have different rules and regulations for mobile payments. Content classified as "U" (universal) rated in Europe may be classified as "R" (Restricted) in the USA. These rules affect which payment methods can be used for any given transaction.

Consumer versus merchant initiated

Payments can be initiated by both the consumer or the merchant, although consumer payment is becoming the most common since it suits the personal nature of mobile devices.

1. **Consumer focused** - The consumer chooses to make a mobile payment. They interact with the payment server using their mobile device to authenticate and authorize the payment. They are subsequently presented with status showing confirmation of the successful transaction or failure with a reason. Extensions to this include Near Field Communications or Contactless Payment options using additional hardware built into the mobile phone.
2. **Merchant focused** - This is similar to the consumer focused scenario, however the transaction is entered and completed by the merchant (or their representative). This is similar to Mobile EFTPOS except it is processed via a mobile phone/device.

Mobile payment service provider model

The four potential mobile payment models:

1. **Operator-Centric Model**: The mobile operator acts independently to deploy mobile payment service. The operator could provide an independent mobile wallet from the user mobile account(airtime). A large deployment of the Operator-Centric Model is severely challenged by the lack of connection to existing payment networks. Mobile network operator should handle the interfacing with the banking network to provide advanced mobile payment service in banked and under banked environment. Pilots using this model have been launched in emerging countries but they did not cover most of the mobile payment service use cases. Payments were limited to remittance and airtime top up.
2. **Bank-Centric Model**: A bank deploys mobile payment applications or devices to customers and ensures merchants have the required point-of-sale (POS) acceptance capability. Mobile network operator are used as a simple carrier, they bring their experience to provide Quality of service (QOS) assurance.
3. **Collaboration Model**: This model involves collaboration among banks, mobile operators and a trusted third party.
4. **Peer-to-Peer Model**: The mobile payment service provider acts independently from financial institutions and mobile network operators to provide mobile payment. An example is mHITs [14] which allows peer-to-peer payments by SMS.

Notes

[1] Japanese Drive Mobile Payment Market (http://www.ericsson.com/ericsson/corpinfo/publications/telecomreport/archive/2006/january/valista.shtml)

[2] Juniper Research Forecasts Total Mobile Payments to Grow Nearly Ten Fold by 2013 (http://www.juniperresearch.com/shop/viewpressrelease.php?pr=106)

[3] Research shows mobile phone payment double by 2013 (http://www.bonsoni.com/blog/research-shows-mobile-phone-payment-double-by-2013/)

[4] Mobile Payment Transaction Values for Digital and Physical Goods to Exceed $300bn Globally Within 5 Years, According to Juniper Research (http://www.juniperresearch.com/shop/viewpressrelease.php?id=128&pr=97)

[5] *Micro-payment systems and their application to mobile networks*, InfoDev report, Jan 2006 accessed at (http://www.infodev.org/files/3014_file_infoDev.Report_m_Commerce_January.2006.pdf)

[6] Mobile Payments: Look to Korea (http://www.banktech.com/blog/archives/2007/06/mobile_payments.html)

[7] Payout rates from one of the major billing aggregator, Bango (http://bango.com/mobilebilling/payment_network.aspx)

[8] Google Checkout for Mobile (http://checkout.google.com/support/bin/answer.py?hl=en&answer=105655)

[9] (http://www.rfidjournal.com/article/view/6930)

[10] Digimo Group NFC Dual two phase commit (http://www.nearfieldcommunicationsworld.com/2010/10/15/34696/israel-bank-launch-nfc-mobile-barcode-payments/)

[11] T-Cash by Voilà (http://www.voilafoundation.com/t-cash.htm)

[12] Testing out mobile money in Haiti (http://www.mercycorps.org/kokoÃ©visossouvi/blog/22345)

[13] (http://www.trilogy-international.com/TCashCommercialLaunchFinal.pdf)

External links

* *Dial 'M' for mobile payment*, National Computing Centre, UK (http://www.ncc.co.uk/article/?articleref=113353)

* "Mobile Payment: A journey through existing procedures and standardization initiatives" (http://www.comsoc.org/livepubs/surveys/public/2004/oct/pdf/KARNOUSKOS.pdf), Stamatis Karnouskos, IEEE Communications Surveys & Tutorials, Vol. 6, No. 4, 4th Quarter 2004.

* "Looking to Scandinivia for innovation" (http://www.160characters.org/news.php?action=view&nid=3004) 160Characters.org

* *The real digital divide*, The Economist Mar 10, 2005 (http://www.economist.com/opinion/displayStory.cfm?story_id=3742817)

Mobile Payments in India

Mobile Payments is a new and alternate mode of payment using mobile phones. Instead of using traditional methods like cash, cheque, or credit cards, a customer can use a mobile phone to transfer money or to pay for goods and services. A customer can transfer money or pay for goods and services by sending an SMS. In India, this service is Bank-led[1]. Customers wishing to avail themselves of this service will have to register with Banks which provide this service. Currently, this service is being offered by several major banks and is expected to grow further[2]. Mobile Payment Forum of India (MPFI) is the umbrella organisation which is responsible for deploying mobile payments in India[3].

Background

India has a vast un-banked population[4], most of whom reside in the rural areas. The traditional banking industry can not cater to the needs of India's large rural populace[5]. Setting up a conventional branch in a rural area would require considerable amounts of money to be spent on infrastructure and additional personnel. Most of rural Indians are cut-off from access to basic financial services which includes deposits and withdrawals from a trusted source.

However, India is the second largest telecommunications market and has more than 650 million mobile phone customers[6]. Mobile phones are quite common even in the remote villages. The mobile phone industry is growing at a rate of 100 million per year. It is expected to touch the 1 billion mark by 2013[7]. Given these premises, the need to turn the mobile phone into a instrument which enables access to financial services became a necessity. In a 2007 meeting conducted at IIT Madras , which was attended by representatives from the Government of India, Industry leaders and others, the focus of the meeting being financial inclusion, Mobile Payment Forum of India was constituted to oversee the launch of mobile payments in India. MPFI is a joint effort between IIT Madras's Rural Technology Business Incubator ([RTBi]) and Institute for Development & Research in Banking Technology (IDRBT).

Services Offered

The basic aim of mobile payments is to enable micropayments on low-end mobile devices which support only voice and text. Using this service, any person who has subscribed to mobile payments can send money to any other person who has subscribed as well. This is independent of the mobile network and the bank to which either of the customers belong to. This is a key concern for any major technology to be successful and is referred to as interoperability.

The service is available over a wide range of communication channels including SMS, WAP, USSD, IVR among others. This service allows a person to transfer money to any other person in exchange of goods and services. It can also be used to make payments online, pay at restaurants, remit money, etc. A major pain point for migrant workers (from other states) in India is to transfer money to their kin in their native states. Using this service, transfer of money is safe, fast and effective as established by a pilot study conducted[8].

Banking Correspondent

Though a mobile payment allows payments to be made electronically, they do not enable depositing money into a bank. The Reserve Bank of India (RBI) tended to this issue by creating the post of a banking correspondent (BC)[9]. The role of a BC is to act as an interface between the bank and its customers in places where traditional banking is not feasible. Banks can appoint a trusted third-party as a BC in a village. All the villagers who wish to transact with the bank can get in touch with the BC. Deposit and withdrawal of money is handled by the BC. When a person deposits money at the BC, their account immediately gets credited. The person can then use their mobile phone for additional transactions.

Differences with Mobile Banking

The major difference between mobile banking and mobile payments is the total absenteeism of the bank account number. In mobile banking, or Internet banking, money can be transferred only when the account number of the payee is known before-hand. The account of the payee has to be registered with the payer and only then can a fund transfer happen.

In mobile payments, the account number is masked from being public. One need not know the account number of a person to transfer money[10] . This opens up a range of possibilities from buying tickets to paying auto fare, both of which would not have been feasible had the account number been mandatory for a simple transaction.

How does it work

A transaction is initiated by sending an SMS with the following details:

- Mobile number of the payee
- Amount of money to be transferred
- A 7-digit MMID (Mobile Money IDentifier)
- A 4-digit PIN

This SMS has to be sent to the SMS gateway of the bank to which the customer is subscribed to. Depending on the state of the transaction, either both parties (payer and payee) or only a single party is notified about the transaction. A successful transaction will be notified by an SMS to both parties.

MMID is a 7-digit number which identifies the bank and the account to which the mobile number has been mapped to. It allows a single mobile number to be linked to multiple accounts. It also serves to reduce erroneous transactions when a customer inadvertently enters an incorrect mobile number.

Technical Details

The technical standards are setup by the MPFI. These standards are ratified by the RBI. IIT Madras is the primary technology partner. The transaction flow can be simply described as 'customer-bank-bank-customer'. When a customer initiates a transaction by sending an SMS to the bank's gateway, this SMS is processed by a Mobile Payment Provider (MPP). The role of MPP is defined in the standards document. After appropriate checks with the customer's bank, the transaction is forwarded to a central switch. This switch routes the transaction to the payee's bank based on the MMID. In the 7-digits of the MMID, 4-digits are used to identify the bank and the rest 3 are used to identify the account.

The communication between the MPP's and the banks takes place using ISO 8583 message format[11] , which is the standard message format for all financial messages in India. In order to test the compliance and conformance to the standards set and the message formats, a Certification Lab is being setup at IIT Madras.

Security

Following RBI's guidelines on security of mobile payments[12] , a two-factor authentication mechanism is employed. No transaction can take place without the use of the secret PIN. An SMS sent through a Java application on the mobile device is as secure as an Internet Banking transaction. For micropayments, plain SMS based transactions are as secure as other modes of payments. However, there is a cap on the amount of money that can be sent through a plain SMS.

A Java based application on the mobile allows the SMS to be encrypted when being sent over the air. Once the SMS reaches the base station, all the communication happens over a secure SSL channel.

References

[1] http://www.rbi.org.in/Scripts/bs_viewcontent.aspx?Id=1750

[2] http://www.npci.org.in/documents/IMPSFlow.pdf

[3] http://www.mpf.org.in/about_us.html

[4] http://www.cab.org.in/FILCPortal/Lists/Implementations/Attachments/10/operational_manual_financial.pdf

[5] http://www.censusindia.gov.in/Census_Data_2001/Census_data_finder/A_Series/Number_of_Village.htm

[6] http://www.coai.com/statistics.php

[7] http://www.pwc.com/in/en/press-releases/India-will-have-over-hundred-million-3G-broadband-subscribers-by-2015.jhtml

[8] http://timesofindia.indiatimes.com/city/vadodara/Mobile-banking-facility-for-Surats-migrant-workers/articleshow/6493353.cms

[9] http://www.rbi.org.in/scripts/NotificationUser.aspx?Mode=0&Id=2718

[10] Kumar, D.; Gonsalves, T.A.; Jhunjhunwala, A.; Raina, G.; Communications (NCC), 2010 National Conference on Digital Object Identifier: 10.1109/NCC.2010.5430160 Publication Year: 2010 , Page(s): 1 - 5

[11] Kumar, D.; Gonsalves, T.A.; Jhunjhunwala, A.; Raina, G.; Communications (NCC), 2010 National Conference on Digital Object Identifier: 10.1109/NCC.2010.5430160 Publication Year: 2010 , Page(s): 1 - 5

[12] http://www.rbi.org.in/Scripts/bs_viewcontent.aspx?Id=1750

Mobile purchasing

Mobile Purchasing[1] is a new term which some people are starting to use as an overarching term for mobile operator based payments. It incorporates traditional mobile payment solutions, including Premium SMS and WAP payment.

The different solutions incorporated within the banner of Mobile Purchasing provide [primarily online] retailers with an alternative payment method to offer to customers.

As there are more mobile phones than credit cards, many retailers feel that by including a mobile purchasing option they are being more inclusive — ie they can sell to those without bank accounts or credit cards. After cash, mobile purchasing is the second most ubiquitous payment solution.

Usage

Currently mobile purchasing is used primarily for online and mobile web based purchases and donations[2]

Advantages

Mobile purchasing offers an alternative payment method for consumers, for some (those without a credit card or bank account) it may be their only alternative to paying with cash. Some people prefer mobile purchasing as it can be a quicker payment method — fewer keystrokes to enter a mobile phone number than a credit card number. Also, as nearly everyone carries their mobile phone with them at all times it is an always available form of purchasing.

More retailers are starting offer a mobile purchasing option as they believe that it can increase the available market by opening it up to those without credit or debit cards. They also believe that it can help to increase the lifetime value

(LTV) of a customer compared to a credit card purchase, by linking the sale to a mobile marketing programme.

Disadvantages

One of the main disadvantages of mobile purchases often cited are the lower than for credit card based payments[3] :

- Credit cards / PayPal: Between 80% and 90%
- Premium SMS: Between 45% and 60%
- Payforit: Between 45% and 89%

Notes

[1] Mobile Purchasing with Payforit (http://www.mxtelecom.com/uk/payforit) (http://www.youtube.com/watch?v=Rwv-antBgSw) (http://wirelessweek.com/Articles/2010/09/Business-Universal-Mobile-Payments-Fragmented-App-Market-Mobile-Content/)

[2] Texting in your campaign donation? (http://www.politico.com/news/stories/0910/42314.html)

[3] Payout rates from one of the major billing aggregator, Bango (http://bango.com/mobilebilling/payment_network.aspx)

MOL AccessPortal

MOL AccessPortal Berhad

Type	E-commerce
Industry	E-commerce
Founded	2000
Headquarters	Malaysia
Key people	Ganesh Kumar Bangah [1]
Website	http://www.mol.com/ [2]

MOL AccessPortal is a payment service providers for games, content and services in Asia.

History

MOL AccessPortal Berhad was incorporated in Malaysia under the Companies Act, 1965 on 9 February 2000 as a private limited company under the name of Superior World Sdn Bhd. It assumed its present name on 8 July 2000 and was converted into a public limited company on 29 April 2002. MOL was officially listed on the MESDAQ Market of Bursa Malaysia Securities Berhad under the Technology Sector on 22 December 2003. It was subsequently privatized by Tan Sri Vincent Tan, Chairman & CEO of Berjaya Corporation, one of the largest conglomerates in Malaysia with an annual turnover of USD3.8 billion in February 2008.

MOL is a MSC Malaysia Status Company that develops and operates payment systems.[1] It leverages on a network of over 540,000 physical and virtual payment channels across more than 75 countries worldwide to operate its key payment products.[2] MOL processes over 4,500,000 transactions per month with a volume of more than USD200 Million a year.

MOL is recognized as one of the Asia Pacific's fastest growing technology companies in the Deloitte Technology Fast 500 Asia Pacific Awards for 2005 & 2006,[3] has won a Merit Award for the Best of E-Commerce Applications in MSC Asia Pacific ICT Awards [4] and is a Microsoft Certified Partner.

Key Products & Services

- MOLePoints- Online Micropayment System For Content and Services
- MOLeTopUp - Electronic Prepaid Distribution Infrastructure
- MOL Freedom – A Multi-Application Prepaid Payment Card [5]
- MOL GamesHive - An Online Game Payment Aggregator [6]

MOLePoints

MOLePoints is the All-In-One online currency for games, content & services. It leverages on MOL AccessPortal's 540,000 physical and virtual payment channels across more than 75 countries worldwide.

References

[1] "Going regional". (http://findarticles.com/p/articles/mi_qn6207/is_20060101/ai_n24909857)

[2] (http://china.mol.com/molap_nr_08index.aspx.)

[3] Deloitte (http://www.deloitte.com/.../content/Tech%20Fast%20500%20Asia%20Pacific%202005%20ranking%20only(1).pdf.)

[4] MSC Asia Pacific (http://www.mscapicta.com.my/images/apicta/page12.pdf)

[5] http://www.lowyat.net/v2/latest/mol-accessportal-launches-mol-freedom-mastercard.html "MOL launches Freedom Mastercard"2007-06-18.

[6] "MOL AccessPortal Signs Astonia 3" (http://www.gamershell.com/news_11258.html) 2004-01-19.

External links

- http://www.mol.com/v2/default.aspx
- http://star-techcentral.com/tech/story.asp?file=/2007/9/20/technology/20070920164928&sec=technology
- http://announcements.bursamalaysia.com/EDMS/AnnWeb.nsf/dfDisplayForm?Openform&Count=-1& form=dfDisplayForm&viewname=LsvAnnsAll&category=MOL+ACCESSPORTAL+BERHAD
- http://www.malaysianwireless.com/2008/11/mol-zone-mobile-payment-application.html
- http://www.computerwire.com/companies/company/?pid=952E537B-2CD5-495F-8906-F70EC13C2F14
- http://www.gamershell.com/news_11258.html
- http://findarticles.com/p/articles/mi_qn6207/is_20060101/ai_n24909857
- http://www.bernama.com/kpdnhep/news.php?id=246800&lang=en
- http://www.snapcard.com/en_gb/news/snap.pdf
- http://ulu_langat.idesa.net.my/index_files/Page2158.htm
- http://www.nst.com.my/Current_News/techNu/Monday/Newsfront/20080720102619/Article/index_html
- http://www.mscmalaysia.my/main_art.php?CategoryID=2&parentID=12073017112685& artID=12081683969953&p_artID=120
- http://www.maybank2u.com.my/myzone/entertainment/mol.html
- http://www.moneycontrol.com/india/news/pressmarket/goldstonetechnologiessoftwaretechnology/ goldstonetechnologiestolaunchiptvservicesmalaysia/market/stocks/article/313150
- http://www.contentasia.tv/feature.php?newsid=3444
- http://biz.thestar.com.my/news/story.asp?file=/2007/9/21/business/18950262&sec=business
- http://www.domain-b.com/industry/Entertainment/20071114_launch.html
- http://www.malaysianwireless.com/2008/05/mol-wings.html

Mondex

Mondex is a smart card electronic cash system which was originally developed by National Westminster Bank in the United Kingdom and subsequently sold to MasterCard International. Mondex launched in a number of markets during the 1990s, expanding from an original trial in Swindon, UK to Hong Kong, Guelph, and New York [1]. It was also trialled on several British university campuses from the late 1990s, including the University of Edinburgh, University of Exeter (between 1997 and 2001), University of York, University of Nottingham, Aston University and Sheffield Hallam University.

Mondex's logo.

The Z notation was used to prove security properties about Mondex, allowing it to achieve ITSEC level E6, ITSEC's highest granted security-level classification.[1] [2]

References

[1] Susan Stepney, David Cooper, and Jim Woodcock, *An Electronic Purse: Specification, Refinement, and Proof* (http://www-users.cs.york. ac.uk/~susan/bib/ss/z/prg126.pdf). Technical Monograph PRG-126 (http://web.comlab.ox.ac.uk/oucl/publications/monos/prg-126. html), Programming Research Group, Oxford University, UK, 2000.

[2] Jim Woodcock, Susan Stepney, David Cooper, John Clark, and Jeremy Jacob, The certification of the Mondex electronic purse to ITSEC Level E6 (http://dx.doi.org/10.1007/s00165-007-0060-5), *Formal Aspects of Computing*, Volume 20, Number 1, pages 5–19, January 2008.

External links

- Mondex.org website (http://www.mondex.org/) dedicated to saving the history of the Mondex card program
- Mondex.com website (http://www.mondex.com/)

Money order

A **money order** is a payment order for a pre-specified amount of money. Because it is required that the funds be prepaid for the amount shown on it, it is a more trusted method of payment than a personal check. The U.S. Postal Service issues money orders for a small charge at any location.

postal money order: Duchy of Brunswick, 1867

History of money orders

The money order system was established by a private firm in Great Britain in 1792, and was expensive and not very successful. In approximately 1836, it was sold to another private firm which lowered the fees, which therefore significantly increased the popularity and usage of the system. The Post Office noted the success and profitability, and it took over the system in 1838. Fees were further reduced and usage increased further, making the money order system reasonably profitable. The only draw-back was the need to send an advance to the paying Post Office before payment could be tendered to the recipient of the order. This drawback was likely the primary incentive for establishment of the Postal Order System on 1 January 1881.[1]

Using money orders

A money order is purchased for the amount desired. In this way it is similar to a certified cheque. The main difference is that money orders are usually limited in maximum face value to some specified figure (for example, the United States Postal Service limits domestic postal money orders to US $1,000.00 as of July 2008) while certified checks are not. Money orders typically consist of two portions: the negotiable check for remittance to the payee, and a receipt or stub that the customer retains for his/her records. The amount is printed by machine or checkwriter on both portions, and similar documentation, either as a third hard copy or in electronic form and retained at the issuer and agent locations.

Money orders were originally issued by the U.S. Postal Service as an alternative to sending cash through the postal system for those who did not have current accounts. They were later offered by many more vendors than just the postal service as a means to pay bills and send money internationally where there were not reliable banking or postal systems. Companies that now offer money orders include 7-11, QuikTrip, Cumberland Farms, Safeway, Western Union, MoneyGram, CVS, and Wal-Mart.

Obtaining a Money order in the US is simple, as they can be purchased with any form of money at any Post Office, and they are sold at many other locations as well.[2]

Drawbacks of money orders

Money orders have limited acceptance in the insurance and brokerage industry because of concerns over money laundering. Because of provisions within the USA PATRIOT Act and the Bank Secrecy Act, money orders have far more regulatory processing requirements than personal checks, cashier's checks, or certified checks. Thus, most brokerage firms, insurance firms, and even many banks will not accept them as payment.

As of 2006, there has been a significant increase in counterfeit postal money orders. Often, such a counterfeit will be sent to an unwitting victim who is instructed, on some pretext, to deposit it at his/her bank and return some of the funds. The victim is more likely to trust an "official" money order than a regular check, for the reasons given above. However, because money orders are paid through the postal service rather than the usual check clearing system, they often take longer to "bounce" than an ordinary check. When this finally occurs it is charged back to the victim, who may already have sent back the funds, for which he or she must take the loss. For this reason banks are now applying increased security to incoming money orders, and are becoming more reluctant to accept them. A safer approach is to cash them at a post office. In this case, the authenticity of the item is immediately determined, and if deemed good, the holder is paid and absolved of further responsibility for the funds.

Money orders around the world

India

In India, a money order is a service provided by the Indian Postal Service. A payer who wants to send money to a payee pays the amount and a small commission at a post office and receives a receipt for the same. The amount is then delivered as cash to the payee after a few days by a postal employee, at the address specified by the payer. A receipt from the payee is collected and delivered back to the payer at his address. This is more reliable and safer than sending cash in the mail.

It is commonly used for transferring funds to a payee who is in a remote, rural area, where banks may not be conveniently accessible or where many people may not use a bank account at all. Money orders are the most economical way of sending money in India for small amounts.[3]

United States

In the United States, money orders are typically sold by third parties such as the United States Postal Service, grocery stores, and convenience stores. Some financial service companies such as banks and credit unions may not charge for money orders to their clients. Money orders remain a trusted financial instrument. In 2005, 889 million money orders were purchased in the United States for a gross transaction volume of $145 billion. (source: Federal Reserve). However, just because a particular business can issue a money order does not necessarily mean that they will cash them.

Postal Money Orders (PMOs) are generally regarded as one of the most difficult financial documents to counterfeit.

- Watermarks. Telltale watermark when held up to the light should reveal images of Benjamin Franklin, repeated on the left side (top to bottom).
- Dark security strip running alongside the watermark (top to bottom), just to the right. If held to the light, a microfiber strip will show tiny letters "USPS" along its length, facing backward and forward.
- Rainbow of inked patterns and tones.
- PMOs are printed on crisp, clean, textured paper stock.
- Maximum value of $1000 for domestic (US) postal money orders, and $700 for International Postal Money Orders.
- Denominations appear in two locations. If the denomination amounts are discolored, that indicates that they have been erased.
- Ultraviolet features include the above mentioned micro-fiber strip that glows red, and the PMO number on the reverse side and the bottom which will also appear red under UV light.

Counterfeiting

Due to the increased public awareness of fraudulent US Postal Money Orders, counterfeiters are using these US Postal and other companies' (see above) money orders to dupe their victims. By obtaining their "mark's" postal zip code, they will draft bogus money orders based on whichever franchises will most likely be in their victim's home area as the familiarity of the store's name offers a sense of security.

Furthermore, money orders are subject to erasing the name and writing in somebody else's name. Money order fraud is specifically not reimbursed by Western Union and the victim is required to go through local police to attempt to recover lost funds. In response, the perpetrator who cashed the money order can simply claim "identity theft" to the investigating detective. Money orders for this purpose can be obtained from places like rent drop boxes.

International money orders

An international money order is very similar in many aspects to a regular money order except that it can be used to make payments abroad. With it, a buyer can easily pay a seller for goods or services if he or she resides in another country. International money orders are often issued by a buyer's bank and bought in the currency that the seller accepts. International money orders are thought to be safer than sending currency through the post because there are various forms of identification required to cash an international money order, often including a signature and a form of photo identification.

When purchasing an international money order, it is important to ensure that the specific type of money order is acceptable in the destination country. Several countries are very strict that the money order be on **pink and yellow paper** and have the words "**international postal money order.**" In particular, the Japan Post (one of the largest banking institutions in the world) requires these features. Most other countries have taken this as a standard when there is any doubt of a document's authenticity.

Alternatives to money orders

In the last decade a number of electronic alternatives to money orders have emerged and have, in some cases, supplanted money orders as the preferred cash transmission method. Many of these alternatives use the ubiquitous Visa/MasterCard payment systems to settle transactions. In Japan, the konbini system enables cash to cash transfers and is available at many of the thousands of convenience stores located in the country. In Italy the PostePay system offered through the Italian post office. In Ireland, 3V is offered through mobile top-up locations, and in the United States, PaidByCash is offered at 60,000 grocery and convenience stores. In the United Kingdom a number of credit card providers have started to provide pre-paid credit cards. These cards can be "topped-up" at any location that uses the Pay-Point system and also at the Post Office for the Post Office card. PayPal has their own branded pre-paid card which can be "topped-up" using a PayPal account, Pay-Points and at the Post Office.

References

[1] Post Office Money Order: Bootle, 1841 (http://www.victorianweb.org/history/letters/bootle.html)

[2] Where to get money orders in the US (http://www.factopo.com/info.php?f=where-to-get-money-order)

[3] Money Order - procedure for sending, charges in India (http://www.money-transfer.in/moneyorder.html)

MoneyGram

MoneyGram International, Inc.

Type	Public (NYSE: MGI [1]
Industry	Aiding products = Financial services
Founded	1940
Headquarters	Dallas, Texas
Website	MoneyGram [2]

MoneyGram International, Inc. (NYSE: MGI [1]) is a US-based, Global Money transfer company, headquartered in Dallas, Texas. It has Global Operations Centers in Saint Louis Park, Minnesota and Brooklyn Center, Minnesota, Global Call Center Operations in Denver, Colorado and regional and local offices around the world.

MoneyGram's business is divided into two categories: Global Fund Transfer and Financial Paper Products. The company offers its services to consumers and businesses through a network of agents and financial institution customers.

Company History

MoneyGram International is a result of two business merging. One company, Minneapolis-based Travelers Express Co. Inc. was founded in 1940 and became the world's largest processor of money orders and a major player in the electronic payments industry. The other company that helped create MoneyGram International was Denver-based Integrated Payment Systems Inc., which entered the international money transfer business in 1988. Travelers Express and MoneyGram Payment Systems joined forces in 1998 when Travelers Express' parent, Viad Corp., purchased MoneyGram Payment Systems. In 2004 Viad spun off the Travelers/MoneyGram group into a new publicly traded company - MoneyGram International Inc.

Headquarters

In September 2010, MoneyGram announced that it will move its global headquarters to the city of Dallas, Texas, although Minneapolis, Minnesota will continue to be the hub for its Global Operations and Information Technology Centers of Excellence, and Denver, Colorado will continue to host its Call Center Operations.[1] The company officially moved its headquarters as of Nov. 1, 2010

Company Facts

- The company, which was founded in Minneapolis as Travelers Express, started as a small money order operation in 1940
- MoneyGram is the second largest money transfer business in the world.
- The company first passed the billion dollar mark in revenue in 2006
- MoneyGram has nearly 210,000 agent locations in more than 190 countries and territories
- MoneyGram has more than twice the locations of McDonald's, Starbucks, Subway and Walmart combined
- More than $18 billion was sent around the world in 2009 using MoneyGram money transfer services
- MoneyGram has as 2,600 employees around the world
- The company's call center and website supports 23 languages

- MoneyGram's money transfer business generated growth in revenue and transaction volume last year and the global agent network increased by 8 percent
- In 2009, the company made revenues of $1.17 billion; Adjusted EBITDA of $247,415
- The company is 82% owned by THL (53%) and Goldman Sachs (29%)

Fraud Prevention

Money transfer systems are many times used by criminals to commit fraud. The company recommends to never send money to someone you don't know.

Some known consumer scams that use money transfer as a vehicle to collect money include:

- Relative in need – sending money to someone who says they are in an emergency and need a significant amount of cash

- Buying a vehicle online – sending a down payment for a car found on an online site

- Romance – sending money to someone met via a romance ad either online or in the paper

- Winning a lottery or sweepstakes – sending a fee in order to collect winnings from an international lottery or sweepstakes

MoneyGram works with local, federal and international authorities to identify and arrest individuals who commit fraud using its money transfer system.

In a press release on July 12, 2009, MoneyGram announced it implemeted a state-of-the-art anti-fraud technology to help identify and stop fraudulent transactions.

"MoneyGram takes fraud very seriously," said Dennis Wildsmith, vice president of transaction services and fraud prevention at MoneyGram. "We have established systems and processes to enhance safe and reliable money transfers, train our agents and employees about fraud, and to educate consumers on ways to safeguard their money. These new technologies are one more step in creating a world-class consumer anti-fraud program."

Global Funds Transfer

- MoneyGram Money Transfer:

Global money transfer service allows consumers to send and receive money worldwide, primarily through a global network of third-party agents that use our money transfer systems. In addition to person-to-person (also known as cash-to-cash), customers have alternatives in money transfer delivery channels such as direct-to-account, ATMs and kiosks for deposit and cash receive, cash-to-a mobile phone and cash-to-card.

- MoneyGram Bill Payments Services:

Bill Payments Services allow consumers to make urgent payments or pay routine bills through our network to certain creditors ("billers"). We maintain relationships with billers in key industries which include the credit card, mortgage, auto finance, telecommunications, corrections, satellite, prepaid card and collections industries. Bill payment services also enable consumers to load and reload prepaid debit cards.

- PropertyBridge:

The Property Bridge Payments Platform offers an integrated, flexible infrastructure that makes it easy for property managers to build out secure, friendly online payments solutions.

Financial Paper Products

- Money Order:

MoneyGram is the second largest money order supplier. Money orders can be purchased at a vast nationwide network of retail and financial institution locations across the United States.

- Official Checks:

MoneyGram offers Official Check Outsource Services which are available to financial institutions in the United States. Official checks are used by consumers where a payee requires a check drawn on a bank and by financial institutions to pay their own obligations.

References

[1] " MoneyGram International Moves Global Corporate Headquarters to Dallas (http://www.businesswire.com/news/home/20100923005281/en/MoneyGram-International-Moves-Global-Corporate-Headquarters-Dallas)." *Businesswire.com*. September 23, 2010. Retrieved on November 4, 2010.

External links

- Official Site (http://www.moneygram.com)
- Official Facebook Page (https://www.facebook.com/moneygram)

Mon€o

WARNING: Article could not be rendered - ouputting plain text.

Potential causes of the problem are: (a) a bug in the pdf-writer software (b) problematic Mediawiki markup (c) table is too wide

Moneo, sometimes branded as mon€o, is an electronic purse system available on FranceFrench bank cards to allow small purchases to be made without cash.The system is aimed at small retailers such as bakeries and cafés and intended for purchases of less than €30. The card is inserted into a handheld Moneo reader by the merchant who enters the transaction amount for the customer. The customer then confirms the purchase by pushing a button on the keypad; the exact amount is debited from the card within a few seconds. As well as the multipurpose bank card version, anonymous cards (also smart cards) are available for the use of people without bank accounts, such as children and tourists. Supported by all French banks, Moneo was tested in Brittany in 2002, and from 2004 Moneo has been added to most French bank cards. External links(French) The official Moneo site

Mopay

mopay Inc.

Industry	Telecommunications Mobile communications Payments
Founded	2000 (as MindMatics)
Headquarters	Palo Alto, California, USA
Products	Electronic payments Mobile Payments
Employees	100
Parent	MindMatics AG
Website	mopay-inc.com [1]

mopay is an internationally leading **mobile payment platform** [1] represented in the USA by mopay Inc. mopay and mopay Inc. are registered trademarks of MindMatics Group, a Germany based mobile marketing expert.

History

The brand mopay was first registered in Germany in 2003 by MindMatics AG. Offering a single payments interface between online merchants and their respective end-customers, mopay from the very beginning was designed as international mobile payment platform.

In 2009 mopay became the central product of the mobile payment division of MindMatics Group. In early 2010 mopay Inc. was founded as the North American branch of mopay. [2]

Product

The international mobile payment platform mopay is addressing vendors of virtual goods and digital goods. It offers a fast and easy billing option for small online purchases through mobile operators accounts. mopay opens up a unique new customer base: unbanked and underbanked individuals who do not have access to credit cards or bank accounts.

By utilizing mobile devices mopay is the most widespread payment option available worldwide. [3] [4] [5] Although mobile payment methods in general still have higher transaction costs than other electronic payments recent studies show that conversion rates improve dramatically with mobile payments. [6]

mopay connects to mobile operators in over 75 countries and thus has a technical reach of 3.3 billion people. [7] .

References

[1] "company profile on Crunchbase" (http://www.crunchbase.com/company/mopay). .

[2] "mopay expands to the U.S." (http://www.insidefacebook.com/2010/02/16/
european-mobile-payments-company-mopay-expands-to-the-united-states). Inside Facebook. 16 February 2010. .

[3] "credit card penetration in selected countries" (http://www.ita.doc.gov/td/finance/publications/creditcards.pdf). .

[4] "mobile network operators of the Americas" (http://en.wikipedia.org/wiki/List_of_mobile_network_operators_of_the_Americas). .

[5] "mopay coverage claim" (http://www.mopay.com/en/mobile-payment/what-is-mobile-payment). .

[6] "mopay conversion rates claim" (http://www.mopay.com/en/mobile-payment/what-is-mobile-payment). .

[7] "mopay coverage list" (http://www.mopay.com/en). .

External links

- mopay Homepage (http://www.mopay-inc.com/)
- mopay demo (http://www.mopay-inc.com/fileadmin/mopay_demo.html)

More

- Mobile payments
- Mobile commerce service provider
- Smscoin
- Fortumo
- Zong mobile payments

MPP Global Solutions

MPP Global Solutions

Type	Private
Industry	Financial Services
Founded	2000
Headquarters	United Kingdom
Products	Payment Gateway, Payment Service Provider
Website	www.mppglobal.com [1]

MPP Global Solutions Ltd are a UK based eCommerce payment solutions provider. They are one of the UK's largest providers of eCommerce payment gateways to businesses to facilitate the transfer of consumer payments.

History

The company was formed in 2000. Paul Johnson CEO has been featured by BBC Radio Manchester discussing the subject of eCommerce[1]

MPP specialise in the Media and Entertainment industries having provided the payment solution for Sky's Player[2] [3] as well as the hotly debated paywall for The Times online site.[4] MPP are also in the process of developing a payment module in conjunction with Vision+Media for the YouView platform [5] [6] [7] and have been selected as the payment provider for the woomi platform across Samsung Connected TV's across the UK and Europe.[8]

Awards

Best eCommerce Tech Company- Northern Tech Awards 2011[9]

References

[1] "BBC Radio Manchester". 13 March 2010.

[2] "TV micropayments" (http://www.nma.co.uk/features/tv-micropayments/3023761.article). *New Media Age.* .

[3] "MPP powered one-click payment transaction with SkyPlayer" (http://kkboss.com/mpp-powered-one-click-payment-transaction-with-skyplayer/). *KKBOSS.* .

[4] "Juggling the Times Paywall Numbers" (http://www.guardian.co.uk/media/organgrinder/2011/mar/29/paywalls-news-corporation). *Guardian.co.uk.* .

[5] "MPP to develop internet TV payment system" (http://menmedia.co.uk/manchestereveningnews/news/business/innovation/s/1420323_mpp-to-develop-internet-tv-payment-system). *Manchester Evening News.* . Retrieved 11 May 2011.

[6] "MPP to Develop YouView Payment Module" (http://www.appmarket.tv/news/1176-mpp-to-develop-youview-payment-module-.html). *App Market TV.* . Retrieved 12 May 2011.

[7] "Vision+Media Selects MPP To Develop YouView Payment Module" (http://sports.tmcnet.com/news/2011/05/10/5498563.htm). *Sports Techy.* .

[8] "MPP to Monetise woomi Platform on Samsung Connected-TV" (http://www.benzinga.com/press-releases/11/05/p1054729/mpp-to-monetise-woomi-platform-on-samsung-connected-tv). *Benziga.* .

[9] "Advanced Television Online" (http://www.advanced-television.com/index.php/2011/03/24/mpp-global-solutions-wins-northern-tech-award/). *MPP Global Solutions wins Northern Tech Award.* .

External links

- Official Site (http://www.mppglobal.com)
- Youtube Page (http://www.youtube.com/mppglobal)
- Twitter (http://www.twitter.com/mppglobal)

NACHA – The Electronic Payments Association

WARNING: Article could not be rendered - ouputting plain text.

Potential causes of the problem are: (a) a bug in the pdf-writer software (b) problematic Mediawiki markup (c) table is too wide

NACHA – The Electronic Payments Association manages the development, administration, and governance of the Automated Clearing HouseACH Network, the backbone for the electronic movement of money and data in the United States. It is funded by the financial institutions it governs. The ACH Network serves as a network for direct consumer, business, and government payments, and annually facilitates billions of payments such as Direct Deposit and Direct Payment. Utilized by all types of financial institutions, the ACH Network is governed by the NACHA Operating Rules, a set of fair and equitable rules that guide risk management and create certainty for all participants. As a not-for-profit association, NACHA represents nearly 11,000 financial institutions via 17 regional payments associations and direct membership. Through its industry councils and forums, NACHA brings together payments system stakeholders to enable innovation that strengthens the industry with creative payment solutions. External links www.nacha.org - Official site www.electronicpayments.org www.payitgreen.org

National Payments Corporation of India

National Payments Corporation of India

Type	Public Company
Industry	Finance
Founded	2008
Headquarters	Mumbai, Maharashtra, India[1]
Key people	AP Hota, Managing Director & CEO[2]
Products	National Financial Switch (NFS), Interbank Mobile Payment Service (IMPS), RuPay, Cheque Truncation System (CTS), Aadhaar Enabled Payment System (AEPS), ACH
Website	Official site [3]

Reserve Bank of India, after setting up of the Board for Payment and Settlement Systems in 2005, released a vision document incorporating a proposal to set up an umbrella institution for all the RETAIL PAYMENT SYSTEMS in the country. The core objective was to consolidate and integrate the multiple systems with varying service levels into nation-wide uniform and standard business process for all retail payment systems. The other objective was to facilitate an affordable payment mechanism to benefit the common man across the country and help financial inclusion.

IBA's untiring efforts during the last three years helped turning this vision a reality. National Payments Corporation of India (NPCI) was incorporated in December 2008 and the Certificate of Commencement of Business was issued in April 2009. It has been incorporated as a Section 25 company under Companies Act and is aimed to operate for the benefit of all the member banks and their customers. The authorized capital has been pegged at ₹ 300 crore (US$66.6 million) and paid up capital is ₹ 60 crore (US$13.32 million) so that the company can create infrastructure of large dimension and operate on high volume resulting payment services at fraction of the present cost structure.

NPCI would function as a hub in all electronic retail payment systems which is ever growing in terms of varieties of products, delivery channels, number of service providers and diverse Technology solutions.

NPCI has a mandate to create a domestic card scheme.The Brand name finalised for the same is RuPay. This scheme would be similar to domestic card schemes one of which is China UnionPay in China. China UnionPay (CUP) was a national agenda for a few years by mandating all domestic transactions to be routed through the national card system. Now China UnionPay cards are accepted in 26 countries. The card base is 1.8 billion. Bulk of the payments are made in China by CUP cards. Although it may not be possible to mandate such transaction flow in India, a domestic card is not a distant dream if all banks work in a co-operative framework. NPCI can reach the scale of China UnionPay by excelling in service quality and by placing the next generation products and services.

Vocalink in UK provides another benchmark for NPCI. Vocalink facilitates money transfer from any bank account to any other bank account in UK on a real time 24 x 7 basis. This implies that the experience of RTGS has been extended to retail payment segment. Now that more than 60,000 bank branches in the country are covered under Core Banking Solution, this is very much a feasible proposition in India and would be known as India MoneyLine.

NPCI would also benchmark against Bankserv in South Africa and KFTC in South Korea in terms of operational efficiency, reach across the country and range of products and services.

Organisation

Presently, there are ten core promoter banks (State Bank of India, Punjab National Bank, Canara Bank, Bank of Baroda, Union bank of India, Bank of India, ICICI Bank, HDFC Bank, Citibank and HSBC). The Board consists of Shri N. R. Narayana Murthy, Chairman, Infosys Technologies Ltd as the Chairman, Nominee from Reserve Bank of India, Nominees from ten core promoter banks and Shri A.P.Hota, Managing Director and Chief Executive Officer, NPCI. The Board for Regulation and Supervision of Payment and Settlement Systems (BPSS) at its meeting held on September 24, 2009 has approved in principle to issue authorisation to NPCI for operating various retail payment systems in the country and granted Certificate of Authorisation for operation of National Financial Switch (NFS) ATM Network with effect from 15 October 2009. NPCI has deputed its officials to IDRBT Hyderabad and NPCI has taken over NFS operations from 14 December 2009. Membership regulations and rules are being framed for enrolling all banks in the country as members so that when the nation-wide payment systems are launched, all would get included on a standardised platform.

A Technical Advisory Committee has also been constituted with two professors of IIT, Mumbai. Prof. N.L.Sarda is the Chairman and Prof. G.Sivakumar is the Co-Chairman of the Technical Advisory Committee. Members in this committees are drawn from banks at the level of Deputy General Manager/ Asst. General Manager.

Services

The corporation service portfolio now and in the future include:

- National Financial Switch(NFS) which connects 76000 ATMs of 55 member banks
- Interbank Mobile Payment Service (IMPS) provided to 20 member banks which have registered more than 10 million customers
- Aadhaar-Enabled Payment System (AEPS) - A payment system for UID based transactions.
- RuPay - Domestic Card Scheme
- Cheque Truncation System (CTS)
- National ACH Service

References

[1] "National Payments Corporation of India" (http://www.npci.org.in/contactus.aspx). Npci.org.in. . Retrieved 2011-03-16.
[2] "Mobile money transfer fee cut to 10p" (http://www.indianexpress.com/news/mobile-money-transfer-fee-cut-to-10p/762456/). Indianexpress.com. . Retrieved 2011-03-16.

External links

- Official site (http://www.npci.org.in/home.aspx)
- CTCircular (http://www.npci.org.in/CTCircular.aspx)

Negotiable instrument

A **negotiable instrument** is a document guaranteeing the payment of a specific amount of money, either on demand, or at a set time. According to the Negotiable Instruments Act, 1881 in India there are just three types of negotiable instruments i.e., promissory note, bill of exchange and cheque.Cheque also includes Demand Draft.

More specifically, it is a document contemplated by a contract, which (1) warrants the payment of money, the promise of or order for conveyance of which is unconditional; (2) specifies or describes the payee, who is designated on and memorialized by the instrument; and (3) is capable of change through transfer by valid negotiation of the instrument.

As payment of money is promised subsequently, the instrument itself can be used by the holder in due course as a store of value; although, instruments can be transferred for amounts in contractual exchange that are less than the instrument's face value (known as "discounting"). Under United States law, Article 3 of the Uniform Commercial Code as enacted in the applicable State law governs the use of negotiable instruments, except banknotes ("Federal Reserve Notes", aka "paper dollars").

Negotiable instruments distinguished from contracts

A negotiable instrument can serve to convey value constituting at least part of the performance of a contract, albeit perhaps not obvious in contract formation, in terms inherent in and arising from the requisite offer and acceptance and conveyance of consideration. The underlying contract contemplates the right to hold the instrument as, and to negotiate the instrument to, a *holder in due course*, the payment on which is at least part of the performance of the contract to which the negotiable instrument is linked. The instrument, memorializing (1) the power to demand payment; and, (2) the right to be paid, can move, for example, in the instance of a 'bearer instrument', wherein the possession of the document itself attributes and ascribes the right to payment. Certain exceptions exist, such as instances of loss or theft of the instrument, wherein the possessor of the note may be a holder, but not necessarily a holder in due course. Negotiation requires a valid *endorsement* of the negotiable instrument. The consideration constituted by a negotiable instrument is cognizable as the value given up to acquire it (benefit) and the consequent loss of value (detriment) to the prior holder; thus, no separate consideration is required to support an accompanying contract assignment. The instrument itself is understood as memorializing the right for, and power to demand, payment, and an obligation for payment evidenced by the instrument itself with possession as a holder in due course being the touchstone for the right to, and power to demand, payment. In some instances, the negotiable instrument can serve as the writing memorializing a contract, thus satisfying any applicable Statute of Frauds as to that contract.

The *holder in due course*

The. rights of a holder in due course of a negotiable instrument are qualitatively, as matters of law, superior to those provided by ordinary species of contracts:

- The rights to payment are not subject to set-off, and do not rely on the validity of the underlying contract giving rise to the debt (for example if a cheque was drawn for payment for goods delivered but defective, the drawer is still liable on the cheque)

- No notice need be given to any party liable on the instrument for transfer of the rights under the instrument by negotiation. However, payment by the party liable to the person previously entitled to enforce the instrument "counts" as payment on the note until adequate notice has been received by the liable party that a different party is to receive payments from then on. [U.C.C. §3-602(b)]

- Transfer free of equities—the holder in due course can hold better title than the party he obtains it from (as in the instance of negotiation of the instrument from a mere holder to a holder in due course)

Negotiation often enables the transferee to become the party to the contract through a contract assignment (provided for explicitly or by operation of law) and to enforce the contract in the transferee-assignee's own name. Negotiation can be effected by indorsement and delivery (order instruments), or by delivery alone (bearer instruments). In addition, the rights and obligations accruing to the transferee can be affected by the *rule of derivative title*, which does not allow a property owner to transfer rights in a piece of property greater than his own.

History

Common prototypes of bills of exchanges and promissory notes originated in China. Here, in the 8th century during the reign of the Tang Dynasty they used special instruments called *feitsyan* for the safe transfer of money over long distances.[1] Later such document for money transfer used by Arab merchants, who had used the prototypes of bills of exchange – suftadja and hawala in 10–13th centuries, then such prototypes had used by Italian merchants in the 12th century. In Italy in 13–15th centuries bill of exchange and promissory note obtain their main features and further phases of its development have been associated with France (16–18th centuries, where the endorsement had appeared) and Germany (19th century, formalization of Exchange Law). In England (and later in the U.S.) Exchange Law was different from continental Europe because of different legal systems.

Classes

Promissory notes and bills of exchange are two primary types of negotiable instruments.

Promissory note

A negotiable promissory note is an unconditional promise in writing made by one person to another, signed by the maker, engaging to pay on demand to the *payee*, or at fixed or determinable future time, certain in money, to order or to bearer. (see Sec.194) Bank note is frequently referred to as a promissory note, a promissory note made by a bank and payable to bearer on demand.

Bill of exchange

A bill of exchange or "draft" is a written order by the *drawer* to the *drawee* to pay money to the *payee*. A common type of bill of exchange is the cheque (*check* in American English), defined as a bill of exchange drawn on a banker and payable on demand. Bills of exchange are used primarily in international trade, and are written orders by one person to his bank to pay the bearer a specific sum on a specific date. Prior to the advent of paper currency, bills of exchange were a common means of exchange. They are not used as often today.

A bill of exchange is an unconditional order in writing addressed by one person to another, signed by the person giving it, requiring the person to whom it is addressed to pay on demand or at fixed or determinable future time a sum certain in money to order or to bearer. (Sec.126)

Bill of exchange, 1933

It is essentially an order made by one person to another to pay money to a third person.

A bill of exchange requires in its inception three parties—the drawer, the drawee, and the payee.

The person who draws the bill is called the drawer. He gives the order to pay money to the third party. The party upon whom the bill is drawn is called the drawee. He is the person to whom the bill is addressed and who is ordered to pay. He becomes an acceptor when he indicates his willingness to pay the bill. (Sec.62) The party in whose favor the bill is drawn or is payable is called the payee.

The parties need not all be distinct persons. Thus, the drawer may draw on himself payable to his own order. (see Sec. 8)

A bill of exchange may be endorsed by the payee in favour of a third party, who may in turn endorse it to a fourth, and so on indefinitely. The "holder in due course" may claim the amount of the bill against the drawee and all previous endorsers, regardless of any counterclaims that may have disabled the previous payee or endorser from doing so. This is what is meant by saying that a bill is negotiable.

In some cases a bill is marked "not negotiable" − see crossing of cheques. In that case it can still be transferred to a third party, but the third party can have no better right than the transferor.

In the Commonwealth

In the commonwealth almost all jurisdictions have codified the law relating to negotiable instruments in a Bills of Exchange Act, e.g. Bills of Exchange Act 1882 in the UK, Bills of Exchange Act 1908 in New Zealand, The Negotiable Instrument Act 1881 in India and The Bills of Exchange Act 1914 in Mauritius. The Bills of Exchange Act:

1. defines a bill of exchange as: 'an unconditional order in writing, addressed by one person to another, signed by the person giving it, requiring the person to whom it is addressed to pay on demand, or at a fixed or determinable future time, a sum certain in money to or to the order of a specified person, or to bearer.
2. defines a cheque as: 'a bill of exchange drawn on a banker payable on demand'
3. defines a promissory note as: 'an unconditional promise in writing made by one person to another, signed by the maker, engaging to pay on demand, or at a fixed or determinable future time, a sum certain in money to or to the order of a specified person or to bearer.'

Additionally most commonwealth jurisdictions have separate Cheques Acts providing for additional protections for bankers collecting unendorsed or irregularly endorsed cheques, providing that cheques that are crossed and marked 'not negotiable' or similar are not transferable, and providing for electronic presentation of cheques in inter-bank cheque clearing systems.

The 1911 Encyclopædia Britannica Eleventh Edition has a comprehensive article on the Bill of Exchange, detailing its history and operation, as understood at the time of its publication.

In the United States

In the United States, Article 3 and Article 4 of the Uniform Commercial Code govern the issuance and transfer of negotiable instruments. The various State law enactments of Uniform Commercial Code §§3-104(a) through (d) set forth the legal definition of what is and what is not a *negotiable instrument*:

> **§ 3-104. NEGOTIABLE INSTRUMENT. (a) Except as provided in subsections (c) and (d), "negotiable instrument" means an unconditional promise or order to pay a fixed amount of money, with or without interest or other charges described in the promise or order, if it:**
>
> **(1) is payable to bearer or to order at the time it is issued or first comes into possession of a holder;**
>
> **(2) is payable on demand or at a definite time; and**
>
> **(3) does not state any other undertaking or instruction by the person promising or ordering payment to do any act in addition to the payment of money, but the promise or order may contain**
>
> **(i) an undertaking or power to give, maintain, or protect collateral to secure payment,**
>
> **(ii) an authorization or power to the holder to confess judgment or realize on or dispose of collateral, or**
>
> **(iii) a waiver of the benefit of any law intended for the advantage or protection of an obligor.**
>
> **(b) "Instrument" means a negotiable instrument.**

(c) An order that meets all of the requirements of subsection (a), except paragraph (1), and otherwise falls within the definition of "check" in subsection (f) is a negotiable instrument and a check.

(d) A promise or order other than a check is not an instrument if, at the time it is issued or first comes into possession of a holder, it contains a conspicuous statement, however expressed, to the effect that the promise or order is not negotiable or is not an instrument governed by this Article.

Thus, for a writing to be a negotiable instrument under Article 3,[2] the following requirements must be met:

1. The promise or order to pay must be unconditional;
2. The payment must be a specific sum of money, although interest may be added to the sum;
3. The payment must be made on demand or at a definite time;
4. The instrument must not require the person promising payment to perform any act other than paying the money specified;
5. The instrument must be payable to bearer or to order.

The latter requirement is referred to as the "words of negotiability": a writing which does not contain the words "to the order of" (within the four corners of the instrument or in endorsement on the note or in allonge) or indicate that it is payable to the individual holding the contract document (analogous to the holder in due course) is not a negotiable instrument and is not governed by Article 3, even if it appears to have all of the other features of negotiability. The only exception is that if an instrument meets the definition of a cheque (a bill of exchange payable on demand and drawn on a bank) and is not payable to order (i.e. if it just reads "pay John Doe") then it is treated as a negotiable instrument.

Negotiation and endorsement

Persons other than the original obligor and obligee can become parties to a negotiable instrument. The most common manner in which this is done is by placing one's signature on the instrument ("endorsement"): if the person who signs does so with the intention of obtaining payment of the instrument or acquiring or transferring rights to the instrument, the signature is called an *endorsement*. There are five types of endorsements contemplated by the Code, covered in UCC Article 3, Sections 204–206 [3]:

- An endorsement which purports to transfer the instrument to a specified person is a *special endorsement*;
- An endorsement by the payee or holder which does not contain any additional notation (thus purporting to make the instrument payable to bearer) is an *endorsement in blank* or *blank endorsement;*
- An endorsement which purports to require that the funds be applied in a certain manner (e.g. "for deposit only", "for collection") is a *restrictive endorsement*; and,
- An endorsement purporting to disclaim retroactive liability is called a *qualified endorsement* (through the inscription of the words "without recourse" as part of the endorsement on the instrument or in allonge to the instrument).
- An endorsement purporting to add terms and conditions is called a *conditional endorsement* – for example, "Pay to the order of Amy, if she rakes my lawn next Thursday November 11th, 2007". The UCC states that these conditions may be disregarded.[3]

If a note or draft is negotiated to a person who acquires the instrument

1. in good faith;
2. for value;
3. without notice of any defenses to payment,

the transferee is a *holder in due course* and can enforce the instrument *without* being subject to defenses which the maker of the instrument would be able to assert against the original payee, except for certain *real defenses*. These real defenses include (1) forgery of the instrument; (2) fraud as to the nature of the instrument being signed; (3) alteration of the instrument; (4) incapacity of the signer to contract; (5) infancy of the signer; (6) duress; (7) discharge in bankruptcy; and, (8) the running of a statute of limitations as to the validity of the instrument.

The *holder-in-due-course rule* is a *rebuttable presumption* that makes the free transfer of negotiable instruments feasible in the modern economy. A person or entity purchasing an instrument in the ordinary course of business can reasonably expect that it will be paid when presented to, and not subject to dishonor by, the maker, without involving itself in a dispute between the maker and the person to whom the instrument was first issued (this can be contrasted to the lesser rights and obligations accruing to mere holders). Article 3 of the Uniform Commercial Code as enacted in a particular State's law contemplate *real defenses* available to purported holders in due course.

The foregoing is the theory and application presuming compliance with the relevant law. Practically, the obligor-payor on an instrument who feels he has been defrauded or otherwise unfairly dealt with by the payee may nonetheless refuse to pay even a holder in due course, requiring the latter to resort to litigation to recover on the instrument.

Usage

While bearer instruments are rarely created as such, a holder of commercial paper with the holder designated as payee can change the instrument to a bearer instrument by an endorsement. The proper holder simply signs the back of the instrument and the instrument becomes bearer paper, although in recent years, third party checks are not being honored by most banks unless the original payee has signed a notarized document stating such.

Alternatively, an individual or company may write a check payable to "Cash" or "Bearer" and create a bearer instrument. Great care should be taken with the security of the instrument, as it is legally almost as good as cash.

Exceptions

Under the Code, the following are not negotiable instruments, although the law governing obligations with respect to such items may be similar to or derived from the law applicable to negotiable instruments:

- Bills of lading and other documents of title, which are governed by Article 7 of the Code
- Deeds and other documents conveying interests in real estate, although a mortgage may secure a promissory note which is governed by Article 3
- IOUs
- Letters of credit, which are governed by Article 5 of the Code
- Securities, such as stocks and bonds, which are governed by Article 8 of the Code

References

[1] Moshenskyi, Sergii (2008). *History of the Weksel* (http://books.google.co.nz/books?id=8UBDndXgNIYC&lpg=PA51& ots=5R0Pl470rd&dq=feitsyan&pg=PA50#v=onepage&q=feitsyan&f=false). Xlibris Corporation. ISBN 978-1-4363-0693-5. .

[2] Uniform Commercial Code - Article 3 (http://www.law.cornell.edu/ucc/3/article3.htm#s3-104)

[3] Article 3, Sections 206(b) (http://www.law.cornell.edu/ucc/3/article3.htm#s3-206)

External links

- Bill of Exchange FAQ on TheBenche.com (https://www.thebenche.com/faq.php?faq=exchang1#faq_bill1)

Netbanx

NETBANX

Type	Public (LSE: NEO)
Industry	Financial Services
Founded	1996
Headquarters	Cambridge, United Kingdom
Products	Payment Gateway, Payment Service Provider
Website	www.netbanx.com [1]

Netbanx allows merchants and retailers to accept and process Web or call centre captured global payments via credit cards, debit cards, pre-paid cards, and a range of other payment types. The company is located in the United Kingdom and has been offering payment services since 1996. Netbanx is a division of global payments company Neovia Financial PLC

Customers

The company indicates it processes online and telephone financial transactions for a range of industries, including government bodies, universities, insurance companies, small and large businesses. Netbanx's customers include: the UK government's business registration agency, Companies House and Environment Agency, Cardsave, npower[1] .

Products and services

Netbanx falls into the payment gateway and payment service provider types of financial services solutions. The company offers card not present (CNP), online, and call centre/interactive voice response (IVR) payment processing. The company's processing service is 3-D Secure[2] and PCI compliant[3] .

The company supports payment through and partners with all the major payment brands and networks, including (in no particular order) Visa, Mastercard, Maestro, Visa Electron, Diners Club, American Express, Visa Debit, JCB, Lloyds TSB Cardnet, Barclaycard, RBS Streamline, HSBC, HBOS, Direct Debit, Giropay, ELV, iDEAL, Poli, DirectPay24, Ukash, Carte Bleue, Carta Si, and the Neteller e-wallet. These relationships allow the company to process payments from most major countries.

Netbanx primarily generates revenue by charging fees to merchants for each transaction that is processed through the company's system.

Netbanx supports companies that already have their own acquiring bank relationships. The company also offers acquiring & bureau services to expedite the process of a new company getting an acquiring relationship/merchant-ID so they can accept payments online.

Security

The company offers a range of fraud, identity and security features[4] to combat online payment and card fraud. These include PCI DSS, 3-D Secure, BIN and IP blocking, and address verification.

Notes

[1] Netbanx clients (http://www1.netbanx.com/content/en/company_our_clients.htm)

[2] Company Website: 3-D Secure (http://www1.netbanx.com/content/en/3d_secure.htm)

[3] Company Website: PCI compliance (http://www1.netbanx.com/content/en/pci_compliance.htm)

[4] Company Website: Fraud and Security (http://www1.netbanx.com/content/en/fraud_and_security_solutions.htm)

External links

- Company's Netbanx site (http://www.netbanx.com)
- Corporate (Neovia Financial) site (http://www.neovia.com)

NetSpend Corporation

NetSpend Corporation (NASDAQ: NTSP [1]**),** is an Austin, Texas-based company that provides processing and marketing services for private and proprietary MasterCard and Visa prepaid debit cards. Oak Investment Partners, is a major shareholder.

netSpend. *America's most trusted provider of Prepaid Card Accounts*

NetSpend Corporation's Logo along with Slogan

History

NetSpend was founded by Roy and Bertrand Sosa, two brothers who were teenagers when their family moved from Mexico to the United States in 1986. Twelve years later in 1998, they launched NetSpend from their one-bedroom apartment with an initial investment of $750. The Sosa brothers believed there was a large market that was left un-served by traditional banking and financial institutions. NetSpend's stated goal is to provide consumers who lack established credit or banking relationships with the security, flexibility and convenience typically associated with debit and credit cards.

Products

The NetSpend product line includes debit cards, cards can be reloaded with funds continuously, gift cards purchased in predenominated values that cannot be reloaded and travel cards that can be reloaded a limited number of times and provide travel protection benefits tied to the cardholder's purchases.

NetSpend, in conjunction with Financial Service Centers of America is the first prepaid card processor to offer a savings account feature with their cards. According to the Austin Business Journal [2] the interest rate on the savings account was increased from .75% to 3% in October 2006.

Recognition

- 2003 "Entrepreneurial Spirit Award" by Minorities in Business Magazine
- 2003 National Association of Small Business Investment Companies (NASBIC) "Portfolio Company of the Year" [3]
- 2004 Entrepreneurs of the Year Award [4] from Ernst & Young
- 2006 Winner, Innovation: The Architect of Ideas Award, Austin Chamber of Commerce [5]

See Also

Payoneer

References

External links

- NetSpend Prepaid Debit Card Website (http://www.netspend.com)
- NetSpend Gift Card Website (http://www.allaccessgift.com)
- NetSpend TravelCard Website (http://www.allaccesstravelmoney.com)
- Financial Consumer Agency of Canada Report on Prepaid Cards (http://www.fcac.gc.ca/eng/publications/other/prepaid/pdfs/prepaid-eng.pdf)

Network Commerce

Established in 1994 by former Microsoft executive Dwayne Walker (first as TechWave and then as ShopNow), Network Commerce Inc. was a technology infrastructure and services company. Network Commerce provided a comprehensive technology and online business services platform that included domain registration, web hosting, e-commerce and online marketing services. Network Commerce was headquartered in Seattle Washington.

Network Commerce started out building e-commerce storefronts including BuySoftware.com and TryAndBuy.com, but several acquisitions, including those of Go Software and Ubarter.com, pushed the company toward payment processing software and B2B electronic commerce. Its consumer flagship website operated under the ShopNow.com domain, and the company umbrella also included the popular entertainment-based website Speedyclick.com. Network Commerce later acquired the Vancouver-based domain registrar Registrars.com and morphed into a registry for domain names and an Internet hosting company. At its height, Network Commerce once employed more than 650 people and had a stock market value over a half a billion dollars[1]. Network Commerce sold shares to the public in September 1999 at $15 per share, and shares traded as high as $23.44 on November 30, 1999.

In January 2001, amid declining revenues, Network Commerce laid off 145 people, shut down its ShopNow.com consumer offering and closed its United Kingdom sales office. Stock price soon began to slump. Shares at this time hovered around $1.50[2], and were soon delisted from NASDAQ.

In March 2002, the company filed suit against Microsoft, accusing them of infringing a patent on a method for selling software, digital music and digital video over the Internet in their Windows Media Player[3].

On November 1, 2002, the company filed a petition for relief under Chapter 11. Shareholders entered into a class-action lawsuit against the company, alleging that they offered misleading offering materials and misrepresented its financial condition so they could attract additional funding. The suit was later dismissed[4].

Todd Terbeek, the former vice president of business development at Network Commerce, said the company was started with the goal of helping people conduct e-commerce. While he believes that was a noble goal, Terbeek acknowledged that the company may have sprinted too fast into new markets.

"It is always sad when something you had a role in starting ends like this," said Terbeek, one of the first 20 employees hired. "But most of all the company ended up being a victim of the times like a lot of other companies."

North American Bancard

North American Bancard

Type	Private
Industry	Financial Services
Founded	1992
Headquarters	Troy, Michigan
Owner(s)	Marc Gardner
Employees	400

North American Bancard (NAB) is a registered merchant services provider and independent sales organization (ISO) with VISA and MasterCard for HSBC Bank USA, N.A., Buffalo, NY and Wells Fargo Bank, N.A., Walnut Creek, CA.[1]

Founded in 1992 by CEO/President Marc Gardner, it is headquartered in Troy, Michigan. Its corporate office employs roughly 400 people. As a merchant services provider, NAB's payment solutions include: credit, debit, EBT, check conversion and guarantee, ATM, gift and loyalty cards, and online payment solutions. The company currently processes over $10 billion per year in electronic transactions for 100,000 merchants in all 50 states.[2]

North American Bancard is also a foundation member of Automation Alley.[3]

History

Since its inception in 1992, North American Bancard has grown into one of the top 50 largest merchant acquirers in the U.S.[4] In 2008, the Michigan Economic Development Corporation (MEDC) recommended the Michigan Economic Growth Authority (MEGA) approve a $21.5 million state tax credit to NAB.[5] The company moved its headquarters to a 105000-square-foot (9800 m^2) building on Stephenson Hwy in fall of 2009.[6]

New corporate headquarters

Awards and nominations

Marc Gardner received the Ernst & Young's Entrepreneur of the Year award in 2008.[7]

North American Bancard was featured a 2002 Green Sheets article[8] and in 2009, founder/CEO/President Marc Gardner was named to Green Sheet Quarterly's Who's Who.[9]

The Detroit Regional Chamber selected Gardner as a guest speaker at the 2009 Mackinac Policy Conference to discuss Michigan's economic future and Gardner's success as an entrepreneur.[10] [11] The panel also included Ari Emanuel, Dennis Archer Jr., and Edward Walker.

The American Heart Association named North American Bancard as a 2010 Fit Friendly Gold Status company for their comprehensive wellness initiatives for their employees.

Current

NAB currently employs over 400 people. It expects to hire 60 more people this year in order to create a total of 1899 jobs over the next decade as part of the MEDC state tax credit.[12]

In June 2010, North American Bancard announced its acquisition of Point and Pay from Vesta Corp as a means to expanding into payment processing for the public sector and non-profits.[13]

As part of Gardner's effort to "expand our established commitment to putting the customer first," North American Bancard launched a redesigned corporate website in June 2010. The new website was expanded to 200+ pages of content and updated to "create a clear, strong and relevant brand identity for North American Bancard".[14]

In January 2011, North American Bancard announced the launch of Pay Anywhere, a mobile payment processing solution. Pay Anywhere is a mobile application and card reader accessory designed so that users can accept credit card payments on their smartphone. The product offers no setup fees, no application fees, no monthly service fees, no cancellation fees, and no monthly minimums.[15]

References

[1] http://usa.visa.com/download/merchants/list-of-registered-independent-sales-organizations.pdf

[2] http://www.nabancard.com/about

[3] http://www.automationalley.com/a2_mbr_Info?id=0016000000JR1cqAAD

[4] http://www.sbnonline.com/Local/Article/14935/72/0/Turning_it_around.aspx

[5] http://www.themedc.org/News-Media/Press-Releases/Detail.aspx?ContentId=34e22ba5-6a3f-44be-81bd-87536327e6c5

[6] http://www.crainsdetroit.com/article/20091109/FREE/911099974

[7] http://www.ey.com/US/en/Newsroom/News-releases/Media-Release-13-06-08ADC

[8] http://www.greensheet.com/gs_archive.php?issue_number=020902&story=3&search_string=marc%20gardner

[9] http://www.marketwire.com/press-release/
     North-American-Bancard-CEO-Marc-Gardner-Featured-in-Green-Sheet-Quarterlys-Whos-Who-1012161.htm

[10] http://mpc.detroitchamber.com/gardner

[11] http://www.prlog.org/10320275-marc-gardner-guest-panelist-at-mackinac-policy-conference.html

[12] http://blog.mlive.com/oak_business_review/2008/03/credit_card_processor_hiring_1.html

[13] http://www.wwj.com/pages/7464356.php?

[14] http://www.prnewswire.com/news-releases/
     north-american-bancard-launches-redesigned-corporate-website-offering-enhanced-customer-experience-96646179.html

[15] http://www.facebook.com/note.php?note_id=128456950553707

External links

- Official North American Bancard site (http://www.nabancard.com)
- North American Bancard blog (http://blog.nabancard.com)
- North American Bancard LinkedIn (http://www.linkedin.com/companies/north-american-bancard)
- Point and Pay site (http://corp.pointandpay.com/default.aspx)
- Pay Anywhere site (http://payanywhere.com/)

Obopay

Obopay, Inc.

Type	Private
Industry	Mobile payment and banking
Founded	United States (2005)
Headquarters	Redwood City, California, United States
Key people	Carol Realini, CEO
Website	obopay.com [1]

Obopay is a company specialized in mobile payment systems and headquartered in Redwood City, California. It was founded in 2005 by Carol Realini, current CEO.

Obopay is a service that allows the transfer of money between mobile phones. Once a customer creates an Obopay account, they can add money from a credit card, debit card, or a bank transfer. From a technical point of view, Obopay service currently works in three ways: via SMS, via Obopay mobile application (requires a smartphone), or via Internet browser (WAP).

History

The business idea came up when Realini was doing volunteer work in Africa, and she realized that many people had a mobile phone even though they did not own a wallet. She came back to USA and founded Obopay in 2005.

Obopay India has a huge partner list now like Yes Bank and UBI. Mobile Money Service has been launched in 6 cities in India in operation with Nokia. This service works on Binary message and is to target the rural area user who actually do not have a bank account. This service is also provide option to withdraw cash from automated teller machines and will be launched across India by the end of 2011.

On March 2008 Obopay launched its services in India through a wholly owned subsidiary.

On March 2009 Nokia announced that it would invest in Obopay, and later in August 2009 unveiled its service Nokia Money.

Obopay was selected as 2010 Technology Pioneer by the World Economic Forum.[1]

References

[1] http://www.forbes.com/feeds/prnewswire/2009/12/03/prnewswire200912030900PR_NEWS_USPR_____NY19933.html

OCMT

OCMT is an abbreviation which stands for *Original currency and amount*. This is a term used for payments between banks.

It is a SWIFT standard code Word part of MT 202. These are messages, which are exchanged between banks after the SWIFT standard.

Deutsche Bank uses such words in its transaction data records (which appears on some types of bank statements).

Octopus card

Octopus Card

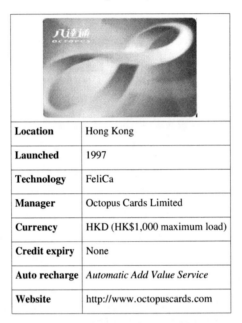

Location	Hong Kong
Launched	1997
Technology	FeliCa
Manager	Octopus Cards Limited
Currency	HKD (HK$1,000 maximum load)
Credit expiry	None
Auto recharge	*Automatic Add Value Service*
Website	http://www.octopuscards.com

The **Octopus card** is a rechargeable contactless stored value smart card used to transfer electronic payments in online or offline systems in Hong Kong. Launched in September 1997 to collect fares for the territory's mass transit system, the Octopus card system was the first contactless smart card system in the world and has since grown into a widely used payment system for virtually all public transport in Hong Kong.[1]

The Octopus is also used for payment at convenience stores, supermarkets, fast-food restaurants, on-street parking meters, car parks, and other point-of-sale applications such as service stations and vending machines.[2]

The Octopus card is recognised internationally, winning the Chairman's Award of the World Information Technology and Services Alliance's 2006 Global IT Excellence Award for being the world's leading complex automatic fare collection and contactless smartcard payment system, and for its innovative use of technologies.[3] According to Octopus Cards Limited, operator of the Octopus card system, there are more than 20 million cards in circulation,[4] nearly three times the population of Hong Kong. The cards are used by 95% of the population of Hong Kong aged 16 to 65, generating over 11 million daily transactions worth a total over HK$100 million (US$12.8 million) everyday.[4]

The slogan of Octopus Card Limited and its products (the cards) is *Making Everyday Life Easier,*[5] which is part of the mission statement of the corporation.[6]

History

The Mass Transit Railway (MTR), one of Hong Kong's railways, adopted a system to recirculate magnetic plastic cards as fare tickets when it started operations in 1979. Another of the territory's railway networks, the Kowloon-Canton Railway (KCR), adopted the same magnetic cards in 1984, and the stored value version was renamed Common Stored Value Ticket. In 1989, the Common Stored Value Ticket system was extended to Kowloon Motor Bus (KMB) buses providing a feeder service to MTR and KCR stations and to Citybus, and was also extended to a limited number of non-transport applications, such as payments at photobooths and for fast food vouchers.[7]

The MTR Corporation eventually decided to adopt more advanced technologies, and in 1993 announced that it would move towards using contactless smartcards. To gain wider acceptance, it partnered with four other major transit companies in Hong Kong to create a joint-venture business to operate the Octopus system in 1994, then known as Creative Star Limited.[8] The Octopus system was launched after three years of trials on 1 September 1997.[9] Three million cards were issued within the first three months of the system's launch. The main reason for the quick success of the system was that the MTR and KCR required that all holders of Common Stored Value Tickets replace their tickets with Octopus cards in three months or have their tickets made obsolete, thus forcing their combined base commuters to switch quickly.[10] Another reason is the coin shortage in Hong Kong in 1997; there was a belief that the older Queen's Head coins in Hong Kong would appreciate in value, so many people hoarded the older coins and waited for their value to increase.[11] [12] The Octopus system was quickly adopted by other Creative Star joint venture partners, and KMB reported that by 2000, most bus journeys were completed using an Octopus card, with few coins used.[13] Boarding a bus in Hong Kong without using the Octopus card requires giving exact change; this is cumbersome compared to using the Octopus card. By November 1998, 4.6 million cards were issued, and this rose to 9 million by January 2002.[10]

In 2000, the Hong Kong Monetary Authority granted a deposit-taking company license to the operator, removing previous restrictions that prohibited Octopus from generating more than 15 percent of its turnover from non-transit related functions, thus allowing the Octopus card to be widely adopted for non-transit-related sales transactions.[14] On 29 June 2003, the Octopus card found another application when the Hong Kong Government started to replace all its 18,000 parking meters with a new Octopus card operated system.[15] The replacement was completed on 21 November 2004.[16]

Etymologies and logo

Octopus card	
Traditional Chinese	八達通
Simplified Chinese	八达通

Transcriptions	
Mandarin	
- Hanyu Pinyin	Bā Dá Tōng
- Wade–Giles	$Pa^1\ Ta^2\ T'ung^1$
Cantonese	
- Jyutping	$baat^3\ daat^6\ tung^1$
- Yale Romanization	baat daaht tùng

The Cantonese name for the Octopus card, *Baat Daaht Tùng* (traditional Chinese: 八達通), translates literally as "eight-arrived pass", where *Baat Daaht* may translate as "reaching everywhere". It was selected by the head of the MTR Corporation, the parent company of Octopus Cards Limited, in a naming competition held in 1996.[17] The number eight is a significant number in Chinese in that it is often used to indicate "many". For instance, the idiom *sei tùng baat daaht* (traditional Chinese: 四通八達) is a common expression loosely translated as "reachable in all directions".[18] It is also considered a lucky number in Chinese culture, and the phrase *baat daaht* can possibly be associated with the similar-sounding *faat daaht*, which means "getting rich" (traditional Chinese: 發達) in the local dialect.

The English name *Octopus card* was also selected from the naming competition,[19] and coincides with the number eight in the Cantonese name, since an octopus has eight tentacles. It is also particularly appropriate since an octopus is able to grab many things at the same time and this ability is conferred to its cardholders who can use it in many different types of transactions.

The logo used on the card features a Möbius strip twisted sideways and into the shape of the Arabic numeral for the number eight, *8*, to indicate the card's "infinite" possibilities. The symbol for infinity, "∞", looks like a sideways *8*.

Types of cards

There are two main types of Octopus card (*On-Loan* and *Sold*), and two less common types (the *Airport Express Tourist* and the *MTR Airport Staff*).

On-Loan cards are issued for usage in day-to-day functions, primarily for fare payment in transport systems. They are further classified into *Child*, *Adult*, *Elder*, and *Personalised* categories, with the first three based on age and different amounts of fare concession.[20] With the exception of the *Personalised* cards, On-Loan cards are anonymous; no personal information, bank account, or credit card details are stored on the card,[21] and no identification is required for the purchase of these cards. If an owner loses a card, only the stored value and the deposit of the card are lost. On-Loan Octopus cards may be purchased at all MTR stations, the KMB Customer Service Centre, New World First Ferry (NWFF) Octopus Service Centres, and the New World First Bus (NWFB) Customer Service Centre.[22] A student on-loan Octopus Card was initially issued, but was discontinued in 2005.[23]

Types of On-Loan Octopus cards

Type	Picture/Colour	Cost and use
Child		Children aged between 3 and 11. This card is sold for HK$70 with an initial value of HK$20. Children's fares are deducted where applicable.
Student		For students attending secondary schools and universities. Discontinued in 2005 and replaced by Personalised Octopus Card.
Adult		The standard version of the Octopus card. This card is sold for HK$150 with an initial value of HK$100. This colour is also used for the logo of Octopus Cards Limited, the operator.
Elder		Eligibility varies between different public transport companies, and even between operating routes of the same type of service—for example, 60 years of age or above for Citybus, 65 for KMB. If no elder fares are available, adult fares are deducted. This card is sold for HK$70 with an initial value of HK$20.
Personalised		The rainbow-coloured *Personalised* card is available on registration. This card is sold for HK$100 with an initial value of HK$30 and a handling charge of HK$20. Students may also qualify for this card at HK$90 with their pictures and names.

The rainbow-coloured *Personalised* card is available on registration. The name and, if opted, a photo of the holder are imprinted on the cards. They can function automatically as a *Child*, *Adult*, or *Elder* card by recognising the cardholder's age stored on the card, hence accounting for different concessionary fares. As of 2003, there were 380,000 holders of *Personalised* Octopus cards.[24] In addition to all the functions of an ordinary card, this card can be used as a key card for access to residential and office buildings.[25] If a *Personalised* card is lost, the holder may report the loss by phone to prevent unauthorised use of the card. A refund would then be issued to the holder of the card for the deposit and the value that remained on the card six hours after the loss is reported, minus a HK$30 card cost and a HK$20 handling fee.[26]

A *Personalised* card with "student status" is available for students in Hong Kong. To be eligible for this card, the applicant must be a full-time Hong Kong student aged between 12 and 25.[27] This type of *Personalised* card is automatically issued to a student who applies for student concessionary privileges. Additionally, they can be used for school administrative tasks such as the recording of student attendance and the management of library loans.[28]

In contrast to On-Loan cards, Sold cards are sponsored and branded cards.[29] They are souvenir cards that are frequently released by Octopus Cards Limited. The designs for these cards usually come from fictional characters in popular culture, or they are inspired by Chinese cultural events such as Chinese New Year. These cards are sold at a premium, have limited or no initial stored

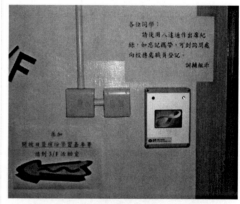

Many schools in Hong Kong use the Octopus card to record student attendance.

value, and cannot be refunded, but they can otherwise be used as ordinary cards. An example of the Sold card is the *Mcmug and Mcdull* collection. It was launched at the end of January 2007 to coincide with the beginning of the Year of the Pig, it features two differently designed versions of the card and is sold for HK$138 per set. Each set comes with an *Adult* Octopus card, with a pouch for the card, a matching strap and a Mcmug or Mcdull ornament.[30] Octopus Cards Limited has launched new collections of these cards for such occasions as the Mid-Autumn Festival, the passing of the year 2004, and the release of the movie *DragonBlade*. Sold Octopus cards may be purchased at selected MTR stations, and all 7-Eleven stores.[22]

The special-purpose card, *Airport Express Tourist Octopus*, was introduced by Octopus Cards Limited to target tourists in Hong Kong. Two versions of this card are offered, a HK$220 card with a free single ride on the Airport

Express, the Mass Transit Railway (MTR) train line that runs between the Hong Kong International Airport and the urban areas of Hong Kong, and a HK$300 card with two free single rides included. The airport journeys are valid for 180 days from the date of purchase. Both versions allow three days of unlimited rides on the MTR and include a HK$50 refundable deposit. Usable value on these cards may be added if necessary. These tourist Octopus cards may be used only by tourists staying in Hong Kong for 14 or fewer days; users may be required to produce a passport showing their arrival date in Hong Kong. *Airport Express Tourist Octopus* is available for purchase at all MTR stations.[31]

The other special-purpose card, the *MTR Airport Staff Octopus*, is available for the staff of Hong Kong International Airport and AsiaWorld-Expo, a convention centre close to the airport, for commuting at a reduced fare between the airport and MTR stations via the Airport Express. Staff who apply for the card may use it for a discount of up to 64 percent for Airport Express single journey fares.[32] The *MTR Airport Staff Octopus* is available upon application via the company for which that a staff member works.[33]

Card usage

The Octopus card was introduced for fare payment on the MTR initially, but the use of the card quickly expanded for multiple other purposes. The card can now be used to pay fares for majority of public transport in Hong Kong and to make purchases for consumer products at many stores in the territory; it is accepted by more than 1,000 merchants. Notable businesses that accept Octopus cards include PARKnSHOP, Wellcome, Watsons, 7-Eleven, Starbucks, McDonald's, and Circle K. The card can be used in many soft drink vending machines, pay phones, photo booths, parking meters, and car parks.[34] Octopus cards also double as access control cards in buildings and for school administrative functions.[25] [28] At certain office buildings,

Octopus reader at an MTR ticket gate

residential buildings, and schools, usage of an Octopus card is required for entry.[35] As of 21 November 2004, all parking meters in Hong Kong had been converted to using the Octopus card as the form of payment.[16]

Payments

Octopus card reader at a McDonald's restaurant in Central

Making or recording a payment using the card for public transport or purchases at Octopus-enabled retailers can be done by holding the card against or waving it over an Octopus card reader from up to a few centimetres away without the user taking out the card. The reader will acknowledge payment by emitting a *beep* sound, and display the amount deducted and the remaining balance of the card.[36] Standard transaction time for readers used for public transport is 0.3 seconds, while that of readers used for retailers is 1 second.[37] When riding the MTR system, the entry point of commuters is noted when a passenger enters, and the appropriate amount based on distance traveled will be deducted when the users show their card again at the exit point.

The MTR charge less for journeys made using an Octopus card instead of conventional single-journey tickets. For example, the adult fare of a single journey from Chai Wan to Tung Chung is HK$20.70 with an Octopus card, and HK$23.50 with a single journey ticket.[38] Other public transport operators also offer intermittent discounts for using

Octopus cards on higher fares and round-trip transits on select routes.[39]

On 6 November 2005, Octopus Cards Limited launched Octopus Rewards, a program that allows cardholders to earn rewards at merchants that are partners in the program. Participating merchants provide consumers with tailor-made offers and privileges.[40] The rewards that the program offers are in the form of points, or *reward dollars*, stored on the card. Once a card is registered for the program, the cardholder may accumulate reward points by making purchases at participating merchants, and payments may be made in the form of cash, credit cards, or Octopus cards themselves.[41] The rate at which reward points are earned per dollar-amount purchase differs by the merchant at which that the purchases are made. At Wellcome, for example, one point is earned for every purchase of HK$200;[42] and at Watsons, points are earned at a rate of 0.5 percent per dollar amount of a purchase.[43] Once these *reward dollars* are accumulated, they may be redeemed as payment for purchases at partner merchants for at least HK$1 per *reward dollar*. To redeem the accumulated *reward dollars*, cardholders must use the entire value amount in whole, and may not elect to use it partially. If the purchase price is lower than the amount of *reward dollars* available, the amount difference remains stored on the card.[44] Founding partners for the Octopus Rewards program include HSBC, UA Cinemas, Watsons, Wellcome, and McDonald's.[45]

Enquiring balances, adding value and refunding

In MTR stations, enquiry machines can be found where cardholders may place their Octopus cards on the machines and the machines will display the balances along with a history of last 10 usages.

Monetary value can be added to the card through a number of ways. Add Value Machines, located at MTR stations, can be used to add more value to the cards. The machines accept cash, and selected machines are also able to accept Electronic Funds Transfer.[46] Alternatively, value may be added with cash at authorised service providers such as PARKnSHOP, Wellcome, Watsons, 7-Eleven, Circle K, and Café de Coral, and also at customer service centres and ticketing offices at other transport stations.[47]

Octopus card enquiry machine

An Octopus card may store a maximum value of HK$1,000,[9] with an On-Loan card having an initial deposit value of HK$50 and a Sold card having no initial deposit value. Negative value is incurred on a card if it is used with insufficient funds—both types of cards may carry a maximum negative value of HK$35 before value needs to be added to them again for use.[48] At the time, the maximum cost of a trip on any of the rail networks except the Airport Express and first class of the MTR East Rail line was HK$34.8, the cost of travelling between East Tsim Sha Tsui Station and Lo Wu Station;[49] [50] the current maximum cost is $47.5, the cost of travelling between Disneyland Resort Station and either Lo Wu Station or Lok Ma Chau Station.

The Octopus Automatic Add Value Service (AAVS) is another method by which cardholders may add value to their cards. This service allows for money to be automatically deducted from a credit card and added to an Octopus card when the value of the Octopus card is less than zero dollars. The credit card used must be one offered by one of 22 financial institutions that participate in AAVS.[51] Participating banks include HSBC, Bank of China, and Hang Seng Bank. HK$250 is added to the card each time value is automatically added; six participating financial institutions offer an option of adding a value of HK$500 instead.[52]

An Octopus card may be returned to any MTR Customer Service Centre for a refund of the remaining value stored on it. A handling fee may be charged for the refund; HK$7 for an anonymous On-Loan card that had been in use for fewer than three months, and HK$10 for a *Personalised* On-Loan card that was issued on or after 1 November 2004.

A refund is immediately provided at the time an anonymous On Loan card is returned, unless it has more than HK$500 stored on it. A *Personalised* On-Loan card or an anonymous On-Loan card with more than HK$500 stored on it needs to be sent back to Octopus Cards Limited for refund processing, in which case, the refund for a *Personalised* On-Loan card would be available in eight days, and that of an anonymous On-Loan card would be available in five days. If a damaged card is returned for refund, a HK$30 levy would be charged to the cardholder.[53]

Technology

The Octopus system was designed by Australia-based company ERG Group. The company was selected in 1994 to lead the development of the Octopus project and was responsible for the building and installation of the components of the Octopus system.[54] Operations, maintenance and development was undertaken by Octopus Cards Limited, and in 2005, it replaced the central transaction clearing house with its own system.[8]

The Octopus card uses the Sony 13.56 MHz FeliCa radio frequency identification (RFID) chip,[55] and Hong Kong is the home of the world's first major public transport system using this technology.[56] This is a "touch and go" system, so users need only hold the card in close proximity of the reader, and thus physical contact is not required. Data is transmitted at up to 212 kbit/s (the maximum speed for Sony FeliCa chips), compared to 9.6 kbit/s for other smart card systems like Mondex and Visa Cash.[56] The card has a storage capacity of 1 KB to 64 KB compared to the 125 bytes provided by traditional magnetic stripe card.[57]

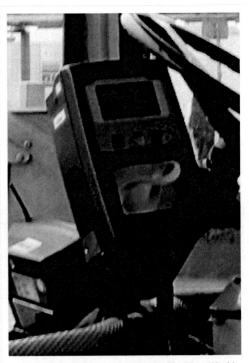

An Octopus reader on a bus operated by New World First Bus

Octopus uses a nonstandard system for RFID instead of the ISO/IEC 14443 standards, since there were no standards in the nascent industry during its development in 1997. The operating range of the reader/writer is between 30 and 100 mm (1.18 and 3.94 in) depending on the type of model being used.[21]

Octopus is specifically designed so that card transactions are relayed for clearing on a store and forward basis, without any requirement for reader units to have realtime round-trip communications with a central database or computer.[58] The stored data about the transaction may be transmitted by network after hours, or in the case of offline mobile readers may be retrieved by a hand held device, for example a Pocket PC.

In practice, different data collection mechanisms are used by different transport operators, depending on the nature of their business. The MTR equips its stations with local area networks that connect the components that deal with Octopus cards—turnstiles, Add Value Machines, value-checking machines and customer service terminals. Transactions from these stations are relayed to the MTR's Kowloon Bay headquarters through a frame relay wide area network, and hence onwards to the central clearing house system (CCHS) for clearing.[59] Similar arrangements are in place for retailers such as 7-Eleven. Handheld devices are used to scan offline mobile readers, including those installed on minibuses. Buses either use handheld devices or a wireless system, depending on operator.[59]

Security

The Octopus card uses encryption for all airborne communication and performs mutual authentication between the card and reader based on the ISO 9798-2 three-pass mutual authentication protocol.[60] In other words, data communications are only established when the card and reader have mutually authenticated based on a shared secret access key. This means that the security of the Octopus card system would be jeopardized should the access key be exposed. A stolen Octopus card reader could be used with stolen Octopus software, for example, to add value (up to HK$1,000) to any Octopus card without authorization.[61] Nevertheless, as of 2003, the Octopus card and system have never been successfully hacked.[62]

Octopus card reader includes a fail-safe that prevents reader from initiating transaction when more than one card is being detected at the same time. On 11 February 2009, *Sing Tao Daily* reported that the fail-safe has been abused for fare evasion through the railway station turnstile. A large amount of dishonest passengers at Sheung Shui Station and Lo Wu Station were stacking up 4 or more cards before breaking through the turnstile, pretending their cards have been touched with the reader correctly but triggering the fail-safe deliberately to avoid card value deduction. Because of this, if they get caught by the station staff, they can make an excuse of a hardware malfunction and offer the Octopus card with an unsuccessful transaction.[63]

Operator

The Octopus card system is owned and operated by Octopus Cards Limited, a wholly owned subsidiary of Octopus Holdings Limited.[64] The company was founded as Creative Star Limited in 1994 to oversee the development and implementation of the Octopus card system, and was renamed as its current name of Octopus Cards Limited in 2002.[8] Creative Star was formed as a joint-venture company by five major transit companies in Hong Kong—MTR Corporation, Kowloon-Canton Railway Corporation, Kowloon Motor Bus, Citybus, and Hongkong and Yaumati Ferry. In January 2001, the shares of Hongkong and Yaumati Ferry in the company was transferred to New World First Bus and New World First Ferry.[65] In the same year, together with MTR Corporation, the company was transformed from its previous non-profit making status to a profit making enterprise.[66]

Due to the expansion of the company's businesses, Octopus Holdings Limited was established in 2005 and Octopus Cards Limited was restructured as its subsidiary. The business of Octopus Cards Limited, being a payment business, is regulated by the Hong Kong Monetary Authority, while Octopus' non-payment businesses are not subjected to such regulation and are operated by other subsidiaries of Octopus Holdings Limited that are independent of Octopus Cards Limited.[64] As of 2007, Octopus Holdings Limited was a joint-venture business owned by five transport companies in Hong Kong; 54.4% by the MTR Corporation, 22.1% by the Kowloon-Canton Railway Corporation, 12.4% by Kowloon Motor Bus, 5% by Citybus, and 3.1% by New World First Bus.[67] Since the Government of Hong Kong owns 76.54% of the MTR Corporation (as of 31 December 2005) and wholly owns the Kowloon-Canton Railway Corporation,[68] [69] it is the biggest effective shareholder of Octopus Holdings Limited, and thus also the biggest effective shareholder of Octopus Cards Limited.

Initially, Octopus Cards Limited, then known as Creative Star Limited, was restricted to having at most 15 percent of Octopus card transactions for non-transport transactions, as it operated under the Hong Kong government's *Banking Ordinance*. On 20 April 2000, the Hong Kong Monetary Authority authorised the company for deposit-taking, which allowed for 50 percent of Octopus card transactions to be unrelated to transport.[14] [70] HK$416 million (US$53.3 million) is deposited in the Octopus system at any given time as of 2000.[71]

Taxis

Although a popular form of transport, taxis in Hong Kong do not accept the Octopus card. On 27 June 2006, after 10 years of negotiations between Octopus Cards Limited and the taxi industry, the first trial of taxis equipped with Octopus card readers was launched in the New Territories with taxis operated by the Yellow Taxi Group.[72] But it was reported on 30 October that of the 20 taxis that participated in the trial, eight had dropped out. Part of the reason was technical—drivers must return to the office every day for accounting. The Octopus card company said it would be upgrading the system to allow automatic account updating in the future.[73] Wong Yu-ting, managing director of the Yellow Taxi Group, also noted that they had been "trying to convince restaurants and retailers" to offer discounts to Octopus taxi passengers, but the Transport Department had been a major obstacle. The Transport Department is against this approach for legal reasons.[73]

Alternative designs

Other than the Octopus card itself, operator Octopus Cards Limited also sells watches and mobile phone covers that function as anonymous Octopus cards. The types of watches available include wrist watches, pocket watches, and watch key chains. The mobile phone covers were specifically designed for Nokia models 3310 and 3330.[74] As with the card itself, these products are used by waving them over a card reader. They may be reloaded with money value the same way as the card itself, including automatic reloading via the Automatic Add Value Service, with the exception that they cannot be reloaded at Add Value Machines due to their shapes.[75] An Octopus watch or mobile phone cover may be stored with a maximum of HK$1,000, but do not have any

A key-chain alternate form of the Octopus Card

initial stored value at the time of its purchase. It may have a maximum negative value of HK$35 as with an Octopus card.[74] These products are not refundable for their costs, but the remaining value stored on them may be refunded if they are damaged, with the damaged product itself also returned to the customer.[75]

In June 2007, a new set of limited edition products was announced, featuring Mini Octopus cards and Child Octopus Wristbands. The Mini Octopus cards, available in Adult and Elder editions, measure 4.7 cm by 3 cm (1.85 in by 1.18 in) and work as regular (anonymous) Adult and Elder, respectively, Octopus cards. The Child Octopus Wristbands are plastic wristbands with a watch-like round face and work as regular Child Octopus cards.[76] The same value-adding abilities and limitations as the aforementioned watches and mobile phone apply.

Outside Hong Kong

Usage of the Octopus card was extended to the Chinese cities of Shenzhen and Macau in 2006. In collaboration with China UnionPay, Octopus Cards Limited introduced Octopus card usage to two Fairwood restaurants in Shenzhen in August 2006.[77] In 2008, five Café de Coral locations in Shenzhen also started accepting Octopus.[78] Value cannot be reloaded to Octopus cards in Shenzhen, but the Automatic Add Value Service is available to automatically deduct money value from a customer's credit card to reload an Octopus card. The two Fairwood restaurants in Shenzhen that were enabled for Octopus card payments are located at Luohu Commercial City and Shenzhen Railway Station.[77] Shenzhen became the first city outside Hong Kong in which Octopus cards may be accepted as payment. In Macau, the Octopus card was introduced in December 2006 when two Kentucky Fried Chicken restaurants in the territory adopted its usage as payment. Similar to its usage in Shenzhen, an Octopus card may not be reloaded in Macau, and the currency exchange rate between the Macanese pataca and the Hong Kong dollar when using an Octopus card is MOP1:HKD1.[79] The two Kentucky Fried Chicken restaurants in Macau that adopted the Octopus card for payment are located at the Rua Do Campo and the Sands Casino.[79]

EPS add-value glitch

In February 2007, it was found that when customers added value to their cards at self-service add-value points located in MTR and KCR stations, their bank accounts would be debited even if the transactions were cancelled.[80] Octopus Cards Limited claimed that the fault was due to an upgrade of communication systems. Initially, two cases were reported. The company then announced that the use of the payment system, Electronic Payment Services (EPS), in add-value service points would be suspended until further notice, and had started investigation of the system's mistake.[81]

Octopus Card Recharging terminal with the now-terminated EPS system

On 27 July 2007, a report was announced that the wrong transactions could be traced back to 2000, and a total of 3.7 million Hong Kong dollars was wrongly deducted from 15,270 cases. The company reported that there may be cases dating before 2000, because only transactions from the past seven years were kept. It stated that it would co-operate with EPS Company Limited, operator of Electronic Payment Services, and banks to contact customers involved and arrange a refund within ten weeks' time.[82]

On 21 December 2007, the company announced to permanently cease all transactions completed using EPS because they cannot guarantee such events from happening again.[83]

Privacy Abuse

On July 15, 2010, despite Octopus' claims to have never sold data, a former employee of the CIGNA insurance company claimed CIGNA purchased records for 2.4 million Octopus users.[84] On July 20, Octopus acknowledged selling customers' personal details to Cigna and CPP, and started an internal review of their data practices.[85] Octopus Holdings made 44 million Hong Kong dollars ($5.7M USD) over 4.5 years.[86] Roderick Woo Bun, Hong Kong's Privacy Commissioner for Personal Data, gave radio interviews and called for transparent investigation, but his term expires at the end of July 2010.[85] Allan Chiang Yam-wang was announced as the incoming Privacy Commissioner. This news was met with protests and international outrage, due to his prior history of privacy invasions involving cameras used to spy on his employees at the Post Office, and disclosing hundreds of job applicants' personal data to corporations.[87] Outgoing Privacy Commissioner Woo pledged to finish a preliminary report on the Octopus privacy abuse before his term ends, and called for a new law making it a criminal offense for companies to sell personal data.[88]

References

[1] "Hong Kong Smart Card System" (http://web.archive.org/web/20070304050613/http://lnweb18.worldbank.org/External/lac/lac.nsf/Sectors/Transport/D5A576A039A802C0852568B2007988AD?OpenDocument). The World Bank Group. Archived from the original (http://lnweb18.worldbank.org/External/lac/lac.nsf/Sectors/Transport/D5A576A039A802C0852568B2007988AD?OpenDocument) on March 4, 2007. . Retrieved 2007-02-13.

[2] "Octopus Products" (http://www.octopuscards.com/consumer/products/en/index.jsp). Octopus Cards Limited. . Retrieved 2007-02-21.

[3] "WITSA Announces 2006 Global IT Excellence Award Winners" (http://www.witsa.org/press/05-04-06_WITSA_AWARDS_rev.doc) (DOC). World Information Technology and Services Alliance. 4 May 2006. . Retrieved 2007-05-01.

[4] "Statistics" (http://www.octopus.com.hk/octopus-for-businesses/benefits-for-your-business/en/index.html). Octopus Cards Limited. . Retrieved 2010-11-14.

[5] "Homepage" (http://www.octopus.com.hk/home/en/index.html). Octopus Cards Limited. . Retrieved 2010-11-14.

[6] "Octopus Holdings Mission" (http://www.octopus.com.hk/mission/en/index.jsp). Octopus Cards Limited. . Retrieved 2009-07-02.

[7] "Our winning card" (http://www.tradelink-ebiz.com/english/331n08or3m9a51l/newscast/ss_0412a.html). Tradelink Electronic Commerce Limited. January 2005. . Retrieved 2007-04-21.

[8] "Our History" (http://www.octopus.com.hk/history/en/index.jsp). Octopus Holdings Limited. . Retrieved 2007-05-17.

[9] Carol L. Clark (2005). "Shopping without cash: The emergence of the e-purse" (http://web.archive.org/web/20070621111847/http://www.chicagofed.org/publications/economicperspectives/ep_4qtr2005_part3_clark_.pdf) (PDF). Federal Reserve Bank of Chicago. pp. 12. Archived from the original (http://www.chicagofed.org/publications/economicperspectives/ep_4qtr2005_part3_clark_.pdf) on June 21, 2007. . Retrieved 2007-03-22.

[10] Lucia L.S. Siu (June 2008). "Coercing Consensus: Unintended success of the Octopus electronic payment system" (http://www.ln.edu.hk/socsp/staff/luciaindex.php#publications). the 6th International Conference on Politics and Information Systems, Technologies and Applications (PISTA). . Retrieved 2008-06-30.

[11] "Supply of new coins will continue" (http://sc.info.gov.hk/gb/www.fstb.gov.hk/fsb/ppr/press/p980218e.htm). Hong Kong SAR Financial Services and the Treasury Bureau. 18 February 1998. . Retrieved 2007-04-25.

[12] "Hong Kong Monetary Authority Annual Report 1997" (http://www.info.gov.hk/hkma/eng/public/ar97/ch04.htm). Hong Kong Monetary Authority. 1997. . Retrieved 2007-04-25.

[13] "Development of KMB's Octopus Payment System" (http://www.kmb.hk/english.php?page=next&file=news/service/news3q03/news2003112701.html). The Kowloon Motor Bus Company. . Retrieved 2007-04-25.

[14] "Survey of electronic money developments" (http://www.bis.org/publ/cpss48.pdf) (PDF). Bank for International Settlements. November 2001. . Retrieved 2007-04-16.

[15] "Octopus-card operated parking meters to launch on 29 June" (http://www.info.gov.hk/gia/general/200306/27/0627317.htm). Hong Kong SAR Government. 27 June 2003. . Retrieved 2007-04-25.

[16] "Octopus operated Parking Meter" (http://web.archive.org/web/20071130032827/http://www.td.gov.hk/transport_in_hong_kong/parking/carparks/octopus_operated_parking_meters/index.htm). Transport Department of the HKSAR. 19 July 2005. Archived from the original (http://www.td.gov.hk/transport_in_hong_kong/parking/carparks/octopus_operated_parking_meters/index.htm) on November 30, 2007. . Retrieved 2007-04-11.

[17] "八達通控股有限公司里程碑 (lit. *Milestones of Octopus Holdings Limited*)" (http://www.octopus.com.hk/milestones/tc/index.jsp) (in Traditional Chinese). Octopus Holdings Limited. . Retrieved 2007-02-28.

[18] "四通八達" (http://dict.idioms.moe.edu.tw/pho/fyb/fyb01352.htm) (in Traditional Chinese). *Dictionary of Chinese Idioms*. Taipei, Taiwan: Ministry of Education, R.O.C.. . Retrieved 2010-06-16.

[19] "Octopus Holdings Milestones" (http://www.octopus.com.hk/milestones/en/index.jsp). Octopus Holdings Limited. . Retrieved 2007-02-28.

[20] "On-Loan Octopus" (http://www.octopuscards.com/consumer/products/cardtype/en/loan.jsp). Octopus Cards Limited. . Retrieved 2007-02-13.

[21] "Hong Kong Octopus financial/transport card, China" (http://rfid.idtechex.com/knowledgebase/en/casestudy.asp?freefromsection=114). The RFID Knowledgebase. 19 November 2006. . Retrieved 2007-02-21.

[22] "How to get Your Octopus" (http://www.octopuscards.com/consumer/products/apply/en/index.jsp). Octopus Cards Limited. . Retrieved 2007-02-21.

[23] "已停售學生八達通 港鐵多扣錢 (lit. *MTR deduces extra fare from the obsoleted Student Octopus card*)" (in Traditional Chinese). Ming Pao. 2 December 2007.

[24] "LCQ4 : Octopus card has a maximum reserved value of $35" (http://www.info.gov.hk/gia/general/200305/21/0521207.htm). Hong Kong SAR Government Information Centre. 21 May 2003. . Retrieved 2007-05-13.

[25] "Access Control" (http://www.octopuscards.com/consumer/other/access/en/index.jsp). Octopus Cards Limited. . Retrieved 2007-02-21.

[26] "Lost Card Reporting" (http://www.octopuscards.com/consumer/help/report/en/index.jsp). Octopus Cards Limited. . Retrieved 2007-02-15.

[27] "Student Travel Scheme (Academic year 2006 / 2007)" (http://web.archive.org/web/20070311043623/http://www.mtr.com.hk/eng/whatsnew/studentoct/studoct0607_e.htm). MTR Corporation. Archived from the original (http://www.mtr.com.hk/eng/whatsnew/

studentoct/studoct0607_e.htm) on March 11, 2007. . Retrieved 2007-02-15.

[28] "School Campuses" (http://www.octopuscards.com/consumer/other/campuses/en/index.jsp). Octopus Cards Limited. . Retrieved 2007-02-21.

[29] "Sold Octopus" (http://www.octopuscards.com/consumer/products/cardtype/en/sold.jsp). Octopus Cards Limited. . Retrieved 2007-02-13.

[30] "Launch of Mcmug and Mcdull Limited Edition Octopus to Greet the Year of the Pig" (http://www.octopus.com.hk/release/detail/en/ 20070129.jsp). Octopus Holdings Limited. 29 January 2007. . Retrieved 2007-02-16.

[31] "Octopus for Tourists" (http://www.octopuscards.com/consumer/help/tourists/en/index.jsp). Octopus Cards Limited. . Retrieved 2007-02-21.

[32] "Panel on Transport Meeting on 26 May 2006 Response to Questions" (http://www.legco.gov.hk/yr05-06/english/panels/tp/papers/ tp0526cb1-1935-1e.pdf) (PDF). Legislative Council. . Retrieved 2010-06-16.

[33] "FAQ: How do I apply for an MTR Airport Staff Octopus?" (http://www.octopuscards.com/consumer/help/faq/en/type.jsp#faq5). Octopus Cards Limited. . Retrieved 2007-02-28.

[34] "Smart Card Case Studies and Implementation Profiles" (http://www.it.iitb.ac.in/~tijo/seminar/Case_Studies_and_Profiles_Report. pdf) (PDF). Smart Card Alliance. December 2003. . Retrieved 2007-02-22.

[35] "View from abroad: Hong Kong's 'Octopus card' technology puts even credit card to shame" (http://badgerherald.com/oped/2004/02/05/ view_from_abroad_hon.php). The Badger Herald. 5 February 2004. . Retrieved 2007-05-31.

[36] "Octopus" (http://web.archive.org/web/20071111155354/http://www.hong-kong-travel.org/Octopus.asp). Hong Kong Travel. Archived from the original (http://www.hong-kong-travel.org/Octopus.asp) on November 11, 2007. . Retrieved 2007-03-11.

[37] "Scrap the coins" (http://web.archive.org/web/20070929202201/http://www.cw.com.hk/computerworldhk/article/articleDetail. jsp?id=316427). Computerworld Hong Kong. 1 April 2006. Archived from the original (http://www.cw.com.hk/computerworldhk/article/ articleDetail.jsp?id=316427) on September 29, 2007. . Retrieved 2007-03-11.

[38] "Journey Time & Fare: Chai Wan to Tung Chung" (http://www.mtr.com.hk/jplanner/eng/planner_index.php?spot=1&start=37& destin=43&x=59&y=18). MTR Corporation. . Retrieved 2008-08-19.

[39] "Citybus & NWFB Offer New Octopus Same Day Return Fare Discounts on Jointly-operated Cross Harbour Tunnel Routes from 1 July" (http://www.nwfb.com.hk/eng/news/database/news05.asp?news_id=1015&yr=2006&cate=A). New World First Bus. 27 June 2006. . Retrieved 2007-05-15.

[40] "Octopus Rewards Grand Launch" (http://www.octopus.com.hk/release/detail/en/20051105.jsp). Octopus Holdings Limited. 5 November 2005. . Retrieved 2007-03-17.

[41] "How It Works" (http://web.archive.org/web/20070210015251/http://www.octopusrewards.com.hk/works/en/index.jsp). Octopus Rewards Limited. Archived from the original (http://www.octopusrewards.com.hk/works/en/index.jsp) on 2007-02-10. . Retrieved 2007-03-17.

[42] "Wellcome" (http://web.archive.org/web/20070526173707/http://www.octopusrewards.com.hk/earning/where/en/ popWellcomeDetails.jsp). Octopus Rewards Limited. Archived from the original (http://www.octopusrewards.com.hk/earning/where/en/ popWellcomeDetails.jsp) on 2007-05-26. . Retrieved 2007-03-17.

[43] "Watsons" (http://web.archive.org/web/20070928080724/http://www.octopusrewards.com.hk/earning/where/en/ popWatsonsDetails.jsp). Octopus Rewards Limited. Archived from the original (http://www.octopusrewards.com.hk/earning/where/en/ popWatsonsDetails.jsp) on 2007-09-28. . Retrieved 2007-03-17.

[44] "Redeeming" (http://www.octopusrewards.com.hk/redeeming/en/index.jsp). Octopus Rewards Limited. . Retrieved 2007-03-17.

[45] "Earning" (http://www.octopusrewards.com.hk/earning/en/index.jsp). Octopus Rewards Limited. . Retrieved 2007-03-17.

[46] "Reload Your Octopus: Overview" (http://www.octopuscards.com/consumer/payment/reload/en/index.jsp). Octopus Cards Limited. . Retrieved 2007-03-19.

[47] "Reload Your Octopus: Other Reload Methods" (http://www.octopuscards.com/consumer/payment/reload/en/other.jsp). Octopus Cards Limited. . Retrieved 2007-03-19.

[48] "FAQ: What is the difference between On-loan Octopus and Sold Octopus?" (http://www.octopuscards.com/consumer/help/faq/en/ type.jsp#faq1). Octopus Cards Limited. . Retrieved 2007-03-22.

[49] "MTR fare chart" (http://www.mtr.com.hk/chi/whatsnew/images/single_journey_fare_chi.pdf) (PDF). MTR Corporation. . Retrieved 2007-05-15.

[50] "KCR East Rail fare table" (http://web.archive.org/web/20060701081739/http://www.kcr.com.hk/html/eng/services/services/ east_rail/fare/images/er_fare.pdf) (PDF). Kowloon-Canton Railway Corporation. Archived from the original (http://www.kcr.com.hk/ html/eng/services/services/east_rail/fare/images/er_fare.pdf) on July 1, 2006. . Retrieved 2007-05-15.

[51] "Automatic Add Value Service" (http://www.octopuscards.com/consumer/payment/reload/en/aavs.jsp). Octopus Cards Limited. . Retrieved 2007-03-25.

[52] "List of Participating Financial Institutions" (http://www.octopuscards.com/consumer/payment/reload/en/financialinst.jsp). Octopus Cards Limited. . Retrieved 2007-03-25.

[53] "FAQ: Refund Procedures" (http://www.octopuscards.com/consumer/help/faq/en/refund.jsp). Octopus Cards Limited. . Retrieved 2007-03-25.

[54] "Projects: Hong Kong" (http://web.archive.org/web/20061110130259/http://www.erggroup.com/projects/hongkong.htm). ERG Group. Archived from the original (http://www.erggroup.com/projects/hongkong.htm) on November 10, 2006. . Retrieved 2007-04-09.

[55] "RFID Smart Cards Gain Ground" (http://www.rfidjournal.com/article/articleview/374/1/1/). RFID Journal. 9 April 2003. . Retrieved 2007-07-08.

[56] "FeliCa" (http://www.sony.net/Products/felica/pdf/data/FeliCa_E.pdf) (PDF). Sony Corporation. . Retrieved 2007-04-11.

[57] "Smart Card Technology" (http://web.archive.org/web/20071015170810/http://www.info.gov.hk/digital21/eng/knowledge/smarttech.html). Hong Kong SAR Government Information Centre. 31 January 2007. Archived from the original (http://www.info.gov.hk/digital21/eng/knowledge/smarttech.html) on October 15, 2007. . Retrieved 2007-04-11.

[58] Kevin Mahaffey (July 2005). "Passive RFID Security" (http://www.blackhat.com/presentations/bh-usa-05/bh-us-05-mahaffey.pdf) (PDF). BlackHat. pp. 20. . Retrieved 2007-04-11.

[59] Jack So. "Integrated Transport and Land Use Planning as a Success Factor for Metros" (http://unpan1.un.org/intradoc/groups/public/documents/APCITY/UNPAN007495.pdf) (PDF). UNPAN. . Retrieved 2007-04-11.

[60] FeliCa Division, Sony Corporation (20 August 2002). "FeliCa RC-S860 Contactless Smart Card Security Target (Public Version)" (http://www.commoncriteriaportal.org/files/epfiles/FeliCaRC.pdf) (PDF). pp. 61. . Retrieved 2008-10-23.

[61] Fong, Loretta; Parry, Simon (18 October 2008). "Drunken pilot stole Octopus machine". *South China Morning Post* (Hong Kong): p. 3.

[62] Peter Winer (13 May 2003). "Security and Authentication Technologies" (http://www.bigchief.com/whitepapers/rfid-world-2003-05-13.pdf) (PDF). Big Chief Partners, Inc.. pp. 20. . Retrieved 2007-04-11.

[63] 李建人 (12 February 2009). "身懷十張八達通 被揭走私記憶卡 蠱惑水客「疊卡」衝閘逃票" (in Traditional Chinese). Hong Kong: Sing Tao Daily. p. 港聞A08.

[64] "Our Company" (http://www.octopus.com.hk/company/en/index.jsp). Octopus Holdings Limited. . Retrieved 2007-04-15.

[65] "Interest in non-controlled subsidiary" (http://www.mtr.com.hk/eng/investrelation/2003frpt_e/F131.pdf) (PDF). MTR Corporation. pp. 27. . Retrieved 2007-04-24.

[66] "Operation of the Octopus Card in Hong Kong" (http://www.legco.gov.hk/yr06-07/english/sec/library/0607in08-e.pdf) (PDF). Legislative Council Secretariat. 2007. . Retrieved 2007-04-25.

[67] "The Joint Venture of Five Major Transport Operators" (http://www.octopus.com.hk/company/en/operators.jsp). Octopus Holdings Limited. . Retrieved 2007-04-15.

[68] "Investors' Information" (http://www.mtr.com.hk/eng/investrelation/shareholder_services.php). MTR Corporation. . Retrieved 2007-04-15.

[69] "History" (http://web.archive.org/web/20070403124553/http://www.kcrc.com/html/eng/corporate/about_kcrc/history/index.asp). Kowloon-Canton Railway Corporation. Archived from the original (http://www.kcrc.com/html/eng/corporate/about_kcrc/history/index.asp) on April 3, 2007. . Retrieved 2007-04-15.

[70] "Legal Service Division Reports on Subsidiary Legislation tabled in the Legislative Council from 7 June to 26 June and on 4 October 2000" (http://www.legco.gov.hk/yr00-01/english/hc/papers/ls-1.pdf) (PDF). Legislative Council of the HKSAR. 4 October 2000. pp. 36. . Retrieved 2007-04-16.

[71] "Octopus Card in Hong Kong" (http://www.china-community.de/index2.php?option=com_content&do_pdf=1&id=45) (PDF). China-community de. . Retrieved 2007-05-15.**(German)**

[72] "Octopus To Be Used In Hong Kong By First Batch of Taxis" (http://www.octopus.com.hk/release/detail/en/20060627.jsp). Octopus Holdings Limited. 27 June 2006. . Retrieved 2007-04-29.

[73] "Setback for Octopus Card Trial in Taxis in HK" (http://web.archive.org/web/20070928200619/http://www.lifeofguangzhou.com/node_10/node_37/node_83/2006/10/31/116225881510438.shtml). Life of GuangZhou. 30 October 2006. Archived from the original (http://www.lifeofguangzhou.com/node_10/node_37/node_83/2006/10/31/116225881510438.shtml) on September 28, 2007. . Retrieved 2007-04-29.

[74] "Other Octopus Products" (http://www.octopuscards.com/consumer/products/other/en/index.jsp). Octopus Cards Limited. . Retrieved 2007-03-27.

[75] "FAQ: Other Octopus Products" (http://www.octopuscards.com/consumer/help/faq/en/other.jsp). Octopus Cards Limited. . Retrieved 2007-03-27.

[76] "Mini Octopus" (http://www.octopus.com.hk/release/detail/en/20070614.jsp). Octopus Cards Limited. . Retrieved 2007-06-25.

[77] "Octopus Joins Forces with Fairwood and China UnionPay to Introduce Octopus to Shenzhen" (http://www.octopus.com.hk/release/detail/en/20060814.jsp). Octopus Holdings Limited. 14 August 2006. . Retrieved 2007-05-01.

[78] "Octopus joins forces with China UnionPay and Café de Coral to Expand Octopus Payment Service in Shenzhen" (http://www.octopus.com.hk/release/detail/en/20080131.jsp). Octopus Holdings Limited. 31 January 2008. . Retrieved 2008-02-03.

[79] "Octopus Extends to Macau with First Acceptance of Octopus Payments at KFC" (http://www.octopus.com.hk/release/detail/en/20061210.jsp). Octopus Holdings Limited. 10 December 2006. . Retrieved 2007-05-01.

[80] "MTR and KCR Octopus EPS Add-Value Services suspended" (http://www.rthk.org.hk/rthk/news/englishnews/20070204/news_20070204_56_376306.htm). RTHK News. 4 February 2007. . Retrieved 2007-07-27.

[81] "Octopus company ordered to submit auditor's report after complaints over EPS add-value losses" (http://gbcode.rthk.org.hk/gb/app2.rthk.org.hk/pda/news/content.php?id=379458). RTHK News. 17 February 2007. . Retrieved 2007-07-27.

[82] "Octopus Card company to refund customers" (http://www.rthk.org.hk/rthk/news/englishnews/20070727/news_20070727_56_419225.htm). RTHK News. 27 July 2007. . Retrieved 2007-07-27.

[83] "Octopus Card company ceased all EPS transactions" (http://www.rthk.org.hk/rthk/news/expressnews/20071221/news_20071221_55_455661.htm) (in Chinese). RTHK News. 21 December 2007. . Retrieved 2008-04-02.

[84] "Octopus in hot water over `sold' personal data claim" (http://www.thestandard.com.hk/news_detail.asp?pp_cat=11&art_id=100560& sid=28905404&con_type=1&d_str=20100715). The Standard. 15 July 2010. . Retrieved 2010-07-29.

[85] "Privacy chief to start Octopus data-sharing probe" (http://www.thestandard.com.hk/news_detail.asp?we_cat=4&art_id=100804& sid=28982591&con_type=1&d_str=20100722&fc=4). The Standard. 22 July 2010. . Retrieved 2010-07-29.

[86] Ng, Jeffrey (27 July 2010). "Hong Kong's Cashless-Payment Operator Under Fire" (http://online.wsj.com/article/ SB10001424052748703292704575393041691058012.html#). WSJ.com. . Retrieved 2010-07-29.

[87] "Postal staff stamp on privacy chief" (http://www.thestandard.com.hk/news_detail.asp?pp_cat=11&art_id=101042&sid=29044821& con_type=1). The Standard. 28 July 2010. . Retrieved 2010-07-29.

[88] "Hong Kong May Outlaw Sale of Consumers' Personal Data" (http://www.bloomberg.com/news/2010-07-29/ hong-kong-may-outlaw-sale-of-consumers-personal-data-apple-daily-reports.html). Bloomberg. 28 July 2010. . Retrieved 2010-07-29.

External links

- Official home page (http://www.octopuscards.com)
- Octopus website case study (http://www.ionglobal.com/casestudy_octopus01.asp)
- Richard MacManus (2 September 2009). "Hong Kong's Octopus Card: Utility Outweighs Privacy Concerns" (http://www.readwriteweb.com/archives/hong_kongs_octopus_card.php) (in en). ReadWriteWeb. Retrieved 2009-09-05.

Official Payments Corporation

Official Payments Corporation, or **OPC** for short, is a source for electronic payment options to the United States government and other organizations. Tier Technologies Inc. wholly owns Official Payments Corporation as a subsidiary. Tier Technologies Inc. is a publicly traded company (NASDAQ:*TIER [1]). Official Payments Corporation enables citizens to use their credit card or debit card to pay anything from parking citations to tax bills.

Contracts with federal, state and local government enable Official Payments Incorporated to collect and process payments from citizens. The company works directly with the government.

Company description

OPC offers "last minute" tax payment options. People located in the U.S. can use their telephone or the web to charge payments to various government entities including federal, state, and local branches. Customers have to choose a payment category and payment type. Various types of bills account for Official Payments Sales. The most poplar include: traffic fines, gas bills, electricity bills, water bills, tuition payments, and property tax bills. The IRS also accounts for a large portion of sales for Official Payments Incorporated.

Company history

Tier Technologies, a California based consulting firm, acquired Official Payments in 2002. Official Payments has been around since 1996. The company has been an IRS payment provider since 1999. Official Payments is a partner with the United States Internal Revenue Services, the District of Columbia, over four hundred colleges and universities, twenty-five state governments, over 2,500 municipal and local government agencies, and public/private interests in all fifty states.

External links

- Official Payments Website [2]
- Tier Technologies [3]

OneVu

OneVu

OneVu [1] is an online service that enables consumers to view, track and pay bills online through their internet bank.

History and ownership

OneVu Ltd is wholly owned by VocaLink, which processes automated payments in the UK.

The company was formed in 2003 as Electronic Bill Presentment & Payment Ltd (EBPP) and changed its name and identity to OneVu Ltd in 2004.

OneVu is in effect part of VocaLink's strategy of continuous enhancement to the UK payments system through online bill payment and paperless billing.

Service principles

OneVu is a consolidated bill management service. It differs from aggregated services that 'scrape' data from other websites, by providing secure authentication which is only achievable via contractual relationships with participating organisations. Further; the OneVu service is housed within the secure infrastructure that ultimately pays 90% of UK salaries.

The service integrates with online banks' websites, largely on a 'white label' basis. Consumers use OneVu as part of everyday online banking. They benefit from the same security that is applied to their current or savings accounts.

Bill information is presented in a table and in chronological order. For each bill, the consumer can drill down to a bill summary and then, if available, to an Adobe Reader PDF version of the full bill. This information is served directly and securely from the biller's website. The consumer does not need to remember or enter additional username or password details.

Using OneVu, it is possible for consumers to manage bills that are paid automatically by Direct Debit and those of a variable nature, such as credit cards. In most cases, consumers may pay bills through the bank's secure payment service. OneVu automatically inserts bill payment reference information, making the process seamless and error-free.

For consumers who are not customers of currently participating banks, OneVu Ltd operates a stand-alone service called MyBillsOnline [2] that provides bill management without a payment facility.

Current position

OneVu is available on the websites of three banks – Lloyds TSB, Royal Bank of Scotland and NatWest – and accessible to almost nine million people who bank online. Around 300 million bills are under management.

The service is known as 'Bill Manager' on the Lloyds TSB online banking website and 'Bill management' on RBS and NatWest.

Around 25 billing organisation brands are part of the OneVu proposition. This list may be seen on the OneVu website [3] and ranges from utilities to loyalty programmes. OneVu Ltd undertakes the task of integration with participating companies' IT and billing systems, a process that typically takes three to four months.

As may be expected, the service is promoted for its convenience and ease of use, lower cost for billers and the environmental advantages associated with reducing waste paper.

Future developments

CheckFree i-series, the technology behind OneVu, is designed to manage services beyond bills. New features, both transactional and informational, will be added to the service in due course. During 2009, for example, OneVu's white-labelled bank services will be rebranded 'MyView' and feature more visibly on the Internet bank sites. The MyView evolution will also include the UK's first Internet bank mobile phone top-up service.

Further banks and billing organisations are expected to join OneVu in line with their plans for online banking and electronic billing.

Awards

In 2007, the OneVu service was voted winner for faster payments in the 'payments innovation' category of The Banker [4] Technology Awards and won the 'most innovative retail or corporate payments service' category in the EPCA/ECR (European Payments Consulting Association/European Card Review) Excellence in Payments Innovations Awards, 2007.

OneVu also was recognised as a Business Superbrand [5], together with Voca (VocaLink's predecessor) in 2005.

Online Banking ePayments

Online Banking ePayments (OBeP) is a type of payments network, developed by the banking industry in conjunction with technology providers, specifically designed to address the unique requirements of payments made via the Internet.[1]

Key aspects of OBeP which distinguish it from other online payments systems are:

1. The consumer is authenticated in real-time by the consumer financial institution's online banking infrastructure.[2]
2. The availability of funds is validated in real-time by the consumer's financial institution.[3]
3. The consumer's financial institution provides guarantee of payment to the merchant.[3]
4. Payment is made as a credit transfer (push payment) from the consumer's financial institution to the merchant, as opposed to a debit transfer (pull payment).[3]
5. Payment is made directly from the consumer's account rather than through a third-party account.[3]

Privacy & Security Features

OBeP systems protect consumer personal information by not requiring the disclosure of account numbers or other sensitive personal data to online merchants or other third parties.[4] During the checkout process, the merchant redirects the consumer to their financial institution's online banking site where they login and authorize charges. After charges are authorized, the financial institution redirects the consumer back to the merchant site. All network communications are protected using industry standard encryption. Additionally, communications with the OBeP network take place on a virtual private network, not over the public Internet.

In order to be positive that your identity, information and other personal features are truly secure, the following cautions should be taken: [5] Make sure a secure browser is being used. Read all privacy policies provided. Many individuals simply skip over such important information that could spell out potential risks. If a risk seems unnecessary and odd, it would be safer to skip this payment rather than take the risk with one's hard earned money. Keep all personal information private. If phone numbers, social security numbers or other private, important information is asked for one should be cautious. Banking information is important information as it is, asking for unnecessary personal information should be a red flag of suspicious behavior. Selecting businesses that are trustworthy is key. Most companies will email a customer with a transaction receipt upon payment. Keeping a record of these is important in order to have proof of purchase or payment. Lastly, checking bank statements regularly is crucial in keeping up-to-date with transactions.

Costs

Costs associated with fraud, estimated at 1.2% of sales by online retailers in 2009[6] , are reported to be dramatically reduced with OBeP, because the issuer bank is responsible for the authentication of the credit transaction and provides guaranteed funds to the merchant.[7]

Because the merchant is not responsible for storing and protecting confidential consumer information, OBeP systems also reduce costs associated with mitigating fraud , fraud screening, and PCI audits.

Transaction fees on Online Banking ePayments vary by network, but are often fixed, and lower than the average 1.9%[8] merchant fees associated with credit card transactions – especially for larger purchases.[9]

Other Benefits

For Consumers

- use of cash-like payment encourages responsible consumerism
- does not require set-up or registration with a third-party payments entity
- presents familiar interface to facilitate online payment
- awareness of funds availability

For Merchants

- improved sales conversion / reduced abandoned carts[10]
- real time authorization of guaranteed ACH payment (good funds)[3]
- offering preferred payment methods may drive repeat transactions

For Financial Institutions

- recapture revenue being lost to alternative payment providers[9]
- encourages consumers to move to online banking, replacing more costly branch and telephone alternatives[9]

Potential Downfalls

The idea of online payments and transactions has led numerous individuals, corporations and groups to be hesitant. Sharing of personal information to such a vast entity, such as the internet, can lead to potential problems. Remaining cautious and careful with what information is shared and to whom it is shared with is key in remaining safe and secure when using ePayments.

- identity theft is prevalent with online transactions
- no face-to-face interaction for help, questions, issues
- website issues can hinder the ability to make payments in a timely manner
- passwords - sometimes remembering a password can be difficult and with something as important as an ePayment website, it is crucial this information is not lost or forgotten

Types & Implementations

OBeP networks may be divided into two categories, based on the network architecture:

1. Multi-Bank – requires that a merchant have a single connection to the OBeP network in order to accept payment from any participating financial institution.

> *Examples include:* EPS [11], IDEAL, Interac Online, Giropay, and Secure Vault Payments [1][11]

2. Mono-Bank – requires that a merchant have a separate connection to each participating financial institution.

> *Examples include:* Nordea e-Payment [13][11]

A third category, also known as "overlay payment solutions" provide a similar consumer experience to Online Banking ePayments, but violate a key tenet of the OBeP definition by requiring the consumer to share their online banking credentials with a third party. Examples include: DIRECTebanking.com [14], sofortüberweisung.de [15], SafetyPay [16], UseMyServices [17] and POLi [18][11]

A fourth category requires that a merchant have a single connection to an alternative payment provider. This alternative payment provider then have connections to multiple online banks. This does not require the consumer to share their online banking credentials, but still offer the same advantages to the merchants as "overlay payment solutions". Examples include: inpay.com [19] and gluepay.

See Also

- Automated Clearing House
- NACHA-The Electronic Payments Association
- E-commerce payment system
- Electronic funds transfer
- Electronic money
- PCI_DSS

References

[1] ["http://icpno.com International Council of Payment Network Operators]

[2] Payments News. Scott Loftesness. July 31, 2010. (http://paymentsviews.com/2010/07/31/obep-oboy)

[3] Payments News. Carol Coye Benson. July 23, 2008. (http://www.paymentsnews.com/2008/07/an-interview--1.html)

[4] FIS News Release. March 18, 2008. (http://fis.mediaroom.com/index.php?s=43&item=352)

[5] May 22, 2011. (http://www.ftc.gov/bcp/edu/pubs/consumer/tech/tec01.shtm)

[6] CyberSource Online Fraud Report 2010. (http://forms.cybersource.com/forms/FraudReport2010NACYBSwwwQ109)

[7] eCommerce Times. Bala Janakiraman. January 26, 2009. (http://www.ecommercetimes.com/story/Alternative-Payments-More-Ways-to-Close-the-Sale-65954.html)

[8] Bloomberg. Peter Eichenbaum. June 17, 2009. (http://www.bloomberg.com/apps/news?pid=newsarchive&sid=aFkFW4ZfxsYk)

[9] SVP Whitepaper by JavelinStrategy & Research. (http://www.securevaultpayments.com)

[10] CyberSource Insiders Guide to eCommerce Payment (http://www.cybersource.com/resources/collateral/Resource_Center/whitepapers_and_reports/insiders_guide.pdf)

[11] Innopay Online Payments 2010 Report. (https://www.ebaportal.eu/_Download/Research and Analysis/2010/Online_payments_2010_Innopay.pdf)

External links

- NACHA - The Electronic Payments Association (http://www.nacha.org)
- International Council of Payment Network Operators (http://www.icpno.com)

Open Payment Initiative

The **Open Payment Initiative**, or **O.P.I.** for short, was launched to standardize the application interface between the EPOS application and any cashless payments solution installed on the EFT/PoS terminal. The specification for this interface focused mainly on international and cross-industry aspects. Today, the interface [1] is already a de facto European standard, which is spreading from Germany to retailing and mineral oil projects throughout Europe.

The specifications, which were first published in 2003, and reference installations are based on the POS EPS specifications from IFSF (International Forecourt Standards Forum), which were developed for the service station industry and to which retail features have been added. The universal O.P.I. interface has made it possible to integrate varying EFT/PoS solutions in European POS projects for the first time.

Versions

Version	Description	Published
1.2	EFT-Standard Interface for POS Applications	Febr. 2003
1.2.1	EFT-Standard Interface for POS Applications	Sept. 2003
1.3	EFT-Standard Interface for POS Applications	Febr. 2005

Technical solution

The O.P.I. interface implementation does not depend on a specific operating system. It is an XML-based interface. Communication takes place via TCP/IP. The XML messages are exchanged over two sockets that are referred to as channels (channel 0 and channel 1). The original OPI/IFSF specification defines three message pairs:

Card Request/Response (channel 0)

Service Request/Response (channel 0)

Device Request/Response (channel 1)

Using the O.P.I. interface gives a payment solution access to the PoS peripherals, e.g. to a PoS printer to print out receipts, a display to output messages to the cashier or cardholder, or a magnetic card reader. Decoupling the interface in this way increases its flexibility for integration in international, solution and industry-specific scenarios for users as well as for PoS and payment solution providers, and therefore also protects their investments.

International installations

Since 2003, the O.P.I. interface has been deployed by various software and EFT/PoS solution providers in numerous projects in Germany, France, Ireland, Austria, Portugal, Switzerland, UK and Denmark.

References

- "Open Payment Initiative" in SOURCE Informationsdienst, Nr. 3, 15. March. 2003 / 10. Jahrg., S. 3
- „Fortschritte bei der Open Payment Initiative" in SOURCE Informationsdienst, Nr. 2, 15. Febr. 2004 / 11. Jahrg., S. 6
- „Der rentable Inventurverlust" in SICHERHEITSHALBER Zeitschrift für Sicherheit in der Supply Chain des Handels, 3 / 2004, ISSN 1612-4774, S. 17
- „OPI sorgt für Flexible Kassen" in Lebensmittelzeitung, 16. April 2004, S. 30
- Horst Rüter: Kartengestützte Zahlungssysteme im Einzelhandel, Ergebnisse der Jahresuntersuchung 2004, Köln 2004, ISBN 3-87257-274-1, S. 12

- Jürgen Manske: „Open Payment Initiative - Länderübergreifender Schnittstellenstandard" in retail technology journal, 3 / 2004, S. 19
- Horst Förster: „Kartenterminals – Die nächste Stufe" in retail technology journal, 1 / 2005, S. 34f
- Cetin Acar, Ulrich Spaan: Kassensysteme 2006, Status Quo und Perspektiven, Köln 2006, ISBN 3-87257-292-X, S. 25f
- „Kartenzahlung bei Karstadt zukunftssicher" in e:view, Ausgabe 1/06, 10. February 2006, ISSN 1862-1643, S. 8f

External links

- International Forecourt Standards Forum: http://www.ifsf.org
- O.P.I. Open Payment Initiative: http://www.wincor-nixdorf.com/internet/com/Products/Software/Retail/StoreITstardard/OPI/Main,version=11.html
- O.P.I. payment interface proves itself internationally: http://www.wincor-nixdorf.com/internet/com/press/pressreleases/06opi/06opi,templateId=BusinessCategoryPressDetail.jsp.html

Optimal Payments

Neovia Financial PLC or Optimal Payments PLC

Type	Public company (LSE: NEO)
Industry	Online banking
Founded	1996
Headquarters	Douglas, Isle of Man
Key people	Mark Mayhew, CEO & president Dale Johnson, Chairman
Products	Electronic money
Revenue	▲ $65 million (2009)
Employees	447 (2009)
Website	neovia.com [1]

Optimal Payments PLC, formerly known as **Neovia Financial PLC**, is a British global payments company based in the Isle of Man and regulated in the United Kingdom. It is the provider of the Netbanx gateway, NETELLER e-wallet, and Net+ debit card products used by merchants and consumers in over 170 countries.

History

The company was formed from the combination of NETBANX and NETELLER. NETBANX was founded in 1996 and NETELLER 1999[1] . The company has been publicly traded on the London Stock Exchange since its initial public offering (IPO) in 2004[2] . In November 2008 the company renamed itself as NEOVIA Financial PLC and changed its stock ticker symbol from NLR to NEO[3] .

In March 2011, the company bought OptimalPayments and rebranded itself as Optimal Payments PLC.

Products and services

The company's products are offered via the software as a service (SaaS) model. NETBANX processes credit- and debit card-not-present and non-card payments for European and Asia global retailers through their online stores, mail-order/telephone order and automated (IVR) phone channels. The service offers both direct processing and acquiring merchant services. NETELLER is an electronic money/e-wallet stored-value service that allows consumers to send and receive money. When a user opens an account with Neteller, all of the transactions are electronically made without any delay or fuss.[4]

U.S. Internet gambling prohibition

As Internet use expanded during the 2000s, the United States government sought to prohibit online gambling by its citizens. As part of this prohibition the U.S. Department of Justice reached agreements with several companies[5] that it believed had provided advertising and payment services to offshore gambling companies including Microsoft, Google, Yahoo, Paypal[6] and Neteller (now part of Neovia Financial). Neteller ceased offering these services to U.S. residents and had the complaint against it by the U.S. Department of Justice dismissed in the summer of 2009[7] .

Notes

[1] Timeline/history (http://www.neovia.com/content/en/about_us_history.htm)

[2] NETELLER IPO Document (http://www.neovia.com/ngroup.file/12.pdf)

[3] Finextra: company renames (http://www.finextra.com/fullpr.asp?id=24594). Finextra.

[4] "Neteller Casino Overview" (http://casinossecurity.com/neteller-overview.htm). . Retrieved 2011-05-24.

[5] Washingtonpost.com: Microsoft, Google, Yahoo Settle Gambling Charges (http://www.washingtonpost.com/wp-dyn/content/article/2007/12/20/AR2007122000047.html)

[6] Cnet.com: PayPal settles over gambling transfers (http://www.news.com/2100-1017_3-5055237.html)

[7] Wall Street Journal: Dismissal Of Complaint, End Of DPA (http://online.wsj.com/article/BT-CO-20090821-702278.html)

External links

- Corporate site (http://www.optimalpaymentsplc.com/)

ORCA Platform

ORCA, Inc.

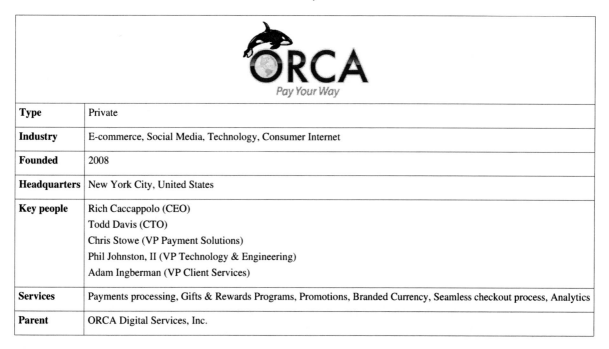

Type	Private
Industry	E-commerce, Social Media, Technology, Consumer Internet
Founded	2008
Headquarters	New York City, United States
Key people	Rich Caccappolo (CEO) Todd Davis (CTO) Chris Stowe (VP Payment Solutions) Phil Johnston, II (VP Technology & Engineering) Adam Ingberman (VP Client Services)
Services	Payments processing, Gifts & Rewards Programs, Promotions, Branded Currency, Seamless checkout process, Analytics
Parent	ORCA Digital Services, Inc.

ORCA (short for **Open Real-Time Currency Application**) is a white-labeled payments and related transactions platform focused on ecommerce via mobile, apps and desktop browsing experiences. It enables merchants to reduce payment processing costs while at the same time grow revenue and profits by utilizing integrated customer acquisition, retention, and monetization features such as Optimized Checkout, Branded Payments, Cost effective processing of Micro-Transactions, Loyalty and Rewards Programs, Digital Gift Cards, and Integrated Analytics. ORCA's open-API enables companies to control the look and feel of transactions, as well as the usage of real and virtual currency, and send marketing messages without third party interference.[1]

History

The **ORCA platform** was created in February 2008, and was launched to the public in July 2009. ORCA is funded by Metamorphic Ventures [2], KPG Ventures [3], and several prominent angels including Geoff Judge [4], Roger Ehrenberg [5], Craig Balsam [6] and John Frankel.[2] [3]

On June 22, 2009 ORCA received $2 million in series A financing.[4] [5] On August 3, 2009 MediaPost published an article about ORCA, calling it an "E-Commerce Killer App."[6]

Currently, ORCA's API is in private beta.[7] [8]

ORCA was founded in 2007[9] and is based in New York City, with additional offices in San Francisco.

Partnerships

Mashery [15], a provider of on-demand API management solutions, works with ORCA to ensure its open APIs integrate and operate smoothly within a community's interface and back office operations. Mashery manages APIs for more than 70 companies including The New York Times and Best Buy. Mashery's on-demand API infrastructure provides the access management, business rules, monitoring, and metrics required to build scalable distribution channels using web services. Launched in 2006, Mashery is backed by First Round Capital, Formative Ventures [16], The Accelerator Group [17], .406 Ventures [18] and many prominent angel investors.

Mashery is based in San Francisco, California.

Products and services

ORCA offers various services within its platform that address different payment, virtual currency and branding solutions.

The platform offers many popular features of major "closed" payment platforms such as iTunes, Amazon, Google Checkout, and Facebook credits in one unified platform. ORCA also manages merchant agreements with payment networks such as VISA, MasterCard, American Express, Discover, GiroPay [5], JCB and other international payment networks on behalf of its digital media companies.

ORCA was first made available in the United States in July 2009. The platform runs on JPOS [19], the prevailing open-source standard for financial software applications used by Chase, Blackhawk, First Data and other major financial services companies.

The extensive functionality is specifically designed for digital media companies with multiple transactions driven business models.

ORCA Pay

ORCA Pay is an online payment processing service aimed at providing digital media companies the functionality to accept online purchases using their own brands. Visitors to a specific website store their credit card, debit card or bank account information in a payment account brand of the website itself, so that users can purchase any e-commerce good at the click of a button.

ORCA Pay differs from major competitors First Data, PayPal, PaymentOne [20] and others in that ORCA allows digital media companies to have full control of the "look & feel" of the transactions process. ORCA Pay is an open-API software platform, allowing developers to integrate ORCA seamlessly into third party applications. Unlike larger competitors, ORCA enables digital media websites to create a payment account and purchase an item seamlessly within the experience on the site instead of having to use shopping cart software or redirecting to another web page of a digital payments company such as PayPal, Moneybookers, or Google Checkout.

ORCA Points

ORCA Points allows developers to create a loyalty program for users to earn points and redeem them for gifts or rewards. Like airline frequent-flyer programs, brands can offer benefits only available to VIP members, making users actively seek out elite status.

The platform is able to convert real money into virtual currency for micro-transactions. The virtual currency may be branded in any way the digital media company chooses, and popular applications include loyalty programs, rewards points, credits, virtual coins. The virtual currency conversion is of the digital media company's choosing - for example one euro might equal 800 virtual currency units, which are then used in the online transaction.

ORCA Pre

ORCA Pre gives digital companies a way for their customers to reserve popular items ahead of time, and allows developers to implement an organized advanced ordering system. The pre-ordering feature allows users to pre-pay for digital goods or content, usually at a discounted price, as they become available. This purchase is made on a digital media company's website. All currently available digital content will automatically download. Anticipated digital content or goods are downloaded automatically as they are released or published.

ORCA Post

ORCA Post helps digital media companies communicate account status and activity with their subscribers through their websites, e-mail, or text messages. Companies can send out low balance alerts, information on sales and discounts or other important information. ORCA Post enables subscribers to stay informed about important activity and also provides user analytics on where, what and when they purchased a digital good or service. ORCA provides digital media companies with an extra layer of protection for subscriber accounts. The platform enables digital media companies to set Euro or Dollar limits for different transactions, including virtual currency activity, frequency of account pre-orders and loyalty or rewards points redemption.

ORCA Pledge

ORCA Pledge is the vehicle through which digital companies can create their own branded virtual currency. Users can upload real money and seamlessly convert it to virtual money which then can be used for any online activity. ORCA Pledge is a stored value payment process, acting as digital version of popular prepaid debit cards and stored-value cards. Subscribers to digital media brands would have money on deposit or "stored" with ORCA Pledge similar to a debit card. One major difference between stored value cards and ORCA-managed accounts is that ORCA accounts are administered in the name of individual account holders, while stored value cards are usually anonymous. The value associated with the ORCA-managed account can be accessed using a mobile phone number and a password.

ORCA Executives

CEO

Richard Caccappolo, an internet industry veteran, serves as CEO. Before joining ORCA, Caccappolo was President of Creative Commerce, LLC [21], an investment and advisory firm. Prior to that, Caccappolo was a member of the senior management team at iVillage, Inc., part of NBC Universal. Prior to joining iVillage, Caccappolo served as the Chief Information Officer of Kodak Polychrome Graphics, the Director of Information Technology for Sun Chemical Europe and a senior manager of Andersen Consulting (now Andersen Consulting Accenture).

Chief Technology Officer

Todd Davis, one of the original co-founders of the company, serves as CTO. Davis was co-founder of Nobel Electronic Transfer [22], a pioneering company (the first full-service transaction processor to move from a mainframe to a server-based technology) in the merchant transaction processing world. Nobel was acquired by TriSource Solutions [23].

Board of directors

Lewis Gersh

Lewis Gersh is a Managing Partner at Metamorphic Ventures [2] which focuses on start-up and early stage companies in digital media and transaction processing technologies in both Web and mobile environments. Prior to Metamorphic, Lewis founded Worldly Information Network [24], which created and provided investment information to both the retail and institutional markets. The company was sold in 2002. Lewis graduated from San Diego State University and earned his JD and Masters in Intellectual Property from Pierce Law [25] and is a member of the NY Bar Association.

Dave Hills

Dave Hills is currently General Partner at KPG Ventures [3] where he uses his strong strategic and operational experience to identify investments and guide KPG's portfolio of companies. Dave has more than 28 years in the media industry and 14 years in online media.

Prior to joining KPG, Dave was President, Chief Executive Officer and Director of LookSmart, Ltd., where he rebuilt the company's ad network, quadrupled audience to LookSmart sites and licensed the company's ad center to sites such as Ask.com. Dave has also served as president of Media Solutions for 24/7 Real Media [26], and CEO and president of sales for About, Inc.

Dave holds an M.S. in communications from Boston University and a B.A. in communications from Bethany College.

Board of Advisors

- **John Frankel**, Advisor for Strategy

John Frankel is President of ff Asset Management [27], an early stage venture fund formed to address the funding gap of early stage companies. Frankel founded ff Asset Management after 21 years at Goldman Sachs, and four years at Arthur Andersen. Frankel was an early stage investor and director of Quigo Technologies, which was purchased by AOL in December 2007. He has also served on the boards of Alerts.com [28] and The Goldman Sachs Trust Company [29], and is currently a director of Patents.com [30] and StrongTech [31], and a member of the board of advisors of Phone.com [32].

- **Geoff Judge**, Advisor for Digital Marketing

Geoff Judge is a venture partner at iNovia [33], and an investor in early stage companies. He is an active member of The New York Angels. Judge was COO of Preclick [34], a digital software firm. Prior to Preclick Judge was COO of Media Solution Services Inc., the market leader in credit card billing insert media.[10] Prior to MSS, Geoff was SVP & GM and a co-founder of 24/7 Real Media [26], which went public in 1998, and was eventually acquired by WPP. Judge was formerly the President and COO of Interactive Imaginations, one of the 3 companies that merged to form 24/7 Media in 1997. He was Vice President: Marketing for iMarket Inc. [36], a venture-backed software company, ranked #27 on the Inc. 500 in 1996.[11] Before iMarket, Judge spent nine years at American Express in the card division in such roles as VP and General Manager, Travel & Corporate Insurance Group and VP Marketing, New Cardmember Group.

- **Steven Rockefeller**, Advisor for Finance

Steven C. Rockefeller, Jr. is founder and CEO of Re-echo Holdings, LLC., a family enterprise specializing in serving a diverse base of high growth companies. Prior, Rockefeller was a Managing Director at Deutsche Bank where he built products and services for poverty alleviation initiatives supported by both the bank and its worldwide client base. Rockefeller seeded the Deutsche Bank Micro-credit Development Fund and initiated another fund for Grameen Foundation that was eventually adopted by Citigroup.[12] The combined support of these funds, through letters of credit to ignite local lending, has brought hundreds of millions of dollars to poor women and their families throughout Asia, Latin America and Africa. Rockefeller also serves on the Board of the Soros Economic Development Fund, the Rockefeller Philanthropy Advisors, is a member of the Rockefeller University Council.

- **Andrew Rees**, Advisor for Electronic Retail

Andrew Rees leads the US Retail and Consumer Products Practice and has substantial operating and strategic experience with leading worldwide consumer brands. Rees was formerly a senior executive at Reebok International, where he was responsible for building Reebok's own retail channel into a substantial and profitable business. Subsequently, he took over responsibility for strategic planning for Reebok worldwide. He also served as an executive at Laura Ashley plc.

- **David Hirsch**, Advisor for Web & Interactive Media

David Hirsch is Managing Partner of Metamorphic Ventures [2]. Hirsch co-founded Metamorphic after eight years at Google where he was on the founding team that launched Google's advertising monetization (Google was generating $3 million in revenue when Hirsch joined). Hirsch co-founded Google's vertical market group which worked with

Fortune1000 companies as well as the top global advertising agencies.

• **Boris Fridman**, Advisor for Mobile & Wireless Media

Boris Fridman is the CEO of Crisp Wireless [39], a provider of mobile content management and delivery solutions for media and entertainment companies. Prior to Crisp, he served as Chief Operating Officer of SJ Labs [40], a developer of award-winning VoIP software products. As founder and CEO of Broadbeam Corporation, he led the company to become a premier supplier of wireless middleware products to enterprises worldwide. Fridman is also an advisory director to RidgeCrest Capital Partners [41]. He co-authored "Wireless Data for the Enterprise: Making Sense of Wireless Business"[13] published by McGraw-Hill and received a patent in the area of wireless access to the Internet.

• **Neil Cohen**, Advisor for Advertising Agencies

Neil Cohen has been creating, building and managing brands for established global companies like Sega, Hilton, Arby's and McDonald's, and for entrepreneurial companies like Ad Auction [43] and Campsix, Inc., for more than 20 years. Cohen was also Vice President of Marketing & Communications for SEGA of America. In 1995 he orchestrated the advertising and media campaign that lead the company to first place in industry market share against Nintendo and Sony, the last time the company has ever achieved that position.

References

[1] http://www.usatoday.com/money/tech/2002-04-19-paypal.htm

[2] http://orcaone.com/orca.php/news/orca-platform-announces-industry-leading-board-of-advisors/

[3] http://www.businesswire.com/portal/site/google/?ndmViewId=news_view&newsId=20090804005926&newsLang=en

[4] http://paidcontent.org/article/419-social-net-payer-onetxt-raises-2-million-first-round/

[5] http://topnews.us/content/25724-2-million-secured-social-media-payment-platform-onetxt

[6] http://www.mediapost.com/publications/?fa=Articles.showArticle&art_aid=110992

[7] http://orcaone.com/orca.php/apply-for-a-beta-api-key

[8] http://www.americanbanker.com/issues/174_124/-383327-1.html

[9] http://venturebeatprofiles.com/company/profile/onetxt

[10] Statement Inserts - Credit Cards (http://www.echo-media.com/mediacat.asp?mediatype=Stmnts - Credit)

[11] http://www.inc.com/inc5000/2007/company-profile.html?id=1996027

[12] Report of Activities: Deutsche Bank Microcredit Development Fund (http://www.community.db.com/downloads/dbmicro_dev_fund.pdf)

[13] "Wireless Data for the Enterprise: Making Sense of Wireless Business, Google Book Result (http://books.google.com/books?id=2UjWBooCNK8C&pg=PA219&lpg=PA219&dq=Wireless+Data+for+the+Enterprise&source=bl&ots=wQVMVLq6uK&sig=AEH7s5RO28DYD5ytu5FKmFcoE5c&hl=en&ei=TnzoStiAN9TtlAfvk9SJCA&sa=X&oi=book_result&ct=result&resnum=1&ved=0CAwQ6AEwAA#v=onepage&q=&f=false)

External links

• ORCA official site (http://www.orcaone.com)

• Mashery Inc., ORCA partner (http://www.mashery.com/)

• Metamorphic Ventures (http://metamorphic.vc/)

• KPG Ventures (http://www.kpgventures.com/)

PA-DSS

The **Payment Application Data Security Standard** (PA-DSS), formerly referred to as the Payment Application Best Practices (PABP), is the global security standard created by the Payment Card Industry Security Standards Council (PCI SSC). [1] PA-DSS was implemented in an effort to provide the definitive data standard for software vendors that develop payment applications. The standard aims to prevent developed payment applications for third parties from storing prohibited secure data including magnetic stripe, CVV2, or PIN. In that process, the standard also dictates that software vendors develop payment applications that are compliant with the Payment Card Industry Data Security Standards (PCI DSS).

Requirements

For a payment application to be deemed **PA-DSS** compliant, software vendors must ensure that their software includes the following 14 protections:[2]

Requirements:

1. Do not retain full magnetic stripe, card validation, code or value, or PIN block data.

2. Protect stored cardholder data.

3. Provide secure authentication features.

4. Log payment application activity.

5. Develop secure payment applications.

6. Protect wireless transmissions.

7. Test payment applications to address vulnerabilities.

8. Facilitate secure network implementation.

9. Cardholder data must never be stored on a server connected to the internet.

10. Facilitate secure remote software updates.

11. Facilitate secure remote access to payment application.

12. Encrypt sensitive traffic over public networks.

13. Encrypt all non-console administrative access.

14. Maintain instructional documentation and training programs for customers, resellers, and integrators.

Governance & Enforcement

PCI SSC has compiled a list of payment applications [3] that have been validated as PA-DSS compliant, with the list updated to reflect compliant payment applications as they are developed. Creation and enforcement of these standards currently rests with PCI SSC via Payment Application-Qualified Security Assessors (PA-QSA). PA-QSAs conduct payment application reviews that help software vendors ensure that applications are compliant with PCI standards.

History

Governed originally by Visa Inc., under the PABP moniker, PA-DSS was launched on April 15, 2008 and updated on October 15, 2008. PA-DSS then became retroactively distinguished as "version 1.1" [3] and "version 1.2"[4] .

Congressional Attention

On March 31, 2009, the United States House of Representatives' Committee on Homeland Security convened to discuss the current PCI DSS requirements.[5] Representatives such as Yvette Clark (D-NY) expressed interest in increasing the strength of standards while others, such as Bennie Thompson (D-Miss.) expressed doubt that industry created standards would be sufficient in the future.[6] While Congressional attention was focused largely on PCI DSS, the criticism of card-issuer standards could eventually bring Congressional or legal focus on PA-DSS and on PCI SSC as an entity.

Future

The future of these standards is somewhat vague, with Congressional attention giving rise to the possibility of governmental intervention. Regardless, meeting standards can prove expensive and time consuming for software vendors, with the current expense of PA-DSS certification outpacing other methods of compliance.[7] Given the cost of compliance and certification, current or as of yet undetermined alternatives could emerge in the PCI standards compliance market.

Supplemental Information

The PCI SSC has published additional materials that further clarify PA-DSS, including the following:

- PA-DSS Requirements and security assessment procedures.[8]
- Changes from past standards.[9]
- General program guide for QSAs. [10]

References

[1] PCI Security Standards Council (https://www.pcisecuritystandards.org/)

[2] PA-DSS Requirements (https://www.pcisecuritystandards.org/pdfs/pci_pa_dss.pdf)

[3] PA-DSS Version 1.1 (https://www.pcisecuritystandards.org/security_standards/pci_pa_dss_v1-1.shtml)

[4] PA-DSS Version 1.2 (https://www.pcisecuritystandards.org/security_standards/pci_pa_dss.shtml)

[5] PCI DSS Congressional Hearing (http://www.homeland.house.gov/hearings/index.asp?ID=185)

[6] Visa, MasterCard In Security Hotseat (http://www.forbes.com/2009/03/31/visa-mastercard-security-technology-security-visa.html)

[7] PA-DSS Certification Vs. Hosted Payments (http://www.elementps.com/software-providers/security/hosted-payments/pa-dss-certification/)

[8] PA-DSS Requirements and Security Assessment Procedures (https://www.pcisecuritystandards.org/pdfs/pci_pa_dss.pdf)

[9] [https://www.pcisecuritystandards.org/pdfs/pci_pa-dss_summary_changes_v11_v12.pdf Summary of PA-DSS Changes]

[10] [https://www.pcisecuritystandards.org/pdfs/pci_pa_dss_program_guide.pdf QSA Program Guide]

PaidByCash

PaidByCash is a cash payment system for Internet retailers allowing them to easily accept cash payment from their e-commerce customers, by exchanging cash for a MasterCard number at a retail location. PaidByCash was started in 2005 and is owned and operated by Retail Expansion Network, Inc [1].

PaidByCash is sold in the United States at 60,000 physical retail locations including Safeway, Inc., Circle K, and Rite-Aid. The shopper "purchases" a MasterCard number at the retail store using cash and a code printed from the website, the MasterCard number can then be used online (or over the phone) anywhere MasterCard is accepted.

The cost for the service varies by retailer and is between $1.95 and $4.95 each time cash is loaded.

Other cash payment e-commerce systems

- Konbini system (Japan)
- PostePay (Italy)
- 3V system (Europe)

Resources

- PaidByCash [2]

PAN truncation

PAN truncation is an anti-fraud measure available on some credit-card-processing POS (point of sale) terminals as part of a merchant account service.

"PAN" is an acronym for Primary Account Number, i.e., the "card number" on either a debit or a credit card. *PAN truncation* simply replaces the card number printed on a customer receipt with a printout of only a few digits, the remainder being replaced usually by asterisks. This hides the card number from anyone who obtains the receipt when discarded, or by other means, while still allowing a card holder with multiple cards to identify which was used, and thus accurately record the transaction.

PAN truncation is a measure to combat credit and debit card fraud, which is increasing dramatically worldwide, flourishing particularly in a global market where CNP (customer not present) transactions are increasingly popular over the Internet, by mail, and by telephone.

Pan-European Automated Clearing House

A **Pan-European Automated Clearing House** (PE-ACH) is an ACH that is able to settle SEPA compliant credit transfers and direct debits across the Eurozone.

At present there is only one PE-ACH in operation - STEP2 - which was established by the Euro Banking Association in April 2003. It is thought that some domestic ACHs will position themselves as PE-ACHs as SEPA is implemented.

Pay at the pump

Pay at the pump is a system used at some filling stations where customers can pay for their fuel by inserting a credit or debit card into a slot on the pump, bypassing the requirement to make the transaction with the station attendant or to walk away from one's vehicle.

The system was introduced in 1982 in Europe, and was first used in the USA by Mobil in 1986. The system allows customers the convenience of not having to walk far from their vehicle, wait in line, or wait for the human station attendant to process the transaction. It also provides the attendants the advantage of being able to

A pay at the pump system

tend to other duties rather than being busy with customers.[1] [2] Only 13 percent of convenience stores had the technology by 1994, but 80 percent of U.S. convenience stores used the technology by 2002, and virtually all stores do today. In 2004, Sheetz was the first to use touch-screen kiosks at the pump where customers can also order in-store foodservice items that they pick up after fueling.[3]

It is seen as a way to keep the cost of gasoline down by reducing the need for employees at filling stations.[4] It is considered to be a major change from the days in which full service was the norm at filling stations, and the attendant not only pumped fuel, but also washed the windshield, and checked the fluids and tire pressure, all while the customer remained in the vehicle[5] (full service is legally mandated in the U.S. states of New Jersey and Oregon).

Issues

Confusion

Some customers are confused with the technology and do not know of any alternatives.[6]

Fraud

Those who use the pay at the pump feature could be putting themselves at risk for fraud, as thieves attach skimmers to the pumps that can steal the information off the cards used to make purchases. Many debit cards can be used to make the purchase either as debit or credit. But those who make the purchases as debit are feeding their information into the skimmers.[7]

Without the human interaction, there is no verification system when credit cards are used to make purchases, and no signature is required. This enables those in possession of stolen or cloned credit cards, or those who are otherwise making unauthorized use of another's card to purchase gasoline without a signature. Many stations now require customers making credit-based transactions to enter their zip code (United States) or equivalent (other countries) in order to be allowed to make a fuel purchase.[8]

The receipts issued by the pumps, if not taken by the customer, often bear the number of the credit card used to make the purchase. If found later by a thief, this could be used to commit fraud against the customer.[9] Laws in some places prohibit the full credit card number from being displayed on the receipt.

Cost to consumers

Some stations will place a temporary block on a certain amount of money in a customer's account following the use of a debit card to make a non-PIN-based purchase, since it takes about three business days to have the accurate amount debited. This could be as little as $1 or as much as $75. While this amount is placed on hold, the customer could be penalized for non-sufficient funds when making other purchases on the same account.[10] Stations are guaranteed to receive up to this $75 on fuel purchases, even if the purchase was made fraudulently and the card-holder is not held liable.[11]

As gas prices have risen during the 2000s, many fill-ups are costing customers more than $75, the maximum amount that can be authorized from a single swipe. Credit card companies have considered raising this limit to accommodate larger purchases.[12]

Cost to employees

The pay at the pump feature has led fewer customers to enter the area of filling stations that sell other items typically sold at convenience stores, thereby hurting the profits stations make from such sales.[13] This is seen as an advantage to the customer not just for saving money, but also by reducing clutter and mess in the vehicle.[14]

The feature is also criticized for causing the loss of some jobs. While stations continue to have an attendant on duty, the customers are performing many of the former tasks of the attendant, thereby leading to less availability of employment.[15] [16]

Some filling stations are totally unattended and only allow customers to purchase fuel by paying at the pump.[17]

References

[1] http://books.google.com/books?id=LkqcpRLrQmMC&pg=PA38&dq=%22pay+at+the+pump%22&as_brr=3&ie=ISO-8859-1& output=html
[2] http://books.google.com/books?id=YwJ2me7RPbUC&pg=PA319&dq=%22pay+at+the+pump%22&as_brr=3&ie=ISO-8859-1& output=html
[3] The History of Gasoline Retailing (http://www.nacsonline.com/NACS/Resources/campaigns/GasPrices_2011/Pages/ 100PlusYearsGasolineRetailing.aspx)
[4] http://books.google.com/books?id=4bMiZSVVaw0C&pg=PA115&dq=%22pay+at+the+pump%22&lr=&as_brr=3&ie=ISO-8859-1& output=html
[5] http://books.google.com/books?id=hZ9frnkOTsQC&pg=RA1-PA287&dq=%22pay+at+the+pump%22&lr=&as_brr=3& ie=ISO-8859-1&output=html
[6] http://books.google.com/books?id=hXy-JLP9ouYC&pg=PA309&dq=%22pay+at+the+pump%22&as_brr=3&ie=ISO-8859-1& output=html
[7] http://www.msnbc.msn.com/id/27201025/
[8] http://www.csdecisions.com/article/1488/cutting-credit-card-fees.html
[9] http://books.google.com/books?id=8w8TYp7gaqAC&pg=PA56&dq=%22pay+at+the+pump%22&lr=&as_brr=3&ie=ISO-8859-1& output=html
[10] http://articles.moneycentral.msn.com/Banking/BetterBanking/HosedAtTheGasPumpByYourDebitCard.aspx
[11] http://www.foxnews.com/story/0,2933,283098,00.html

[12] http://www.washingtonpost.com/wp-dyn/content/article/2008/06/20/AR2008062003060_pf.html

[13] http://www.accessmylibrary.com/coms2/summary_0286-8361445_ITM

[14] http://books.google.com/books?id=0XzUgPXAWT0C&pg=PA289&dq=%22pay+at+the+pump%22&lr=&as_brr=3&ie=ISO-8859-1&output=html

[15] http://books.google.com/books?id=uR6fp1-hYB0C&pg=PA34&lpg=PA34&dq=%22pay+at+the+pump%22&lr=&as_brr=3&ie=ISO-8859-1&output=html

[16] http://books.google.com/books?id=mFH2NIHJfBEC&pg=PA64&dq=%22pay+at+the+pump%22&lr=&as_brr=3&ie=ISO-8859-1&output=html

[17] http://books.google.com/books?id=NorSiqCb9mMC&pg=PA249&dq=%22pay+at+the+pump%22&lr=&as_brr=3&ie=ISO-8859-1&output=html

Pay card

A **pay card** is a notation system or device used in some nightclubs to indicate the value of the drinks or services (like coat check fees) consumed by or used by a patron. Pay cards are chip cards, hole cards, or a piece of paper card with several fields which servers mark with special pens, pencils, or clippers.

When patrons leaves the nightclub, they remit their pay card to a cashier, who decodes it, and the required payment is displayed on the checkout box. The pay card is most often the property of the nightclub and stays in the cashbox for future use. Patrons losing or damaging the paycard have to pay a maximum price indicated on the paycard.

Issues

Nightclubs use paycards because it facilitates payment; staff do not have to carry change, and servers do not have to walk about the restaurant with hundreds of dollars in cash. Some nightclub owners use paycard systems because they believe that patrons drink more than in clubs that do not use paycards.

There are some disadvantages for nightclubs that use paycards. There are often long queues at the exit, especially when the club closes and is crowded. Paycards can be damaged by foam parties. Some unsophisticated paycards can be manipulated by the patron.

Paycards give patrons an incentive to escape through emergency exits, so these, in such clubs, are safeguarded by alarms.

Pay with a Tweet

Pay with a Tweet is a social media marketing system that lets content creators give away access to their content in exchange for a promotional message in form of a tweet on Twitter or a wall post on Facebook. It was founded by the advertising creative team Leif Abraham and Christian Behrendt, aka Innovative Thunder, and debuted in June, 2010 with the release of their book "OH MY GOD WHAT HAPPENED AND WHAT SHOULD I DO?" that people were able to download for free, if they would "pay with a Tweet."[1]

References

[1] OH MY GOD WHAT HAPPENED AND WHAT SHOULD I DO? - Website (http://www.ohmygodwhathappened.com)

Notes

- *Pay with a Tweet* website (http://www.paywithatweet.com)
- *Innovative Thunder* founder's website (http://www.innovativethunder.com)
- *Internet Retailer* site review (http://www.internetretailer.com/2010/07/08/will-consumers-pay-tweet)
- *Social Commerce Today* site review (http://socialcommercetoday.com/pay-with-a-tweet-pay-with-a-like-new-social-payments-platforms/)
- *ABC* about the founders (spanish) (http://www.abc.es/hemeroteca/historico-29-06-2010/abc/Medios_Redes/el-primer-libro-que-cuesta-un-tuit_140330022131.html)

PayDirect

Yahoo! PayDirect was the name of a person-to-person money transfer service by Yahoo! via HSBC, competing with Billpoint and PayPal.

Yahoo launched PayDirect in March 2000 after purchasing Athas, a provider of electronic billing services. Athas' dotBank.com service allowed customers to make online bill payments and to exchange money with other customers. When Yahoo! took over the site, the accounts were managed by international bank HSBC.

In 2000, Yahoo extended the Yahoo! PayDirect service to mobile phones, as part of its Yahoo Everywhere initiative.

The Yahoo! PayDirect service was discontinued effective November 22, 2004, leaving only a web page (biz.yahoo.com/paydirect/index.html [1]) showing "The PayDirect service and web site is closed and now unavailable."

Payment card

The term **payment card** covers a range of different cards that can be presented by a cardholder to make a payment.

Types

Typically a payment card is backed by an account holding funds belonging to the cardholder, or offering credit to the cardholder. Payment cards can be classified into types depending on how this account is managed. Different types of payment cards are described in following sections.

Example of two credit cards

Credit card

A credit card is part of a system of payments named after the small plastic card issued to users of the system. It is a card entitling its holder to buy goods and services based on the holder's promise to pay for these goods and services.[1] The issuer of the card grants a line of credit to the consumer (or the user) from which the user can borrow money for payment to a merchant or as a cash advance to the user.

A credit card is different from a charge card, where a charge card requires the balance to be paid in full each month. In contrast, credit cards allow the consumers to 'revolve' their balance, at the cost of having interest charged. Most credit cards are issued by local banks or credit unions, and are the shape and size specified by the ISO/IEC 7810 standard as ID-1. This is defined as 85.60 × 53.98 mm in size.

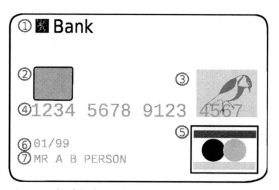

An example of the front of a typical debit card: Issuing bank logo EMVEMV chipHologramCredit card numberCard numberCard brand logo Expiration date Cardholder's name

Debit card

A debit card (also known as a *bank card* or *check card*) is a plastic card that provides an alternative payment method to cash when making purchases. Functionally, it can be called an electronic cheque, as the funds are withdrawn directly from either the bank account, or from the remaining balance on the card. In some cases, the cards are designed exclusively for use on the Internet, and so there is no physical card.[2] [3]

The use of debit cards has become widespread in many countries and has overtaken the cheque, and in some instances cash transactions by volume. Like credit cards, debit cards are used widely for telephone and Internet purchases, and unlike credit cards the funds are transferred from the bearer's bank account instead of having the bearer to pay back on a later date.

Debit card

Debit cards can also allow for instant withdrawal of cash, acting as the ATM card for withdrawing cash and as a cheque guarantee card. Merchants can also offer "cashback"/"cashout" facilities to customers, where a customer can withdraw cash along with their purchase.

Charge card

A charge card is a means of obtaining a very short term (usually around 1 month) loan for a purchase. It is similar to a credit card, except that the contract with the card issuer requires that the cardholder must each month pay charges made to it in full—there is no "minimum payment" other than the full balance. Since there is no loan, there is no official interest. A partial payment (or no payment) results in a severe late fee (as much as 5% of the balance) and the possible restriction of future transactions and risk of potential cancellation of the card.

Stored-value card

A stored-value card refers to monetary value on a card not in an externally recorded account and differs from prepaid cards where money is on deposit with the issuer similar to a debit card. One major difference between stored value cards and prepaid debit cards is that prepaid debit cards are usually issued in the name of individual account holders, while stored value cards are usually anonymous.

The term *stored-value card* means the funds and or data are physically stored on the card. With prepaid cards the data is maintained on computers affiliated with the card issuer. The value associated with the card can be accessed using a magnetic stripe embedded in the card, on which the card number is encoded; using radio-frequency identification (RFID); or by entering a code number, printed on the card, into a telephone or other numeric keypad.

Fleet card

A fleet card is used as a payment card most commonly for gasoline, diesel and other fuels at gas stations. Fleet cards can also be used to pay for vehicle maintenance and expenses at the discretion of the fleet owner or manager. The use of a fleet card also eliminates the need for cash carrying, thus increasing the level of security felt by fleet drivers. The elimination of cash also makes it easier to prevent fraudulent transactions from occurring at a fleet owner or manager's expense.

Fleet cards are unique due to the convenient and comprehensive reporting that accompanies their use. Fleet cards enable fleet owners/managers to receive real time reports and set purchase controls with their cards helping them to stay informed of all business related expenses.

Other

Other types of payment cards include:

- Gift card
- Electronic purse

Technologies

Magnetic stripe card

A magnetic stripe card is a type of card capable of storing data by modifying the magnetism of tiny iron-based magnetic particles on a band of magnetic material on the card. The magnetic stripe, sometimes called a *magstripe*, is read by physical contact and swiping past a reading head. Magnetic stripe cards are commonly used in credit cards, identity cards, and transportation tickets. They may also contain an RFID tag, a transponder device and/or a microchip mostly used for business premises access control or electronic payment.

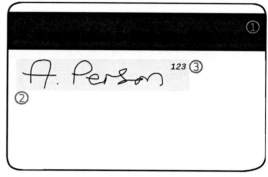

An example of the reverse side of a typical debit card:
Magnetic stripe#Financial cardsMagnetic stripeSignature strip
Card Security Code

A number of International Organization for Standardization standards, ISO/IEC 7810, ISO/IEC 7811, ISO/IEC 7812, ISO/IEC 7813, ISO 8583, and ISO/IEC 4909, define the physical properties of the card, including size, flexibility, location of the magstripe, magnetic characteristics, and data formats. They also provide the standards for financial cards, including the allocation of card number ranges to different card issuing institutions.

Smart card

A smart card, chip card, or integrated circuit card (ICC), is any pocket-sized card with embedded integrated circuits which can process data. This implies that it can receive input which is processed — by way of the ICC applications — and delivered as an output. There are two broad categories of ICCs. Memory cards contain only non-volatile memory storage components, and perhaps some specific security logic. Microprocessor cards contain volatile memory and microprocessor components. The card is made of plastic, generally PVC, but sometimes ABS. The card may embed a hologram to avoid counterfeiting. Using smart cards is also a form of strong security authentication for single sign-on within large companies and organizations.

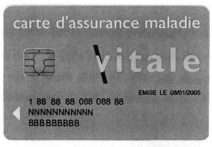

Smart card used for health insurance in France

EMV is the standard adopted by all major issuers of smart payment cards.

Proximity card

Proximity card (or prox card) is a generic name for contactless integrated circuit devices used for security access or payment systems. It can refer to the older 125 kHz devices or the newer 13.56 MHz contactless RFID cards, most commonly known as contactless smartcards.

Modern proximity cards are covered by the ISO/IEC 14443 (proximity card) standard. There is also a related ISO/IEC 15693 (vicinity card) standard. Proximity cards are powered by resonant energy transfer and have a range of 0-3 inches in most instances. The user will usually be able to leave the card inside a wallet or purse. The price of the cards is

A proximity card

also low, usually US$2–$5, allowing them to be used in applications such as identification cards, keycards, payment cards and public transit fare cards.

Security

Credit card fraud

Credit card fraud is a wide-ranging term for theft and fraud committed using a credit card or any similar payment mechanism as a fraudulent source of funds in a transaction. The purpose may be to obtain goods without paying, or to obtain unauthorized funds from an account. Credit card fraud is also an adjunct to identity theft. According to the Federal Trade Commission, while identity theft had been holding steady for the last few years, it saw a 21 percent increase in 2008. However, credit card fraud, that crime which most people associate with ID theft, decreased as a percentage of all ID theft complaints for the sixth year in a row.[4]

The cost of card fraud in 2006 were 7 cents per 100 dollars worth of transactions (7 basis points).[5] Due to the high volume of transactions this translates to billions of dollars. In 2006, fraud in the United Kingdom alone was estimated at £535 million,[6] or US$750–830 million at prevailing 2006 exchange rates.[7]

International credit card data theft

Credit card data theft is often a crime of international scope. The cost of credit card fraud reaches into billions of dollars annually. In 2006, fraud in the United Kingdom alone was estimated at £535 million,[6] or US$750–830 million at prevailing 2006 exchange rates.[7]

References

[1] Sullivan, arthur; Steven M. Sheffrin (2003). *Economics: Principles in action* (http://www.pearsonschool.com/index. cfm?locator=PSZ3R9&PMDbSiteId=2781&PMDbSolutionId=6724&PMDbCategoryId=&PMDbProgramId=12881&level=4). Upper Saddle River, New Jersey 07458: Pearson Prentice Hall. pp. 261. ISBN 0-13-063085-3. .

[2] Säkra kortbetalningar på Internet I Nordea.se (http://www.nordea.se/Privat/Kort+och+betalningar/Kort/SÄ¤kra+kortbetalningar+pÃ¥+ Internet/205784.html)

[3] e-kort (http://www.swedbank.se/sst/inf/kort-och-betalningar/0,,135189,00.html)

[4] http://www.ftc.gov/sentinel/reports/sentinel-annual-reports/sentinel-cy2008.pdf

[5] [www.sas.com/news/analysts/mercator_fraud_1208.pdf Credit Card Issuer Fraud Management, Report Highlights, December, 2008]

[6] "Plastic card fraud goes back up" (http://news.bbc.co.uk/2/hi/business/7289856.stm). BBC. 2008-03-12. . Retrieved 2010-05-22.

[7] USDGBP=X: Basic Chart for USD to GBP — Yahoo! Finance (http://finance.yahoo.com/q/bc?s=USDGBP=X&t=2y)

Payment gateway

A **payment gateway** is an e-commerce application service provider service that authorizes payments for e-businesses, online retailers, bricks and clicks, or traditional brick and mortar. It is the equivalent of a physical point of sale terminal located in most retail outlets. Payment gateways protect credit card details by encrypting sensitive information, such as credit card numbers, to ensure that information is passed securely between the customer and the merchant and also between merchant and the payment processor.

How payment gateways work

A payment gateway facilitates the transfer of information between a payment portal (such as a website, mobile phone or IVR service) and the Front End Processor or acquiring bank. When a customer orders a product from a payment gateway-enabled merchant, the payment gateway performs a variety of tasks to process the transaction:

1. A customer places order on website by pressing the 'Submit Order' or equivalent button, or perhaps enters their card details using an automatic phone answering service.
2. If the order is via a website, the customer's web browser encrypts the information to be sent between the browser and the merchant's webserver. This is done via SSL (Secure Socket Layer) encryption.
3. The merchant then forwards the transaction details to their payment gateway. This is another SSL encrypted connection to the payment server hosted by the payment gateway.
4. The payment gateway forwards the transaction information to the payment processor used by the merchant's acquiring bank.
5. The payment processor forwards the transaction information to the card association (i.e., Visa/MasterCard)
    1. If an American Express or Discover Card was used, then the processor acts as the issuing bank and directly provides a response of approved or declined to the payment gateway.
    2. Otherwise, the card association routes the transaction to the correct card issuing bank.
6. The credit card issuing bank receives the authorization request and sends a response back to the processor (via the same process as the request for authorization) with a response code. In addition to determining the fate of the payment, (i.e. approved or declined) the response code is used to define the reason why the transaction failed (such as insufficient funds, or bank link not available)
7. The processor forwards the response to the payment gateway.
8. The payment gateway receives the response, and forwards it on to the website (or whatever interface was used to process the payment) where it is interpreted as a relevant response then relayed back to the cardholder and the merchant.
9. The entire process typically takes 2–3 seconds
10. The merchant submits all their approved authorizations, in a "batch", to their acquiring bank for settlement.
11. The acquiring bank deposits the total of the approved funds in to the merchant's nominated account. This could be an account with the acquiring bank if the merchant does their banking with the same bank, or an account with another bank.
12. The entire process from authorization to settlement to funding typically takes 3 days.

Many payment gateways also provide tools to automatically screen orders for fraud and calculate tax in real time prior to the authorization request being sent to the processor. Tools to detect fraud include geolocation, velocity pattern analysis, delivery address verification, computer finger printing technology, identity morphing detection, and basic AVS checks.

Security

- Since the customer is usually required to enter personal details, the entire communication of 'Submit Order' page (i.e. customer - payment gateway) is often carried out through HTTPS protocol.
- To validate the request of the payment page result, signed request is often used - which is the result of the hash function in which the parameters of an application confirmed by a «secret word», known only to the merchant and payment gateway.
- To validate the request of the payment page result, sometimes IP of the requesting server has to be verified.
- There is a growing support by acquirers, issuers and subsequently by payments gateways for Virtual Payer Authentication (VPA), implemented as 3-D Secure protocol - branded as Verified by VISA, MasterCard SecureCode and J/Secure by JCB, which adds additional layer of security for online payments. 3-D Secure promises to alleviate some of the problems facing online merchants, like the inherent distance between the seller and the buyer, and the inability of the first to easily confirm the identity of the second.

Payment processor

A **payment processor** is a company (often a third party) appointed by a merchant to handle credit card transactions for merchant banks. They are usually broken down into two types: front-end and back-end.

Front-end processors have connections to various card associations and supply authorization and settlement services to the merchant banks' merchants. Back-end processors accept settlements from front-end processors and, via The Federal Reserve Bank, move the money from the issuing bank to the merchant bank.

In an operation that will usually take a few seconds, the payment processor will both check the details received by forwarding them to the respective card's bank issuing bank or card association for verification, and also carry out a series of anti-fraud measures against the transaction.

Additional parameters, including the card's country of issue and its previous payment history, are also used to gauge the probability of the transaction being approved.

Once the payment processor has received confirmation that the credit card details have been verified, the information will be relayed back via the payment gateway to the merchant, who will then complete the payment transaction. If verification is denied by the card association, the payment processor will relay the information to the merchant, who will then decline the transaction.

References

Payment service provider

A **payment service provider** (**PSP**) offers merchants online services for accepting electronic payments by a variety of payment methods including credit card, bank-based payments such as direct debit, bank transfer, and real-time bank transfer based on online banking. Some PSPs provide unique services to process other next generation methods (Payment systems) including cash payments, wallets such as PayPal, prepaid cards or vouchers, and even paper or e-check processing.

Typically, a PSP can connect to multiple acquiring banks, card, and payment networks. In many cases, the PSP will fully manage these technical connections, relationships with the external network, and bank accounts. This makes the merchant less dependent on financial institutions and free from the task of establishing these connections directly - especially when operating internationally.

Furthermore, a full service PSP can offer risk management services for card and bank based payments, transaction payment matching, reporting, fund remittance and fraud protection in addition to multi-currency functionality and services.

PSP fees are typically levied in one of two ways: as a percentage of each transaction or a low fixed cost per transaction.

US-based on-line payment service providers are supervised by the **Financial Crimes Enforcement Network** (or **FinCEN**), a bureau of the United States Department of the Treasury that collects and analyzes information about financial transactions in order to combat money laundering, terrorist financiers, and other financial crimes.

Payment Services Directive

The **Payment Services Directive** (PSD, 2007/64/EC) is a regulatory initiative from the European Commission (Directorate General Internal Market) which will regulate payment services and payment service providers (as defined in the Directive) throughout the European Union (EU) and European Economic Area (EEA). The purpose is to increase pan-European competition and participation in the payments industry (also from non-banks), as well as to provide for a level playing field by harmonising consumer protection and the rights/obligations for payment providers and users.[1] The final adopted text of the Directive (2007/64/EC)[2] was officially published on 5 December 2007, to be transposed into national legislation by all EU (and EEA) Member States by 1 November 2009 at the latest.[3] Although the PSD is a maximum harmonisation Directive, certain elements still allow for different options/choices[4] by individual countries.

Overview

Whereas SEPA (Single Euro Payments Area) is a self-regulatory initiative by the banking sector of Europe (represented in the European Payments Council − EPC) which defines the harmonisation of payment products, infrastructures and technical standards (Rulebooks for Credit Transfer/Direct Debit, BIC, IBAN, ISO 20022 XML message format, EMV chip cards/terminals), the PSD is driven by regulators and provides for the necessary legal framework within which all payment service providers will operate.

The PSD contains two main sections: the market rules for payment service providers and the business conduct rules.

The market rules defined in the PSD describes which type of organisations can provide payment services. Next to credit institutions (i.e. banks) and certain authorities (e.g. Central Banks, government bodies), the PSD mentions Electronic Money Institutions (EMIs), created by the E-Money Directive (EMD) in 2000, and also creates the new category of Payment Institutions with its own prudential regime rules. Organisations that are not credit institutions or EMIs, can apply for an authorisation as a PI (certain capital and risk management requirements apply) in any EU country of their choice (where they are established) and then passport their payment services into other Member States across the EU without additional PI authorisation requirements.

The business conduct rules specify the requirements around transparency of information to be provided by payment service providers to payment users, including any charges, exchange rates, transaction references and maximum execution time. It also stipulates the rights and obligations for both payment service providers and users, including how to authorise and execute transactions, liability in case of unauthorised use of payment instruments, refunds on payments, revoking payment orders, maximum execution time and value dating of payments.

Each country must designate a Competent Authority to provide prudential supervision[5] of the PIs and to monitor compliance with the business conduct rules, as transposed into national legislation.

Key dates

- March 2000: Through the Lisbon Agenda Europe's leaders decide to make Europe "the world's most competitive and dynamic knowledge-driven economy" by 2010
- Dec 2001: Regulation EC 2560/2001 on cross-border payments in euro
- 2002: Creation of the European Payments Council (EPC) by the banking industry, driving the Single Euro Payments Area initiative to harmonise the main non-cash payment instruments across the Euro area (by end 2010)
- 2001–2004: Consultation period and preparation of a Directive to create a New Legal Framework for payment services in the EU
- Dec 2005: Proposal for Directive by DG Internal Market Commissioner McCreevy
- 5 Dec 2007: Official publication of the adopted Payment Services Directive
- 1 Nov 2009: deadline for implementation of PSD in national legislation

Key implications[6]

- Removal of barriers to access by payment service providers to any EU country (cross-border service offering becomes much easier)

External links

- European Union PSD official website [7]
- European Payments Council [8]
- SEPA and the Payment Services Directive references from the Financial Services Club [9]
- 2009 EU Payment Services Directive microsite from HSBC [10]

References

[1] Payments Services Directive: Complexities on the Road to Harmonisation, Edgar, Dunn & Company White Paper (http://www.edgardunn.com/uploads/100030_english/100260.pdf)

[2] Text from the Official Journal of the European Union (http://eur-lex.europa.eu/LexUriServ/LexUriServ.do?uri=OJ:L:2007:319:0001:01:EN:HTML)

[3] Transposition status by country (http://ec.europa.eu/internal_market/payments/framework/transposition_en.htm)

[4] Member State options (http://ec.europa.eu/internal_market/payments/framework/options_en.htm)

[5] List of currently designated Competent Authorities (http://ec.europa.eu/internal_market/payments/docs/framework/transposition/authorisation_supervision_en.pdf)

[6] PSD – Business opportunities and challenges for different players (presentation at Edgar, Dunn & Company Cards & Payments Council, Frankfurt, June 12th, 2008) (http://www.edgardunn.com/uploads/100023_english/100272.pdf)

Payments Council

The **Payments Council** is an organisation of financial institutions in the United Kingdom that sets strategy for UK payment mechanisms.[1]

DRIVING CHANGE IN UK PAYMENTS

Payments Council logo

History

In his 2003 Pre-Budget Report, the Chancellor announced that the Office of Fair Trading (OFT) would lead a new Payments Systems Task Force. The OFT recommended to the Chancellor in 2006 that the Task Force should establish a new body responsible for the integrity and efficiency of co-operative payment systems in the UK. This was set up as the Payments Council in 2007.[2] [3]

By the time of a planned 2-year OFT review in 2009, the Payments Council had taken over some activities from the Association for Payment Clearing Services (APACS), which no longer exists. One of the tasks of the Payments Council has been to implement a phased roll-out the Faster Payments Service, taking clearing times in the UK from among the slowest to among the fastest in the world. Critiques have been made about delays and shortcomings in delivery and for inability to ensure Faster Payments members promptly pass on benefits to their customers.[2]

Closure of Cheque Clearing

The first major move of the Payments Council, in 2009, was to agree to a target of 2018 for the closure of cheque clearing in the UK.[4] [5] It also announced that the cheque guarantee card scheme would end in June 2011.

The Payments Council advised a Treasury Select Committee inquiry in February 2010 that cheques were in "terminal decline", down to 3.5 million per day in 2009 from a peak of 11 million in 1990.[4] After lobbying from the charity sector, the Council reaffirmed in October 2010 that the 2018 closure is conditional on adequate alternatives being in place by 2016.[6]

However, in April 2011 the Select Committee reopened its inquiry into the 2018 target date, after receiving a large volume of correspondence from small businesses, voluntary organisations and older people who were still using cheques.[7] The inquiry will also consider the structure and performance of the Payments Council, including whether it is sufficiently accountable for the impact of its decisions on consumers.[4] [8]

The chair of the inquiry, Andrew Tyrie MP, stated, "The Payments Council has not thought through its arguments carefully enough and its first piece of work on the cost-benefit of abolishing cheques was clearly defective."[4] The Payments Council welcomed the opportunity to reassure the public that cheques would not be banned before acceptable alternatives were available.[9]

Structure

Board

The Board of the Council includes an independent Chair. As a further safeguard for the public interest, four more independent members, when voting together, have a right of veto over the other 11 Board members who represent the payments industry.[2]

Membership

The Payments Council is a voluntary membership organisation, with 30 members (correct on 03 May 2011):

- Allied Irish Bank (GB)
- American Express Services Europe Ltd
- Bank Machine Limited
- Bank of America N.A.
- Bank of England
- Bank of Ireland
- The Bank of New York Mellon
- Bank of Tokyo-Mitsubishi UFJ , Ltd.
- Barclays Bank plc
- Citibank NA (London Branch)
- Clydesdale Bank plc
- Co-operative Bank plc (The)
- Danske Bank
- Deutsche Bank AG
- Group 4 Securicor
- Handelsbanken
- HSBC Bank plc
- ING Direct
- JPMorgan Chase Bank N.A. (London Branch)
- Lloyds TSB Bank plc
- Nationwide Building Society
- Northern Rock plc
- PayPal (Europe) Limited
- Post Office Limited
- Royal Bank of Scotland plc
- Santander UK plc
- Standard Chartered Bank
- Voice Commerce Group
- Wells Fargo

Other bodies such as SWIFT hold associate membership.[10] [11]

Contracts

On behalf of the UK payments industry as a whole, the Payments Council operates contracts with service providers such as BACS, CHAPS, Cheque and Credit Clearing Company Limited and the LINK ATM Scheme.[2]

References

[1] Payments Council (http://www.ukpayments.org.uk/uk_payment_schemes/payments_council/) outline at UK Payments Administration

[2] Review of the operations of the Payments Council (OFT1071) (http://www.oft.gov.uk/shared_oft/reports/financial_products/oft1071. pdf), OFT, March 2009

[3] 'Payments Council': The new name setting payments strategy in the UK (http://www.paymentscouncil.org.uk/media_centre/ press_releases/-/page/585/), Payments Council press release, 2007

[4] King, Mark. Abolition of cheques to be reconsidered (http://www.guardian.co.uk/money/2011/apr/14/ abolition-cheques-reconsidered-payments-council), *The Guardian*, 14 April 2011

[5] 2018 target date set for closure of central cheque clearing (http://www.paymentscouncil.org.uk/media_centre/press_releases/-/page/855/), Payments Council press release, 16 December 2009

[6] Mair, Vibeka. Abolition of cheques in 2018 not definite, says Payments Council (http://www.civilsociety.co.uk/finance/news/content/ 7641/abolition_of_cheques_in_2018_not_definite_says_payments_council), *Civil Society*, 29 October 2010

[7] Moore, Elaine; Ross, Alice. Inquiry reopened into ban on cheques (http://www.ft.com/cms/s/2/ 0ba42456-667e-11e0-ac4d-00144feab49a.html). *Financial Times*, 14 April 2011. Retrieved 19 April 2011. Archived (http://www. webcitation.org/5y3lIpNFR) April 19, 2011 at WebCite

[8] The future of cheques (http://www.parliament.uk/business/committees/committees-a-z/commons-select/treasury-committee/news/ new-inquiry-the-future-of-cheques/), Commons Select Committee, 14 April 2011

[9] Cheque abolition to be examined by MPs (http://www.bbc.co.uk/news/business-13080850), BBC News, 14 April 2011

[10] SWIFT joins the Payments Council (http://www.bobsguide.com/guide/news/2011/Apr/11/SWIFT_joins_the_Payments_Council. html), press release, 11 April 2011. Retrieved 19 April 2011.

[11] Associate Member List (http://www.paymentscouncil.org.uk/our_members/associate_membership/associate_member_list/), Payments Council. Retrieved 19 April 2011.

External links

- Payments Council (http://www.paymentscouncil.org.uk)

Payoneer

Payoneer

Type	Online Payment, International Money Transfer and Prepaid Debit Cards
Founded	New York, New York (2005)
Headquarters	New York, New York
Website	Payoneer.com [1]

Payoneer is an Internet-based financial services business that allows users to transfer money and receive payments through re-loadable prepaid MasterCard debit cards. The company focuses on specific payment solutions, primarily affiliate, mass payments, Local Electronic Funds Transfer (EFT), merchant accounts, and payout programs in countries with underdeveloped banking systems.

Payoneer is a registered Member Service Provider (MSP) of MasterCard worldwide. The Company is headquartered in New York City with R&D offices in Tel Aviv, Israel. Payoneer has received venture funding from Greylock Partners, Carmel Ventures, and Crossbar Capital.[1] [2]

Alternative payments

Many card Issuing Banks issue prepaid Visa Inc. or MasterCard debit cards either directly or through Member Service Providers (MSPs). In order to compete, many of these organizations target specific markets, where they can differentiate their products. Payoneer pursues a number of markets by providing salary and commission payout solutions for industries like affiliate marketing [3], summer camps,[4] freelancers,[5] direct selling and clinical trials.[6]

Techcrunch described Payoneer as a competitor to Paypal, having an "advantage over Paypal in the micro-payments arena" because "it makes international payments easier by not requiring a bank account for verification."[1] According to *The New York Observer*, a large share of the traffic to Payoneer's web site comes from Russia and Central Asian countries like Krgyzstan, Uzbekistan and Kazakhstan.[7] Payoneer has a partnership with the freelance-marketplace firm Guru.com; 85% of Guru.com pay card holders are from outside USA.[8]

The New York Observer reports that Payoneer uses Belize's Choice Bank Limited and the Iowa's MetaBank for some of its services, after it has used the First Bank of Delaware in the past.[7]

Questions in al-Mabhouh assassination

Dubai police reported that Payoneer cards were used in financial operations behind the assassination of Mahmoud al-Mabhouh, Hamas militant, in 2010.[9] Payoneer's management and funding connections to former Israeli army and special forces soldiers fueled conjecture around potential conspiracy.[7] [10] The incident resulted in Payoneer and others in the prepaid card industry to review and improve security around the movement of funds through their systems.

References

[1] Schonfeld, Erick (2008-07-24). "Payoneer Raises $8 million Series B From Greylock And Carmel" (http://techcrunch.com/2008/07/24/payoneer-raises-8-million-series-b-from-greylock-and-carmel). TechCrunch. . Retrieved 2011-02-28.

[2] Chowdhry, Amit (2007-03-26). "Greylock Partners Leads $4 Million Series A Investment In Payoneer" (http://pulse2.com/2007/03/26/greylock-partners-leads-4-million-series-a-investment-in-payoneer/). Pulse2. . Retrieved 2011-02-28.

[3] "Avangate Pays Vendors and Affiliates Using the new Avangate Prepaid MasterCard Powered by Payoneer" (http://www.prweb.com/releases/avangate/prepaid-debit-mastercard/prweb1865714.htm). PRWeb. 2009-01-15. . Retrieved 2011-03-03.

[4] Shifrin, Peter (2010-03-02). "Paying with Plastic: Camping Style" (http://www.acacamps.org/content/paying-plastic-camping-style). Camping Magazine. . Retrieved 2011-02-28.

[5] "oDesk Expands Provider Payment Options with Payoneer and the oDesk Debit MasterCard" (http://www.odesk.com/w/ odesk-expands-provider-payment-options-payoneer-debit-mastercard). oDesk. 2007-04-30. . Retrieved 2011-02-28.

[6] "New York Hospital Uses Prepaid Cards to Pay Study Participants" (http://www.centerwatch.com/news-resources/clinical-trials-today/ headline-details.aspx?HeadlineID=853). CenterWatch. 2010-03-23. . Retrieved 2011-02-28.

[7] Abelson, Max (2010-03-09). "New York City's Assassination Connection" (http://www.observer.com/2010/wall-street/ new-york-citys-assassination-connection). The New York Observer. . Retrieved 2011-02-15.

[8] Heet, LaRita (2009-09-29). "More employees say 'hello' to payroll cards" (http://www.creditcards.com/credit-card-news/ payroll-cards-pay-cards-walmart-1271.php). CreditCards.com. . Retrieved 2011-02-28.

[9] McGregor, S.; Walter, V., Setrakian, L. (2010-02-24). "Dubai Police Release New Suspects in Hit Squad Killing" (http://abcnews.go.com/ International/Blotter/dubai-police-release-suspects-hit-squad-killing/story?id=9930164). ABC News. . Retrieved 2011-02-15.

[10] Murphy, Brian (2010-02-24). "Dubai police allege assassination team in Hamas commander's slaying used credit cards issued by Iowa bank" (http://thegazette.com/2010/02/24/ dubai-police-allege-assassination-team-in-hamas-commanders-slaying-used-credit-cards-issued-by-iowa-bank/). Gazette.com (SourceMedia). . Retrieved 2011-02-15.

External links

- Payoneer homepage (https://www.payoneer.com/)

PayPal

PayPal Inc.

Type	Subsidiary of eBay Inc.
Founded	Palo Alto, California USA (1998)
Founder	Ken Howery Max Levchin Elon Musk Luke Nosek Peter Thiel
Headquarters	San Jose, California USA
Area served	Worldwide
Key people	Scott Thompson, President Patrick Dupuis, CFO
Revenue	US$2.23 billion (2009)
Owner	eBay Inc.
Website	PayPal.com [1]
Alexa rank	31 [1]
Advertising	Yes
Registration	Optional
Available in	Multilingual
Current status	Active

PayPal is an e-commerce business allowing payments and money transfers to be made through the Internet. Online money transfers serve as electronic alternatives to traditional paper methods such as cheques and money orders.

A PayPal account can be funded with an electronic debit from a bank account or by a credit card. The recipient of a PayPal transfer can either request a cheque from PayPal, establish their own PayPal deposit account or request a transfer to their bank account.

PayPal performs payment processing for online vendors, auction sites, and other commercial users, for which it charges a fee. It may also charge a fee for receiving money, proportional to the amount

eBay's North First Street satellite office campus (home to PayPal's corporate headquarters)

received. The fees depend on the currency used, the payment option used, the country of the sender, the country of the recipient, the amount sent and the recipient's account type.[2] In addition, eBay purchases made by credit card through PayPal may incur extra fees if the buyer and seller use different currencies.

On October 3, 2002, PayPal became a wholly owned subsidiary of eBay.[3] Its corporate headquarters are in San Jose, California, United States at eBay's North First Street satellite office campus. The company also has significant operations in Omaha, Nebraska; Scottsdale, Arizona; and Austin, Texas in the U.S., Chennai, Dublin, Kleinmachnow (near Berlin) and Tel-Aviv. As of July 2007, across Europe, PayPal also operates as a Luxembourg-based bank.

On March 17, 2010, PayPal entered into an agreement with China UnionPay (CUP), China's bankcard association, to allow Chinese consumers to use PayPal to shop online.[4] PayPal is planning to expand its workforce in Asia to 2,000 by the end of the year 2010.[5] [6]

Between December 4–9, 2010, PayPal services were disrupted due to denial-of-service attacks organized by Anonymous in retaliation for PayPal's decision to freeze the account of WikiLeaks citing terms of use violations over the publication of leaked US diplomatic cables.[7] [8] [9] [10]

History

Beginnings

The current incarnation of PayPal is the result of a March 2000 merger between Confinity and X.com.[11] Confinity was founded in December 1998 by Max Levchin, Peter Thiel, Luke Nosek, and Ken Howery, initially as a Palm Pilot payments and cryptography company.[12] X.com was founded by Elon Musk in March 1999, initially as an Internet financial services company. Both Confinity and X.com launched their websites in late 1999.[13] Both companies were located on University Avenue in Palo Alto. Confinity's website was initially focused on reconciling beamed payments from Palm Pilots[14] with email payments as a feature and X.com's website initially featured financial services with email payments as a feature.

At Confinity, many of the initial recruits were alumni of *The Stanford Review*, also founded by Peter Thiel, and most early engineers hailed from the University of Illinois at Urbana-Champaign, recruited by Max Levchin. On the X.com side, Elon Musk recruited a wide range of technical and business personnel, including many that were critical to the combined company's success, such as Amy Klement, Sal Giambanco, Roelof Botha[15] of Sequoia Capital, Sanjay Bhargava and Jeremy Stoppelman.[16]

To block potentially fraudulent access by automated systems, PayPal used a system (see CAPTCHA) of making the user enter numbers from a blurry picture, which they coined the Gausebeck-Levchin test.[17]

eBay watched the rise in volume of its online payments and realized the fit of an online payment system with online auctions. eBay purchased Billpoint in May 1999, prior to the existence of PayPal. eBay made Billpoint its official payment system, dubbing it "eBay Payments," but cut the functionality of Billpoint by narrowing it to only payments made for eBay auctions. For this reason, PayPal was listed in many more auctions than Billpoint. In February 2000, the PayPal service had an average of approximately 200,000 daily auctions while Billpoint (in beta) had only 4,000 auctions.[18] [19] [20] By April 2000, more than 1,000,000 auctions promoted the PayPal service.[21] PayPal was able to turn the corner and become the first dot-com to IPO after the September 11 attacks.[22]

Acquisition by eBay

In October 2002, PayPal was acquired by eBay for $1.5 billion.[23] PayPal had previously been the payment method of choice by more than fifty percent of eBay users, and the service competed with eBay's subsidiary Billpoint, Citibank's c2it, whose service was closed in late 2003, and Yahoo!'s PayDirect, whose service was closed in late 2004. Western Union announced the December 2005 shut down of their BidPay service but subsequently sold it in 2006 to CyberSource Corporation. BidPay subsequently ceased operations on December 31, 2007. Some competitors which offer some of PayPal's services, such as Google Checkout, Wirecard, and Moneybookers remain in business, despite the fact that eBay now requires everyone on its Australian and United Kingdom sites to offer PayPal.[24] [25] eBay Australia was subsequently forced to moderate its position by the Australian Competition & Consumer Commission, mandating that sellers on eBay Australia offer PayPal as one of the (but not necessarily the only) payment methods.[26] These accepted payment methods include bank deposit, cheques and money orders, escrow, and credit cards (processed by other than PayPal).[27]

In January 2008, PayPal agreed to acquire Fraud Sciences, a privately-held Israeli start-up company with expertise in online risk tools, for $169 million, in order to enhance eBay and PayPal's proprietary fraud management systems and accelerate the development of improved fraud detection tools.[28] In November 2008, the company acquired Bill Me Later, an online payments company offering transactional credit at over 1000 online merchants in the US.[29]

PayPal's total payment volume, the total value of transactions, was US$ 60 billion in 2008, an increase of 27 percent over the previous year,[30] and US$ 71 billion in 2009, an increase of 19 percent over the previous year.[31] The company continues to focus on international growth and growth of its Merchant Services division, providing e-payments for retailers off eBay.

Business today

Currently, PayPal operates in 190 markets, and it manages more than 232 million accounts, more than 87 million of them active. PayPal allows customers to send, receive, and hold funds in 24 currencies worldwide.[30] These currencies are the Australian dollar, Brazilian real, Canadian dollar, Chinese renminbi yuan (only available for some Chinese accounts, see below), Euro, pound sterling, Japanese yen, Czech koruna, Danish krone, Hong Kong dollar, Hungarian forint, Israeli new sheqel, Malaysian Ringgit, Mexican peso, New Zealand dollar, Norwegian krone, Philippine Peso, Polish zloty, Singapore dollar, Swedish krona, Swiss franc, New Taiwan Dollar, Thai Baht and U.S. dollar. PayPal operates locally in 21 countries.

Residents in 194 markets can use PayPal in their local markets to send money online.

PayPal revenues for Q1 2009 were $643 million, up 11 percent year over year. 42 percent of revenues in q1 2009 were from international markets. PayPal's Total Payment Volume (TPV), the total value of transactions in Q1 2009 was nearly $16 billion, up 10 percent year over year.[32]

In 2008, PayPal's TPV off eBay exceeded volume on eBay for the first time. PayPal's Total Payment Volume in 2008 was $60 billion representing nearly 9 percent of global e-commerce and 15 percent of US e-commerce.[33]

At an analyst day on March 11, 2009, eBay CEO John Donahoe announced that PayPal could be a larger driver of revenue than the eBay marketplaces business.[34] RIM announced that PayPal will be the only payment mechanism for its Blackberry App World, which launched on April 1, 2009.[35]

PayPal launched Student Accounts for teens in August 2009 allowing parents to set up a student account, transfer money into it, and obtain a debit card for student use. The program provides tools to teach teens how to spend money wisely and take responsibility for their actions.[36] [37]

In November 2009 PayPal opened its platform, allowing other services to get access to its code and to use its infrastructure in order to enable peer-to-peer online transactions.[38]

Although PayPal's corporate headquarters are located in San Jose, PayPal's operations center is located near Omaha, Nebraska, where the company employs more than 2,000 people as of 2007.[39] PayPal's European headquarters are in Luxembourg and international headquarters in Singapore. In October of 2007, PayPal opened a data service office on the north side of Austin. The company also recently opened a technology center in Scottsdale, Arizona, and Chennai, India.

PayPal Operations Center and main office outside Omaha, NE

PayPal business model evolution

PayPal's success in terms of users and volumes was the product of a three-phase strategy described by eBay CEO Meg Whitman: *"First, PayPal focused on expanding its service among eBay users in the U.S. Second, we began expanding PayPal to eBay's international sites. And third, we started to build PayPal's business off eBay".*[40]

Phase-1

In the first phase, payments volumes were coming mostly from eBay auction web-site. The system was very attractive to auction sellers, most of which were individuals or small businesses that were unable to accept credit card, and for consumers as well. In fact, many sellers could not qualify for a credit card "merchant account" because they lacked a commercial credit history. The service also appealed to auction buyers because they could fund PayPal accounts using credit cards or bank account balances, without divulging credit card numbers to unknown sellers. PayPal employed an aggressive marketing campaign to accelerate its growth, depositing $10 in new users' PayPal accounts (+$10 for each new user they referred).

Phase-2

The biggest challenge in 2000 remained PayPal's unsustainable business model. Initially, PayPal offered its service free of charge, planning to earn interest on funds in users' PayPal accounts (i.e., the "float"). However, most recipients withdrew their funds immediately. Furthermore, a large majority of senders funded their payments using credit cards, which cost PayPal roughly 2% of payment value, rather than relying on electronic transfers from bank accounts, which were much less costly.

In order to boost its user base over eBay, both in US and internationally, PayPal decided to lever some of the ever existing concerns of sellers and buyers dealing with the virtual world, simplifying and easing the procedures regarding litigations, frauds and liabilities (transaction losses borne by PayPal also included the cost of buyer and seller protection programs. In fact, when merchants went bankrupt—not rare events in online retailing—PayPal was liable for any outstanding chargebacks related to credit card-funded PayPal payments. As with credit cards, buyers were protected against unauthorized use of their PayPal accounts. In addition, eBay buyers using PayPal received up to $1,000 in fraud protection (with a limit of three refunds per year) for items never delivered or materially misrepresented, but only if the seller had high eBay feedback ratings. Finally, subject to a $5,000 annual cap, merchants with business accounts qualified for seller protection against losses due to chargebacks, provided that they complied with reimbursement policies (e.g., retaining traceable proof of shipping to a confirmed address or requiring a signature receipt for items valued over $250).

Phase-3

After fine-tuning PayPal's business model and increasing its domestic and international penetration on eBay, PayPal started its off-eBay strategy. Strong growth in active users growth by adding users across multiple platforms, despite the slowdown in on-eBay growth and low-single-digit user growth on the eBay site. A late 2003 reorganization created a new business unit within PayPal—Merchant Services—to provide payment solutions to small and large e-commerce merchants outside the eBay auction community. Starting in the second half of 2004, PayPal Merchant Services unveiled several initiatives to enroll online merchants outside the eBay auction community, including:

- Lowering its transaction fee for high-volume merchants from 2.2% to 1.9% (while increasing the monthly transaction volume required to qualify for the lowest fee to $100,000)
- Encouraging its users to recruit non-eBay merchants by increasing its referral bonus to a maximum of $1,000 (versus the previous $100 cap)
- Persuading credit card gateway providers, including CyberSource and Retail Decisions USA, to include PayPal among their offerings to online merchants.
- Hiring a new sales force to acquire large merchants such as Dell, Apple's iTunes, and Yahoo! Stores, which hosted thousands of online merchants
- Reducing fees for online music purchases and other "micropayments"
- Launching PayPal Mobile, which allowed users to make payments using text messaging on their cell phones

Local restrictions

China

In China PayPal offers two kinds of accounts:

- PayPal.com accounts, for sending and receiving money to/from other PayPal.com accounts. All non-Chinese accounts are PayPal.com accounts, so these accounts may be used to send money internationally.
- PayPal.cn accounts, for sending and receiving money to and from other PayPal.cn accounts.

It is impossible to send money between PayPal.cn accounts and PayPal.com accounts, so PayPal.cn accounts are effectively unable to make international payments. For PayPal.cn, the only supported currency is the renminbi.

Japan

In late March 2010, new Japanese banking regulations forced PayPal Japan to suspend the ability of personal account holders registered in Japan from sending or receiving money between individuals and as a result are now subject to PayPal's business fees on all transactions.[41] [42]

Taiwan

As of mid July 2010, users in Taiwan have noticed that the "Personal" tab for sending money has been omitted without notice. There is no longer an option to send personal payments, thus forcing all recipients to pay a fee.

Brazil

As of mid-November 2010, users in Brazil also have noticed that the "Personal" tab for sending money has been omitted without notice. There is no longer an option to send personal payments, thus forcing all recipients to pay a fee. Balance transfers between PayPal accounts of the same account holder incur an additional 6.4% fee.

As of beginning January 2011, Brazilian users are no longer allowed to withdraw money using credit/debit cards.

India

As of March 2011, PayPal made changes to the User Agreement for Indian users to comply with Reserve Bank of India regulations [44]. Notable changes to the agreement were:

- Export related payments for goods and services may not exceed $500.
- Any balance or future payments must not be used to buy goods or services but transferred to a bank account within 7 days from the receipt of payment.
- Credit/Debit cards must be used to pay through Paypal.

PayPal Labs

PayPal's innovation environment, PayPal-Labs.com,[43] hosts several outreach and experimental projects such as the storefront application,[44] the MySpace and Facebook donation widgets, and the PayPal blog.[45]

Bank status

Peter Thiel, the founder of PayPal, has stated that PayPal is not a bank because it does not engage in fractional-reserve banking.[46] Rather, PayPal's funds that have not been disbursed are kept in commercial interest-bearing checking accounts.[47]

In the United States, PayPal is licensed as a money transmitter on a state-by-state basis.[48] PayPal is not classified as a bank in the United States, though the company is subject to some of the rules and regulations governing the financial industry including Regulation E consumer protections and the USA PATRIOT Act.[49]

Commencing 2 July 2007, as PayPal (Europe) S.à r.l. & Cie, S.C.A., PayPal moved its European operations from the UK to Luxembourg. As a Luxembourg entity, it is since regulated as a bank by the Commission de Surveillance du Secteur Financier (CSSF) and provides PayPal service throughout the European Union.

Safety and protection policies

The PayPal Buyer Protection Policy states that the customer may file a buyer complaint within 45 days if they did not receive an item or if the item they purchased was significantly not as described. If the buyer used a credit card, they might get a refund via chargeback from their credit-card company. However, in the UK, where such a purchaser is entitled to specific statutory protections (that the credit card company is a second party to the purchase and is therefore equally liable in law if the other party defaults or goes into liquidation) under Section 75 Consumer Credit Act 1977, the purchaser loses this legal protection if the card payment is processed via PayPal.

According to PayPal, it protects sellers in a limited fashion via the Seller Protection Policy.[50] In general the Seller Protection Policy is intended to protect the seller from certain kinds of chargebacks or complaints if seller meets certain conditions including proof of delivery to the buyer. PayPal states the Seller Protection Policy is "designed to protect sellers against claims by buyers of unauthorized payments and against claims of non-receipt of any merchandise". The policy includes a list of "Exclusions" which itself includes "Intangible goods", "Claims for receipt of goods 'not as described'" and "Total reversals over the annual limit". There are also other restrictions in terms of the sale itself, the payment method and the destination country the item is shipped to (simply having a tracking mechanism is not sufficient to guarantee the Seller Protection Policy is in effect).[51] The PayPal Seller Protection Policy does not provide the additional consumer protection afforded by UK consumer legislation (e.g. Sale of Goods

Act) and in addition it cannot be enforced in the Courts because PayPal operates from Luxembourg, outside all three of the UK legal jurisdictions.

Security

Security key

In early 2006, PayPal introduced an optional security key as an additional precaution against fraud. A user account tied to a security key has a modified login process: the account holder enters their login ID and password, as normal, but is then prompted to press the button on the security key and enter the six-digit number generated by it. For convenience, the user may append the six-digit to their password in the login screen. This way they are not prompted for it on another page. Using this method is required for some services, such as when using PayPal through the eBay application on iPhone.

This two-factor authentication is intended to make account compromise by a malicious third party without access to the physical security key difficult, although it does not prevent so-called Man in the Browser (MITB) attacks. However, the user (or malicious third party) can alternatively authenticate by providing the credit card or bank account number listed on their account. Thus, the PayPal's implementation does not offer the security of true two-factor authentication.

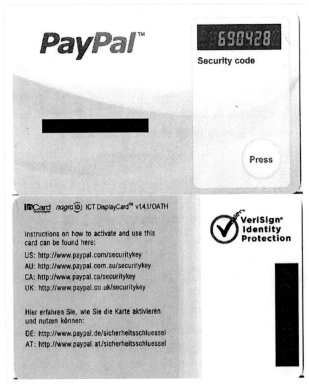

A credit-card sized alternative to the keychain security token, the PayPal Keycard generates a temporary login code to authenticate the user.

The key currently costs US$29.95 for all users with no ongoing fees.[52] The option of using a security key with one's account is currently available only to users registered in Australia, Germany, Canada, the United Kingdom and the United States.[53]

MTAN

It is also possible to use a mobile phone to receive an MTAN (Mobile Transaction Authentication Number) via SMS.[54] Like all security measures, there have been reports of vulnerabilities to older mobile handsets.[55]

Regulation

In Europe, PayPal is registered as a bank in Luxembourg under the legal name PayPal (Europe) Sàrl et Cie SCA, a company regulated centrally by the Luxembourg bank authority, the Commission de Surveillance du Secteur Financier (CSSF)[56] (note that all of the company's European accounts were transferred to the PayPal's bank in Luxembourg on July 2, 2007.[57]) Prior to this move, PayPal had been registered in the UK as PayPal (Europe) Ltd, an entity which was licensed as an Electronic Money Issuer with the UK's Financial Services Authority (FSA) from 2004. This ceased in 2007, when the company moved to Luxembourg.[58] [59] It is therefore not possible for UK customers to obtain legal redress from the company in the English, Scottish, or Northern Irish Courts.

In the US, although PayPal has an extensive User Agreement,[60] PayPal is not directly regulated by the U.S. federal government, because it serves as a payment intermediary.[61] The law is unclear as to whether PayPal is a bank, narrow bank, money services business or money transmitter. PayPal could also be subject to state regulation, but state laws vary, as do their definitions of banks, narrow banks, money services businesses and money transmitters. The most analogous regulatory source of law for PayPal transactions comes from P2P payments using credit and debit cards. Ordinarily, a credit card transaction, specifically the relationship between the issuing bank and the cardholder, is governed by the Truth in Lending Act (TILA) 15 U.S.C. §§ 1601-1667f as implemented by Regulation Z, 12 C.F.R. pt. 226, (TILA/Z). TILA/Z requires specific procedures for billing errors, dispute resolution and limits cardholder liability for unauthorized charges.[62] Similarly, the legal relationship between a debit cardholder and the issuing bank is regulated by the Electronic Funds Transfer Act (EFTA) 15 U.S.C. §§ 1693-1693r, as implemented by Regulation E, 12 C.F.R. pr. 205, (EFTA/E). EFTA/E is directed at consumer protection and provides strict error resolution procedures.[63] However, because PayPal is a *payment intermediary* and not otherwise regulated directly, TILA/Z and EFTA/E do not operate exactly as written once the credit/debit card transaction occurs via PayPal. Basically, unless a PayPal transaction is funded with a credit card, the consumer has no recourse in the event of fraud by the seller.

In India, as of January 27, 2010, PayPal has no cross-border money transfer authorization. In The New York Times article "India's Central Bank Stops Some PayPal Services", Reserve Bank of India spokesman Alpana Killawalla stated: "Providers of cross-border money transfer service need prior authorization from the Reserve Bank under the Payment and Settlement Systems Act, PayPal does not have our authorization."[64] PayPal is not listed in the "Certificates of Authorisation issued by the Reserve Bank of India under the Payment and Settlement Systems Act, 2007 for Setting up and Operating Payment System in India".[65]

Fraud

If an unauthorized third party obtains and uses someone's PayPal login information and completes a transaction using the accountholder's debit or credit card, EFTA/E and TILA/Z make PayPal responsible for the breach. There are, of course, fact specific exceptions to this rule. One is if funds are illicitly withdrawn from a PayPal deposit account. In that situation, neither PayPal nor the bank is required to return the funds, because the agreement between a consumer and PayPal makes those types of transactions *authorized*.[66]

PayPal account holders' private information is marginally protected under one federal law. Since PayPal is a *financial institution* under the Gramm-Leach-Bliley Act (GLB), it cannot disclose its account holders' non-public personal information to third parties unless account holders opt in to those disclosures.[67]

If an account is subject to fraud or unauthorized use, PayPal puts the "Limited Access" designation on the account. At this point, the account holder must:

- Log in
- Reset their password
- Develop a set of security questions (based on the subjective and not fact — e.g. "What is your favorite ice cream?" *not* "What is your mother's maiden name?")
- Verify location by phone or by mail

Phishing

PayPal presents anti-phishing advice on their website[68] for identifying and reporting phishing. PayPal encourages consumers to report all phishing emails to them.

Criticism and limitations

The current (2011/04/15 09:17 CST) PayPal user agreement is a 34 page long pdf document[69]. If one buys an item from a PayPal merchant, one is agreeing to an additional layer of arbitration beyond the merchant himself. Thus even if the merchant has acted improperly, PayPal has not violated their own policy until the user has gone through an extra arbitration process with PayPal. According to their 34-page (single-spaced) user agreement, "If a sender of a payment files a Chargeback, the credit card issuer, not PayPal, will determine who wins the Chargeback," which confirms that a user can employ the normal (legally mandated) dispute resolution process with his credit card issuer, instead of following PayPal's procedures. A user who reads section 13.7 (on page 27) finds notice that the user may have chargeback rights independent of the dispute resolution procedure privileges granted by the PayPal UA. Section 14.1 is entitled "Contact PayPal First" indicates that in case of a dispute, the user must contact PayPal first.

In September 2005, Richard Kyanka, owner of the website Something Awful, set up an account to collect donations for Hurricane Katrina to be given to the Red Cross. Owing to the high rate at which donations were made, the account was automatically frozen, and Kyanka criticized the time and difficulty involved in getting PayPal's customer service to unfreeze the account. In response to the concerns of Something Awful members over the charity used by PayPal, United Way, Kyanka finally opted to have the money refunded to the donors so that they could donate directly to their charities of choice, though PayPal did not refund exchange and handling fees for international donors.[70] [71]

In March 2008, Australian current affairs show Today Tonight aired a segment criticising PayPal, with regard to safety, freezing accounts and customer service.[72]

Several PayPal gripe sites have been created complaining of problems such as the freezing of accounts of eCommerce stores if they experience rapid growth, preventing them from being able to pay suppliers and fulfill orders.[73] One such site, Paypalsucks.com,[74] ranked third on a Forbes Magazine listing of "Top Corporate Hate Web Sites" in 2005 based on "hostility" and "entertainment value" of web forum postings and other criteria.[75]

In June 2008, the Australian Competition and Consumer Commission found that, "The evidence available does not support the view that PayPal is the most secure method of payment, or offers the best service for all transactions."[76]

In February 2010, PayPal stopped or reversed all "personal" transactions in or out of India without prior notice. Funds already transferred and transactions that had previously been "completed" were reversed leaving many vendor accounts over-drafted. Companies, contractors and service providers throughout India were left in debt to PayPal for services they had already provided when PayPal, without warning or consent, returned funds vendors had already received and withdrawn.[77]

In spite of its international reach, PayPal has limited functionalites for multi-country users, most notably the impossibility to have bank accounts in several countries, or to have a shipping address in a different country than one's bank account / credit card.

In March 2010, PayPal froze donations to Cryptome, seizing over $5300 of in-transit donations.[78] PayPal refused to inform Cryptome of the reason for this action, claiming that to disclose why the donations had been confiscated would violate Cryptome's own privacy.[79] A week later, PayPal offered an apology, which was rejected by Cryptome founder John Young as "insulting and unacceptable".[80]

In September 2010, PayPal froze the account of Markus Persson, developer of independent video game Minecraft. His account contained around €600,000.[81] [82]

Also in September 2010, PayPal froze the account of the open-source revision control software TortoiseSVN. The lead developer compared the situation to a car shop that "decides not to do business with you anymore. ... But then the shop owner tells you that they keep your car for half a year first because that's their policy."[83]

In December 2010, PayPal permanently restricted an account used to raise funds for WikiLeaks citing it was in violation of the PayPal Acceptable Use Policy. At a conference in Paris, a PayPal VP, in response to an attendee's question, stated the account was restricted after PayPal was allegedly pressured by the U.S. State Department.[84] Afterwards, PayPal reiterated the decision was based on violation of PayPal's Acceptable Use Policy. This was followed by cyber attack on the paypal.com website and a small boycott of PayPal, in which some users closed their PayPal account in protest.

Litigation

In 2002, CertCo filed a suit against PayPal claiming patent infringement concerning the use of distributed computing systems that process micropayments, or small cash amounts. In April 2002, CertCo dropped the suit and stated that they had come to a settlement involving, "a non-consequential payment and mutual releases."[85]

In March 2002, two PayPal account holders separately sued the company for alleged violations of the Electronic Funds Transfer Act (EFTA) and California law. Most of the allegations concerned PayPal's dispute resolution procedures. The two lawsuits were merged into one class action lawsuit (In re: PayPal litigation). An informal settlement was reached in November 2003, and a formal settlement was signed on June 11, 2004. The settlement requires that PayPal change its business practices (including changing its dispute resolution procedures to make them EFTA-compliant), as well as making a US$9.25 million payment to members of the class. PayPal denied any wrongdoing.[86]

In May 2002, Tumbleweed Communications filed a lawsuit against PayPal (and later expanded it to include eBay) claiming that PayPal had violated its patents for sending personalized links through e-mail, which PayPal uses to alert its customers about financial transactions. In January 2004, the two parties came to an agreement, but didn't disclose the financial terms of their licensing agreement.[87]

In June 2003, Stamps.com filed a lawsuit against PayPal and eBay claiming breach of contract, breach of the implied covenants of good faith and fair dealing, and interference with contract, among other claims. In a 2002 license agreement, Stamps.com and PayPal agreed that Stamps.com technology would be made available to allow PayPal users to buy and print postage online from their PayPal accounts. Stamps.com claimed that PayPal did not live up to its contractual obligations and accused eBay of interfering with PayPal and Stamps.com's agreement, hence Stamp.com's reasoning for including eBay in the suit.[88]

In August 2002, Craig Comb and two others filed a class action against PayPal in, *Craig Comb, et al. v. PayPal, Inc.*. They sued, alleging illegal misappropriation of customer accounts and detailed ghastly customer service experiences. Allegations included freezing deposited funds for up to 180 days until disputes are resolved by PayPal, and forcing customers to arbitrate their disputes under the American Arbitration Association's guidelines (a costly procedure). The court stated that "the User Agreement and arbitration clause are substantively unconscionable under California law," noting their unjustifiable one-sidedness and explicit prohibition of class actions produces results that "shock the conscience" and indicate PayPal was "attempting to insulate itself contractually from any meaningful challenge to its alleged practices" and ruled against PayPal.[89]

In September 2003, PayPal filed suit against Bank One Corporation for patent infringement. PayPal claimed that Bank One's online bill-payment system was an infringement against PayPal's online bill-payment patent, issued in 1998. PayPal filed the suit after a warning to the bank's lawyers in February went unheeded.[90]

In November 2003, AT&T filed suit against eBay and PayPal claiming that their payment systems infringed an AT&T patent, filed in 1991 and granted in 1994.[91]

In March 2004, PayPal and New York state's Attorney General, Eliot Spitzer, came to an agreement to require PayPal to disclose clients' rights and liabilities more accurately and to pay $150,000 to the state of New York for penalties and the costs of the investigation.[92]

In April 2007, one of two anti-trust lawsuits was filed against eBay/PayPal by Michael Malone of Texas.[93] This suit claims that the monopolistic relationship between eBay and PayPal violates United States anti-trust laws.

References

[1] "Paypal.com - Traffic Details from Alexa" (http://www.alexa.com/siteinfo/paypal.com). Alexa Internet, Inc. . Retrieved 2011-03-19.

[2] "Paypal.com" (https://www.paypal.com/us/cgi-bin/webscr?cmd=xpt/UserAgreement/ua/USUA-outside#fees-policy). Paypal.com. 2011-01-07. . Retrieved 2011-01-20.

[3] Troy Wolverton (2002-10-03). "It's official: eBay weds PayPal" (http://news.com.com/Its+official+eBay+weds+PayPal/2100-1017_3-960658.html). CNet. . Retrieved 2007-05-07.

[4] "PayPal and China UnionPay Announcement" (https://www.paypal-media.com/press-releases/20100317005661). PayPal Press Center. . Retrieved 2011-05-20.

[5] "PayPal Expands in Asia, Announces Partnership with China UnionPay" (http://www.auctionbytes.com/cab/cab/abn/y10/m03/i17/s00). Auctionbytes.com. . Retrieved 2011-01-20.

[6] "PayPal Expands Services In Asia" (http://payments.banking-business-review.com/news/paypal_expands_services_in_asia_100318/). Payments.banking-business-review.com. . Retrieved 2011-01-20.

[7] "PayPal Freezes WikiLeaks Account" (http://www.wired.com/threatlevel/2010/12/paypal-wikileaks). Wired, Inc. . Retrieved 2010-12-05.

[8] "PayPal Cuts Off WikiLeaks Account" (http://www.npr.org/2010/12/04/131813224/paypal-cuts-off-wikileaks-account). NPR. . Retrieved 2010-12-05.

[9] "Hackers take down website of bank that froze WikiLeaks funds" (http://www.rawstory.com/rs/2010/12/hackers-website-bank-froze-wikileaks-funds/). . Retrieved 7 December 2010.

[10] "Wikileaks defended by Anonymous hacktivists" (http://www.bbc.co.uk/news/technology-11935539). *BBC News*. . Retrieved 7 December 2010.

[11] "FindlawDocumentation" (http://contracts.corporate.findlaw.com/agreements/paypal/confinity.mer.2000.03.01.html). 2006-12-31. .

[12] "Wired Article-PayPal Puts Dough in Your Palm" (http://www.wired.com/news/technology/0,1282,20958,00.html). 2006-12-31. .

[13] Plotkin, Hal (September 8, 1999). "Beam Me Up Some Cash" (http://www.halplotkin.com/cnbcs029.htm). *CNBC.com (web)*. .

[14] "Wired Article" (http://www.wired.com/science/discoveries/news/1999/07/20958). 1999-07-27. .

[15] "Roelof Botha - Venture Capitalist - Sequoia Capital" (http://www.sequoiacap.com/people/roelof-botha/). Sequoiacap.com. 2010-09-27. . Retrieved 2011-01-20.

[16] "PayPal: An alternate history according to Elon Musk" (http://valleywag.com/tech/paypal/an-alternate-history-according-to-elon-musk-230076.php). Valleywag.com. 2007-01-19. . Retrieved 2011-01-20.

[17] "How PayPal Works" (http://money.howstuffworks.com/paypal.htm/printable). . Retrieved 2010-10-23.

[18] "Siliconinvestor.advfn.com" (http://siliconinvestor.advfn.com/readreplies.aspx?subjectid=22496&nonstock=False&msgid=12963552). Siliconinvestor.advfn.com. 2000-02-26. . Retrieved 2011-01-20.

[19] "Shvoong.com" (http://www.shvoong.com/internet-and-technologies/1658346-paypal/). Shvoong.com. . Retrieved 2011-01-20.

[20] "Theanalystmagazine.com" (http://www.theanalystmagazine.com/10120.htm). Theanalystmagazine.com. . Retrieved 2011-01-20.

[21] "Siliconinvestor.advfn.com" (http://siliconinvestor.advfn.com/readmsg.aspx?msgid=13474497). Siliconinvestor.advfn.com. 2000-04-20. . Retrieved 2011-01-20.

[22] "Ecommercetimes.com" (http://www.ecommercetimes.com/story/16639.html). Ecommercetimes.com. . Retrieved 2011-01-20.

[23] Kane, Margaret (July 8, 2002). "eBay picks up PayPal for $1.5 billion" (http://www.news.com/2100-1017-941964.html). *CNET News.com* (CNET Networks). . Retrieved 2007-11-13.

[24] "eBay announcement March 24, 2008 09:00AM GMT" (http://www2.ebay.com/aw/uk/200803211515302.html). .ebay.com. . Retrieved 2011-01-20.

[25] "eBay Australia announcing PayPal will be the exclusive payment method from June 17, 2008" (http://pages.ebay.com.au/useprotection/changes.html). Pages.ebay.com.au. . Retrieved 2011-01-20.

[26] "eBay International AG - Notification - N93365" (http://www.accc.gov.au/content/index.phtml/itemId/823668). www.accc.gov.au. . Retrieved 2008-04-11.

[27] eBay Australia payment options, which include methods other than PayPal. (http://pages.ebay.com.au/securitycentre/payment-options.html)

[28] "Tagedge.com" (http://tagedge.com/2008/01/28/paypal-acquires-fraudsciences/). Tagedge.com. . Retrieved 2011-01-20.

[29] "Paypal-Media.com" (https://www.paypal-media.com/releasedetail.cfm?ReleaseID=346724). Paypal-Media.com. . Retrieved 2011-01-20.

[30] "Paypal-Media.com" (https://www.paypal-media.com/documentdisplay.cfm?DocumentID=2260). Paypal-Media.com. 2008-03-25. . Retrieved 2011-01-20.

[31] "Paypal-Media.com" (https://www.paypal-media.com/common/download/download.cfm?companyid=PAY&fileid=114524& filekey=3de5bbd9-e30b-4fd6-95c2-11bb0deb3566&filename=PAY_WebDoc_2260.pdf) (PDF). . Retrieved 2011-01-20.

[32] "Shareholder.com" (http://files.shareholder.com/downloads/ebay/423749529x5130933x289176/ f4b1d2f8-f565-408d-9b58-54a5280ab957/eBay_Q109_EarningsRelease.pdf) (PDF). . Retrieved 2011-01-20.

[33] PayPal corporate fact sheet Paypal-Media.com (https://www.paypal-media.com/documentdisplay.cfm?DocumentID=2260)

[34] "Digitaltransactions.net" (http://www.digitaltransactions.net/newsstory.cfm?newsid=2197). Digitaltransactions.net. 2008-10-06. . Retrieved 2011-01-20.

[35] Blackberrynews.com (http://www.blackberrynews.com/2009/03/31/blackberry-app-world-active-now-over-350-apps-online/)

[36] "PayPal Student Accounts - Giving Teens Their Own Spending Power" (https://student.paypal.com/us/cgi-bin/ marketingweb?cmd=_render-content&content_ID=marketing_us/student_accounts&nav=1.2.2). Student.paypal.com. 2010-11-05. . Retrieved 2011-01-20.

[37] PayPal Creates Student Accounts for Teens (http://news.softpedia.com/news/PayPal-Creates-Student-Accounts-For-Teens-118965. shtml). Retrieved 23 October 2010.

[38] "PayPal's (Partially) Open Platform to Usher in New Payment Models & Apps: Tech News and Analysis «" (http://gigaom.com/2009/11/ 03/paypals-partially-open-platform-to-usher-in-new-payment-models-apps/). Gigaom.com. 2009-11-03. . Retrieved 2011-01-20.

[39] Virgil Larson, "Local building, global growth: PayPal opens facility, plans to expand staff to keep up with business," *Omaha World-Herald*, March 8, 2007, 1D.

[40] "Wall Street Folly: Ebay: Conference call transcript - 1/18/06" (http://wallstfolly.typepad.com/wallstfolly/2006/01/intel_conferenc. html). Wallstfolly.typepad.com. . Retrieved 2011-01-20.

[41] Martyn Williams, PayPal to halt some remittance services in Japan (http://www.computerworld.com/s/article/9174359/ PayPal_to_halt_some_remittance_services_in_Japan), Compuserve, March 30, 2010 03:16 AM ET

[42] New regs force PayPal to stop Japanese personal payments (http://www.finextra.com/news/fullstory.aspx?newsitemid=21238), Finextra, 30 March 2010

[43] "PayPal-Labs.com" (https://www.paypal-labs.com). PayPal-Labs.com. . Retrieved 2011-01-20.

[44] "storefront application" (http://storefront.paypallabs.com). Storefront.paypallabs.com. . Retrieved 2011-01-20.

[45] "PayPal blog" (https://www.thepaypalblog.com). PayPal blog. . Retrieved 2011-01-20.

[46] Ecdev.stanford.edu (http://ecdev.stanford.edu/authorMaterialInfo.html?mid=1036)

[47] Money.cnn.com (http://money.cnn.com/2008/02/26/smbusiness/paypal_float.fsb/)

[48] Wolverton, Troy, FDIC decides PayPal's no bank (http://news.zdnet.com/2100-9595_22-858445.html), *ZDNet News*, 2002-03-13. Retrieved 2008-03-19.

[49] Uniting and Strengthening America by Providing Appropriate Tools Required to Intercept and Obstruct Terrorism (USA Patriot Act) Act of 2001, Pub. L. No. 107-56, 115 Stat. 272 (2001)

[50] User Agreement for PayPal Service (https://www.paypal.com/us/cgi-bin/webscr?cmd=p/gen/ua/policy_spp-outside) (it reads in part: "Credit card chargeback rights, if they apply, are broader than PayPal Buyer Protection")

[51] The in-line paypal URL in this section. Disputes between Buyers and Sellers - Buyer Protection Programs. (https://www.paypal.com/ cgi-bin/webscr?cmd=p/gen/ua/policy_buyer_complaint-outside#pbp-policy)

[52] "Hardware and Software Security" (https://cms.paypal.com/cgi-bin/marketingweb?cmd=_render-content&content_ID=security/ hardware_software_protection#logging_in-security_key). Paypal.com. . Retrieved 2011-05-10.

[53] PayPal Help Center Paypal.com (https://www.paypal.com/helpcenter/main. jsp;jsessionid=HtXJGK2vmnXLYrk1hQQhWLqYFJkv2TtkjbvcbtMwpZPdR8V8qBnL!-36873408?locale=en_US&_dyncharset=UTF-8& countrycode=US&cmd=_help&serverInstance=9006&t=solutionTab&ft=browseTab&ps=solutionPanels&solutionTopic=20167& solutionId=11333&isSrch=Yes)

[54] "PayPal Security Key - PayPal" (https://www.paypal.com/cgi-bin/webscr?cmd=xpt/Marketing_CommandDriven/securitycenter/ PayPalSecurityKey-outside). . Retrieved 2009-08-18.

[55] "Investigators Replicate Nokia 1100 Online Banking Hack - Business Center - PC World" (http://www.pcworld.com/businesscenter/ article/165326/investigators_replicate_nokia_1100_online_banking_hack.html). www.pcworld.com. . Retrieved 2009-05-25.

[56] "Paypal.com" (https://www.paypal.com/uk/cgi-bin/webscr?cmd=xpt/cps/general/LUXMigrationFAQ-outside). Paypal.com. . Retrieved 2011-01-20.

[57] Holahan, Catherine (2007-06-15). "Businessweek.com" (http://www.businessweek.com/technology/content/jun2007/ tc20070614_606853.htm?chan=technology_technology+index+page_top+stories). Businessweek.com. . Retrieved 2011-01-20.

[58] "FSA.gov.uk" (http://www.fsa.gov.uk/register/firmBasicDetails.do?sid=99095). FSA.gov.uk. . Retrieved 2011-01-20.

[59] Stevenson, Tom (2007-05-15). "Telegraph.co.uk" (http://www.telegraph.co.uk/money/main.jhtml?xml=/money/2007/05/15/ cnpaypal15.xml). Telegraph.co.uk. . Retrieved 2011-01-20.

[60] "Paypal.com" (https://www.paypal.com/us/cgi-bin/webscr?cmd=xpt/UserAgreement/ua/USUA-outside). Paypal.com. 2011-01-07. . Retrieved 2011-01-20.

[61] "Bepress.com" (http://law.bepress.com/cgi/viewcontent.cgi?article=1153&context=expresso). . Retrieved 2011-01-20.

[62] Margaret Jane Radin et al., Internet Commerce The Emerging Legal Framework 1174-1175 Foundation Press (2d ed. 2006)

[63] Margaret Jane Radin et al., Internet Commerce The Emerging Legal Framework 1176 Foundation Press (2d ed. 2006)

[64] NYtimes.com (http://www.nytimes.com/2010/02/11/business/global/11paypal.html) The New York Times, India's Central Bank Stops Some PayPal Services, by Heather Timmons and Claire Cain Miller, February 10, 2010

[65] RBI.org.in (http://rbi.org.in/scripts/PublicationsView.aspx?id=12043) Certificates of Authorisation issued by the Reserve Bank of India under the Payment and Settlement Systems Act, 2007 for Setting up and Operating Payment System in India

[66] Margaret Jane Radin et al., Internet Commerce The Emerging Legal Framework 1189-1190 Foundation Press (2d ed. 2006)

[67] Margaret Jane Radin et al., Internet Commerce The Emerging Legal Framework 1188 Foundation Press (2d ed. 2006)

[68] "Security Center" (https://www.paypal.com/us/cgi-bin/webscr?cmd=_security-center-outside). Paypal.com. 2010-11-05. . Retrieved 2011-01-20.

[69] "PayPal User Agreement" (http://www.webcitation.org/5ySkNOJHn). Paypal.com. 2010-11-01. Archived from the original (https://cms.paypal.com/cms_content/US/en_US/files/ua/ua.pdf). Error: If you specify |archiveurl=, you must also specify |archivedate=. . Retrieved 2011-04-15.

[70] Cyrus Farivar. "Wired News" (http://www.wired.com/science/discoveries/news/2005/09/68788). Wired.com. . Retrieved 2011-01-20.

[71] "E-Commerce News: Security: Feds Investigating Fraudulent Katrina-Related Web Sites" (http://www.ecommercetimes.com/story/46325.html). Ecommercetimes.com. . Retrieved 2011-01-20.

[72] "Youtube video of news report on eBay and PayPal aired March 2008 on an Australian news TV show called Today Tonight" (http://youtube.com/watch?v=KAlM0E-zrhM). Youtube.com. . Retrieved 2011-01-20.

[73] "AboutPayPal.com Website" (http://paypalsucks.com/). 2008-04-23. .

[74] "PayPal Alternative - Pay Pal Lawsuits, PayPal Complaints & Fraud" (http://www.paypalsucks.com). Paypalsucks.com. . Retrieved 2011-01-20.

[75] Charles Wolrich (2005-03-08). "Special Report:Top Corporate Hate Web Sites" (http://www.forbes.com/2005/03/07/cx_cw_0308hate.html). Forbes Magazine. .

[76] "Draft Notice in respect of a notification lodged by eBay International A.G." (http://www.accc.gov.au/content/trimFile.phtml?trimFileName=D08+54179.pdf&trimFileTitle=D08+54179.pdf&trimFileFromVersionId=833795). Australian Competition and Consumer Commission. 2008-06-12. . Retrieved 2008-07-03.

[77] "Paypal India Outage — No Payments to or from India" (http://www.pluggd.in/paypal-india-outage-no-payments-to-or-from-india-297/). Paypal India Outage — No Payments to or from India. 2010-02-05. . Retrieved 2010-02-05.

[78] Orlowski, Andrew (2010-03-08). "Theregister.co.uk" (http://www.theregister.co.uk/2010/03/08/paypal_cryptome_ko/). Theregister.co.uk. . Retrieved 2011-01-20.

[79] Orlowski, Andrew (2010-03-10). "Theregister.co.uk" (http://www.theregister.co.uk/2010/03/10/cryptome_paypal/). Theregister.co.uk. . Retrieved 2011-01-20.

[80] Orlowski, Andrew (2010-03-16). "Theregister.co.uk" (http://www.theregister.co.uk/2010/03/16/cryptome_paypal/). Theregister.co.uk. . Retrieved 2011-01-20.

[81] Sep 10 2010 Tweet (2010-09-10). "on a Friday update, crying over paypal" (http://notch.tumblr.com/post/1096322756/working-on-a-friday-update-crying-over-paypal). Notch.tumblr.com. . Retrieved 2011-01-20.

[82] "PayPal Freezes MineCraft Dev's 600k Euros" (http://www.rockpapershotgun.com/2010/09/10/paypal-freezes-minecraft-devs-600k-euros/). Rock, Paper, Shotgun. . Retrieved 2011-01-20.

[83] "How PayPal screws open source projects" (http://tortoisesvn.net/howpaypalscrewsopensourceprojects.html). Tortoisesvn.net. 2010-09-17. . Retrieved 2011-01-20.

[84] Addley, Esther; Halliday, Josh (2010-12-08). "Operation Payback cripples MasterCard site in revenge for WikiLeaks ban" (http://www.guardian.co.uk/media/2010/dec/08/paypal-us-pressure-wikileaks-mastercard). The Guardian (London). .

[85] "CertCo Drops PayPal Patent Suit" (http://www.internetnews.com/bus-news/article.php/1023191). 2008-04-23. .

[86] "Settlement Agreement" (http://paypalsucks.com/files/PayPalSettlementAgreement.pdf). 2004-06-11. .

[87] "EBay Settles Patent Lawsuit With Tumbleweed Communications" (http://www.crn.com/it-channel/18840325). 2008-04-23. .

[88] "Stamps.com Asserts Breach of Contract Claim Against PayPal and eBay" (http://www.stamps.com/company/news/20030625p/). 2008-04-23. .

[89] "Comb v. PayPal Inc." (http://pub.bna.com/eclr/021227.htm). 2007-01-21. .

[90] "Internet: PayPal Sues Bank One Over Patent Infringement" (http://query.nytimes.com/gst/fullpage.html?res=9C0DEFD91F3DF932A35753C1A9659C8B63). The New York Times. 2008-04-23. .

[91] Festa, Paul (2008-04-23). "AT&T sues eBay, PayPal over patent" (http://news.com.com/2100-1032_3-5110038.html). .

[92] "Spitzer Obtains Agreement With E-Payment Service" (http://www.webcitation.org/5gd9LOmMk). 2008-04-23. Archived from the original (http://www.oag.state.ny.us/media_center/2004/mar/mar08a_04.html) on a date that you can find on the archiveurl which makes requiring this field seem entirely nonsensical to me.. .

[93] "Justia.com" (http://dockets.justia.com/docket/court-candce/case_no-5:2007cv01882/case_id-190774/). Dockets.justia.com. . Retrieved 2011-01-20.

External links

- PayPal (https://www.paypal.com/)
- PayPal Australia (http://www.paypal.com.au/au)
- PayPal Canada (https://www.paypal.ca/ca/cgi-bin/webscr?cmd=_home&locale.x=en_US) **(English)**
- PayPal UK (http://www.paypal.co.uk/uk)
- PayPal Labs (https://www.paypal-labs.com/paypal-labs/)
- PayPal Group Collect (https://www.paypal-collect-money.com/)

PayPoint

PayPoint plc

Type	Public limited company
Traded as	LSE: PAY [1]
Industry	Payment systems
Founded	1996
Headquarters	Welwyn Garden City, UK
Key people	David Newlands, (Chairman) Dominic Taylor, (CEO)
Revenue	£212.1 million (2008)
Operating income	£29.2 million (2008)
Net income	£21.0 million (2008)
Website	[2]

PayPoint plc is a British business offering a system for paying bills in the United Kingdom and Republic of Ireland. The company is listed on the London Stock Exchange and is a former constituent of the FTSE 250 Index.

History

The PayPoint network was set up in 1996 providing a convenient place for customers to pay towards a limited range of utility companies' payment schemes: it was first tested in Northern Ireland[1] The Company launched its system to the media in 1997.[1] In 1998 the system was first offered to British Gas plc customers wanting to pay their bills; in 2000 it was also offered to Vodafone customers and in 2001 it was extended to Scottish Power, Manweb and Orange customers.[1] The Company was first listed on the London Stock Exchange in 2004.[2] The system was first extended to TV Licences in 2006.[1]

In November 2006 and February 2007 PayPoint acquired internet payment service providers Metacharge[3] and SECPay,[4] respectively. These ventures were merged and rebranded as PayPoint.net, providing a secure debit and credit card payment system for web-merchants, in July 2008.[5]

Operations

The Company provides the following services:[6]

- It allows customers to make cash payments at any one of its 20,750 PayPoint outlets (in the UK) to settle their gas, electricity or water bills, or to pay for their TV licence, Council Tax or London congestion charge or to top-up pay-as-you-go mobile phones.
- Shop Direct is one of the mail order companies that use the system to allow nominated convenience shops to scan-in goods for return to them by courier at the mail order company's expense, using a posted or emailed label with a PayPoint bar code. The scheme is managed by Collect+ [9] who also allow the public to buy bar-code labels for courier delivery of parcels between network shops.
- It allows customers to make cash payments to re-charge their gas or electricity keys and then use those keys in place of coin-based electricity meters
- It operates in-store ATMs connected to the LINK network
- It operates in-store credit/debit card processing facilities with Chip and PIN compliance.

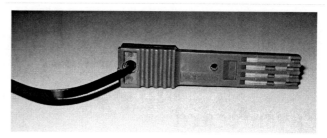

Electricity key

Competitors

Rivals to PayPoint include the Post Office Ltd (in the UK), Payzone and An Post's PostPoint network (in Ireland) all of which offer similar services.

References

[1] PayPoint: History (http://www.paypoint.com/companyhistory.htm)

[2] PayPoint IPO fits the bill (http://findarticles.com/p/articles/mi_hb6602/is_/ai_n26014447) Investors Chronicle, September 2004

[3] "Paypoint buys internet payment provider Metacharge for 8.4 mln stg" (http://www.forbes.com/markets/feeds/afx/2006/11/01/afx3136105.html). Forbes.com. 1 November 2006. . Retrieved 2008-11-28.

[4] "PayPoint acquires SECPay Limited" (http://www.24dash.com/news/Central_Government/2007-02-26-PayPoint-acquires-SECPay-Limited). 24dash.com. 26 February 2007. . Retrieved 2008-11-28.

[5] Customers benefit from Comodo PayPoint.net Agreement (http://www.hostpulse.com/hosting/news/CV1-5455.html) Hostplus, 31 December 2008

[6] PayPoint: What can I pay? (http://www.paypoint.co.uk/whatcanipay.htm)

External links

- Official site (http://www.paypoint.com)
- PayPoint Ireland (http://www.paypoint.ie)
- PayPoint.net (http://www.paypoint.net)
- Collect+ (http://www.collectplus.co.uk)

PaySafe

PaySafe was the first Secure Electronic Payment System for Credit Cards over the Internet.

PaySafe was conceived in Australia in 1991 by Dennis Charter and developed by a group of computer programmers headed by Justin Fanning and included others such as the renowned international security consultant and PGP encryption inventor Phil Zimmerman. In 1996 PaySafe was launched in the United States. Its creators had such belief in its security that a US$10 Million 'prize' was offered to anyone who could hack the PaySafe security portal. No one made claim to the prize.

Dennis Charter's Secure Electronic Payment invention for the internet is the foundation of all internet based electronic transactions today. This single invention is one of the most commercially significant inventions of the 1990's. Not a single transaction over the internet today is performed without a Secure Electronic configuration of some description.

References

- The Inventors "Secure Electronic Payment System" [1]

Paysafecard

Paysafecard is an electronic payment method for predominantly online shopping and is based on a pre-pay system. Paysafecard is based in Vienna, Austria and has been in existence since 2000. Exchanging cash for Electronic Money (for use online) is facilitated through paysafecard in many countries worldwide.

Since 2006 paysafecard has been involved with the eTEN programme (Project description) [1] promoted by the European Union.

Advantages

Buying with cash at online stores is gradually becoming more commonplace with the emergence of services like paysafecard. Historically, most web shops have only accepted card payments for online purchases. For the majority of online consumers card payments are simple and convenient, while web shops are reassured by obtaining an immediate payment authorisation from the consumer's card issuer.

However, many consumers are concerned about entering their financial details online while shopping, and in some cases consumers simply don't have a credit card to use online. In these cases the ability to use cash online can be beneficial to web merchants and their customers.

How it works

In order to purchase a Paysafecard in the UK, customers pay cash (£10, £25, £50 or £75) at any retailers linked to PayPoint and thus receive a secure 16 digit PIN printed on a card. In other countries paysafecards are mostly available at newsagents, petrol stations, chemists or kiosks. When paying in an online shop, the user enters the 16 digit number and the amount tendered is deducted from the paysafecard balance. For larger sums it is possible to combine up to ten Paysafecard PINs up to a total amount of £1.000. [1]

Twelve months after purchasing a paysafecard for the first time, and no later than 24 months after the production date printed on each card, customers will be charged an administrative fee of £2 per month, which will be automatically deducted from their credit. [2]

The current balance of each paysafecard as well as its transaction history and production date can also be viewed at the official site [4] by entering the respective 16 PIN code.

Where it can be used

Paysafecards are normally sold as eVouchers (uniquely numbered receipts from in-store sales terminals) in Argentina, Austria, Belgium, Cyprus, the Czech Republic, Denmark, France, Germany, Greece, Ireland, Italy, Luxembourg, the Netherlands, Norway, Poland, Portugal, Romania, Slovakia, Slovenia, Spain, Sweden, Switzerland and the United Kingdom. According to paysafecard.com, there are over 280,000 sales terminals worldwide [5]. [3]

Further, there are more than 3,500 webshops [7] accepting paysafecard from across the world. Those fall mainly into the following categories: online games/gaming (including browser games, skill games, community games), music download sites, telecommunication services, gambling sites and travel. [4]

Financial Services Authority Register listing

Paysafecard.com Limited is an electronic money institution authorised and regulated by the Financial Services Authority in the United Kingdom FSA Register Details [9] (Register number: 475502). The Financial Services Authority's Register can be accessed through www.fsa.gov.uk/register [5]

Paysafecard is permitted to issue electronic money in all 28 European Economic Area countries under "The Financial Services and Markets Act 2000 (EEA Passport Rights) Regulations 2001" FSA Passport Details [11].

External links

- http://www.paysafecard.com
- http://www.paysafecard.com/uk/
- European Union - project description [1]
- FSA Register Details [9]
- FSA Passport Details [11]
- Exchange of Paysafecard [12]

References

[1] (http://www.paysafecard.com/uk/general/faqs/#c977faq_458), how is this possible with cards of £75 and a maximum of ten per purchase?

[2] http://www.paysafecard.com/uk/general/faqs/#c977faq_456

[3] http://www.paysafecard.com/uk/buy/sales-outlets/

[4] http://www.paysafecard.com/uk/pay/

[5] http://www.paysafecard.com/uk/(bottom of page)

- Párhonyi, Róbert, study on micropayment systems: http://wwwhome.cs.utwente.nl/~pras/publications/ 2005-I3E-2ndgeneration-payments.pdf

PayXpert

PayXpert BV

Type	Besloten Vennootschap
Industry	Payment Service Provider
Founded	Hoofddorp, Netherland (2009)
Founder(s)	E. Preitschopf
Headquarters	Hoofdorp, Netherland
Area served	Europe, South America
Key people	E. Preitschopf (Founder, CEO)
Parent	Digital Media Synergies
Website	www.payxpert.com

PayXpert is an international Payment Service Provider supplying PCI level-1 payment gateways and banking intermediation to low and high risk e-commerce merchants. The company helps merchants to open merchant accounts in its partner banks, and transfers payments from end-users to these merchant accounts through an SSL-encrypted network. PayXpert is also McAfee's website-security software supplier for Europe.

References

- McAfee
- http://www.digitalmediasynergies.com/
- http://www.theregister.co.uk/2010/06/30/pci_compliance/

External links

- PayXpert.com (http://payxpert.com/)
- PayXpert.es (http://payxpert.es/)
- List of on-line payment service providers

Peppercoin

Peppercoin is a cryptographic system for processing micropayments. **Peppercoin Inc.** was a company that offers services based on the peppercoin method.

The peppercoin system was developed by Silvio Micali and Ron Rivest and first presented at the RSA Conference in 2002[1] (although it had not yet been named.) The core idea is to bill one randomly selected transaction a lump sum of money rather than bill each transaction a small amount. It uses "universal aggregation", which means that it aggregates transactions over users, merchants as well as payment service providers. The random selection is cryptographically secure -- it cannot be influenced by any of the parties. It is claimed to reduce the transaction cost per dollar from 27 cents to "well below 10 cents."[2]

Peppercoin, Inc. was a privately held company founded in late 2001 by Micali and Rivest based in Waltham, MA. It has secured about $15M in venture capital in two rounds of funding.[3] [4] Its services have seen modest adoption.[5] [6] Peppercoin collects 5-9% of transaction cost from the merchant.[7] Peppercoin, Inc. was bought out in 2007 by Chockstone for an undisclosed amount.[4]

References

[1] S. Micali and R. L. Rivest. *Micropayments revisited* (http://citeseer.ist.psu.edu/micali02micropayments.html). In B. Preneel, editor, Proc. Cryptography Track at RSA Conference 2002, pages 149–263. Springer, 2002. Lecture Notes in Computer Science No. 2271.

[2] 2003 press release (http://www.peppercoin.com/press/pressreleases/2003/0929.shtml)

[3] Company history (http://www.peppercoin.com/company/history.shtml)

[4] Micro-payment's Peppercoin Bought Out (http://www.thealarmclock.com/mt/archives/2007/04/micropayments_p.html)

[5] Peppercoin picked by Wurld Media for P2P payment system (http://masshightech.bizjournals.com/masshightech/stories/2005/03/28/daily9.html)

[6] Peppercoin scoops up customer for loyalty program (http://boston.bizjournals.com/boston/stories/2006/07/24/story10.html)

[7] Peppercoin, Inc. Response to the Request for Information By the Joint Committee of the Higher Education and Entertainment Communities Technology Task Force (http://www.educause.edu/elements/attachments/rfi/rfi_2/Peppercoin_summary.pdf)

Piano Media

Piano Media based in Bratislava, Slovakia, is a subscription-based media content payment system started on May 2, 2011

Founded by partners in Etarget,[1] a Slovak-based targeted online media advertising company, and NextBig,[2] a Czech-Slovak new media consultancy company, Piano Media provides major media publishers in Slovakia with a secure group-payment system for their customers.

Using Piano, participating publications place all, or a portion, of their content behind a pay-wall with a €2.90 flat-fee. Piano's users receive unlimited access to all participating publications, similar to a cable-TV package model. User payments are split between publications according to how much time each user spends on an individual site.

Nine major Slovak publishers are participating (see list below) in the first-wave of the project. These participants include Slovakia's most popular news portal, all three national daily broadsheet newspapers, two highly influential Slovak magazines and two online video services.

Publishers choose what content is put behind the pay-wall and what benefits users will receive. Some publishers provide ad-free versions of their content, while other offer premium access to their content before it is released to the public later in the day. Charges for discussion forums and archived articles are among other paid content options publishers provide.

Slovakia is the first market world-wide where the majority of publishers have agreed to join a common payment system. In the future Piano will offer the benefits of this concept to other single-language European markets.

How Piano Media Systems work

On participating publisher's sites, a registration bar appears below the menu bar in a reader's browser. This bar allows a reader to register, or show that he has already signed in with Piano and continue on to reading content on the publisher's site. Readers pay a flat-fee, either weekly, monthly or yearly and receive full, unfettered access to all participating media's content. All a publisher's content remains on the his websites rather than being pushed onto Piano's site.

Publishers are compensated not by the number of clicks their stories receive but rather by the amount of time a user spends on a publisher's site. This encourages publishers to come up with better content rather than just flashy headlines. Slovak publishers feel well served as well. "We will earn some money through the project which is better than nothing," said Matus Kostolny, SME's editor-in-chief. "Only our unique content is locked and the rest is free, which enables us to keep traffic on the website." [3]

Initial Reactions

Although Piano has only been operational in Slovakia since May 2, 2011 the reaction by participating publications has been positive. Discussion forums, which were open to anyone before, are now only available after purchasing a Piano Subscription, reducing both spam and inane comments on publications' discussion forums. "Our discussions were cleaned up from inappropriate and stupid posts," [4] Tyzden's editor Štefan Hríb says.

Page views, which typically drop after the implementation of a pay-wall, have not dipped as much as had been anticipated. "We have lost some traffic although it is not yet significant," says says deputy editor of the SME Constantine Čikovský." [5] He noted that in the third week of May Medialne.sk [6] had 43,000 hits while the average weekly hits prior to Piano's implementation was 56,000.

History of Piano Media Systems

In the summer of 2010, Marcel Vašš, the CEO of ETarget, a targeted online media advertising company, was thinking about how to monetize major media content and invited Tomáš Bella, former deputy editor of Slovakia's bigger news portal SME and then a consultant at NextBig to help him flesh out the idea. The two came up with a plausible plan and were quickly approached by an angel investor who agreed to provide first round funding to set up the project in Slovakia, do market research in the rest of Europe and lead Piano to a second round of funding.

The idea Vašš and Bella formulated was a cross between a micro-payment scheme and a pay-tv subscription. Excellent contacts within the Slovak publishing industry enabled the duo to quickly conclude pay-wall agreements with nine major Slovak publishers. On April 18, 2011 Piano's nationwide pay-wall went up, although as a free two-week trail. On May 2, 2011 Piano's pay-wall was erected.

Participating Publications

- SME [7] - Slovakia's leading broadsheet newspaper
- Tyzden [8] - Slovakia's Award Winning weekly newsmagazine
- Hospodarske noviny [9] - Slovakia's daily business newspaper
- Pravda [10] -Slovakia's oldest daily newspaper
- Dennik Sport [11] - Slovakia's biggest sports newspaper
- Medialne [12] -A Slovak media business site run by Trend, a business weekly
- MeToo [13] - Slovak video portal
- PC Revue [14] -Slovak monthly IT magazine
- JOJ and Huste.tv [15] - Slovakia's #2 TV station and video site

Company personnel

- Tomáš Bella [16] - CEO
- Marcel Vašš [17] - Supervisory Board Member

References

[1] Etarget (http://www.etarget.eu/)

[2] NextBig (http://www.nextbig.eu/)

[3] Bloomberg, "Slovak Media Follow Murdoch by Pushing Online Paywall Plan," May 13, 2011 (http://www.bloomberg.com/news/2011-05-12/slovak-media-follow-murdoch-in-online-paywall.html/)

[4] SME.sk ,Piano vyhnalo z webu zlých diskutérov," May 30, 2011 (http://ekonomika.sme.sk/c/5914747/piano-vyhnalo-z-webu-zlych-diskuterov.html/)

[5] SME.sk ,Piano vyhnalo z webu zlých diskutérov," May 30, 2011 (http://ekonomika.sme.sk/c/5914747/piano-vyhnalo-z-webu-zlych-diskuterov.html/)

External links

- Official website of Piano Media (http://www.pianomedia.eu/)
- Piano Media systems on Twitter (http://twitter.com/pianosystem/)
- Piano Media systems on Facebook (http://facebook.com/pianomedia/)
- Piano Media systems on Linked In (http://www.linkedin.com/company/1884071?goback=.fcs_*2_Piano+Media_false_*2_*2_*2_*2_*2_*2_*2_*2_*2_*2_*2_*2&trk=ncsrch_hits/)
- Piano Media in the New York Times (http://www.nytimes.com/2011/04/25/business/media/25cache.html?ref=world/)
- Piano Media on the BBC (http://news.bbc.co.uk/2/hi/programmes/click_online/9476374.stm/)

- Piano Media AP coverage (http://www.google.com/hostednews/ap/article/ALeqM5g7uc_BzTW0lnTxvTDDUvsIpiv0CQ?docId=d855a267a5b94d8dae3290304fdfe12a/)
- Piano Media in the WSJ (http://blogs.wsj.com/emergingeurope/2011/04/27/slovak-entrepreneurs-to-test-charging-for-news-online/?mod=google_news_blog/)
- Piano Media in Spain's ABC (http://www.abc.es/20110512/medios-redes/abcp-prensa-eslovaca-lanza-modelo-20110512.html/)
- Piano Media on Bloomberg's wire (http://www.bloomberg.com/news/2011-05-12/slovak-media-follow-murdoch-in-online-paywall.html/)

Pivotal Payments

Pivotal Payments

Type	Privately Owned
Industry	Financial Services
Founded	2003
Headquarters	Melville, New York, USA, Montreal, Quebec, Canada
Key people	Philip Fayer, Lester Fernandes, Frank LoSchiavo, Patrick Huynh
Products	Financial services, Merchant accounts, Payment processing
Owner(s)	Philip Fayer
Employees	300 (*2010*)
Website	Official Website [1]

Pivotal Payments is an independent payment processing provider, offering a full range of merchant services to small, medium and large-sized retail businesses, governmental agencies and not-for-profit organizations across North America and the United Kingdom, such as retailers, chain stores, franchises, restaurants, dealerships, mail and telephone order merchants, and e-commerce stores.[1] .

History

Pivotal Payments was established in 2003 when President and CEO Philip Fayer had difficulties in getting payment processing because like many entrepreneurs, he had no money or credit. This realization made him start the company to provide payment processing to small and mid-sized businesses, and has grown to provide merchant services to large customers.

In 2006, the company received funding from Goldman Sachs. In 2009, the company created about 80 jobs (over 350 employees and over 1,000 agents in 2011) and doubled its net income during a recession.

Acquisitions

The company achieved strategic acquisitions like Cardex Corporation in 2007, a Canadian ISO/MSP, Tangarine Payment Solutions Corp in 2008, POS Card Systems and National Credit Card Processing, both divisions of Vision Bankcard, Inc, in 2010.

Partnerships

Pivotal Payments is building business relationships with other companies as part of its strategy to grow. Partnerships include New Edge Networks, provider of network solutions to businesses through direct and wholesale channels, 411.ca, a Canadian phone lookup and business directory search engine, VeriSign, a digital certificates provider, and VirtueMart, an open source e-commerce solution.

Headquarters

Pivotal Payments USA 200 Broadhollow Road, Suite 207 Melville, New York 11747, USA

Pivotal Payments Canada 685 Cathcart Street, Suite 1000 Montreal, Quebec H3B 1M7, Canada

Management

Philip Fayer is the Chief Executive Officer and President

Programs

- **ISO/Agent Program** that allows Independent Sales Organizations (ISOs) and independent agents to resell Pivotal Payments merchant service products[2].
- **VAR Program**. Allows Value Added Resellers or 3rd party resellers to distribute Pivotal Payments' payment processing products and services [3].
- **E-Commerce Partner Program** Referral partner program that allows web hosting companies, web development companies, e-commerce VARs and e-commerce technology companies to earn extra revenue by providing their clients with payment processing services[4].

Notable Clients

- Honda
- Pizza Hut
- Best Western
- Pennzoil

References

[1] Financial Post Pivotal Payments CEO interview (http://www.financialpost.com/related/topics/Thinking+small+forges+payoff/ 2773933/story.html)
[2] ISO/Agent Program (http://www.isoagentprogram.com)
[3] VAR Program (http://www.pivotalpayments.com/agent-programs/value-added-resellers/)
[4] E-Commerce Partner Program (http://www.pivotalepayments.com/partner-programs/become-a-partner/)

External links

- Pivotal Payments Website (http://www.pivotalpayments.com)
- Pivotal E-Payments (http://www.pivotalepayments.com)
- ISO/Agent Program (http://www.isoagentprogram.com)

Point of sale

Points of sale at a Target store.

Marketing
Key concepts
Product • Pricing Distribution • Service • Retail Brand management Account-based marketing Marketing ethics Marketing effectiveness Market research Market segmentation Marketing strategy Marketing management Market dominance
Promotional content
Advertising • Branding • Underwriting Direct marketing • Personal Sales Product placement • Publicity Sales promotion • Sex in advertising Loyalty marketing • Premiums • Prizes
Promotional media
Printing • Publication Broadcasting • Out-of-home Internet marketing • Point of sale Promotional merchandise Digital marketing • In-game In-store demonstration Word-of-mouth marketing Brand Ambassador • Drip Marketing

Point of sale (POS) (also sometimes referred to as **Point of purchase (POP)**) or **checkout** is the location where a transaction occurs. A "checkout" refers to a POS terminal or more generally to the hardware and software used for checkouts, the equivalent of an electronic cash register.

A POS terminal manages the selling process by a salesperson accessible interface. The same system allows the creation and printing of the receipt.

History

Software prior to the 1990s

Early electronic cash registers (ECR) were controlled with proprietary software and were very limited in function and communications capability. In August 1973 IBM announced the IBM 3650 and 3660 Store Systems that were, in essence, a mainframe computer packaged as a store controller that could control 128 IBM 3653/3663 point of sale registers. This system was the first commercial use of client-server technology, peer-to-peer communications, local area network (LAN) simultaneous backup, and remote initialization. By mid-1974, it was installed in Pathmark Stores in New Jersey and Dillard's Department Stores.

The first microprocessor-controlled cash register was built by William Brobeck and Associates in 1974, for McDonald's Restaurants. Each station was controlled by an Intel 8008, a very early microprocessor. There was one button for every item -- for example [2 Vanilla Shake], [1 Chocolate Shake], etc. By pressing the [Grill] button, a second or third order could be worked on while the first transaction was in progress. When the customer was ready to pay, the [Total] button would calculate the bill, including sales tax. This made it accurate for McDonald's and very convenient for the servers. Up to eight stations could be interconnected and printed reports, prices, and taxes handle from a single station in "Manager Mode."

Programmability allowed retailers to be more creative. In 1979 Gene Mosher's Old Canal Cafe in Syracuse, New York was using POS software written by Mosher that ran on an Apple II to take customer orders at the restaurant's front entrance and print complete preparation details in the restaurant's kitchen. In that novel context, customers would often proceed to their tables to find their food waiting for them already. This software included real time labour and food cost reports. In 1986 Mosher used the Atari ST and bundled NeoChrome paint to create and market the first graphical touchscreen POS software

Modern software (post 1990s)

In 1992 Martin Goodwin and Bob Henry created the first point of sales software that could run on the Microsoft Windows platform named IT Retail.[1] Since then a wide range of POS applications have been developed on platforms such as Windows and Unix. The availability of local processing power, local data storage, networking, and graphical user interface made it possible to develop flexible and highly functional POS systems. Cost of such systems has also declined, as all the components can now be purchased off-the-shelf.

The key requirements that must be met by modern POS systems include: high and consistent operating speed, reliability, ease of use, remote supportability, low cost, and rich functionality. Retailers can reasonably expect to acquire such systems (including hardware) for about $4000 US (2009) per lane.

Hardware interface standardization (post 1990s)

Vendors and retailers are working to standardize development of computerized POS systems and simplify interconnecting POS devices. Two such initiatives are OPOS and JavaPOS, both of which conform to the UnifiedPOS standard led by The National Retail Foundation.

OPOS (OLE for POS) was the first commonly-adopted standard and was created by Microsoft, NCR Corporation, Epson and Fujitsu-ICL. OPOS is a COM-based interface compatible with all COM-enabled programming languages for Microsoft Windows. OPOS was first released in 1996. **JavaPOS** was developed by Sun Microsystems, IBM, and NCR Corporation in 1997 and first released in 1999. JavaPOS is for Java what OPOS is for Windows, and thus largely platform independent.

There are several communication protocols POS systems use to control peripherals. Among them are

- EPSON Esc/POS
- UTC Standard
- UTC Enhanced
- AEDEX
- ICD 2002
- Ultimate
- CD 5220
- DSP-800
- ADM 787/788.

There are also nearly as many proprietary protocols as there are companies making POS peripherals. EMAX, used by EMAX International, was a combination of AEDEX and IBM dumb terminal.

Most POS peripherals, such as displays and printers, support several of these command protocols in order to work with many different brands of POS terminals and computers.

Web based POS (post 2000s)

Web based POS software can be run on any computer with an Internet connection and supported browser, without additional software. The POS software is hosted on secure servers in multiple data centers with real-time backups.

Industry

Retail industry

The retailing industry is one of the predominant users of POS terminals.

A Retail Point of Sales system typically includes a computer, monitor, cash drawer, receipt printer, customer display and a barcode scanner, and the majority of retail POS systems also include a debit/credit card reader. It can also include a weight scale, integrated credit card processing system, a signature capture device and a customer pin pad device. More and more POS monitors use touch-screen technology for ease of use and a computer is built in to the monitor chassis for what is referred to as an all-in-one unit. All-in-one POS units save valuable counter space for the retailer. The POS system software can typically handle a myriad of customer based functions such as sales, returns, exchanges, layaways, gift cards, gift registries, customer loyalty programs, BOGO (buy one get one), quantity discounts and much more. POS software can also allow for functions such as pre-planned promotional sales, manufacturer coupon validation, foreign currency handling and multiple payment types.

The POS unit handles the sales to the consumer but it is only one part of the entire POS system used in a retail business. "Back-office" computers typically handle other functions of the POS system such as inventory control, purchasing, receiving and transferring of products to and from other locations. Other typical functions of a POS system are to store sales information for reporting purposes, sales trends and cost/price/profit analysis. Customer information may be stored for receivables management, marketing purposes and specific buying analysis. Many retail POS systems include an accounting interface that "feeds" sales and cost of goods information to independent accounting applications.

Hospitality industry

Hospitality point of sales systems are computerized systems incorporating registers, computers and peripheral equipment, usually on a computer network. Like other point of sale systems, these systems keep track of sales, labor and payroll, and can generate records used in accounting and book keeping. They may be accessed remotely by restaurant corporate offices, troubleshooters and other authorized parties.

Point of sales systems have revolutionized the restaurant industry, particularly in the fast food sector. In the most recent technologies, registers are computers, sometimes with touch screens. The registers connect to a server, often referred to as a "store controller" or a "central control unit." Printers and monitors are also found on the network. Additionally, remote servers can connect to store networks and monitor sales and other store data.

The efficiency of such systems has decreased service times and increased efficiency of orders.

Another innovation in technology for the restaurant industry is Wireless POS. Many restaurants with high volume use wireless handheld POS to collect orders which are sent to a server. The server sends required information to the kitchen in real time.

Hair and Beauty Industry

Point of sale systems in the hair and beauty industry have become very popular with increased use of computers. In order to run a salon efficiently it is essential to keep all appointments, client, employee roster and the checkout in a system where you can create performance reports for. The nature of salons and spas vary depending on the setup of the business and products offered in addition to the business. This is why POS comes along with most salon software.

Restaurant business

Restaurant POS refers to point of sale (POS) software that runs on computers, usually touch screen terminals or wireless handheld devices. Restaurant POS systems assist businesses to track transactions in real time.

Typical restaurant POS software is able to print guest checks, print orders to kitchens and bars for preparation, process credit cards and other payment cards, and run reports. In addition, some systems implement wireless pagers and electronic signature capture devices.

In the fast food industry, registers may be at the front counter, or configured for drive through or walk through cashiering and order taking. Front counter registers take and serve orders at the same terminal, while drive through registers allow orders to be taken at one or more drive through windows, to be cashiered and served at another. In addition to registers, drive through and kitchen monitors may be used by store personnel to view orders. Once orders appear they may be deleted or recalled by "bump bars", small boxes which have different buttons for different uses. Drive through systems are often enhanced by the use of drive through wireless (or headset) systems which enable communications with drive through speakers.

POS systems are often designed for a variety of clients, and can be programmed by the end users to suit their needs. Some large clients write their own specifications for vendors to implement. In some cases, POS systems are sold and supported by third party distributors, while in other cases they are sold and supported directly by the vendor.

Wireless systems consist of drive though microphones and speakers (often one speaker will serve both purposes), which are wired to a "base station" or "center module." This will, in turn broadcast to headsets. Headsets may be an all-in-one headset or one connected to a belt pack.

Hotel business

POS software allows for transfer of meal charges from dining room to guest room with a button or two. It may also need to be integrated with property management software.

Checkout system

A checkout system generally involves the following components:

- General computer hardware
- General computer software
- Checkout hardware
- Checkout software
- Miscellaneous store hardware

A Checkout in a Guatemalan supermarket.

Because of the expense involved with a POS system, the eBay guide recommends that if annual revenue exceeds the threshold of $700,000, investment in a POS system will be advantageous.[2]

POS systems are manufactured and serviced by such firms as Fujitsu, IBM, MICROS Systems, Panasonic, Radiant Systems, Sharp, Squirrel Systems, and Vectron POS among others (see the point of sale companies category for complete list).

Point of sales systems in restaurant environments operate on DOS, Windows or Unix environments. They can use a variety of physical layer protocols, though Ethernet is currently the preferred system.

Checkout hardware

Specific to the POS industry, generally including:

- USB Credit card reader
- USB Receipt printer
- Cash drawer
- USB Barcode scanner
- USB PIN pad with Integrated Card Swipe
- Stands on which the payment devices are held/mounted/posted

Checkout software

Top software, based on U.S. Install Base:

- Radiant/Aloha: 24%
- Internally Developed: 15%
- MICROS: 14%[3]

Accounting forensics

Tax fraud

POS systems record sales for business and tax purposes. Illegal software dubbed "zappers" is increasingly used on them to falsify these records with a view to evading the payment of taxes.

References

[1] Kaplan, Karen. "Do-It-Yourself Solution: Small Grocery Chain Has Big Plans for Its Retailing Software", "Los Angeles Times", November 29, 1995, accessed December 10, 2010.

[2] "Point of Sale (POS) Systems Buying Guide" (http://pages.ebay.com/buy/guides/point-of-sale-pos-system-buying-guide/). . Retrieved 2009-07-23.

[3] *Source: Chain Store Guide 2004 Market Study of FoodService Technology - Top 768 chains, counted by Company*

Post-dated check

In banking, **postdated** refers to checks which have been written by the drawer for a date in the future. In the United States, postdated items are described in Article 3, Section 113 of the Uniform Commercial Code.[1] Postdated checks are often used in conjunction with payday loans.

Many banks will honor postdated checks, even if they are deposited before the postdate. In the United States, national banks are permitted to pay checks even though payment occurs prior to the date of the check. According to the Comptroller of the Currency: "A check is a negotiable instrument—the payee, the person to whom the check is written, may negotiate it through the banking system at any time".[2] Nonetheless, if the bank has been given proper notice of the post-dating, the Uniform Commercial Code requires that the notice be honored, or the bank be held liable for damages.[3]

In the United Kingdom post-dating a cheque carries no legal weight and therefore such a cheque can be cashed before the due date. However a bank can refuse to accept them if the post-date is spotted; if it isn't, the payer has no right to take any form of legal action against the bank for letting the check be processed.[4]

References

[1] 3 UCC 113 from the Cornell Law Center's online version of the Uniform Commercial Code (http://www.law.cornell.edu/ucc/3/article3.htm#s3-113)

[2] "Answers About Cashing Checks" (http://www.helpwithmybank.gov/faqs/banking_check_cashing.html#drop02). Comptroller of the Currency, Administrator of National Banks. . Retrieved 2008-11-25.

[3] http://www.law.cornell.edu/ucc/4/4-401.html

[4] http://www.chequeandcredit.co.uk/faqs/-/page/can_i_post-date_a_cheque/

Postal Order

In the United Kingdom (UK), a **Postal Order** is used for sending money through the mail. In the United States, this is known as a Postal money order. Postal Orders are not legal tender, but a type of promissory note, similar to a cheque.

History and use of the Postal Order

The Postal Order is a direct descendent of the money order which had been established by a private company in 1792. During World War I and World War II, British Postal Orders were temporarily declared legal tender to save paper and labour. Postal Orders can be bought and redeemed at post offices in the UK, although a crossed Postal Order must be paid into a bank account.[1] Until April 2006 they came in fixed denominations but due to increased popularity they were redesigned to make them more flexible and secure. They now have the payee and value added at the time of purchase, making them more like a cheque. The fee for using this form of payment falls into one of three bands - details are available on the Post Office website. The maximum value of Postal Order available is £250.00 with the fee capped at £10.[2] It was a safe method in times past, but nowadays offers very little advantage over cheques or electronic funds transfer. However, Postal Orders have regained popularity, especially as a form of payment for shopping on the Internet, as they are drawn on the Post Office's accounts so a vendor can be certain that they will not bounce. The use of Postal Orders (or postal notes in some countries) was extended to most countries that are now part of the Commonwealth of Nations, plus to a few foreign countries such as Jordan, Egypt and Thailand.

One of the most famous postal orders in history - the one alleged to have been cashed by George Archer-Shee.

Irish 9 shilling postal order with additional stamp used in 1969. Used postal orders are seldom seen because most were destroyed when they were redeemed or cashed at the post office or bank.

Collecting

Postal Orders are gaining in popularity as collectables, especially among numismatists who are actively collecting banknotes.

There is an active numismatic organisation in Great Britain called the Postal Order Society that was established in 1985 and which has members from both Great Britain and overseas. They hold twice-yearly postal auctions of Postal Orders and related material from across the British Commonwealth.

References

[1] "Frequently Asked Questions" (http://www.postoffice.co.uk/portal/po/content1?catId=73500709&mediaId=73500713). Post Office Ltd.. 2008. . Retrieved 2008-05-12.

[2] "Fee structure" (http://www.postoffice.co.uk/portal/po/jump1?catId=86500737&mediaId=73500709). Post Office Ltd.. 2009. . Retrieved 2009-04-19.

Postal orders around the world

- British Forces Post Office postal orders
- Postal Orders of Brunei
- Postal Orders of Canada
- Postal Orders of Cyprus
- Postal Orders of Gibraltar
- Postal Orders of Great Britain
- Postal Orders of Hong Kong
- Postal Orders of Ireland
- Postal Orders of New Zealand
- United States postal notes

External links

- Malaysian Postal Order images - RM1 to RM100. (http://www.pos.com.my/v1/?c=/v1/retailservices/poscounter/postalo.htm)

Pranasys

Pranasys is a technology company that develops solutions and services based on information and communication technologies. The products offered are based on software and electronic devices of their own design. Pranasys core business is mobile commerce and especially the electronic recharge of prepaid mobile phones.[1] Pranasys was founded in 1999 and has offices in Mexico, United States and Uruguay. Additionally, Pranasys develops business in Argentina, Paraguay, Bolivia and Venezuela. Pranasys is member of the NAMA (*National Automatic Merchandising Association*) [2] and is the first and only company of South America and the second company of Latin America registered at the EVA (*European Vending Association*) [3].[2]

Products

Pranasys main products are Vyana, PhoneCash!, Telcovending and Udana.

Vyana is the evolution of the **AtiendoRetail** platform of Pranasys. Vyana is a high performance transactional multi-platform switch that provides native support for 8583 ISO standard. Its implementation is based on PCI [5] security standards. Vyana enables computer systems like those located in a cash register or an ATM to sale intangible products (eg electronic recharge of prepaid mobile phones, parking tickets, gambling tickets, shows tickets, etc.) or interfaces with different financial institutions in order to obtain an online authorisation for the transaction (credit card, debit card, loyalty programs, etc.).

PhoneCash! is the later version of the **Atiendo!** platform of Pranasys. Phonecash! is a mobile commerce platform that provides to the user and the merchant a secure way to complete a transaction using the mobile phone instead of cash as payment method. Additionally, in combination with Vyana it allows the purchase of intangible products to end users by means of different interfaces (Web, mobile phone, etc.).

Telcovending is a platform for vending machines operators. The platform is based on **Udana**, an electronic device developed by Pranasys that is installed in the vending machine and enables new services. In the first place, it incorporates new means of payment (mobile phones, credit cards, meal tickets) to the sale of traditional products (hot and cold drinks, candies, snacks, etc.). In the second place, it allows the sales of intangible products in the vending machine. Finally, it offers the possibility to manage the business in a more efficient way, providing stock control, remote monitoring, real-time information, etc.[3] [4]

Awards

In 2003, United Nations organised the World Summit on the Information Technology (WSIS 2003) and selected some SMEs companies from all over the world to participate. From Latin America, only three were selected and Pranasys was one of them.[5]

In 2005, Pranasys received the 2005 National Innovation Award in Uruguay. The prize is awarded annually by Red ProPymes [9]. [6]

In 2009, Pranasys was included in the Uruguay Showcase of Excellence by the SOLAR-ICT project. According to the project website: "The SOLAR-ICT Showcase of Excellence gathers best practices in the ICT sector coming from Latin American to illustrate the latest innovative developments carried out in the region".[7]

External links

- Pranasys website. [12]
- "Con mayor presencia internacional." [13]. El País. October 23, 2003. Retrieved February 8, 2010.
- "El celular se convierte en billetera virtual." [14]. El País. May 19, 2005. Retrieved February 8, 2010.
- "Investigación + Desarrollo. ¡Claro que se Puede!" [15]. Noticias desde la DICyT. September 4, 2006. Retrieved February 10, 2010.
- "Billeteras Virtuales." [16]. La República. February 26, 2007. Retrieved February 8, 2010.

References

[1] [lDirección de Inonvación, Ciencia y Tecnología para el desarrollo, DICyT (http://www.dicyt.gub.uy/)] (2006). *Investigación + Desarrollo. ¡Claro que se puede! V.* pp. 13–15. ISBN 9974-36-064-1.

[2] [lEuropean Vending Association, EVA (http://www.vending-europe.eu/)] (2008), *Data Transfer Standard EVA DTS 6.1* (http://www. vending-europe.eu/documents/standards/09appendixbmanufcodesjanuary10_v2.pdf), pp. B5, , retrieved April 5, 2010

[3] Cardozo, Alvaro; Rodríguez, Gustavo; Katzenstein, Martín; Oreggioni, Julián (2009), "Platform to Perform Remote Commercial Transactions by Means of Vending Machines" (http://appft.uspto.gov/netacgi/nph-Parser?Sect1=PTO2&Sect2=HITOFF&p=1&u=/netahtml/PTO/ search-bool.html&r=1&f=G&l=50&col=AND&d=PG01&s1=12/341724&OS=12/341724&RS=12/341724), *US Patent Application number 20090164043,*

[4] Katzenstein, Martín; Oreggioni, Julián; Cardozo, Alvaro (2009), "Electronic Device for the Sale of Intangible Products in Vending Machines" (http://appft.uspto.gov/netacgi/nph-Parser?Sect1=PTO2&Sect2=HITOFF&p=1&u=/netahtml/PTO/search-bool.html&r=2&f=G& l=50&col=AND&d=PG01&s1=Pranasys&OS=Pranasys&RS=Pranasys), *US Patent Application number 20090177319,*

[5] "Final list of participants." (http://www.itu.int/wsis/docs/geneva/summit_participants.pdf). *World summit on the information society.* January 28, 2004. pp. 187. . Retrieved February 8, 2010.

[6] "Premio a la pyme innovadora." (http://www.elpais.com.uy/05/09/16/pciuda_174060.asp). El País. September 16, 2005. . Retrieved February 8, 2010.

[7] "*Promoting FP7 in each target country - Uruguay Showcase.*" (http://www.solar-ict.eu/Default.aspx?tabid=226). *The SOLAR-ICT Project.* . Retrieved February 8, 2010.

Prepaid

Prepaid refers to services paid for in advance. Examples include tolls, pay as you go cell phones, and stored-value cards such as gift cards and preloaded credit cards. Prepaid accounts are assets, and they are increased by debiting the account(s).

Prepaid services and goods are sometimes targeted to marginal customers by retailers. Prepaid options can have substantial cost reductions over postpaid counterparts because they allow customers to monitor and budget usage in advance.

Unlike postpaid or contract based services, prepaid accounts can be obtained with cash. As a result, they can be established by people who have minimal identification or poor credit ratings. Minors, immigrants, students, defaulters, and those on low incomes are typical prepaid customers.

Prepaid mobile phones

Recent statistics (OECD *Communications Outlook* 2005) indicate that 40% of the total mobile phone market in the OECD region consists of prepaid accounts. This service was invented by Portuguese provider TMN, while researching for a means to increase penetration of mobile technology by allowing anyone to buy a fully working (usually requiring a quick and simple activation process) mobile phone on any supermarket or electronics store. By removing the complications inherent to the contract system, this allowed the mobile communications user base to grow incredibly fast. In many countries this type of service became the predominant one, shortly after introduction, by providing both consumers and service providers with considerable advantages over the traditional method. In some countries, such as Italy or Mexico, market share of prepaid can be as high as 90%. In other countries, such as Finland or South Korea, the figure drops to about 2%.

A Prepaid Call (or even Calling Card) is actually established through two calls, and the first is either through an 800 Toll Free Number, and even some from the big telephone companies have them available with international toll free numbers , or you will find many that offer calling through a local phone number, usually printed on the back that offer cheaper rates but the first call costs are passed on to you, the consumer.

You place this first call to get to the providers platform, and once connected you are authenticated via a PIN or as seen in Europe or around other parts of the world the card may have an electronic chip on it, like you may have seen on the American Express Blue card. If you use the local number provided from your home or cell phone you pay for the cost of the first call, you can see this on your bills even if you don't get connected. The reason that 800 toll free is more expensive is because the Prepaid Calling Card Company pays for the attempts and even when you just call to check your balance, you only pay when you are actually connected. Many Local Telephone Companies don't show local usage so you may not see that you are paying for a local call every time you make an attempt. This is not true when you call a toll free number from a land line but with Cell phones you do use air time. With most local phone companies you can get call detail to support this.

Once you are authenticated you are usually presented with your balance then prompted for your destination number (the second call), and usually given the time left on your card based on the number you just dialed. Then you are connected.

With smaller companies beware the hidden charges when the rates are too low to be true. They mave have hidden fees or poorly advertised fees, like 3 minute rounding, connection fees, monthly, weekly, daily, or even maintenance fees. Look around when you buy these smaller name brands to make sure you know what you are buying.

The pseudonymity enabled by prepaid services has recently become a concern with law enforcement agencies that consider it a safe haven for criminals and terrorists. As a result, a number of countries including Australia, Germany, Indonesia, Japan, Malaysia, Mozambique, Norway, Singapore, South Africa, Switzerland, and Thailand have passed laws to require that all prepaid customers register their personal information with their mobile carrier.

In some countries the law requires that customers notify their mobile carrier when transferring ownership of a prepaid phone or SIM card.

In Australia, the prepaid registration policy is part of a larger law enforcement initiative that includes the creation and maintenance of an Integrated Public Number Database.

Energy

In 1999, Texas deregulated the energy industry by allowing third-party affiliates to offer electricity services. As a result, a handful of Texas companies are offering the ability to prepay your electricity, with the balance going toward the posted kilowatt hours rate. [1]

External links

- Privacy Rights and Prepaid Communications Services in Canada [2]
- Australia's Integrated Public Number Database scheme [3]

References

[1] http://www.paylesspower.com/texas-power-company.html Texas Power Company News

ProPay

ProPay, Inc is an American financial services company headquartered in Lehi, UT. The company provides payment solutions that include merchant accounts, payment processing, ACH services, pre-paid cards and other payment-related products. ProPay also provides end-to-end encryption and tokenization services. ProPay is a privately held company located in Lehi, UT.

History

Founded in 1997, ProPay has boarded more than 1.3 million merchants. Along with PayPal, Moneybookers, and Paymate, ProPay is one of the select few payment solutions authorized for use on the online auction site Ebay.[1] In 2008, the payments industry began calling for a service to remove payment data from the merchant environment in order to reduce the risk of compromise. In 2009, ProPay was among a handful of companies that began to offer an end-to-end encryption and tokenization service.[2] At that time, ProPay also introduced the MicroSecure Card Reader®, allowing small merchants to securely accept card present transactions.[3] In 2010, ProPay received the Independent Sales Organziation of Year award from the Electronic Transaction Association.[4]

Current Executive Team

- Gary Goodrich, Chief Executive Officer, President and Director
- Gregori Pesci, Chief Operating Officer
- Bryce Thacker, Executive Vice President of Sales and Marketing
- Mark Johnson, Chief Information Officer
- Chris Jensen, Executive Vice President, Treasurer and Secretary
- Chris Mark, Executive Vice President, Data Security and Compliance
- Lance Rich, Executive Vice President, Risk
- Frank Anthony Allen, Executive Vice President, Corporate Counsel

References

[1] ProPay Reveals Details of New PayPal Alternative on eBay, AuctionBytes, October 19, 2008.

[2] ProPay Unlocks ProtectPay Encrypted Credit Card Processing, TMC.net 02/20/2009

[3] Pocket Credit Card Reader Takes Transactions on the Go, PC World 01/07/2009

[4] ProPay Receives 2010 Electronic Transaction Association ISO of the Year Award, Silicone Slopes 04/20/2010

External links

- ProPay website (http://www.propay.com/)
- Patent Assigned to ProPay: Method and apparatus for credit card processing via facsimile (http://patft.uspto. gov/netacgi/nph-Parser?Sect1=PTO2&Sect2=HITOFF&p=1&u=/netahtml/PTO/search-bool.html&r=1& f=G&l=50&col=AND&d=PTXT&s1=propay.ASNM.&OS=AN/propay&RS=AN/propay)
- Patent Assigned to ProPay: Linking a merchant account with a payment card (http://patft.uspto.gov/netacgi/ nph-Parser?Sect1=PTO2&Sect2=HITOFF&p=1&u=/netahtml/PTO/search-bool.html&r=1&f=G&l=50& col=AND&d=PTXT&s1=ProPay.ASNM.&OS=AN/ProPay&RS=AN/ProPay)

QC Record Format

The **QC record format** is one of the two standard formats used for the interchange of financial transactions in the New Zealand banking system. The other standard format is BACHO.

QC-format transactions are primarily used in batch processing systems running on MVS mainframe computers.

A QC record consists of a fixed 23-byte header (containing record type codes, destination account details, and the transaction amount) followed by zero or more optional fields, each of which is of variable size.

Kamal Quadir

Kamal Quadir	
	Quadir in 2008
Occupation	CEO of bKash Limited [1][1] Founder of CellBazaar Inc. [3][2]

bKash Limited

Industry	Financial Services
Website	www.bkash.com [5]

CellBazaar Inc.

Industry	Mobile Telecommunication
Website	www.cellbazaar.com [6]

Kamal S. Quadir is a Bangladeshi American entrepreneur and artist best known as the creator of CellBazaar, a mobile phone based electronic marketplace which, after reaching 4 million users, was acquired by Norwegian telecommunications operator Telenor in 2010.[3]

Kamal is currently heading bKash which provides financial services through an extensive network of community-based agents and existing technology, including mobile phones.[4]

Kamal is one of the most-cited (recently in the *Wall Street Journal*[5]) thinkers in mobile innovations who has been credited for "grass-root level market creation"[6] with emerging technologies.

Kamal is a founding member of Open World Initiatives, a Lausanne, Switzerland based organization of young thinkers.[2] He is involved with *Anwarul Quadir Foundation* which recognizes innovations in developing countries. He is a First Mover Fellow of The Aspen Institute. In 2009, TED selected Kamal a TEDIndia Fellow[7] and the World Economic Forum recognized him as a Young Global Leader.[8]

Early life

Quadir was an intern at Insight Venture Partners in New York, led the Business Development Division of Occidental Petroleum's initiative in Bangladesh and worked for New York City's Chamber of Commerce. He was also the co-founder and creative director of *GlobeKids Inc.*, an animation company.

Kamal has a BA from Oberlin College and an MBA from the MIT Sloan School of Management.

He is also an accomplished artist whose art works are in the permanent collection of the Bangladesh National Museum and the Liberation War Museum.

bKash

bKash Limited is a joint venture between BRAC Bank Ltd., Bangladesh, and Money in Motion LLC, USA. ensuring access to a broader range of financial services for the people of Bangladesh is the ultimate objective of bKash. It has a special focus to serve the low income people of the country and promote sustainable micro-savings to achieve broader financial inclusion by providing financial services that are convenient, affordable and reliable.

bKash is working both as an extension of BRAC Bank and as a full-scale mobile phone-based payment switch. This will highly benefit the country as 83% of the population lives under $2 a day and access to finance can help in improving their economic situation. Less than 15% of Bangladeshis are connected to the formal financial system whereas 44% of total population are having mobile phones. Providing financial services using this mean can make the service more accessible and cost effective for the vast population of Bangladesh.[9]

CellBazaar

CellBazaar is an electronic marketplace, launched in 2006 in Bangladesh, that allows buyers and sellers to connect with one another and buy and sell goods and services using their mobile phones or computers.

Limited communication has always been a hindrance for performing business, especially in developing countries. In Bangladesh, the isolated and uninformed farmers and traders have little bargaining power with exploitative middlemen. CellBazaar enables entrepreneurs and small businesses in Bangladesh to start and grow operations in a market that wouldn't otherwise be available in their local community, thereby creating jobs, stimulating the economy, and delivering products and services that improve the lives of millions of poor people. CellBazaar has been credited as a revolutionary service in mobile telecommunications to have the potential to significantly contribute to socioeconomic development particularly in developing countries due to the ability to bridge non-existing wired telecommunications and transportation infrastructure and delivering various services directly to the end-user.[10] Nokia, in their Expanding Horizons magazine, accredited CellBazaar as a door opener to mobile commerce.[11]

The CellBazaar marketplace is available to more than 25 million people in Bangladesh, including farmers that use the service to sell their harvest at fair market prices and struggling students that find and connect with tutors.

The service is accessible via Text message (SMS), WAP or Internet enabled handset, Computer or Web and Voice (IVR), each of which connects to one customer-generated marketplace. Users pay only the standard SMS or Internet charges for accessing the service on mobile, and there are no monthly or posting fees.

It is alleged that the idea of CellBazaar was originally conceived by Syed Rayhan, a Bangladeshi born US citizen, who approached Kamal's brother, Iqbal Quadir; but later the brothers implemented it without Syed's consent.[12]

Awards

- Year 2009
  - "Young Global Leader (YGL)" by the World Economic Forum of Davos [13]
- Year 2008
  - Global Mobile Award of the GSM Association in the category of "Best Use of Mobile for Social & Economic Development" [14]
  - Telecom Asia's "Asian Innovation of the Year" Award [15]
  - India's Manthan Award for "Best E-Content for Development" [16]
- Year 2007
  - Tech Award for "Applying Technology to Benefit Humanity" [17]
- Year 2005
  - MIT Ideas Award [18]

References

[1] http://www.thedailystar.net/newDesign/news-details.php?nid=175903

[2] Highlighted Profiles of the Young Global Leaders, World Economic Forum (http://www.weforum.org/en/Communities/Young Global Leaders/Whoweare/index.htm)

[3] http://www.vilcap.com/making-markets-mission-markets-and-better-world-books

[4] http://www.thedailystar.net/newDesign/news-details.php?nid=175903

[5] http://online.wsj.com/article/SB122081673203508037.html

[6] http://www.livemint.com/2008/12/18222207/Making-markets-with-mobiles.html

[7] http://www.ted.com/pages/view?id=305

[8] http://new.oberlin.edu/office/creativity/speakers-and-symposia/entrepreneurship-week.dot

[9] http://www.bkash.com/About.php

[10] Revolutionary service in mobile telecommunications

[11] Expanding Horizons by Nokia & Nokia Siemens Network (http://expandinghorizons.nokia.com/issues/?issue=ExpandingHorizonsQ22008&page=13)

[12] http://blog.syedrayhan.com/2009/12/they-stole-my-startup-idea.html

[13] http://www.weforum.org/en/media/Latest%20Press%20Releases/PR_YGL2009

[14] http://www.globalmobileawards.com/history/index.shtml

[15] (http://www.telecomasia.net/content/closing-divide-humble-phone-0)

[16] http://www.manthanaward.org/section_full_story.asp?id=667

[17] http://www.techawards.org/laureates/stories/index.php?id=164

[18] http://web.mit.edu/newsoffice/2005/awards-ideas-0601.html

External links

- Anuwarul Quadir Foundation (http://www.quadir.org)
- The Tech Award page (http://www.techawards.org/laureates/stories/index.php?id=164)
- GSMA Global Mobile Award page (http://www.globalmobileawards.com/history/index.shtml)
- Telecom Asia's award page (http://www.telecomasia.net/content/closing-divide-humble-phone-0)
- India's Manthan award page (http://www.manthanaward.org/section_full_story.asp?id=667)
- World Economic Forum's Young Global Leader (YGL) of 2009 (http://www.weforum.org/en/media/Latest Press Releases/PR_YGL2009)
- MIT Ideas award page (http://web.mit.edu/newsoffice/2005/awards-ideas-0601.html)
- Wall Street Journal article (http://online.wsj.com/article/SB122081673203508037.html)
- Livemint.com article (http://www.livemint.com/2008/12/18222207/Making-markets-with-mobiles.html)
- Kamal Quadir at Crunchbase (http://www.crunchbase.com/person/kamal-quadir)
- CellBazaar at Crunchbase (http://www.crunchbase.com/company/cellbazaar)
- The Business of Art, Oberlin.edu (http://www.oberlin.edu/alummag/oamcurrent/oam_winter99/profile.html)

- WTO Public Symposium 2003: Session IV - "Cancun: Next Stop on the Road to the 2015 Millennium Development Goals" (http://www.cid.harvard.edu/cidtrade/geneva/sessions/session04.html)
- CellBazaar portfolio at Omidyar.com (http://www.omidyar.com/portfolio/cellbazaar)
- Corporate page at CellBazaar.com (http://corp.cellbazaar.com)
- Comapny page of bKash Limited (http://www.bkash.com)

Quick Wertkarte

Quick is an electronic purse system available on Austrian bank cards to allow small purchases to be made without cash. The history of the Quick system goes back to 1994.

The system is aimed at small retailers such as bakeries, cafés, drink and parking automats (but even small discount shops such as Billa accept it) and intended for purchases of less than €400. The card is inserted into a handheld Quick reader by the merchant who enters the transaction amount for the customer. The customer then confirms the purchase by pushing a button on the keypad, the exact amount debited from the card within a few seconds.

As well as the multipurpose bank card version, anonymous cards (also smart cards) are available for the use of people without bank accounts, such as children and tourists. At ATMs, one can transfer money for free between bank cards and the Quick chip (either on a standalone smart card, or contained in the bank card).

Currently the scheme is operated by Europay Austria and most of the Maestro cards in use contain Quick support, but new ones are not issued without it.

External links

- The official Quick site (in German) [1]
- Quick, Austria's electronic purse [2]

Ready Financial

Ready Financial

Type	Private
Industry	Finance
Founded	2006
Founder(s)	Will Tumulty
Headquarters	Boise, Idaho, USA
Products	Debit card
Website	www.readyfinancial.com [1]

Ready Financial, headquartered in Boise, Idaho, is the creator of the ReadyDebit Visa Inc. prepaid debit card and online bill payment and check writing service. Ready Financial was founded by Will Tumulty and has received substantial investments by private equity group Rockbridge Growth Equity LLC, founded by Dan Gilbert.[1] The company provides consumers lacking established credit with the security and convenience associated with debit and credit cards. The card offers the Path2Credit Score Tracker that helps consumers watch their credit score rise over time.

Notes

[1] "Ready Financial Secures $7.0 Million Series B Funding to Provide Consumers with Affordable Alternatives to High-Fee Checking Accounts" (http://www.businesswire.com/news/home/20091118005116/en/Ready-Financial-Secures-7.0-Million-Series-Funding)

External links

- Ready Financial (http://www.readyfinancial.com)
- ReadyDebit (http://www.readydebit.com)
- Review of ReadyDebit card (http://www.getdebit.com/prepaid-debit-card/readydebit-prepaid-debit-visa-select/)

Real Time Gross Settlement

Real time gross settlement systems (RTGS) are funds transfer systems where transfer of money or securities[1] takes place from one bank to another on a "real time" and on "gross" basis. Settlement in "real time" means payment transaction is not subjected to any waiting period. The transactions are settled as soon as they are processed. "Gross settlement" means the transaction is settled on one to one basis without bunching or netting with any other transaction. Once processed, payments are final and irrevocable.

Existing systems

Below is a listing of countries and their RTGS systems:

- Albania - AECH, RTGS
- Australia - RITS (Reserve Bank Information and Transfer System)
- Bulgaria - RINGS (**R**eal-time **IN**terbank **G**ross-settlement **S**ystem)
- Brazil - STR (Sistema de Transferência de Reservas)
- Canada - LVTS (Low Value Transfer System) (This is actually an RTGS *Equivalent* system. Final settlement happens in the evening.)
- China - China National Advanced Payment System ("CNAPS") (also called "Super Online Banking System)[2]
- Chile - LBTR/CAS (Spanish: *Liquidación Bruta en Tiempo Real*)
- Croatia - HSVP (Croatian: *Hrvatski sustav velikih plaćanja*)[3]
- Czech Republic - CERTIS (Czech Express Real Time Interbank Gross Settlement System)
- Hong Kong - Clearing House Automated Transfer System (CHATS)
- Hungary - VIBER (Hungarian: *Valós Idejű Bruttó Elszámolási Rendszer*)
- India - RTGS
- Indonesia - Sistem Bank Indonesia Real Time Gross Settlement (BI-RTGS)
- Iran - SATNA (⬚ ▮▮▮⬚⬚⬚ ⬚⬚⬚▮▮▮ ⬚⬚ , Real-Time Gross Settlement System)
- Israel - Zahav (Credit and Transfers in Real Time)[4]
- Japan - BOJ-NET (Bank of Japan Financial Network System)[5]
- Kenya - Kenya Electronic Payment and Settlement System (KEPSS)
- Kuwait - KASSIP (Kuwait's Automated Settlement System for Inter-Participant Payments)
- Macedonia - MIPS (Macedonian Interbank Payment System)[6]
- Malaysia - RENTAS (Real Time Electronic Transfer of Funds and Securities)
- Mexico - SPEI (Spanish: *Sistema de Pagos Electrónicos Interbancarios*) [7]
- New Zealand - ESAS (Exchange Settlement Account System)
- Nigeria - NAGSS (Nigerian Automated Gross Settlement System)
- Peru - LBTR (Spanish: *Liquidación Bruta en Tiempo Real*)
- Philippines - PhilPaSS [8]
- Poland - SORB[9]
- Russia - BESP system (Banking Electronic Speed Payment System)[10]
- Romania - ReGIS system [11]
- Saudi Arabia - (Saudi Arabian Riyal Interbank Express) SARIE [12]
- Singapore - MEPS+ (MAS Electronic Payment System Plus)
- South Africa - SAMOS (The South African Multiple Option Settlement) [13]
- Switzerland - SIC (Swiss Interbank Clearing) [14]
- Thailand - BAHTNET (**B**ank of Thailand Automated **H**igh value **T**ransfer **Net**work)
- Turkey - EFT (Electronic Fund Transfer)
- United Kingdom - CHAPS (Clearing **H**ouse Automated **P**ayment **S**ystem)

- United States - Fedwire

RTGS systems covering multiple countries:

- TARGET resp. TARGET2 (**T**rans-European **A**utomated **R**eal-time **G**ross Settlement **E**xpress **T**ransfer System) in 26 countries of the European Union

TARGET2 [15] is the Real Time Gross Settlement system for the Euro currency, and is offered by the Eurosystem, which comprises the European Central Bank and the National Central Banks of those countries that have adopted the Euro currency. The Eurosystem and the European System of Central Banks will co-exist as long as there are EU Member States outside the Euro area.

TARGET2 is used for the settlement of central bank operations, large-value Euro interbank transfers as well as other euro payments. TARGET 2 provides real-time financial transfers, debt settlement at central banks which is immediate and irreversible.

Mechanism

This "electronic" payment system is normally maintained or controlled by the Central Bank of a country. There is no physical exchange of money; the Central Bank makes adjustments in the electronic accounts of Bank A and Bank B, reducing the amount in Bank A's account by $1000 and increasing the amount of Bank B's account by the same.

The RTGS system is suited for low-volume, high-value transactions. It lowers settlement risk, besides giving an accurate picture of an institution's account at any point of time.

Such systems are an alternative to systems of settling transactions at the end of the day, also known as the *net settlement* system such as BACS. In the net settlement system, all the inter-institution transactions during the day are accumulated. At the end of the day, the accounts of the institutions are adjusted. Extending the example above, say another person deposits a check drawn on Bank B in Bank A for $500. At the end of the day, Bank A will have to "electronically" pay Bank B only $500 ($1000 - $500).

The implementation of RTGS systems by Central Banks throughout the world is driven by the goal to minimize risk in high-value electronic payment settlement systems.

In an RTGS system, transactions are settled across accounts held at a Central Bank on a continuous gross basis. Settlement is immediate, final and irrevocable. Credit risks due to settlement lags are eliminated.

RTGS does not require core banking to be implemented across participating banks, since transactions are direct, with no central processing or clearing operations. Any RTGS employs two sets of queues: one for testing outgoing funds availability on a chronological FIFO basis with the option of prioritizing specific inquiries, while the other queue is for processing debit/credit requests received from the central bank's Integrated Accounting System.

References

[1] Committee on Payment and Settlement Systems of the central banks of the Group of Ten countries (March 1997). *Real-Time Gross Settlement Systems* (http://www.bis.org/publ/cpss22.pdf). Bank for International Settlements. p. 14. .

[2] "China's 'Super Online Banking System' Launches on Monday" (http://en.21cbh.com/HTML/2010-8-30/1MMDAwMDE5NDg1MA. html). *Business China*. August 30, 2010. . Retrieved September 3, 2010.

[3] http://www.hnb.hr/platni-promet/medubankovni-platni-statistika/hsvp/h-sustav-velikih-placanja.htm

[4] The Zahav System (http://israbank.gov.il/zahav/pc_e.htm) Bank of Israel website

[5] Bank of Japan (2003). *Payment systems in Japan* (http://www.boj.or.jp/en/type/release/zuiji/kako03/set0305a.pdf). Bank of Japan. . Retrieved Jun.17,2010.

[6] (http://www.nbrm.gov.mk) National Bank of Macedonia website

[7] (http://www.banxico.org.mx/sitioingles/sistemasdepago/inforgeneral/sistemasPagoAltoValor/SegundoNivel/SPEI.htm) - Banxico's SPEI

Recurly

Recurly, Inc.

Type	Payment service provider
Industry	Software Industry, Finance
Founded	2009
Headquarters	San Francisco, California
Key people	Isaac Hall, CEO Dan Burkhart, President James Michels, V.P. Engineering
Employees	7
Website	recurly.com [1]

Recurly is a software as a service company that provides recurring billing management as an outsourced service. Founded in September, 2009[1] and made available as a public beta in January, 2010.[2] Companies with subscription business models commonly encounter errors from payment gateways, acquiring banks, issuing banks, or credit card associations. Recurly remediates credit card payment errors on behalf of merchant customers, and automates customer communications related to subscription billing. In July, 2010, Recurly raised $1.6MM in seed fundraising, led by Polaris Venture Partners,[3] and a number of individual angel investors[4] Recurly is a Level 1 PCI-DSS compliant service provider.

References

[1] Online subscription billing is a pain Recurly wants to alleviate (http://techcrunch.com/2009/11/17/ online-subscription-billing-is-a-pain-recurly-wants-to-alleviate-it/)
[2] Recurly public beta (http://techcrunch.com/2010/01/19/recurly-public-beta/)
[3] DogPatch Labs unveils new brood (http://techcrunch.com/2010/05/01/dogpatch-labs-unveils-new-brood/)
[4] Recurly raises $1.6 million to help companies manage subscription billing (http://techcrunch.com/2010/08/03/ recurly-raises-1-6-million-to-help-companies-manage-subscription-billing/)

External links

- Recurly website (http://recurly.com/)
- Crunchbase (http://www.crunchbase.com/company/recurly)

Red Wing Software

History

Red Wing Software was founded as Red Wing Business Systems in 1979 as primarily an agricultural software developer and distributor. As the company grew, it began to create and market additional accounting software products for businesses as well. In 2001, Red Wing Business Systems merged with Champion Business Systems and FMS/Harvest. Software products included in the company merger were Champion Controller Accounting, Profit and Profit Gold Accounting (Champion Business Systems), Perception Accounting Software (FMS/Harvest), AgCHEK, Red Wing DOS Accounting and Payroll, and Red Wing Windows Accounting and Payroll (Red Wing Business Systems). [1] In 2003, the merged company was purchased by the management team and has since operated as Red Wing Software, Inc. Today, Red Wing Software develops and distributes five products: CenterPoint Accounting Software, TurningPoint Accounting Software, CenterPoint Accounting Software for Agriculture, CenterPoint Fund Accounting Software, and CenterPoint Payroll Software.

External links

Red Wing Software Company Web site [2]

References

- Hest, D. "Software to Count On" [1], "Farm Industry News", March 1, 2002.
- CenterPoint Payroll Software, 2008 CPA Technology Advisor Review, 5 Star Rating [3] (September 2008)
- CenterPoint Payroll Software, 2007 CPA Technology Advisor Review, 5 Star Rating [4] (September 2007)
- TurningPoint Accounting Software, 2009 CPA Technology Advisor Review, 4.5 Star Rating [5] (June 2009)
- TurningPoint Accounting Software, 2009 Web CPA Mid Range Accounting Software Review [6] (January 2009)
- TurningPoint Accounting Software, 2008 Web CPA Top 100 Products [7] (December 2008)
- TurningPoint Accounting Software, 2008 CPA Technology Advisor Review, 4.5 Star Rating [8] (September 2008)
- TurningPoint Accounting Software, 2008 Web CPA Mid Range Accounting Software Review [9] (January 2008)
- TurningPoint Accounting Software, 2007 CPA Technology Advisor Review, 4.5 Star Rating [10] (September 2007)
- TurningPoint Accounting Software, 2006 CPA Technology Advisor Review, 4.5 Star Rating [11] (September 2006)
- CenterPoint Accounting Software, 2009 CPA Technology Advisor Small Business Accounting Software Tier II Review [12] (June 2009)
- CenterPoint Accounting Software, 2009 Web CPA New Products [13] (February 2009)
- CenterPoint Fund Accounting Software, 2008 Web CPA Tech Bulletin Briefs [14] (June 2008)
- CenterPoint Accounting Software for Agriculture, 2006 Delta Farm Press [15] (May 2006)

Revolution Money

Revolution Money Inc.

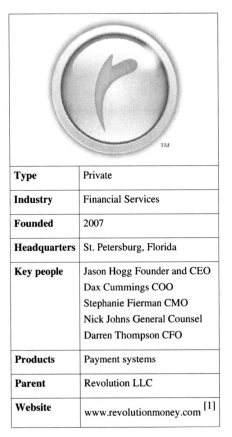

Type	Private
Industry	Financial Services
Founded	2007
Headquarters	St. Petersburg, Florida
Key people	Jason Hogg Founder and CEO Dax Cummings COO Stephanie Fierman CMO Nick Johns General Counsel Darren Thompson CFO
Products	Payment systems
Parent	Revolution LLC
Website	www.revolutionmoney.com [1]

Revolution Money is a financial services company whose products include a PIN-based credit card, online person-to-person payments service with a linked stored value card, and gift card. Revolution Money is the first new payment brand introduced in the United States since Discover Network in 1985, and is the only credit card that does not charge retailers interchange fees.

Revolution Money's site was visited by only 33,000 people in the U.S. even in February, down from a marketing-fueled high of 742,000 a year before in March, 2008. Revolution Money is based in St. Petersburg, Florida.[1]

Revolution Money has three products: RevolutionCard, Revolution MoneyExchange and RevolutionGift. RevolutionCard is a credit card. Revolution MoneyExchange provides free online money transfers between members and the card linked to the account can be used at retailers and ATMs. Revolution MoneyExchange accounts are issued by First Bank and Trust.

On November 18th, 2009, American Express announced that it would acquire Revolution Money for 500 million USD and finally did for 300 million USD.[2]

Products

RevolutionCard

RevolutionCard (click on this page [4] for card image) is a PIN-based credit card. The card itself has no name, signature, or account number so, if lost or stolen, it cannot be used unless the PIN is known. 150,000 merchants currently accept RevolutionCard, and it is projected that 1 million locations will accept it by the end of 2008. In 2009, that plateau hasn't been reached, but Revolution Money expect to do it with a new partnership with Chase. Even accepted on many merchants, Revolution Money still an under suscribed system due to its low income to banks, and in certain cases losses. Consumers receive a credit approval decision instantly when applying for the RevolutionCard. RevolutionCard works with multiple banks to providing a broad spectrum of interest rates for card applicants. RevolutionCard charges merchants a 0.50% transaction processing fee and no interchange fee. Revolution Money then helps retailers turn some of their savings into rewards or discounts for consumers. RevolutionCard's network is built on a rules-based, proprietary technology using the Internet as the backbone for transactions.

Revolution MoneyExchange

Revolution MoneyExchange is an online payments service that lets users send and receive money. There are no fees charged for online transfers between accounts. The Revolution MoneyExchange Card is a stored-value card that allows accountholders to access their funds for purchases at merchant locations on the RevolutionCard network and for cash withdrawals at ATMs nationwide. Revolution MoneyExchange is available only to people in the United States.

RevolutionGift

RevolutionGift is a prepaid PIN-based gift card. Like the RevolutionCard, there is no account number printed on the card. RevolutionGift card must be activated before use.

Revolution LLC

Revolution Money is a division of Revolution LLC and Mirage Investments, LLC, an investment firm founded by Steve Case, the founder of AOL and co-CEO of Mirage Investments, LLC.

Partners

- Yahoo! Sports
- Fifth Third Bank
- List of many retailers accepting the RevolutionCard [5]

References

[1] https://www.revolutioncard.com/WebSite/about_us.aspx

[2] http://finance.yahoo.com/news/American-Express-to-buy-apf-2466608827.html?x=0&sec=topStories&pos=2&asset=&ccode=

- Squires, Paula (June 1, 2008). "Steve Case searches for another iconic brand" (http://www.virginiabusiness.com/index.php/news/article/steve-case-searches-for-another-iconic-brand/893/). *Virginia Business*. Retrieved 2008-07-22.

- Graham, Jefferson (2007-11-06). "Talkin' 'bout a Revolution in transferring money online" (http://www.usatoday.com/tech/techinvestor/corporatenews/2007-11-06-ted-leonis-steve-case_N.htm). *USA Today*. Retrieved 2008-07-22.

- "Revolution Money - Formerly GratisCard" (http://www.paymentsnews.com/2007/09/revolution-mone.html). *Payments News*. Retrieved 2008-07-22.

- "Revolution Money offers online payment alternative" (http://www.gizmag.com/go/8124/). *gizmag.com*. October 12, 2007. Retrieved 2008-07-22.

- "Revolutionary Money: Upstart Challenges the Credit Card Industry" (http://www.portfolio.com/views/blogs/the-tech-observer/2008/07/01/revolutionary-money-upstart-challenges-the-credit-card-industry). *Portfolio.com*. 2008-07-01. Retrieved 2008-07-22.

- "Revolution Money Aims for 1 Million Merchants, Cardholders by Year End" (http://www.digitaltransactions.net/newsstory.cfm?newsid=1820). *Digital Transactions*. June 20, 2008. Retrieved 2008-07-22.

- Burnsed, Brian (June 20, 2008). "Top News: To Save Money at the Gas Pump, Pay Cash. Filling stations are offering a 6¢-a-gallon discount for cash customers, to incentivize the use of cash, cutting back on hefty credit-card fees" (http://www.businessweek.com/bwdaily/dnflash/content/jun2008/db20080619_083558.htm). *BusinessWeek*. Retrieved 2008-07-22.

- Gonsalves, Antone (November 8, 2007). "Revolution Online Money Transfer Service Pits Itself Against PayPal. The company is marketing its new RevolutionCard credit card payment service as a more secure option to traditional credit cards from MasterCard or Visa." (http://www.informationweek.com/news/internet/showArticle.jhtml?articleID=202804023). *InformationWeek*. Retrieved 2008-07-22.

- "St. Pete payments firm strikes deal with Fifth Third" (http://news.moneycentral.msn.com/provider/providerarticle.aspx?feed=ACBJ&date=20080205&id=8140775). *MSN Money*. 2008-02-05. Retrieved 2008-07-22.

- Cauley, Leslie (2007-09-23). "Account number, name not on this credit card" (http://www.usatoday.com/money/perfi/credit/2007-09-23-revolution-credit_N.htm). *USA Today*. Retrieved 2008-07-22.

- Manning, Margie (August 17, 2007). "St. Petersburg credit card company launches a Revolution" (http://tampabay.bizjournals.com/tampabay/stories/2007/08/20/story7.html). *Tampa Bay Business Journal*. Retrieved 2008-07-22.

- Hundley, Kris (October 27, 2007). "Get ready for credit card 2.0. The name of the St. Petersburg company sums it up, say the founders of Revolution Money." (http://www.sptimes.com/2007/10/27/Business/Get_ready_for_credit_.shtml). *St. Petersburg Times*. Retrieved 2008-07-22.

- "AOL co-founder backs new online payment firm" (http://www.washingtonpost.com/wp-dyn/content/article/2007/09/25/AR2007092501899_pf.html). *The Washington Post*. 2007-09-25. Retrieved 2008-07-22.

- Regan, Keith (January 9, 2008). "A Host of Hot Niches on the E-Commerce VC Trail" (http://www.ecommercetimes.com/story/61104.html). *E-Commerce Times*. Retrieved 2008-07-22.

Revolution MoneyExchange

Revolution MoneyExchange is an online bank that bills itself as an alternative to PayPal and its chief competitor, Google Checkout. It was founded by Jason Hogg and Patrick Graf as GratisCard in April 2007 [1]. Ted Leonsis and Steve Case are on its board of directors. [2]

Revolution MoneyExchange is backed by Citi, Morgan Stanley, and Deutsche Bank AG, as well as its parent company, Revolution LLC. [3]

Among some of its features are money sending over AOL Instant Messenger. [4]

Presently (as of November, 22nd 2010), Revolution MoneyExchange does not accept new user registrations.

References

[1] "Revolution Money Exchange" (http://geek-news.net/2008/02/revolution-money-exchange.html). *Geek-News.Net*. 2008-02-10. . Retrieved 2008-07-15.

[2] "Small Correction" (http://ted.aol.com/category.php?catID=650). *Ted's Take*. 2008-02-11. . Retrieved 2008-07-15.

[3] "Revolution MoneyExchange: New Person-to-Person Payment System and $25 Bonus Promotion" (http://www.mymoneyblog.com/archives/2008/01/revolution-moneyexchange-new-person-to-person-payment-system-and-25-bonus-promotion.html). *MyMoneyBlog*. 2008-01-31. . Retrieved 2008-07-15.

[4] "You've Got Payments - AOL Founder Backs P-to-P Start-Up" (https://www.revolutionmoney.com/PressUpdates/YouveGotPayments-AOLFounderBacksP-to-PStart-Up.pdf). *American Banker*. 2007-09-25. . Retrieved 2008-07-15.

External links

- Website (http://www.revolutionmoneyexchange.com/)
- A review of Revolution MoneyExchange (http://geek-news.net/2008/05/great-paypal-alternative-revolution.html)

Ripple monetary system

Ripple is an open-source software project for developing and implementing a protocol for an open decentralized payment network. In its developed form (it is not substantially implemented), the Ripple network would be a peer-to-peer distributed social network service with a monetary honour system based on trust that already exists between people in real-world social networks; this form is financial capital backed completely by social capital. Another possible direction

for implementation is extension of the existing hierarchical banking system, providing alternate payment routes that do not pass through a central bank.

Background

Modern monetary systems are built on obligations of the participants to each other. Cash and bonds are government obligations, and loan agreements are the personal obligations of borrowers. Bank account balances are bank obligations, backed by borrower and government obligations. For an obligation to have value, the holder must trust that the issuer can supply that value. Thus the banking network can be described as a trust network.

The primary method of making payment to another participant in the system is by transferring ownership of bank obligations electronically over a chain of accounts in the banking network from payer to recipient. The banking network is essentially hierarchical, with banks acting as sole intermediary between its account-holders, and central banks acting as sole intermediary between banks. This structure means that it is simple to route payments to and from any participants, but is inherently full of Single points of failure, which may also be characterized as *single points of control*.

Principle

The core idea of Ripple is that it should be possible to route payments through an open, arbitrary trust network, similar to how the internet routes packets of data through an open, arbitrary computer network. The advantages of such a system would be that it wouldn't be reliant on a small decision-making body at the center to set monetary policy for the entire nation; instead, it would be set in a more democratic fashion by all participants, and in theory be more responsive to regional and community needs. There would be no need for a tightly regulated institutional trust hierarchy to control the behaviour of those participants near the center: like the internet, but unlike the existing global monetary system, the Ripple network would be designed to weather the collapse of a large number of its nodes.

Note that the Ripple protocol itself wouldn't preclude a hierarchical payment structure evolving, it just allows for the possibility of other structures.

Put another way, Ripple is a system of free banking that separates the payment routing function from the credit aggregation function.

Comparison with existing payment systems

Other alternative (to standard public clearing houses such as ACH) payment/monetary systems already exist, including internet currencies such as PayPal, currency networks like KlickEx, or local currencies such as LETS. Ripple is fundamentally different from hierarchical models in that it provides a level playing field that treats all participants equally. Both PayPal and LETS are modelled on a single central authority that issues obligations based on its policy and handles the accounting of payments between leaf nodes. In Ripple, no node has any greater or lesser capability than any other node -- this is acknowledgement that every participant in a debt-based monetary system does in fact issue their own currency (or obligations). A node's connectedness in Ripple is based on the trust of the other participants and nothing else.

In a sense, every Ripple node is like a LETS or a PayPal unto itself. Ripple could be used to connect existing alternative and mainstream payment systems into a single network.

References

- WOT for WAT: Spinning the web of trust for peer-to-peer barter relationships , K Saito - IEICE Transactions on Communications, 2005 - IEICE
- Local production, local consumption peer-to-peer architecture , K Saito, E Morino, Y Suko, T Suzuki, J Murai - Applications and the Internet Workshops, 2007.

External links

- Ripple project home page [1]
- Ripplepay.com: a demonstration of Ripple concept as a standalone social network website [2], source code available [3]
- Ripplexchange: classifieds using Ripple [4]
- Video of Dave Hales talking about the Ripple Project and other P2P related concepts, at the European Complex Systems Conference, Dresden, Oct. 2007 [5]
- The original paper by Ryan Fugger about Ripple [6]
- according to Google Scholar, Ripple has been cited by at least 2 peer-reviewed published papers [7]

RuPay

RuPay

Operating area	India
Founded	April 2011

RuPay is an Indian domestic card scheme launched by National Payments Corporation of India.[1] It is a domestic payment scheme on the lines of global gateways such as Visa and MasterCard, and is based on China UnionPay.[2]

History

The Reserve Bank of India in 2009, had asked the Indian Bank Association to launch a non-profit payment solutions company to meet the requirements of domestic banks. After two years of planning, NPCI has finalized the name of the proposed card as RuPay.[3]

RuPay card

RuPay card would be soon launched

References

[1] http://articles.timesofindia.indiatimes.com/2011-03-21/india-business/29170858_1_debit-cards-credit-card-market-npci

[2] http://www.livemint.com/2011/04/11235814/India8217s-payment-gateway.html

[3] http://blogs.forbes.com/greatspeculations/2011/04/06/indian-rupay-card-causes-trouble-in-asia-for-mastercard-visa/

SADAD Payment System

SADAD Payment System (SADAD) was established by the Saudi Arabian Monetary Agency (SAMA) to be the national Electronic Bill Presentment and Payment (EBPP) service provider for the Kingdom of Saudi Arabia (KSA). The core mandate for SADAD is to facilitate and streamline bill payment transactions of end consumers through all channels of the Kingdom's Banks. SADAD was launched on October 3, 2004.

SADAD links the commercial sector and local banks, offering the ability to collect customer payments electronically through all the banking channels in the kingdom 24 hours a day.

History & Background

SAMA mandated that all banks must accept bill payments at their branches from anyone. The payer does not have to be a customer of the bank. Pre-SADAD economics of bill payment placed an unduly large burden on banks; it was inefficient and slow. Banks recovered a small portion of the cost through keeping the collected money for varying periods of 7–30 days after the bill was paid.

Approximately 60-70% of bills were paid in cash at bank branches. Due to the high number of bills generated in the Kingdom, this results in high costs for banks in front office, payment processing, IT integration and reconciliation. In addition, consumers queue for a long time at banks' front office desks before paying their bills. Bill presentment and collection is largely manual and paper-based creating significant inefficiencies and overheads for billers and banks.

Large billers formed bilateral agreements with banks in order to enhance bill payments collection. This enabled consumers to use their bank channels to view and pay bills (without any bill consolidation). It required every biller to connect to the 12 different banks operating in KSA and from banks to connect separately to every biller they are under contract with.

SAMA chose to integrate these connections through SADAD, which is a single platform that links different billers and banks to enable the consumers to use the electronic channels of any bank. SADAD is now facilitating the payment of high-volume periodic bills (such as utility bills and phone bills) and customer initiated payments, such as traffic fines.

How Sadad Works

1. Billers send summary bills information to SADAD at a pre-determined schedule
2. SADAD validates data received and uploads it into its database
3. SADAD notifies Billers of any discrepancies
4. Customer requests bill(s) information through Bank channels(1)
5. The Bank forwards the request received to SADAD
6. SADAD retrieves bill information from its database and forwards it to customer
7. Customer selects the bill(s) to be paid and the respective amount(s)
8. The Bank debits the customer account and confirms the transaction
9. SADAD updates its database based on the Bank's confirmation(2)
10. SADAD notifies relevant Biller(s) accordingly
11. At the end of the day, SADAD initiates settlement instructions through SARIE
12. At the end of the day, Billers receive reconciliation reports from SADAD showing a breakdown of all transactions processed by SADAD
13. SADAD updates bills status to "settled"

SADAD Vision

- SAMA's initiative aim to establish an electronic platform to streamline the bill payment process in the Kingdom
- The electronic platform will act as an intermediary between billers and banks
- The intermediary will be the core to a trusted payment brand in the Kingdom
- A trusted payment process will use leading edge technology to provide efficient and effective customer service to the people of the Kingdom
- Leading edge technology will provide cost effective bill payment wherever and whenever the customer desires

External links

- http://www.sadad.com/English/(English Version)

Saudi Payments Network

The **Saudi Payments Network** (**SPAN**) is the only and major payment system in the kingdom of Saudi Arabia. It connects all ATM and point of sale (POS) terminals throughout the country to a central payment switch which in turn re-routes the financial transactions to the card issuer, (local bank, VISA, AMEX or MasterCard). All Banks in Saudi Arabia are required by the Saudi Arabian Monetary Agency (SAMA) to issue ATM cards fully compatible with the network. All services are provided to the customer free of charge, regardless of the ATM used, its operator, or the customer's card issuer.

There are now more than 6,000 ATMs and 55,000 POSs connected to the network and in 2006 more than 340 million transactions went through SPAN, with a total value of 160 billion SR (42.5 billion USD).

The network has recently been upgraded to SPAN2 which is compliant with EMV standards and implements a higher capacity infrastructure and therefore less processing time, especially at POS terminals, resolving a major problem of the first generation SPAN system.

Member banks in the network

1. Al-Rajhi Bank
2. Al Bilad Bank
3. Arab National Bank
4. Bank AlJazira
5. Emirates Bank International
6. National Commercial Bank
7. Riyad Bank
8. SABB
9. Saudi Hollandi Bank
10. Saudi Fransi Bank
11. Saudi Investment Bank
12. Samba Financial Group
13. National Bank of Kuwait
14. Bank Muscat

External links

- SPAN home page [1]

Secure POS Vendor Alliance

Secure POS Vendor Alliance	
SPVA SECURE POS VENDOR ALLIANCE delivering comprehensive payment security experience	
Abbreviation	SPVA
Formation	2009
Type	Non-Profit
Purpose/focus	Payment Industry Security
Region served	Global
Chairman	Paul Rasori
Main organ	Board of Directors
Website	http://www.spva.org/

The **Secure POS Vendor Alliance** (SPVA) is a non-profit organization created to increase awareness of, and improve, payment security in the electronic point-of-sale industry.[1] The SPVA was founded by Hypercom, Ingenico and VeriFone, the three largest suppliers of point-of-sale payment terminals.[2]

Membership

General membership is open to any organization whose primary focus is the development of secure POS payment terminals. Specifically, any organization that manufactures at least one payment terminal on PCI-SSC's list of approved personal identification number entry devices may become a general member.

Associate membership is open to organizations that have products or services that interact with secure POS payment terminals, such as processors, issuers, acquirers, merchants, and credit card brands.[3]

Governance

The SPVA is governed by a management committee consisting of five directors: a Chairman, a Chief Technology Officer, a Secretary/Treasurer, and two representatives, one for the general members and one for the associate members. Each of the permanent members (Ingenico, Hypercom and VeriFone) are allotted one of the three officer positions. The other two directors are elected by their respective membership groups.[4]

Technical Working Groups

One of the primary purposes of the SPVA is to create technical working groups, which are collaborations of industry experts focused on specific issues within the electronic point-of-sale industry.[5]

The four current working groups focus on a variety of issues pertaining to industry wide standards, such as the growing need for a common interpretation of the various global security requirements for payment processing and standardized implementation of POS terminals in conjunction with the SEPA initiative. They also are addressing technical issues such as better tracking measures for POS terminals throughout their lifecycle, and a more coherent approach to security throughout the entire terminal to host payment process.[6]

When the working groups have sufficiently developed their standards and guidelines, the SPVA intends to facilitate an official compliance program through which vendors can apply for SPVA approval. Approved devices could then bear the SPVA logo, informing retailers and consumers that they adhere to the SPVA's security standards.[7]

References

[1] *Secure POS Vendor Alliance is launched by Hypercom, Ingenico and VeriFone* (http://www.ecommerce-journal.com/news/ 14854_secure_pos_vendor_alliance_is_launched_by_hypercom_ingenico_and_verifone), ECommerce Journal, 2009,

[2] Joanna Seow (May 10, 2009), *Consistent security standards* (http://www.straitstimes.com/Breaking+News/Singapore/Story/ STIStory_375022.html), The Straits Times,

[3] *Terminal Rivals Cooperate on Plan for Card Data Security* (http://www.digitaltransactions.net/newsstory.cfm?newsid=2189), Digital Transactions, 2009,

[4] *SPVA Builds Membership to Accelerate Enhanced Security Guidelines* (http://www.marketwatch.com/story/ spva-builds-membership-to-accelerate-enhanced-security-guidelines), Market Watch, 2009,

[5] *Hypercom, Ingenico, VeriFone Launch SPVA Secure Payment Alliance* (http://www.paymentsnews.com/2009/04/ hypercom-ingenico-verifone-launch-spva-payment-security-alliance.html), Payments News, 2009,

[6] *New Consumer Research From The Secure POS Vendor Alliance Underscores Need For Greater Payment Security Measures* (http://www. itreselleronline.com/article.mvc/New-Consumer-Research-From-The-Secure-POS-0001?VNETCOOKIE=NO), IT Reseller Online, 2009,

[7] Jay Roach (June 15, 2009), *New Non-Profit To Take On Retailers' Payment Security Woes* (http://www.retailsolutionsonline.com/article. mvc/Non-Profit-To-Take-On-Payment-Security-Woes-0001?VNETCOOKIE=NO), Retail Solutions Online,

External links

- SPVA (http://www.spva.org/index.aspx)
- PCI Security Standards Council (https://www.pcisecuritystandards.org/)
- EMVco (http://www.emvco.com//)

SecurityMetrics

SecurityMetrics

Type	Privately held
Founded	Orem, Utah, U.S.
Headquarters	Orem, Utah, United States
Area served	United States, United Kingdom
Key people	**Brad Caldwell** (CEO) **John Bartholomew** (VP of Sales) **Wenlock Free** (VP of Business Development) **Rich Running** (VP of Marketing)[1]
Products	Site Certifcation No-Internet Site Certification Quarterly Penetration Testing On-site Assessments IDS/IPS Security Appliances Forensics Incident Response
Website	SecurityMetrics [2]

SecurityMetrics is a full service payment card industry (PCI) Data Security Standard (DSS) vendor headquartered in Orem, Utah.[2]

Overview

Founded in 2000 in a one-room office space, SecurityMetrics has grown to nearly 300 employees. The company is listed as a Qualified Security Assessor (QSA) by the PCI Security Standards Council[3] and is a member of the Electronic Transactions Association.[4] As a QSA, SecurityMetrics is a leading PCI DSS vendor with working relationships with major payment processing companies such as First Data, Global Payments Inc. and others. SecurityMetrics currently has the largest support staff in the PCI industry worldwide, fielding over 100,000 calls a month.[5] [6]

SecurityMetrics assists merchants in obtaining PCI compliance, a requirement of the PCI Data Security Council and the major payment card associations. SecurityMetrics is certified as a security assessor for all four major card associations in the United States: Visa, MasterCard, American Express, and Discover.[7] [8] SecurityMetrics works closely with global acquiring banks and other electronic payment leaders to provide PCI solutions for their merchants.[9] SecurityMetrics helps protect these organizations and their retail customers from security breaches and data theft.

SecurityMetrics serves the preferred PCI compliance vendor for the First Data payment processor for its "Level 4" program for merchants running fewer than 20,000 Visa e-commerce transactions per year.[10] [11]

Services

SecurityMetrics' products include technology tailored to PCI DSS compliance requirements such as the certification to perform PCI scans (ASV), Qualified Security Assessment (QSA), Payment Application Data Security Standard audits, MasterCard point of sale terminal security program audits and penetration tests. The company is a Qualified Incident Response Assessor (QIRA).[12]

Products

SecurityMetrics' security technology addresses vulnerability assessment, intrusion detection and intrusion prevention capabilities. To address the compliance needs of both e-commerce and non e-commerce merchants, SecurityMetrics has two different site certifications: certification no-Internet and certification with quarterly scanning.[13]

References

[1] Management - SecurityMetrics (https://www.securitymetrics.com/management.adp) (accessed 5 August 2010)

[2] About Us - SecurityMetrics (https://www.securitymetrics.com/aboutus.adp) (accessed 5 August 2010)

[3] Qualified Security Assessors (https://www.pcisecuritystandards.org/pdfs/pci_qsa_list.pdf) (accessed 5 August 2010)

[4] ETA Member Companies (http://www.electran.org/content/view/676/377/) (accessed 17 August 2010)

[5] First Data - Payment Card Industry Data Security Standard Compliance (http://www.firstdata.com/downloads/marketing-merchant/fd_pci_ss.pdf) (accessed 25 August 2010)

[6] Global Payments Inc. - PCI DSS Program (http://www.globalpaymentsinc.com/USA/customerSupport/industryInit/PCI_DSS_Program.html) (accessed 25 August 2010)

[7] Laws and Regulations for Credit Card Processing Security (http://www.shift4.com/CC_security.cfm) (accessed 17 August 2010)

[8] Merchant Services - PCI Compliance (http://www.merchantsvcs.com/pci_compliance) (accessed 17 August 2010)

[9] ISO Launches PCI Compliance Program, Sees Strong Interest Among Merchants (http://www.paymentssource.com/news/Sterling-Payment-PCI-Compliance-Merchant-3001553-1.html) (accessed 17 August 20100

[10] Payment Card Industry Non-Compliance (http://www.merchantinsider.com/merchantresources/datasecurity/noncompliance) (accessed 18 March 2011)

[11] First Data working with SecurityMetrics to keep your customer's information secure (http://bhdnews.blogspot.com/2009/08/diear-data-working-with-security.html) (accessed 18 March 2011)

[12] Visa Inc. Qualified Incident Response Assessor (QIRA) List (http://usa.visa.com/download/merchants/cisp_qualified_cisp_incident_response_assessors_list.pdf) (accessed 19 August 2010)

[13] Products and Services - SecurityMetrics (https://www.securitymetrics.com/products.adp) (accessed 17 August 20100

External links

- SecurityMetrics (https://www.securitymetrics.com/)

Self checkout

Self checkout machines provide a mechanism for customers to pay for purchases from a retailer without direct input to the process by the retailer's staff. They are an alternative to the traditional cashier-staffed checkout. They have been implemented most often in grocery stores and other large-scale stores.

A woman operates the NCR FastLane self checkout at a Wal-Mart store.

History

The first supermarket self-checkout system in the world was installed in 1992 in the Price Chopper Supermarkets in Clifton Park, New York.[1] The system was invented by Dr. Howard Schneider,[2] [3] as described in United States patents 5083638 and 5,168,961, which were granted in 1992. Schneider called the self-checkout machines "robots," thinking that a new class of "service robots" would perform service work and provide a platform for his ideas on artificial intelligence. The company, Optimal Robotics, was founded in Montreal in 1991 (in Schneider's garage, the same address listed on the patents[2]) to design, build and market these service robots.

The Optimal Robotics "self-checkout robots" performed well at Price Chopper Supermarkets and in the 1990s was implemented in the Kroger chain, and then in many supermarket chains throughout the U.S, Canada, U.K., and Australia. Optimal Robotics went public on NASDAQ in the mid 1990s with a new management and Dr. Schneider leaving the company. Eventually Optimal Robotics sold the technology to NCR and to Fujitsu[4] and got out of the robot/self-checkout business and changed their name to the Optimal Group.[5]

NCR first prototyped their self-checkout machines in 1997.[6] [7] By 2003, these automated checkouts had become widespread, with most being supplied by NCR, Fujitsu/ICL and IBM.[8]

There has been little improvement since the 1990s in the design or operation of the typical self checkout systems used in the retail environment. For example, a recent United States Patent No. 7,516,819[9] issued on April 14, 2009 to Michael Johnson and co-inventors at IBM, is extremely similar to the prior patents issued for self-checkout. In this recent patent, titled, "Self-checkout system with plurality of capacity-detecting loading stations" the invention claims a multiple of scales and if a wrong weight occurs the scanner is shut down and won't scan the next item (something that the Optimal Robotics original supermarket checkout machine did, and something that current NCR and Fujitsu models do).[10] [11]

As of the end of 2008, there were 92,600 self checkout units worldwide. The number is estimated to reach 430,000 units by 2014.[12]

Description

In self-checkout systems, the customer is permitted to scan the barcodes on their own items, and manually identify items such as fruits and vegetables (usually with a touchscreen display), which are then weighed where applicable, and place the items into a bagging area. The weight observed in the bagging area is verified against previously stored information to ensure that the correct item is bagged, allowing the customer to proceed only if the observed and expected weights match.[13]

There is considerable technology, both electronic and software (artificial intelligence) involved in the operation of the machines. For example, the main reason the Optimal Robotics self-checkout system, based on Schneider's patents, did so well compared to the other model on the market at the time, e.g., the CheckRobot model marketed by IBM in the 1990s,[14] is because it had self-learning functions, i.e., it didn't have to be programmed with the weight, color, etc. of a new product, but learned these features on its own. The first time the Optimal machine scanned a new product, it actually allowed the customer to scan and bag the product without interference and assumed the customer was honest (the customer would not know it was the first time it was presenting an item to the machine and would not want to try to steal something fearing an alarm would be triggered and the item rejected), and it accumulated data on the product. As the machine saw the items more times it learned what the weight tolerances of this product were, what the color tolerances were (there were color cameras overhead on the early Optimal machines), etc. This information was passed on to other self checkout machines. So in essence the machines learned on their own, and provided seemingly reliable service to the supermarket with little intervention on behalf of the supermarket. As well, similar computer routines were required to keep the machine functioning smoothly. For example, in United States Patent No. 5,125,465 awarded to Dr. Howard Schneider of Optimal Robotics on June 30, 1992, a mechanism to allow the customer to keep scanning one item after another quickly, i.e., more quickly than the scales could mechanically react to, is given:[15]

In some self-checkout systems, rather than weighing items in the bagging area, a conveyor belt moves items from the barcode scanner to the bagging area. In such a system, the item is verified while it is on the conveyor belt.

Normally, an attendant watches over several self checkout machines, to provide assistance, prevent theft through exploitation of the machines' weaknesses, and enforce payment. Attendant assistance is also required for purchase of age-restricted items.

Payment on these machines can be accepted by various methods: card via EFTPOS, debit/credit cards, electronic food assistance cards, cash via coin slot and bank note scanner, and in-store gift cards where applicable. Most coupons also have barcodes and can be scanned the same way that items are scanned although some require attendant entry.

Advantages

The benefit to the customer is in the reduced checkout time because stores are often able to run two to six self checkout units efficiently where it normally would have had one cashier. Some customers appreciate the ability not to have to deal with anyone. Self checkout may create an illusion of privacy and anonymity, when in fact the self checkout attendant can track the progress of customers on all machines via a separate terminal known as a RAP (Remote Attendant Post).[10] [11]

The benefit to the retailer in providing self checkout machines is in reduced staffing requirements since one attendant is all that is required to run 4 to 6 checkout lanes at one time.[10] [11]

Disadvantages

The time efficiency requires that the machine be operating efficiently and effectively, and the customers using the machine be reasonably competent.

An inexperienced customer can cause even more delays than an inexperienced cashier on a conventional register, and older customers may expect the attendant to assist them directly with scanning items, preventing the attendant from dealing with other customers who actually require intervention.

As the weight observed in the bagging scale is checked to allow the customer to proceed only if the observed and expected weights match, it is difficult to reconcile with the use of environmentally preferable alternatives to shop-provided bags, for example, baskets, rucksacks, and other reusable (but heavier) carriers. Conveyor belt-based verification avoids this problem.

Another frequent problem is the bagging scale failing to register properly the weight of the items purchased. The systems often falsely report that unscanned items have been bagged, or that scanned items were not placed in the bag. These false alerts halt the checkout process and require the store attendant to come and approve the weight exception, often eliminating any time savings that could have been realized by using self-checkout instead of waiting in line for a regular register. This issue sometimes occurs because of weight fluctuations on the bag scale caused by the platter being improperly positioned or calibrated, or with items of varying weight (e.g. 10 lemons for a certain price apiece may not weigh exactly the same).

Self-checkout is vulnerable to some shoplifting techniques. However, in many cases the machine will pick up the attempt to steal or else cause the shopper to alter behavior (e.g., put an item not on the scales but somewhere else where it should not be put and will be noticed by the system supervisor). For example, in 2007, a man was charged with replacing the tag of a plasma TV with a $4.88 DVD, and trying to purchase it through self-checkout.[16]

It has also been noted that the experience of using self-checkout tills has been dehumanizing for customers, particularly the elderly.[17]

Alternative system

An alternative system consists of a portable barcode scanner that is used by the customer to scan and bag items while shopping. When the customer has finished shopping, the scanner is brought to a checkout kiosk, where the information from the barcode scanner is downloaded to the kiosk, usually in conjunction with a customer loyalty card. The customer pays and receives a receipt at the checkout kiosk. The integrity of the system is maintained through the use of random audits or RFID.

EasyShop system at Martin's

Theft on these services is reduced by a combination of a high barrier to entry, and occasional audits of customers' shopping, where customers chosen at random are taken to a specialised till and have their shopping scanned in the usual way.[18]

Open systems

In 2010, the *open-source-self-check* open source project was announced. By using readily obtainable hardware and opensource software, the self checkout system costs less than one-tenth of the commercial version.[19] [20]

Criticisms

BBC news recently reported on the rise of self service tills and how even the error messages like 'unexpected item in the bagging area' are becoming part of the new shopping experience and even given rise to t-shirts in tribute to these new machines.[21] [22]

References

[1] "Roger Clarke's 'Price Chopper Supermarkets'" (http://www.rogerclarke.com/EC/PriceChopper.html). Roger Clarke. . Retrieved 2009-10-09.

[2] "United States Patent: 5168961" (http://patft.uspto.gov/netacgi/nph-Parser?Sect1=PTO2&Sect2=HITOFF&p=1&u=/netahtml/PTO/search-bool.html&r=2&f=G&l=50&col=AND&d=PTXT&s1=supermarket.TI.&s2=checkout.TI.&OS=TTL/supermarket+AND+TTL/checkout&RS=TTL/supermarket+AND+TTL/checkout). United States Patent and Trademark Office. . Retrieved 2009-10-09.

[3] "United States Patent: 5083638" (http://patft.uspto.gov/netacgi/nph-Parser?Sect1=PTO1&Sect2=HITOFF&d=PALL&p=1&u=/netahtml/PTO/srchnum.htm&r=1&f=G&l=50&s1=5083638.PN.&OS=PN/5083638&RS=PN/5083638). United States Patent and Trademark Office. . Retrieved 2009-10-09.

[4] http://www.fujitsu.com/us/news/pr/ftxs_20040412.html

[5] "Optimal Group Inc. / Groupe Optimal Inc" (http://www.optimalgrp.com/). Optimalgrp.com. . Retrieved 2009-10-09.

[6] . http://nl.newsbank.com/nl-search/we/Archives?p_product=PI&s_site=philly&p_multi=PI&p_theme=realcities&p_action=search&p_maxdocs=200&p_topdoc=1&p_text_direct-0=0EB32E48EF4616D2&p_field_direct-0=document_id&p_perpage=10&p_sort=YMD_date:D&s_trackval=GooglePM.

[7] "Star Tribune: Express lane; Grocers counting on technological improvements for greater efficiency" (http://www.highbeam.com/doc/1G1-62609852.html). Highbeam.com. 1997-05-07. . Retrieved 2009-10-09.

[8] "Union Tribune: Grocery clerks' real nightmare" (http://www.signonsandiego.com/news/business/20031228-9999_mz1b28clerks.html). Signonsandiego.com. 2003-12-28. . Retrieved 2009-10-09.

[9] "United States Patent: 7516819" (http://patft.uspto.gov/netacgi/nph-Parser?Sect1=PTO1&Sect2=HITOFF&d=PALL&p=1&u=/netahtml/PTO/srchnum.htm&r=1&f=G&l=50&s1=7516819.PN.&OS=PN/7516819&RS=PN/7516819). United States Patent and Trademark Office. . Retrieved 2009-10-09.

[10] http://www.fujitsu.com/us/services/retailing/self/

[11] http://www.ncr.com/products_and_services/point_of_sale/self_checkout/index.jsp

[12] http://www.selfserviceworld.com/article.php?id=22715

[13] Daniella Miletic (April 22, 2008). "A new way to shop — check it out for yourself" (http://www.theage.com.au/news/national/a-new-way-to-shop-151-check-it-out-for-yourself/2008/04/21/1208742852723.html?page=fullpage). Melbourne: The Age. . Retrieved 2008-09-02.

[14] "Uniquest Inc. of Jacksonville, Fla., plans to acquire CheckRobot Inc. | North America > United States from" (http://www.allbusiness.com/technology/computer-software/271824-1.html). AllBusiness.com. . Retrieved 2009-10-09.

[15] "United States Patent: 5125465" (http://patft.uspto.gov/netacgi/nph-Parser?Sect1=PTO1&Sect2=HITOFF&d=PALL&p=1&u=/netahtml/PTO/srchnum.htm&r=1&f=G&l=50&s1=5125465.PN.&OS=PN/5125465&RS=PN/5125465). United States Patent and Trademark Office. . Retrieved 2009-10-09.

[16] "Man Pays $4.88 for Plasma TV at Wal-Mart" (http://www.sfgate.com/cgi-bin/article.cgi?f=/n/a/2007/06/28/national/a141024D56.DTL). Sfgate.com. 2007-06-29. . Retrieved 2009-10-09.

[17] Cunningham, Tessa (2011-04-07). "Unexpected item in the bagging area: a human!" (http://www.dailymail.co.uk/femail/article-1374183/Unexpected-item-bagging-area-human.html?ito=feeds-newsxml). London: dailymail.co.uk. . Retrieved 2011-04-12.

[18] http://kiosknews.blogspot.com/2008/05/giant-easyshop-gives-self-checkout-new.html

[19] open-source-self-check (http://code.google.com/p/open-source-self-check/)

[20] Self-Check Kiosk from Scratch: Iowa Librarian's Coding Skills Prove Valuable (http://www.libraryjournal.com/lj/community/managinglibraries/853685-273/self-check_kiosk_from_scratch_iowa.html.csp)

[21] "The problem with self-service checkouts" (http://news.bbc.co.uk/1/hi/8399963.stm). *BBC News*. 2009-12-09. .

[22] http://www.unexpectediteminthebaggingarea.com/

Shared Check Authorization Network

Shared Check Authorization Network (SCAN) is a comprehensive database of bad check writers in the United States. The database is used by retailers in order to reduce the number of bad checks received. The database keeps track of those who have written outstanding bad checks to any retailer using the system, and retailers can determine, based on these records, whether or not to accept a check from a particular accountholder.

Retailers using the SCAN system have at least one scanner in the store, and often one at every register, that is used to scan checks that are written. The scanner reads the account number and compares it with the database of checking account numbers for which bad checks have been written to any participating retailer and not repaid. If the account number matches one in the system, the retailer will be notified, and will not likely accept the check.

SCAN also operates a collection service on bad checks that are written.

External links

- ArjayData.com [1]

Shift4

Shift4 Corporation

Type	Private
Industry	Payment Processing
Founded	1994
Headquarters	Las Vegas, Nevada and St. George, Utah, USA
Key people	CEO: J. David Oder, COO: Katherine A. Oder, CTO: J.D. Oder II
Products	DOLLARS ON THE NET, IT'S YOUR CARD, FraudSentry, 4Go, i4Go
Revenue	N/A
Operating income	N/A
Net income	N/A
Employees	120+ (2010)
Website	Shift4 [1]

Shift4 Corporation is a provider of financial transaction and payment processing services based in Las Vegas, Nevada. The company's core product is a merchant-centric Application Service Provider (ASP) banking and payment gateway solution.

History

Shift4 started as a spinoff of an accounting software application firm for which Shift4 founders J. David Oder, Katherine A. Oder, Kevin Cronic, Steven Sommers, and J.D. Oder II worked in Irvine, California. Seeing that most of their early customers were Las Vegas megaresorts, the Oder family relocated their company and incorporated as Shift4 in Las Vegas, Nevada in 1994.

For its first product offering, Shift4 took on the design concept of auditing credit card transactions prior to their submission to a merchant bank, and developed the Microsoft DOS application *$$$ In the Bank* (Dollars in the Bank). This software provided the ability to pre-authorize transactions, void transactions later if necessary and to send full data to banks during the authorization of credit cards. The auditing capabilities of this software appealed directly to "high ticket average" businesses, such as hotels and casinos, for its potential to lower the discount rate of business transactions.

In 1998, Shift4 released *$$$ In The Bank* for Windows. The intended use of this software was to fully integrate Point of Sale software with credit card authorization software.

Shortly thereafter, Shift4 introduced Virtual Leased Line for traditional "card-present" brick and mortar businesses to process card-present credit card transactions over the Internet, as opposed to telephone lines or leased lines. The only use of the Internet for processing credit cards before this offering was from website-based, card-not-present shopping cart software. Neither version of *$$$ In The Bank* is still available, and as of the end of 2003 *$$$ In The Bank* for DOS was fully phased out of support.

In 2000, Shift4 developed what is now their core product, DOLLARS ON THE NET, a web-based payment gateway between a POS or property management system and a bank or processor. This payment processing solution was developed using a Software as a service model, [1] and utilizes VPN technology to enable companies with an Internet connection to connect to the gateway. The gateway is used to obtain authorizations in real-time and conduct pre-settlement audits.

In recent years, Shift4 has been a proponent for removing cardholder data from payment systems by using a process called Tokenization, a term the company coined in 2005. [2] The company has been focusing their efforts on developing cardholder data (CHD) replacement technologies to remove that data from merchants' locations and computer systems. These technologies are slightly controversial, however, as their adoption would require a paradigm shift in the way people and organizations look at using and securing electronic payment transactions. [3]

Origin of Company Name

Shift4 describes their company name in the following excerpt borrowed from their webpage: "To solve the Shift4 riddle, hold down your "SHIFT" key while pressing the "4" key. What do you see? A dollar sign. [4]

Reliability

In a 2004 article by Paul Demery published in Internet Retailer said:

> The only system downtime that occurred in 2004 was a pre-scheduled 3-hour window during which Shift4 brought live its new state-of-the-art data center. A second data center, with an even larger load capacity, will be brought online later this year, though no downtime will be associated with that go live date. Together, these two, completely redundant data centers will bring Shift4's system availability close to its ultimate goal of five-nines (99.999% availability), or in layman's terms, less than five and a half minutes of downtime per year.[5]

References

[1] Shift4 Introduces New E-Payment Gateway (http://www.pressreleasepoint.com/ shift4-introduces-new-epayment-gateway-and-asp-server-spring-internet-world)

[2] (http://epx.com/blog/?p=89)

[3] Opposition to Tokenization (http://www.storefrontbacktalk.com/securityfraud/opposition-to-tokenization-a-lot-more-than-token/)

[4] Shift4 - credit card processing software (http://www.shift4.com/about_us.htm)

[5] http://www.internetretailer.com/2004/08/02/shift4-corporation-leads-payment-gateway-industry-in-reliability

External links

- Shift4 Homepage (http://www.shift4.com)
- Shift4's Facebook Page (http://www.facebook.com/shift4corp)

Single Euro Payments Area

The Single Euro Payments Area (SEPA) initiative for the European financial infrastructure involves the creation of a zone for the euro or any currency whose member state wishes to notify participation,[1] e.g. the Swedish krona[2] , in which all electronic payments are considered domestic, and where a difference between national and intra-European cross border payments does not exist. The project aims to improve the efficiency of cross border payments and turn the fragmented national markets for euro payments into a single domestic one: SEPA will enable customers to make cashless euro payments to anyone located anywhere in the area using only a single bank account and a single set of payment instruments.[3] The project includes the development of common

The 32 member states of the Single Euro Payments Area and two non-members

financial instruments, standards, procedures, and infrastructure to enable economies of scale. This should in turn reduce the overall cost to the European economy of moving capital around the region (estimated today as 2%–3% of total GDP).[4]

Overview

There are two major milestones for the establishment of SEPA:

- Pan-European payment instruments for credit transfers started 28 January 2008. Direct debits and debit cards will be available later (before 2011).
- At the end of 2010, all present national payment infrastructures and payment processors should be in full competition to increase efficiency through consolidation and economies of scale.

For direct debits, the first milestone has been missed due to delay in the implementation of enabling legislation, the Payment Services Directive (PSD), in the European Parliament. Direct debits became available in November 2009. This has put severe pressure on the second milestone.[5]

The European Commission has established the legal foundation through the Payments Services Directive (PSD). The commercial and technical frameworks for payment instruments are being developed by the European Payments Council (EPC), made up of European banks, and are mostly finalised as of July 2007. The EPC is committed to delivering three pan-European payment instruments:

- For credit transfers: *SCT – SEPA Credit Transfer*
- For direct debits: *SDD – SEPA Direct Debit*. Banks started to offer this service from 2 November 2009.[6]
- For cards: *SEPA Cards Framework*

To provide end-to-end straight through processing (STP) for SEPA-Clearing the EPC committed to delivering Technical Validation Subsets of ISO 20022. Whereas bank-to-bank messages (pacs) are mandatory for use, customer-to-bank message types (pain) are not; they are strongly recommended however. Because there was tolerance left for interpretation, it is expected that several pain-specifications will be published across SEPA-countries.

Businesses, merchants, consumers and governments are also interested in the development of SEPA; the European Associations of Corporate Treasurers (EACT), TWIST, the European Central Bank, the European Commission, the European Payments Council, the European Automated Clearing House Association (EACHA), payments processors and pan-European banking associations (European Banking Federation, EBF; European Association of Co-operative Banks, EACB; European Savings Banks Group, ESBG) are playing an active role in defining the services which SEPA will deliver.

Since January 2008, banks are migrating customers over to the new payment instruments. By 2010, the majority should be on the SEPA framework. As a result, banks throughout the SEPA area (not just the Eurozone) will need to invest heavily in technology with the capacity to support SEPA payment instruments.

Multi-national businesses and banks have the opportunity to consolidate their payments processing onto common platforms across the Eurozone. They will benefit from substantial efficiencies by choosing among competing suppliers offering a range of solutions and operating across borders.

The introduction of SEPA will increase the intensity of competition among banks and corporates for customers across borders within Europe. For consumers and organizations, SEPA could mean cheaper, more efficient and faster payments transfer when moving Euro from one Eurozone country to another.

Territorial coverage

SEPA consists of 32 countries:

- the 17 members of European Economic Area (EEA) and EU that are in the Eurozone
- the 10 members of EEA and EU that are not in the Eurozone,
- the 3 members of the EEA that are not in the EU: Liechtenstein, Iceland and Norway (Svalbard is not part of the EEA[7])
- 1 non EU country that uses the Euro by agreement with the EU, but is not officially part of the Eurozone: Monaco[8]
- Switzerland.

It includes the following territories that are considered to be part of the EU in accordance with Article 299 of the Treaty of Rome: Martinique, Guadeloupe, French Guiana, Réunion, Gibraltar, Azores, Madeira, Canary Islands, Ceuta and Melilla and Åland Islands.[9]

Despite usage of Euro as official currency by agreement with the EU the Vatican City and San Marino are not part of SEPA and as of March 2011 the Vatican City isn't even using IBAN.[10] [11] The principality of Andorra also is not part of SEPA, despite its de facto adoption of the euro as its currency, because it does not have an official currency.[12]

Montenegro and Kosovo that use the Euro as their official currency without an agreement with the EU are not part of SEPA.

Organisation

SEPA is an initiative of the European Payments Council. It is supported by the European Central Bank and the European Commission, the latter strongly involved via the Payment Services Directive.

Misconceptions

There is a common misconception that all credit transfers in the SEPA are free to the consumer, either by scheme rules or national transposition of the Payments Services Directives. However, the European Parliament merely mandated that a bank charge the same amount for SEPA credit transfers (which may be cross border) as they charge for domestic credit transfers in euro's. Banks and payment institutions still have the option of charging a credit transfer fee of their choice, as long as it is charged uniformly to all SEPA-reachable participants, banks or payment institutions, domestic or foreign.[13] This is specifically relevant for countries that do not use the euro, as domestic transfers in euro by consumers are extremely uncommon there, so inflated fees might be charged.

Main objectives

The main objectives of SEPA are:

* Standardization of euro payments: equal time limits, equal fraud-risk levels, equal processes, all-electronic straight through processing, no differences between national and international payments in the SEPA area; strengthening trust and reliability on a pan-European basis.
* Competition in respect to higher number of competitors, fewer niches or special fields or incompatibilities through standardization.
* Reduction of costs of electronic money and of payment transactions through competition at the side of payment providers and banks − both are considered as the biggest losers of the SEPA standardization process at an estimated € 40,000,000,000 per year).
* Reduction of cash money and increase of electronic money through reduction of costs of electronic money.
* Increasing surveillance of (electronic) money flow particularly regarding money laundering (unofficially also for surveillance of illicit work [10–30% of GDP's], organized crime and taxes).

Key dates

1957	Treaty of Rome creates a European Community
1992	Maastricht Treaty creates the Euro
1999	Introduction of the euro as an electronic currency, including introduction of the RTGS system TARGET for large-value transfers
2000	Lisbon Agenda. The meeting creates a European Financial Services Action Plan
2001	EC Regulation 2560/2001 harmonises fees for cross-border and domestic euro transactions
2002	Introduction of Euro banknotes and coins
2003	First pan-European ACH (PE-ACH) goes live. EC Regulation 2560/2001 comes into force for Euro transactions up to €12,500
2006	EC Regulation 2560 cap increases Euro transactions up to €50,000
2008	SEPA pan-European payment instruments become operational in parallel to domestic instruments on 28 January.[14]
2009	PSD − Payment Services Directive (PSD) to be implemented in national laws by November
2010	SEPA payments will become the dominant form of electronic payments
2011	SEPA payments will replace all national payments in the Eurozone

Progress Report

Official progress report in published here http://www.ecb.europa.eu/paym/sepa/about/indicators/html/index. en.html In November 2008, the European Central Bank published its 6th progress report on SEPA (see links below)

In barely disguised diplomatic language, the ECB expressed frustration at the lack of clarity on many aspects of the SEPA, and implored the banks, regulators, and the software industry to get on with the job. It has set out ten questions for which it wants answers, and has set out a timetable for those answers. The questions mainly require clear and unambiguous decisions at European level, but given the multi-national nature of SEPA, the collective answer requires national commitment in each country.

The main ECB criticism is of the SEPA governance process, which is poorly resourced, lacking in clarity, and failing to involve a sufficiently wide range of interested parties.

The European Central Bank regards SEPA as an essential element to advance the usability and maturity of the Euro currency. SEPA went live in Jan 2008, but as of late 2010, only 13.9% of credit transfers within Europe are executed according to SEPA standards.

The main points presented in the 39-page report are:

1. Banks must create greater awareness of SEPA, and must offer better products, based upon the SEPA infrastructure. Government should accelerate programs to adopt SEPA as the standard for its disbursements.
2. The banking industry must commit to work together to remove obstacles which might compromise the 1 Nov 2009 launch date of the SEPA Direct Debit. Debates on the launch date, the validity of existing DD mandates, and interchange fees must be closed out rapidly.
3. Bank systems need to be improved to enable end-to-end straight-through-processing, originated by files submitted or by e-payment, e-invoicing, and m-payments.
4. The ECB wants to see a target end date for migration to SEPA products, and for exiting out of older credit transfer and direct debit.
5. The SEPA card framework in its current form has not yet delivered the reforms which the ECB wants. In particular, ECB wants to see a European card scheme emerging.
6. The ECB perceives a lack of consistency in card standards. It wants to ensure that a clear set of standards are adopted and promoted throughout the industry.
7. A common, high level of security for Internet banking, card payments and online payments is needed.
8. Clearing and settlement organisations in many countries have made good progress on SEPA, and several are upgrading from national to pan-European.
9. The banking industry, and its representative body, the EPC have not sufficiently involved other stakeholders. Furthermore, the EPC itself does not have sufficient resources or support to enable it to complete its task.

In this situation, the ECB has set out 10 issues which it wants to see resolved, and has set deadlines by which it wants to see clear responses.

- Deadline end-March 2009
  - How will the legal continuity of Direct Debit mandates be ensured?
  - In the longer term, what is the proposal for the methodology of the multilateral interbank arrangement for national and crossborder SEPA Direct Debits? (In simpler terms, where two banks are involved in a SDD transaction, what fee will be payable by one bank to the other?)
- Deadline end-June 2009
  - A review and revision of Regulation 2560/2001/EU should be agreed for implementation by November 2009 to coincide with the Payment Services Directive and the launch of the SEPA Direct Debit. Regulation 2560 limits the pricing of cross-border transactions.
  - When will today's legacy Credit Transfer systems be turned off and fully replaced by the SEPA Credit Transfer?

- Deadline 1 – November 2009
  - Will we have a situation where all banks which currently offer Direct Debits will offer SEPA Direct Debits?
  - Will we have the Payment Services Directive transposed into national law in all of the SEPA countries? Will banks and other service providers have achieved full compliance?
- Deadline end-December 2009
  - What is the agreed framework for future e-invoicing systems?
  - When will today's Direct Debit systems be turned off and fully replaced by the SEPA Direct Debit?
  - A clear declaration is required regarding the creation of additional European SEPA-compliant card schemes.
- Deadline end-December 2010
  - Full-scale implementation of "SEPA for cards". Among other things, this will require an EMV chip on all cards issued in SEPA countries.

References

[1] Regulation (EC) No 924/2009 on cross-border payments (http://eur-lex.europa.eu/LexUriServ/LexUriServ. do?uri=CELEX:32009R0924:EN:NOT), Article 14: Application to currencies other than the euro

[2] Extension of Regulation (EC) No 2560/2001 to Swedish Kronor (http://ec.europa.eu/internal_market/payments/crossborder/archive_en. htm#SEK), Official Journal, 11 July 2002

[3] "Solution: SEPA, the single euro payments area" (http://web.archive.org/web/20080320033946/http://www.ecb.europa.eu/paym/ sepa/about/solution/html/index.en.html). European Central Bank. Archived from the original (http://www.ecb.europa.eu/paym/sepa/ about/solution/html/index.en.html) on 20 March 2008. . Retrieved 28 January 2008.

[4] "Agreement reached on cross-border banking" (http://www.rte.ie/news/2007/0327/banking.html). RTÉ News. 27 March 2007. . Retrieved 28 January 2008.

[5] "EU Press Release on implementation of PSD" (http://europa.eu/rapid/pressReleasesAction.do?reference=IP/07/550&format=HTM). Europa (web portal). . Retrieved 26 April 2011.

[6] EUROPA – Press Releases – Single Euro Payments Area (SEPA): cross-border direct debits now a reality (http://europa.eu/rapid/ pressReleasesAction.do?reference=IP/09/1665&format=HTML&aged=0&language=EN&guiLanguage=fr) EUROPA, published 3 November 2009, accessed 4 February 2011

[7] "Lov om gjennomføring i norsk rett av hoveddelen i avtale om Det europeiske økonomiske samarbeidsområde (EØS) m.v. (EØS-loven)." (http://www.lovdata.no/all/tl-19921127-109-0.html) (in Norwegian). Lovdata. 10 Aug 2007. . Retrieved 24 March 2010.

[8] Press release regarding the acceptance of Monaco in the SEPA. (http://www.gouv.mc/304/wwwnew.nsf/1909$/ 5983c9b47267edfac12575e5004db3cdgb?OpenDocument&2Gb). The Ministry of State of the Principality of Monaco

[9] "EPC , About SEPA – SEPA Vision and Goals" (http://www.europeanpaymentscouncil.eu/content.cfm?page=sepa_vision_and_goals). Europeanpaymentscouncil.eu. 16 December 2010. . Retrieved 26 April 2011.

[10] IBAN Registry, May 2010 (http://www.swift.com/solutions/messaging/information_products/bic_downloads_documents/pdfs/ IBAN_Registry.pdf)

[11] "IBAN Registry, March 2011" (http://www.swift.com/dsp/resources/documents/IBAN_Registry.pdf) (PDF). . Retrieved 26 April 2011.

[12] Usual currency of the Principality of Andorra (http://www.andorra.be/en/8_2_2.htm). The Embassy of Andorra to the Benelux, Denmark and Slovenia

[13] Regulation (EC) No 2560/2001 of the European Parliament and the Council of the European Union (http://eur-lex.europa.eu/LexUriServ/ LexUriServ.do?uri=CELEX:32001R2560:EN:NOT).

[14] "Single Euro Payments Area kicks in , EU – European Information on Financial Services" (http://www.euractiv.com/en/ financial-services/single-euro-payments-area-kicks/article-169861). EurActiv.com. 28 January 2008. . Retrieved 26 April 2011.

External links

- http://eurodebit.com/
- The EPC Official SEPA Adherence directory (http://epc.cbnet.info/content/adherence_database)
- SEPA and Switzerland (http://www.sepa.ch)
- SEPA and Ireland (http://www.sepa.ie)
- The European Payments Council (EPC) is the decision-making and coordination body of the European banking industry in relation to payments. (http://www.europeanpaymentscouncil.eu)
- SEPA and the Payments Services Directive (PSD): Reference materials from the Financial Services Club (http://thefinanser.co.uk/fsclub/sepa/)
- The Payments Services Directive (PSD): Complexities on the Road to Harmonisation (Edgar Dunn & Company white paper) (http://www.edgardunn.com/uploads/100030_english/100260.pdf)
- Book: The Future of Finance after SEPA (http://www.amazon.com/dp/0470987820)
- 6th Progress report on SEPA (ECB) (http://www.ecb.europa.eu/pub/pdf/other/singleeuropaymentsarea200811en.pdf)
- SEPA Payment Cards discussion (http://www.italkcash.com/forum/i-talk-cash-news/246416-monnet-credit-card-alternative-visa-mastercard.html)
- XMLdation.com offers SEPA-XML validation service (http://www.XMLdation.com)
- http://wiki.XMLdation.com
- www.payfits.com (http://en.payfits.com/) PayFITS offers validation as well as easily creation and testsupport services for ISO 20022 based SEPA messages.

Sistema de Pagamentos em Moeda Local

SML, **Sistema de Pagamentos em Moeda Local** (en: *Local Currency Payment System*)

The SML was established on October 3, 2008. It allows that payment orders are paid and received in local currency. Initially, the SML was used only in transactions between Brazil and Argentina, but recently Brazilian Central Bank is studying the expansion of the system to other countries like Uruguay [1] and Paraguay. More countries, like Russia, India and China have shown interest in adopting the system in bilateral trade with Brazil. [2]

Senders and recipients have the option of paying or receiving payment in their own local currency. This supposedly makes life easier for small producers, which until then were used to sell and buy goods only in their own currencies. They don't have to fix their prices in US-Dollars or calculate exchange-rates their own currency and the currency of the other country, intermediating with the US-dollar.

The system includes by the central banks authorized financial institutions. Transactions are made between the financial institutions and the Central Banks. The importers and exporters fix their prices using the SML-rate published by the Central Banks.

In the first year brazilians and argentines only used the SML in transactions involving goods, [3] but central banks are considering enable operations of trade in services and payments of social benefits.

References

[1] http://epocanegocios.globo.com/Revista/Common/0,,EMI100451-16359,00-BRASIL+E+URUGUAI+VAO+INTEGRAR+
    SISTEMA+DE+PAGAMENTOS+EM+MOEDA+LOCAL.html

[2] http://g1.globo.com/Noticias/Economia_Negocios/0,,MUL1253389-9356,00-PARA+MEIRELLES+BRASIL+JA+SAIU+DA+
    RECESSAO.html

[3] http://jus2.uol.com.br/doutrina/texto.asp?id=13180

External links

- Brazilian Central Bank (http://www.bcb.gov.br/?sml)
- Argentinean Central Bank (http://www.bcra.gov.ar)

Sleekpay

SleekPay is an online Payment gateway for Kenya that allows businesses/individuals to accept secure payments from customers -- 24 hours a day, 365 days a year. Merchants and buyers use the SleekPay virtual payment gateway to pro-actively manage, authorize and settle transactions in real time.

Introduction

SleekPay is owned and operated by Sleekpay Limited, a registered technology company in Kenya. The online system was designed and developed to fully introduce E-Commerce in Kenya and the East African Region. The system's development is supervised by Mr. Alex Bengo, who is the Chief Technology Officer at Sleekpay Limited.

The company is currently in partnership with Ebits Online [1] to develop, host and market professional E-Commerce websites for all its clients. Sleekpay Ltd is partnering with many service providers and e-commerce website owners in Kenya and the region to enable them sell online and get paid securely. The system currently supports MPESA M-Pesa, ZAP Zap, YUCASH [2], Cash, Wire Transfer and Cheque with Western Union Money Transfer soon to be introduced as forms of account top-up methods, to make the whole process flexible for the online buyer.

Products and Services

Merchant Account

SleekPay provides Internet Merchant Accounts to e-commerce website owners that allows them to accept payments online. The online payment processor uses sophisticated technology to process online transactions and provide relevant reporting to both merchants and customers. The web-based merchant interface allows one to view all transactions, configure account settings, view account statements, generate reports and much more. Services

Personal account

SleekPay Personal Account is completely free. There are no charges by SleekPay for using the system to make online payments to their accredited merchants. SleekPay provides dual email communication from the systems to facilitate confirmation and tracking of transactions, which means that you will confirm your order and pay for it from your account instantly.

Money Transfer

You can instantly send money to another SleekPay member, all you need is their email address. There is no limit to the amount being sent (at the moment) or frequency of sending. A fee of Ksh 10 is charged for this process.

Topup methods

Topup is made using MPESA, ZAP, YUCASH, Wire Transfer, Cheque, bank deposit, bank transfer or Cash at the office (or specified agents), the minimum topup amount is Ksh 500.

Support

Sleekpay employs a very effective support team available 24/7 to provide support via email, telephone or Online chat. A ticketing system is also available for effective tracking and resolving issues.

Security

The system runs on a 256 bit Secure, encrypted, SSL (Secure Socket Layer) environment that provides encryption between the users' web browser and our web server allowing information to be transmitted over the Internet securely. Furthermore it has its own inbuilt security engine. SleekPay Accounts (Personal and Merchant) are completely secured, both at the server and browser level.

External links

1. SleekPay Limited [3]

SMS banking

SMS banking is a technology-enabled service offering from banks to its customers, permitting them to operate selected banking services over their mobile phones using SMS messaging.

Push and pull messages

SMS banking services are operated using both push and pull messages. Push messages are those that the bank chooses to send out to a customer's mobile phone, without the customer initiating a request for the information. Typically push messages could be either Mobile marketing messages or messages alerting an event which happens in the customer's bank account, such as a large withdrawal of funds from the ATM or a large payment using the customer's credit card, etc. (see section below on Typical Push and Pull messages).

Another type of push message is One-time password (OTPs). OTPs are the latest tool used by financial and banking service providers in the fight against cyber fraud. Instead of relying on traditional memorized passwords, OTPs are requested by consumers each time they want to perform transactions using the online or mobile banking interface. When the request is received the password is sent to the consumer's phone via SMS. The password is expired once it has been used or once its scheduled life-cycle has expired.

SMS Banking Message No. 4

Your account 'Save 1' was credited with $ 999.98 on Wed 22 Nov 2006

Ref. 2390809CR

Call 800800 for assistance, if required.

Thank you for SMS Banking with ABC Bank.

1:20 pm 22 Nov 2006

Screenshot of a typical SMS Banking message on a mobile screen

Pull messages are those that are initiated by the customer, using a mobile phone, for obtaining information or performing a transaction in the bank account. Examples of pull messages for information include an account balance enquiry, or requests for current information like currency exchange rates and deposit interest rates, as published and updated by the bank.

The bank's customer is empowered with the capability to select the list of activities (or alerts) that he/she needs to be informed. This functionality to choose activities can be done either by integrating to the internet banking channel or through the bank's customer service call centre.

Typical push and pull services offered under SMS banking

Depending on the selected extent of SMS banking transactions offered by the bank, a customer can be authorized to carry out either non-financial transactions, or both and financial and non-financial transactions. SMS banking solutions offer customers a range of functionality, classified by push and pull services as outlined below.

Typical push services would include:

- Periodic account balance reporting (say at the end of month);
- Reporting of salary and other credits to the bank account;
- Successful or un-successful execution of a standing order;
- Successful payment of a cheque issued on the account;
- Insufficient funds;
- Large value withdrawals on an account;
- Large value withdrawals on the ATM or EFTPOS on a debit card;
- Large value payment on a credit card or out of country activity on a credit card.
- One-time password and authentication

Typical pull services would include:

- Account balance enquiry;
- Mini statement request;
- Electronic bill payment;
- Transfers between customer's own accounts, like moving money from a savings account to a current account to fund a cheque;
- Stop payment instruction on a cheque;
- Requesting for an ATM card or credit card to be suspended;
- De-activating a credit or debit card when it is lost or the PIN is known to be compromised;
- Foreign currency exchange rates enquiry;
- Fixed deposit interest rates enquiry.

Concerns and skepticism about SMS banking

There is a very real possibility for fraud when SMS banking is involved, as SMS uses insecure encryption and is easily spoofable (see the SMS page for details). Supporters of SMS banking claim that while SMS banking is not as secure as other conventional banking channels, like the ATM and internet banking, the SMS banking channel is not intended to be used for very high-risk transactions.

Quality of service in SMS banking

Because of the concerns made explicit above, it is extremely important that SMS gateway providers can provide a decent quality of service for banks and financial institutions in regards to SMS services. Therefore, the provision of Service Level Agreement(SLA) is a requirement for this industry; it is necessary to give the bank customer delivery guarantees of all messages, as well as measurements on the speed of delivery, throughput, etc. SLAs give the service parameters in which a messaging solution is guaranteed to perform.

The convenience factor

The convenience of executing simple transactions and sending out information or alerting a customer on the mobile phone is often the overriding factor that dominates over the skeptics who tend to be overly bitten by security concerns.

As a personalized end-user communication instrument, today mobile phones are perhaps the easiest channel on which customers can be reached on the spot, as they carry the mobile phone all the time no matter where they are. Besides, the operation of SMS banking functionality over phone key instructions makes its use very simple. This is quite different from internet banking which can offer broader functionality, but has the limitation of use only when the customer has access to a computer and the Internet. Also, urgent warning messages, such as SMS alerts, are received by the customer instantaneously; unlike other channels such as the post, email, Internet, telephone banking, etc. on which a bank's notifications to the customer involves the risk of delayed delivery and response.

The SMS banking channel also acts as the bank's means of alerting its customers, especially in an emergency situation; e.g. when there is an ATM fraud happening in the region, the bank can push a mass alert (although not subscribed by all customers) or automatically alert on an individual basis when a predefined 'abnormal' transaction happens on a customer's account using the ATM or credit card. This capability mitigates the risk of fraud going unnoticed for a long time and increases customer confidence in the bank's information systems.

Compensating controls for lack of encryption

The lack of encryption on SMS messages is an area of concern that is often discussed. This concern sometimes arises within the group of the bank's technology personnel, due to their familiarity and past experience with encryption on the ATM and other payment channels. The lack of encryption is inherent to the SMS banking channel and several banks that use it have overcome their fears by introducing compensating controls and limiting the scope of the SMS banking application to where it offers an advantage over other channels.

Suppliers of SMS banking software solutions have found reliable means by which the security concerns can be addressed. Typically the methods employed are by pre-registration and using security tokens where the transaction risk is perceived to be high. Sometimes ATM type PINs are also employed, but the usage of PINs in SMS banking makes the customer's task more cumbersome.

Technologies employed for SMS banking

Most SMS banking solutions are add-on products and work with the bank's existing host systems deployed in its computer and communications environment. As most banks have multiple backend hosts, the more advanced SMS banking systems are built to be able to work in a multi-host banking environment; and to have open interfaces which allow for messaging between existing banking host systems using industry or de-facto standards.

Well developed and mature SMS banking software solutions normally provide a robust control environment and a flexible and scalable operating environment. These solutions are able to connect seamlessly to multiple SMSC operators in the country of operation. Depending on the volume of messages that are require to be pushed, means to connect to the SMSC could be different, such as using simple modems or connecting over leased line using low level communication protocols (like SMPP, UCP etc.). Advanced SMS banking solutions also cater to providing failover mechanisms and least-cost routing options.

Smscoin

smscoin

Main website page

URL	http://smscoin.net
Commercial?	yes
Type of site	mobile payments
Registration	free of charge
Available language(s)	Russian, English
Launched	July 2006

SMSCOIN is a mobile payment systems provider which specializes in SMS payments in particular, and provides premium SMS services in 88 countries supporting hundreds of mobile carrier networks worldwide. The main goal of the project was, and still is to cover as many countries worldwide as possible. Currently, SmsCoin project is the leading company on the mobile payments market that offers its services in 88 countries worldwide.

History

2006

SmsCoin project was launched in July 2006 with only 4 countries (Russia, Ukraine, Kazakhstan, Israel) offering 3 of the following services: sms:chat, sms:key and sms:bank. During month of November additional service called sms:transit was developed, and closer to the end of the year 13 countries became available.

2007

The beginning of 2007 was marked by adding a few more countries as well as developing innovative extensions for browsers and a MIDlet that made it easier for SmsCoin' partners to access the statistics of their websites using mobile phones. English version of the website was presented in February. Its anniversary SmsCoin celebrated with 5 different sms:services across 18 countries worldwide working with over 5 thousand partners and processing more than a million SMS messages.

2008

Year 2008 began with presenting a new program for developing ready-to-use modules for popular CMS, 10 of which were published on the website as well as brand new service sms:content was launched. In April SmsCoin announced the connection of 30 countries worldwide. During this harsh period caused by a fierce competition on mobile payments market the project prospered due to higher payouts as well as enabling partners to choose their own short codes. Additionally, across Russia the payouts were made in rubles, and partners could request their revenue share payout once every 5 days which than was quite extraordinary. Throughout October till November additional achievements were presented - first of all a global support was launched unifying all means of contact using Instant messaging. Secondly, SmsCoin now offered its services across so much as 40 countries.

2009

In march 2009 SmsCoin announced a series of events starting with even greater coverage - 50 countries, connecting several Latin American countries at once, next 6 Middle Eastern countries followed in May. 3rd anniversary celebration opened with a brand new and refreshing website design and structure improvement which made it much more convenient to work with [1] . Immediately a new service called sms:donate was launched. Towards the end of the year SmsCoin project covered as much as 65 countries including its latest "acquisitions": China, Taiwan, Hong Kong. Throughout 2009 ready-to-use scripts library was considerably expanded as part of an improvement plan that began in 2008 and continues to this day forward.

2010

Good karma came in the beginning of 2010 when SmsCoin project connected the following countries India and Cyprus which considered to be unique on the mobile payments market [2] . Moreover, during the summer of 2010 SmsCoin has connected 9 additional countries: Italy, Vietnam, Guatemala, Honduras, Dominican Republic, El Salvador, Nicaragua, Panama, Paraguay, and by achieving that finally establishing itself a unique key leader within the mobile payments market. By November 2010 SmsCoin connected 87 countries[3] .

Unique features

SmsCoin is a public open-source project with entirely free registration, and provides several unique and innovative features both on Russian and international markets as follows:

- extensive coverage in more than 86 countries, some of which cannot be found on any other similar service
- complete library of ready-to-use modules for various CMS and instant solutions for various ideas

As highly-qualified competitor SmsCoin project have captured the attention of various well-known projects such as HeroCraft, Odnoklassniki, Alawar Entertainment, Depositfiles

Review

SmsCoin service has been used repeatedly for the purposes of fraud, and despite the fact that all fraud attempts have been blocked, the service has been often criticized for its simplified registration process and services setup and maintenance.

More

- Mobile payments
- Mobile commerce service provider
- Fortumo
- Zong mobile payments
- Mopay

References

[1] "Celebrating the 3rd anniversary of SmsCoin project Agregator Ltd. reviews and concludes its activities for the past year" (http://world. procontent.ru/node/366/). .

[2] "Catch good Karma – SmsCoin connected India" (http://world.procontent.ru/node/431/). .

[3] "SmsCoin reaches new heights – 87 countries connected" (http://world.procontent.ru/node/464/). .

Links

- Official website (http://smscoin.net)

SparkBase

SparkBase LLC

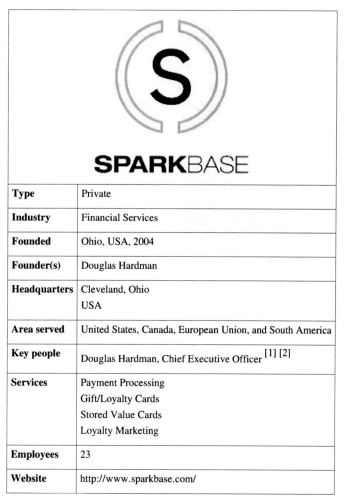

Type	Private
Industry	Financial Services
Founded	Ohio, USA, 2004
Founder(s)	Douglas Hardman
Headquarters	Cleveland, Ohio USA
Area served	United States, Canada, European Union, and South America
Key people	Douglas Hardman, Chief Executive Officer [1] [2]
Services	Payment Processing Gift/Loyalty Cards Stored Value Cards Loyalty Marketing
Employees	23
Website	http://www.sparkbase.com/

SparkBase, LLC (*SparkBase* or *SB*) is a stored-value and gift card transaction processor located in Cleveland, Ohio, USA.[3] It provides private-label, stored-value, specialty gift cards, customer loyalty, and community rewards programs to Independent Sales Organizations (independent companies used by banks to develop new merchant relationships on their behalf).[2] ISOs may then sell these gift and loyalty products to merchant customers along with credit card services and processing equipment.[4]

Sparkbase currently manages gift card processing for over 12 million alternate payment system cards, with an average daily balance of approximately $120 million.[5] The company develops its own network code in-house, with twenty-three developers on staff, and operates its own servers and Tier V data center on site, with off-site secondary and tertiary backup data centers.

History

The company was founded in 2004 by software developer Douglas Hardman as a division of Technology Imaging Services [6], and purchased by Hardman in early 2007. Hardman was the CTO of *SparkBase* prior to his acquisition of the company.[6] [7]

SparkBase's offices in Cleveland, Ohio

Place in the Prepaid Card Industry

SparkBase is in the closed system prepaid card part of the gift card industry, offering a software as a service stored-value payment processing network for specialty gift cards, customer loyalty programs, and community rewards programs. *SparkBase* does not service merchants directly, but rather acts as a private-label service through third parties, such as Independent Sales Offices (ISOs), loyalty marketing companies, financial institutions, and banks. These entities then market their own version of *SparkBase's* gift and loyalty platform to their merchants in conjunction with credit card services and processing equipment.[4]

The gift card network provided by *SparkBase* is a private-label or white label system that allows the third party (typically an ISO), to brand the company's stored-value network and associated gift cards with the third party's own logo and other identifying information.[8]

Industry Services Originating with SparkBase

GetYourBalance.com

GetYourBalance.com [10] is a tool offered by *SparkBase* which allows customers to register their gift cards, and check their balances online. The API toolset permits ISOs and merchants to create a registration and gift card balance portal directly on their own branded site. Through that portal, merchants can then access contact and other information about their customers acquired through the registration process, and use this information in e-mail, SMS messaging, and other marketing efforts.[8]

Text Messaging Gateway

In October 2008, *SparkBase* launched the first SMS (short messaging service) gateway integration, allowing merchants to reach individual gift card holders directly through SMS text messaging.[9]

The text messaging service offered by *SparkBase* may be used as a marketing vehicle and a means of payment, and provides end-users a mechanism to check loyalty card balances and otherwise conduct loyalty card transactions directly through their cell phone.[8] This service also offers merchants the ability to send electronic coupon codes, special offers, and rewards messages directly to their customers.[10]

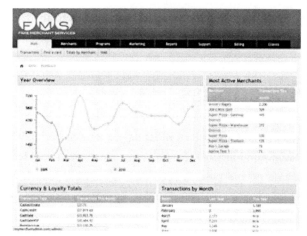

Screenshot of mock customer analytics page for *SparkBase's* private-label merchant services

Awards

- In 2009, founder Douglas Hardman received the *Smart Business Network "Rising Star" Award* in relation to *Sparkbase*.
- In 2011, *Sparkbase's* smart phone-enabled mobile payment service, Paycloud®, won the *Technology Innovation Award* at the Electronic Transactions Association's Annual Meeting.[11]

References

[1] "Emerging leaders talk about what Cleveland could be" (http://www.cleveland.com/business/index.ssf/2009/10/emerging_leaders_talk_about_wh.html). *The Plain Dealer*. . Retrieved 2010-02-18.

[2] "A new era in digital marketing" (http://greensheet.com/emagazine.php?issue_number=100101&story_id=1737&search_string=hardman&search_string2=). The Green Sheet 2.0. . Retrieved 2010-02-18.

[3] "Sparkbase's loyalty card services expected to create jobs in Cleveland area" (http://www.hivelocitymedia.com/innovationnews/Sparkbase10_22_09.aspx). hiVelocity. . Retrieved 2010-02-18.

[4] "Catching Fire: How Douglas Hardman is taking Sparkbase LLC to the next level" (http://www.sbnonline.com/Local/Article/18057/65/0/Catching_fire.aspx). Smart Business Magazine. . Retrieved 2010-02-18.

[5] "Doug Hardman of Cleveland's SparkBase on what he looks for in employees: Talk With the Boss" (http://www.cleveland.com/business/index.ssf/2009/12/doug_hardman_of_clevelands_spa.html). *The Plain Dealer*. . Retrieved 2010-02-18.

[6] "SparkBase of operations" (http://www.greensheet.com/company_profiles.php?flag=display_profile&id=323). The Green Sheet 2.0. . Retrieved 2010-02-18.

[7] "SparkBase CTO becomes Owner" (http://www.sparkbase.com/sparkbase-cto-becomes-owner/). Sparkbase website. . Retrieved 2010-02-18.

[8] "Gift card network at your service" (http://greensheet.com/emagazine.php?issue_number=090402&story_id=1321&search_string=hardman&search_string2). The Green Sheet 2.0. . Retrieved 2010-02-18.

[9] "SparkBase Launches SMS Gift Card Portal" (http://www.pr.com/press-release/108935). PR.com. . Retrieved 2011-05-19.

[10] "SMS Gift Card system powered by Inspiton Logistics" (http://www.ecommerce-journal.com/news/sms_gift_card_system_powered_by_inspiton_logistics). eCommerce Journal. . Retrieved 2010-02-18.

[11] "SparkBase's Paycloud® Mobile Wallet Wins 2011 Technology Innovation Award" (http://www.sfgate.com/cgi-bin/article.cgi?f=/g/a/2011/05/19/prweb8458033.DTL). San Francisco Chronicle. . Retrieved 2010-02-18.

External links

- SparkBase (http://www.sparkbase.com) website
- GetYourBalance.com (http://www.getyourbalance.com) website

Speedpass

Speedpass is a keychain RFID device introduced in 1997 by Mobil Oil Corp. (which merged with Exxon to become ExxonMobil in 1999) for electronic payment. It was originally developed by Verifone. As of 2004, more than seven million people possess Speedpass tags, which can be used at approximately 10,000 Exxon, Mobil and Esso gas stations worldwide. At one point, Speedpass was deployed experimentally in fast-food restaurants and supermarkets in select markets. McDonald's alone deployed Speedpass in over 400 Chicago area restaurants. Additionally, Stop & Shop grocery chain tested Speedpass at their Boston area stores and removed the units in early 2005. The test was deemed a failure and McDonald's removed the scanners from all their restaurants in mid 2004. Speedpass has also been previously available through a Speedpass Car Tag and Speedpass-enabled Timex watch.

Speedpass was one of the first widely deployed consumer RFID payment systems of its kind, debuting nationwide in 1997 far ahead of today's VISA and MasterCard RFID trials, and the RFID/EPC (Electronic Product Code) privacy controversy.

Technology behind the Mobil Speedpass

The ExxonMobil Speedpass is based on the Texas Instruments TIRIS RFID platform. It was originally designed by Verifone in two configurations; one intended for installation inside the fuel dispensing "pump", and a convenience store model known as the Verifone RF250 (which was a redesign of the SC250 reader for smart cards).

Speedpass with Spanish Pieces of Eight, money forms that span the history of the United States.

Security of the Mobil Speedpass

The ExxonMobil Speedpass uses a cryptographically-enabled tag with a Digital Signature Transponder (DST) which incorporates a weak, proprietary encryption scheme to perform a challenge-response protocol. On Jan 29th 2005, RSA Security and a group of students from Johns Hopkins University broke the proprietary encryption algorithm used by the Exxon-Mobil Speedpass. [1] They were able to successfully copy a Speedpass and use the copied RFID tag to purchase gas.

In an attempt to prevent fraud, Speedpass users are now required to enter their zip code into scanners at some gas stations. [2]

During the 1998 development of the RF250 convenience store reader some prototype units were shipped from Verifone in Rocklin, CA, USA to a Verifone office in Florida, USA. The units did not arrive on time and were thought to be lost in transit. They were later found, and despite each unit having a Verifone logo and being encased in boxes showing the Verifone logo; the shipping company had nothing in their lost goods database showing that name. Rather, the units turned up via a query for "flying red horse", apparently since the units displayed a small Mobil logo—and the Mobil logo was and is a red Pegasus. The internal codename for the project was thus changed to "Flying Red Horse".

External links

- ExxonMobil Speedpass site [3]
- ExxonMobil Speedpass Location Finder site [4]
- *Business Week*, Mar. 10, 1997 [5] (Retrieved May 30, 2007)

Square (payment service)

Square, Inc.

Type	Private
Founder	Jack Dorsey Jim McKelvey
Headquarters	San Francisco, California, U.S.
Area served	United States
Key people	Jack Dorsey (CEO) Keith Rabois (COO)
Website	[1]
Type of site	Mobile payments
Launched	May 2010

Square is an electronic payment service, and the name of the card-reading device it uses. Square allows users in the United States to accept credit cards through their mobile phones, either by swiping the card on the Square device or by manually entering the details on the phone.

Introduced in early 2010 by Square Inc.,[1] the Square application is available for the iPhone, iPod Touch, iPad and Android-based mobile phones.[2] Square was co-founded by Twitter creator Jack Dorsey and Jim McKelvey.[1] Dorsey also serves as CEO, Keith Rabois as COO.[1]

In March 2011, rival payment company VeriFone claimed that the Square system was insecure, and that a "reasonably-skilled" programmer could write a replacement app which could conceivably use the Square device to skim a credit card and return its details. VeriFone posted a demonstration video and sample skimming app to its website.[3] Dorsey called VeriFone's claims "neither fair nor accurate", noted that the card data could be gathered visually from the card, and said that the claims ignored the fraud protection provided by card issuers.[4]

At the TechCrunch Disrupt conference in May 2011, Square announced the release of two new apps, Card Case and Register. Card Case allows customers to view merchant menus, do mobile payments, receive virtual receipts, and discover other Square-enabled merchants. Square Register is point of sale software aimed at replacing traditional credit card terminals and cash registers.

References

[1] "About Square" (https://squareup.com/about). Square Inc.. . Retrieved 2011-03-15.
[2] Mark Milian (May 11, 2010). "Square begins taking orders for free credit card reader" (http://latimesblogs.latimes.com/technology/2010/05/square.html). *Los Angeles Times*. . Retrieved 2010-05-14.
[3] Hsu, Tiffany (March 9, 2011). "Square's mobile credit card reader easily hacked, says VeriFone" (http://latimesblogs.latimes.com/technology/2011/03/squares-mobile-credit-card-reader-easily-hacked-says-verifone.html). *Los Angeles Times*. . Retrieved March 11, 2011.
[4] Olivarez-Giles, Nathan (March 10, 2011). "Square answers VeriFone's accusations on security of mobile credit card reader" (http://latimesblogs.latimes.com/technology/2011/03/square-answers-verifones-accusations-on-security-of-mobile-credit-card-reader.html). *Los Angeles Times*. . Retrieved March 11, 2011.

External links

• Official website (https://squareup.com/)

Standing order (banking)

A **Standing Order (or a Standing Instruction)** is an instruction a bank account holder gives to his bank to pay a set amount at regular intervals to another account. The instruction is sometimes known as a **banker's order**.

They are typically used to pay rent, mortgage or other fixed regular payments. Because the amounts paid are fixed, a standing order is not usually suitable for paying variable bills such as credit card, or gas and electricity bills.

Standing orders are available in the banking systems of several countries, including Germany, the United Kingdom, Barbados, the Republic of Ireland, Netherlands, Russia and presumably many others. In the United States, and other countries where cheques are more popular than bank transfers, a similar service is available, in which the bank automatically mails a cheque to the specified payee.

Country differences

Germany

A standing order *(Dauerauftrag)* can run for a set number of payments, a set period of time, or until cancelled.

The Netherlands

Standing orders *(periodieke overboekingen)* are not available for a set period of time. They run until cancelled.

South Korea

A standing order *(납부자자동이체)* runs until cancelled. They can be cancelled at the account holder's request. The bank charges fees (average 300KRW) per transfer.

Spain

A standing order can be set up to run for a set period of time, not indefinitely. They can be cancelled at the account holder's request.

UK and Ireland

A standing order can be set up to run for a set period of time, or indefinitely, and can be cancelled at the account holder's request. Standing orders are standardized by the trade body APACS. In 2008 a number of banks began to introduce Faster Payments as the method of transfer for standing orders when available, in place of the slower BACS system; with this method payments reach the receiving account the same day, rather than after a delay of three days or more.[1]

Difference with direct debit

Standing orders are distinct from direct debits; both are methods of setting up repeated transfers of money from one account to another, but they operate in different ways. The fundamental difference is that standing orders send payments arranged by the *payer,* while direct debits are specified and collected by the *payee.*

- A standing order can only be set up and modified by the payer, and is for amounts specified by the payer to be paid at specified times (usually a fixed amount at a specified interval). The amount can be paid into any bank account, which need not belong to an organisation vetted by the payer's bank.

- A direct debit requires the payer to instruct the bank to honour direct debit requests from a specified payee; the payee can then take a direct debit for any amount at any time. The payer has no direct control over these payments, but can cancel the direct debit at any time, with no reason required, and require the return of disputed payments. It is not possible to authorise an individual to take direct debits; only organisations that have a contract with the payer's bank, or have been vetted by it, can do this. For details and country differences, see direct debit.

References

[1] "APACS - Standing Orders" (http://www.apacs.org.uk/payment_options/automated_payments_1.html). ., APACS

Stored-value card

A **stored-value card** refers to monetary value on a card not in an externally recorded account and differs from prepaid cards where money is on deposit with the issuer similar to a debit card.[1] One major difference between stored value cards and prepaid debit cards is that prepaid debit cards are usually issued in the name of individual account holders, while stored value cards are usually anonymous.

The term *stored-value card* means the funds and or data are physically stored on the card. With prepaid cards the data is maintained on computers affiliated with the card issuer. The value associated with the card can be accessed using a magnetic stripe embedded in the card, on which the card number is encoded; using radio-frequency identification (RFID); or by entering a code number, printed on the card, into a telephone or other numeric keypad.

Typical applications

Typical applications of stored-value cards include transit system farecards and telephone prepaid calling cards. Typical applications of a prepaid card include payroll cards, incentive cards, HSA cards, gift cards, and travel cards. The U.S. Department of the Treasury manages three stored-value card programs (EZpay, EagleCash, and Navy Cash) which are used by the U.S. military as electronic alternatives to cash in areas characterized by difficult access and limited banking / telecommunications infrastructure.

Closed system prepaid cards

Closed system prepaid cards have emerged and replaced the traditional gift certificate and are commonly known as merchant gift cards. "Closed system" means the cards are only accepted at a single merchant. Purchasers buy a card for a fixed amount and can only use the card at the merchant that issues the card. Generally, few if any laws govern these types of cards. Card issuers or sellers are not required to obtain a license. Closed system prepaid cards are not subject to the USA PATRIOT Act, as they generally cannot identify a customer. As debts owed to consumers who purchased the card, these purchases remain on the books of a merchant as a liability rather than an asset. Consequently, gift certificates and merchant gift cards have fallen under state escheat or abandoned property laws (APL). However, the emergence of closed system prepaid cards has blurred the applicability of APL. North Carolina and Illinois have excluded these types of cards from APL provided the card has no expiration date or a service fee. Maine and Virginia require the issuer to pay the state when the cards are abandoned. In Connecticut an issuer is required to identify the residence of the gift card owner. Since most merchant gift cards are anonymous, the residence of the card's owner is deemed to be the state's treasurer's office.

A vending machine sells farecards for the Washington Metro subway.

Presently, no law exists that requires an issuer to provide refunds for lost or stolen cards. Whether a refund is possible is specified in an issuer's cardholder agreement. In addition, most closed system cards cannot be redeemed for cash. When a cardholder redeems all but an insignificant portion of the card on merchandise, that amount is generally lost and is absorbed by the issuer.

Such cards are increasingly becoming a way for Mexican drug cartels to smuggle money across the border without repercussions.[2]

Semi-closed system prepaid cards

Semi-closed system prepaid cards are similar to closed system prepaid cards. However, cardholders are permitted to redeem the cards at multiple merchants within a geographic area. These types of cards are issued by a third party, rather than the retailer who accepts the card. Examples include university cards and mall gift cards. The laws governing these types of cards are unsettled. Depending on the state, the issuer may or may not be required to have a money transmitter license or other similar license. In addition to the District of Columbia, the states that require a license include Connecticut, Florida, Illinois, Iowa, Louisiana, Maryland, Minnesota, Mississippi, North Carolina, Oregon, Texas, Vermont, Virginia, West Virginia, Washington, and Wyoming. Note, these states explicitly require licensing for card issuers. Other states may have more subtle licensing laws. Under 18 USC section 1960, it is a crime for an issuer to conduct a money transmitting business without a license. Cardholders generally suffer from the same redressability problems that closed system card holders suffer. It is unclear whether or not Chapters 7 and 11 of the Bankruptcy code are applicable to these types of cards.

Open system prepaid cards

Open System Prepaid Cards or network branded prepaid cards are not credit cards, although they are sometimes marketed as "prepaid credit cards". No credit is offered by the card issuer and the cardholder spends money which has been prepaid to a card. Therefore, these cards are also marketed as "prepaid debit cards". The value is not physically stored on the card instead, the card number uniquely identifies a record in a central database, where the balance is recorded. These cards are similar to closed system prepaid cards, but are endorsed by a retail electronic payments network such as Visa, Visa Electron, MasterCard, or Maestro and can, unlike gift cards, be used anywhere debit cards with the same logo may be used. They are very similar to a debit card except that they don't require a checking account. They have been heavily marketed in the United States as a safe and responsible means for parents to give their children some spending power which is why they sometimes are referred to as teen cards. Whilst in the United Kingdom, they have been heavily marketed as a convenience tool and budgeting aid for global usage. Market participants such as Kalixa,[3] Caxton FX,[4] Travelex [5] and My Travel have used these cards to stimulate the adoption and appeal of open system prepaid cards in the UK. These cards have seen a $10 - 15\%$ growth since they appeared in the UK market six years ago.[6] These cards are also sometimes referred to as "open loop" cards.

These cards have been marketed to consumers with poor credit, who are unable to qualify for the line of credit that backs a mainstream credit card.[7] The fees associated with these cards are often very high. These have been criticized as unjustified, because the issuer is not taking any credit risk. The Financial Consumer Agency of Canada describes prepaid credit cards as "an expensive way to spend your own money"[8].

A variation on this are the PaidByCash virtual cards in the United States and the 3V cards issued in the Republic of Ireland. These consist only of a card number plus expiry date and verification number, so can only be used for customer not present transactions.

The Tobacco Card has undergone testing and is scheduled for nationwide introduction in Japan in 2008. It will contain an IC with information about the cardholder's age, and will be required for purchasing cigarettes from vending machines. It will have stored-value capability.

Generally these cards are afforded similar characteristics as "open system prepaid cards". Similar to credit cards, these cards may carry an expiration date, an account number, and a verification number. They also may carry with them service fees and other fees associated with use, or non use of the card. The money on the card can be redeemed for goods only, and is not redeemable for cash. These cards are generally issued by a "money services business"(MSB) or an FDIC banking institution. The type of issuer depends on the law governing them. MSB's are only required to obtain a money transmitter license if they sell more than $1,000 per person per day. Cards issued by an MSB generally are governed by the laws governing "closed system cards" and "semi-closed system laws". Cards issued by an FDIC bank are covered under the Federal Reserve Act and afford cardholders much more protection and opportunity to assert claims. The cardholder should be aware of the network's agreement and rules and regulations set forth by these networks.

Another example of open system prepaid cards is the Payroll card. Payroll cards are used by employers to pay employees. The employee is issued a card that permits access to an account established by the employer. At the end of each pay period, the employee's ability to draw money from that account is increased by the amount of his or her wages. The card may be used at an Automated Teller Machine (ATM) to obtain cash, and may be used at a store to pay for purchases. The payroll card is particularly useful for employees who do not have a regular checking or savings account at a financial institution because they can access their wages conveniently. Also, if there is no charge for using an ATM, they avoid fees charged for cashing checks. The advantage to the employer is low cost of paying wages and efficiency. These cards are subject to Chapters 7 and 11 of the Bankruptcy Code, as well as the Electronic Funds Transfer Act (Regulation E). They are also subject to the Federal Deposit Insurance Reform Act.

Money laundering

There is growing concern that drug traffickers and other criminals worldwide are using stored-value cards to move the proceeds from drug transactions and other criminal activities across international borders. In the United States, it is legal for anyone to enter or leave the country with money that is stored on these cards, and (unlike cash in high amounts) does not have to be reported to customs or another government entity. Some members of the U.S. Congress are considering creating laws that would require travelers crossing entering or leaving the country to report these cards.[8]

The Financial Crimes Enforcement Network of the U.S. Department of the Treasury, has published a notice of proposed rulemaking on stored-value cards in the June 28, 2010 edition of the *Federal Register*. The proposed rules would require sellers of prepaid cards to register with the government and keep records on transactions and customers.[9]

References

[1] Dlabay, Les R.; Burrow, James L.; Brad, Brad (2009). *Intro to Business*. Mason, Ohio: South-Western Cengage Learning. p. 433. ISBN 9780538445610.

[2] "Assessment: Prepaid Stored Value Cards" (http://www.justice.gov/ndic/pubs11/20777/index.htm). Johnstown, PA: National Drug Intelligence Center. October 31, 2006. . Retrieved December 16, 2009.

[3] Kalixa Prepaid MasterCard (http://www.kalixa.com)

[4] Caxton FX Cards (http://www.caxtonfxcard.com/)

[5] [www.cashpassport.com//Travelex]

[6] Growth among UK market participants is noted at http://www.scluk.com/ roundtable-concludes-the-uk-prepaid-market-is-alive-and-very-much-kicking Global foreign exchange

[7] Credit Cards and You: About Pre-paid Cards (http://www.fcac-acfc.gc.ca/eng/publications/CreditCardsYou/PrepaidCards_e.asp)

[8] Reuters, March 26, 2010, Drugs, terrorism and shadow banking, http://blogs.reuters.com/great-debate/2010/03/26/ drugs-terrorism-and-shadow-banking/

[9] http://edocket.access.gpo.gov/2010/pdf/2010-15194.pdf

Notes

- Hughes, Sarah Jane, Stephen T. Middlebrook, and Broox W. Peterson. "Developments In The Law Concerning Stored Value and Other Prepaid Payment Products". *Business Lawyer*, November 2006.

- Rinearson, Judith and Chris Woods. "Beware Strangers Bearing Gift Cards". *Business Law Today*. Nov/Dec 2004, Vol. 14, Num. 2

- "A Conversation with Terry Goddard, *Washington Post*: http://www.washingtonpost.com/wp-dyn/content/ article/2009/04/03/AR2009040301909.html

Substitute check

Front view of a substitute check

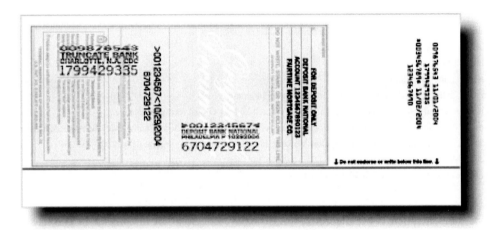

Rear view of a substitute check

A **substitute check** (also called an **Image Replacement Document** or "**IRD**")[1] is a negotiable instrument used in the United States to represent the digital reproduction of an original paper check. As a negotiable instrument, a substitute check maintains the status of a "legal check" in lieu of the original check as authorized under the United States law *Check Clearing for the 21st Century Act* (Check 21 Act). Instead of presenting the original paper checks, financial institutions and payment processing centers electronically transmit data from substitute checks for settlement through the Federal Reserve System.[2]

Substitute checks are recognized as legal checks as long as the instruments meet specific requirements. These requirements include the faithful reproduction of the paper check and warranty of the instrument by the reconverting bank—the bank that created the substitute checks or the first bank that transferred or presented them during the check clearing process.[3] Substitute checks are also subject to the Uniform Commercial Code (UCC), existing federal and state check laws, and regulations specific to consumer rights that affect the acceptance of these instruments.[4] Although substitute checks are subject to the UCC and existing state and federal check laws, the Check 21 Act takes precedence over these other laws and regulations for substitute checks.[5]

General

Under the Check 21 Act, payment instruments that are eligible for conversion into substitute checks include consumer (personal) checks, commercial (business) checks, money orders, traveler's checks and treasury checks.[6] The Check 21 Act permits any financial institution (such as a commercial bank or credit union) that participates in the check collection process to remove or "truncate" the original check from the forward collection or return process without first requiring an existing agreement between the bank of first deposit (BOFD) and the paying bank.[4] [6] The elimination of the original paper checks from the clearing process saves the banking industry the costs of handling, sorting, transporting, storing, guarding, and mailing paper checks. After the bank truncates the original checks in favor of substitute checks, the bank can store or archive the paper checks, return them to its customers according to state law, or later destroy the checks.

Legal requirements

A properly prepared substitute check is considered the *legal equivalent* of the original paper check that can be accepted for payment or proof of payment in the same manner as the original check. Every substitute check must adhere to the following requirements before it can be recognized as the legal equivalent of the original check:

1. The substitute check must accurately represent all information depicted on the front and back of the original check at the time the financial institution truncates the original check. The information includes the names of the payor and payee, courtesy and legal amounts, endorsements, and encoding information, among other details.
2. The substitute check must accurately represent the MICR line of the original check.
3. The substitute check must bear the legend "This is a legal copy of your check. You can use it the same way you would use the original check."
4. The financial institution or processor must provide a warranty for the substitute check when it removes or "truncates" the original paper check from the forward collection or return process and converts the paper check into a substitute check.
5. The financial institution or processor that truncated the original check must follow ASC X9 standards in the capture of check images and MICR data when it produces the substitute check.[2]

Image statements that include pictures or images of the original paper checks and/or substitute checks, photocopies of the original checks, and images of checks posted online are not recognized as the legal equivalents of substitute checks.[7] Unlike a substitute check, a photocopy of a check cannot be presented through the check clearing process for settlement because the photocopy of the check does not adhere strictly to the requirements for substitute checks under the Check 21 Act.[4]

Since substitute checks are considered legal "checks," substitute checks are subject to existing check laws and regulations. Other laws and regulations that govern substitute checks in the United States include the Expedited Funds Availability Act, Article 3 (Negotiable Instruments),[8] and Article 4 (Bank Deposits and Collections)[9] of the Uniform Commercial Code (UCC), along with a variety of state and federal regulatory laws. U.S. federal laws that also affect substitute checks include Federal Reserve regulations that provide for recrediting the amount of the substitute check in the case of fraud and duplicate payments caused by settlement of both the substitute check and the original check used for creating the substitute check.[2] [4] [6] If any state law, federal law, or provision of the UCC conflicts with the Check 21 Act, the Check 21 Act takes precedence to the extent of the inconsistencies among those laws and provisions.[5]

Clearing process

Each substitute check processed for forward collection is encoded with a "4" as the External Processing Code or "EPC" in position 44 of the MICR line.[10] An example of the forward collection process for substitute checks involves the following steps:[2]

1. The payee endorses the original paper check and presents it to the depository bank or bank of first deposit.
2. The bank of first deposit or "BOFD" (Bank 1) stamps its endorsement on the rear of the original check.
3. Bank 1 as the "truncating" bank captures an image of the front and back of the original check and the MICR line data from the front of the check. Bank 1 then removes (truncates) the original check from the clearing process.
4. Bank 1 electronically transmits the check image and the MICR line data captured from the original check to its correspondent or intermediary bank (Bank 2). If no agreement exists between Bank 1 and Bank 2 to exchange check images and data, Bank 1 must provide either the original check or the legal equivalent of the substitute check to Bank 2.
5. Bank 2 as the "reconverting" bank adds its electronic endorsement for the item to the record. The reconverting bank then uses the check image, MICR data, its own electronic endorsement, and the electronic endorsements received from Bank 1 to create a substitute check.
6. Bank 2 presents the check image and MICR data to the paying bank (Bank 3) for settlement. If no agreement exists between Bank 2 and Bank 3, Bank 2 must provide Bank 3 with either the original check or a legal equivalent of the substitute check for the item.
7. The paying bank (Bank 3) uses check image and MICR data or information from the substitute check received from the reconverting bank (Bank 2) to process the item during the normal course of settlement.
8. After the settlement process, Bank 3 provides a copy of the substitute check to the customer who wrote the original check or includes information about the substitute check in that customer's monthly or periodic statement.

Any financial institution that participates in the forward collection (or return) process can become the reconverting bank if that bank creates the substitute check for transmittal and settlement.

If a substitute check must be returned unpaid because of insufficient funds, the paying bank (Bank 3) stamps the item NSF (non-sufficient funds) as the reason for the return. In this case, Bank 3 encodes a "5" as the EPC on the MICR line, along with the routing number of the depository bank and the dollar amount of the substitute check. Bank 3 encodes this information on a return strip, perforated strip, or carrier document that the bank attaches to the unpaid substitute check.[10] The paying bank then returns the unpaid substitute check through the routing process to the BOFD (Bank 1) for further handling. Once Bank 1 receives the returned substitute check, the bank issues a charge back notice to its customer who deposited or offered the check for settlement.[2]

References

[1] "Frequently Asked Questions: 10. What is the difference between an Image Replacement Document (IRD) and a substitute check?" (http://www.ffiec.gov/exam/check21/faq.htm#General). Federal Financial Institutions Examination Council. (n.d.). . Retrieved May 2, 2011.

[2] "Check Clearing for the 21st Century Act Foundation for Check 21 Compliance Training" (http://www.ffiec.gov/exam/check21/Check21FoundationDoc.htm). Federal Financial Institutions Examination Council. (n.d.). . Retrieved May 28, 2009.

[3] About Check Clearing for the 21st Century Act (http://www.federalreserve.gov/paymentsystems/truncation). (2006, March 1). U.S. Federal Reserve Board. Retrieved January 16, 2007.

[4] "Consumer Guide to Check 21 and Substitute Checks" (http://www.federalreserve.gov/pubs/check21/consumer_guide.htm#whatis). U.S. Federal Reserve Board. (2004, February 16). . Retrieved May 28, 2009.

[5] Substitute checks. (http://edocket.access.gpo.gov/cfr_2009/janqtr/12cfr229.59.htm) 12 C.F.R. § 229.59 (2009). Retrieved October 4, 2009.

[6] "The Check Clearing for the 21st Century Act ("Check 21"): Frequently Asked Questions" (http://www.usdoj.gov/ust/eo/private_trustee/library/chapter07/docs/check21/Check21FAQs-final.pdf). U.S. Department of Justice. (2004, October 28). . Retrieved May 30, 2009.

[7] "Check 21: Q's and A's" (http://www.occ.gov/Consumer/check21.htm). U.S. Comptroller of the Currency. (n.d.). . Retrieved May 30, 2009.

[8] Negotiable instrument. (http://www.law.cornell.edu/ucc/3/3-104.html) 3 U.C.C. § 104 (2009). Retrieved October 11, 2009.

[9] Electronic presentment. (http://www.law.cornell.edu/ucc/4/4-110.html) 4 U.C.C. § 110 (2009). Retrieved October 11, 2009.

[10] "Check 21 Resource Document" (http://www.eccho.org/check21_resource.php). Electronic Check Clearing House Organization. (2009). . Retrieved May 28, 2009.

External sources

- Accredited Standards Committee (ASC) X9 Financial Industry Standards: Statement on Check 21 adoption (October 23, 2004) (http://www.x9.org/news/pr031028)
- Anatomy of a substitute check. (http://www.frbservices.org/files/eventseducation/pdf/SubstituteCheck.pdf) (2004). Federal Reserve Financial Services.
- Ways to Use Check 21. (http://www.eccho.org/check21_aids_uses.php) (March 2004). Electronic Check Clearing House Organization (ECCHO)
  (diagram of the check clearing and return processes for a substitute check)
- Substitute Checks: Development of Processing & Quality Standards. (http://www.eccho.org/pdf/ CTA_Standards.pdf) Electronic Check Clearing House Organization (ECCHO)
  (callouts to identify parts of a substitute check from the forward collection and return processes included at the end of the document)

Swreg

Digital River

Type	Public NASDAQ: DRIV [1]
Industry	software
Founded	1987
Founder(s)	Steve Lee
Headquarters	Eden Prairie, Minnesota, United States
Area served	global
Key people	Jessy Jex
Products	digital software delivery
Website	http://www.swreg.org/

SWREG Inc is an US customer-focused payment processing company whose clientele are software and service publishers.

The company is a global e-commerce solution designed to provide software and shareware authors a convenient method of selling products online, with special features for direct software downloads. SWREG offers multiple payment options, complete customisation, flexibility, and distribution into international markets.

Payment options include: Mastercard, Eurocard, VISA, Delta, JCB, Switch, Solo, Discover, American Express, Diner's Club, US personal check, International Money Orders, bank wires and PayPal. The checkout process allows users to purchase with their currency of preference.[1]

History

Founded in 1987, SWREG Inc is now part of the Digital River family of companies and is also headquartered in Eden Prairie, Minnesota.

Originally part of Compuserve, SWREG was purchased by Steve Lee's Atlantic Coast PLC in England who employed Cyrus Maaghul (who had previously owned Digibuy) as managing director in order to sell the business to Digital River.[2] Steve Lee then left. Digital River's SWREG acquisition was announced on 18 May 2005.[3]

References

[1] http://www.swreg.org/overview_company.htm
[2] http://www.npsoft.org/article42.html
[3] http://www.allbusiness.com/company-activities-management/operations-customer/5045717-1.html

External links

- SWREG website (http://www.swreg.org)

Talking ATM

A **Talking ATM** is a type of automated teller machine (ATM) that provides audible instructions so that persons who cannot read an ATM screen can independently use the machine. All audible information is delivered privately through a standard headphone jack on the face of the machine or a separately attached telephone handset. Information is delivered to the customer either through pre-recorded sound files or via text-to-speech speech synthesis.

History

The world's first talking ATM for the blind was an NCR machine unveiled by the Royal Bank of Canada on October 22, 1997 at a bank branch on the corner of Bank Street and Queen Street in Ottawa, Ontario. The talking ATM was a result of concerns Chris and Marie Stark, two blind customers, raised with the bank beginning in 1984. Their concerns turned into a discrimination complaint with the Canadian Human Rights Commission in 1991.[1] The machine was manufactured by NCR and adapted by Ottawa based T-Base Communications at a cost of about $500,000 Canadian dollars.[2]

Usage

A user plugs a standard headset into the jack, and can hear instructions such as "press 1 for withdrawal", "press 2 for deposit." There is an audible orientation for first time users, and audible information describing the location of features such as the number keypad, deposit slot, and card slot.[3]

Talking ATMs in Australia

National Australia Bank and Westpac have deployed talking ATMs.[4]

Talking ATMs in Canada

By 2002 Royal Bank had 15 talking ATMs in operation and announced an additional 250 units would be installed.[5]
[6]

Relevant legislation and standards

- Canadian Human Rights Act
- Canadian Standards Association:CAN/CSA-B651.1-01 (R2006)- Barrier-Free Design for Automated Banking Machines[7]

Talking ATMs in the Philippines

Metrobank uses talking ATMs.

Talking ATMs in Turkey

Yapı ve Kredi Bankası [8] implemented Talking ATMs first time in Turkey starting on December 2010. The Talking ATM function is specifically designed for visually impaired or partially sighted Yapi Kredi or other bank's customers. Utilising the text-to-speech technology, customers can perform cash withdrawal or balance inquiry transactions via Talking ATMs. The audible transaction starts when headphone plug is connected to the Talking ATM's headphone jack and when it is disconnected from the jack, transaction is ended for security. Optionally, the customer may select to mask the account information on the ATM screen.

Talking ATMs in the UK

Many of the larger banks in the United Kingdom have begun to deploy talking ATMs. Most recent machines used by banks such as Barclays include a standard audio jack for blind persons to interact with the machine.

Talking ATMs in the US

The first public actions in the United States to achieve ATM access for the blind occurred in June 1999. On June 3, Mellon Bank and PNC Bank were sued in federal courts in Philadelphia and Pittsburgh respectively.[8] On June 25, 1999, Wells Fargo became the first major bank in the United States to commit to installing talking ATMs. In a legal settlement with blind community leaders, the bank agreed to install a talking ATM at all of its 1,500 ATM locations in California. The company has subsequently installed talking ATMs at all ATM locations in all states.[9] In July 1999, Citibank agreed to pilot five talking ATMs in and around San Francisco and Los Angeles. The Citibank machine represented a unique engineering and research challenge as it uses a touch screen interface and has no function keys to offer access to the blind. All Citibank locations with this kind of machine have been adapted with talking functionality.[10]

The first talking ATM in the United States was a Diebold machine installed on October 1, 1999 in San Francisco's City Hall by the San Francisco Federal Credit Union. Like the Royal Bank machine, it was adapted by T-Base Communications.[11] In March 2000, Bank of America became the first financial institution to commit to installing a talking ATM at all of its ATM locations nationwide. A legal settlement called for the installation of hundreds of machines with later negotiations for a schedule for the remainder.

By 2005 there were approximately 30,000 Talking ATMs in the United States.

Relevant legislation and standards

• Americans With Disabilities Act

Talking ATMs today

With the increasing processing power available inside ATMs today, most ATM manufacturers provide the ability to connect headsets to their ATMs. Speech features are now available from lower-cost ATM producers, which means that the technology should gradually appear in off-premise ATM installations as equipment wears out and is replaced.

References

[1] (http://blindcanadians.ca/publications/index.php?id=624) Alliance for Equality of Blind Canadians

[2] Ottawa Sun, October 23, 1997

[3] (http://www.afb.org/afbpress/pub.asp?docID=aw040106) American Foundation for the Blind

[4] Web search (http://www.e-accessibility.com/issues/2003/mar2003.txt)

[5] (http://www.atmmarketplace.com/news_story.htm?i=12393) www.atmmarketplace.com

[6] Edmonton Journal January 28, 2003.

[7] (http://www.csa-intl.org/onlinestore/GetCatalogItemDetails.asp?mat=2414474&Parent=2562) Canadian Standards Association

[8] (http://www.dimenet.com/disnews/archive.php?mode=P&id=1083) The Philadelphia Inquirer June 4, 1999 (via National Council on Disability Document Archive)

[9] (http://www.gdblegal.com/resources.php?menuItem=61&article=32) Goldstein, Demchak, Baller, Borgen & Dardarian law firm

[10] (http://www.dredf.org/press_releases/citibankatms.html) Disability Rights Education and Defense Fund (DREDF)

[11] (http://www.dimenet.com/dpolicy/archive.php?mode=N&id=34) The San Francisco Examiner (via National Council on Disability Document Archive)

Telegraphic transfer

Telegraphic Transfer or **Telex Transfer** , often abbreviated to **TT**, is an electronic means of transferring funds overseas. A transfer charge is collected while sending money.

A banking term commonly called "T/T," meaning a cable message from one bank to another in order to effect the transfer of money.[1]

It is most often used in UK Banking to refer to a CHAPS transfer; that is a payment made via the Clearing House Automated Payments System.

The term is also used to describe other electronic funds transfer methods and, incorrectly, BACS (Bankers Automated Clearing Services) and AFTS (Automated Funds Transfer System) payments.

References

[1] Glossary, International Trade Services, First National Bank (http://www.firsttradenet.com/its/glossary/index.jsp?area2=gloss&letter=T)

Scott Thompson (businessman)

Scott Thompson is President of PayPal.[1] Scott previously served as PayPal's senior vice president and chief technology officer where he oversaw information technology, product development, and architecture for PayPal.

Prior to PayPal, Scott worked for Inovant,[1] a subsidiary of Visa formed to oversee global technology for the organization. As executive vice president of technology solutions at Inovant, he was responsible for all development, support and maintenance of Visa's global payment system.

Scott was also chief information officer of Barclays Global Investors,[1] where he implemented a new strategic technology platform and global infrastructure. In addition, he has worked with Coopers and Lybrand, delivering information technology solutions to leading financial services clients such as Wells Fargo.

Scott received a bachelor's in accounting and computer science from Stonehill College.[1]

References

[1] "Scott Thompson: Executive Profile & Biography" (http://investing.businessweek.com/research/stocks/people/person. asp?personId=20480823&ticker=EBAY:US). BusinessWeek. . Retrieved 12 July 2010.

Threshold pledge system

The **threshold pledge** or **fund and release** system is a way of making a fundraising pledge as a group of individuals, often involving charitable goals or financing the provision of a public good. An amount of money is set as the goal or *threshold* to reach for the specified purpose and interested individuals will pitch in, keeping the donation in an escrow fund. When the threshold is reached, the contributions are retired from the escrow fund and a contract is formed so that the collective good is supplied. This system is often applied to creative works, both for financing new productions and for buying out existing works; in the latter cases, it's sometimes known as **ransom publishing model** or **Street Performer Protocol** (SPP).

Sometimes contributions are refunded to the donors if the threshold amount is not reached as of some expiration date, and no contract is signed: this variation is known as an assurance contract. Contributions to an assurance contract may also be collected as pledges which are only called-in when the threshold is reached.

When used to fund the creation of artistic works, the threshold pledge is quite dependent on the reputation of the artist, so that the artist is known for producing valued works and that the artist will live up to the terms of the contractual agreement. It therefore assumes that the artists will have built up this reputation by previously released works, such as previous chapters in a serial.

Street Performer Protocol

Street Performer Protocol is the origin of the threshold pledge system. SPP is the threshold pledge system encouraging the creation of creative works in the public domain or copylefted, described by the cryptographers John Kelsey and Bruce Schneier[1] (although the underlying idea is much older). This assumes that current forms of copyright and business models of the creative industries will become increasingly inefficient or unworkable in the future, because of the ease of copying and distribution of digital information.

Under the SPP, the artist announces that when a certain amount of money is received in escrow, the artist will release a work (book, music, software, etc.) into the public domain or under a free content license. Interested donors make their donations to a publisher, who contracts with the artist for the work's creation and keeps the donations in escrow, identified by their donors, until the work is released. If the artist releases the work on time, the artist receives payment from the escrow fund. If not, the publisher repays the donors, possibly with interest. As detailed above, contributions may also be refunded if the threshold is not reached within a reasonable expiring date. The assessed threshold also includes a fee which compensates the publisher for costs and assumption of risks.

The publisher may act like a traditional publisher, by soliciting sample works and deciding which ones to support, or it may only serve as an escrow agent and not care about the quality of the works (like a vanity press).

Ransom Model in Software

In software, source code escrow is a publishing model that applies the SPP to source code (often involving existing proprietary software) which is eventually released under an open source or free software license.

History

The Street Performer Protocol is a natural extension of the much older idea of funding the production of written or creative works through agreements between groups of potential readers or users.

Mozart and Beethoven, among other composers, used subscriptions to premiere concerts and first print editions of their works. Unlike today's meaning of *subscription*, this meant that a fixed number of people had to sign up and pay some amount before the concert could take place or the printing press started.

"These three (piano) concertos K413-415 (...) formed an important milestone in his career, being the first in the series of great concertos that he wrote for Vienna, and the first to be published in a printed edition. Initially, however, he followed the usual practice of making them available in manuscript copies. Mozart advertised for subscribers in January 1783: "These three concertos, which can be performed with full orchestra including wind instruments, or only a quattro, that is with 2 violins, 1 viola and violoncello, will be available at the beginning of April to those who have subscribed for them (beautifully copied, and supervised by the composer himself)." Six months later, Mozart complained that it was taking a long time to secure enough subscribers. This was despite the fact that he had meanwhile scored a great success on two fronts:..."[2]

However, there are a number of differences between this traditional model and the SPP. The most important difference is that traditionally, the subscribers would be among the first to get access, and would do so with the understanding that the work would likely always be a "rare" good; thus there was some status in owning a copy, as well as the prestige of being among the patrons. Additionally, subscriptions were generally sold at a set price, though some wealthy subscribers may have given more in order to be a patron. In the modern SPP, each funder chooses the amount they want to pay, and the work is released to the public and freely reproduced.

In 1970, Stephen Breyer argued for the importance of this model in *The Uneasy Case for Copyright*.[3]

The Street Performer Protocol was successfully used to release the source code and brand name of the Blender 3D animation program. After NaN Technologies BV went bankrupt in 2002, the copyright and trademark rights to Blender went to the newly created NaN Holding BV. The newly created Blender Foundation campaigned for donations to obtain the right to release the software as free and open source software software under the GNU General Public License. NaN Holding BV set the price tag at 100,000 Euros. More than 1,300 users became members and donated more than 50 Euros each, in addition to anonymous users, non-membership individual donations and companies. On October 13, 2002, Blender was released on the Internet as free/open source software.[4]

Variations of the SPP include the Rational Street Performer Protocol [5] and the Wall Street Performer Protocol [6].

References

[1] John Kelsey; Bruce Schneier. " The Street Performer Protocol (http://schneier.com/paper-street-performer.html)" USENIX Press, *The Third USENIX Workshop on Electronic Commerce Proceedings*, November 1998.

[2] Robert Philip , Sleeve Notes - *Mozart: Piano Concertos 11 12 & 13; Susan Tomes (piano), The Gaudier Ensemble* (http://www. hyperion-records.co.uk/al.asp?al=CDH55333&f=Mozart: Piano Concertos 11). Hyperion Records, *Helios* (2004).

[3] Stephen Breyer, "The Uneasy Case for Copyright: A Study of Copyright in Books, Photocopies and Computer Programs", *Harvard Law Review* (http://www.harvardlawreview.org) 84(2) 1970.

[4] "Blender.org history" (http://www.blender.org/blenderorg/blender-foundation/history/). Amsterdam. 2009-07. .

Further reading

• Steven Schear, COPYLEFT: Rethinking Intellectual Property in the Digital Age (http://web.archive.org/web/20040624034123/http://freedom.orlingrabbe.com/lfetimes/copyleft.htm), 2(16), 1998.

• John Kelsey and Bruce Schneier, The Street Performer Protocol and Digital Copyrights (http://firstmonday.org/htbin/cgiwrap/bin/ojs/index.php/fm/article/view/673/583), *First Monday* 4(6), 1999.

• Crosbie Fitch, The Digital Art Auction (http://digitalartauction.com/history/essay.htm) - March 2001.

• Chris Rasch, The Wall Street Performer Protocol (http://firstmonday.org/htbin/cgiwrap/bin/ojs/index.php/fm/article/viewArticle/865/774), *First Monday* 6(6), 2001. (tROT)

• Karl Fogel: The Promise of a Post-Copyright World (http://questioncopyright.org/promise#threshold_pledge) - QuestionCopyright.org, October 2005

TIPANET

TIPANET (Transferts Interbancaires de Paiement Automatisés) is an international payment system set up by the European cooperative banks. Its shareholders were Natexis Banques Populaires, France; Banca Popolare Commercio e Industria, Italy; Istituto Centrale delle Banche Popolari Italiane, Italy; Banco Popular de España, Spain; Crédit Professionnel, Belgium; The Cooperative Bank plc, United Kingdom; Österreichische Volksbanken AG, Austria; Geno Group, Germany (DG BANK, GZ-Bank, WGZ-Bank), and Caisse Centrale Desjardins Quebec, Canada.

Its commercial counterpart and partner was UNICOPAY which failed in 2004 because it was overtaken by technological innovations such as the advent of SWIFT FileAct facilities and the creation of STEP2. The UNICOPAY principals were Caisse National de Crédit Agricole-Indosuez, France; Istituto Centrale delle Banche di Credito Cooperativo, Italy; KBC Bank (formerly CERA), Belgium; Lloyds TSB Bank, United Kingdom; OKOBANK, Finland; Rabobank, Netherlands; Raiffeisen Zentralbank, Austria and DG BANK, Germany.

Tipanet was founded in 1993 in order to manage, develop and run an efficient cross-border clearing system, in order to fulfill the "7 ECB objectives" issued around 2001 which were:

- Enhanced systems/services
- Priority for cross-border credit transfers
- Lower prices for cross-border credit transfers
- Settlement time should be comparable for domestic and cross-border payments
- Fees borne by the originator (OUR-payments)
- Access to cross-border retail payment systems
- Standard implementations

Each TIPANET member is free to seek out the most suitable international partners in the light of its business interests, its business traditions and its international trade relations, and these arrangements are made known to other members.

The local TIPANET agent collects payment instructions and converts them into the TIPANET message format, which complies with the SWIFT MT 102+ message structure. The TIPANET format handles credit transfers and money-cheques. After collecting the payment orders,the local agent compiles payment blocks and sends composite instructions to the respective foreign agents, who then convert the TIPANET message format into its domestic equivalent for local execution. The latest time for the exchange of files on any working day is 4 p.m. local time of the receiving bank for next-day execution. Therefore the beneficiary's account is normally credited two working days after the order is placed.

PDF Reference Documents

Downloadable 25 March 2010

European Central Bank Conference: TOWARDS A DOMESTIC PAYMENT INFRASTRUCTURE FOR THE EURO AREA Frankfurt am Main 7 February 2001 Elektronische. Transaktions-und Zahlungssysteme http://www.ecb.int/events/pdf/conferences/04Malz_tipa.pdf

European Central Bank Blue Book, August 2007 http://www.ecb.int/pub/pdf/other/ecbbluebookea200708en.pdf

CPSS - Red Book - 2003 Payment systems in the euro area http://www.bis.org/publ/cpss53p04eu.pdf

EC Regulation 2560/2001: study of competition for cross-border payment services final report. Project n° markt/2004/11/f, prepared for the European Commission Internal Market and Services Directorate-General http://ec.europa.eu/internal_market/payments/docs/reg-2001-2560/competition_en.pdf

ToDDaSO

ToDDaSO is an electronic payments service in the UK for the transfer of retail customer payment arrangements between different bank accounts in UK banks. ToDDaSO is an acronym that stands for *Transfer of Direct Debits and Standing Orders*.

The service allows UK retail banks to electronically request the transfer of Direct Debit and Standing Order payments arrangements, on behalf of new customers, wishing to transfer payment arrangements from a previous bank accounts. The scheme is also known as the *Inter Bank Transfer of Direct Debit Instructions* [1] service and is governed by BACS (also known as Voca), the UK's automated payments clearing scheme.

ToDDaSO is also commonly referred to in the UK as the *Switching Bank Account Service* [2].

Background

This service was first established in the mid 1990s, and then improved in 2005 as an industry response to criticisms of consumer banking services, contained in Section 4 of Don Cruickshank's *Review of Banking Services in the UK* [3], published by the HM Treasury. This government report highlighted the competitive difficulties faced by retail customers in being able to switch between retail account providers.

External links

- BACS - UK Bank Switching Service [4]
- Direct Debit - Direct Credit [5]
- Voca [6]
- APACS, the UK Payments Association [6]

References

[1] "Direct Debit Glossary" (http://web.archive.org/web/20070224162740/http://www.bacs.co.uk/BPSL/directdebit/resources/ glossary). BACS Payment Schemes Limited. 2005. Archived from the original (http://www.bacs.co.uk/BPSL/directdebit/resources/ glossary) on 2007-02-24. . Retrieved 2007-03-20.

[2] "About Voca" (http://web.archive.org/web/20070104133924/http://www.voca.com/Voca/About+us/About+Voca/History/). Voca Limited. Archived from the original (http://www.voca.com/Voca/About+us/About+Voca/History/) on 2007-01-04. . Retrieved 2007-03-20.

[3] "Review of Banking Services in the UK" (http://www.hm-treasury.gov.uk/documents/financial_services/banking/bankreview/ fin_bank_reviewfinal.cfm). HM Treasury. . Retrieved 2007-03-20.

TPS Pakistan

TPS Pakistan

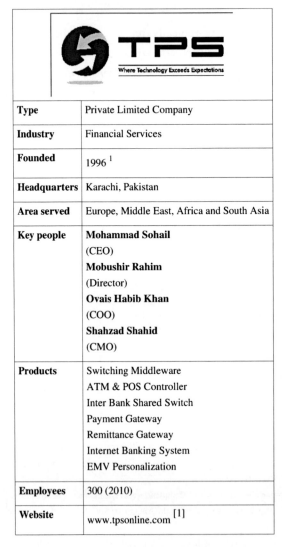

Type	Private Limited Company
Industry	Financial Services
Founded	1996 [1]
Headquarters	Karachi, Pakistan
Area served	Europe, Middle East, Africa and South Asia
Key people	**Mohammad Sohail** (CEO) **Mobushir Rahim** (Director) **Ovais Habib Khan** (COO) **Shahzad Shahid** (CMO)
Products	Switching Middleware ATM & POS Controller Inter Bank Shared Switch Payment Gateway Remittance Gateway Internet Banking System EMV Personalization
Employees	300 (2010)
Website	www.tpsonline.com [1]

TPS Pakistan is a Pakistan based technology firm established in 1996 by two entrepreneurs Mohammed Sohail and Mobushir Rahim. TPS is credited with the establishment of the ebanking infrastructure in Pakistan and is powering 80% of the banks in Pakistan and the largest inter bank shared switch - 1LINK[1].

Since its inception in 1996, TPS has developed cutting edge solutions from Pakistan and currently employs around 300 employees in its Karachi based Head Quarters. TPS has a sister concern in Middle East by the name of TPS Middle East FZ LLC which looks after the area of Middle East and North Africa (MENA). Whereas TPS Pakistan looks after the area of Europe, Africa (except North Africa) and South Asia.

TPS is currently present in more than 70 countries through its resellers and has 135 customers in 35 of those countries. TPS solutions are packaged with some customizations for each customer and are focused on the electronic banking area only. The solutions are for ATM, POS, Inter Bank and Multi Bank Switching & Controllers, Internet Banking, Inward & Outward Remittance Systems, Reconciliation and Settlement and a variety of other related solutions.

TPS is one of the largest IT firms in Pakistan.

ATM and other alternate delivery channels are fast becoming a common thing in Pakistan with many people using the ATMs and POS for various purposes which includes withdrawals, purchases and bill payments.

TPS is also the technology behind Telenor Pakistan[2] Pakistan's EasyPaisa bill payment hub and Ufone[3] USSD based multi-bank mobile banking hub. EasyPaisa has now become the single largest bill payment and funds transfer hub in Pakistan with a transaction volume that exceeds that of the national bill payment hub at 1LINK with a factor of 1 to 100. After the success of 1LINK, TPS was selected to implement an Inter Bank Shared Switch in Bangladesh (OMNIBUS). The OMNIBUS Inter Bank Shared Switch has currently 6 banks connected for reciprocation of ATM related services.

Recently TPS IRIS Multi Institution Financial Middleware was selected by Group BPCE[4] for its operations in Africa starting from Cameroon and Republic of Congo. TPS IRIS is also running Doha Bank's operations in 3 countries and is powering the Commercial Bank of Kuwait's electronic banking infrastructure as well. Network International UAE uses TPS Prepaid Card Management System for its hosted prepaid card services, the first bank to go live with this system is ENBD UAE.

Headquarters

TPS Pakistan's headquarters are located at TPS Tower in Karachi, Pakistan

TPS Pakistan's headquarters were located in Business Avenue Karachi, Pakistan. In 2008 TPS Pakistan announced that it was moving its headquarters from Business Aveneue to a bigger and spacious building named as TPS Tower in Karachi, Pakistan.

History

TPS Pakistan started of as a two man operation in 1996 by the name of Transaction Processing Systems, it gradually grew and eventually was incorporated with the Securities and Exchange Commission of Pakistan as TPS Pakistan Private Limited in 2003.

References

[1] 1LINK, p.1
[2] Telenor Pakistan, p.2
[3] Ufone, p.3
[4] Group BPCE, p.4

Notes

External links

- TPS Expands its frontiers (http://pashanews.org/?p=250)
- Telenor (http://www.telenor.com)
- Group BPCE selects IRIS (http://www.tpsonline.com/website/news/archive/news2009.php)
- UBL Upgrades its technology infrastructure (https://www.ubl.com.pk/news/UBL_Banking_Technology_Upgrades.asp)
- e-peak systems signs up as TPS distributor (http://www.e-peaksystems.com/partners.aspx)
- Launch of IRIS (http://ciopakistan.com/2008/11/tps-pakistan)
- TPS website (http://www.tpsonline.com)

Transit check

A **transit check** or **not on-us check** is a negotiable item (check) which is drawn on another bank than that at which it is presented for payment.

For example, a check drawn on Bank of America, presented for deposit at Wells Fargo Bank, would be considered a transit item by Wells Fargo, while the same item presented for cash or deposit at Bank of America would be an on-us check. Routing numbers, as well as the bank name printed on the check, help to determine an item's classification.

TRANZ 330

TRANZ 330

Manufacturer	VeriFone
Type	General-purpose Point of Sale (POS) device
Operating system	Proprietary VeriFone TCL
Power	9VAC, 1A
CPU	Zilog Z80
Display	16-character vacuum fluorescent display
Input	Card reader, two serial ports, optional bar code or PIN pad device
Touchpad	16-key numeric keypad
Connectivity	Modem (300/1200 baud), two serial ports

The **TRANZ 330** is a popular point-of-sale device manufactured by VeriFone in 1985. The most common application for these units is bank and credit card processing, however, as a general purpose computer, they can perform other novel functions. Other applications include gift/benefit card processing, prepaid phone cards, payroll and employee timekeeping, and even debit and ATM cards. They are programmed in a proprietary VeriFone TCL language (Terminal Control Language), which is unrelated to the Tool Command Language used in UNIX environments.

Traveler's cheque

A **traveler's cheque** (also **traveller's cheque**, **travellers cheque**, **traveller's check** or **traveler's check**) is a preprinted, fixed-amount cheque designed to allow the person signing it to make an unconditional payment to someone else as a result of having paid the issuer for that privilege.

Usage

As traveler's cheques can usually be replaced if lost or stolen (if the owner still has the receipt issued with the purchase of the cheques showing the serial numbers allocated), they are often used by people on vacation in place of cash.

Traveler's cheques are available in several currencies such as U.S. dollars, Canadian dollars, Pounds sterling, Japanese yen, Chinese Yuan and Euro; denominations usually being 20, 50, or 100 (x100 for Yen) of whatever currency, and are usually sold in pads of five or ten cheques, e.g., 5 x €20 for €100. Traveler's cheques do not expire, so unused cheques can be kept by the purchaser to spend at any time in the future. The purchaser of a supply of traveler's cheques effectively gives an interest-free loan to the issuer, which is why it is common for banks to sell them "commission free" to their customers. The commission, where it is charged, is usually 1-2% of the total face value sold.

In 2005, American Express released the *American Express Travelers Cheque Card*, a stored-value card that serves the same purposes as a traveler's cheque, but can be used in stores like a credit card. It however discontinued the card in October 2007. A number of other financial companies went on to issue stored-value or pre-paid debit cards containing several currencies that could be used like credit or debit cards at shops and at ATMs, mimicking the traveler's cheque in electronic form. One of the major examples is the Visa TravelMoney card.[1]

History

Traveler's cheques were first issued on 1 January 1772 by the London Credit Exchange Company for use in ninety European cities,[2] and in 1874 Thomas Cook was issuing 'circular notes' that operated in the manner of traveler's cheques.[3]

American Express was the first company to develop a large-scale traveller's cheque system in 1891,[4] and is still the largest issuer of traveler's cheques today by volume.

American Express's introduction of traveler's cheques is traditionally attributed to employee Marcellus Flemming Berry, after company president J.C. Fargo had problems in smaller European cities obtaining funds with a letter of credit.

Terminology

Legal terms for the parties to a traveler's cheque are the **obligor** or **issuer**, the organization that produces it; the **agent,** the bank or other place that sells it; the **purchaser,** the natural person who buys it, and the **payee,** the entity to whom the purchaser writes the cheque for goods and/or services. For purposes of clearance, the obligor is both **maker** and **drawee**.

Use and acceptance

Upon obtaining custody of a purchased supply of traveler's cheques, the purchaser should immediately write his or her signature once upon each cheque, usually on the cheque's upper portion. The purchaser will also have received a receipt and some other documentation that should be kept in a safe place other than where he or she carries the cheques.

When wanting to cash a traveler's cheque while making a purchase, the purchaser should, in the presence of the payee, date and countersign the cheque in the indicated space, usually on the cheque's lower portion (if at a restaurant, it may be helpful to ask the waiter to watch and wait for this to be done).[5]

Applicable change for a purchase transaction should be given in local currency as if the cheques were banknotes.

Several travellers cheques have been created; the most widely accepted travellers cheques are:

- Thomas Cook Group
- American Express

Security concerns

It is a reasonable security procedure for the payee to ask to inspect the purchaser's picture ID; a driver's license or passport should suffice, and doing so would most usefully be towards the end of comparing the purchaser's signature on the ID with those on the cheque. The best first step, however, that can be taken by any payee who has concerns about the validity of any traveler's cheque, is to contact the issuer directly; a negative finding by a third-party cheque verification service based on an ID check may merely indicate that the service has no record about the purchaser (to be expected, practically by definition, of many travelers), or at worst that he or she has been deemed incompetent to manage a personal chequing account (which would have no bearing on the validity of a traveller's cheque).

Black market

One of the main advantages travellers cheques provide is the replacement if lost or stolen. This feature has also created a black market where swindlers buy travellers cheques, sell them at 50% of their value to other people (such as travellers) and falsely report their travellers cheque stolen with the company where the cheque has been obtained. As such, they get back the value of the travellers cheque and make 50% of the value as profit.[5]

Deposit and settlement

A payee receiving a traveler's cheque should follow its normal procedures for depositing cheques into its bank account: usually, endorsement by stamp or signature and listing of the cheque and its amount on the deposit slip. The bank account will be credited with the amount of the cheque as with any other negotiable item submitted for clearance.

In the United States, if the payee is equipped to process cheques electronically at point of sale (*see:* Check 21 Act), they should still take custody of the cheque and submit it to a financial institution, particularly to avoid any confusion on the part of the purchaser.

References

[1] "Visa TravelMoney Cards" (http://europeforvisitors.com/europe/articles/amex-travelfunds-visa-travelmoney-cards.htm). europeforvisitors.com. . Retrieved January 3, 2011.

[2] On this day - January 3 (http://archive.thisislancashire.co.uk/2005/1/3/452155.html)

[3] http://www.competition-commission.gov.uk/rep_pub/reports/1995/fulltext/361c3.pdf

[4] Host With The Most (http://www.time.com/time/magazine/article/0,9171,866900-7,00.html), Time Magazine, 9 April 1956 issue

[5] Handboek voor de Wereldreiziger by Frans Timmerhuis

External links

- American Express Traveler's Cheques merchant site (http://www10.americanexpress.com/sif/cda/page/0,1641,18540,00.asp?)

Truck system

A **truck system** is an arrangement in which employees are paid in commodities or some currency substitute (referred to as *scrip*), rather than with standard money. This limits employees' ability to choose how to spend their earnings—generally to the benefit of the employer. As an example, scrip might be usable only for the purchase of goods at a "**company store**" where prices are set artificially high.

While this system had long existed in many parts of the world, it became widespread in the eighteenth and nineteenth centuries, as industrialisation left many poor, unskilled workers without other means to support themselves and their families. The practice has been widely criticised as exploitative and similar in effect to slavery, and has been outlawed in many parts of the world. Variations of the *truck system* have existed worldwide, and are known by various names.

The practice is ostensibly one of a free and legal exchange, whereby an employer would offer something of value (typically goods, food or housing) in exchange for labor, with the result being the same as if the laborer had been paid money and then spent the money on these necessities. The word *truck* came into the English language within this context, from the French *troquer*, meaning 'exchange' or 'barter'. A truck system differs from this kind of open barter or payment in kind system by creating or taking advantage of a closed economic system in which workers have little or no opportunity to choose other work arrangements, and can easily become so indebted to their employers that they are unable to leave the system legally. The popular song "Sixteen Tons" dramatizes this scenario, with the narrator telling Saint Peter (who would welcome him to Heaven upon his death) "...I can't go; I owe my soul to the company store."

Truck systems came under increasing criticism, and laws were passed in many jurisdictions that made it illegal for payment to be made other than in lawful money, and to specify how or where employees spent their pay.

Origin of the saying "I'll have no truck with that" to mean "I will have nothing to do with that system".

References

- Anderson, Adelaide M. (1899), "Truck Legislation in England and on the Continent" (http://books.google.com/?id=CUcBAAAAYAAJ), in MacDonnell, John, *Journal of the Society of Comparative Legislation*, London, pp. 395–406, retrieved 2008-06-01
- Burton, John Hill (1847), "Truck System" (http://books.google.com/?id=pYMDAAAAQAAJ), *Manual of the Law of Scotland (The Law of Private Rights and Obligations)* (2nd ed.), Edinburgh: Oliver & Boyd, p. 265
- Gaskell, P. (1833), "Truck and Cottage Systems" (http://books.google.com/?id=etFGvcK-dYwC), *The Manufacturing Population of England*, London: Baldwin and Cradock, pp. 342–361, retrieved 2008-05-31
- Lauchheimer, Malcolm H. (1919), "The Terms of Employment (in the Labor Law of Maryland)" (http://books.google.com/?id=lNsOAAAAYAAJ), *Johns Hopkins University Studies in Historical and Political Science*, **XXXVII**, Baltimore: The Johns Hopkins Press, pp. 106–112
- M'Culloch, J. R. (1852), "Truck System" (http://books.google.com/?id=tGpCAAAAIAAJ), in Vethake, Henry, *A Dictionary, Practical, Theoretical, and Historical, of Commerce and Commercial Navigation.*, **II**, Philadelphia: A. Hart, pp. 684–86
- Morgan, James Appleton (1881), "Illegality of contracts for the payment of work otherwise than in current coin. — The truck system." (http://books.google.com/?id=fjI9AAAAIAAJ), *A Treatise on the Law of Contracts by Charles Greenstreet Addison*, **I**, Jersey City: Frederick D. Linn & Co., pp. 434–36
- Ruegg, Alfred Henry (1901), "Changes in the Law of England Affecting Labour (The Truck System)" (http://books.google.com/?id=j1czAAAAIAAJ), *A Century of Law Reform*, London: MacMillan and Co, pp. 254–257, retrieved 2008-05-31

- Commissioners appointed to Inquire into the Truck System, ed. (1871), *Truck; or, Semi-Serfdom in the Shetland (Zetland) Isles* (http://books.google.com/?id=obkHAAAAQAAJ) (2nd ed.), London: Elliot Stock
- Manufactories, Commissioners for Inquiring Into the Employment and Condition of Children in Mines and (1842), "Of the Hiring, and the Wages Paid to Persons Employed in Mines" (http://books.google.com/?id=TS1vx7eHjUkC), *The Condition and Treatment of the Children Employed in the Mines and Collieries of the United Kingdom*, London: William Strange, pp. 84–85
- "The Truck-System" (http://books.google.com/?id=G0RRPgJbU-kC), *The British and Foreign Review*, **XV**, London: Richard and John Edward Taylor, 1842 (published 1843), pp. 79–100

TSYS

Total System Service s, Inc.

	TSYS
Type	Public (NYSE: TSS [1])
Industry	Credit Card
Founded	Columbus, Georgia (1983)
Headquarters	Columbus, GA, USA
Key people	Philip W. Tomlinson, Chairman & CEO Troy Woods, President
Products	TS1,TS2
Revenue	$2 billion
Website	www.tsys.com [2]

Total System Services, Inc. (NYSE: TSS [1]) (commonly referred to as **TSYS**) is the largest processor of merchant acquirers and bank credit card issuers. Creators of TS2 and TS1. TSYS is located in Columbus, Georgia, United States. TSYS acquired a leading prepaid card processor, Clarity Payment Solutions, Inc. in 2004 and rebranded it TSYS Prepaid.

History

In 1959 TSYS started as a division of Columbus Bank and Trust (CB&T). In 1974, CB&T started processing credit cards for other banks. In 1983, TSYS became a separate publicly traded company, although majority ownership remained with CB&T and its successor, Synovus. In 1991, TSYS began development on the next generation of processing platforms. Then in 1994, TSYS launched TS2. On September 24, 1999 TSYS opened up its new Riverfront Campus in Downtown Columbus.[1] On October 25, 2007, TSYS and Synovus (holding 81% of shares at the time) announced a spin-off that was completed as of the end of 2007.[2]

Total System Services Inc. Announced the acquired majority stake in First National Bank of Omaha's merchant acquisition business for $150.5 million.[3]

Cost-Saving Strategies

On January 20, 2010, TSYS announced a cost-reduction plan to close a revenue gap which resulted from the global recession. The result would be a 5% staff reduction, primarily in the US, by the end of February 2010. A global hiring freeze was also announced. Merit increases in pay were suspended and discretionary contributions to the employees' retirement plans were eliminated.

Subsidiaries

- INFONOX, A TSYS Company, Pune, India, formerly Infonox Software Pvt. Ltd.
- TSYS do Brazil
- TSYS Healthcare
- TSYS Analytics

- TSYS Card Tech, formerly Card Tech Ltd
- TSYS Prepaid, formerly Clarity
- TSYS Acquiring Solutions, formerly Vital
- TSYS Debt Management, also known as TDM
- TSYS Loyalty, formerly ESC Loyalty
- TSYS Merchant Solutions, formerly First National Merchant Solutions

Joint ventures

- CUP Data
- GP Net Japan
- TSYS de Mexico
- TSYS Managed Services EMEA, also known as BPM

Partners

- China UnionPay
- Ontario Systems, LLC
- Telrock

External links

- TSYS Official Website [6]
- TSYS Acquiring Website [7]
- TSYS Press Releases [8]
- Infonox Website [9]

References

[1] " TSYS History (http://www.tsys.com/company/history.htm)." Retrieved on January 16, 2008.

[2] " TSYS Board Approves Agreement with Synovus for Spin-Off (http://www.tsys.com/news/Releases/20071025agreementspinoff.cfm)." Retrieved on March 11, 2011.

[3] "Total Systems acquires part of Bank of Omaha unit" (http://www.businessweek.com/ap/financialnews/D9EQCDR00.htm). 1 April 2010. . Retrieved 5 April 2010.

- Boyce, Christopher (October 14, 2004). "Columbus, Ga.-based credit account processor completes J.P. Morgan deal." (http://www.accessmylibrary.com/article-1G1-123233177/columbus-ga-based-credit.html). *Columbus Ledger-Enquirer* (Columbus, GA). Retrieved 2 January 2010.

UK Payments Administration

The **UK Payments Administration Ltd (UKPA)** (previously APACS, the **Association for Payment Clearing Services**) is a United Kingdom trade organisation that brings together all payment systems organisations and gives banks, building societies and card issuers a

forum where they can work together on non-competitive issues. It covers most forms of payments within the UK including cash, credit cards, debit cards, cheques, and automated payments such as direct debits, salary payments and online/phone transactions.

It has been responsible for the creation of rules regarding customer liability in cases of card and cheque fraud and starting in 2004 oversaw and guided the transition of debit cards to Chip and PIN.

UKPA was created on the July 6, 2009, as a direct successor of the 'Association for Payment Clearing Services' (APACS) to act as a portal company for each of the respective sectors of UK payment services such as BACS, CHAPS, the Cheque and Credit Clearing Company and other businesses.

Standards

The UKPA standards define both procedural and technical practice for:

- Debits (including cheques)
- Standing order mandates
- Coin packaging and banknote wrappers
- Magnetic media interchange
- Interchange data formats
- EFTPOS device communications
- Other services

UKPA members

- Abbey National
- Alliance & Leicester
- Bank of America
- Bank of England
- Bank of Ireland
- Bank of Scotland
- Barclays Bank
- Capital One
- Citigroup

- Co-operative Bank
- Deutsche Bank
- DnB NOR Bank
- Egg
- GE Capital
- HFC Bank
- HSBC
- JPMorgan
- Lloyds TSB

- MBNA
- Morgan Stanley
- NAB
- Nationwide Building Society
- National Westminster Bank
- Northern Rock
- Royal Bank of Scotland
- Royal Mail
- Standard Chartered Bank
- Wachovia

Initiatives

In 1994 APACS commissioned Bacs Limited to develop and deliver a networked service known as IBDE (Inter-Bank Data Exchange) to facilitate the clearance of cheques between the member banks.

In the late 1990s — in an effort to counter the growing problem of 'skimming' which is fraudulently copying a credit card for criminal purposes — APACS pioneered the development of credit cards containing a computer chip. The early APACS work proved the viability of 'chip cards', and helped in the creation of the common EMV (Europay, Mastercard, VISA) standards for such cards.

In December 2005, the association of banks started the Faster Payments Service initiative to improve the speed of lower value consumer and business transactions, to be used in parallel with the CHAPS and Bacs systems.

As APACS, it managed Card Watch, a UK banking industry initiative that aimed to raise awareness of card fraud prevention,[1] now superseded by Financial Fraud Action UK.

References

[1] Card Watch (http://replay.waybackmachine.org/20090604165821/http://www.cardwatch.org.uk/), copy at the Internet Archive

External links

- UKPA official website (http://www.ukpayments.org.uk/)
- Cheque and Credit Clearing Company (http://www.chequeandcredit.co.uk) - the organisation that manages cheque clearing in the UK
- Financial Fraud Action UK (http://www.financialfraudaction.org.uk/)

Unfunded loan commitments

Unfunded loan commitments are those commitments made by a Financial institution that are contractual obligations for future funding. They should not be confused with Letters of credit which require certain trigger events before funding is needed. Increasingly, originating lending institutions are selling Senior loans and related funded or unfunded commitments to institutional investors like Investment management firms, mutual funds and insurance companies.

Typically, unfunded commitments are separated into two categories:

- Multiple Advance, Closed End: This type of loan (typically a construction loan) advances incremental amounts up to a certain limit, based upon some criteria such as inspection and approval of a draw request. Any principal reductions received during the loan period are **not** available to be drawn on, but rather have paid down the loan balance.
- Revolving or Open End: This type of loan (known informally as a Line of credit) allows the borrower to continue to borrow up to the original loan amount. Principal reductions are immediately available for future advances.

Banks are required to report unfunded commitments on schedule RC-L of the quarterly Report of Condition and Income (Call Report).

External links

• FDIC Call Report Information [1]

Uniform Customs and Practice for Documentary Credits

The **Uniform Customs and Practice for Documentary Credits** (UCP) is a set of rules on the issuance and use of letters of credit. The UCP is utilised by bankers and commercial parties in more than 175 countries in trade finance. Some 11-15% of international trade utilises letters of credit, totalling over a trillion dollars (US) each year.

Historically, the commercial parties, particularly banks, have developed the techniques and methods for handling letters of credit in international trade finance. This practice has been standardized by the ICC (International Chamber of Commerce) by publishing the UCP in 1933 and subsequently updating it throughout the years. The ICC has developed and moulded the UCP by regular revisions, the current version being the UCP600. The result is the most successful international attempt at unifying rules ever, as the UCP has substantially universal effect. The latest revision was approved by the Banking Commission of the ICC at its meeting in Paris on 25 October 2006. This latest version, called the UCP600, formally commenced on 1 July 2007.

ICC and the UCP

A significant function of the ICC is the preparation and promotion of its uniform rules of practice. The ICC's aim is to provide a codification of international practice occasionally selecting the best practice after ample debate and consideration. The ICC rules of practice are designed by bankers and merchants and not by legislatures with political and local considerations. The rules accordingly demonstrate the needs, customs and practices of business. Because the rules are incorporated voluntarily into contracts, the rules are flexible while providing a stable base for international review, including judicial scrutiny. International revision is thus facilitated permitting the incorporation of the changing practices of the commercial parties. ICC, which was established in 1919, had as its primary objective facilitating the flow of international trade at a time when nationalism and protectionism threatened the easing of world trade. It was in that spirit that the UCP were first introduced – to alleviate the confusion caused by individual countries' promoting their own national rules on letter of credit practice. The aim was to create a set of contractual rules that would establish uniformity in practice, so that there would be less need to cope with often conflicting national regulations. The universal acceptance of the UCP by practitioners in countries with widely divergent economic and judicial systems is a testament to the rules' success.

UCP600

The latest revision of UCP is the sixth revision of the rules since they were first promulgated in 1933. It is the fruit of more than three years of work by the ICC's Commission on Banking Technique and Practice.

The UCP remain the most successful set of private rules for trade ever developed. A range of individuals and groups contributed to the current revision including: the UCP Drafting Group, which waded through more than 5000 individual comments before arriving at this final text; the UCP Consulting Group, consisting of members from more than 25 countries, which served as the advisory body; the more than 400 members of the ICC Commission on Banking Technique and Practice who made pertinent suggestions for changes in the text; and 130 ICC National Committees worldwide which took an active role in consolidating comments from their members.

During the revision process, notice was taken of the considerable work that had been completed in creating the International Standard Banking Practice for the Examination of Documents under Documentary Credits (ISBP), ICC

Publication 645. This publication has evolved into a necessary companion to the UCP for determining compliance of documents with the terms of letters of credit. It is the expectation of the Drafting Group and the Banking Commission that the application of the principles contained in the ISBP, including subsequent revisions thereof, will continue during the time UCP 600 is in force. At the time UCP 600 is implemented, there will be an updated version of the ISBP to bring its contents in line with the substance and style of the new rules.

Note that UCP600 does not automatically apply to a credit if the credit is silent as to which set of rules it is subject to. A credit issued by SWIFT MT700 is no longer subject by default to the current UCP – it has to be indicated in field 40E, which is designated for specifying the "applicable rules".

Where a credit is issued subject to UCP600, the credit will be interpreted in accordance with the entire set of 39 articles contained in UCP600. However, exceptions to the rules can be made by express modification or exclusion. For example, the parties to a credit may agree that the rest of the credit shall remain valid despite the beneficiary's failure to deliver an instalment. In such case, the credit has to nullify the effect of article 32 of UCP600, such as by wording the credit as: "The credit will continue to be available for the remaining instalments notwithstanding the beneficiary's failure to present complied documents of an instalment in accordance with the instalment schedule."

eUCP

The eUCP was developed as a supplement to UCP due to the strong sense at the time that banks and corporates together with the transport and insurance industries were ready to utilise electronic commerce. The hope and expectation that surrounded the development of eUCP has failed the UCP600 and it will remain as a supplement albeit slightly amended to identify its relationship with UCP600.

An updated version of the eUCP came into effect on 1 July 2007 to coincide the commencement of the UCP600. There are no substantive changes to the eUCP, merely references to the UCP600.

CDCS

The Certified Documentary Credit Specialist is a qualification awarded by IFSA US and IFS UK and endorsed by ICC Paris as the only International qualification for Trade Finance Professionals, recognising the competence, and ensuring best practice. It requires Re-Certification every Three years. UCP 600 rules will be included from April 2008 examinations only. CDCS requires some 4–6 months of independent study and a pass in 3 hour examination of 120 multiple choice questions as well as 3 in basket exercises with questions which demonstrate skill in real-world applications of UCP.

External links

- International Chamber of Commerce [1]
- ICC Publications [2]

Universal Air Travel Plan

Universal Air Travel Plan, Inc. (UATP) is a global corporate travel payment network issued by 14 major airlines and accepted by over 250 merchants around the world for air, rail and cruise travel. Established in 1936, UATP is the first charge card issued.

UATP also connects airlines to alternative forms of payment brands such as Acculynk, BillMeLater, Cash-Ticket, HomeATM, Moneta, PayPal, Stored Value Solutions and Ukash.

UATP is expanding its merchant network to include hotels and car rental vendors.

Locations

Headquarters: Washington, D.C.

Regional offices: Los Angeles, Miami, São Paulo, Geneva, Beijing, Singapore, Tokyo

Products

Products offered:

- UATP Corporate Card
- Travel Protection Plans
- UATP Settlement Services
- UATP University
- ATCAN
- ATCAN-ICH

External links

UATP Website [1]

Virgin Voucher

The Virgin Voucher

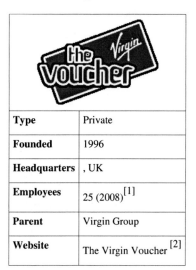

Type	Private
Founded	1996
Headquarters	, UK
Employees	25 (2008)[1]
Parent	Virgin Group
Website	The Virgin Voucher [2]

The **Virgin Voucher** is a monetary voucher available in four denominations of £5, £10, £20 and £50.

History

The Virgin Group launched the Virgin Voucher in 1995 and it became available from 1996[2] [3] . It can be purchased and used at over forty locations[4] .

References

[1] "Virgin Voucher" (http://www.virgin.com/Companies/TheVirginVoucher/TheVirginVoucher.aspx). Virgin Group. . Retrieved 2008-05-27.

[2] "Virgin launches vouchers offer" (http://www.accessmylibrary.com/coms2/summary_0286-6327887_ITM). Access Library. 1995-02-09. . Retrieved 2008-05-27.

[3] "The Virgn Voucher" (http://www.virgin.com/Companies/TheVirginVoucher/TheVirginVoucher.aspx). Virgin Group. . Retrieved 2008-05-27.

[4] "Where can I spend my voucher" (http://web.archive.org/web/20080523150118/http://www.thevirginvoucher.co.uk/info/where-can-i-spend-my-vouchers,28,AR.html). The Virgin Voucher. Archived from the original (http://www.thevirginvoucher.co.uk/info/where-can-i-spend-my-vouchers,28,AR.html) on 2008-05-23. . Retrieved 2008-05-27.

External links

- The Virgin Voucher UK (http://www.thevirginvoucher.co.uk)

Visa Buxx

Visa Buxx is a prepaid card intended for use by teenagers. The program was Visa's first prepaid card product and was launched in 2001. Visa Buxx is not a credit card; instead, it is a prepaid card that enables parents to repeatedly load the card online or over the phone and monitor spending, so parents can work with their teen to review their spending habits. The teen must be at least 13 years old to sign up.[1] [2]

Distributors

- PAYjr Visa Buxx[3]
- US Bank[4]
- Sandy Spring Bank[5]
- Wachovia[6]
- Navy Federal Credit Union[7]
- Prepaid cards issued inside a Visa Buxx BIN but not using the "Buxx" name are issued by MetaBank, for example the UPside Visa cards[8]

Fees

A Visa Buxx card is typically $9.95 but costs $19.95 for custom designed cards.

References

[1] "Be a parent to college student, not a human ATM" (http://www.chicagotribune.com/business/yourmoney/ sns-yourmoney-0808onthemoney,1,5358375.story?coll=chi-health-hed). Chicago Tribune. August 8, 2004. .

[2] Savage, Terry (August 29, 2002). "New Visa card gives parents teen control" (http://www.suntimes.com/business/savage/ 30964,cst-fin-terry-146.savagearticle). Chicago Sun-Times. .

[3] PAYjr Visa Buxx Prepaid Custom Card Designer (http://www.buxx.com/)

[4] Visa Buxx Prepaid Teen Card from U.S. Bank (http://usbank.visabuxx.com/)

[5] Sign Up for VIsa Buxx with one of these Card Providers (http://usa.visa.com/personal/cards/prepaid/buxx_sign_up.html)

[6] Wachovia Visa Buxx (https://www.visaprepaidprocessing.com/Wachovia/VisaBuxx/Pages/Home.asp)

[7] Navy Federal Visa Buxx (https://www.visaprepaidprocessing.com/NavyFederal/VisaBuxx/Pages/Home.aspx)

[8] http://www.upsidevisa.com

External links

- Visa Corporate Website (http://usa.visa.com/personal/cards/prepaid/visa_buxx.html)

Visa Cash

Visa Cash is a smart card electronic cash system owned by VISA.

Trialled in various locations Worldwide (including Leeds, UK in 1997), the system works via a 'chip' embedded in a bank card, and looks similar to the so-called 'Chip and PIN' cards issued, among other countries, in Europe.

The card is 'loaded' with cash via specialized ATMs, and the cash can later be 'spent' by inserting the card into the retailer's card-reader and pressing a button to confirm the amount. Neither PIN entry nor a signature is required, which makes for a speedy transaction for the card's owner.

Other competing cashless payment systems for micro-payments (small amounts) include Mondex.

A more successful smart card electronic cash system is the Octopus card system in Hong Kong.

External links

- VisaCash.org [1] a website dedicated to saving the history of the Visa Cash card program.

Voluntary Collective Licensing

VCL (Voluntary Collective Licensing) is the framework by which most Reproduction Rights Organisations (RROs) in the English speaking world operate. In voluntary collective licensing, the RRO issues licenses to copy protected material on behalf of those rights holders who have given it a mandate to act on their behalf. Since the right of reproduction is an exclusive right, it is natural to establish the collective management of reprographic reproduction rights on a voluntary basis.

RROs obtain licensing authority from mandates given by national rights holders, and the international repertoire through bilateral agreements with RROs in other countries. These bilateral agreements are based on the principle of reciprocal representation. Many RROs, especially in the Anglo-American (common law) tradition, base their activities generally on voluntary contracts.

In the United States, collective licensing through Copyright Clearance Center (CCC) is based solely on non-exclusive contracts. Authors and publishers determine which works are to be included in different licensing programmes. In some programmes they can set the prices individually for each work.

Even in the case of voluntary licensing, copyright legislation may include stipulations that govern the activities of the RRO. The Copyright Licensing Agency Limited (CLA) in the United Kingdom operates under the following provisions of the Copyright Act:

- CLA must be officially recognised as the national RRO
- In cases where licences are available, free use provisions such as in the field of education ('fair dealing') cease to apply
- A Government Minister oversees licensing schemes and licensing bodies, and may extend the scope of existing licensing schemes
- A Copyright Tribunal adjudicates in disputes between users and licensing bodies

In Japan, the Copyright Law provides for the author's right of reproduction with certain limitations on this right. The Special Law on Management Business of Copyright and Neighbouring Rights has been in effect as from October 2001. Under this law, the Japan Reprographic Rights Center (JRRC) was registered and designated as a management business operator in 2002.

In Colombia, Centro Colombiano de Derechos Reprográficos (CEDER) obtained governmental recognition as a collective management organisation in 2000, and the necessary authorisation for operation was granted in 2002 by the relevant government authority (Dirección National de Derecho de Autor). These allow CEDER to act as a reproduction rights organisation in Colombia.

There are countries where legislation clearly encourages rights holders to establish reproduction rights organisations. For instance, the Jamaica Copyright Act of 1993 allows for certain limitations and exceptions in the right of reproduction, in cases where voluntary licensing is not readily available. After the establishment of Jamaican Copyright Licensing Agency (JAMCOPY) such photocopying became subject to a licence.

Noank Media, a US corporation which provides access to audio, video, still image, and document files also uses Voluntary Collective Licensing. Berkman Center for Internet & Society also launched *Digital Media Exchange (DMX)*, a P2P content service, operated as a non-profit cooperative which uses the same concept. [1]

References

[1] Digital Media Project (http://cyber.law.harvard.edu/media/projects/dmx)

External links

- Description and white paper at EFF Website (http://www.eff.org/share/collective_lic_wp.php)
- "Building the Tools to Legalize P2P Video-Sharing" by JANKO ROETTGERS, NY Times: May 9, 2009 (http://mindfirst.com/?p=266)

Voucher

A **voucher** is a bond which is worth a certain monetary value and which may be spent only for specific reasons or on specific goods. Examples include (but are not limited to) housing, travel, and food vouchers. The term voucher is also a synonym for receipt and is often used to refer to receipts used as evidence of, for example, the declaration that a service has been performed or that an expenditure has been made.

The term is also commonly used for education vouchers, which are somewhat different.

In tourism

Vouchers are used in the tourism sector primarily as proof of a named customer's right to take a service at a specific time and place. Service providers collect them to return to the

This British Army Forces Voucher, issued to soldiers in Germany following World War II, may be used only in canteens or other specified transactions.

tour operator or travel agent that has sent that customer, to prove they have given the service. So, the life of a voucher is as below:

1. Customer receives vouchers from tour operator or travel agent for the services bought
2. Customer goes to vacation site and forwards the voucher to related provider and asks for the service to be given
3. Provider collects the vouchers
4. Provider sends collected vouchers to the agent or operator that sends customers from time to time, and asks for payment for those services
5. Uncollected vouchers do not deserve payment

This approach is most suitable for free individual tourist activities where pre-allocation for services are not necessary, feasible or applicable. It was customary before the information era when communication was limited and expensive, but now has been given quite a different role by B2C applications. When a reservation is made through the internet, customers are often provided a voucher through email or a web site that can be printed. Providers customarily require this voucher be presented prior to providing the service.

Accounts payable

A voucher is an accounting document representing an internal intent to make a payment to an external entity, such as a vendor or service provider. A voucher is produced usually after receiving a vendor invoice, after the invoice is successfully matched to a purchase order. A voucher will contain detailed information regarding the payee, the monetary amount of the payment, a description of the transaction, and more. In Accounts Payable systems, a process called a "payment run" is executed to generate payments corresponding to the unpaid vouchers. These payments can then be released or held at the discretion of an Accounts Payable supervisor or the company Controller. The term can also be used with reference to accounts receivable, where it is also a document representing intent to make an adjustment to an account, and for the general ledger where there is need to adjust accounts within that ledger; in that case it is referred to as a journal voucher....

Mobile phones

A voucher is a recharge number sold to a customer to recharge their SIM card with money and to extend the card's availability period. Vouchers are typically sold at retail outlets, such as phone stores run by the mobile operator or by distributors, grocery stores, and gas stations. Vouchers can also be purchased online at distributor sites such as PandaPhone [1] in China, or PrepaidWireless[2] in the US. These services email a voucher to the purchaser, typically in the form of a 16-digit PIN that is then entered into the phone. Online recharge sites may charge fees and require registration or a payment approval process before accepting Customer Not Present online payments. After payment acceptance, the purchaser is then sent a confirmation letter including the PIN code and recharge instructions.

Other options for online recharge of prepaid mobile phones Prepaid mobile phone do not require a voucher and may or may not charge fees. ezRecharge.in [3] providing instant online recharge services without vouchers. Whereas fastrecharge.com [4] is another online recharge services based on vouchers. The problem with vouchers is validity period and the possibility of thefting/generating the recharge code. Freecharge.in [5] has brought a unique model to this business and gives free discount vouchers of Indian retail stores along with every online recharge. Mobikwik [6] in India offers a "Recharge with SMS" feature where after depositing a balance into a Mobikwik account, purchasers call the company for activation. Purchasers can then recharge for any amount without fees by sending an SMS. Aryty [7] is also based in India and accepts online payments from around the world and from the US and Canada for recharge to mobile phones in India using SMS. Another online recharge service that does not require vouchers and does not charge fees is Prepaid.com[8]. Www.prepaid.com is based in the US and accepts payments such as Visa or MasterCard credit or debit cards to recharge mobile phones in Mexico. Prepaid.com does not require registration and recharges the recipients phone immediately.

Vouchers are the prevalent form of recharge for prepaid mobile phones in many countries such as Italy and Spain where well over 90% of consumers use vouchers, and the UK where over 60% buy vouchers at retail.[1] In other countries such as the United States, Ireland, and many Nordic countries, there is a growing trend of customers using Card Not Present recharge options such as online payments, or by using their mobile handsets to call the operator and recharge with a representative (CSR) or through their IVR (Interactive Voice Response) system. [1] A growing number of prepaid mobile operators such as Meteor[2] in Ireland and T-Mobile USA[3] are offering the option to send an SMS (text to pay), or use handset applications such as WAP or BREW technology.[1] in the notrthwren times

Internet

A voucher can also be used online in the form of an e-voucher. These types of vouchers can be entered when shopping online and the relevant vouchers value added to your order. It can take the form of any code. Many companies have opted to use voucher codes for the last few years but with a massive incline in use towards the end of 2008/early 2009. There are many internet websites devoted to promoting these deals and vouchers online, as well as Facebook groups offering items such as student discounts and 2-for-1 restaurant voucher deals.

There is a small number of sites that use a disreputable method of click to reveal method for dropping cookies on the consumer's computer, which has led to the introduction of guidelines for voucher use in Internet Marketing.

Most video game special editions come with a voucher for exclusive content in-game. For example, the Gran Turismo 5 Collector's Edition comes with a voucher for 5 exclusive DLC "Chrome Line" cars for the full game. Also, pre-ordering games at certain shops may get you vouchers to content only available if you pre-order at that store.

References

[1] Time to Top-Up the Prepaid User Experience: How an effective top-up strategy can improve operator performance metrics and accelerate mobile payments. Northstream White Paper, June 2009 http://northstream.se/wp-content/uploads/2009/06/Prepaid_Whitepaper_Jun_2009.pdf

[2] http://en.wikipedia.org/wiki/Meteor_%28mobile_network%29

[3] http://en.wikipedia.org/wiki/T-Mobile_USA

Voucher privatization

Voucher privatization is a privatization method where citizens are given or can inexpensively buy a book of vouchers that represent potential shares in any state-owned company. Voucher privatization has mainly been used in the early-to-mid 1990s in the transition economies of Central and Eastern Europe - countries such as Russia, Poland, Bulgaria, Slovenia and Czechoslovakia.

A way in which vouchers are used for partial privatization is the government requiring taxpayers to pay for a service whether they use it or not and allowing them to choose their service provider. Each

Privatization voucher used in Czechoslovakia

citizen is given vouchers allowing them to use that service (or a certain amount of it) at government expense. Examples include education vouchers and shadow tolling. A disadvantage of this type of system, relative to full privatization, is that there is no incentive for citizens to seek to reduce the cost of the service they use below the voucher amount.

External links

- David Ellerman, "*Lessons From East Europe's Voucher Privatization*" [1], The Capital Ownership Group (virtual think tank).

Warrant of payment

In financial transactions, a **warrant** is a written order from a first person that instructs a second person to pay a specified recipient a specific amount of money or goods at a specific time.[1] The warrant may or may not be negotiable and may authorize payment to the warrant holder on demand or after a maturity date. Governments may choose to pay wages and other accounts payable by issuing warrants instead of checks.

History

In the 18th century, **warrants** were used by the military to authorize payments to soldiers and suppliers. George Washington, for example, signed warrants that ordered quartermasters to deliver money or acquire supplies. [2] These warrants were used by quartermasters to issue vouchers to acquire food, supplies, munitions, clothing, transportation, etc. for the use of the American military and to maintain Washington's headquarters. Warrants could be redeemed by the army paymasters, but most often they were used like cash by the recipient. Warrants, like bills of exchange and vouchers, were often heavily discounted and depreciated in value. The fortunes of war could be traced through the discount rates on warrants, vouchers, and Continental dollars.

In the early days of the colony at Sydney Cove in Australia, the merchant Robert Campbell was one of the first merchants to attempt to trade, but lacked sufficient currency. When he first sailed into Sydney aboard his company's ship the *Hunter* in 1798,[3] Campbell was forced to sell his first consignment of goods to a syndicate of military officers in return for *Paymaster's Bills* drawn on London, which were like warrants.[4]

The term warrant may continue to be used broadly as an order to pay or an order to deliver goods.

Modern warrants

Sample Registered Warrant

In government finance, a **warrant** is an order to pay that instructs a federal, state, or county government treasurer to pay the warrant holder on demand or after a maturity date. Such warrants look like checks and clear through the banking system like checks, but are not drawn against cleared funds in a checking account (demand deposit account). Instead they may be drawn against "available funds" or "out of fund 0027" so that the issuer can collect interest on the float or delay redemption. If the warrant is conditional on funds being available, the warrant is not a negotiable debt instrument. In the U.S., warrants are issued by government entities such as the military and state and county governments. Warrants are issued for payroll to individual employees, accounts payable to vendors, to local governments, to taxpayers receiving tax refunds, to recipients of unemployment benefits, and to owners of unclaimed money. A warrant differs from a check in that the warrant is not drawn on a checking account, is not necessarily payable on demand, and may not be negotiable.[5] [6]

Warrants deposited in a bank are routed (based on the MICR routing number) to a collecting bank which processes them as collection items like maturing treasury bills and presents the warrants to the government entity's treasury department for payment to the bank each business day.

Regular warrants are redeemable by the government treasurer after they are issued. "Registered Warrants" bear interest and need not be redeemed by the treasurer until the warrant maturity date.[7] If warrants cannot be immediately redeemed by the issuing entity, the collecting bank may accept the warrants as short term debt instruments and collect interest when redeemed in accordance with a prior agreement. The collecting bank may refuse to accept a warrant issue, in which case other banks may also refuse to accept them. [8]

"The warrants of a municipal corporation are not negotiable instruments. They do not constitute a new debt, or evidence of a new debt, but are only the prescribed means devised by law for drawing money from the treasury."[9]

The U.S. Securities and Exchange Commission said on July 9, 2009 that California's Registered Warrants are "securities" under federal securities law and will be regulated as municipal securities by the Municipal Securities Rulemaking Board.[10] Under these regulations anybody who profits by buying and reselling warrants must be registered as a municipal securities broker-dealer.[11]

Although Registered Warrants are evidence of a municipality's obligation to pay, because they demonstrate an intent to disburse funds when those funds become available, the US Supreme Court has ruled that a holder of a valid warrant cannot obtain a writ of mandamus for specific performance of the obligation to pay, enforced against a treasurer or other employee of the municipality.[12]

Warrants can be replaced with substitute checks under the Check 21 Act.[13] Such substitute checks show the MICR routing numbers that identify them as warrants.

In the United Kingdom

In the UK, warrants are issued as payment by the *NS&I* when a *Premium Bond* is chosen.

The difference between a warrant and a cheque is that a cheque usually places no explicit time frame on when the amount is to be paid.

References

[1] Oxford English Dictionary, 1971.

[2] Revolutionary War Warrant Books of George Washington, 1775-1776 (http://memory.loc.gov/ammem/gwhtml/gwseries5.html)

[3] Steven, Margaret (2006). "Campbell, Robert senior (1769 - 1846)" (http://adbonline.anu.edu.au/biogs/A010190b.htm). Australian Dictionary of Biography, ANU. . Retrieved 7 June 2010.

[4] Binney, Keith Robert (2005). "The Merchants" (http://books.google.com.au/books?id=0xYF0v8doEgC). *Horsemen of the first frontier (1788-1900) and the Serpent's legacy*. Volcanic Productions. pp. 72. ISBN 0-646-44865-X. . Retrieved 2010-06-28.

[5] "Check" (http://a-z-dictionaries.com/glossaries/Accounting_Glossary.html#check). *Glossary of Accounting terms*. A-Z-Dictionaries.com. 2005. . Retrieved 26 May 2009. See also "Warrant"

[6] "Warrant" (http://a-z-dictionaries.com/glossaries/Accounting_Glossary.html#warrant). *Glossary of Accounting terms*. A-Z-Dictionaries.com. 2005. . Retrieved 26 May 2009. See also "Check"

[7] Frequently Asked Questions about Registered Warrants (http://www.sco.ca.gov/5935.html)

[8] California IOU holders (http://www.reuters.com/article/rbssBanks/idUSN0733020720090707)

[9] First National Bank v. Cook, 43 Neb. 318, 61 N.W. Rep. 693. 12 B.L.J. 151.

[10] SEC press release (http://www.sec.gov/news/press/2009/2009-154.htm)

[11] California IOUs considered securities SEC says (http://www.marketwatch.com/story/story/print?guid=EB33BA40-5890-437C-9993-458D5B54B339)

[12] Raton Waterworks Co. v. Raton, 174 US 360.

[13] Substitute Checks - Frequently Asked Questions - Section B.8 (http://www.eccho.org/check21_aids_faq.php)

External links

- California law on Registered Warrants (http://caselaw.lp.findlaw.com/cacodes/gov/17270-17280.2.html)
- Country regulations for Registered Warrants (http://www.clallam.net/Board/assets/applets/522_Registered_Warrants.pdf)
- Frequently Asked Questions about Registered Warrants (IOUs) (http://www.sco.ca.gov/5935.html)
- Responses to questions from California banks (http://www.calbankers.com/pdf/responses to registered warrants cba bank questions.pdf)

WePay

WePay, Inc.

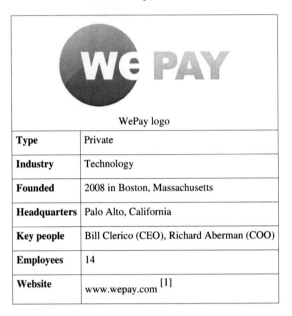

WePay logo

Type	Private
Industry	Technology
Founded	2008 in Boston, Massachusetts
Headquarters	Palo Alto, California
Key people	Bill Clerico (CEO), Richard Aberman (COO)
Employees	14
Website	www.wepay.com [1]

WePay is an online payment service for groups and organizations in the United States. The company creates lightweight, shareable accounts -insured by the Federal Deposit Insurance Corporation with functionality that permits payments into and out of those accounts.[1] [2] Founded in 2008 in Boston, WePay is based in Palo Alto, California.

The company profits through commissions, where it receives either 50 cents or 3.5% of the total transaction depending on whether the payment was made with a credit card or bank account.

The company has a partnership with 1000Memories, an online memories website, in which WePay gives free accounts to 1000Memories users. This allows visitors to donate money in the names of the deceased using WePay's service.

History

The company was founded by Rich Aberman and Bill Clerico in 2008 in Boston, Massachusetts, and is based in Palo Alto, California.[3] The inspiration for WePay originated when Aberman found he had difficulty fundraising for his brother's bachelor party. He had to amass $4,200 from 14 men spread across the United States to pay bottle service at a club, rent for a beach house in Florida, and food such as burgers and chips. Little by little, he was able to collect the needed money after a few weeks of nagging. Aberman believed that there was a more efficient way of accomplishing this.[4] After he studied PayPal's weaknesses, he invited Clerico to join him in the establishing WePay.[5] To devote his energy to WePay, Clerico stopped working at an investment banking job and Aberman postponed a scholarship to law school at New York University.[4]

Because Aberman and Clerico did not get into the Techstars Boston program, and because they were accepted by Y Combinator in California, they relocated to California. On the West Coast, they have received monetary support from Max Levchin, a cofounder of PayPal, and Ron Conway, an angel investor.[3] The company received $1.65 million from August Capital during initial fundraising efforts; by August 2010, it received an additional $7.5 million from Highland Capital Partners and August Capital.[6] By December 2010, WePay had raised $9 million in funding.[3] Other investors include Steve Chen, a cofounder of YouTube, and Eric Dunn, a former CTO of Intuit.[4]

Profits

WePay earns a profit through commissions. Contingent on if users are using their credit cards or bank accounts, the company will receive "either a flat 50 cents or 3.5% of the total".[4] WePay allows group leaders to see how much money fellow members are paying so that the late paying can be reminded through email.[4]

Partnership and competitors

In August 2010, WePay partnered with 1000Memories, a website that allows users to craft online memories for the deceased. The partnership gives users of 1000Memories the opportunity to create free WePay accounts, where visitors can use a credit card or bank card to donate in the names of the deceased.[7]

WePay's competitors include PayPal[6] and Authorize.Net. According to CNNMoney.com, PayPal could pose trouble for WePay. Were the "behemoth" PayPal, which has 85 million active users, to alter its current "system for multi-party transactions", WePay would be in danger.[4] Dave McClure, a former employee of PayPal and the founder of 500Startups which provides financial support to WePay, stated that he did not believe WePay was in trouble. McClure said that PayPal does not "mov[e] as fast as startups".[4]

References

[1] Schultz, Jennifer Saranow (2010-06-28). "A New Way to Get Money for Group Events" (http://www.webcitation.org/5vcVoT4Sm). *The New York Times*. Archived from the original (http://bucks.blogs.nytimes.com/2010/06/28/a-new-way-to-get-money-for-group-events/) on 2011-01-09. . Retrieved 2011-01-06.

[2] McMahan, Ty (2010-08-13). "From Boston College Mascot To Venture-Backed CEO" (http://www.webcitation.org/5vcfxxwHW). *Wall Street Journal*. Archived from the original (http://blogs.wsj.com/venturecapital/2010/08/13/from-boston-college-mascot-to-venture-backed-ceo/) on 2011-01-09. . Retrieved 2011-01-06.

[3] Kirsner, Scott (2010-12-20). "Born in Boston, growing in Calif." (http://www.webcitation.org/5vcWjqmI3). *Boston Globe*. Archived from the original (http://www.boston.com/business/technology/articles/2010/12/20/born_in_boston_growing_in_calif/) on 2011-01-09. . Retrieved 2011-01-09.

[4] Alsever, Jennifer (2010-10-12). "WePay is the anti-PayPal" (http://www.webcitation.org/5vca4TWN7). CNNMoney.com. Archived from the original (http://money.cnn.com/2010/10/12/technology/wepay/index.htm) on 2011-01-09. . Retrieved 2011-01-09.

[5] "WePay set out to kill PayPal" (http://www.webcitation.org/5vcZ2XzUl). *OneIndia*. 2010-10-16. Archived from the original (http://news.oneindia.in/2010/10/16/paypal-killer-wepay-new-online-paymenent-service.html) on 2011-01-09. . Retrieved 2011-01-09.

[6] Barbierri, Cody (2010-08-12). ""Group" paying service WePay gets $7.5M boost" (http://www.webcitation.org/5vcXCu1Hu). *VentureBeat* (Reuters). Archived from the original (http://www.reuters.com/article/idUS186110615820100813) on 2011-01-09. . Retrieved 2011-01-09.

[7] Barbierri, Cody (2010-08-10). "Raise Money in Memory of a Loved One With 1000Memories" (http://www.webcitation.org/5vcXzSlaS). *The New York Times*. Archived from the original (http://www.nytimes.com/external/venturebeat/2010/08/10/10venturebeat-raise-money-in-memory-of-a-loved-one-with-10-89246.html?dbk) on 2011-01-09. . Retrieved 2011-01-09.

External links

- Official website (http://www.wepay.com/)

White Label ABMs in Canada

White Label ABMs in Canada provide alternative source of cash dispensing vis-à-vis traditional automatic banking machines (ABMs) from banks.

Background

In Canada, the major financial institutions have their own branded ABMs located throughout the country. These ABMs prominently display the logo of the banks. A "white label" or "no name" ABM, which are usually located in non-traditional places, display no major bank labels on the actual ABM. Before 1997, only banks and other deposit taking financial institutions were allowed to be part of the Interac network. After 1997, independent operators were allowed to operate ABMs, not owned by major financial institutions.

In 2006, a little more than half of the 51,000 ABMs in operation in Canada were "white label".

White label fees

Customers usually pay an added fee to use these ABMs, which can be split between the private provider and the owner of the property hosting the machine.

According to the Financial Consumer Agency of Canada (FCAC), fees for using a "white-label" ATM can add up to over $6.00 per transaction.[1] The same agency states that private (white-label) operators are "not required to adhere to a minimum or maximum limit", meaning that the fee amount is up to the operator.[2] The operator is obliged, however, to disclose the fee to be charged and give the consumer the option of cancelling the transaction.[1]

CIBC has been criticized for creating a wholly owned subsidiary white label company, "Ready Cash". While many CIBC customers have free access to transactions with official CIBC accounts, as Ready Cash is not a CIBC bank, they are charged twice, once by Ready Cash and once by CIBC.[1]

Local small establishment retailers such as gas stations, bars/pubs, & restaurants are common for putting in the private White Label ATM's to receive a fee for each transaction made at the ATM. Most white-label ATM's charge a minimum C$1.50 for the use of the machine with approximately 50% of that going to the retailer. The C$1.50 is above and beyond what the cardholders financial institution may charge.

Notification of Fees

A warning message will appear at some point prior to accepting to withdraw funds, advising the cardholder what the cost of the service is. There is always an opt out function to cancel the transaction and avoid paying the fees.

Private operators

Some of the providers in Canada include:

- Money Plus Express/ Money Plus Xpress of Toronto - 2011 - http://www.moneyplusgrp.com
- ATM Canada Inc. - Since 1997 - http://www.atmcanadainc.com
- Flex-Touch Canada Inc. - International Sales, Services, Leasing, Processing, Wireless Solutions - http://www.flextouch.ca -
- ATM Systems Ltd. of Toronto - 2000 http://www.atm4Canada.com
- Cash N Go Ltd of Edmonton AB & Hamilton ON - 1998 http://www.cashngo.com
- Direct Cash ATM of Calgary AB - 1998
- Ezee ATM of Toronto ON
- Frisco-Bay ATMs of Montreal QC is unit of Frisco-Bay Industries Ltd of Montreal - 1997 http://www.friscoatms.com"

- Inkas Group of Toronto ON - 1998 http://www.inkas.ca
- King Cash Corp. of Edmonton AB - 2001 http://www.kingcash.ca
- Triton Canada Ltd of Calgary AB - 1997
- Laser Cash owned by Threshold Financial of Mississauga ON http://www.threshold-fti.com
- ClearCard is a National service provider of ATMs http://www.clearcard.ca
- Canada Cash ATM's Ltd. in Atlantic Canada
- Canada Card Processing - http://www.canadacardprocessing.com/related-products/atm-machine-services/

References

[1] ATM fees (http://www.cbc.ca/marketplace/pre-2007/files/money/atm/), CBC Marketplace

Wire transfer

Wire transfer or **credit transfer** is a method of Electronic funds transfer from one person or institution (entity) to another. A wire transfer can be made from one bank account to another bank account or through a transfer of cash at a cash office. Wire transfer systems are intended to provide more individualized transactions than bulk payment systems such as ACH and Check21.

Different wire transfer systems and operators provide a variety of options relative to the immediacy and finality of settlement and the cost, value, and volume of transactions. Central bank wire transfer systems, such as the Federal Reserve's FedWire system in the United States are more likely to be Real time gross settlement (**RTGS**) systems. RTGS systems provide the quickest availability of funds because they provide immediate "real-time" and final "irrevocable" settlement by posting the gross (complete) entry against electronic accounts of the wire transfer system operator. Other systems such as CHIPS provide net settlement on a periodic basis. More immediate settlement systems tend to process higher monetary value time-critical transactions, have higher transaction costs, and a smaller volume of payments. Currency transaction risk (because of market fluctuations) may be reduced (in part) by immediacy of settlement.

Wire transfer is not the only kind of electronic transfer of funds. Most people are more likely to see EFTS or ACH transfers than wire transfers. See "Other Electronic Transfers" below.

Process

Bank wire transfers are often the most expedient method for transferring funds between bank accounts. A bank wire transfer is effected as follows:

1. The entity wishing to do a transfer approaches a bank and gives the bank the order to transfer a certain amount of money. IBAN and BIC codes are given as well so the bank knows where the money needs to be sent.
2. The sending bank transmits a message, via a secure system (such as SWIFT or Fedwire), to the receiving bank, requesting that it effect payment according to the instructions given.
3. The message also includes settlement instructions. The actual transfer is not instantaneous: funds may take several hours or even days to move from the sender's account to the receiver's account.
4. Either the banks involved must hold a reciprocal account with each other, or the payment must be sent to a bank with such an account, a correspondent bank, for further benefit to the ultimate recipient.

Banks collect payment for the service from the sender as well as from the recipient. The sending bank typically collects a fee separate from the funds being transferred, while the receiving bank and intermediate banks through which the transfer travels deduct fees from the money being transferred so that the recipient receives less than what the sender sent.

Regulation and price

In 2002, the European Commission relegated the regulation of the fees that a bank may charge for payments in euros between European Union member countries down to the domestic level,[1] resulting in very low or no fees for electronic transfers within the Eurozone. Wire transfers between the Eurozone and external areas can be expensive.

In 2005, Iceland, Liechtenstein, and Norway joined the EU regulation on electronic transfers. However, this regulation is intended to be superseded by the Single Euro Payments Area (SEPA), consisting of 32 European countries.

In 2009 EC published a new regulation (EC) No 924/2009 [2] on cross-border payments in the Community and repealing Regulation (EC) No 2560/2001 (the text of which is no longer available). The new regulation (EC) No 924/2009 Article 1 (q.v., Ref.4) states that an IBAN/BIC transfer within SEPA must not cost more than a national transfer, no matter which currency is used. But receiving bank can charge for exchanging to local currency. However, according to Article 7 any current arrangements (made between payment services before November 1, 2009) can be honored up to November 1, 2012.

In the United States wire transfers are costly and seldom if ever used by consumers. As an example of the cost, Bank Of America as of February 2010 charged $25 to send a wire and $12 to receive one within the US. For international transfer, it charged $35–$45 outgoing, $16 incoming. However, fees may vary from bank to bank.

In the United States, domestic wire transfers are governed by Federal Regulation J[3] and by Article 4A of the Uniform Commercial Code.[4]

Security

Bank-to-bank wire transfer is considered the safest international payment method. Each account holder must have a proven identity. Chargeback is unlikely, although wires can be recalled. Information contained in wires is transmitted securely through encrypted communications methods. The price of bank wire transfers varies greatly, depending on the bank and its location; in some countries, the fee associated with the service can be costly.

Wire transfers done through cash offices are essentially anonymous and are designed for transfer between persons who trust each other. It is unsafe to send money by wire to an unknown person to collect at a cash office: the receiver of the money may, after collecting it, simply disappear. This scam has been used often, especially in the so-called *419 scam.*

International transfers involving the United States are subject to monitoring by the Office of Foreign Assets Control (OFAC), which monitors information provided in the text of the wire to ascertain whether money is being transferred to terrorist organizations or countries or entities under sanction by the United States government. If a financial institution suspects that funds are being sent from or to one of these entities, it must block the transfer and freeze the funds.[5]

SWIFT or IBAN wire transfers are not completely free of vulnerabilities. Every intermediate bank that handles a wire transaction can take a fee directly out of the wire payload (the assets being transferred) without the account holders knowledge or consent. In many places, there is no legislation or technical means to protect customers from this practice. If bank S is the sending bank (or brokerage), and bank R is the receiving bank (or brokerage), and banks I1, I2, and I3 are intermediary banks, the client may only have a contract with bank S and/or R, but banks I1, I2, and I3 can (and often do) take money from the wire without any direct arrangement with the client. Clients are sometimes taken by surprise when less money arrives at bank R. Contrast this with cheques, the amount transferred is guaranteed in full, and fees (if there are any) can be charged only at endpoint banks.,[6] Europe offers some partial protection from this practice by prohibiting European intermediate banks from taking a fee out of the amount being transferred, even for transatlantic transfers. However, it's still common practice for a European brokerage firm to state that they charge no transfer fee, and then contract their bank to take an unpublished fee from the amount transferred as a means to compensate their bank with their clients assets. E.g. CMC Markets implements this policy in partnership with Natwest.

European privacy law may be breached by some USA operators such as SWIFT, so EU users are sometimes required by their service provider to make an explicit declaration that seeks to circumvent EU privacy regulations.

Methods

Currency transaction risk

When a corporation or person engages in a transfer of currency that will occur in the future, they are at risk of market fluctuations. Each currency pair can fluctuate from 1 - 3 pennies daily. For every $100,000 USD contract, each penny represents $1000 of risk on average. Therefore a $100,000 purchase of goods overseas could cause the contract to fluctuate $1000 − $3000 per day due to the fluctuation of the market. Importers and exporters hire or outsource a currency planner to evaluate the risk of the future transaction and to suggest currency hedge options that best suit the cash flow position of the company.

Planning currency transfers

When establishing a currency plan, it is important to understand the average fluctuation of the currency pair transferring to and from within the time frame of the contract. If the transfer is to occur in 3 months from now, it is good to understand what the average monthly fluctuation is. After which, it is advised to begin taking steps to hedge the transfer to prevent loss. A good currency hedge is designed to reduce risk and still maximize upside potential of the currency fluctuation.

Import / export / manufacturing and foreign currency transfers

Importing goods or products from another country sometimes require the purchase of the goods to be in the currency of the country importing from. Corporations may also pay in their currency and allow the exporter to convert the currency. Negotiations can be made between importers and exporters on which currency will be used. When negotiating paying in another currency, discounts can be negotiated for the party who has to convert the currency. These discounts can reach up to 5% of the contract price for taking on the risk associated with a future contract and the work associated with performing the physical transaction. A currency planner is often hired to assess risk of the contract and to suggest a forex hedge.

Manufacturers who sell direct to buyers in other countries are also subject to the same negotiations and discounts if they are savvy about how the market works. Larger corporations typically hire a currency planner, while smaller corporations outsource individual contracts to companies who specialize in planning currency transactions.

Common terms relating to currency hedging

Spot - A spot transaction is an immediate transfer. It will sometimes take up to a day or two using a conventional banking system. Modern technology and a good discount broker allows us to make spot contracts that are effective immediately. This type of trade represents a "direct exchange" between currencies, has the shortest time frame, involves cash rather than contract, and interest is not included in the agreed-upon transaction. If speed is a priority and you need to transfer money fast at the best exchange rates, spot contracts is the right option. Once you verbally or online agree a rate with your chosen currency specialist, your currency can be transferred as soon as you have paid for the contract.[7]

Forward - A forward contract is a deal that enables a client to buy foreign currency based on current market rates, for a delivery at a pre-determined date in the future (up to one year ahead). The transaction occurs on that date, regardless of what the market rates are then. The duration of the trade can be one day, one week, one month or even one year or more. Usually the rate is decided by both parties, and a forward contract is a negotiated agreement between the two parties.

Forward contract can take form of part or full delivery of their currency at an earlier date (Drawdown), or if business circumstances dictate, defer payment and delivery of the currency (Rollover) to a later date. A deposit will be required for each forward deal which acts as security and is deducted from part or full settlement of the trade.[7]

Future - A future contract is an exchange traded forward contract with standard contract sizes and maturity dates. Futures are standardized and are usually traded on an exchange created specifically for this purpose. Futures contracts are usually inclusive of any interest amount and are typically 3 months in length.

Swap - A swap is the most common type of a forward contract. In a swap, two parties exchange currencies for a certain length of time and agree to reverse the transaction at an agreed upon date. Swaps are not traded on exchanges and are not standardized contracts.

Option - A foreign exchange option (also known as an FxOption) is a derivative where the owner has the right but not the obligation to exchange money denominated in one currency into another currency at an agreed upon rate on a specified date. FxOptions are the deepest most liquid market for options of any kind in the world. FxOptions are also looked at as insurance, where if the purchaser of the option does not like the exchange rate at the time before the option comes due, they can essentially forfeit their initial investment into the option.

FX global transfer

The key to low cost is the exchange rate offered. When one transfers funds, one is selling one currency and buying another. Currency dealers mark up the exchange rate by adding a spread: this is the difference between the price at which one can sell one's primary currency and what ones has to pay to buy the delivery currency.

Retail money transfers

One of the largest companies that offer wire transfer is Western Union, which allows individuals to transfer or receive money without an account with Western Union or any financial institution.[8] Concern and controversy about Western Union transfers have increased in recent years, because of the increased monitoring of money-laundering transactions, as well as concern about terrorist groups using the service, particularly in the wake of the September 11, 2001 attacks. Although Western Union keeps information about senders and receivers, some transactions can be done essentially anonymously, for the receiver is not always required to show identification.[8]

Another option for consumers and businesses transferring money internationally is to use specialised brokerage houses for their international money transfer needs.[9] Many of these specialised brokerage houses can transfer money at better exchange rates compared to banks, thus saving up to 4%.[9] These providers can offer a range of currency exchange products like Spot Contracts, Forward Contracts and Regular payments.[10]

International

Most international transfers are executed through SWIFT, a co-operative society founded in 1974 by seven international banks, which operate a global network to facilitate the transfer of financial messages. Using these messages, banks can exchange data for the transfer of funds between financial institutions. SWIFT's headquarters are in La Hulpe, on the outskirts of Brussels, Belgium. The society also acts as a United Nations–sanctioned international standards body for the creation and maintenance of financial-messaging standards. See SWIFT Standards.

Each financial institution is assigned an ISO 9362 code, also called a *Bank Identifier Code* (*BIC*) or *SWIFT Code*. These codes are generally eight characters long.[11] For example: Deutsche Bank is an international bank with its head office in Frankfurt, Germany, the SWIFT Code for which is *DEUTDEFF*:

- *DEUT* identifies Deutsche Bank.
- *DE* is the country code for Germany.

- *FF* is the code for Frankfurt.

Using an extended code of 11 digits (if the receiving bank has assigned extended codes to branches or to processing areas) allows the payment to be directed to a specific office. For example: DEUTDEFF500 would direct the payment to an office of Deutsche Bank in Bad Homburg.

European banks making transfers within the European Union also use the International Bank Account Number, or IBAN.

United States of America

Banks in the United States use SWIFT to send messages to notify banks in other countries that a payment has been made. Banks use the CHIPS or Fedwire system to actually effect the payment.

Domestic bank-to-bank transfers are conducted through the Fedwire system, which uses the Federal Reserve System and its assignment of routing transit number, which uniquely identify each bank.

Other electronic transfers

There are forms of electronic transfer that are distinct from wire transfer. Electronic funds transfer system (EFTS) is one such system. This is the system one uses when one gives one's bank account number and routing information to someone one owes money and that party transfers the money from one's account. It is also the system used in some payments made via a bank's online bill payment service. EFTS transfers differ from wire transfers in important legal ways. An EFTS payment is essentially an electronic personal check, whereas a wire transfer is more like an electronic cashier's check.

In the United States, such EFTS transfers are often called "ACH transfers," because they take place through Automated Clearing House.

One important way ACH transfers differ from wire transfer is that the recipient can initiate it. There are of course restrictions, but this is the way people often set up automatic bill payment with utility companies, for example.

References

[1] Regulation (EC) No. 2560/2001 (http://eur-lex.europa.eu/LexUriServ/LexUriServ.do?uri=OJ:L:2001:344:0013:0016:EN:PDF). European Parliament and the Council of the European Union

[2] Regulation (EC) No 924/2009 (http://eur-lex.europa.eu/LexUriServ/LexUriServ.do?uri=OJ:L:2009:266:0011:0018:en:PDF).

[3] Regulation J - Check Collection and Funds Transfer (http://www.bankersonline.com/regs/210/210.html). BankersOnline.com

[4] Section 4A of Universal Commercial Code (http://www.law.cornell.edu/ucc/4A/overview.html). Legal Information Institute.

[5] OFAC facts (http://ofacscout.gus.net/OFACFacts.htm)

[6] "Correspondent Bank Fees" (http://www.openoffshorebankaccountsfornonresidents.com/Wire_transfer_correspondent_fees.htm). Openoffshorebankaccountsfornonresidents.com. . Retrieved 2010-07-01.

[7] "Foreign Exchange contract definitions" (http://www.fxcompared.com/Content/FAQs.php). Fxcompared.com. .

[8] "Western Union Money Transfer Options" (http://www.westernunion.com/info/osMoneyTransferOptions.asp). Westernunion.com. . Retrieved 2010-07-01.

[9] "Money Transfer South Africa" (http://www.moneytransfersouthafrica.org/starting-information/). MoneyTransferSouthAfrica.org. . Retrieved 2011-01-01.

[10] "Currency Specialists" (http://www.franceforex.com/currency-specialists-â-rapidly-growing-participants-in-the-foreign-exchange-industry-fxcompared-com-â-âgolden-pagesâ-of-the-industry/). franceforex.com. . Retrieved 2011-01-01.

[11] http://www.swift.com/biconline/index.cfm?fuseaction=display_aboutbic

External links

- IBAN (http://www.ecbs.org/iban.htm)

Wirecard

Wirecard AG

	wirecard
Type	Aktiengesellschaft
Traded as	FWB: WDI [1]
Industry	Financial services, technology
Founded	1999
Headquarters	Grasbrunn, Germany
Key people	Markus Braun (CEO), Wulf Matthias (Chairman of the supervisory board)
Products	Payment processing, electronic payment services, banking, card issuance, credit checking
Revenue	€271.6 million (2010)[1]
Operating income	€67.4 million (2010)[1]
Profit	€54.0 million (2010)[1]
Total assets	€549.9 million (end 2010)[1]
Total equity	€289.8 million (end 2010)[1]
Employees	500 (end 2010)[1]
Website	www.wirecard.com [3]

Wirecard AG is a global financial services and technology company headquartered in Grasbrunn, Munich, Germany. The company provides payment processing, card issuing and risk management services to more than 10.000 corporate customers worldwide. Its Internet payment service competes with PayPal and Western Union. Wirecard Bank AG operates under a German Banking License and is a Principal Member of VISA, MasterCard and JCB. Wirecard AG is listed on the Frankfurt Securities Exchange.

Financial information

According to preliminary figures, Group sales revenues of the Wirecard AG were up by 16 percent, from 196.8 million euros in the previous year to 228.3 million euros in 2009. Earnings before interest, taxes, depreciation and amortization (EBITDA) increased by 16 percent, from 52.4 million euros to 60.8 million euros. Earnings before interest and taxes (EBIT) were up by 15.7 percent, from 49.0 million euros to 56.7million euros.[2].

Wirecard AG is listed on the TecDAX [3] index of Deutsche Börse since September 18, 2006 and now ranks among the 30 largest German technology companies below the DAX.

Products and services

In November 2006, Wirecard launched an Internet payment service called "Wirecard" [6]. By registering online the consumer opens an account at Wirecard Bank which he can load by cash, cards, direct debit, wire transfer or various local payment schemes. The service includes a free virtual prepaid MasterCard for consumers that can be used to pay at millions of MasterCard locations worldwide. In addition to standard MasterCard products, the Wirecard system also enables users to send each other money in real-time. An optional physical MasterCard enables users to pay at 24.7 million MasterCard brick&mortar acceptance points and to withdraw cash at nearly 1 million ATMs worldwide.

Wirecard AG's electronic payment processing and risk management platform supports more than 85 local and international payment and fraud protection schemes. Wirecard AG is a member of ADP CardClear and IATA.

Wirecard's Supplier and Commission Payments (SCP) product enables automated global settlement of payments to suppliers and sales agents. The service is based on an automated issuing of "virtual" credit cards by Wirecard Bank AG. Supplier or commission payouts to be transferred internationally (e.g. payment of intermediary commissions by hotels to travel agencies) can be processed and settled by electronic dispatch of single- and restricted-use "virtual" credit card numbers.

Wirecard Bank AG provides card acquiring services to corporate clients for VISA, MasterCard and JCB. Various types of credit and debit cards are issued for private and corporate customers.

The largest german virtual shopping mall Yatego and Wirecard concluded a contract to improve the credit card acceptance in 2009.[4]

Bank status

Since January 1, 2006 Wirecard Bank AG [8] is part of the Wirecard Group. Wirecard Bank holds a full banking license [9] and is a Principal Member of VISA, MasterCard and JCB. The bank's deposits are secured by the Deposit Protection Fund [10] of the Association of German Banks (Einlagensicherungsfonds deutscher Banken e.V).

Wirecard Bank operates a virtual branch [11] inside the 3-D virtual world Second Life.

Wirecard Bank has purchased a license from Mindark, the operators of the Entropia Universe virtual world, to operate a bank within the Entropia Universe, but has as of April 2009 not yet opened their virtual bank.

References

[1] "Annual Report 2010" (http://irpages2.equitystory.com/download/companies/wirecard/Annual Reports/ DE0007472060-JA-2010-EQ-E-00.pdf). Wirecard. . Retrieved 22 April 2011.

[2] "Wirecard AG / Annual Report 2007" (http://ir.wirecard.com/dl/dl.ssp?id=273646). .

[3] "Deutsche Börse / Official listing of TecDAX member companies" (http://deutsche-boerse.com/dbag/dispatch/en/isg/gdb_navigation/ home?active=constituents&module=InConstituents_Index&wp=DE0007203275&wplist=DE0007203275&foldertype=_Index& wpbpl=ETR). .

[4] "Yatego enters into Framework Agreement with Wirecard" (http://www.wirecard.com/press/press-releases/press-reports-singleview/ article/yatego-enter.html). .

External links

- Official website (http://http://www.wirecard.com)

WorldPay

WorldPay

WorldPay	
Type	Private
Industry	Electronic Payment Services
Founded	1989 (as Streamline)
Services	Payment Services
Parent	Consortium of Advent International and Bain Capital 80.01% The Royal Bank of Scotland Group 19.99%
Website	www.worldpay.com [1]

WorldPay (formerly **RBS WorldPay**) is a payment processing company. It provides payment services for mail order and internet retailers, as well as point of sale transactions. Customers are a mix of multinational, multichannel retailers, with the majority being small business merchants in the UK. WorldPay started as an electronic payment provider called Streamline in 1989 but has extended into Mail Order/Telephone Order, "unattended" payments and handling secure payments over the internet through merger and acquisition of several other companies.[1]

WorldPay first provided internet payment services in 1994, making it one of the first providers of such services in the world. In 2009 it was combined with seven leading retail payment solutions brands: Streamline, Streamline International, PaymentTrust, Bibit, RiskGuardian and RBSLynk. WorldPay is the largest merchant acquirer in Europe and one of the largest globally, operating in more than 40 countries, 120 transaction currencies and 14 settlement currencies. In 2007, WorldPay processed 4.4 billion transactions worldwide.[2]

On 3 November 2009 it was announced that RBS WorldPay had to be sold by the RBS Group despite being a profitable business, as this was part of the terms negotiated to join the UK Government's asset protection scheme. The company was said to have had around 40 interested buyers and the sale was planned to be completed by the end of April 2010.[3] On 6 August 2010, Advent International and Bain Capital agreed to acquire WorldPay for £2.025bn including a £200m contingent consideration. The RBS group will retain a 19.99% stake in the newly-independent business.[4]

The sale completed on 1 December 2010. RBS WorldPay was renamed WorldPay as part of the deal.[5]

References

[1] WorldPay - About Us (http://www.worldpay.com/about_us/index.php?page=history&c=WW)

[2] WorldPay - Media Centre (http://www.worldpay.com/media/index.php?page=archive&sub=rbs&c=WW)

[3] RBS starts auction for Williams & Glyn's bank (http://business.timesonline.co.uk/tol/business/industry_sectors/banking_and_finance/article7050315.ece) Marcus Leroux. The Times. 4 March 2010

[4] RBS Announces WorldPay Sale (http://www.pehub.com/79205/rbs-announces-worldpay-sale/) PEHub. August 2010

[5] WorldPay (1 December 2010). "RBS completes sale of RBS WorldPay" (http://www.worldpay.com/media/index.php?page=archive&sub=rbs-complete-sale-of-rbsworldpay&c=UK). . Retrieved 25 January 2011.

External links

- worldpay.com (http://www.worldpay.com/)

XIPWIRE

XIPWIRE Inc.

Founded	Philadelphia USA (2009)
Founder	Sharif Alexandre
Headquarters	Philadelphia USA
Area served	USA
Website	www.xipwire.com [1]
Alexa rank	2,791,697[1]
Advertising	None
Registration	partial
Available in	English
Current status	Active

Xipwire is a mobile payment service provider allowing payments and money transfers to be made with mobile devices using simple text messages. Mobile money transfers serve as electronic alternatives to traditional paper methods such as checks and money orders.

A Xipwire account can be funded with an electronic debit from a bank account or by a credit card. The mobile-to-mobile service allows consumers and merchants to send and receive money through text messages, protected by a PIN. Xipwire is free for users in 2010 but will start charging a flat 10 cent fee per transaction in 2011. Businesses will be charged one percent of each transaction amount in 2011, compared to the 2 to 2.5 percent credit charged for card fee transactions.[2] [3]

The fee does not apply to donations to FOSS projects.[4] On 7 December 2010 Xipwire announced it will also be accepting donations on behalf of the website WikiLeaks free of charge.[5]

References

[1] "xipwire.com - Traffic Details from Alexa" (http://www.alexa.com/siteinfo/xipwire.com). Alexa Internet, Inc. . Retrieved 2010-12-08.

[2] Vanessa Martinez (2010-04-28). "XIPWIRE lets students on the go pay with texts" (http://www.dailypennsylvanian.com/article/students-go-can-now-pay-texts). The_Daily_Pennsylvanian. . Retrieved 2010-12-08.

[3] Chris Harnick (2010-01-08). "Xipwire targets tech-savvy college students for mobile payments" (http://www.mobilecommercedaily.com/xipwire-targets-tech-savvy-college-students-for-mobile-payments/). Mobile_Commerce_Daily. . Retrieved 2010-12-08.

[4] Lisa Hoover (2010-03-01). "Xipwire Helps FOSS Projects Collect Donations for Free" (http://ostatic.com/blog/xipwire-helps-foss-projects-collect-donations-for-free). Ostatic. . Retrieved 2010-12-08.

[5] Joe Petrucci (2010-12-07). "Philly mobile payment startup Xipwire to collect donations for WikiLeaks" (http://www.flyingkitemedia.com/features/xipwirewikileaks1207.aspx). flyingkitemedia.com. . Retrieved 2010-12-08.

External links

- XIPWIRE website (http://www.xipwire.com)

Yang Cheng Tong

Yang Cheng Tong

Location	Guangzhou, Guangdong, ██ China
Launched	2001
Manager	Guangzhou Yang Cheng Tong Limited
Currency	CNY
Credit expiry	None
Auto recharge	*Automatic Add Value Service*
Website	card.gzyct.com/ [1]

Yang Cheng Tong, (Chinese: 羊城通; pinyin: *Yáng chéng tōng*; literally "Ram City Pass") is a contactless rechargeable stored value smartcard designed for paying the travel fares in the metro, buses, taxis and ferries in Guangzhou, China and surrounding cities, namely Foshan, Huadu, Zengcheng and Panyu. It was developed and managed by Guangzhou Yang Cheng Tong Limited (广州羊城通有限公司), Guangzhou Public Transport Data Control Center (tentative English translation of 廣州市公共運輸數據管理中心) and Guangzhou Metro Corporation.

The card is also sometimes accepted by city merchants, zoos, restaurants, parking meters, and in other establishments as payment. With the card holder's personal information stored in the Yang Cheng Tong, further functions can be applied, such as access control of buildings and roll call in school. The system was successfully launched in 30 December, 2001. According to the official statistics announced by its operator, the circulation of Yang Cheng Tong is over 5 million cards and 2.2 million transactions per day. [1]

Yang Cheng Tong literally means *Ram City Pass*, since the *Five Rams*, Chinese: 五羊; pinyin: *wǔ yáng*) statue is one of the important landmarks in Guangzhou. *Wu Yang Cheng* or *Yang Cheng* are both well-known nicknames of Guangzhou among Chinese people.

Type of cards

There are different types of the Yang Cheng Tong card, but their functions are basically the same.

- **Standard card**, sold for 80RMB and containing deposit value of 30RMB. Deposit will be refunded when the card is returned.
- **Memorial card**, deposit not included and refund of this type is prohibited. For example, the designs of these cards in 2006 are travel spots-themed, sold for 20RMB each card. When showing this card to relative spot box office, 10% discount would be offered for admission.
- **Xeno-card** is a wrist watch, key chain or cell phone lanyard which is implanted with the chip used in Yang Cheng Tong cards. These products may derive from the idea of Octopus watch.
- **Enterprise card.**
- **Joint card.**

Yang Cheng Tong Reader in taxi

A Yang Cheng Tong Card

Criticism

Compared to other contactless smartcards in use, the data transmission of Yang Cheng Tong is criticized by commuters that it takes 1~2 seconds between the card and reader to complete the transaction, though the operator claims that the data communication only costs 0.5 seconds in its official site. [2]

Moreover, there are insufficient facilities to refill the card value with cash. Currently there are only two Yang Cheng Tong customer service centers, a few 7-Eleven stores and a small number of Guangzhou Metro stations accepting the cash for recharging value to Yang Cheng Tong card. Otherwise, a bank card is required for using automatic self-service add-value terminals located at each Guangzhou Metro station and in joint banks, McDonald's restaurants, car parks, etc. [3]

You can load cash to your Yang Cheng Tong at every 7-eleven, many other small retailers that accept the card for payment. This means there is literally no building block without a facility to load your card.

The reaction of the turnstiles of the metro to swiping your card is immediately and does not cause delays.

An issue with the Guangzhou Yang Cheng Tong smart card is, however, that the system seems to be very old in terms of IT systems. It was first used in the late nineties of the twentieth century. That is why the card does not support fare integration with other modes of transport, e.g. when you do a trip with multiple interchanges between bus and metro, you will have to pay again at every transfer from one to another mode of transport.

References

[1] **(Chinese)** 欢迎光临！进入-广州羊城通有限公司 (http://www.gzyct.com/about.asp)

[2] http://www.gzyct.com/fanwei_info.asp?pid=23&ppid=7&pmc=□□□&ppmc=□□□&id=720

[3] **(Chinese)** 欢迎光临！进入-广州羊城通有限公司 (http://www.gzyct.com/kefu2.asp)

External links

- **(Chinese)** Yang Cheng Tong official website (http://www.gzyct.com)

Zimswitch

Zimswitch, operated by Uniswitch, is a Zimbabwean third party transaction acquiring business launched in the 1990s. Zimswitch is affiliated with 13 commercial banks which operate a network of over 300 point of sale terminals.[1] [2]

External links

- Uniswitch, 'About Ecommerce Services' [3]

References

[1] "Zimbabwe: Zimswitch System Failure Inconveniencing Consumers" (http://allafrica.com/stories/200807150158.html). *The Herald (Harare) via allafrica.com.* July 15, 2008. . Retrieved 2008-09-24.

[2] Chirove, Liberty (September 15, 2003). "Zimswitch Transactions Spiral As Public Turns to 'Plastic Money'." (http://www.accessmylibrary. com/coms2/summary_0286-24415315_ITM). *Zimbabwe Standard - AAGM via Asia Africa Intelligence Wire.* . Retrieved 2008-09-24.

Article Sources and Contributors

Payment card industry *Source*: http://en.wikipedia.org/w/index.php?oldid=432039126 *Contributors*: AlephGamma, Alynna Kasmira, Artgib, Aspects, Bazzargh, Beland, Bwpach, Glatk, Hbrandon, ICameToSee, Ignorance is strength, Jcoveney1, Joekucker, Knguyeniii, Kulikovsky, Martensjd, Mitch Ames, Mwalsh34, Pci expert, Pnm, R0pe-196, Random name, Richrdnit, Sargdub, Scottdimmick, Sfoak, Sliman89, Spatulacity, SteveLoughran, Stymiee, Tnspartan, Woohookitty, Zaraxas, 33 anonymous edits

Payment Card Industry Data Security Standard *Source*: http://en.wikipedia.org/w/index.php?oldid=432855181 *Contributors*: Abadger2k6, Akshaymathur, Alangh, AlephGamma, Andy Dingley, Andybarratt, AntonChuvakin, Artgib, Arvindn, Beland, BiT, Bixgal, Bkell, Blackgorge, Bogey97, Capricorn42, Classof96, CliffC, Coachjpg, Danbriley, Debresser, Desanu, Digital fuel, Discospinster, Djptechie, Doctorallan, Donalcampbell, Falcon8765, Flowanda, Frap, Fredhopper, G Clark, Glatk, Hbrandon, Hga, Iain Cheyne, JJC1138, Jehnidiah, Jeltz, Jestep, Jimmyshaft, Jojo-schmitz, Jonralton, JukoFF, Kaihsu, Kashifsohail, Katana0182, Kehrbykid, KelleyCook, Knguyeniii, Kravietz, Kuru, Lazydaisy, Leeatcookerly, Liquidnexxus1, Midnight Madness, Mikaey, Mindmatrix, MrDolomite, MrOllie, Neilhenry, OnebadGTR, Pcimonkey, Poweron, Pradameinhoff, Quadrature, R'n'B, Random name, Raoulhira, Reconscout94, Revolutionwifi, Rich Farmbrough, Ronz, Scottdimmick, Securityphreaks, Sfoak, Sh00tr, Sliman89, Snori, Stagalj, Steve Baner-Mann, SteveLoughran, Stevehughes, Stymiee, TastyPoutine, Tdurden77007, Technopat, TerraFrost, Tessian, Tnxman307, UncleDouggie, Vmp2009, William Avery, Yhabibzai, 218 anonymous edits

GRCM *Source*: http://en.wikipedia.org/w/index.php?oldid=432110547 *Contributors*: Angus Lepper, Bwpach, Canis Lupus, Corp Vision, Gil Gamesh, ICameToSee, Rjwilmsi, Woohookitty

Payment system *Source*: http://en.wikipedia.org/w/index.php?oldid=426254503 *Contributors*: AS, Andres, Anon lynx, Barek, Beetstra, Beland, Bongomatic, Btphelps, Cellular, Ciotog, Elkman, Fayenatic london, Gogo Dodo, Hmains, Instantpc, Jokin1981, Josh Parris, Michael Hardy, Nirvana2013, Nzseries1, Piano non troppo, R'n'B, RBBrittain, Rj, SDC, Searchme, Shaddack, Tsavage, VladGenie, Vpovilaitis, WissensDürster, Wistex, ZimZalaBim, Zrinski hr, Zzuuzz, 19 anonymous edits

1LINK *Source*: http://en.wikipedia.org/w/index.php?oldid=425595718 *Contributors*: 1LINKPAK, Anon lynx, Arpingstone, Awg1010, Betacommand, DGG, Drbreznjev, Dsp13, Firsfron, Fratrep, Gracenotes, Hariswaheed, Kathleen.wright5, Koavf, Kslall8765, Rehanhi, Rich Farmbrough, Sarsdran, ScottMainwaring, UsernameRedacted, Zaidiwaqas, Zlerman, 5 anonymous edits

3V (payment solution) *Source*: http://en.wikipedia.org/w/index.php?oldid=398156999 *Contributors*: Boothy443, Cahk, Darklilac, DocendoDiscimus, Ewlyahoocom, Exsanguinated5, Firsfron, Jtm12345, Martarius, Ohconfucius, OisinisiO, Paradoxian, SimonP, Steroberts89, Stifle, The Baroness of Morden, Vegaswikian, Woohookitty, 53 anonymous edits

Aadhar-enabled payment system *Source*: http://en.wikipedia.org/w/index.php?oldid=432125730 *Contributors*: Randhirreddy, 1 anonymous edits

Acquirer *Source*: http://en.wikipedia.org/w/index.php?oldid=396566475 *Contributors*: Abune, Ajuk, Andrew c, Asaladinozi, Bartlettbill, Bill.albing, BowChickaNeowNeow, Caerwine, Calltech, Captain Disdain, Cliffb, Cmdrjameson, Dryanstephens, Ed!, Flowanda, HPS28213, Hirak 99, Jmabel, Miernik, Radagast83, Sbonsib, Stymiee, SueHay, Thiseye, Tim Barber, Tnxman307, VZakharov, WAJWAJ, Yworo, Zaian, 24 anonymous edits

Acquiring bank *Source*: http://en.wikipedia.org/w/index.php?oldid=378157508 *Contributors*: Arthena, Carabinieri, Cornellrockey, Echuck215, Fbooth, Flowanda, Gogo Dodo, Jmabel, Leeatcookerly, LilHelpa, Mkns, Radagast83, Rwgardencity, SueHay, Sukee2, Tim Barber, VZakharov, Yakudza, Zamsinus, 17 anonymous edits

Adyen *Source*: http://en.wikipedia.org/w/index.php?oldid=390149789 *Contributors*: Apenstaartje, Fallschirmjäger, J9s, ZooFari, 5 anonymous edits

Allstar (fuel card) *Source*: http://en.wikipedia.org/w/index.php?oldid=428046559 *Contributors*: Almufasa, Alvin Seville, Arwel Parry, Beagel, Bearcat, Iridescent, Leopheard, Locklock

Alternative payments *Source*: http://en.wikipedia.org/w/index.php?oldid=430797808 *Contributors*: 2kcharge, Akerans, Bobby Tables, Malcolma, Marketada, Nono64, Parkerdr, Rettetast, Superk1a, Tassedethe, Woohookitty, ウルトラ大不況, 1 anonymous edits

American Express *Source*: http://en.wikipedia.org/w/index.php?oldid=433283549 *Contributors*: 7elevin, Abtract, Admrboltz, Alex43223, AlexandergordonNYC, Alexius08, Ali ringo, Alikaalex, Alison9, AllanVS, Amasa walker III, Amcl, Andymadigan, Anon lynx, Apmolde, Arie, Astrader, Astronautics, Atropos lee, BD2412, Barryob, Beetstra, Beland, Belovedfreak, Ben5082, Bender235, Bento00, Biker Biker, Biruitorul, Bmalicoat, Bobblewik, Bohlia123, Bongwarrior, Boothy443, Bovineone, Brandon5485, Brian Brockmeyer, Brian0101, Brianga, Brougham96, Buckeyebrain, Buttmunch101, ButtonwoodTree, CORNELIUSSEON, CPAScott, Calltech, Camelbinky, Cantarevolare, Carl.bunderson, Catdude, Centpacrr, Centrx, Chadlupkes, ChemGardener, Chetfarmer, Chowbok, Chris the speller, ChrisRuvolo, Ckorhonen, Classicrockfan42, Coffee4binky, Comayagua99, CommonsDelinker, Complicated73, Conrad.pramboeck, CoolKid1993, Coolhawks88, Crocodile Punter, Crysb, Cuvtixo, Cyclops 396, DECIUM, DIEXEL, DMCer, DMG413, Dajanes, Dallasphil, Dandison, Darkieboy236, David.Monniaux, Delirium, Deutschemarine723, Dfarmer, Dihard, Discospinster, DocWatson42, Dr. Blofeld, Dr.alexwright, Dreaded Walrus, Dsarokin, DubaiTerminator, DubbaG, Dubkiller, EPadmirateur, Ecveteran, Edward, Either way, Ejohnsequilar, Elcarmean, Elkman, Elvira100, Empoor, Erc, Ertemplin, Esperant, Esrever, Eustress, ExecutiveWatch, Ezeu, Faitdodo, Falcon8765, Financial Zorro, FireOcean, Firsfron, Flowanda, Fortdj33, Fourthords, Frederick Slade 2440, Funandtrvl, Furrykef, Future Perfect at Sunrise, Gabe0505, Gaius Cornelius, Gazpacho, Glorithm, Gogo Dodo, Gr1st, GraemeL, Grain co, GreenReaper, Greenshed, Ground Zero, Grouse, Gurch, Guydoesit, Gwernol, HJ Mitchell, HaeB, Hagrinas, HairyWombat, HalJor, Halgin, Harksaw, Hassocks5489, Hawaiian717, Hbdragon88, Hedgey42, Helmandsare, Honbicot, Hoof Hearted, Husond, Hyacinth, Ian3055, Ibbn, Iceman 347, Idontknowbob, Inarius, Ironist, Ivymike21, J.delanoy, JASpencer, JIP, Jackk, Jamcib, JamisBraucher, Jason6149, Jbl1975, Jeff Silvers, Jeffq, Jerryseinfeld, Jfwald, Jiang, Jim.henderson, John, John K, Jonasaurus, Jonniewags, Jpgordon, Jsayre64, Jum4, Jvcdude, Kaganer, Kent Wang, Khalid hassani, Kiden Nixon 413, Kiiron, Kilo-Lima, Kirjtc2, Kitch, Kkm010, Kmccoy, Kukini, Kurieeto, Kuru, Kwammi, Kwertii, Kylerwilliams, Lakemirror, Laurascudder, Levineps, Ligulem, LilHelpa, Linkspamremover, Listre, LordXenu2009, Lorem Ipsum, Lotje, Lucidwind, Lukobe, Luna Santin, M@sk, MFfan310, MONGO, MOhistory, Ma'ame Michu, Maddy1123, Madhero88, Mahanga, Malepheasant, Marsp, Martarius, Martin451, Mauls, MaybeBoo, Merbabu, Mindmatrix, Misthos, Mitch Ames, Mjdimino, Mm1972, Mooinglemur, Mordicai, Mroach, Murtoa, N328KF, Navy Blue, NawlinWiki, NeilN, Neutrality, Newyork4me, Nigholith, Nivix, Nnatmc2007, Numbersinstitute, Nurg, Nyelvmark, OHFM, Ohnoitsjamie, Oneevent, Opiance, Oroso, Pafcool2, PamD, Paranomia, Parkwells, Pascal666, Patlocke, Patrickballoonman, Patstuart, PaulHanson, Pcannella, PeterCooperJr, Phatom87, Phoe, Platypus222, Pottsf, Powerlifter450, Prayspot, ProhibitOnions, Pumeleon, RM-Taylor, RadicalBender, Raeky, Rcawsey, Red marquis, Reinhardheydt, Rettetast, Rfraleigh, Rhallanger, Rich Farmbrough, Rj, Rjwilmsi, Rlaager, Rnrkrishnan, Ronz, RyanGerbil10, SQGibbon, Saint-Paddy, Sam Hocevar, Samtheboy, Samuel Curtis, Samuell, Sardanaphalus, Satori Son, Scott Sanchez, SebRovera, Sergei Kravinoff 7982, Sfomspphl, Sfphotocraft, Shadowcat 148, Shanedidona, Shawnc, Sherool, Shortride, Shriprasanna, SidP, Silencethefire, SilkTork, SirSadiq, Skarebo, Skionxb, SkylineEvo, Sloman, Sneakers55, Solarisworld, Southfork, Spangineer, Splash, Spud29, Sreekesh, Steelbeard1, Stevenplunkett, Stifle, Stv2999, SunCreator, Sushi Tax, Swat671, Swizzlez, T 22779, Taifarious1, TeaganMago, Teapotgeorge, Tellumo, The undertow, The wub, Thepangelinanpost, Thesammy12, Thumperward, Timc, Tinton5, Tnetzel, Tokenizeman, Tomasf, TopGun51, Topnews, Torc2, Toreau, Travisl, TubularWorld, USA 5000, Ujjval10, Ulric1313, UltraMagnus, Urbanrenewal, User27091, Uvaduck, Vegas949, Versageek, WLU, Wannger27, Weetjesman, WikHead, WikiDon, Wildball, Will Beback, Willking1979, WinTakeAll, Wiutstudent, Www.crossprofit.com, X-factor, X736e65616b, Xenonvision, Xlrisk, Xorr the God-Jewel 2211, Yerbaandyayo, Ykral, Ypetrachenko, Yuliya7, Zak089, Zzuuzz, 口口口口口口.24, 584 anonymous edits

Antedated cheque *Source*: http://en.wikipedia.org/w/index.php?oldid=433110818 *Contributors*: Akendall, Deadflagblues, Drutt, Joeblakesley, Joshua Issac, Nbarth, Pascal.Tesson, PatrickFlaherty, Piotrus, Tingrin87, 1 anonymous edits

Argentum album *Source*: http://en.wikipedia.org/w/index.php?oldid=218282800 *Contributors*: Alvin-cs, Brian0918, Outriggr, Pegship

AS 2805 *Source*: http://en.wikipedia.org/w/index.php?oldid=400301972 *Contributors*: Dkam, Icd, JaGa, Miracle Pen, Mitch Ames, 1 anonymous edits

ATM usage fees *Source*: http://en.wikipedia.org/w/index.php?oldid=429946542 *Contributors*: Agent L, Aitias, Anna Lincoln, Auntof6, Biglovinb, Blanchebaum, Buhin, Crocodile Punter, Dansiman, Dcandeto, Denisgomes, EDCAlistairGates, Flarn2006, Gaius Cornelius, Glic16, GoingBatty, Gorgan almighty, Gpvos, Greenbough, Guidod, Justjoy, Kslall8765, Little Professor, Mask-13, Mclay1, Mihitha, Miken2005, Mild Bill Hiccup, Muttster, Pascal666, Pimlottc, Pkoistin, PrimroseGuy, Psiphiorg, Rfc1394, Ribamar23, Rjwilmsi, Ruatoriapies, Sam5154, Scarykitty, Signalhead, Sillybilly, Stifle, Supreme Deliciousness, Swizzlez, Tawker, Tetzcatlipoca, Thincat, Tigeron, Timrollpickering, Twgwneatl, Uhanu, Winchelsea, Woohookitty, Zariane, ZimZalaBim, 96 anonymous edits

Automated Clearing House *Source*: http://en.wikipedia.org/w/index.php?oldid=432094294 *Contributors*: 1ForTheMoney, Adam850, Afadeyi, Afed, AlanDupree, Albanaco, Avivs, Babigos, Barek, Barte, Beland, Boing! said Zebedee, CR85747, Calltech, Centrx, Chaldor, Chmod007, Chris the speller, Cliffb, Cobaltbluetony, Commander Keane, ConradPino, Dingar, Displague, DocendoDiscimus, EastTN, Erielhonan, Fantumphool, FishSpeaker, Flavious27, Flowanda, Gbleem, Greensburger, Itai, JREVA, JackS333, Jamesday, JayMay023, JeremyStein, Kcrossover, Mag410, Mang kiko, Markber, Marrante, Mdkarazim, Miernik, Mindmatrix, Nonesuch13, Olegos, OsamaBinLogin, Pankajdynamic, PaulHanson, PeterJohnson, Ph.eyes, Pnm, Profchris, Pseudomonas, Qst, R Math, RBBrittain, RayGates, Rj, Sach1220, Seanamcelroy, Sebmol, SimonP, Sjordan26, Slaniel, Someareemoreequal, Supaplex, Superm401, Tgiphil, Vargob, Virgil Vaduva, Waltonob, Warfin, Welsh, Zac11485, Zencv, 120 anonymous edits

Automated teller machine *Source*: http://en.wikipedia.org/w/index.php?oldid=432973646 *Contributors*: 159753, 259, 842U, A1ACo, Acdx, Adambisset, Adrie7, Aheppenh, Ahoerstemeier, Airisatm, Airodyssey, AlaaT, Alansohn, Albert Gonzalez, Aldie, Ales Hakl, Ali@gwc.org.uk, AllanVS, Amd, Andonic, AndrewWTaylor, Andrewpmk, Andycjp, AnemoneProjectors, Anglokurisu, Anish qw1, Antandrus, AppleMan1, Arctic Night, Armoreno10, ArnoldReinhold, Arthurfbi, Arwel Parry, Ashdurbat, Astronaut, Astrotrain, Atmsecurity, Attilios, Az1568, AzaToth,

BIL, BRUTE, Babbage, Babu01, Bacchus87, Bagpuss, Bapho, Barek, Barek-public, Barrykas, Batmann99, Bauani, Bbatiz64, Bbatsell, Bcartolo, Beland, Ben Ben, Bender235, Benhughes, Bhou, BillC, BillStratford03, Bishbi, Blakes20, Blaxthos, Bobblewik, Bobo192, Bradeos Graphon, Bremerenator, Briaboru, Brian Schlosser42, Brian426uk, Brittany Ka, Britzfritz, BroadSt Bully, Brsanthu, Burto88, CBM, Cadpah, CalendarWatcher, Calicat, Can't sleep, clown will eat me, Candis Rochelle, CanisRufus, Canley, Captian Falcon, CaribDigita, Carp3, Ccacsmss, Cheezmeister, Cherkash, Chitoryu12, Chocolateboy, Chowbok, ChrisErbach, Chrisieboy, Chrislk02, Cliffb, Cluth, Cobaltbluetony, CommonsDelinker, ComplsMyRx, Conversion script, Coolcaesar, Crispmuncher, Crocodealer, Cutler, Cvalda, DARTH SIDIOUS 2, Dainis, Damian Yerrick, DamianFinol, DamonH2, Daniel C. Boyer, Darwin-rover, Dawkeye, Dbenbenn, Dekimasu, DerHexer, Deville, Dgtsyb, Dmsar, DocWatson42, Doctor Whom, Dominic, Dominichirsch, Doppelzoo, Down10, Downfall2209, DreamsAreMadeOf, Drmagic, Drsatman, Drunkasian, Ds02006, Dutfield, Duude, Dwp49423, Dysepsion, Dysprosia, E rulez, ERIC TAARGÜS, Earldelawarr, Earle Martin, Ed Poor, Edmilne, Edward, EdwinHJ, Eliyak, Epbr123, EpsilonOmega, Erebus555, Esperant, Essexmutant, Eurosong, Evil Monkey, Evil saltine, Evillan, Ewlloyd, Excirial, Excretion, Eyreland, FA Jon, Facts707, Fadyfadl6, FaerieInGrey, Fansipans, Fayenatic london, Feedmecereal, Ferkelparade, Filanca, FisherQueen, FloK, Florentino floro, Frank Robinson, Franklee83, Frap, Frazzydee, Freakofnurture, Frenchman113, Furrykef, Gaius Cornelius, Galoubet, Gbrandt, GeneralBelly, GeorgHH, Gidonb, Gilliam, Glacier Wolf, Gobonobo, GoingBatty, Graham Chapman, Graham87, GreatWhiteNortherner, Greensburger, Gregfitzy, GregorB, Grundle2600, Gsarwa, Guinness2702, Gwk, H005, Hadal, Hairy poker monster, Halfalah, Harry491, Haseo9999, Heathen, Hellfire83, Hellno2, Henry Flower, Hi878, Homer Landskirty, Howardmcn, Hu12, Hyad, Ian3055, Icd, Ida Shaw, Igoldste, Ikescs, Indon, IntoCom, Iridescent, Isher, Isidore, J.delanoy, JForget, JNW, JPMcGrath, JPZingher, JaGa, Jack324, JackLumber, Jambornik, Jan1nad, Jasondmath, Jcairns78, Jeff G., Jeroen.pelgrims, Jesster79, Jkeene, JohnInDC, JonHarder, JonRoma, Joncnunn, Jondel, Jordav, Jpbowen, Jpers36, Jpgordon, Jpp42, JuJube, Juliancolton Alternative, KSinitski, KapilTagore, Kathleen.wright5, Kchishol1970, Kcordina, Ke4roh, Kendickens, Kenyon, Ketil3, Kevin McE, Khalid hassani, Khatru2, Khendon, Khoikhoi, Kingpin13, Kinou, Kittoo, KnowledgeOfSelf, Koavf, Krkas, Kylesandell, Leeyc0, LennartBolks, Lerdsuwa, LewisHamiltonTR, Lightmouse, Lilac Soul, Ling.Nut, Liquidnexxus1, Little_guru, Livajo, Longhair, Lost tourist, Lovely Chris, Luna Santin, Lunar Jesters, Mac, MacGyverMagic, Mafmafmaf, Magnus Manske, Mais oui!, Makingitbetter7, Malcohol, Malleus Fatuorum, Malvineous, Mani1, Mardus, Markt3, Martin Hogbin, Martinoei, Martyburr, MaryCSki, Masamunecyrus, Masterofpsi, Matticus78, Media Research, Medvedenko, Meelar, Meesterturner, Melamed katz, Menchi, Meowy, Mfc, Mhockey, Michael Hardy, Michael Zimmermann, Michael.chlistalla, Mifter, MikeMass, Milnivlek, Mindmatrix, Minesweeper, Mmccalpin, Moh man742, Molinari, Momet, MrOllie, Msp0, Muchness, Mulad, Mullety2, Mummyboi, Mwalcoff, Myfanwy, N7912, NFH, NJR ZA, Nachdenklich, Nagy, Nagytibi, NapoliRoma, Nathan Hamblen, NathanBeach, Nbk, Nenyedi, Networld1, Neverquick, NewYork1956, NickBush24, Nickreed60s, Nigholith, Nightstallion, Njbob, Noisy, Nono64, Norm, Not a dog, NotAnonymous0, Notnebalum, Octahedron80, Off!, Ohnoitsjamie, OlEnglish, Oli2140, Oliver202, Onorem, Oreo Priest, Orourkek, OscarMeyerWienerdog, Ossido, PM800, Patrick, PatrickFisher, Pekinduck, PeteVerdon, Peyna, Phatom87, Philip Cross, Philip Trueman, Php2rh, Phydend, Pigman, Pilotguy, Plinkit, Plop, Pnot, Portsaid, Ppntori, PrimroseGuy, ProhibitOnions, Propound, Prvc, Psychless, PubliusFL, Pudelek, Queeg, R'n'B, Raccoon Fox, Radagast, Rama, Ramanpotential, RaseaC, Rata7, Raven4x4x, Rbaumy, Rdht, Reedy, Retired username, Revth, Rfc1394, Rhobite, Rhombus, Rhyshuw1, Rich Farmbrough, Rich257, Rjwilmsi, Rl, RobyWayne, Roche-Kerr, Rrlc, Rronline, Russ, Ryank808, Ryulong, SAUNDERS, SE16, Sadettin, Sayedt, Sc147, Scjessey, Scott Sanchez, Scouseftw, Sdedeo, Searchme, Securetech, Sevela.p, Seyon, Sherurcij, Shijaz, Shizhao, Sietse Snel, Signalhead, Silly rabbit, Simon-in-sagamihara, SimonP, SirJibby, Sky Harbor, Slipperyweasel, Sloman, Smerus, Smjg, Snickerdo, Snigbrook, Snillet, SoCalSuperEagle, Solid State, Solipsist, Son, Sonett72, South Bay, SpaceFlight89, Spaceboy492, Spookfish, Sport woman, Squeed, Srajangupta, Stassats, StephenDawson, Sterio, Stickhouse, Stifle, Superm401, TKKIAEU, Tabletop, Tad Lincoln, Tahaarifali, TakuyaMurata, Tankostar, Tarcus, Tarret, Technopat, Teryx, The Anome, The Rambling Man, The undertow, Thebeginning, Theo10011, TheoClarke, Thereruns, Thomas von der Lippe, Thompson.matthew, Thumperward, TimmyJnr, Tizaj, Tokek, Tom-, TomGreen, Tomjager, Tomtefarbror, Triona, Tunapul, TutterMouse, Ugenius, Ukexpat, Ultimaga, Unreal7, Urbanrenewal, User5050, Valhalla, Vancouverguy, Vanhoabui, Vatlieb, Vegaswikian, Velella, Vicki Rosenzweig, VictorianMutant, Vincesiy99, Vistet, Voidvector, Vssun, Ward3001, Wernher, Wfeidt, Wfwiki, Wikikwon, Will Beback, Winodhello, Wk muriithi, Woohookitty, Wrh1973, Wutsje, X736e65616b, X96lee15, XandroZ, Xneilj, Xyzzyplugh, Zarxos, Zcsala021, Zundark, आशीष भटनागर, 大西洋鮭, 1007 anonymous edits

Autopass Card *Source*: http://en.wikipedia.org/w/index.php?oldid=405665190 *Contributors*: Either way, Fernvale, Gaius Cornelius, Improv, Jacklee, Joshua, Kappa, Mr Tan, PigFlu Oink, Sovietmole, Takamaxa, Terence, Xaiver0510

BACHO record format *Source*: http://en.wikipedia.org/w/index.php?oldid=247616140 *Contributors*: MacSpon, 1 anonymous edits

BACS *Source*: http://en.wikipedia.org/w/index.php?oldid=425846141 *Contributors*: Alex9788, Baden Cottage, Biscuittin, Chase me ladies, I'm the Cavalry, Chp-flms, Chriscf, Chrisd10, D6y, DJromT, Danno uk, David Biddulph, Edw400, Ian3055, Ieuan Friend, Ioeth, Johnkenyon, Johnwalton, JulesN, LouiseMcNeil, Lradrama, Mandtplatt, Mervyn, Miracle Pen, Mosaicsoftware, Mrh30, Naive rm, NathanBeach, PANONIAN, PeteVerdon, Pigsonthewing, Pommygranite, Quiensabe, RetiredUser2, Rickybling, Robidy, SEPAMAN, Sargdub, SchuminWeb, The.Edmund, Thumperward, Uklondoner, Vivenot, Vocalink.Marketing, Widefox, YorkshireM, 72 anonymous edits

Bad Check Restitution Program *Source*: http://en.wikipedia.org/w/index.php?oldid=417460636 *Contributors*: Alan Liefting, Betsup, Bumchecks, Cliffb, Eastlaw, Hellno2, Noble Story, Sperril, Stifle, Tylerbag, VladimirReshetnikov, WRK, 22 anonymous edits

Banker's draft *Source*: http://en.wikipedia.org/w/index.php?oldid=432389616 *Contributors*: Davidbod, Itai, LeeG, Rajah, Robocoder, Smoke003723, Tabletop, Theo10011, 18 anonymous edits

Bankers' clearing house *Source*: http://en.wikipedia.org/w/index.php?oldid=418184221 *Contributors*: Greensburger, Hmains, Marrante, Nbarth, Nick Number, Sargdub

Bankgiro *Source*: http://en.wikipedia.org/w/index.php?oldid=203986695 *Contributors*: Arsenikk, GoAirForce, Logictheo, Rettetast, Tkynerd

Bartercard *Source*: http://en.wikipedia.org/w/index.php?oldid=411360256 *Contributors*: BarterBoy, BarterTruth, Bartermedia, Bluedogbeer, Chad Zani, Davluong, Fourohfour, Icestorm815, JohnPMurphy, Miracle Pen, Nn123645, Nzflag.info, Paxse, Rjwilmsi, Scarykitty, Vgranucci, 9 anonymous edits

BASE24 *Source*: http://en.wikipedia.org/w/index.php?oldid=392602775 *Contributors*: Anon lynx, Dawynn, Nagytibi, R'n'B, YUL89YYZ, 6 anonymous edits

The Benefit Company *Source*: http://en.wikipedia.org/w/index.php?oldid=365402014 *Contributors*: Dsp13, Fabrictramp, Glengyron, GrahamHardy, LilHelpa, Phatom87, Seektrue, 2 anonymous edits

Bilhete Único *Source*: http://en.wikipedia.org/w/index.php?oldid=431177001 *Contributors*: Ah Liveto Domun, Dantadd, David Santos, Dbacellar, Edson Rosa, Eduardo Sellan III, Edudobay, Frap, IsObaricOhiO, John of Reading, MCBastos, Mild Bill Hiccup, Mmorsello, Opraco, Queenmomcat, Victor Lopes, WOSlinker, Woohookitty, 13 anonymous edits

Bill Me Later *Source*: http://en.wikipedia.org/w/index.php?oldid=428861013 *Contributors*: Aspects, CR85747, David H Braun (1964), Debresser, Dthomsen8, Hellno2, Ihcoyc, JasonHockeyGuy, Shortride, Skrimgeour, Zahidncst, 30 anonymous edits

Bill of credit *Source*: http://en.wikipedia.org/w/index.php?oldid=422066335 *Contributors*: BD2412, Dave Smith, Magicpiano, Mysdaao, NuclearWarfare, Perceval, Woohookitty, 2 anonymous edits

Billpoint *Source*: http://en.wikipedia.org/w/index.php?oldid=397044583 *Contributors*: AA, Aezram, Antriver, ChrisLamb, Davehard, DragonflySixtyseven, Good Olfactory, Hmains, Hydrargyrum, Jeodesic, Meandmyself, Mecanismo, Mrzaius, Night Gyr, Nobody of Consequence, Pearle, Pegship, R18e05h08, RJFJR, Rjwilmsi, Rmm813, Singularity, Stev0, Thegn, Wikidenver, Xaosflux, 6 anonymous edits

BitPass *Source*: http://en.wikipedia.org/w/index.php?oldid=322518959 *Contributors*: 2bar, BesigedB, Bryan Derksen, Caknuck, Canley, Dragonfiend, Epolk, GDallimore, Gokusandwich, GraemeL, Hu12, Ifenn, Jaraalbe, Johnmcombs, Rettetast, Srice13, Stepheng3, TakuyaMurata, The wub, Tim1357, WatchAndObserve, 16 anonymous edits

Blank cheque *Source*: http://en.wikipedia.org/w/index.php?oldid=431889027 *Contributors*: Adashiel, Alvis, Arminius, Bduddy, Bigjonnyg, Branddobbe, Ccady, ChrisP2K5, Citz, Ckatz, Clawed, Coolcaesar, Cwolfsheep, DJ Clayworth, Ed Fitzgerald, Elkman, Exor674, Fuhghettaboutit, Furrykef, Gh87, Gilliam, Goodnightmush, GreetingsEarthling, Ground Zero, Hucz, Husky, Ianblair23, Jeff3000, Jeni, KelisFan2K5, Korg, Laurinavicius, Mboverload, Mexaguil, Mgaert, Nbarth, NeilFraser, NeilTarrant, Ohpilot, Otolemur crassicaudatus, Pete142, Proud Ho, Rich Farmbrough, Rifleman, Rlconkl, Rmrfstar, Samw, Schrödinger's Neurotoxin, Sherool, Skooma2112, Slipperyweasel, Stefanomione, Stephenb, TenOfAllTrades, TheLimbicOne, TheOuthouseMouse, Theo10011, UnitedStatesian, User2004, Valkyryn, Vzbs34, Zondor, 55 anonymous edits

Bluecorner *Source*: http://en.wikipedia.org/w/index.php?oldid=270540772 *Contributors*: LaurenMcMillan, Malcolma, PatrickFlaherty, Rich Farmbrough, Secretlondon, Tim Ivorson

BPAY *Source*: http://en.wikipedia.org/w/index.php?oldid=418949159 *Contributors*: 1exec1, Afromcbenny, Bonadea, Bongwarrior, Cgotz, Dkam, Dougweller, Energizer07, Galaxiaad, JamesBWatson, Jmchugh, Justinsullivan, Leginag, MER-C, Scalene, Ukexpat, Yossarian223, 22 anonymous edits

Card association *Source*: http://en.wikipedia.org/w/index.php?oldid=408413745 *Contributors*: Daltxn, EdH, Flowanda, Giraffedata, GoingBatty, Sadads, Tim Barber, Versus22, 4 anonymous edits

CardIt *Source*: http://en.wikipedia.org/w/index.php?oldid=371655256 *Contributors*: Flowanda, Pmikal, Rjwilmsi, Tim1357, Vegaswikian, Work permit, 1 anonymous edits

CarIFS *Source*: http://en.wikipedia.org/w/index.php?oldid=410370417 *Contributors*: CaribDigita, Tassedethe, 1 anonymous edits

Cash advance *Source*: http://en.wikipedia.org/w/index.php?oldid=422577011 *Contributors*: Bearcat, CWenger, Hellno2, Little Mountain 5, Longhair, Magioladitis, Philip Trueman, Rd232, Rich Farmbrough, Santryl, Scott Ritchie, Stifle, Tide rolls, 8 anonymous edits

Cashier's check *Source*: http://en.wikipedia.org/w/index.php?oldid=430705236 *Contributors*: Akendall, Allen3, Andrea105, AshishG, BarretBonden, Beland, Betacommand, Bobk, Booyabazooka, Bumm13, Click23, DMG413, Dabagboy, Eastlaw, Ellsworth, Epbr123, Evil Monkey, Fracturing, Freetech, Gaius Cornelius, Gentgeen, Harland1, Harryboyles, Hasel001, IRP, Isnow, JaGa, Jacroe, Jcortes66, Jigen III, Julesd, Kalmia, Kencf0618, Manishearth, Marianocecowski, Mdanh2002, Prevention19, Robocoder, Rotbloodi, RoySmith, Ryguasu, Sbeck, Scott Sanchez, Slaniel, Stifle, StuRat, Tabletop, Themfromspace, Theo10011, Tommy2010, TylerA97, Uriah923, Uvaduck, WinTakeAll, 92 anonymous edits

Cashplus *Source*: http://en.wikipedia.org/w/index.php?oldid=429699294 *Contributors*: 6birc, Adamrowlandagrp, Aitias, Andrewfanner, Anon lynx, Astraphael, Cahk, Catchpole, Comparemoney, Crocodile barbecue, DuncanHill, Flowanda, Fratrep, Gary King, Gruffy, Jamespyer, Jfire, JulesH, Kuru, O keyes, Ohnoitsjamie, Paxse, Phatom87, RasterFaAye, Shajure, Southlondonlife, Spectrumps, WikHead, Wimt, 21 anonymous edits

CashU Inc *Source*: http://en.wikipedia.org/w/index.php?oldid=359059763 *Contributors*: LilHelpa, Mawald

CCBill *Source*: http://en.wikipedia.org/w/index.php?oldid=430746079 *Contributors*: Bearcat, Canley, D6, Dread333, JoeFredricks, Justjennifer, MaesterTonberry, Malcolma, PoeticVerse, Power182, SLKarlsen, Seb az86556, Waynem37, Xlbnushk, 23 anonymous edits

Central Securities Depository *Source*: http://en.wikipedia.org/w/index.php?oldid=432650809 *Contributors*: Bmathis, Cander0000, Doldrums, Emersoni, Epeefleche, Finansvalp, Gonzalo Diethelm, Good Olfactory, Little saturn, NJgeezer, Naive rm, PigFlu Oink, Protothyas, Rgnewbury, Roland2, Sargdub, Skalmier, SueHay, TVDP, Tabletop, Tzeeb, Vivenot, Will Beback Auto, 16 anonymous edits

Centricom *Source*: http://en.wikipedia.org/w/index.php?oldid=355704206 *Contributors*: 2005, Centricom, Chris the speller, LilHelpa, Miracle Pen, Smartse

Certified check *Source*: http://en.wikipedia.org/w/index.php?oldid=420677895 *Contributors*: Airodyssey, AllanHainey, Cybercobra, DocWatson42, Ebeisher, Fkmiami, Garrybowers, JYi, JackLumber, Jorge331, Jusdafax, Kwsn, Oxo, P.F.O.S.B., Plastikspork, Salon Essahj, SethTisue, Shastamcdayna, Stephenb, StuRat, Uvaphdman, Yuckfoo, 25 anonymous edits

Certified Funds *Source*: http://en.wikipedia.org/w/index.php?oldid=418548306 *Contributors*: Anomalocaris, Ebeisher, GoingBatty, Katharineamy, Rigadoun, Samuel Blanning, Shastamcdayna, 10 anonymous edits

Certified Payment-Card Industry Security Auditor *Source*: http://en.wikipedia.org/w/index.php?oldid=341318225 *Contributors*: Krausedw, Sfoak, Vicky Ng, 2 anonymous edits

Certified Payment-Card Industry Security Manager *Source*: http://en.wikipedia.org/w/index.php?oldid=393368582 *Contributors*: Cerebellum, Krausedw, Rjwilmsi, Sfoak, Vicky Ng, 7 anonymous edits

CHAPS *Source*: http://en.wikipedia.org/w/index.php?oldid=429701334 *Contributors*: Aelfthrytha, Fabiform, FerdinandFrog, HongQiGong, Ian3055, JDAWiseman, Mandtplatt, Mark83, Mauls, Montanabw, Naive rm, Opabinia regalis, RKT, Wierzba, 23 anonymous edits

Charge card *Source*: http://en.wikipedia.org/w/index.php?oldid=415076034 *Contributors*: Airodyssey, B0at, Beano ni, Bingoboyy, CommonsDelinker, Crocodile Punter, Dondon83, DrVeghead, Ency, Esrever, Fourthords, Frispar, Future Perfect at Sunrise, J.delanoy, Jeff Muscato, John Broughton, Johnjreiser, Jtg920, Kencaesi, Mauls, Mintaru, Plasma, Preslethe, ProhibitOnions, RadiantRay, Radiojon, Rich Farmbrough, Rifleman 82, Rjwilmsi, Rrburke, Saltlakejohn, Scott Sanchez, Stifle, TeaganMago, Tide rolls, UkPaolo, Winner 42, 48 anonymous edits

ChargeSmart *Source*: http://en.wikipedia.org/w/index.php?oldid=401695038 *Contributors*: DavidScubadiver, Flowanda, Grafen, Pmikal, Quentin X, Rjwilmsi, Tim1357

Chargify *Source*: http://en.wikipedia.org/w/index.php?oldid=432803627 *Contributors*: Casieg, MacMog

Chase Paymentech *Source*: http://en.wikipedia.org/w/index.php?oldid=427557483 *Contributors*: Asaladinozi, Woohookitty, 1 anonymous edits

Check 21 Act *Source*: http://en.wikipedia.org/w/index.php?oldid=426426816 *Contributors*: Ad sotomayor, Akendall, ArcAngel, Armsmi01, Ashdc77, Bankreform, Beland, Blender50, Bradrules, CSTAR, Caltrop, Chops76, Chris the speller, Christopherlin, Cjewell, DavidLevinson, Decora, Dustman81, EagleFan, Eastlaw, Edcolins, EoGuy, Eyreland, Fuhghettaboutit, G Clark, GDallimore, GraemeL, Greensburger, Hellno2, JREVA, JTimmins, JamesBWatson, Jed234, Jfromcanada, Jim Cook, Jschecks, Kbailey1, Keetonwill, Kiand, LilHelpa, Lucaq, Lwalt, Magog the Ogre, Markles, Marstead, Maximus Rex, MrDolomite, Narsil, Nonesuch13, NormBograham, Nowa, PRRfan, Paddysmyth, PaulHanson, Philip Trueman, Pmrobert49, Poccil, Rjstreet, Sam Hocevar, Sapphic, Sargdub, Schalicto, Scootey, Scott Sanchez, Seaphoto, SmartGuy, Sme, Targetpuller, Tony1, Trödel, Vectro, Vi.agarwal, Wesha, 91 anonymous edits

Check card *Source*: http://en.wikipedia.org/w/index.php?oldid=387637730 *Contributors*: Bearcat, Jeodesic, Rror, Sidesrural, Waltpohl, 10 anonymous edits

Cheque *Source*: http://en.wikipedia.org/w/index.php?oldid=432702517 *Contributors*: 159753, 6mat1, Aaerial, Abscissa, Abscond, Adam78, Ahoerstemeier, Ahpook, Airodyssey, Akendall, Alan Au, Alandavidson, Alex43223, Alexrexpvt, AllanHainey, Alon, Amir85, Andrewpmk, Andrus Kallastu, Anna Lincoln, Anwar saadat, Artemis on Mars, Arthena, Avalon, BD2412, BKCI, Bagatelle, Bdelisle, Bearian, BearingArms, Behmod, Beland, Bigjonnyg, Bkonrad, BlueZenith, Bodragon, Bratch, Brideshead, BrokenMirror, BrokenMirror2, Brossow, CR85747, Cahk, Cameron Nedland, CanadianLinuxUser, CarbonLifeForm, Centrx, Cfso2325, Chester Markel, Chochopk, Choster, Chris the speller, Chrisd10, Christopherlin, Ckatz, Clawed, Cleared as filed, Computer97, Curious1i, Czalex, DW805366597GB, DXRAW, Dadado1, Daffodillman, Dave9190, David Cohen, David Levy, Dcandeto, Decora, Deli nk, Delldot, Djheini, DocWatson42, Dolek, Donatus, Donfbreed, DragonflySixtyseven, Drake Wilson, Dt2chow, Dulciana, Duncanogi, EVula, Eatcacti, Ehrenkater, Ekarulf, El C, Ellsworth, Elvey, Emana, Enviroboy, Ephebi, Erc, Espoo, Etrigan, Evice, Evil Monkey, Excretion, Exxolon, Eyreland, Fangz, Feedmecereal, Felix Wan, Flavious27, Foolswisdom, Francis Tyers, Frank Anchor, Fratrep, Funandtrvl, Funkysapien, GVnayR, Gail, Galoubet, Gareth Aus, GentlemanGhost, Gerhard51, Ghane, GordonUS, Gpvos, Gravitan, Greensburger, Hairy Dude, Hauskalainen, Heartagram man, HenryLi, Herbertxu, Historychecker, Hmains, Hohum, Hova1278, Huey45, II MusLiM HyBRiD II, Ianmacm, Igorpetchorine, Iridescent, Ironholds, Ixfd64, JackLumber, Jagged 85, Jamesontai, Jayapura, Jeff G., JeffJ, Jfurtner, Jkstark, John Nevard, Jonsafari, JulesH, Kanrahk, Kbh3rd, KingShakota, Kingal86, Kintetsubuffalo, Kinu, Koenbeek, Kolonuk, Kostisl, Ksyrie, LachlanA, Lacrimosus, Lairor, Lambiam, Legis, Levin, Liftarn, LilHelpa, Lincolnite, Lotje, Lowellian, Luckyherb, MAG1, MER-C, Mailer diablo, Mani1, MarkSutton, Martinjakubik, Materialscientist, Mauls, Maxí, Mazin07, Melsaran, Mexaguil, Michael Hardy, Michael Zimmermann, Mirageous, Mkooiman, Mmustafa, Mmw09, Montrealais, Morken, Mosca, Mr. Wheely Guy, MrNonchalant, Mrschimpf, Mspraveen, Mukerjee, Myria, N5iln, NFH, Naudefj, NawlinWiki, Nazgul533, Nbarth, Ndkartik, Nesher, Nickshanks, Nikopoley, Nina98765, Nk, Nlaporte, Noisy, Nonky, Nono64, Novacatz, Novium, Nuance13x, OLP1999, OMBG, Ohconfucius, Orange Suede Sofa, OsamaBinLogin, Ost316, PBurns, Palica, Paradoxian, Pauls32822, Pepijn Schmitz, PeterR, Philip Trueman, Phuzion, Piano non troppo, Pinethicket, Potosino, Psychonaut, Ptschett, Pwt898, RBBrittain, RM21, Random832, Ranveig, Rdavout, RedCoat10, Rees11, Reyk, Rfc1394, Rivalarrival, Rjd0060, Rjwilmsi, Roastytoast, Rob625, RockMFR, Rod Dobson, Ryanminier, SDC, Sargdub, Sasdrtx, Schzmo, Scott Sanchez, Scriberius, Scrouds, Sean.hoyland, Search4Lancer, Searchme, Secator, Shoeofdeath, Siddharth9200, Simon-in-sagamihara, Simon123, Skäpperöd, Sligocki, Slipperyweasel, Smack, Smiteri, Smoke003723, Snowy150, Sonett72, Songdog, SteinbDJ, Stephan Leeds, Stifle, Struthious Bandersnatch, Sumsum2010, Tawker, Teotwawki-je, The Grand Rans, Thedreamdied, Theflyingman, Thirty-seven, Thomas Larsen, Thumperward, Tide rolls, Tigga en, Tomyhoi, Toon05, TradeMe, Trovatore, Turkeyphant, Twin Bird, Unreal7, ValerioC, Vicarious, Viciouslime, Violetriga, Void2258, W5848, WadeSimMiser, What123, Wlodzimierz, Wnpaul, Wongm, Woohookitty, Wpktsfs, Wyoskier, Xp54321, Yellow Element, Yst, यात्रिक, ☻, 454 anonymous edits

Cheque guarantee card *Source*: http://en.wikipedia.org/w/index.php?oldid=426519295 *Contributors*: Airodyssey, Chrisieboy, Fayenatic london, Gpvos, Grobertson, Hairy Dude, JimWhitaker, Nbarth, Pne, Rich Farmbrough, Scott Sanchez, Wflynn, 14 anonymous edits

Cheque truncation *Source*: http://en.wikipedia.org/w/index.php?oldid=419104738 *Contributors*: ClamDip, Irish Payments Services Organisation, John of Reading, Khangrah, Lwalt, Nbarth, Sargdub, 1 anonymous edits

Cheque truncation system *Source*: http://en.wikipedia.org/w/index.php?oldid=426165036 *Contributors*: Angamk, FiachraByrne, Garima.rai30, Mr Sheep Measham

Chip and PIN *Source*: http://en.wikipedia.org/w/index.php?oldid=430989675 *Contributors*: AJR, Accounting4Taste, Acolston, Admrboltz, Adw2000, Ajuk, Antaeus Feldspar, Baibeigui, Barek, BillG, Brockert, Carbonix, Cjnewbs, Dah31, Dave2, Davidsteed, Dennisc24, Dhollm, Digitalme, Djegan, Dwheeler, ENeville, ESkog, Earlgrey, Edward, Extra999, Favonian, Fish and karate, FisherQueen, Georgeslegloupier, GregX102, Hairy Dude, Harrykitten, Heron, I do not exist, IMSoP, IainP, Islander, JK125, JameiLei, Jazzygeof, JoeSmack, Jomsborg, Jvlm.123, Kaihsu, Kgaughan, L-Zwei, Leeatcookerly, Luckyeye13, Martian, MartinRe, Mh96, Mitch Ames, Mojo-chan, Motley Crue Rocks, Mr WR, Mrmuk, Mwsealey, Neal ricketts, NerdyNSK, Nishkid64, Ojw, Olipro, Omgosh30, Parisnparis, Pastore Italy, PatrikR, Plop, Pluke, Pmytch, Pol098, Prunesqualer, Putney Bridge, R Lowry, Rapido, Rbrwr, Rd232, Rheumatictangle, Rich Farmbrough, Rjwilmsi, Robindch, SJMurdoch, SLi, Sargdub, Setanta747, Sjakkalle, Slow Riot, Socrates2008, Solair2020, Stephan Leeds, SteveLoughran, Stickee, Stuwee, Sunholm, The Anome, The Thing That Should Not Be, TheIntersect, Thingg, Tjq, Tom-, Tommy2010, Trounce, TurboForce, VictorianMutant, Vrenator, WatchAndObserve, Wjousts, Woohookitty, Zootm, 171 anonymous edits

Chip Authentication Program *Source*: http://en.wikipedia.org/w/index.php?oldid=428757060 *Contributors*: Compressionignition, CrossHouses, Danorton, Jjasi, Jomsborg, LeoNerd, Little Professor, Max Naylor, Mitch Ames, Mrph, Niayre, Olipro, Petergullberg, Quixoticgeek, Scottmacpherson, Tassedethe, Tcnuk, Vimalp, Woohookitty, 44 anonymous edits

Choice (credit card) *Source*: http://en.wikipedia.org/w/index.php?oldid=389527008 *Contributors*: ProhibitOnions, Rjwilmsi, SchuminWeb, 1 anonymous edits

Circular note *Source*: http://en.wikipedia.org/w/index.php?oldid=411233442 *Contributors*: CorbinSimpson, Gregbard, ToyotaPanasonic, Wwoods, 1 anonymous edits

Clearstream *Source*: http://en.wikipedia.org/w/index.php?oldid=432165053 *Contributors*: ADM, AK Auto, Alast0r, AlexLevyOne, Amohren, Andreas Toth, Atmfixer, Avaiki, Avant Guard, Awiseman, Barticus88, Bastin, Bejnar, Betacommand, BorgQueen, Brenont, Brunorossignol, CambridgeBayWeather, Cenarium, Chendy, Circeus, Cmdrjameson, D6, DabMachine, DickSummerfield, District Nein, Ed Fitzgerald, Edward, EmanWilm, Epeefleche, Erianna, Fiachra10003, Gaius Cornelius, Gloriamarie, Good Olfactory, GregorB, Gwernol, Haus, Hooiwind, Info.abstracta, Janawar, JeDi, JohnInDC, Johnbod, Joseph Solis in Australia, Kessler, Klearstream, Ksnow, LAk loho, Ligulem, LilHelpa, Lkomisar, M3taphysical, Maher27777, Mailer diablo, Marc Tobias Wenzel, Marudubshinki, Marysunshine, Matrask, Matt 314, Mervyn, Messie Français, Mikaelbook, Mike McGregor (Can), Mion, Myk60640, Neurillon, One, PatrikR, Plasticup, Plymouthpictures, Pvazz, Quadell, RJFJR, Ricky81682, Rjwilmsi, Sargdub, Simon12, Softron, Spejic, Stereo, Steven J. Anderson, TJive, Tazmaniacs, The Thing That Should Not Be, Theo10011, Thomas Blomberg, Travelbird, Truetom, Vivenot, WikiLaurent, Will Beback, Woohookitty, Xavier Sylvestre, 105 anonymous edits

Cleeng *Source*: http://en.wikipedia.org/w/index.php?oldid=422564352 *Contributors*: Bearcat, Donald.res, Gildo GD, Nick Wilson, Yworo, 11 anonymous edits

ClickandBuy *Source*: http://en.wikipedia.org/w/index.php?oldid=433037844 *Contributors*: Faceman98, Leo141, Moonriddengirl, Top Jim, VernoWhitney

CNG Processing A/S *Source*: http://en.wikipedia.org/w/index.php?oldid=415106638 *Contributors*: Bluiee, Neurolysis, Reedy, Sargdub, The Thing That Should Not Be, Xe7al, 1 anonymous edits

Collect on delivery *Source*: http://en.wikipedia.org/w/index.php?oldid=418393558 *Contributors*: AgentPeppermint, Alx xlA, Ashley Pomeroy, Calwiki, Hairy Dude, Hrsn, Ike9898, Jackfork, Krich, Lord Cornwallis, Michael Romanov, Montana's Defender, Morio, Pil56, PohTayToez, Polylerus, Radiojon, RainbowCrane, RedWolf, Sc147, Scarykitty, Silvonen, Tassedethe, Tercio28, Vranak, Yidisheryid, 19 anonymous edits

Concord EFS, Inc. *Source*: http://en.wikipedia.org/w/index.php?oldid=386179103 *Contributors*: Alvin Seville, Bearcat, GregorB, Hsbrent, Sweetmoose6, 1 anonymous edits

Confinity *Source*: http://en.wikipedia.org/w/index.php?oldid=424636326 *Contributors*: Crystallina, Elonka, Eptin, Funandtrvl, Gazpacho, Hmains, Korenzhang2244, Monkeyblue, Nobody of Consequence, Rjwilmsi, Scott Illini, 9 anonymous edits

Corporate travel management *Source*: http://en.wikipedia.org/w/index.php?oldid=432654978 *Contributors*: Ajgw-nyc, Beta16, EagleFan, EnOreg, Funandtrvl, Jackelfive, Malcolma, Penbat, R'n'B, RHaworth, Ravigoel06, Vicky Ng, 5 anonymous edits

Cougar Mountain Software *Source*: http://en.wikipedia.org/w/index.php?oldid=428492785 *Contributors*: Cander0000, Craw-daddy, Dparvin, EnviroGranny, Fiftyquid, Haakon, Hmains, Joebray, Malcolma, Masiano, Mvching, R'n'B, Rcawsey, ReneeEG, S.K., Timneu22, 8 anonymous edits

Crossing of cheques *Source*: http://en.wikipedia.org/w/index.php?oldid=430541878 *Contributors*: Bender235, Canis Lupus, Dawningthunder, Fabrictramp, Funandtrvl, Markiewp, Nbarth, Skruhkui775, Taliska, TinribsAndy, Wloveral, Wonglokking, 11 anonymous edits

Crowd funding *Source*: http://en.wikipedia.org/w/index.php?oldid=432773360 *Contributors*: Adrian J. Hunter, Ahannula, Alexzabbey, Allthingsonline, Ashappy, Barek, BenRG, BenediktG, Bernark2010, Billsaysthis, Classicalecon, CliffC, Connor2nz, Dazwest, Dennis Bratland, Dgeertz, Edwell, Elbradio, ErCradel, Erianna, Everton137, Gary King, Geertz, GetMKWearMKFly, Grafen, Hmbr, Hugh Mason, Indywood, Jamesderin, Jarry1250, Jeremymclain, Karl.brown, Kevinlawton, Kittycats74, Madsy19, Matdewas, Mathewvwalker, MatthiasGutfeldt, Mikomaniac, Nahum Reduta, Nestorvc, Nowa, Ohnoitsjamie, Olliemmc, Owaine1, Pde, Piledhigheranddeeper, Piotrus, Pnm, Quasar1000, Rjwilmsi, Sameerthahir, Shadowjams, Sopoforic, Spaxbuilder, Startupman1, Steven Walling, Supramannz, The Interior, Themfromspace, Vgregv, Victor985, WebHamster, Wikidemon, Wjmcn, Xc87slc, Zainfidel, Île flottante, 158 anonymous edits

Currence *Source*: http://en.wikipedia.org/w/index.php?oldid=431390228 *Contributors*: Sargdub

CyberCash, Inc. *Source*: http://en.wikipedia.org/w/index.php?oldid=423109168 *Contributors*: Blaisorblade, Bobo192, Curps, Elvey, Honus, LtPowers, RJFJR, RazorICE, Robertjm, 18 anonymous edits

Debit card *Source*: http://en.wikipedia.org/w/index.php?oldid=432776403 *Contributors*: (, .mdk., 123music, 64.229.89.xxx, 842U, A Softer Answer, Accurizer, Adashiel, Ageekgal, Airplaneman, Akohler, AlexJ, Alexf, Alexius08, Alhizar, Alice Mudgarden, Altzinn, Androl, Angelicarulez, Ansett, Antiussentimnet, Appleseed, Arthena, Asclepius, Auric, Azrin619, Azuresky63, BIL, Baa, Bdelisle, Beland, BenShade, Berkland, Bfortega, Bilz0r, Biscuittin, Bloodgod884, Bluemoose, Bmgoau, Bonadea, Brandongohwh, Brian Katt, Brianga, Buddha24, Buybooks Marius, COMPFUNK2, CUSENZA Mario, Cab88, Caerbannog, Cahk, Carlosguitar, Cashonthebeach, Caspertheghost, Catgut, CesarB, Ceyockey, Cfaerber, Chadsamaniego, Chensiyuan, Chowbok, Chrisieboy, Christopherlin, Ciotog, Clearduty, Colourshield, Comp25, Computor, Confession0791, Conversion script, CowboyBear, Crazycomputers, Crocodile Punter, Crossmr, Curlyjimsam, Cyber Sayers, Cyberplant, DVD R W, Da monster under your bed, DanielEng, Dantadd, Danusch, Dave314159, Dbpgroup, Dcandeto, De728631, Debresser, DeeMusil, Deli nk, DerHexer, Dethme0w, Devil deadman, Djegan, Dolovis, Dominic, DopefishJustin, Dopeslax, DrVeghead, Dub8lad1, Dude444, E Wing, Earthlyreason, EdH, Edward, ElKevbo, Emmanuel JARRI, Epark129, Evanluxzenburg, Evice, Evil Monkey, Ewawer, Excirial, Excretion, Faizhaider, Faradayplank, FinalRapture, Flex125, FlowR, Furrykef, Fvasconcellos, Gaius Cornelius, Geoffg, Glane23, GoingBatty, GoldRenet, Gombang, GraemeL, Grant M, GreenJoe, Greenbough, Grick, Gsarwa, Gwernol, HDokins, HalfShadow, Hammer1980, Hanii Puppy, Hellno2, Hello350, Hmains, Hongkonghusain, Hoo man, Hotsaucedude, Hroðulf, Inata, Intermittentgardener, Inzy, J, J.delanoy, JBellis, JFM, JForget, JSellers0, Jackster, Jamesofur, Janke, Jasondmath, JavierMC, Jedi Davideus, Jerryseinfeld, John Quincy Adding Machine, John of Reading, Johnbradleytlh, Johnnie ong, Joostik, Jopemon, JoshFarron, Joshua, Joy, Kashmiri, Katt, Kedi the tramp, Kenyon, Kfkowa63, Kikumbob, Killervogel5, Kimiko, Kirjtc2, Kjd, Knutux, Kozuch, Kremmen, Kungfuadam, Kurt Jansson, Kurykh, L Kensington, Lan3y, Lcmortensen, Legion fi, Lester112, Lirane1, Logan, Loganberry, Lstanley1979, Luci Sandor, Lupo, Macktheknifeau, Malatesta, Mapletip, Marek69, MarkS, Markb, Martarius, Materialscientist, Maxf, Mbstone, Mdoubledragon, Mendaliv, Micru, Midnightcomm, Miernik, MikeKn, Minimac, Mkl12, Montegorx, Mr Stephen, MrWeeble, Mrubin22, Mulder416, MyLoveLife, Myanw, Myscrnnm, Mz20g7, NFH, Nachdenklich, Naive rm, NawlinWiki, Neal ricketts, Neelix, Niayre, Nivix, Noelgsan, NotMuchToSay, O1ive, ONUnicorn, OlEnglish, OwenBlacker, Oystermind, P.B. Pilhet, Paradoxsociety, Paranomia, Patrick, PaulHanson, Pavel Vozenilek, Pearle, Peripitus, Phatom87, Philip Trueman, Pjessen, Pointillist, Pontificalibus, Poochy, Prashanthns, ProhibitOnions, Prowler08, Pt, Qsecofr, Quadell, R. S. Shaw, RBBrittain, RLEEG, Raanoo, Racingmom, Radagast, Radiant chains, RadiantRay, Realmgic, Recognizance, Reinoutr, ResidueOfDesign, Rettetast, RetypePassword, Rfc1394, Rich Farmbrough, Richard Arthur Norton (1958-), Rimshot, Rivalarrival, Rjd0060, Rjstott, Rjwilmsi, RobertMfromLl, RobyWayne, Ronhjones, Rufus843, Sabbath1993, Samuelsl01, Sargdub, Saros136, Scarequotes, Scott Sanchez, Scoub, Sea0818, Seanth123, Seaphoto, Searchme, Secretlondon, Sega381, SergioGeorgini, Shadowlink1014, Silroquen, Simon123, Sjakkalle, Smalljim, Smallman12q, Snowolf, Sockatume, Solsticedhiver, Sonett72, South Bay, Spag85, SpiderJon, Staffwaterboy, Starionwolf, Starkhorn, Stefan2, Stifle, Stuskiv, Superflush, Tetrahedron93, The Anome, The Thing That Should Not Be, TheTechieGeek63, Thelawnchair, Tide rolls, Timichal, Tingrin87, Tins128, Tresiden, Uncle G, Unisubs, UseMyBank, VISIONTEKTELE, Victor, Vidyasagara, Voice99, Vuo, Waffle, Wednesdayblues, Welshie, Western west, Westleyd, Weyes, WikHead, WillMcC, Willuknight, Wizard191, Woohookitty, Wt90401, X-Biiz, Xandern, Xpanzion, Yamaguchi先生, Yamamoto Ichiro, Yintan, Ynhockey, Zeuscho, Zippanova, Zollerriia, 恐龙 1971, 719 anonymous edits

Decoupled debit card *Source*: http://en.wikipedia.org/w/index.php?oldid=335505611 *Contributors*: Funandtrvl, Hu12, L'Aquatique, Mmpartee, Rjwilmsi, 1 anonymous edits

Demand draft *Source*: http://en.wikipedia.org/w/index.php?oldid=396976750 *Contributors*: Betacommand, Delldot, Eugene-elgato, Fishnet37222, GregorB, Hbent, Hitomi, Iball, Instantpc, Instantpc1, Jlygrnmigt, LilHelpa, MaximvsDecimvs, PenguiN42, Seanstickywiki, Someguy1221, Spellcast, Stifle, ZimZalaBim, 9 anonymous edits

Depository Trust & Clearing Corporation *Source*: http://en.wikipedia.org/w/index.php?oldid=428897780 *Contributors*: Awdamle, Barticus88, Beardo, Beta m, BillyTheWiz, Bmathis, Bobblewik, Chase me ladies, I'm the Cavalry, Cla68, DocendoDiscimus, Duedilly, ERcheck, Edward, Eliz81, Epeefleche, Ethelh, Feco, Feeeshboy, Feldmang, Figureofnine, Funandtrvl, Fvasconcellos, Gaius Cornelius, Giraffedata, Grafikm fr, Ground Zero, Hu12, Huw Powell, Imasud, J Conmy, Jamesdin, JohnnyB256, JoshuaZ, Joy, JzG, KoshVorlon, Larry Bergman, Lawrence Cohen, Leifern, Lesliepear, Lousypoetry, MZMcBride, Magioladitis, Maurreen, Mickster810, Pearle, Ph.eyes, Piperdown, QuiteUnusual, R.D.H. (Ghost In The Machine), Radiant!, RegentsPark, Rich Farmbrough, Rjwilmsi, Rrius, Samiharris, Sargdub, Sarregouset, Shortride, Skalmier, Smallbones, Softgirl, Solbris, Stjen, Timothylord, Tregoweth, Trident13, Twang, Waggers, Watson272, Watson45, Will Beback, Woohookitty, 126 anonymous edits

Dexit *Source*: http://en.wikipedia.org/w/index.php?oldid=358723908 *Contributors*: Everyking, Ground Zero, Indefatigable, Kurieeto, Lectonar, Mihoshi, Pstegs, SarahEmm, TheoClarke, Timc, YUL89YYZ, 4 anonymous edits

DigiCash *Source*: http://en.wikipedia.org/w/index.php?oldid=433318090 *Contributors*: Ampatarini, Andy Dingley, Davidshq, Dawynn, Huan086, Phyzome, Robofish, Silpol, Tagishsimon, 7 anonymous edits

Digital wallet *Source*: http://en.wikipedia.org/w/index.php?oldid=431565935 *Contributors*: Bsadowski1, Chris83, Danathompson, Donnabella11, Dweller, Elonka, Frap, Gogo Dodo, GoingBatty, Jpbernier, L3lackEyedAngels, Lmkahn, Malcolma, MrOllie, Pharaoh of the Wizards, Prezence, Rich Farmbrough, Robinramm, Spoirier, TwistOfCain, 39 anonymous edits

Diners Club International *Source*: http://en.wikipedia.org/w/index.php?oldid=432145118 *Contributors*: 205ywmpq, Adambro, Airodyssey, Ajraddatz, Alvis, Andris, Anon lynx, BlueRyan1975, Branddobbe, Brougham96, Buybooks Marius, CambridgeBayWeather, Celarnor, Crocodile Punter, D3gtrd, Damian Yerrick, Davemcarlson, Deb, Diners Club, Dismas, EagleOne, Esrever, Fergie4000, Flowanda, Friedo, Ground Zero, HiFiGuy, Ida Shaw, IndyMustang, IvanLanin, Jamcib, Jaraalbe, Jerryseinfeld, Jusily, Jxan3000, Kbdank71, Kevintoronto, Khalid hassani, Lucasreddinger, Luckyluke, M@sk, MSTCrow, Malepheasant, Nargalzius, NatTerner2, NeonMerlin, Neutrality, Pauli133, Peterhgregory, Pmlineditor, Postdlf, ProhibitOnions, Qwyrxian, Rees11, Rintrah, Scott Sanchez, Shii, Shirley Locks, TJMELIS, TheNewPhobia, Tinton5, Valentino, Vargklo, Versageek, Viperazzi, WideArc, Wistex, Zhxy 519, 124 anonymous edits

Direct corporate access *Source*: http://en.wikipedia.org/w/index.php?oldid=425991536 *Contributors*: Beardtwizzle, Chase me ladies, I'm the Cavalry, Egonavis, Fabrictramp, Pigsonthewing, Rickybling, SchuminWeb, Sophus Bie, Top Jim, YUL89YYZ, 13 anonymous edits

Direct debit *Source*: http://en.wikipedia.org/w/index.php?oldid=431294457 *Contributors*: After Midnight, Ale And Quail, Alex.muller, All4peace, Andrus Kallastu, Andysta, AstroMark, Balfa, Beland, Beria, Betacommand, Blazius, BreakfastTime, Camw, Celique, Cfaerber, DDexpert, Daniel Lawrence, Dkam, Dynam1te3, EditorInTheRye, Elwell, FloreatAntiquaDomus, Flowanda, Fuzheado, Gavinl2001, Gerhard51, Goudzovski, Hairy Dude, Harcombe10, Hmains, J Di, Jamiegodwin, Japo, Jennydoop, Lexicon, Lordbufonte, Mandarax, Mccready, Miernik, Mitchellj, NFH, NMTower, Naive rm, Necrothesp, Nemo bis, Neuro, Neutrality, Oashi, Olegos, Pallas44, Peoplehub, Pgr94, Php2rh, Reesmf, Rjstott, Roughana, S473599, Shepard, Sicherlich, Simon123, SimonArlott, Smjg, Stefan2, SteveCrook, Stifle, Sturm55, TastyPoutine, Tiger888, TimBenjamin, Twilsonb, Valeriegirl23, Vic Halom, Vytis1, Welshie, Xabier Cid, 98 anonymous edits

Disney's Fastpass *Source*: http://en.wikipedia.org/w/index.php?oldid=431929825 *Contributors*: 68DANNY2, Afrank99, AmericaSings, Bellagio2, Boyd888, Brian Kendig, Chardish, Crispy1995, DavidLevinson, DerHexer, Derktar, Elf, Epolk, Etoile, Evil saltine, FA Jon, Gaius Cornelius, Hawaiian717, Herehy, Herlehy, IloveHKDL, Jedi94, Jonnny, LordBleen, MHarrington, McDoobAU93, Mike411, Monotonehell, Napnet, Perimosocordiae, Polyman586, RadioFan2 (usurped), Rjwilmsi, SFGiants, SchmuckyTheCat, SchuminWeb, Seinfreak37, Speedway, SpikeJones, Summerhawk, The Wiki ghost, Themeparkagent, Themeparkgc, ThunderBlue, Tiggerjay, Tpwc12, Tregoweth, Valedc03ls, WestJet, Weston96, Xezbeth, Zepheus, 49 anonymous edits

Double-spending *Source*: http://en.wikipedia.org/w/index.php?oldid=432628267 *Contributors*: Catdude, Cesium 133, Chronulator, Nbarth, 1 anonymous edits

Dynamic currency conversion *Source*: http://en.wikipedia.org/w/index.php?oldid=419650395 *Contributors*: Aruanda12, Barek-public, Brianfrey, D.M, DabMachine, Dippa3000, Edward, FXreviewer, Fram, Fxrate, GoingBatty, Jcockrem, Jgombos, Jraftery, Keithmccabe2, Kring, LilHelpa, Middayexpress, Mpeylo, Mr. Laser Beam, NFH, Radiojon, SLi, Seanwood7, Smcelroy, Smiker, Soylentyellow, Stefan2, TerrySav, ThorstenS, Tj-sav, Tom Foolery, Vicky Ng, Woohookitty, 79 anonymous edits

e-gold *Source*: http://en.wikipedia.org/w/index.php?oldid=433339822 *Contributors*: -jkb-, Albyva, AlexE, Angelguy, Artemis.Dreamseeker, Asadqureshy, AshtonBenson, Astronaut, Ati7, Atlastawake, Atreyu42, AxelBoldt, Basilwhite, Bbird, Bigger Woulds, Birdhombre, Bookandcoffee, Butlerm, Cadwallader, Can't sleep, clown will eat me, Chasemcc, Cheque some, Chowbok, CommonsDelinker, Crucible Guardian, Crystallina, Da Vynci, Damian Yerrick, David-Sarah Hopwood, Db26, Dbollard99, Dbrisinda, Der Eberswalder, Dick Lepre, Dissipate, Dkameleon, Dodonov, Drew-rox-u, Dylan Lake, Dysprosia, Eb.eric, Emperorbma, Enwik, Epimetreus, Eric Shalov, Erwin, Eshui2007, Eurobas, Ewlyahoocom, Eyreland, Eztli, Flowanda, Foobaz, FusionKnight, Gasy, Gene Nygaard, GoingBatty, Gokusandwich, Gonvaled, GraemeL, GregorB, Haakon, Hayabusa future, Hemanshu, Heycam, Highway of Life, Hit bull, win steak, I already forgot, Ideamakingmach, Idleguy, Insider-network, J Di, JDezoer, Jdavidb, Jdlh, JeremyStein, Jiang, John Broughton, John Quiggin, John Vandenberg, Jonahtrainer, Kelly clan, Kevin143, Kingboyk, Krimm99, Kuru, Leafyplant, Leuko, M5, MMTbureau, Madchester, Magasin, Mendaliv, Miernik, Miked84, Mild Bill Hiccup, MisterHand, Monkeyman, MrJones, Mx3, N1h1l, N5iln, Night Gyr, NintendoWiki, Nirvana2013, Norm, Ohwell32, Omegatron, Oneiros, Pamri, Panthos304, Pelister, Philwelch, Psb777, Qrsdogg, Rapido, RevRagnarok, Rick7425, Rio, Rjwilmsi, Roadrunner, Rob T Firefly, Rockfang, Romaeus, Scott Burley, Search4Lancer, Searchme, Seneca91, Sferrier, Shaddack, Shii, Shlomke, Simple Bob, SnowFire, Sobec, Soylentyellow, Stephen e nelson, Storkk, TMSTKSBK, Terjepetersen, Texture, Thadius856AWB, TheSeer, Thoerin, Trivialist, Trufonz, Turkeyphant, Veinor, Versageek, Versus22, VeryVerily, WhisperToMe, White 720, Witzcowitz, Xyzzyplugh, Yosemite1967, Ypicurve@yahoo.ie, Yserarau, Zarutian, Zotel, 498 anonymous edits

E-toll *Source*: http://en.wikipedia.org/w/index.php?oldid=404289077 *Contributors*: DiiCinta, Hippietrail, Jll, Merbabu, Mfa fariz, SatuSuro, SimonTrew, 5 anonymous edits

Eagle Cash *Source*: http://en.wikipedia.org/w/index.php?oldid=428151650 *Contributors*: Art LaPella, Beland, Blueviper99, Chris the speller, Funandtrvl, Haemo, Hmains, Joshua Scott, LorenzoB, Rafaelgoogle, 5 anonymous edits

Earnest payment *Source*: http://en.wikipedia.org/w/index.php?oldid=418301274 *Contributors*: Allycallas, AnakngAraw, Anwar saadat, Aristitleism, Brian0918, Cyrius, David Haslam, Delldot, Edwardaretz, Ewlyahoocom, Grutness, H Padleckas, J3ff, John hartley, Kalbasa, Karmafist, Michaelbluejay, NatePhysics, PullUpYourSocks, Reflex Reaction, Rklawton, Shaneatx, Sonett72, Surv1v4l1st, Visviva, Viva-Verdi, Zvar, 24 anonymous edits

Ebillz *Source*: http://en.wikipedia.org/w/index.php?oldid=390123906 *Contributors*: Canis Lupus, Hm2k, Joaquin008, Woohookitty, Zardari1, 54 anonymous edits

EBPP *Source*: http://en.wikipedia.org/w/index.php?oldid=425500944 *Contributors*: 2710-4E-809, Axlq, Cahk, Chomphosy, Dilip8708, DouglasEBraun, ESkog, Espoo, Funandtrvl, Greenrd, Jdmcnaul, JonathanY08, Joncwarner, Kinu, Kuru, Nitoszka, Octopus-Hands, Phatom87, Philriordan, Pical, Radiojon, Roleplayer, Saudss, Stevegrifftx, Ziplock3600, 9 anonymous edits

ecash *Source*: http://en.wikipedia.org/w/index.php?oldid=429958179 *Contributors*: Andy Dingley, Apoc2400, Bensin, Daniel11, DanielPharos, Frap, Gzornenplatz, Ironic goat, LittleDan, Markulf, Miracle Pen, Pratyeka, RobertMfromLI, Rudykog, Scientus, Searchme, Tim Pritlove, Yishiuan, 37 anonymous edits

EDesk *Source*: http://en.wikipedia.org/w/index.php?oldid=423674692 *Contributors*: Chonchonr, Funezn, Khangrah, RadioFan, Tassedethe, The Elves Of Dunsimore, Woohookitty, 1 anonymous edits

eFaktura *Source*: http://en.wikipedia.org/w/index.php?oldid=283617176 *Contributors*: Arsenikk, Pilum, Rettetast, Superbeecat, 3 anonymous edits

EFTPOS *Source*: http://en.wikipedia.org/w/index.php?oldid=430274566 *Contributors*: (, Abeorch, Aenar, Alexwcovington, Ansett, Beetle120, BenShade, Blue520, Bobo192, Boyroma80, Ceyockey, ChrisCork, ClementSeveillac, Cmdrjameson, Conversion script, DazMan07, Deanm nz, Dkam, Domster, Doomaxe54, Drstuey, Elkman, Epbr123, Erebus555, Ewawer, Farah99, Favonian, Fbriere, Gaius Cornelius, Galaxiaad, Gezrah, GringoInChile, Hobscrottle, Itai, Jedkiwi, Jey1432, John Quincy Adding Machine, Joy, Joyous!, Jwissick, Kaijan, Kewp, Khalid hassani, Lanma726, Laurawaring, Lee Carre, Lofor, Lupin, Marek69, Martarius, Meand, Mitch Ames, MoondyneAWB, Mprovost, Mrath, NathanBeach, Nlu, Nunganunga, Onursendag2, Phatom87, Phil-hong, PrimroseGuy, Rich Farmbrough, Rlgwilliams, Ryanminier, Sargdub, Scott Sanchez, Sean Heron, Simon123, SimonP, Snickerdo, Snori, Srushe, Tawker, Terence, Thomas Hambleton, Ttwaring, UkPaolo, VxP, WikHead, Wistex, YUL89YYZ, Yamaguchi先生, Youngtwig, Zaian, Ziggurat, 161 anonymous edits

Electronic Benefit Transfer *Source*: http://en.wikipedia.org/w/index.php?oldid=409823935 *Contributors*: 2, AMC0712, Akerans, Avij, Beeblebrox, Beland, Blastarr, Caeden1966, Calwatch, Dosman, E. Fokker, Edward, Frank Anchor, Gbleem, Gospelnous, Gracenotes, Jonnycando, Kiand, Minivet, Mrbrown, Owen, PaulHanson, Pnm, RBBrittain, Rufus843, SFHomeless, Steveparsons98, SuperHamster, Thumperward, Tom-, Tyrol5, 33 anonymous edits

Electronic bill payment *Source*: http://en.wikipedia.org/w/index.php?oldid=419365573 *Contributors*: 2, Beland, Danntm, Funandtrvl, Greensburger, Oashi, Phatom87, Pnm, Radiojon, Rifleman 82, Rjwilmsi, Ron Ritzman, Scott Sanchez, Steinsky, Vuo, WKCole, ZimZalaBim, 9 anonymous edits

Electronic billing *Source*: http://en.wikipedia.org/w/index.php?oldid=416946533 *Contributors*: 2710-4E-809, Axlq, Barek, Beland, Billingmaster, Cburnett, Chewy m, Chomphosy, Christian75, Cliffb, CourtneyLBrewer, Ellery, Espoo, Firsfron, Hoo man, Hu12, Jeffco, Jim0115, John Quiggin, Jpbowen, Kenrick.koo, Lsjzl, Mbh66, MrOllie, Nitoszka, Nricardo, Octopus-Hands, Oxymoron83, Pearrari, Pgillman, RBBrittain, Radiojon, Reinoutr, Saganaki-, Silverdoctor, SiobhanHansa, Stevegrifftx, UberScienceNerd, 26 anonymous edits

Electronic Check Council *Source*: http://en.wikipedia.org/w/index.php?oldid=426377042 *Contributors*: Chris83, Colonies Chris, Mikeblas, Pearle, Pegship, RBBrittain, RJFJR, Rj, Sargdub, Woohookitty

Electronic funds transfer *Source*: http://en.wikipedia.org/w/index.php?oldid=428581227 *Contributors*: 1ForTheMoney, A2Kafir, Ansett, Arsenikk, Avihu, Barek, Beland, Can't sleep, clown will eat me, Closedmouth, Correogsk, Cyber Sayers, Danielwfisher, Darth Mike, DougsTech, Epipelagic, Flowanda, Fmheir, Fru1tbat, Greensburger, Gurch, Gzkn, HDokins, Hu, Iulius, Joy, KSinitski, LizardJr8, Mazarin07, Mild Bill Hiccup, Mindmatrix, Mosmof, MrOllie, Paradox CT, Ph.eyes, Pnm, Praveen kodali, Prowriter16, R, R Math, Rcalvert, Sargdub, Schutz, Srushe, Templarion, The Thing That Should Not Be, Thunderboltz, Tomkliff, Unisubs, Versageek, Vpay, Weirdgaybigal, Willjasen, Winodhello, Zac11485, Zaian, 105 anonymous edits

Electronic money *Source*: http://en.wikipedia.org/w/index.php?oldid=433252419 *Contributors*: 12sa, 1dragon, 2D, 33rogers, A.Hamza, Ahmad Yasin, Aldie, Anaxial, Aneeraj007, Angr, Arctic Night, Atreyu42, AvicAWB, Beland, BenAbuyah, Bracton, CZmarlin, Cahk, Calebrw, Carom, Chronulator, CommonsDelinker, Creditz, Cromalter, Csenly, DBigMac, Danny, Dduane, Denisarona, Dreaded Walrus, Dskaushik, Ed Fitzgerald, Elockid, Excirial, FMax, Frap, Fredrik, Freewol, Fuzheado, Gaius Cornelius, Galathrax, Georgesawyer, Giwt goa, Gogo Dodo, Gonzonoir, GraemeL, Greudin, Grondilu, H1523702, Haemo, Hankyu, Haydont, Henrik, Holron, Hroðulf, Hselig01, Hu, HughMor, I am Me true, Ironic goat, Isaacsurh, Ixfd64, J-Star, Jackie, Jackriter, JamesBWatson, Jasonwacker, John of Reading, Kaskaad, Khalid hassani, Korath, Kragen, Kyrosho, Libertaar, Limideen, Listlist, MER-C, Macavity23, Marianna1407, Matt Crypto, Matt.smart, Maurreen, Mawald, Mazarin07, Mendel123, Merovingian, Meste, Miami33139, MickeyDuckling, Mindmatrix, Mitch Ames, Mkabalen, Monkeyman, MrOllie, Mydogategodshat, Neal ricketts, Newone, Nicks100, Nikai, Nirvana2013, NormanGorman, Notinasnaid, Novum, Ohnoitsjamie, Paalantam, Pcb21, Philip Trueman, Pkaram, Pratyeka, PurpleInkWriter, Quercus basaseachicensis, R Math, RJII, Rachel1234321, Ragnar1, Randwicked, Rashidjaved99, RasputinAXP, Rchamberlain, Reggionh, Remy B, Risi, Rjwilmsi, Roadrunner, Rwwww, SYSS Mouse, SchuminWeb, Scientus, SeanDuggan, Searchme, Shaddack, Shadow1, Shalom Yechiel, Shenme, Sioln, Sjjupadhyay, Sky Captain, Speculatrix, Sree34, Stv666, SunCreator, Swedenborg, TakuyaMurata, Teilolondon, Tiak, Timrichardson, Triquetra, Ukexpat, Vegetator, Versageek, Watsonladd, WhiteDragon, Whufc48, Xyzzyplugh, Yaronf, Yartiles, Yiannistsiounis, ZimZalaBim, Zimage, Zotel, Zro, Zzuuzz, 259 anonymous edits

Electronic Money Association *Source*: http://en.wikipedia.org/w/index.php?oldid=432500309 *Contributors*: Ajdlinux, Andrew lenaghan, Apoc2400, Bill william compton, Giraffedata, Ian Dalziel, Villabear, 7 anonymous edits

Electronic Payment Services *Source*: http://en.wikipedia.org/w/index.php?oldid=425282473 *Contributors*: Cellular, Ciotog, Eps2010, Excirial, Gm33223, HenryLi, Hydrogen Iodide, Instantpc, LG4761, Rayyung, SDC, Takamaxa, Un3creation, ZimZalaBim, Zzuuzz, 12 anonymous edits

Elektronisches Lastschriftverfahren *Source*: http://en.wikipedia.org/w/index.php?oldid=374569974 *Contributors*: PamD, Pratyeka

EPAS *Source*: http://en.wikipedia.org/w/index.php?oldid=411174056 *Contributors*: Adw2000, Anadyr, Ben.c.roberts, Cjdevane, Edcolins, Equens, Geozapf, Ioannes Pragensis, JennyRad, John Vandenberg, Leolaursen, PigFlu Oink, PrimroseGuy, So mok wi dat, 25 anonymous edits

Eurocheque *Source*: http://en.wikipedia.org/w/index.php?oldid=413140745 *Contributors*: Akhristov, Cfaerber, Dzsi, Fursten, Hairy Dude, Jemiller226, John Nevard, Michael Zimmermann, Mintaru, Mobius, NFH, NuclearWarfare, PrimroseGuy, Rjwilmsi, Searchme, 16 anonymous edits

The Everything Card *Source*: http://en.wikipedia.org/w/index.php?oldid=391677150 *Contributors*: Anon lynx, GrahamHardy, ProhibitOnions, 1 anonymous edits

Eway *Source*: http://en.wikipedia.org/w/index.php?oldid=429647253 *Contributors*: Bearcat, BurlyBower, Drmies, Glenfarclas, Grahamec, Jenncrudup, Jjimagery, JoSafBridge, Mhockey, Mortense, Reach Out to the Truth, Ttonyb1, 2 anonymous edits

EWise *Source*: http://en.wikipedia.org/w/index.php?oldid=410335156 *Contributors*: Anticipation of a New Lover's Arrival, The, Carltonsouthby, Derekwong32, Dreadstar, JForget, Jevansen, Mekm, Mhockey, Razzatk, Searchme, 2 anonymous edits

Express Payment System *Source*: http://en.wikipedia.org/w/index.php?oldid=422430906 *Contributors*: Chris the speller, Dbpgroup, Deor, Ginsengbomb, Lightmouse, S1to1c1km1iles1, Sky Harbor, 1 anonymous edits

Faster Payments Service *Source*: http://en.wikipedia.org/w/index.php?oldid=426341627 *Contributors*: 100phil, Agsnu, Baden Cottage, Bazj, Berk, Bgpaulus, Blarg99, Bobathon71, Chase me ladies, I'm the Cavalry, Chrisbloe, Chrisd10, Chrisjj3, Datamonkey5, Download, Egonavis, EoGuy, EssJayEll, Flyingscot, Fpseditor, Gt94sss2, Harry The Bustard, Kipoc, Kuru, Leszek Jańczuk, MRSC, Mandtplatt, Manne marak, Mayalld, NathanBeach, Neilf4321, Nzseries1, Olipro, Out there 101, Overett1, PaulHanson, Pauldoust, Phil-welch, Pol098, Pommygranite, Rcalvert, Rich Farmbrough, Rjwilmsi, SchuminWeb, Smjg, Stannered, Stiofan.walsh, Stokesd3, SurreyPanda, Thumperward, Timrollpickering, Vox Rationis, 297 anonymous edits

First Data *Source*: http://en.wikipedia.org/w/index.php?oldid=430835864 *Contributors*: Alex43223, Amcl, Arthur Smart, AznBurger, Beland, Ben5082, Bongomatic, CliffC, Cmiller173, Crocodile Punter, Csaenzs, DShantz, DamienMorris, Damiens.rf, Earlthepearl2, Gidzz, Greenshed, Gturpin, Hellno2, IronGargoyle, Kjohnson200, Kozuch, Lukobe, Maestrosync, MainFrame, Mason746, Mikejamesgrant, Nick Dillinger, Noswadmot, Nowa, Nutcracker, OSborn, PaulHanson, Pegship, Pig of Wig, Pretzelpaws, QueueNut, Reflex Reaction, Rich Farmbrough, Rjwilmsi, Salvio giuliano, Scott Illini, Scrouds, Shawnc, Shortride, Solarisworld, Sunny5414, Sweet-pea-1981, The wub, Thepangelinanpost, UnitedStatesian, Urbanrenewal, Walshga, Whaas2, WhisperToMe, Xnatedawgx, Александр Мотин, 117 anonymous edits

Flattr *Source*: http://en.wikipedia.org/w/index.php?oldid=432934566 *Contributors*: Bensin, Cander0000, Clamiax, CommonsDelinker, Cuaxdon, Devourer09, Eeekster, Greenrd, HaeB, Hontogaichiban, IGEL, Intgr, InverseHypercube, Jacob Lundberg, Jamiew, Jbening, Kocio, Mabdul, Malcolma, Manuelzs, MatiasSingers, MichaelSchoenitzer, Mortense, Nsaa, Obhave, OlivierMehani, PabloCastellano, Piglop, Polarbearjack, Rjwilmsi, Robbo1337, Ruud Koot, Skizzik, Smartse, Sonicsuns, Stassats, SuNotísima, Toussaint, Tuggler, Uwe Dedering, WakiMiko, Xeno, 14 anonymous edits

FloristWare POS System *Source*: http://en.wikipedia.org/w/index.php?oldid=404471679 *Contributors*: Camillia, Fabrictramp, Gaius Cornelius, Katharineamy, Mhockey, Mstuartanderson, Rjwilmsi, Warmfuzzygrrl, 1 anonymous edits

Freight payment service *Source*: http://en.wikipedia.org/w/index.php?oldid=431952024 *Contributors*: Cander0000, Colonies Chris, Fredsmith2, Lewisgoh, Mogmios, MrOllie, Nanzilla, Open2universe, Power piglet, Queerbubbles, SMasters, Steve.hill, Wafp1, 32 anonymous edits

FreshBooks *Source*: http://en.wikipedia.org/w/index.php?oldid=429113856 *Contributors*: Benvca, Hm2k, Jerome Charles Potts, JustinRossi, Kuru, LinguistAtLarge, Mortense, Rockfang, Sandybremer, Satori Son, Sonjaaa, Zeke72791, 15 anonymous edits

Fuel card *Source*: http://en.wikipedia.org/w/index.php?oldid=432003552 *Contributors*: 21655, Abbey fuelcards, Alynna Kasmira, Arwel Parry, BettyBoo2, Bobby588, Cdowning707, ColinAppleby, Custacquisition, DerHexer, Dimon2005, Download, Drieux, Drunkenmonkey, Ebyabe, Editproper, Emtl97, EncMstr, Environnement2100, Flowanda, Fox, Fremlin, Frogthing, Fuelcards, Guy Peters, Hellno2, Homiachok7, Incisivebusiness, JNW, KurtRaschke, Kuru, Legokid, Leopheard, Logan, Matthuxtable, Maxlapiovra, Mild Bill Hiccup, Nick, Peterfollows, Rich Farmbrough, Rich257, Rjwilmsi, Ross7, Runningonbrains, Seolake15, Sepeople, Springnuts, Stevejohnclarke, Swim900, Tony Hobbs, Tony2380, Vegaswikian, VictorianMutant, Xeolyte, 67 anonymous edits

Gift card *Source*: http://en.wikipedia.org/w/index.php?oldid=432769086 *Contributors*: Alfiewashere, Andymadigan, Ang258, Archaniz, Artur Perwenis, Atif.t2, Balibones, Benhebert, Bennyo1976, BozMo, Cadsuane Melaidhrin, Cahk, Cardtech, Chris the speller, Comp25, Compuandy, Courcelles, Crumley, DandyDan2007, Daniel Case, Ekem, Eldacan, Empty Buffer, FlyingPenguins, Giftcardbin, Giftcardideas, Giftsms, Gilliam, Glane23, Goldsteinal, GraemeL, Graham87, Grovecom, Ham Pastrami, Haus, Hellno2, Hemidemisemiquaver, Henning Makholm, Houldieson, Incomecows, J04n, Jabraha7, JamesBWatson, Jim.henderson, Jmart805, JoshXF, Jweiss11, Kuru, MER-C, MFP187, Malloryloren, Muimi, Nakon, NewEnglandYankee, Oda Mari, Ohnoitsjamie, Onyx0tel88, RHaworth, RadioFan, Radiojon, Rjwilmsi, Romaine, Shugal, Stifle, Stybn, Svick, Tide rolls, Tinahenson, Tjackwilliams, Uncle Milty, Vampirerocks123, Woohookitty, YUiCiUS, 77 anonymous edits

Gilbarco Veeder-Root *Source*: http://en.wikipedia.org/w/index.php?oldid=432074624 *Contributors*: Beetstra, Chowbok, DinosaursLoveExistence, Kjp993, Megan5522, Woohookitty, 20 anonymous edits

Giro *Source*: http://en.wikipedia.org/w/index.php?oldid=433029152 *Contributors*: ABX, Ahenobarb, Antandrus, Beland, Bensin, Branddobbe, Chetvorno, Chinorm, Chrisieboy, Cuppy, Daniel Newby, Didoshaaban, DocendoDiscimus, Doctorfluffy, ElKevbo, Encyclops, Frediculous biggs, GS3, Gbleem, Girobastart, Goldendaisy, Greensburger, Gribeco, Guidod, HTUK, Hairy Dude, Hallerin, Hauskalainen, Heff01, Ike9898, Japo, Johnny Sumner, Joseph Solis in Australia, KIMSEUNGWON, Kwamikagami, Lectonar, Lee M, Lucky 6.9, Macrakis, Mark Foskey, Markt3, Martarius, Maury Markowitz, Michael Hardy, Mickey d, Mkweise, Nakkiel, NoisyJinx, Now3d, Petri Krohn, PhotoBox, Profoss, RBBrittain, Radagast, Rilkas, Robert K S, Scott Sanchez, Severinus, Simon123, Skapur, SteveW, Sumirati, T-rex, THEN WHO WAS PHONE?, Tawlboy, The Noodle Incident, The Yowser, Ubermonkey, Vuo, WWC, Warofdreams, Wenkai31, West.andrew.g, Wikipelli, Woohookitty, Xanzzibar, 51 anonymous edits

Girocard *Source*: http://en.wikipedia.org/w/index.php?oldid=432752868 *Contributors*: Anon lynx, Cfaerber, Chris the speller, Guidod, Kju, LMB, Nachdenklich, Sargdub, Tomeasy, 5 anonymous edits

Giropay *Source*: http://en.wikipedia.org/w/index.php?oldid=407842504 *Contributors*: Basket of Puppies, Mintaru, Pratyeka, Rich Farmbrough, Rpyle731, Tabletop, 2 anonymous edits

Global Payments Inc. *Source*: http://en.wikipedia.org/w/index.php?oldid=347881583 *Contributors*: Beland, Cander0000, CliffC, Discospinster, Jmalik2, Jmejedi, The Thing That Should Not Be, 8 anonymous edits

Google Wallet *Source*: http://en.wikipedia.org/w/index.php?oldid=433315341 *Contributors*: Bayonetblaha, Breawycker, Caseyh, Daxterminator, Gary King, Modamoda, Psantora, Sandman8888, Scarce, Shaolinx, Skizzik, Smbius, 4 anonymous edits

GreenZap *Source*: http://en.wikipedia.org/w/index.php?oldid=401762290 *Contributors*: Baileypalblue, Beltz, Bmicomp, Brokshen, Brownh2o, Busy Stubber, Captainstarbucs, ChicanoJ, Darklilac, ESkog, Evrik, Gavin.collins, Gurch, Jbamb, Jehochman, JeremyWJ, Kerowyn, MBisanz, Paul August, ReyBrujo, Rozaleenda, Skepicalcynic, Slicing, Tartan, UnitedStatesian, Viriditas, Wickethewok, Wyldraven, Xiahou, 65 anonymous edits

GrIDsure *Source*: http://en.wikipedia.org/w/index.php?oldid=403329766 *Contributors*: Ajuk, Carlossuarez46, Darkwind, Ettrig, Fabrictramp, Gareth Jones, Igoldste, Jfire, Johnwishart, Merrybrit, Neils.place, Nono64, Pakaraki, Pigman, Prnrm, Steve Smith, TehPoep, XDanielx, 25 anonymous edits

Honesty bar *Source*: http://en.wikipedia.org/w/index.php?oldid=408265603 *Contributors*: Autarch, JimTS, Lmartenot, MCB, SimonTrew, Tysto, V111P, Vegaswikian, Woohookitty, 1 anonymous edits

Honesty box *Source*: http://en.wikipedia.org/w/index.php?oldid=413241669 *Contributors*: AlasdairBailey, Beeblebrox, DJ Clayworth, GerhardNL, Guidod, Joshua, RainbowOfLight, Robofish, SimonTrew, SqueakBox, The Thing That Should Not Be, Waindigo, Xhin, 8 anonymous edits

Hundi *Source*: http://en.wikipedia.org/w/index.php?oldid=431719053 *Contributors*: Arjaay, Bobrayner, Indian Chronicles, Itai, Rowreduced, Sagarkhanna2211, Shyamsunder, Wavehunter, Xyn1, Zenwort

i2c Inc *Source*: http://en.wikipedia.org/w/index.php?oldid=426243357 *Contributors*: Arif-Sajjad, Auntof6, CliffC, Grutness, Haus, Jpbowen, Materialscientist, Pahari Sahib, Ser Amantio di Nicolao, Stepheng3, Tahirakram, TsAr1983, WebHamster, Woohookitty, Wrelwser43, 30 anonymous edits

iDEAL *Source*: http://en.wikipedia.org/w/index.php?oldid=418123479 *Contributors*: -cide, Anetode, Azzmodan, DGG, DaProx, Dryke, Effeietsanders, Gaius Cornelius, Garion96, Good Muslim, HAl, Ideal34, J9s, Markthemac, Mhsb, Mintaru, Nikosgreencookie, Onceler, Otolemur crassicaudatus, Pcmadman, PeterSymonds, Rudolphous, SK-luuut, Shuki, Stormie, Styath, Techfast50, Woohookitty, 12 anonymous edits

IMF Balance of Payments Manual *Source*: http://en.wikipedia.org/w/index.php?oldid=382722941 *Contributors*: Cerberus0, Dougie WII, Finnancier, Gary King, MBisanz, Michael Hardy, RDipp, The Siktath, 6 anonymous edits

InteliSpend Prepaid Solutions *Source*: http://en.wikipedia.org/w/index.php?oldid=425525639 *Contributors*: NDSteve10, 3 anonymous edits

Interac *Source*: http://en.wikipedia.org/w/index.php?oldid=426319318 *Contributors*: Airodyssey, Alexwcovington, Andrewpmk, Anon lynx, Arifsaha, Awbrennan, Bearcat, Bill.albing, Bremen, BroMonque, Buck Mulligan, Charlie T, Chealer, Ckatz, Cleduc, ConsultRick, Crittervan, Dadam10, Deetdeet, Dhodges, Duja, Dustinasby, Ericleb01, Eyreland, Frysun, Gary King, GreenJoe, Greenbough, Hu, Iain44, Itai, Jeffpontes, Kbarry-cwood, Kevs, Kirjtc2, Koman90, Kurieeto, LSX, Mindmatrix, Mrosscan, NorthernThunder, Not a dog, Phatom87, Phil-hong, PrimroseGuy, Prowsej, Qutezuce, Radagast, Remember the dot, Rjwilmsi, Royalguard11, Rufus843, Sargdub, Schnits, Scott Sanchez, Simon123, Sky Harbor, Snickerdo, Spinboy, Tabletop, Tawker, TheDrew, Themepark, Timrollpickering, UTSRelativity, Vaolath, Writerguy, YUL89YYZ, 45 anonymous edits

Interac e-Transfer *Source*: http://en.wikipedia.org/w/index.php?oldid=420021108 *Contributors*: Adolson, Airodyssey, Capit, Cconrad, Charlie T, Dawnep, Deetdeet, Dubious Irony, Feureau, Oldtimer6, Remember the dot, RoyBoy, 23 anonymous edits

Interbank Mobile Payment Service *Source*: http://en.wikipedia.org/w/index.php?oldid=428542435 *Contributors*: Sapna81

Interbank Mobile Payment System *Source*: http://en.wikipedia.org/w/index.php?oldid=428542092 *Contributors*: KuwarOnline, LilHelpa, Pnm, Randhirreddy, Sapna81

Internet currency *Source*: http://en.wikipedia.org/w/index.php?oldid=402880047 *Contributors*: Anonymous Dissident, Brianhe, Cromson, Leowatson, Rjwilmsi, TheNewPhobia, Toyokuni3, WaldoJ, Yiannistsiounis, 1 anonymous edits

Irish Payment Services Organisation *Source*: http://en.wikipedia.org/w/index.php?oldid=409680488 *Contributors*: Edward, Gert7, IPSO Ltd, Irish Payments Services Organisation, Pdcook

ISO 8583 *Source*: http://en.wikipedia.org/w/index.php?oldid=428736130 *Contributors*: A.Hamza, Bill.albing, Bmannaa, Cheef000, Ciphers, Crazycomputers, DabMachine, Dmprantz, Elwell, Ga mtn man, Greensburger, GregorB, Grlea, Hydro, Informad, JZavel, Jpp, Jubal, Kgx, Kmorozov, Koshatul, Linzhuf, Mandarax, MarkNorman, Mitch Ames, Nasa-verve, NathanBeach, Ninchisl, Osanderson, Petrb, Rcalvert, Reggionh, Robindch, Rror, Saifulalam, SalientNZ, Searchme, Seba5618, Shadowjams, Sharmabrij, Stack, Thumperward, Vi.agarwal, Waldir1977, Zaian, 215 anonymous edits

Issuing bank *Source*: http://en.wikipedia.org/w/index.php?oldid=404742233 *Contributors*: Betacommand, Tim Barber

K-CASH *Source*: http://en.wikipedia.org/w/index.php?oldid=267118048 *Contributors*: Excretion, Jaysopher, Malcolm, Pegship, 2 anonymous edits

Legal Electronic Data Exchange Standard *Source*: http://en.wikipedia.org/w/index.php?oldid=413100129 *Contributors*: Altruistguy, Cander0000, Everyking, Isheden, Jpbowen, Kbdank71, Manix24, Minorpeace, Nricardo, Rich Farmbrough, Romanc19s, Rschroeder001, Spongewilly Squarewheels, 6 anonymous edits

M-Pesa *Source*: http://en.wikipedia.org/w/index.php?oldid=417096252 *Contributors*: Astanhope, Bearcat, Beland, Btphelps, CommonsDelinker, Dgwbirch, Ensconsed, Erjaeger, Gonzonoir, Hirsch30, JamBlam, JamesBWatson, Jasond09, Julius Sahara, Karl.brown, Lordmwesh, MatthewVanitas, Msafiriwiki, Nfarrow, Npoulton, R2-T2, Rich Farmbrough, Smithy2204, Tomwansa, Vartikashuk, 31 anonymous edits

Macau Pass *Source*: http://en.wikipedia.org/w/index.php?oldid=425617341 *Contributors*: Cybercobra, Dragonfly730, Eliyak, Ghfj007, Jpbowen, Marcadana, Swsleep, 8 anonymous edits

Malaysian Electronic Payment System *Source*: http://en.wikipedia.org/w/index.php?oldid=429048233 *Contributors*: Aspects, Auntof6, Hismad, Hytar, Masba1812, Mfa fariz, NJA, Not a dog, Ph.eyes, PrimroseGuy, Ridhwanrosli, Sky Harbor, Stkhoo, Takamaxa, 14 anonymous edits

Manual fare collection *Source*: http://en.wikipedia.org/w/index.php?oldid=409649668 *Contributors*: Coinswede, CrossHouses, Eekerz, LtPowers, MickMacNee, Nudecline, Pne, SJ Morg, Sebwite, Swarve, 17 anonymous edits

Medi Script *Source*: http://en.wikipedia.org/w/index.php?oldid=351957187 *Contributors*: Ettrig, Jreferee, RockMFR

Mefo bills *Source*: http://en.wikipedia.org/w/index.php?oldid=431827927 *Contributors*: Altenmann, Amy jo2, Barticus88, Bender235, Chochopk, Domino theory, Eric Shalov, Hadžija, Hongooi, Jaraalbe, Jhobson1, Mordemur, Pottsf, Quebec99, Rich Farmbrough, SimonP, Surfingslovak, That Guy, From That Show!, The Land, Tschild, Xufanc, 12 anonymous edits

Merchant account *Source*: http://en.wikipedia.org/w/index.php?oldid=426001012 *Contributors*: Abc518, Acroterion, Adamarthurryan, Ajuk, Aksera, Appraiser, Aurum 20, BeatenByJacks, Beland, Biker Biker, Bluiee, Bobthejobman, BrainStain, Brian1979, Businessinc, CPHIPPSAAPCTP, Calltech, Card1234, Cbunk, Ckatz, Cmskog, Cometstyles, Damianlaw, Danieljosephprice, Darrenmv, Davefish23, Devinma, Directbancard, DocWatson42, Donnahunt, Evanchaney, Evershade, Fallsend, Firsfron, Fljackson4, Funandtrvl, Geniac, GreenReaper, HPS28213, Harvestchristian, Hawaiian717, Henry.nutter, I already forgot, Imprus, Insanephantom, Izcool, Jason.bordeaux, Jayszop, Jestep, Jmabel, Joekucker, John254, Johnnrep, Jpgordon, Katchar, Kiberlain, Knilez, KnowledgeOfSelf, Livefeeordie, Marcperkel, Marthyvp, Marx0728, Mattcbruno, MerchantAccount, Mike411, Mild Bill Hiccup, Mindmatrix, Monerisexec, Mrweeje, N7912, Nbscp, Niayre, Nisewon, Nono64, Ohnoitsjamie, Orangysb, Pajawa, Paulballen, Pearle, Pedro, Philclarke123, Pwiskell7, Quadell, Rcoulam, Rimshot, Ryanminier, STCL, Samet10, Saturday, Scottdimmick, Scottwilleke, Securus, Shalom Yechiel, Sjordan26, Stargat, Stymiee, Synchrite, Tercio28, TerraFrost, The former 134.250.72.176, ThoriumBoy, Tim Barber, Tizaj, Tr40404, Trusilver, Tylerdee, Uncle Milty, Us.bhupathi, Veinor, Ventdog, Vinautomatic, WAJWAJ, WadeSimMiser, Warut, Wrockca, Yintan, Yiosie2356, Yserarau, ZimZalaBim, Zzuuzz, 309 anonymous edits

Mergers & Acquisitions International Clearing House *Source*: http://en.wikipedia.org/w/index.php?oldid=385045506 *Contributors*: Cander0000, Flaming, Gonzalo Diethelm, Good Olfactory, Sargdub, Woohookitty, Worm That Turned, YUL89YYZ, 1 anonymous edits

MHITS *Source*: http://en.wikipedia.org/w/index.php?oldid=370975197 *Contributors*: Blowdart, Issac 37, LilHelpa, Mhitslimited, 3 anonymous edits

Micropayment *Source*: http://en.wikipedia.org/w/index.php?oldid=431836535 *Contributors*: 041744, 2bar, Adrian J. Hunter, Alex.g, Alvin-cs, Andreaspizsa, Angela, Arvindn, AuroraStars, Azttboy, Bogdangiusca, Boxpay, CGameProgrammer, Cameron Scott, Cander0000, Chp-flms, Connorferster, Consequencefree, CosineKitty, Cwookie21, Daedelus, Danbloch, Darkwind, David Gerard, Dbfirs, Dduane, Demiurge, Dissipate, Doume, EAi, Edward, Erianna, Eric Shalov, Error, Evan.carrigan, Fewill, FlamingSilmaril, Fleetham, Futuremania, GB fan, Gallens, Gary King, Gbleem, GeeJo, Gnewf, Gobonobo, Gold21, Goldenbushel, GraemeL, HadmarFreiherrvonWieser, HaeB, Hmbr, Hongooi, Hwfhwf, Iainscott, Imrananwar, JNeal, Jesterjje, Jo.witte, Jtatum, Ken Arromdee, Khalid hassani, Khym Chanur, Kowey, KrakatoaKatie, Loren.wilton, Lowellian, MER-C, Madsmith, MagneticFlux, MatiasSingers, Mav, Mereda, Merope, Michael Hardy, Michal Nebyla, Mild Bill Hiccup, Mindmatrix, Mitar, MobileGeek81, Mooncatx, Mpearl, MrOllie, Mydogategodshat, Naima.fatimi, NeonMerlin, Nifboy, Night Gyr, Obhave, Ourai, Paine Ellsworth, Peter Greenwell, Peter Grey, Phyzome, Pseudo account, QuiteUnusual, R'n'B, Rettetast, Rkomatsu, Robofish, Royalguard11, Rsxbase, Ruud Koot, Sbluen, Schandi, Scott McNay, Shaunfensom, Sjl, Snori, Sohmc, Suntech0, Tagus, Tassedethe, Teerawat, The Anome, The real dan, Thinboy00P, Tiles, Tim Barber, Tommy, Tony Myers, Uruiamme, Vbs, WatchAndObserve, Woohookitty, 182 anonymous edits

Military Payment Certificate *Source*: http://en.wikipedia.org/w/index.php?oldid=428150083 *Contributors*: Aatombomb, Daxmac, Diderot, DieYuppieScum, Funandtrvl, Hmains, JavierMC, Jrvz, Kchishol1970, LorenzoB, Mikedelsol, Mwtoews, Pyvanet, TerraHikaru, Woohookitty, 17 anonymous edits

MM code *Source*: http://en.wikipedia.org/w/index.php?oldid=395770265 *Contributors*: Contributor23, D.M.N., Jomsborg, Markus Kuhn, Mayalld, Mitch Ames, Uncle G, 3 anonymous edits

MNET *Source*: http://en.wikipedia.org/w/index.php?oldid=370991619 *Contributors*: Moonriddengirl

Mobile payment *Source*: http://en.wikipedia.org/w/index.php?oldid=432938359 *Contributors*: Abovingdon, Adrianski, Akis, Alexpashanov, Alfred1520, Angela, Antonioeram, Arho, Arpingstone, Ashokpundit, Auntof6, Beginner info, Blanchardb, Bldiddy, Blogster21, Bvanmaele, CaribDigita, Chandrahas9, Chevalierblanc, Chmyr, Chris the speller, ChrisCork, Cmari06,

ConstantineSerafim, Cracked acorns, Crazytales, Cromson, Cyberbram, Dariel 01, David Haslam, Dawaters, Donnabella11, DrTheNewWay, Edward, Eficach, Elo80ka, Epallares1961, Fox, Galoubet, Gogo Dodo, Gonhidi, Goplett, Gsarwa, HANNAMAN, HaeB, Hu12, Imberner, Iridescent, Jackdbristow, JamBlam, Javaboyjunior, JimAyson, Johnvdh, JonHarder, Jraftery, Juzcat, Jvs.cz, Karl.brown, Khym Chanur, Kukini, Kuru, Kzaral, MER-C, Mike.i.bradford, MilkMiruku, Mindmatrix, MobileGeek81, Mocle, Mojodaddy, Moldova1979, Mrzaius, Mutunzi, Notinasnaid, Nposs, Olivepick, Overflorian, OwenX, Paywithyourmobile, Petri Krohn, R'n'B, REnDuikd2, Ramymora, RayneVanDunem, Rfidconsultants3, RoyBoy, Rrius, Servant Saber, SimonP, Skerr, Somno, Sosweet san, Stevebor1, Steven Zhang, TastyPoutine, ToastyKen, Top Jim, Upaid, Vegaswikian, Versity, Versus22, Vikas Kumar Ojha, Wafulz, Wikidavem, Zamsinus, Zinnmann, 180 anonymous edits

Mobile Payments in India *Source*: http://en.wikipedia.org/w/index.php?oldid=421124317 *Contributors*: Chandrahas9, Sudhir h, Wayne Slam, Woodshed, Woohookitty, 1 anonymous edits

Mobile purchasing *Source*: http://en.wikipedia.org/w/index.php?oldid=408535575 *Contributors*: HaeB, MatthewVanitas, Melaen, Paulpaterson, Sachinvenga, 3 anonymous edits

MOL AccessPortal *Source*: http://en.wikipedia.org/w/index.php?oldid=426693620 *Contributors*: Biglovinb, CommonsDelinker, Gary King, JohnI, Kamosuzo, Katharineamy, Molglobalpr, Movingboxes, Ninjahello, Rich Farmbrough, Tancolin, Techfast50, Tnxman307, Woohookitty, YUL89YYZ, 41 anonymous edits

Mondex *Source*: http://en.wikipedia.org/w/index.php?oldid=414974257 *Contributors*: -alx, Adament, Aitias, Amcfreely, Ancheta Wis, Beao, Bearcat, DNewhall, Dawynn, ExpatEgghead, Gogo Dodo, HarrisX, Instantnood, Iridescent, Ishabamf, Jpbowen, Juntung, Lmcelhiney, Marudubshinki, Michael Slone, MrWideMouth, Mushin, Pegship, Pstegs, Rjwilmsi, Svencb, Track n Field, UkPaolo, 37 anonymous edits

Money order *Source*: http://en.wikipedia.org/w/index.php?oldid=431766913 *Contributors*: 28bytes, AAAAA, Adukfat, Alansohn, Alias777, Amitkinger, AnOddName, Anþony, Bhuck, BigrTex, Bkell, BrianGV, Cab88, Calmer Waters, Cassowary, Chris Roy, Cluth, Cohesion, Com2kid, Crusoe8181, DARTH SIDIOUS 2, DVD R W, DarkfireTaimatsu, Darwinek, Debresser, Dmitri Yuriev, Doldrums, Eastlaw, Elkman, Ellsworth, Eric.weigle, Filpaul, Findingcitations, Francs2000, Frazzydee, Furrykef, GVOLTT, Galoubet, Garr1984, Geni, Go for it!, Hagerman, Haseo9999, Ike9898, J.delanoy, JCrazy84, Jackkalpakian, Jason Quinn, Jenks1987, Jusjih, K-UNIT, Kidlittle, LeaveSleaves, LorenzoB, Lowellian, Mab2112, Markbyrn, Marknagel, MarshallKe, Mas2265, Matteh, Maximus Rex, Metallurgist, Miaers, Michael Romanov, Mirokado, Moonlight Mile, Myanw, Mysdaao, Newmanbe, Nkour, No Guru, Notinasnaid, Now3d, Nufy8, Ohnoitsjamie, Paul August, Peruvianllama, Pie4all88, Plebeian, Poshua, RBBrittain, Ramymora, Rchamberlain, Retired username, Rfc1394, Rhetth, Rich Farmbrough, Rizalninoynapoleon, RobJ1981, SJP, Scott Sanchez, ScottAlanHill, Shanel, Shimgray, Simon123, Simonmatt1100, Smyth, SpK, SwanSZ, Tckma, TedPavlic, Teryx, The Thing That Should Not Be, The undertow, Theboss48506, Tiptoety, TradeMe, Traveler100, Trivialist, UU, Versus22, VictorianMutant, Wernher, Wik, Wtshymanski, 201 anonymous edits

MoneyGram *Source*: http://en.wikipedia.org/w/index.php?oldid=430555293 *Contributors*: Alai, Alvin-cs, B. Jennings Perry, Betacommand, Billymac00, Binksternet, Cch101, DancingPenguin, DavidLevinson, DocendoDiscimus, Dreadstar, EnWikinombre, Geniac, Gohiking, Hooperbloob, Jsl2586, K. Annoyomous, Korath, Marcika, MattTM, Mauls, Maurreen, Muhandes, Nestorius, One, One more night, PaulHanson, Pcpcpc, Pearle, Ph.eyes, Pill, Pontificake, Properwithanedge, RBBrittain, Reinyday, Schwarzseher, Scott Burley, Taladita, Thomaskibu, Toby464, Vegaswikian, Wabten, Weirdgaybigal, WhisperToMe, Why217, Wind-ru, Xnatedawgx, 73 anonymous edits

Mon€o *Source*: http://en.wikipedia.org/w/index.php?oldid=364210162 *Contributors*: Alai, Axic, Bluemoose, Cahk, ClementSeveillac, Fang Aili, Greudin, Khalid hassani, Mgill, Nono64, Severo, Spacepotato, Thewayforward, Thryduulf, Toitoine, Woohookitty, 4 anonymous edits

Mopay *Source*: http://en.wikipedia.org/w/index.php?oldid=395981051 *Contributors*: E258, Graeme Bartlett, Hmains, Meankeeper, Tias1999

MPP Global Solutions *Source*: http://en.wikipedia.org/w/index.php?oldid=432331547 *Contributors*: Armbrust, Bearcat, Chzz, CommonsDelinker, Jamesaeddleston, Jarkeld, 9 anonymous edits

NACHA – The Electronic Payments Association *Source*: http://en.wikipedia.org/w/index.php?oldid=432967668 *Contributors*: 478jjjz, Ceyockey, Cobaltbluetony, CraSH, Deleteme42, DocendoDiscimus, Ehn, Elizium23, NACHAEmployee, Pearle, Pegship, Pnm, RBBrittain, Renesis, Rj, Sargdub, Tevildo, Wikipedian2, 16 anonymous edits

National Payments Corporation of India *Source*: http://en.wikipedia.org/w/index.php?oldid=428545566 *Contributors*: Jovianeye, KuwarOnline, Mild Bill Hiccup, Randhirreddy, Sapna81, Shyamsunder, 9 anonymous edits

Negotiable instrument *Source*: http://en.wikipedia.org/w/index.php?oldid=432820158 *Contributors*: 2D, AJR, Andymadigan, Aranel, Atyphoon, BD2412, Bjornstrom, Bspatafora, Caelarch, Cbmccarthy, Chris the speller, Clerk at work, DS1953, DavidBrooks, Deor, Dialectic, DocendoDiscimus, Donatus, Donreed, Dpr, Eastlaw, Eldumpo, Ellsworth, Ewlyahoocom, Excirial, Fayenatic london, Feco, Gaius Cornelius, Gladyslouden, Greensburger, Gregalton, Hahbie, Ida Shaw, Inotnuts, JNW, JPP355, JdwNYC, Jeff3000, Jh51681, John Z, Jrauff, Kaihsu, Karl Dickman, Kazvorpal, Kzzl, LaidOff, Lawyer2b, LilHelpa, Lisiate, Magioladitis, MidgleyC, Modify, Nbarth, Olaffpomona, Olegwiki, Physchim62, Pinethicket, Piotrnikitin, Pjrich, Pnm, RJFJR, Rcsheets, Robofish, RoyBoy, Rysz, Sander87, Sargdub, Scott Sanchez, TFOWR, THEN WHO WAS PHONE?, The Nut, Theodoranian, Triddle, Unara, Vanka5, VodkaJazz, W1 m2, Walshga, Wikipism, Wordwright, 172 anonymous edits

Netbanx *Source*: http://en.wikipedia.org/w/index.php?oldid=386401302 *Contributors*: Andimok, Darkieboy236, DinosaursLoveExistence, Inthelionsden, Jimmyjazz22, SmartGuy, VinceBowdren, 6 anonymous edits

NetSpend Corporation *Source*: http://en.wikipedia.org/w/index.php?oldid=428727758 *Contributors*: AOL Alex, Addere, Bonadea, Browncom, Consumerviewpoint, Discospinster, Drdak, Faizanalivarya, Flowanda, Fraize, Gaius Cornelius, HDokins, Hot Sexy Beast, Kbdank71, Kmb480, Neurolysis, Niayre, Ohnoitsjamie, ST47, SlackerMom, Someguy1221, Urbanrenewal, Vindows, Warmclimate, William Ortiz, Xlsupert, Yandman, Zldoty, 43 anonymous edits

Network Commerce *Source*: http://en.wikipedia.org/w/index.php?oldid=413779732 *Contributors*: El C, Kevinmooney, Mhockey, Rjwilmsi, Robofish, 5 anonymous edits

North American Bancard *Source*: http://en.wikipedia.org/w/index.php?oldid=420167108 *Contributors*: Airsquid, Ebyabe, Elinnab, Falcon8765, Jthrem01, Moonriddengirl, MuffledThud, Pascal666, PhilKnight, Welsh, 16 anonymous edits

Obopay *Source*: http://en.wikipedia.org/w/index.php?oldid=432461440 *Contributors*: Diarmuidmallon, GoingBatty, JamBlam, Lintrouvable, Ohnoitsjamie, Prashanttyagi, 1 anonymous edits

OCMT *Source*: http://en.wikipedia.org/w/index.php?oldid=399745480 *Contributors*: Goldenrowley, MagicalTux, Mclay1, Twp

Octopus card *Source*: http://en.wikipedia.org/w/index.php?oldid=429678685 *Contributors*: 08chujj1, 84denniswong, 8teve, AOL Alex, Aidasvaidas, Ajho61, Akirste, Alanmak, Alasdair, Alerante, Alex Shih, Aliwalla, Ancheta Wis, Andrewong813, ArnoldReinhold, Ascánder, Avenue, Bender235, Benjwong, Betacommand, Bobblewik, Bogdangiusca, Borfo, Bourquie, Broux, Bunnyhop11, Bz2, C S, CRGreathouse, Cahk, CaliforniaAliBaba, CesarB, Chezhiyan, Chris j wood, Christopher Parham, ClementSeveillac, Colonies Chris, CommonsDelinker, Cybercobra, Da Vynci, Denmise, Dismas, Don Ellis, Dralwik, Dreaded Walrus, Dsp13, Dylan Lake, Dynotec, Earthlyreason, Edo-biscuit, Edward, Ef651100, Enochlau, Ewc21, Excirial, F, Filthybutter, Fleung, Fred Bradstadt, Fuzheado, Gadfium, Gakmo, Gavia immer, Ginkgo100, Glenibaby06, Hadoooookin, Haseo9999, Hello32020, HenryLi, Herenthere, Heron, HkCaGu, HongQiGong, Huaiwei, Ian3055, Jesanephantom, Instantnood, Iten, JPG-GR, Jackl, Jarsyl, JiMidnite, Jiang, Johnnyspastic, JonMoore, Juntung, K.C. Tang, KTC, KX675, Kanags, Kcordina, KelvSYC, Kfsung, King of Hearts (old account 2), KojieroSaske, Kwamikagami, Lahiru k, Leeyc0, Leolisa1997, Leujohn, LilHelpa, Loudenvier, Lr4087, Luckyluke, LuisVilla, Lupin, MD1026, MER-C, Mailer diablo, Malcolm, Maork, Mark Yen, Marskell, Martpol, Master of the Oríchalcos, Matt Crypto, Mattisse, Mboverload, Mcy jerry, Meelar, Metamagician3000, Michael Devore, Michael Hardy, Miles Lee, Mindmatrix, Minghong, Mintchocicecream, MisfitToys, Mitch Ames, Mom2jandk, Mortein, Muhandes, Natgoo, Neutrality, Nick Moss, Nikai, Niteowlneils, Novacatz, Novum, NuclearWarfare, Oblivious, OhanaUnited, Ohconfucius, Olivier, Omicronpersei8, Optim, P3Pp3r, Paddles, Paradacomics, Paranoid, Patrick, Patrickov, PeregrineAY, Pharos, Phoenix-forgotten, Piccolissima, PierreAbbat, Plasticup, Plop, Pne, Pureeminences, R.K.Himura, RHaworth, Reinthal, Reward, RexNL, Rich Farmbrough, Rjwilmsi, Robert Merkel, RobertG, Ropers, Roux, Ruinia, Rye1967, SYSS Mouse, Sameboat, SandyGeorgia, Sat84, Saxsux, Searchme, Shanes, Shinjiman, Shizhao, Singaporean, Sirap bandung, Sl, Smiley.toerist, Solidman051, Starwiz, SusanLai, Ta bu shi da yu, Tawker, Tbhotch, Telso, The Thing That Should Not Be, Thewinchester, Thumperward, Thuresson, Tlrmq, Tokpok, Tom-, Tomasso, Tony1, Tonyngkh, Toyotaboy95, Trevor Andersen, Trevor MacInnis, Typhoonchaser, UCLARodent, Umofomia, Urumartin, Vikkileung, Waphle, WibblyLeMoende, Wikipeditor, Winhunter, Wshun, X1987x, Xavier114fch, Xmnemonic, Yellowdesk, Zepheus, 244 anonymous edits

Official Payments Corporation *Source*: http://en.wikipedia.org/w/index.php?oldid=303972675 *Contributors*: MLauba, Metropolitan90, Tomfort

OneVu *Source*: http://en.wikipedia.org/w/index.php?oldid=395268182 *Contributors*: Chase me ladies, I'm the Cavalry, JonathanY08, Mhockey, 3 anonymous edits

Online Banking ePayments *Source*: http://en.wikipedia.org/w/index.php?oldid=430420049 *Contributors*: Cemelody, Comm12yay, ICPNO, Marketada, Methecooldude, Mhockey, Payment2010, Phantomsteve, Thor202, Wuhwuzdat, 3 anonymous edits

Open Payment Initiative *Source*: http://en.wikipedia.org/w/index.php?oldid=428567203 *Contributors*: Lefschetz, Mhockey, PrimroseGuy, So mok wi dat, Welsh, Yanngeffrotin, 8 anonymous edits

Optimal Payments *Source*: http://en.wikipedia.org/w/index.php?oldid=430665566 *Contributors*: 2005, Abra63, Anthony Appleyard, Bbx, Benhamin9029, Cahk, Centricom, Darkieboy236, DennyColt, Deuce-daddy, DifiCa, EdX20, Exitsforeandaft, FisherQueen, Flowanda, FreplySpang, Gilliam, Gloriamarie, Gobonobo, GoingBatty, Inthelionsden, Jcc1, Jimmyjazz22, Kellen`, Kingboyk, Lightmouse, Ling.Nut, LukeHoC, Maralia, Mbbs, Meandmyself, Meisterkoch, Mexeno1, Mhockey, Mike Payne, Mr.mengkai, Neelix, Night Gyr, Nssdfdsfds, Poweron, Randall00, Reedy, ST47, Sirex98, SmartGuy, Stev0, Tellyaddict, ThePointblank, Veinor, Wiskedjak, 117 anonymous edits

ORCA Platform *Source*: http://en.wikipedia.org/w/index.php?oldid=425885828 *Contributors*: Ahoerstemeier, Bearcat, Chrisamichaels, Chzz, Colonies Chris, FetchcommsAWB, Gary King, Ilnyc8, Mhockey, Rd232, Ron Ritzman, Webpoet, YUL89YYZ, 7 anonymous edits

PA-DSS *Source*: http://en.wikipedia.org/w/index.php?oldid=387922427 *Contributors*: Nono64, Orangegardens, Pichpich, Plasticspork, Topbanana, 1 anonymous edits

PaidByCash *Source*: http://en.wikipedia.org/w/index.php?oldid=395271776 *Contributors*: 6birc, Ariel., Bocafoos, Mhockey, Mmarubio, Mom2jandk, Nirvana2013, Rhobite, Searchme, Wenli, 10 anonymous edits

PAN truncation *Source*: http://en.wikipedia.org/w/index.php?oldid=415514795 *Contributors*: Abhorsen327, Akihabara, DynamicDes, Erechtheus, Kyoko, Mmutilva, Pol098, RegRCN, 8 anonymous edits

Pan-European Automated Clearing House *Source*: http://en.wikipedia.org/w/index.php?oldid=382565165 *Contributors*: Nick Number, Somearemoreequal, 1 anonymous edits

Pay at the pump *Source*: http://en.wikipedia.org/w/index.php?oldid=427931819 *Contributors*: Floquenbeam, Flowanda, Hellno2, Ncmvocalist, Symplectic Map, TorW, TreoBoy680, 4 anonymous edits

Pay card *Source*: http://en.wikipedia.org/w/index.php?oldid=432453606 *Contributors*: Cadsuane Melaidhrin, CairoTasogare, Deon, Gilliam, Hq3473, Midhart90, Mykolas OK, OnBeyondZebrax, Outlook, RainbowOfLight, Randomcombooflettters, SchuminWeb, Zonk43, 2 anonymous edits

Pay with a Tweet *Source*: http://en.wikipedia.org/w/index.php?oldid=429650257 *Contributors*: Holics12, RayneVanDunem, Salvio giuliano, YUL89YYZ

PayDirect *Source*: http://en.wikipedia.org/w/index.php?oldid=395271379 *Contributors*: Alynna Kasmira, BuickCenturyDriver, Cliffb, DNewhall, Jtalstad, Mhockey, Nobody of Consequence, Shadowjams

Payment card *Source*: http://en.wikipedia.org/w/index.php?oldid=433020056 *Contributors*: Kozuch, Leopheard, Mitch Ames, Mormegil, Ranveig, Sepeople, Yupik, Zaian, 13 anonymous edits

Payment gateway *Source*: http://en.wikipedia.org/w/index.php?oldid=432330833 *Contributors*: AJR, Abune, Alkamins, Amese, Andrew c, Angr, Aravind20, Bartlettbill, Bennyn, Black Kite, Bluiee, Calltech, Casper n, Cjkporter, CliveAnsley, Commercehelper, DeadEyeArrow, Dialie, Dina Jones, Dreftymac, Edupedro, Ematters, Ffidler, General Rommel, Ginajetten, Giwt goa, Gogo Dodo, GoingBatty, GrahamSmith, GrandMoffVixen, Gregwooten, Gurock, Hackajar, ITS REN, Ianpell, Ignacioerrico, Ipso2, JSpung, Jasonkhanlar, Jaysweet, Jestep, Jimmyjazz22, Jjimagery, John2wiki, Kiberlain, Kracker, Kuchiguchi, L Kensington, Lerdthenerd, Les boys, Manfi, Mayalld, Mhockey, Mnalin, Mobile88, Moldova1979, MuffledThud, Mwhitecybs, Nightsource, Ohnoitsjamie, OnebadGTR, Ouroboros hr, Owenob, Paalantam, Parhamr, Pedro, Phatom87, Phoenix Hacker, Plohich, Psangitrao, Qef, R'n'B, RHaworth, Rbrown@mydtx.com, Rchamberlain, Reformedegyptian, Ruconcept.lucy, Ryratt, SGGH, Shakespeareanpie, Shift4SMS, Stawrogin, Stegop, Stormie823, Stymiee, Sujata1212, Thumperward, Timneu22, Tlineshill, Touol, Treemonster19, Triciahill, Tsunaminoai, Veinor, Versageek, WaldoJ, Wcquidditch, Whenitcounts, Wrockca, Xionbox, Zamsinus, Zzuuzz, 272 anonymous edits

Payment processor *Source*: http://en.wikipedia.org/w/index.php?oldid=403396695 *Contributors*: Alkamins, Americasroof, Caseyallen0, Christopher Kraus, Fabrictramp, Flowanda, Ianeversley, Jmalik2, John2wiki, Katharineamy, Ma8thew, Ohnoitsjamie, Open2universe, RenegadeMonster, Tizaj, Wuhwuzdat, 2 anonymous edits

Payment service provider *Source*: http://en.wikipedia.org/w/index.php?oldid=416964652 *Contributors*: Ahvahsaa, Alkamins, Alvin-cs, Amandlaman, Aurum 20, Barek, Bluiee, Capricorn42, Cybersource, Dina Jones, Euryalus, Ffidler, Flewis, Ginajetten, Gogo Dodo, Hetakaushal, Historiene, Hmains, Ianpell, Ipso2, J9s, Jeremy.gumbley, Jimmyjazz22, Jumama, Katnels, Kiberlain, Knilez, Luciddreaming, Mazarin07, MightyWarrior, Mindscraper, Mjm uk 123, Mkns, Nemesisa, Nemo bis, Ohnoitsjamie, Olafgeurs, Paalantam, Pegship, Piet Delport, Radagast83, S473599, Ssuresh.rks1, Stymiee, TastyPoutine, Terrytrident, Thorpe, Touol, Veinor, Versageek, Wlaup97, 70 anonymous edits

Payment Services Directive *Source*: http://en.wikipedia.org/w/index.php?oldid=417582203 *Contributors*: A2800276, Blardibla, DJromT, EDCAlistairGates, Ehn, Gadget850, Gladiool, TheAllSeeingEye, 18 anonymous edits

Payments Council *Source*: http://en.wikipedia.org/w/index.php?oldid=428390717 *Contributors*: Aboutmovies, Alast0r, Chrisd10, Doriena, Eastmain, Fayenatic london, Sargdub, Smyth

Payoneer *Source*: http://en.wikipedia.org/w/index.php?oldid=431968736 *Contributors*: Alpha Quadrant, Avanu, Bbb23, Cirt, Flowanda, FuFoFuEd, HDokins, Hhcaas, Hu12, JulieAnna77, Kuru, Meshatz, Michaelregnal, Michts, Mogmios, Taltalk, 6 anonymous edits

PayPal *Source*: http://en.wikipedia.org/w/index.php?oldid=432167488 *Contributors*: 0612, 16@r, 2005, A3RO, ALiEN, ANONYMOUS COWARD0xC0DE, ARC Gritt, Aardark, Aaron Brenneman, AaronWL, Acalamari, Acedip, Achromatic, Aeon1006, Agamemnon2, Ageekgal, Ahudson, Airamerica, Akeleven, Aksmth, Alansohn, Alanthehat, Alex63, Alias2, Alien123456, Allstarecho, Alsocal, Alvin-cs, Alvis, Amalas, Amilator, Anaraug, Andrejj, Andypandy.UK, Anetode, Anomo, Ansett, Anson Stark, Antandrus, AnthonyTo, Antiope66, Anujnayar, Anwar saadat, Aoco, Appraiser, Arcdigital, Archibald Heatherington Nastiface, Arifulnr, Artherd, Arthur Rubin, Artsmith, Asarelah, Asbucher, Ascorbic, Ash, Asim91, Aspro, Badboyjames, Badn3wz, Baeksu, Banhammer, Barek, Barneypell, Battle Ape, Bballvinoguy, Bcballard, Beano, Bedel23, Beland, Bellthorpe, Beltz, Bgnuf, Bgpaulus, Bhadani, Bigar, Biguana, Birdhombre, Bkkbrad, BlackTerror, Blackmissionary, BloodDoll, BlueSkyMan, Bobblewik, Bobo192, Bobonmynuts, Bokkura, Bombaymix, Bonadea, Bongwarrior, Bordello, Bovineone, Brazucs, BrekekekexKoaxKoax, Brewcrewer, Britlooks97, Brothejr, Brother Dave Thompson, Brujo, Brun8, Brycefafster, Btilm, Bunnyhop11, Burntsauce, C.Fred, CIreland, CR85747, Cadsuane Melaidhrin, Caknuck, Caltas, Calton, CalumH93, Calwatch, Cambrasa, CambridgeBayWeather, Canadian-Bacon, Canihaveacookie, Canterbury Tail, Capricorn42, CardinalDan, Cat10001b, Catdude, Centrx, CesarDominguez, Cetot, Cghfhgfhgfhgcfxgf, Charles Nguyen, Chowbok, Chris the speller, Chrisef, Chrislk02, Cjjcjjc, Cjkporter, Ckatz, ClanCC, Clicketyclack, CliffC, Cliffb, Closedmouth, Cmdrjameson, Cmskog, Cohesion, CommonsDelinker, Computerjoe, Cool110110, CoolKid1993, Coolcaesar, Coolslko, Craigbrass, CrazyLegsKC, Crazymotherfunk, Crossmr, Cryellow, Ctjf83, Cumulus Clouds, Cupidvogel, CutOffTies, Cyktsui, DVD R W, DaBler, DanMatan, Danlev, Darrell Greenwood, Davehi1, Davemc500hats, Dbeastly1, Dclondons, Defsac, Dejvid, Dekisugi, Delldot, DelosHarriman, Deltabeignet, DemonKyoto, Digied21, Dipskinny, DirkvdM, Dirthvader, Discospinster, Djinn Mark, Doc9871, DocWatson42, DogStar5, DominicConnor, DooStang3, DopefishJustin, Dr.K., Dralithi, Drat, Drugonot, Dtobias, Duck1, EH74DK, Echuck215, Ed Poor, Edit Fixer, Edward, Egil, El C, Eleschinski2000, Eleven even, Elvey, Emanresu27, Emoscopes, EndlessMike, Erianna, Espoo, Estoy Aquí, Evil saltine, EwokiWiki, Excirial, Exxazz, Ezemovie, F.torri, Fabricationary, Fagiolonero, Falcon Kirtaran, Falcon8765, Famspear, FelisLeo, Felixhonecker, Fernkes, Feureau, Fiach6383, Finalius, Finalnight, Flapdragon, FlashSheridan, Flowanda, FlyingToaster, Franzwu, Frecklefoot, FreplySpang, Frog186, Fudoreaper, Fullstop, Funnyfarmofdoom, Furrykef, Gaius Cornelius, Gargaj, Gary King, Gershwinrb, GioCM, GiovanniS, Gldlvr, Globepay, Gloriamarie, Gngngn, Go slowly, Goatasaur, Gobonobo, Gogo Dodo, GoingBatty, Good Olfactory, Goodralph, GraemeL, Gramoun kal, Grantos1, Greenshed, Grk99, Gronky, Grouse, Groyolo, Guernica, Gurch, Guthrie, Gwernol, Hadal, Haipa Doragon, Hamtechperson, Hankwang, Harry the Dirty Dog, Harumphy, Havardnh, Havoc29, Haza-w, Hdcolo, Heimstern, Hermaja, Hi878, Hkelkar, Homerjay, Hope(N Forever), Hornet35, Hurricane Floyd, Hyacinth, I already forgot, IRP, IanA, Icezinhu, Icseaturtles, IdleRich, Ijustam, Ike-bana, Ilikerps, Insanephantom, Int21h, IronCannibal, Israel28, Itom2010, Ivansanchez, Ixfd64, Ixparamentex, J.delanoy, JD, JForget, JPLeonard, JackLumber, Jackfork, Jackingram, Jamesooders, Jann2010, Janschejbal, Jaranda, Jasonreina, Jatgill7, Jawed, Jayjg, Jcarle, Jdavidb, Jdock1, Jeffrey Mall, Jfromcanada, Jimscott13, Jive Dadson, Jmchuff, JoeSmack, Johann Wolfgang, John Fader, John254, JohnCD, Johndburger, Johnnrep, JohnnyTwain, Johnuniq, Jollyroger87, Jonphamta, Jooler, Joseph Solis in Australia, Jossi, Jovianeye, Joyous!, Jpbowen, Jpgordon, Jules7484, Justellian, Jweiss11, Kaiken, Karam.Anthony.K, KarenFischer, Kashmiri, Kejoxen, Kevin Saff, Khalid hassani, Khalidkhattak, Kintetsubuffalo, Kirachinmoku, Kkm010, Kmccoy, Konstable, Kozuch, Kralizec!, Krellis, Kroeger579, Ksyrie, Kulikovsky, Kuru, Kwokie, L Kensington, L0b0t, Larrymcp, Lavanga, Lcarscad, LeaW, Lee J Haywood, Legend78, Lequis, Liam Skoda, Lifung, Lightmouse, Lilac Soul, LindsayH, LittleSmall, Longhair, Lotje, Lowellian, Lproven, Lpython, Lucanos, Lucydovan, Luisg2513, Lukas0907, Lukeaw, Luna Santin, Luther93, LynnWider, MARRYTHENIGHT, MC10, MK8, Madvac2005, MagicBez, Mapletip, Marbruk, MarcelS, Marchije, Marcus Qwertyus, MarkSG, Marmusek, Martin451, Marysunshine, Mastervikram, MathiasRav, Matt4077, MattTM, MattieTK, Mazarin07, Mbc362, Mehudson1, Menthaxpiperita, Mets501, Mgiganteus1, Mhagerman, Michael Hardy, Midnightcomm, Mikeabundo, Mikie333, Minesweeper, Minimac, Minimac's Clone, Minitrue, Mjbourquin, Moday777n, Mokkawokka, Moncrief, Mooquackwooftweetmeow, Morven, Mountainclyde, Mountpanorama, Mr Adequate, Mr.moyal, Mrhuba, Mrschimpf, Multixfer, Mvjs, Mydogategodshat, Mygerardromance, Myself488, Mysid, N2e, N419BH, NaBUru38, Naive cynic, Nakon, Nelchee, Neurolysis, Neutral777, Nirvana2013, Nitroblu, Njyoder, Nobody of Consequence, Noel877, Novum, Nsaa, Nsgaeverine, Ntt ng, NuclearWarfare, Nufta, Nunh-huh, Oberiko, Odea, Off2riorob, Ohnoitsjamie, OmegaZero Alpha, Omegatron, Ongar the World-Weary, Ooohsnaaap, Opelio, Oracle21, Osidenate, Otto Knell, OverlordQ, P.G.Davies, Paalantam, PaigePhault, Patriarch, Paul Arthur Martin, Paypal2, Paypalinc, Pdspatrick, Pengo, Peter McGinley, Petmal, Philip Trueman, Philthecow, Piano non troppo, Pikasaur, Pinethicket, Piotrus, Plasticup, Pleasantville, Plrk, Pne, Polis4rule, Portalian, Powerangers, Pr0gr4mm3r, PrestonH, Prince256, Prj, Promethean, PrometheusX303, Protosot, QuasiAbstract, RJaguar3, Raven4x4x, Rchamberlain, Rdavout, Redvers, Reinyday, Repetition, Rettetast, RexNL, Rhobite, Rich Farmbrough, RichSatan, RichardRosse, Richiau, Richthe4th, Risker, Rjwilmsi, Rmarsden, RobertHuaXia, Rockfang, Ron Ritzman, Ronark, Ronhjones, Rookkey, Rossami, Router, Rozaleenda, Rror, Ryan Knight, SJP, Sagaciousuk, SalineBrain, Sam Barsoom, Samisuccar, Samsoncity, Samuel Blanning, Samwb123, Sango123, Saopaulo1, Sasank, Satanoid, Saturday, Scott Illini, Scottbell, Sdornan, Seaphoto, Searchme, Sengkang, Sf46, Sferrier, Shadow demon, Shadowjams, ShawnIsHere, Shii, Shoeofdeath, Shoppingcart, Sintaku, Sir Nicholas de Mimsy-Porpington, Sjl, SkyWalker, SkylineEvo, SlamDiego, Sligocki, Slt517, SmartGuy, Smartse, Smileyborg, Smooth08, Smyth, Snaxe920, Soap, Someastroturfer, Someguy1221, Sonicsuns, SpaceFlight89, Spec, Spiel496, Splash, Spondoolicks, Spuddock, Squash Racket, SqueakBox, Staborama, StarTrekkie, StaticGull, Stefan2, Stephen Gilbert, Stephen Hui, StephenBuxton, Stepheng3, Steven Zhang, Stevertigo, Stifle,

Stupidguy24, Stwalkerster, Subdolous, Subsolar, SunCreator, Sundown 7, SuperTycoon, Superm401, Supran, SusanLesch, Svick, Sweet Rocket, Swid, Sydneyfong, Syrthiss, T71024, THDju, THEunique, TJJFV, Tannin, TaranRampersad, Tarquin, Tassedethe, Tbg connor, Tcalves, That Guy, From That Show!, The Evil Spartan, The Haunted Angel, The Thing That Should Not Be, The wub, TheMan232, TheNewPhobia, TheSuave, Thejaswi.puthraya, Themoneymultiplier, Thessaysno, Thomas Larsen, Tills, Tim Barber, Timc, Timrollpickering, Tingrin87, Tommy2010, Tstrobaugh, Tsukamasa, TubularWorld, Turkey2020, Ukexpat, Uncle Dick, Uncle G, Usbswiper, Utcursch, VMS Mosaic, Vary, Vegaswikian, Veinor, Versageek, Vicki Rosenzweig, Vicky Ng, Vikizh, Viridae, Vorratt, Vrenator, Vtarasov, WOTWA, Walkiped, Walt Byars, WarFox, Wdfarmer, Weopgon, Wesha, Wik, Wiki332, Wikibofh, Wikidemon, Wikinewguy, William Graham, William Ortiz, Williethenewguy, Wmahan, Wnt, Wossi, Wrivenbark, Wtmitchell, Wuhwuzdat, XVreturns, Xaosflux, Xarok, Xavier Peniche, Xionbox, Xkoalax, Xp54321, Xtm, Yamla, Yboord028, Yerpo, Ykhwong, Yoghurt, Yonskii, Yopienso, Yourfreestuff, Yserarau, Zabadab, Zarutian, ZayZayEM, Zigger, Zikalify, ZimZalaBim, Zoe, Zondor, Zpb52, Zuckermaul, Zzuuzz, Ævar Arnfjörð Bjarmason, Óðinn, 1515 anonymous edits

PayPoint *Source*: http://en.wikipedia.org/w/index.php?oldid=431154574 *Contributors*: AndrewHowse, Ark25, AvicAWB, Bastin, Cahk, Carlossuarez46, Chris the speller, Dormskirk, Edward, Ezetop, Gr1st, Huon, IMSoP, Ian Pitchford, Jisatsusha, Mankind 2k, Mauls, Pegship, PrimroseGuy, Ptheb61, Qasdfdsaq, R.carroll, Rdd, RxS, Secretlondon, Tappyea, Thomas Blomberg, Tnxman307, Trident13, Veganline, Woohookitty, YorkshireM, Zzuuzz, 12 anonymous edits

PaySafe *Source*: http://en.wikipedia.org/w/index.php?oldid=395271022 *Contributors*: Bearcat, Cahk, EdgeOfEpsilon, Fram, Hello Control, Mhockey, Omicronpersei8, Quatloo, RobertandKathy, 11 anonymous edits

Paysafecard *Source*: http://en.wikipedia.org/w/index.php?oldid=427457072 *Contributors*: AkiraRavenNights, Cpopa, Davecrosby uk, EarthFurst, Greengiant1966, Greenrd, Innv, Mazarin07, Mhockey, Timbach2, 58 anonymous edits

PayXpert *Source*: http://en.wikipedia.org/w/index.php?oldid=408053068 *Contributors*: Bearcat, Bourrafond, Crazycomputers, SarahStierch, WOSlinker, 1 anonymous edits

Peppercoin *Source*: http://en.wikipedia.org/w/index.php?oldid=415024469 *Contributors*: Arvindn, Bearly541, Bihzad, FloydRTurbo, Keenan Pepper, Kupojsin, Mangojuice, 12 anonymous edits

Piano Media *Source*: http://en.wikipedia.org/w/index.php?oldid=432639531 *Contributors*: Dbrauchli, 1 anonymous edits

Pivotal Payments *Source*: http://en.wikipedia.org/w/index.php?oldid=432218516 *Contributors*: Charles Edward, Chevymontecarlo alt, DGG, Odisha1, Pivotalpayments, Seaphoto, Socialpiv, Tassedethe, 21 anonymous edits

Point of sale *Source*: http://en.wikipedia.org/w/index.php?oldid=432305881 *Contributors*: 1982zico, 7, A. B., Aboltinsh, Adwait k123, Ahoerstemeier, Aiingel, Akbarc, Alan leee, Alberrosidus, Alexei aus, Alpha 4615, Alx 91, AmericanDad, Amnewsboy, Andonic, Andrewism, Anna Lincoln, Apobilgin, Archana 3600, Ausgangskontrolle, Barticus88, Baryonic Being, Bearsharexx, Beetstra, Bigdumbdinosaur, Bilky asko, Blaxthos, Blender09, Bloodshedder, Bobo192, Bongwarrior, Burn, CVBS1, Caatkinson, Cab.jones, CanadianLinuxUser, Cancun771, CanisRufus, Capricorn42, Carbuncle, Careful Cowboy, Carlryds, Christopherlin, Clickedon, Codyfinke6, Coffee, Correogsk, Csbirchby, DGG, Da1999, Danlev, Davidpdx, Denelson83, Dispenser, DonScorgie, Dreadstar, Dysprosia, EagleOne, Eaolson, Edward, Egg-fire, Ejrrjs, Eliz81, ElliotThomas, Emj, Failtrainhardcore, Fan-1967, Faradayplank, Favonian, FeyFre, Fiftyquid, Frap, Frehley, Frymaster, Garion96, Gobonobo, Goog, GraemeL, Haef, Half jesus, Hengkc, Hephaestos, Hmains, Hu12, Il MusLiM HyBRiD II, ITurtle, Imnotminkus, Isaac Sanolnacov, Itesso, Ixfd64, JadaKim, Jason7t1, Jeffrey Scott Maxwell, Jennavecia, Johnuniq, Jok2000, Josamm, Jswagman, Jvcdude, Kertrats, Khalid hassani, Kmorozov, Krfh30, Krkas, Kukini, Kzzl, Lectonar, Leeatcookerly, LefTSouth, Logical Cowboy, Lowellian, Lukerh18, Luna Santin, Lynnstanikmas, M1sm1, MER-C, Malo, MarkGallagher, Markymarc1981, Marsland, Martin451, Maureen, Maury Markowitz, Mav, Maxwellterry, Mazca, Mdmatney, Meand, Megan5522, Memescc, Mktgassistant, Monkeylover34, Moon7308, MorganaFiolett, Mparak, Mrath, Mushroom, Myanw, Mydogategodshat, Neils.place, NerdyScienceDude, Neverquick, Nistra, Nono64, Nonsequiturmine, Nufy8, Oatmeal batman, Ohnoitsjamie, Oli2140, Omicronpersei8, Opksrj, Oxymoron83, POS maid, POSSuperhero, Pak21, PamD, Panadolmomo, Panchurret, PandaAdventures, Pathfinder500, Patrick, PaulKaye, Peruvianllama, PeterKoegel, Piano non troppo, Piercetp, Planobe, Plazie, Plinkit, Possystemca, PrimroseGuy, R Math, Rac082, Radiojon, Rasssd, RedWolf, Redoctober312, Retired username, Ricobandito, Rjwilmsi, RobertG, Rudyvalencia, Sandstein, SarekOfVulcan, Sargdub, Sarranduin, SchuminWeb, ScottSteiner, Sdaniel, Shadowjams, Sleekwog, Snackwell, Socrates2008, Somecrowd, Sottolacqua, SpeedLine, Sploot, Spud1, Stbalbach, Stephenb, Stifle, Stihdjia, Strait, Tevildoii, The Anome, The Rationalist, Thisara.d.m, Thniels, Thumperward, Timneu22, Tkondaks, Tktktk, Tobias Bergemann, Topsfield99, Tr00st, Ubcule, Uberuser2037, UkPaolo, UnTillHospitality, Velella, Versus22, ViperSnake151, Vishalmaintech, Wiechert, WikiLeon, WikipedianMarlith, Wimt, Winbuyer, Wongm, Ww2censor, Xs935, Youngtwig, Zantolak, ZioNicco, Zkrige, 466 anonymous edits

Post-dated check *Source*: http://en.wikipedia.org/w/index.php?oldid=422195768 *Contributors*: Akendall, Beto, Bfigura, Cybercobra, From the North, GJArguello, Gavia immer, Hmains, Hucz, Joeblakesley, Koine, Nbarth, OffsBlink, Ozzykhan, Pascal.Tesson, Rconan, SimonP, Tingrin87, Woohookitty, 7 anonymous edits

Postal Order *Source*: http://en.wikipedia.org/w/index.php?oldid=432920768 *Contributors*: 159753, Aidan Work, Anomenat, Caesura, Crusoe8181, Deathphoenix, Fabiform, Fys, Gaius Cornelius, Gnj, Hu, Johann Wolfgang, John, Kmellem, Lincspoacher, Maidonian, Man vyi, Michael Romanov, Mom2jandk, Moonlight Mile, Nick1nildram, Ohconfucius, Phiellaep, RJFJR, Radagast83, Random832, RichardJohn, Rjwilmsi, Searchme, Sjorford, Sonett72, Squigish, Tyom, Ww2censor, Yosri, 20 anonymous edits

Pranasys *Source*: http://en.wikipedia.org/w/index.php?oldid=426295802 *Contributors*: Codf1977, Joreggioni, Pink Bull, Rjwilmsi, Tnxman307, Woohookitty

Prepaid *Source*: http://en.wikipedia.org/w/index.php?oldid=430035372 *Contributors*: Ajuk, Anakin101, AnnaAniston, Bobblewik, Bwilkins, Calvinhrn, CanadianCaesar, Canthusus, Ckatz, Colonies Chris, Danielleevandenbosch, EagleFan, Elfguy, Flowanda, Gaius Cornelius, Gogo Dodo, Hardush, Hlop83, Hqb, Ianeversley, Jaxl, Kompere, Kyfer, Ma8thew, Malcolma, Mauls, Nunocordeiro, Ohnoitsjamie, Pagrashtak, Romaine, Severo, SiobhanHansa, Southlondonlife, Splash, Starbois, TimRoe1203, Tokek, Utcursch, Wimt, Yasth, 47 anonymous edits

ProPay *Source*: http://en.wikipedia.org/w/index.php?oldid=431118754 *Contributors*: Chop2, DGG, Drvanthorp, Fewill, Johnpacklambert, Mean as custard, Mhockey, Sgroupace, Tbennert, Virgy, ZimZalaBim, 6 anonymous edits

QC Record Format *Source*: http://en.wikipedia.org/w/index.php?oldid=288191966 *Contributors*: MacSpon, Surv1v4l1st, 1 anonymous edits

Kamal Quadir *Source*: http://en.wikipedia.org/w/index.php?oldid=433201497 *Contributors*: Bellayet, Felix Folio Secundus, Fuadcse, H8erade, Irtizaur, Joaquin008, Nasmtih, Nawsher, Salamlemon, 3 anonymous edits

Quick Wertkarte *Source*: http://en.wikipedia.org/w/index.php?oldid=392166276 *Contributors*: Axic, BillC, Monomyth, Woohookitty, 1 anonymous edits

Ready Financial *Source*: http://en.wikipedia.org/w/index.php?oldid=421567810 *Contributors*: Hut 8.5, Jezhotwells, Squiddles11

Real Time Gross Settlement *Source*: http://en.wikipedia.org/w/index.php?oldid=427592776 *Contributors*: Antiselfdual, Asheikh73, Ashishsheth, Bongomatic, CanisRufus, Ceefour, Closedmouth, El C, Ennio morricone, Flo sibiu, Future Perfect at Sunrise, Gfis, GregorB, Haardik, HongQiGong, Jackeapen, KelvinMo, Kukini, Limbergchero, Lukejmorrison, Matt.ellis, Mrtrey99, Naveenpf, Novacatz, Ph.eyes, Phil websurfer@yahoo.com, Pnm, Qwyrxian, Randhirreddy, Reach tanvir, Ruzbehraja, Sargdub, Savidan, Severo, Shadowphrogg32642342, Siroxo, Skalmier, Tadpole9, Timpo, Tsavage, Winodhello, Wk muriithi, Yabbadab, 82 anonymous edits

Recurly *Source*: http://en.wikipedia.org/w/index.php?oldid=431271084 *Contributors*: Deekomalley, Mhockey, Raerae7133, Wilhelmina Will

Red Wing Software *Source*: http://en.wikipedia.org/w/index.php?oldid=358423401 *Contributors*: Sjelsen, Teapotgeorge

Revolution Money *Source*: http://en.wikipedia.org/w/index.php?oldid=423246123 *Contributors*: Amire80, Awtribute, Eastmain, Emitchell62000, FiveDentists, HitroMilanese, Ironholds, Josephgrossberg, Leszek Jańczuk, NellieBly, Nieuwenhuis, Pedro, Rjwilmsi, Rnb, Robsavoie, YUL89YYZ, 43 anonymous edits

Revolution MoneyExchange *Source*: http://en.wikipedia.org/w/index.php?oldid=398270770 *Contributors*: Luvcraft, Mhockey, PamD, Raymie, Wesha

Ripple monetary system *Source*: http://en.wikipedia.org/w/index.php?oldid=430076270 *Contributors*: Altenmann, Atreyu42, Beefman, Captain Awesome Power, ColdFeet, DNewhall, DO11.10, Fasten, GrantNeufeld, L0b0t, Lycurgus, Miami33139, Mårten Berglund, Nirvana2013, Noddycr, Rfugger, Rgrant, RomualdoGrillo, Rougieux, Skomorokh, Spoirier, Touisiau, TouristPhilosopher, Toussaint, VanGore, 39 anonymous edits

RuPay *Source*: http://en.wikipedia.org/w/index.php?oldid=429067053 *Contributors*: Randhirreddy, Sapna81, Woohookitty

SADAD Payment System *Source*: http://en.wikipedia.org/w/index.php?oldid=406723618 *Contributors*: CommonsDelinker, Farmanesh, Jtafas, Mhockey, Mnoohu, SueHay, Supertouch, Zizo1st, 7 anonymous edits

Saudi Payments Network *Source*: http://en.wikipedia.org/w/index.php?oldid=423311144 *Contributors*: Aelfthrytha, Ahoerstemeier, Big Zee, BigHaz, Carabinieri, CiaranG, Ciotog, Daemonic Kangaroo, Eagleamn, Gscshoyru, Jim62sch, John Vandenberg, Michael Hardy, Mikespedia, Miracle Pen, NickelShoe, Not a dog, Phatom87, PrimroseGuy, RanjithMN, Seektrue,

SelfStudyBuddy, Turkeyphant, Vgranucci, Z yousef, □□□.□□□.24, 23 anonymous edits

Secure POS Vendor Alliance *Source*: http://en.wikipedia.org/w/index.php?oldid=411843994 *Contributors*: JamesBWatson, Ldurfee, Leeatcookerly, Nono64, Ver, Vicky Ng

SecurityMetrics *Source*: http://en.wikipedia.org/w/index.php?oldid=419461640 *Contributors*: A. B., Access Denied, Faustus37, Hairhorn, Msbaxter22, SecurityMetrics, 2 anonymous edits

Self checkout *Source*: http://en.wikipedia.org/w/index.php?oldid=431531242 *Contributors*: 5 albert square, A Softer Answer, Agnesknosis, Alphaboi867, Andycjp, Apl2007, Avianwind, Babbage, Barrylb, Belovedfreak, Blahma, Busy Stubber, Camann, Ccacsmss, Closedmouth, Cometstyles, Crookesmoor, Cyclingbrian, Dachannien, Edauchy, Elkman, Epson291, Erianna, Etherelly, Fcar, Groyolo, HiLo48, Hmains, Hu12, IRP, Islander, J.delanoy, Jake Wartenberg, Jasmina.mesic, Jesseadyer, Johnuniq, Joshcating, Jroddi, Ken Gallager, KenFehling, KodakFilm, LilHelpa, Luna Santin, Man vyi, Manishearth, Markb, MiLo28, Moogleluvr, Mr.weedle, Mrschimpf, Nihiltres, Nonexistant User, OverlordQ, OwenX, PamD, Philspil, Quantpole, R'n'B, Raysonho, RedRiverGorge, Rich Farmbrough, Riki, Rjwilmsi, Runnau, SchuminWeb, Securetech, Smellmyfingaz, Sorsha76, Soupyjnr, SpK, Spiral5800, Stifle, Synergy, Takeel, Tasquith, Teimu.tm, Th1rt3en, The Thing That Should Not Be, The wub, TheCoffee, TheTruthiness, Thompson.matthew, TravisKKircher, Tsimshatsui, Virtualerian, Walpole, Wt90401, Yerpo, 141 anonymous edits

Shared Check Authorization Network *Source*: http://en.wikipedia.org/w/index.php?oldid=315922620 *Contributors*: Hellno2, Lotje, 1 anonymous edits

Shift4 *Source*: http://en.wikipedia.org/w/index.php?oldid=424980369 *Contributors*: Alkamins, CambridgeBayWeather, Casper n, CaustiCutie, Chowbok, Closedmouth, Drmies, Echuck215, Firsfron, Flowanda, Hackajar, Hmains, ITS REN, Jbf99, Mhockey, Scarykitty, Spitfire, Struway, Stymiee, Vegaswikian, WLS567, Warut, Welsh, Woodshed, Zorrik, 78 anonymous edits

Single Euro Payments Area *Source*: http://en.wikipedia.org/w/index.php?oldid=432142426 *Contributors*: 101chris, A1r, Alinor, Baden Cottage, Bdnz, Bz2, Cbdorsett, Charl39, Chase me ladies, I'm the Cavalry, Colonies Chris, DJromT, DerKetzer, Dima1, Djegan, Dulciana, Dzsi, EDCAlistairGates, EH101, Echoray, Eiger Systems, Emosssays, Eyreland, Frank1101, Gadget850, GluonBall, Golffies, Gugganij, Hu12, Huaä, Iain Cheyne, Ian3055, IanHarkins, Indon, JLogan, Jayapura, Jgombos, Johnderham, Jushi, Kaihsu, Kelsklan, Kku, Lavecchia, LippyTheLip, Loonybin345, Markus0408, MartEves, Maticgrobelsek, Mucks26, NathanBeach, Nightstallion, O Fenian, Ohconfucius, Oneiropagides, Ospalh, PatrikR, Ph.eyes, Pierremc, RScheiber, Rjwilmsi, Roger Pearse, Romainz, SEPAMAN, Saibo, SchuminWeb, Snappy, Snowolf, Somearemoreequal, Stefan2, Stifle, SunTecSBS, Tabletop, TalerConvention, Tocogano, Unifits, Varlagas, Versus22, Vlad, Wini1, Yha68, Æåm Fætsøn, 122 anonymous edits

Sistema de Pagamentos em Moeda Local *Source*: http://en.wikipedia.org/w/index.php?oldid=431117584 *Contributors*: J-archer, Johnpacklambert, Malcolma, Rettetast, Thedarxide, 1 anonymous edits

Sleekpay *Source*: http://en.wikipedia.org/w/index.php?oldid=382184929 *Contributors*: Vipinhari, Zeddarn, 1 anonymous edits

SMS banking *Source*: http://en.wikipedia.org/w/index.php?oldid=414355612 *Contributors*: Aleenf1, Anticipation of a New Lover's Arrival, The, Artem.batkovsky, BesnikBelegu, Brianski, Deafakos, Fleohau, Iosef, Jpbowen, Karl.brown, Kuru, Manuelamsp, MarkS, Nuttycoconut, Oli Filth, R Math, Sosh, Sujit Sivanand, Tanthalas39, TastyPoutine, Wikipageperson, Winnie007, Winnieliang007, 12 anonymous edits

Smscoin *Source*: http://en.wikipedia.org/w/index.php?oldid=418140555 *Contributors*: BRUTE, LilHelpa, Meankeeper, Moldova1979, Orlodrim, 7 anonymous edits

SparkBase *Source*: http://en.wikipedia.org/w/index.php?oldid=431037048 *Contributors*: AkankshaG, Blu3vibe, Chaler, CptTripps, Fred the Oyster, Levdr1, Lifebaka, Phearson, Pinkychanti, Rd232, Rich Farmbrough, Themfromspace

Speedpass *Source*: http://en.wikipedia.org/w/index.php?oldid=433176631 *Contributors*: Alan W, Ardenn, Azumanga1, Calicat, DabMachine, Dachshund, Dfmock, Dtwitkowski, Eastlaw, Edcolins, Good Olfactory, GraemeL, Grm wnr, Hellno2, Jafet, Joel7687, Lupinelawyer, Pascal666, Patken4, Potus52, Rob86TA, SDC, Speciate, Spinboy, Startstop123, Tawker, Tharsaile, The Anome, Tregoweth, Uberhill, Vicky Ng, Vybr8, Woohookitty, 11 anonymous edits

Square (payment service) *Source*: http://en.wikipedia.org/w/index.php?oldid=431932615 *Contributors*: 336, Canley, Casablanca2000in, English06, JRStutler, PRRfan, Pbhj, Phattcityusa, Shawnleejayz, Tbhotch, Timneu22, ToastIsTasty, 8 anonymous edits

Standing order (banking) *Source*: http://en.wikipedia.org/w/index.php?oldid=427839630 *Contributors*: Adhominem, Al.locke, Baje Tiger, Bender235, Cadr, Euryalus, Gpvos, Ian3055, J.delanoy, Jamesjiao, Jsnx, Lordbufonte, Martarius, NNemec, Naive rm, Nbarth, Pol098, Qxz, THEN WHO WAS PHONE?, Wikipongdia, 36 anonymous edits

Stored-value card *Source*: http://en.wikipedia.org/w/index.php?oldid=427045763 *Contributors*: AkankshaG, Alarichus, Amakuru, Berkebaydu, Bobrayner, Cab88, Candice45, CanisRufus, Carlymullan, Cerebellum, CptTripps, Crocodile Punter, DMG413, DagnyB, Dforest, Dina, Discospinster, Dreaded Walrus, DuncanHill, EDCAlistairGates, Edward, Ellogo, Elmsat, Elynnia, Fg2, Flowanda, Futurecards, Glane23, GraemeL, Greenbough, Grstain, Hairy Dude, Hraefen, I am Me true, JamesBWatson, Jkeene, Jtata, Kinerry, Kuru, Lensovet, Matthewgoldman, Mbstone, Michael Hardy, Monkeyman, Mrubin22, Mughaleazam123, Myk60640, NE2, Neutrality, OhioTrivium, Old Moonraker, Olegos, Opportunity0007, Pakaran, Quadell, RafaelRGarcia, Saelion11, Sam Hocevar, Scristaldi, SheikYerBooty, Smartse, Snigbrook, Somearemoreequal, Spainerd, StevenPhillips, Stifle, Surv1v4l1st, Tacticus, TerraHikaru, Tim Ivorson, Tom Foolery, Tribalthunder, UkPaolo, UncleDouggie, Unkx80, Vegaswikian, Wiki Kedar, Winterhalder, 121 anonymous edits

Substitute check *Source*: http://en.wikipedia.org/w/index.php?oldid=429837984 *Contributors*: Barek-public, Beland, Decora, Dthomsen8, Edge3, Emana, Gpvos, Greensburger, Iridescent, Jgombos, Jimp, John of Reading, Koavf, Lwalt, Maethordaer, NielsenGW, Pegship, Pnm, RBBrittain, Relyco, Sargdub, Starionwolf, 7 anonymous edits

Swreg *Source*: http://en.wikipedia.org/w/index.php?oldid=431092879 *Contributors*: 7h3dud3, Alanthehat, Falcon8765, GoingBatty, J04n, Johnnrep, Jumbocruiser, MuZemike, 10 anonymous edits

Talking ATM *Source*: http://en.wikipedia.org/w/index.php?oldid=432460772 *Contributors*: ChrisGriswold, GoingBatty, LilHelpa, Midhart90, Nightstallion, Nordeide, Oatmeal batman, Omnipaedista, PrimroseGuy, Tarret, Vegaswikian, Yakdo, 14 anonymous edits

Telegraphic transfer *Source*: http://en.wikipedia.org/w/index.php?oldid=379908752 *Contributors*: DavidFarmbrough, Dekisugi, Dwayne, Foolip, Gbleem, Jamesontai, Jpp, Leeyc0, Marek69, Martinsabo, Nakon, Neo-Jay, Onewaystreet 89, PhilKnight, Randhirreddy, Rrose Selavy, The Thing That Should Not Be, Wiki-uk, 10 anonymous edits

Scott Thompson (businessman) *Source*: http://en.wikipedia.org/w/index.php?oldid=421685180 *Contributors*: Alvin Seville, Dbeastly1, Drmies, EdoDodo, Graeme Bartlett, Gscshoyru, Mandarax, Richardcavell, Ttonyb1, VasilievVV, Vel110, 6 anonymous edits

Threshold pledge system *Source*: http://en.wikipedia.org/w/index.php?oldid=415197331 *Contributors*: Alan Pascoe, Anthony Appleyard, BD2412, Beroal, BrandonSeifert, Bunyk, Charivari, Classicalecon, Comrade Graham, CrosbieFitch, David Cooke, DewiMorgan, Eldred, Ethnopunk, Everything counts, Furrykef, Grafen, GregorB, Guyjohnston, HaeB, Hugh Mason, Jacj, JohnOwens, Jonkerz, Kfogel, Kimiko, Lexein, Malcolma, Marudubshinki, Matt Crypto, Michael Hardy, Micru, Mike Schwartz, Morten Blaabjerg, Palfrey, Pde, Perey, R'n'B, Rl, Sega381, Shadowmage13, ShaunMacPherson, Skomorokh, Snoyes, Steven.schear, Tmrwolf, Veikk0.ma, WaltBusterkeys, Willscrlt, 41 anonymous edits

TIPANET *Source*: http://en.wikipedia.org/w/index.php?oldid=373423538 *Contributors*: John of Reading, Katharineamy, Malcolma, Timpo

ToDDaSO *Source*: http://en.wikipedia.org/w/index.php?oldid=389683606 *Contributors*: Clicketyclack, Maerkmaerk, MikeKHants, MrRadioGuy

TPS Pakistan *Source*: http://en.wikipedia.org/w/index.php?oldid=422189030 *Contributors*: Dondegroovily, Hariswaheed, LilHelpa, Mar4d, Timneu22, Ttonyb1, Woohookitty, 5 anonymous edits

Transit check *Source*: http://en.wikipedia.org/w/index.php?oldid=332216295 *Contributors*: Akendall, Kross, Simon123

TRANZ 330 *Source*: http://en.wikipedia.org/w/index.php?oldid=413873605 *Contributors*: Hawaiian717, John Vandenberg, Kernel Saunters, Nekohakase, Reswobslc, 2 anonymous edits

Traveler's cheque *Source*: http://en.wikipedia.org/w/index.php?oldid=432581303 *Contributors*: Anastrophe, Andrewpayneaqa, Bdesham, Ben5082, Bentogoa, COMPFUNK2, CWenger, Chochopk, Cjohnzen, Correogsk, Cphilp, Crocodile Punter, David.Monniaux, Dennis Bratland, Esrever, Excirial, Gerweck, Gilliam, GregAsche, Halosix, Ilike2edit, IvanLanin, Jigen III, Joshua Issac, Mark Foskey, Mauls, Mochi, Myscrnnm, Nonsequiturmine, Privacy, RBBrittain, Randhirreddy, Resurgent insurgent, Rmhermen, Rror, Sargdub, Scott Sanchez, Spliffy, Sudosiko, TerraHikaru, Thaifriend, Thbarnes, TinyClanger, Tiyang, Vary, VincentPang8888, Wereon, Wikipelli, Woohookitty, Xredsox14x, □□□, 91 anonymous edits

Truck system *Source*: http://en.wikipedia.org/w/index.php?oldid=389388953 *Contributors*: Ahoerstemeier, Altenmann, Aplomado, Charles Matthews, Chenopodiaceous, Conscious, Doradus, Ekedolphin, Fredrik, Gavia immer, Graham Moss, Grant65, JasonAQuest, Jonne, JovanCormac, Mattisse, Meco, Mukadderat, N1h11, Notuncurious, PamD, Rjwilmsi, Romainz, Scottb1, Serpentnight, SimonP, Slightsmile, Snori, Squids and Chips, Thumperward, Ufwuct, Valfontis, Van helsing, Verdatum, Wdyoung, Wolfgang glock, Yvwv, 20 anonymous edits

TSYS *Source*: http://en.wikipedia.org/w/index.php?oldid=418376426 *Contributors*: Alphapotato, AmandaMcC, Camryn, CliffC, Crkey, Discdrivedj, Eastmain, Fbraski, Gaurav1627, Htanna, I-be-da-man, Kmorozov, Lhman12, M.e, Noswadmot, Orangemike, Pearrari, R'n'B, RadioFan, Soxford69, Srikanth2384, Steevo714, Straykat99, TexasAndroid, Tsyscom, Wapdat, 39 anonymous edits

UK Payments Administration *Source*: http://en.wikipedia.org/w/index.php?oldid=431897853 *Contributors*: Akibitzer, Alast0r, BenShade, Carabinieri, Chrisd10, Chrisieboy, Clerkcosts, Eddie.willers, Fayenatic london, Flahmz, Funandtrvl, JukoFF, Kreb, Malcolma, Mauls, Michael Hardy, Million Little Gods, NathanBeach, Nbarth, Olipro, Owen, PaulHanson, Royan, Sargdub, Tabletop, TehGrauniad, TheAllSeeingEye, Tim Ivorson, 18 anonymous edits

Unfunded loan commitments *Source*: http://en.wikipedia.org/w/index.php?oldid=313043821 *Contributors*: CRoetzer, Laxrulz777, Malcolma, Robofish, Snigbrook

Uniform Customs and Practice for Documentary Credits *Source*: http://en.wikipedia.org/w/index.php?oldid=432252617 *Contributors*: 5618, Alandavidson, Beland, Bleagle, BrownHairedGirl, CambridgeBayWeather, Dav999, Dinobuddy, Edward130603, EstelSnow, Gaius Cornelius, Gregalton, Gsmc2100, Guenael, Khalil Matar, Kinayath, MarkS, Miyagawa, Pubby2010, Rjwilmsi, Samfreed, Splowey, TreasuryTag, Versageek, 37 anonymous edits

Universal Air Travel Plan *Source*: http://en.wikipedia.org/w/index.php?oldid=417071822 *Contributors*: Btphelps, Cosmoboricua, Fabrictramp, Katharineamy, MuffledThud, Raymond, 1 anonymous edits

Virgin Voucher *Source*: http://en.wikipedia.org/w/index.php?oldid=390087197 *Contributors*: Digifiend, LemonTimer, OjWollig, TubularWorld, 1 anonymous edits

Visa Buxx *Source*: http://en.wikipedia.org/w/index.php?oldid=406042055 *Contributors*: Brownie Charles, Devster310, EikwaR, Greensburger, Jkeene, Jone5050, PatricePeyret, Paul A, PhilKnight, Rich Farmbrough, Serpent's Choice, THEN WHO WAS PHONE?, 17 anonymous edits

Visa Cash *Source*: http://en.wikipedia.org/w/index.php?oldid=417739939 *Contributors*: A boardley, Bigtophat, Dordoy, E Wing, Fences and windows, Fujiyama17, Greganddorne, Grutness, Instantnood, Juntung, Korg, MER-C, Msablic, PeregrineAY, Pstegs, 23 anonymous edits

Voluntary Collective Licensing *Source*: http://en.wikipedia.org/w/index.php?oldid=427213983 *Contributors*: Adrian, Bryan Derksen, Dawynn, Feedmecereal, Grocer, Haakon, Kuru, Loisbray, Olegwiki, Physicistjedi, Woohookitty, 5 anonymous edits

Voucher *Source*: http://en.wikipedia.org/w/index.php?oldid=430712802 *Contributors*: 6502programmer, Ahoerstemeier, Ajuk, Alma Pater, Anomalocaris, Arationalguy, BillCook, Blaxthos, Bluelightcard, Born2cycle, Born2lead u, Can't sleep, clown will eat me, Cemka, Crystallina, DARTH SIDIOUS 2, Demitsu, Dtplovell, Elagatis, Ewlyahoocom, Gaius Cornelius, Gfoley4, Gons, Guy Peters, Heatherdavies1990, J.delanoy, JHarrNL, JdwNYC, Jpwink1, Koolkyle123, Lasersharp, Metatron's Cube, NawlinWiki, Nekohakase, Nyttend, Papercrab, Petr Kopač, Prhartcom, Psychonaut, Rateruk, Raujibhai, Rrius, Scoops, Sergei Kazantsev, Sharoncollinsr, Skippy le Grand Gourou, Skully.jj, Sn0wflake, TastyPoutine, Thegreenj, Tinton5, Tomchiukc, Transity, Wabschke, Woohookitty, 73 anonymous edits

Voucher privatization *Source*: http://en.wikipedia.org/w/index.php?oldid=418441180 *Contributors*: Adam Zivner, Aldrich Hanssen, Colchicum, Digwuren, Ida Shaw, JanSuchy, Kozuch, Mrmuk, Pavel Vozenilek, Petri Krohn, Rd232, Rios, Sergei Kazantsev, Shaddack, Tim!, TouristPhilosopher, 5 anonymous edits

Warrant of payment *Source*: http://en.wikipedia.org/w/index.php?oldid=432298403 *Contributors*: BassJapas, Cybercobra, Dana boomer, Greensburger, Hmains, John Chamberlain, Majormax, Muhandes, Neutrality, The359, TheBigZzz, 3 anonymous edits

WePay *Source*: http://en.wikipedia.org/w/index.php?oldid=432528752 *Contributors*: Billclerico, Cunard, Grondemar, Ground Zero, JEH, Kimse, Od Mishehu, Opal8164, Piledhigheranddeeper, Truthanado, Wikidemon, Wuhwuzdat, 4 anonymous edits

White Label ABMs in Canada *Source*: http://en.wikipedia.org/w/index.php?oldid=432460941 *Contributors*: AlbertR, BillC, Carrionluggage, Chris the speller, Deetdeet, Ettrig, GoingBatty, Greenbough, Kaiden2007, Kevlar67, Kurieeto, Louipc, Mindmatrix, Nmajdan, PrimroseGuy, Rillian, Samuell, Themightyquill, YUL89YYZ, 36 anonymous edits

Wire transfer *Source*: http://en.wikipedia.org/w/index.php?oldid=431852637 *Contributors*: Accuruss, Admiral Norton, Ahoerstemeier, Akjarvis0, Aleator, AlexanderTechnique, Alexsegre, Alvis, Arsenikk, Baldwin040, Beland, Blanchardb, Blinkzedd, Calwiki, Canthony3, Carlymullan, Cataphract, Chrisbw, Chrylis, Ckatz, ClockworkLunch, Codyrank, Correogsk, Cpl Syx, Cyrillic, DMCer, Debresser, Eagleamn, Edward, Elmsat, Espoo, Eyreland, Flowanda, Frans Fowler, Fred zen, Fxrainman, GWBeasley, Gbleem, Gerhard51, Giraffedata, Goeie, GraemeL, Greenmind, Greensburger, HaeB, HarveyWireman, Haxwell, Heman, Hmains, Imarcaide, IndiQuest, Infrogmation, JPMcGrath, Jgombos, Jleedev, John of Reading, Jorunn, Jushi, KenT, Kuru, Kymacpherson, Liftarn, Longhorn90, Lupin, Luxdormiens, Markber, Materialscientist, May0104, MegaHasher, Mfwitten, Michael Hardy, Mmdoogie, Morpheusoptic, MuffledThud, NFH, Ndenison, Neo-Jay, NickBurns, Nicolas39, Odeliaj, OverlordQ, Paolo1979, Petri Krohn, Piercetheorganist, Preslethe, Ramymora, ReubenGarrett, Rjwilmsi, Rnbc, Roger J Cooper, Rschmertz, S0aasdf2sf, Salocin, San004, Sargdub, Scott Sanchez, Scriberius, Sloani10, Sourpearpirate, Speight, Stuart P. Bentley, Swanner, Teeschmid, The Grumpy Hacker, Thumperward, Tomseddon, UBJ 43X, Vicki01761, Whufc48, WikiLaurent, Wikipelli, Winodhello, Wiredabc, Wladi001, Woohookitty, Worldbanker123, Xionbox, Ynhockey, 171 anonymous edits

Wirecard *Source*: http://en.wikipedia.org/w/index.php?oldid=425338124 *Contributors*: AndrewHowse, Ary29, Bender235, Bernburgerin, Cander0000, Codiak, Dsp13, Eavesdropper, Ehn, Gr1st, Grzegorz Dąbrowski, Gwernol, Janus III, Massingasetta, Phatom87, SergioGeorgini, WhiteWriter, Zencv, Zuckermaul, ^demon, 67 anonymous edits

WorldPay *Source*: http://en.wikipedia.org/w/index.php?oldid=430820036 *Contributors*: Asav, Bearcat, HaeB, Kateshortforbob, Oxfordmale, Sc0974, TubularWorld, Warren.singer

XIPWIRE *Source*: http://en.wikipedia.org/w/index.php?oldid=401634555 *Contributors*: LuxorMG, Spitzl

Yang Cheng Tong *Source*: http://en.wikipedia.org/w/index.php?oldid=400797148 *Contributors*: ASDFGH, Andrei Stroe, BanyanTree, BradBeattie, Heimstern, Jpatokal, Malcolm, Rjwilmsi, SDC, Sameboat, Typhoonchaser, Visik, 3 anonymous edits

Zimswitch *Source*: http://en.wikipedia.org/w/index.php?oldid=395277949 *Contributors*: Beeblebrox, Eastmain, Mhockey, Mr Accountable, PamD, Tatendataona, Vegaswikian

Image Sources, Licenses and Contributors

Image:Portal-puzzle.svg *Source*: http://en.wikipedia.org/w/index.php?title=File:Portal-puzzle.svg *License*: Public Domain *Contributors*: User:Eubulides

File:BritishChequeAnnotated.png *Source*: http://en.wikipedia.org/w/index.php?title=File:BritishChequeAnnotated.png *License*: Creative Commons Attribution-Sharealike 3.0 *Contributors*: Sargdub

File:Romania Basarabia Chisinau telegraph money order counterfoils.jpg *Source*: http://en.wikipedia.org/w/index.php?title=File:Romania_Basarabia_Chisinau_telegraph_money_order_counterfoils.jpg *License*: Public Domain *Contributors*: unknown

File:Sweet success.jpg *Source*: http://en.wikipedia.org/w/index.php?title=File:Sweet_success.jpg *License*: Creative Commons Attribution 2.0 *Contributors*: michael kooiman

File:Ansari X-Prize Check.jpg *Source*: http://en.wikipedia.org/w/index.php?title=File:Ansari_X-Prize_Check.jpg *License*: GNU Free Documentation License *Contributors*: Belb, Benchill, Foroa, Ingolfson, Kbh3rd, Maksim, Wikipeder, 1 anonymous edits

File:Cheque guarantee.jpeg *Source*: http://en.wikipedia.org/w/index.php?title=File:Cheque_guarantee.jpeg *License*: Fair Use *Contributors*: Chrisieboy

Image:Subcheck FRONT.png *Source*: http://en.wikipedia.org/w/index.php?title=File:Subcheck_FRONT.png *License*: Public Domain *Contributors*: U.S. Federal Reserve Board

Image:Subcheck BACK.png *Source*: http://en.wikipedia.org/w/index.php?title=File:Subcheck_BACK.png *License*: Public Domain *Contributors*: U.S. Federal Reserve Board

Image:Chipandpin.png *Source*: http://en.wikipedia.org/w/index.php?title=File:Chipandpin.png *License*: Fair Use *Contributors*: User:82.114.94.13, User:BetacommandBot, User:Cydebot, User:Islander, User:Neal ricketts, User:Ossmann, User:PoccilScript, User:Polbot, User:Strangerer

Image:Chip and PIN Ireland.png *Source*: http://en.wikipedia.org/w/index.php?title=File:Chip_and_PIN_Ireland.png *License*: Fair Use *Contributors*: User:Djegan

Image:Chipandpin.jpg *Source*: http://en.wikipedia.org/w/index.php?title=File:Chipandpin.jpg *License*: Creative Commons Attribution-Sharealike 2.5 *Contributors*: JK125

image:Barclays pinsentry.jpg *Source*: http://en.wikipedia.org/w/index.php?title=File:Barclays_pinsentry.jpg *License*: Creative Commons Attribution-Sharealike 3.0 *Contributors*: Asim18

Image:Nordea_e-kod.jpg *Source*: http://en.wikipedia.org/w/index.php?title=File:Nordea_e-kod.jpg *License*: Creative Commons Attribution 3.0 *Contributors*: Petergullberg

Image:nationwide-CAP-reader.jpg *Source*: http://en.wikipedia.org/w/index.php?title=File:Nationwide-CAP-reader.jpg *License*: Creative Commons Attribution-Sharealike 3.0 *Contributors*: Beao, LeoNerd, Stifle

Image:ChoiceCardLogo.png *Source*: http://en.wikipedia.org/w/index.php?title=File:ChoiceCardLogo.png *License*: Fair Use *Contributors*: User:ProhibitOnions

File:PD-icon.svg *Source*: http://en.wikipedia.org/w/index.php?title=File:PD-icon.svg *License*: Public Domain *Contributors*: Various. See log. (Original SVG was based on File:PD-icon.png by Duesentrieb, which was based on Image:Red copyright.png by Rfl.)

file:Clearstream.gif *Source*: http://en.wikipedia.org/w/index.php?title=File:Clearstream.gif *License*: Fair Use *Contributors*: Sargdub, We hope

File:ClickandBuy.JPG *Source*: http://en.wikipedia.org/w/index.php?title=File:ClickandBuy.JPG *License*: Public Domain *Contributors*: ClickandBuy International Ltd

File:Flag of the United Kingdom.svg *Source*: http://en.wikipedia.org/w/index.php?title=File:Flag_of_the_United_Kingdom.svg *License*: Public Domain *Contributors*: Original flag by James I of England/James VI of ScotlandSVG recreation by User:Zscout370

Image:CNG Headquarter.jpg *Source*: http://en.wikipedia.org/w/index.php?title=File:CNG_Headquarter.jpg *License*: Public Domain *Contributors*: Bluiee, Neurolysis

Image:Smartcard2.png *Source*: http://en.wikipedia.org/w/index.php?title=File:Smartcard2.png *License*: Creative Commons Attribution-Sharealike 3.0 *Contributors*: Channel R

Image:CCardFront.svg *Source*: http://en.wikipedia.org/w/index.php?title=File:CCardFront.svg *License*: Public Domain *Contributors*: Alexander Jones

Image:CCardBack.svg *Source*: http://en.wikipedia.org/w/index.php?title=File:CCardBack.svg *License*: Public Domain *Contributors*: Alexander Jones

File:Demand_draft.jpg *Source*: http://en.wikipedia.org/w/index.php?title=File:Demand_draft.jpg *License*: Creative Commons Attribution-Sharealike 3.0 *Contributors*: Hitomi22

File:Decrease2.svg *Source*: http://en.wikipedia.org/w/index.php?title=File:Decrease2.svg *License*: Public Domain *Contributors*: Sarang

Image:Diners Club Logo3.svg *Source*: http://en.wikipedia.org/w/index.php?title=File:Diners_Club_Logo3.svg *License*: Fair Use *Contributors*: Esrever, Vargklo, Vegaswikian

Image:Disney FASTPASS.svg *Source*: http://en.wikipedia.org/w/index.php?title=File:Disney_FASTPASS.svg *License*: Fair Use *Contributors*: FA Jon

Image:Credit Card Slip DCC.png *Source*: http://en.wikipedia.org/w/index.php?title=File:Credit_Card_Slip_DCC.png *License*: Creative Commons Zero *Contributors*: Mpeylo

File:Img etollcard.jpg *Source*: http://en.wikipedia.org/w/index.php?title=File:Img_etollcard.jpg *License*: Fair Use *Contributors*: Mfa fariz

Image:Eaglecash.jpg *Source*: http://en.wikipedia.org/w/index.php?title=File:Eaglecash.jpg *License*: Public Domain *Contributors*: US Department of the Treasury

File:Smart card 001.jpg *Source*: http://en.wikipedia.org/w/index.php?title=File:Smart_card_001.jpg *License*: Public Domain *Contributors*: Blueviper99

Image:Usingeaglecash.jpg *Source*: http://en.wikipedia.org/w/index.php?title=File:Usingeaglecash.jpg *License*: Public Domain *Contributors*: US Department of the Treasury

Image:Efaktura logo.png *Source*: http://en.wikipedia.org/w/index.php?title=File:Efaktura_logo.png *License*: Fair Use *Contributors*: Arsenikk

Image:EFTPOS Logo.gif *Source*: http://en.wikipedia.org/w/index.php?title=File:EFTPOS_Logo.gif *License*: Public Domain *Contributors*: Ansett, 1 anonymous edits

File:Eftpos-paymark-nz-logo.PNG *Source*: http://en.wikipedia.org/w/index.php?title=File:Eftpos-paymark-nz-logo.PNG *License*: Fair Use *Contributors*: Sargdub

Image:Eftpos-nz-logo.gif *Source*: http://en.wikipedia.org/w/index.php?title=File:Eftpos-nz-logo.gif *License*: Fair Use *Contributors*: Sargdub, Sfan00 IMG, 2 anonymous edits

Image:Eurocheque logo.jpg *Source*: http://en.wikipedia.org/w/index.php?title=File:Eurocheque_logo.jpg *License*: Fair Use *Contributors*: Mintaru

Image:Ec-bankkarte.jpg *Source*: http://en.wikipedia.org/w/index.php?title=File:Ec-bankkarte.jpg *License*: Creative Commons Attribution-Sharealike 3.0 *Contributors*: Christian 'VisualBeo' Horvat

File:EWAYLogo.gif *Source*: http://en.wikipedia.org/w/index.php?title=File:EWAYLogo.gif *License*: Public Domain *Contributors*: This is the company logo

Image:EPS Merchants.png *Source*: http://en.wikipedia.org/w/index.php?title=File:EPS_Merchants.png *License*: Fair Use *Contributors*: Sky Harbor

Image:Faster payments logo.png *Source*: http://en.wikipedia.org/w/index.php?title=File:Faster_payments_logo.png *License*: Fair Use *Contributors*: User:Chrisd10, User:FairuseBot, User:MBisanz

Image:FirstData Logo 2008.jpg *Source*: http://en.wikipedia.org/w/index.php?title=File:FirstData_Logo_2008.jpg *License*: Fair Use *Contributors*: Gturpin

Image:Flattr.svg *Source*: http://en.wikipedia.org/w/index.php?title=File:Flattr.svg *License*: Public Domain *Contributors*: Flattr

File:Gift card assortment.jpg *Source*: http://en.wikipedia.org/w/index.php?title=File:Gift_card_assortment.jpg *License*: Creative Commons Attribution 2.0 *Contributors*: Tom Eppenberger Jr. Color-corrected and cropped by Daniel Case

Image:Gilbarco Veeder-Root forwikipedia.jpg *Source*: http://en.wikipedia.org/w/index.php?title=File:Gilbarco_Veeder-Root_forwikipedia.jpg *License*: Public Domain *Contributors*: MPence

Image:Girocard.svg *Source*: http://en.wikipedia.org/w/index.php?title=File:Girocard.svg *License*: Fair Use *Contributors*: Cfaerber, Melesse

File:Google-Wallet-logo.png *Source*: http://en.wikipedia.org/w/index.php?title=File:Google-Wallet-logo.png *License*: Fair Use *Contributors*: Caseyh

File:Roadside unattended jam stall, Stoke by Nayland - geograph.org.uk - 233767.jpg *Source*: http://en.wikipedia.org/w/index.php?title=File:Roadside_unattended_jam_stall,_Stoke_by_Nayland_-_geograph.org.uk_-_233767.jpg *License*: Creative Commons Attribution-Share Alike 2.0 Generic *Contributors*: Ingolfson

Image:I2c-inc-logo.jpg *Source*: http://en.wikipedia.org/w/index.php?title=File:I2c-inc-logo.jpg *License*: Fair Use *Contributors*: MBisanz, Tahirakram, 2 anonymous edits

File:Flag of the United States.svg *Source*: http://en.wikipedia.org/w/index.php?title=File:Flag_of_the_United_States.svg *License*: Public Domain *Contributors*: Dbenbenn, Zscout370, Jacobolus, Indolences, Technion.

File:Flag of Pakistan.svg *Source*: http://en.wikipedia.org/w/index.php?title=File:Flag_of_Pakistan.svg *License*: Public Domain *Contributors*: Abaezriv, AnonMoos, Badseed, Dbenbenn, Duduziq, F. F. Fjodor, Fry1989, Gabbe, Himasaram, Homo lupus, Juiced lemon, Klemen Kocjancic, Mattes, Mollajutt, Neq00, Pumbaa80, Rfc1394, Srtxg, TFCforever, ThomasPusch, Túrelio, Zscout370, 9 anonymous edits

Image:I2c-pakistan.jpg *Source*: http://en.wikipedia.org/w/index.php?title=File:I2c-pakistan.jpg *License*: Creative Commons Attribution 3.0 *Contributors*: Takbot

Image:Interac.svg *Source*: http://en.wikipedia.org/w/index.php?title=File:Interac.svg *License*: Fair Use *Contributors*: Koman90

Image:K-cash logo.jpg *Source*: http://en.wikipedia.org/w/index.php?title=File:K-cash_logo.jpg *License*: Fair Use *Contributors*: ESkog, Eastmain, Excretion, Zyxw

Image:Macaupass green.jpg *Source*: http://en.wikipedia.org/w/index.php?title=File:Macaupass_green.jpg *License*: Fair Use *Contributors*: Ghfj007

Image:MEPS New Logo.png *Source*: http://en.wikipedia.org/w/index.php?title=File:MEPS_New_Logo.png *License*: Copyrighted free use *Contributors*: MEPS

File:Schaffnertasche mit galoppwechsler.jpeg *Source*: http://en.wikipedia.org/w/index.php?title=File:Schaffnertasche_mit_galoppwechsler.jpeg *License*: Creative Commons Attribution-ShareAlike 3.0 Unported *Contributors*: Infrogmation, LosHawlos, Pfctdayelise

Image:Credit card terminal.jpg *Source*: http://en.wikipedia.org/w/index.php?title=File:Credit_card_terminal.jpg *License*: Public domain *Contributors*: Original uploader was Izcool at en.wikipedia

License

Lightning Source UK Ltd.
Milton Keynes UK
175782UK00001B/3/P